Anonymous

Hutchinson's Indianapolis City Directory

embracing an alphabetical list of citizens' names, a business directory, street

directory, church directory, shippers' guide, post office list, and an appendix of

much useful information

Anonymous

Hutchinson's Indianapolis City Directory
embracing an alphabetical list of citizens' names, a business directory, street directory,
church directory, shippers' guide, post office list, and an appendix of much useful information

ISBN/EAN: 9783337291426

Printed in Europe, USA, Canada, Australia, Japan

Cover: Foto ©Andreas Hilbeck / pixelio.de

More available books at **www.hansebooks.com**

HUTCHINSON'S

Indianapolis City Directory,

EMBRACING AN

ALPHABETICAL LIST OF CITIZENS' NAMES,

A BUSINESS DIRECTORY,

STREET DIRECTORY, CHURCH DIRECTORY, SHIPPERS'
GUIDE, POST OFFICE LIST, AND AN APPENDIX
OF MUCH USEFUL INFORMATION.

PUBLISHED ANNUALLY.

INDIANAPOLIS:
SENTINEL STEAM PRINTING ESTABLISHMENT,
1870.

CONTENTS.

INDEX TO ADVERTISEMENTS.

ALPHABETICAL DIRECTORY

OF THE

STREETS, AVENUES AND ALLEYS

OF INDIANAPOLIS.

The principal Streets crossing Washington Street are divided into North and South; those crossing Meridian Street into East and West. The four principal Avenues extend in four diagonal directions, from near the center to the limits of the City.

AGNES, north and south from New York to North, twelve blocks west of Meridian.

ALABAMA, north and south, three blocks east of Meridian.

ALLEGHANEY ALLEY, east and west from Tennessee, bet. Vermont and Michigan.

ANN, from Macauley to Catherine, bet. Tennessee and Mississippi.

ARCH, east and west, bet. Jackson and Noble, nine blocks north of Washington.

ARCHER, from Michigan to St. Clair, four blocks east of corporation.

ARSENAL, from east National road to Michigan, one-quarter mile east of corporation.

ASH, from Massachusetts av. to Home av., bet. Bellefontaine and Oak.

ATHON, north and south from Rhode Island to Indiana av., ten blocks west of Meridian.

BARNHILL, north and south from Elizabeth to Coe, sixteen blocks west of Meridian.

BATES, east and west, from Noble to corporation east, four blocks south of Washington.

BEATY, from Buchanan to McCarty, bet. Noble and Greer.

BELLEFONTAINE, from corporation to Home av., between Peru and Ash.

BENTON, north and south, from Harrison to Market, bet. Noble and Cady.

BICKING, east and west, from Delaware to East, two blocks south of McCarty.

BIDDLE, east and west, bet. Winston and corporation east, seven blocks north of Washington.

BLACKFORD, north and south, from National road to North, seven blocks west of Meridian.

BLAKE, north and south, from National road to Indiana av., ten blocks west of Meridian.

BLUFF ROAD, terminus south Meridian.

BRADSHAW, east and west, from Beaty to Virginia av., bet. Buchanan and McCarty.

BRETT, east and west, beyond corporation, west of Michigan road.

BRIGHT, north and south, from Ohio to North, eight blocks west of Meridian.

BROADWAY, from St. Clair to Home av., bet. Plum and Jackson.

BROOKS, north and south, from First to Drake, bet. Michigan road and Fall creek.

BUCHANAN, east and west, from East to Virginia av., bet. Dougherty and McCarty.

BUTLER, east and west, from Fort Wayne av. to College av., twelve blocks north of Washington.

CADY, north and South, from Harrison to Market, one block east of Benton.

CALIFORNIA, north and south, from Washington to St. Clair, six blocks west of Meridian.

CAMP, from St. Clair to First, west of Canal.

CAMPBELL, east and west, east of corporation, six blocks north of Washington.

CATHARINE, east and west, from Mississippi to West, bet. Merrill and McCarty.

CEDAR, north-east and south-west, from Dillon to Virginia av., bet. Grove and Pine.

CENTER, east and west, from Douglass to Ellen, bet. North and Elizabeth.

CHADWICK, from McCarty to city limits south, bet. Missouri and West.

CHARLES, from St. Clair to John, east of Noble.

CHATHAM, from Massachusetts av. to St. Clair, bet. East and Noble.

CHERRY, east and west, bet. Ft. Wayne av. and Charles, ten blocks north of Washington.

CHESTNUT, from Georgia to Morris, bet. Delaware and Pennsylvania.

CHESAPEAKE ALLEY, east and west, from Mississippi to West, bet. Maryland and Georgia.

CHOPTANK ALLEY, from Washington to St. Clair, bet. New Jersey and East.

CHRISTIAN AVENUE, east and west, from Ft. Wayne av. to Peru R. R., eleven blocks north of Washington.

CIRCLE, crossing of Meridian and Market, one block north of Washington.

COBURN, east and west, from East to Short, bet. Dougherty and corporation south.

COE, east and west, west of corporation line, ten blocks north of Washington.

COLLEGE AVENUE, from Christian av. to Home av. bet. Ash and Broadway.

COLUMBIA ALLEY, north and south, from Georgia to Michigan, bet. West and Missouri.

COTTRELL, from Louisiana to Georgia, bet. Missouri and West.

COURT, east and west, bet. Washington and Market, from Pennsylvania to Delaware.

CRANE, east and west, from Arsenal to Seymour, two blocks north of Washington.

CROSS, east and west, bet. Peru and Bellefontaine R. R., eleven blocks north of Washington.

CRUSE, from Washington to Highland, near Cady.

DACOTA, from Rockwood to city limits south, bet. West and White river.

DAVIS, north-east and south-west, from Indiana av. to Fall creek, twelve blocks north of Washington.

DELAWARE, north and south, two blocks east of Meridian.

DILLON, north and south, from Harrison to corporation south, on corporation line east.

DORMAN, from Michigan to St. Clair, one block east of corporation.

DOUGHERTY, east and west, from East to Virginia av., bet. Buchanan and Coburn.

DOUGLAS, north and south, from Ohio to Indiana av., nine blocks west of Meridian.

DOWNEY, east and west, from Bluff road to Japan, fourteen blocks south of Washington.

DRAKE, east and west, beyond corporation, west of Michigan road.

DUNCAN, east and west, from Delaware to New Jersey, bet. South and Merrill.

DUNLOP, east and west, from Bluff road to Japan, fifteen blocks south of Washington.

EAST, north and south, five blocks east of Meridian.

EAST CUMBERLAND, east and west, from Delaware to East, one-half block south of Washington.

EAST NATIONAL ROAD, terminus east Washington.

ECKERT, from Kentucky av. to Merrill, bet. West and Kentucky av.

EDDY, from Merrill to South, bet. Illinois and Tennessee.

EIGHTH, east and west, eighteen blocks north of Washington.

ELIZABETH, east and west, from Blake to Ellen, eight blocks north of Washington.

ELK, north-east and south-west, from Dillon to Virginia av., bet. Dillon and Virginia av.

ELLEN, north and south, from North to Indiana av., eight blocks west of Meridian.

ELLIS, from Georgia to Maryland, bet. West and Helen.

ELLSWORTH, north and south, from New York to Vermont, bet. Missouri and Mississippi.

ELM, north-west and south-east, from Noble to Dillon, bet. Virginia av. and Huron.

ERIE ALLEY, from Washington to St. Clair, bet. Alabama and New Jersey.

FAYETTE, north and south, from North to St. Clair, bet. Missouri and West.

FIFTH, east and west, fifteen blocks north of Washington.

FIRST, east and west, west of Meridian, eleven blocks north of Washington.

FLETCHER AVENUE, north-west and south-east, from Noble to Dillon, bet. Forest av. and Huron.

FOREST AVENUE, north-west and south-east, from Harrison to Dillon, bet. Harrison and Fletcher av.

FORT WAYNE AVENUE, north-east and south-west, from Pennsylvania and North, to city limits north-east.

FORT WAYNE ROAD, terminus Fort Wayne av.

FOURTH, east and west, fourteen blocks north of Washington.

FRANKLIN, from Morris to city limits south, bet. Wallace and Japan.

GARDEN, east and west, from Mississippi to Pennsylvania, bet. South and Merrill.

GEISENDORFF, north and south, from National road to New York, nine blocks west of Meridian.

GEORGIA, east and west, two blocks south of Washington.

GRANT, bet. West and Kentucky av., one block south of Merrill.

GREER, from Buchanan to Stevens, bet. East and Beaty.

GREGG, east and west, bet. New Jersey and Jackson, nine blocks north of Washington.

GROVE, north-east and south-west, from Dillon to Virginia av., bet. Elk and Cedar.

HARRISON, east and west, from Noble to corporation east, four blocks south of Washington.

HELEN, from Maryland to Louisiana, bet. Ellis and White river.

HENDERSON, north and south, terminus of North Illinois.

HENRY, east and west, from Missouri to Mississippi, bet. South and Merrill.

HIGH, from McCarty to corporation south, bet. New Jersey and Alabama.

HOME AVENUE, east and west, from Fort Wayne av. to Peru R. R., thirteen blocks north of Washington.

HOSBROOK, north-west and south-east, from Cedar to Dillon, bet. Virginia av. and Elm.

HOWARD, north and south, from First to Seventh, bet. Lafayette and Mill.

HUDSON ALLEY, from Ohio to Walnut, bet. Delaware and Alabama.

HURON, east and west, from Virginia av. to Noble, one block south of South.

HURON, north-west and south east, from Noble to Dillon, bet. Fletcher av. and Elm.

ILLINOIS, north and south, one block west of Meridian.

INDIANA AVENUE, north-west and south-east, from corner Ohio and Illinois to city limits north-west.

JACKSON, from St. Clair, to Home av., bet. Broadway and East.

JAPAN, north and south, extension of south East.

JOHN, east and west, bet. Peru and Bellefontaine R. R., ten blocks north of Washington.

JONES, east and west, from West to Dacota, six blocks south of McCarty.

KANKAKEE ALLEY, from Michigan to North, bet. Illinois and Tennessee.

KANSAS, east and west, from Meridian to Minnesota, thirteen blocks south of Washington.

KENTUCKY AVENUE, north-east and south-west, from corner Washington and Illinois, to city limits south-west.

KINGAN, east and west, from West to White river, two blocks south of McCarty.

LAFAYETTE, north and south, from First to city limits, bet. Mississippi and Howard.

LAFAYETTE ROAD, terminus Indiana av.

LENOX, north and south, from Seventh to Ninth, bet. Lafayette and Mill.

LIBERTY, north and south, six blocks east of Meridian.

LOCKERBIE, east and west, from East to Liberty, bet. New York and Vermont.

LOCUST, from McCarty to Morris, bet. Meridian and Union.

LORD, east and west, from Noble to corporation east, bet. Louisiana and Harrison.

LOUISIANA, east and west, three blocks south of Washington.

MACAULEY, east and west, from Ann to Missouri, one block south of McCarty.

MADISON AVENUE, north-west and south-east, from corner South and Meridian to city limits.

MADISON ROAD, terminus Madison av.

MAPLE, from Ray to Morris, bet. Tennessee and Illinois.

MARGARET, east and west, south of City Hospital.

MARIA, east and west, east of City Hospital.

MARKET, east and west, one block north of Washington.

MARYLAND, east and west, one block south of Washington.

MASSACHUSETTS AVENUE, north-east and south-west, from corner of Ohio and Pennsylvania, to city limits north-east.

MAXWELL, north and south, from Elizabeth to Davis, fourteen blocks west of Meridian.

MAYHEW, east and west, beyond corporation, west of Michigan rd.

MEEK, east and west, from Noble to corporation east, two blocks south of Washington.

MEIKEL, from McCarty to city limits south, bet. Mississippi and Missouri.

MERIDIAN, north and south, through Govenor's circle, bet. Pennsylvania and Illinois, south terminus per canvass, McCarty st.

MERRILL, east and west, six blocks south of Washington.

MIAMI ALLEY, east and west, bet. Ohio and New York.

MICHIGAN, east and west, five blocks north of Washington.

MICHIGAN ROAD, terminus north-west.

MICHIGAN ROAD, (east,) east terminus, Washington, ten blocks east of Meridian.

MILL, north and south, from Fifth to city limits, bet. Howard and Michigan road.

MINERVA, north and south, from Ohio to North, eleven blocks west of Meridian.

MINNESOTA, from Morris to city limits south, bet. Tennessee and West.

MISSISSIPPI, north and south, three blocks west of Meridian.

MISSOURI, north and south, four blocks west of Meridian.

MOBILE ALLEY, east and west, from Meridian to Mississippi, bet. Georgia and Louisiana.

MORRIS, east and west, twelve blocks south of Washington.

MORRISON, east and west, bet. Delaware and Alabama, twelve blocks north of Washington.

MULBERRY, from McCarty to Morris, bet. Union and Chestnut.

MUSKINGUM ALLEY, from Louisiana to First, bet. Tennessee and Illinois.

McCARTY, east and west, eight blocks south of Washington.

McGILL, from Louisiana to South, bet. Mississippi and Missouri.

McGINNIS, from McCarty to Ray, bet. Tennessee and Mississippi.

McINTIRE, east and west, beyond corporation, west of Michigan rd.

McKERNAN, from Buchanan to corporation south, bet. Short and Wright.

McNABB, east and west, from Illinois to Meridian, bet. Louisiana and South.

NEW JERSEY, north and south, four blocks east of Meridian.

NEW YORK, east and west, three blocks north of Washington.

NINTH, east and west, nineteen blocks north of Washington.

NORTH, east and west, six blocks north of Washington.

NOBLE, north and south, seven blocks east of Meridian.

OAK, from Massachusetts av. to Christian av., bet. Ash and Plum.

OHIO, east and west, two blocks north of Washington.

OREGON, north and south, from First to Pratt. bet. Brooks and Michigan rd.

OSAGE ALLEY, north and south, from Georgia to Pratt, bet. Missouri and Mississippi.

OXFORD, east and west, bet. Charles and corporation east, nine blocks north of Washington.

PACA, from St. Clair to First, west of Canal.

PATTERSON, north and south, from Vermont to Elizabeth, thirteen blocks west of Meridian.

PEARL, east and west, from Illinois to Pennsylvania, half-block south of Washington.

PECK, bet. old and new cemetery, terminus Kentucky av.

PENDLETON PIKE, terminus Massachusetts av.

PENNSYLVANIA, north and south, one block east of Meridian.

PERU, from North to Home av., nine blocks east of Meridian.

PHIPPS, east and west, from Meridian to Pennsylvania, bet. Merrill and McCarty.

PINE, north-east and south-west, from Harrison to Virginia av., one block east of Noble.

PITTSFIELD, from Seventh to Tenth, nr. Canal.

PLUM, from St. Clair to Christian av., bet. Oak and Broadway.

POPLAR, east and west, from Union to Chestnut, two blocks south of McCarty.

POTOMAC ALLEY, east and west, bet. Washington and Market, nr. West.

PRATT, east and west, nine blocks north of Washington.

RAILROAD, from Market to Massachusetts av., bet Spring and Davidson.

RAY, east and west, from McGinnis to Chestnut, two blks south of McCarty.

RHODE ISLAND, east and west, eight blocks north of Washington.

RIVER, south of old cemetery.

ROANOKE ALLEY, north and south, from Ohio to First, bet. Tennessee and Mississppi.

ROBSON, from National Road to Arsenal.

ROCKWOOD, east and west, from West to Dacota, three blocks south of McCarty.

ROOT, east and west, from West to White river, one block south of McCarty.

ROSE, bet. West and White river, two blocks south of Merrill.

RUSSELL, north and south, from Meridian to Illinois, bet. McCarty and Merrill.

SAND, southeast, from Kentucky av., to White River, one block west of West.

SANDERS, east and west, from Shelbyville road to terminus of Wright, at terminus of Virginia av.

SCHOOL, north and south, from South to Huron, bet. Noble and Virginia av

SCIOTO ALLEY, from Washington to New York, bet. Meridian and Pennsylvania.

SECOND, east and west, twelve blocks north of Washington.

SEVENTH, east and west, seventeen blocks north of Washington.

SEVERN ALLEY, north and south, from Louisiana to Second, bet. Meridian and Illinois.

SEYMOUR, from east National rd. to Crane, one-quarter mile east of corporation.

SHARPE, east and west, from Eckert to Missouri, bet. South and Merrill.

SHELBYVILLE ROAD, terminus Virginia av.

SHORT, from Dougherty to city limits south, bet. McKernan and Virginia av.

SILVAN, from Vermont to Elizabeth, west of Canal.

SINKER, east and west, from Alabama to East, one block north of McCarty.

SIXTH, east and west, sixteen blocks north of Washington.

SMITH, north and south, from Rhode Island to Indiana av., eleven blocks west of Meridian.

SOUTH, east and west, four blocks south of Washington.

SPRING, from Market to St. Clair, bet. Noble and Railroad.

STEVENS, east and west, from East to Virginia av., one block north of McCarty.

SUSQUEHANNA ALLEY, from Washington to North, bet. Pennsylvania and Delaware.

ST. CLAIR, east and west, eight blocks north of Washington.

ST. JOSEPH, east and west, ten blocks north of Washington.

ST. MARYS, east from Delaware, eleven blocks north of Washington.

TENNESSEE, north and south, two blocks west of Meridian.

TENTH, east and west, twenty blocks north of Washington.

THIRD, east and west, thirteen blocks north of Washington.

THOMAS, east and west, from West to Dacota, five blocks south of McCarty.

TINKER, east and west, seventeen blocks north of Washington.

TIPPECANOE ALLEY, east and west, from Tennessee to Illinois, bet. Vermont and New York.

TORBET, east and west, from Fall Creek to Michigan rd., beyond corporation.

UNION, from Merrill to Morris, bet. Meridian and Chestnut.

VERMONT, east and west, four blocks north of Washington.

VINE, east and west, bet. Jackson and Charles, nine blocks north of Washington.

VINTON, east and west, from West to Dacota, four blocks south of McCarty.

VIRGINIA AVENUE, north-west and south-east, from corner Washington and Pennsylvania to city limits.

WABASH ALLEY, east and west, bet. Market and Ohio.

WALLACE, from Morris to city limits south, bet. Madison rd. and Franklin.

WALNUT, east and west, seven blocks north of Washington.

WASHINGTON, east and west, length of city, first street south of Governor's Circle.

WATERS, from Stevens to McCarty, bet. Greer and Virginia av.

WESSON, east and west, from Arsenal to Seymour, one block north of Washington.

WEST CUMBERLAND, east and west, from Tennessee to White river, one-half block south of Washington.

WEST NATIONAL ROAD, east and west, west White river bridge.

WESTFIELD PIKE, terminus north Illinois.

WILKINS, east and west, from Tennessee to Chestnut, three blocks south of McCarty.

WILLIAMS, north from Washington near east corporation.

WILLARD, from Merrill to Garden, bet. Tennessee and Mississippi.

WILLARD, north and south, south side east National rd., one-half mile east of corporation.

WILSON, north and south, from Elizabeth to Davis, fifteen blocks west of Meridian.

WINSTON, from Ohio to Walnut, ten blocks east of Meridian.

WISCONSIN, east and west, from West to Meridian, fourteen blocks south of Washington.

WOOD, north and south, from Michigan to North, bet. Missouri and Mississippi.

WRIGHT, from Buchanan to corporation south, one block west of McKernan.

WYOMING, east and west, from Delaware to East, one block south of McCarty.

YEISER, east and west, from Bluff road to Japan, thirteen blocks south of Washington.

ABBREVIATIONS.

al. alley.
bet. between.
bds. boards.
bldg. building.
blk. block.
(col'd) colored.
cor. corner.

clk. clerk.
E. east.
es. east side.
lab. laborer.
N. north.
ne. north-east.
nr. near.

ns. north side.
P. O. post office.
rd. road.
r. residence.
S. south.
se. south-east.

ss. south side.
sw. south-west.
W. west.
ws. west side.
whol. wholesale.
(wid) widow.

ABB

ABBETT C. H. (L. & C. H. Abbett) 35 Virginia av., r. same.

Abbett Chas. H., traveling agent, American Saw Works, bds. Pyle House.

Abbett Jas. M., tinner, Munson & Johnston's, r. 386 W. New York.

Abbett John B., Grand Scribe Sons of Temperance, r. 164 Virginia av.

Abbett L. (L. & C. H. A.) r. 221 N. Tennessee.

ABBETT L. & C. H., physicians, 35 Virginia av.

Abbot Frederic M., clk., bds. Pyle House.

Abbott J. D., photographer, 94 E. Washington, r. 221 N. Tennessee.

Abbott Wesley, (col'd) lab., r. Ninth, near canal.

Abel Charles, lab. Schmidt's brewery, r. 401 S. Delaware.

Aborne Mary J. Mrs., teacher 9th ward school, r. 116 Broadway.

Aborn Orrin, Dr., 74 E. Market, r. 116 Broadway.

Abrahams James, ostler, 163 W. Washington, bds. Nagle House.

Abrams John, book keeper, r. 129 N. Noble.

Abrams John, (col'd) lab., r. 260 Indiana av.

Abrams Maggie Mrs., r. 419 N. East.

ACK

Abrams Milton, engineer Journal Office, bds. 98 N. East.

ABROMET A., agent Ætna Fire and Life Insurance Co., office Ætna bldg. N. Pennsylvania, r. 126 W. Maryland.

Academy of Music, se. cor. Ohio and Illinois, Butsch, Dickson & Co., proprietors.

ACADEMY OF MUSIC SALOON, under Academy of Music, Philip Fahrbach, prop.

Achelles Thomas, turner, works 23 E. South.

Achey American, expressman, r. 589 Maple.

Achey James, bds. 17 Kentucky av.

Achey John, r. 17 Kentucky av.

Achey Mary, (wid. Henry) r. 17 Kentucky av.

Ackerman Andrew, Western Furniture Company.

Ackerman August, printer, Daily Telegraph, r. 28 W. Georgia.

Ackerman John, bridge builder, r. 83 W. South.

Ackert G. F., with Asher & Adams, r. 221 E. Michigan.

Ackles Mollie Mrs., dressmaker, r. 322 E. Washington.

2

H. H. LEE

Makes a Specialty of

CHOICE GOLDEN RIO,

AND

OLD GOVERNMENT JAVA COFFEES.

Ackley Isaac, engineer Vincennes R. R., bds. 61 S. Noble.

Adam William, teamster, r. cor. Noble and Michigan.

Adam William, teamster, r. 312 N. New Jersey.

Adams Aaron, (col'd) lab. r. 247 N. West.

Adams Alex., boarding house, 268 E. St. Clair.

Adams B. F. (J. F. & B. F. A.) r. 17½ Virginia av.

Adams Charles, cooper, r. 3 Bates.

Adams Charles E., clk. 49 and 53 W. Washington.

Adams D. O. (A. & Davis) photographers, 2½ W. Washington.

ADAMS EXPRESS CO., 16 N. Meridian, new Sentinel bld'g, J. H. Ohr, agent.

Adams F. J. (F. J. & B. F. A.), r. 17½ Virginia av.

Adams F. J. & B. F., dry goods and notions, 180 E. Washington.

Adams George F. (G. F. A. & Co.), r. 175 E. Market.

Adams George, clk. J. W. Adams, bds. 430 N. Illinois.

Adams George M., brakeman C. C. & I. C. R. R., r. 318 E. Georgia.

ADAMS G. F. & CO. (G. F. Adams & George H. Batty) Housekeepers' Emporium, 32 S. Meridian.

ADAMS HARRY C., Deputy Sheriff, r. 115 S. New Jersey.

Adams Hubert S., policeman, r. 380 S. East.

Adams Isaac, (col'd) porter, C. Dickson & Co.

Adams J. W., boots and shoes, 49 and 53 W. Washington, r. 430 N. Illinois.

Adams Jesse, brick maker, r. 346 N. New Jersey.

Adams John H., groceries and provisions, 198 W. South, r. same.

Adams Mary W. (wid. Reuben) r. 115 S. New Jersey.

Adams Samuel, attorney at law, 17½ W. Washington, r. 297 N. Delaware.

Adams S. C., brick maker, r. 297 N. Delaware.

Adams Wesley M., carpenter, res. 42 Fletcher av.

Adams William C., brick moulder, bds. 163 Spring.

Adams William L. (Hume & A.) r. 384 N. New Jersey.

Adams & Davis, (D. O. Adams and T. G. Davis) photographers, 2½ W. Washington.

Addison Anna, (col'd, wid. Henry) r. African al., bet. Sixth and Seventh.

Adkins M. V. B., conductor C. C. C. & I. R. R., r. 346 N. Noble.

Adkinson John, carpenter, r. 206 Huron.

Adsit Charles J., cl'k, 40 S. Meridian, bds. 179 N. Alabama.

Aebker Henry, cabinet maker, r. 580 E. Washington.

Aebker William, cabinet maker, r. 580 E. Washington.

ÆTNA FIRE INS. COMPANY, room 1 Ætna Building. N. Pennsylvania, A. Abromet, Ag't.

Ætna Life Ins. Co. of Hartford, A. Abromet. Ag't.

Affanger, S. J., groceries, 199½ Indiana av, r. 215 W. North.

Aftune Andrew, book and news stand, 26 S. Delaware, r. 277 S. New Jersey.

Ahlders Ahlrich, harness maker, r. 29 W. McCarty.

Ahnrfelt William, carpenter, r. 381 Virginia av.

Aikin J. B., Ins. Ag't, r. 649 N. Tennessee.

Aikin L. G., trav. ag't L. Ludorff & Co., r. 649 N. Tennessee.

Aikins Milton, teamster, bds. 121 Huron.

Aikman John B. (Kimble, Aikman & Co.) r. 382 N. Tennessee.

Aker Ellis L., carpenter, cor. South and Delaware, r. 116 Elm.

Albany City Fire Ins. Co., Albany, N. Y., R. E. Beardsley, Ag't.

ALBERSHARDT H. F., boots and shoes, 139 E. Washington, r. same.

Albersmeier Daniel, wks T. H. & I. R. depot, r. 172 Union.

Albert J. W., carriage trimmer, r. 110 N. Delaware.

Albert Lawson H., baggage man, Union Depot, r. 211 N. Missouri.

Albertson A. C., printer, Journal office, bds. 98 N. East.

Albras James, ostler, E. S. Alverd, r. same.

Albray Clinton, painter, 18 S. Meridian.

Albrecht George, varnisher, Cabinet Makers' Union, r. 182 North Davidson.

Albro Henry O., foreman Chandler & Taylor's foundry, r. 160 Blackford.

Alcon Albert, (Alcon & Co.) r. 90 N. East,

Alcon & Co. (Albert A., J. M. Carron, and J. M. Washington) botanic and patent medicines, 27 S. Illinois.

Aldag August, shoemaker, r. 617 E. Washington.

Aldag Charles, boots and shoes, 175 E. Washington, r. same.

Aldag Charles, r. E Court, bet. New Jersey and East.

Aldag C. L., shoemaker, r. 119 N. New Jersey.

Aldag Louis, shoemaker, r. Court, bet. New Jersey and East.

Alden Charles, railroader, r. 326 E. Michigan.

Aldendorf Henry, porter, Murphy, Johnston & Co. bds. Globe House.

Aldrich Alex. W. with B. F. Haugh & Co. r. 15 College av.

Aldrich Chauncey, carpenter, r. 425 E. St. Clair.

Aldrich Frank, (Aldrich & Gay) r. 362 N. West.

Aldrich Isaac R., night policeman, r. 63½ S. Illinois.

Aldrich John D., stairsbuilder, 73 E. Washington, r. 17 College av.

Aldrich L. A. Rev., pastor Olivet Presbyterian Church, r. 248 S. Meridian.

Aldrich & Gay, (Frank A. and Alfred G.) wood yard, cor. Indiana av. and Canal.

Alexander Alvira, (wid. Archibald) r. 319 S. Delaware.

Alexander Emma B. (wid.), r. 332 E. Ohio.

Alexander Eugene, hardware clk, bds. Ray House.

Alexander George, barber, r. 181 W. Washington.

ALEXANDER G. W., real estate agent, 2½ W. Washington, r. 596 N. Illinois.

Alexander Joseph, carpenter, r. 173 Huron.

Alexander Mary Miss, clk. at Trade Palace, bds. 129 N. Illinois.

Alexander Nort. E., traveling agent Indiana Sentinel bds. 129 N. Illinois.

Alexander Theodore, T. salesman W. P. Bingham & Co. r. se. cor. Indiana av. and Vermont.

Alexander William, farmer, r. 233 N. Winston.

Alford Henry A., salesman, 77 S. Meridian, r. 175 N. Alabama.

Alford T. G. (Alford, Talbot & Co) r. 175 N. Alabama.

ALFORD, TALBOT & CO., (T. G. Alford, R. L. Talbot, J. P. Patterson, J. A. Moore, and W. H. Morrison) wholesale grocers, 123 S. Meridian.

Alfrey Maria Mrs. (wid.) r. 141 W. Washington.

Algeo John (Howe Sewing Machine Co.) r. 40 Lord.

BENHAM BRO'S,

36 E. Washington St.,

AGENTS FOR THE

INDIANAPOLIS MANUFACTURING CO.'S

PIANOS.

Algeo John, canvasser, r. 321 E. Ohio.

Algeo Samuel, salesman, r. 159 N. Munson.

Alhand John, wagon maker, r. 490 S. West.

Allaire Andrew, blacksmith, r. Clinton, bet. East and New Jersey.

Allaire James P., brickmason, r. 95 Jackson.

Allaire Peter, brickmason, r. 465 N. East.

Allbright Frank, (col'd) barber, r. 182 W. Washington.

Alleby James, veterinary surgeon, r. 92 E. New York.

Allen A. C., r 181 N. Delaware.

Allen A. W., general agent Lamb Knitting Machine 18 N. Delaware, bds. cor. Tennessee and Kentucky av.

Allen Byron, lab., r. 74 Massachusetts av.

Allen Edward, (col'd) lab., r. 173 Douglass alley.

Allen Fannie H. Miss, r. 35 N. California.

Allen George, (col'd) laborer, r. 154 Huron.

Allen George W. lab., r. 184 N. Winston.

ALLEN HENRY, livery, sale, and boarding stable, 25 and 26 E. Pearl, r. 130 W. Vermont.

Allen H. R., M. D., Indiana Surgical Institute, r. 340 N. Meridian.

Allen H. S., salesman, Trade Palace, bds. at Palmer House.

Allen Jacob, bricklayer, r. 44 Douglass.

Allen James, printer, bds. 31 W. Georgia.

Allen James R., wks. at C. C. & I. C. shop, r. 217 Mass. av.

Allen Jerome, lab., with W. P. Fishback, E. Washinton, nr. Asylum.

Allen John,(col'd) lab., r. Howard, bet. Third and Fourth.

Allen John, (col'd) lab., r. 44 Harrison.

Allen Martha Mrs., r. 134 Virginia av.

ALLEN NANA M. MRS., dress and cloak making, rooms 36½ E. Washington, bds. at Bates House.

Allen O. M., Ag't Lamb Knitting Machine, bds. at 44 S. Tennessee.

Allen Robert, machinist, r. 31 W. Georgia.

Allen T. C., operator, W. U. Tel., bds. 181 N. Delaware.

THE CHINA TEA STORES

Have the NAME of being the

MOST ATTRACTIVE STORES IN THE WEST.

No. 7 Odd Fellows Hall

AND

ACADEMY OF MUSIC CORNER.

Allen Thomas (col'd) cook at Macy House, bds. same.

Allen William, foreman Eagle Machine Works.

Allen William A., office 36½ E. Washington, bds. at Bates House.

Allen W. L., cooper, bds. 38 Hellen.

Allendorf J. H., porter, Murphy, Johnson & Co., bds. at California House.

Allison Joseph E., plasterer, r. 48 Fletcher av.

Allison Mary Mrs., r. 52 N. Pennsylvania.

Allison Robert, cl'k, 5 W. Washington, bds. 52 N. Pennsylvania.

Allison Thomas S., plasterer, bds. cor. Christian av. and Ash.

Allred Garrison W., Coroner Marion county, r. 215 W. South.

Altenburger Jacob, watchman Coffin's pork house, r. nr. same.

Altenheiner John, lab., r. 497 S. New Jersey.

Althoff Ernst, miller, Ætna Mills, bds. S. end East.

Altland Hiram, constable, r. 150 Fort Wayne av.

Altland Samuel F., carpenter, 176 E. Court, r. 179 Spring.

Altman Herman (H. A. & Co.), r. cor. Ray and Meridian.

ALTMAN HERMAN & CO. (H. A., Wm. Sogimeir & W. Meyer), groceries, saloon, and feed store, cor. Ray and Meridian.

Alto James, paper maker, r. 300 S. Missouri.

Alvey James H. (Carr & Alvey), r. 548 N. Tennessee.

Alvord E. S., pres't Citizens Street R. R. Co., r. 94 N. Pennsylvania.

Alvord James C., sec'y Citizens Street R. R. Co., office cor. Louisiana and Tennessee.

Alvord Mary Mrs. (wid. E. B.,) r. 334 N. Illinois.

Alward Samuel, with Stoneman, Pee & Co., r. 322 N. Illinois.

Amberg Charles, engineer, r. 166 N. Davidson.

Ambrose Morris, lab., I. C. & L. R. R. shops.

Ambrose S., fireman, I. C. & L. R. R.

American Leg and Arm Co., 172 E. Washington.

American Merchants Union Express Co., 42 E. Washington, J. A. Butterfield, agent.

Amicable Mutual Life Insurance Co., of New York, Mark Poore, gen. agt., 45½ E. Washington.

Amos Isaac, (Amos & Co.) r. cor. Lafayette R. R. and First.

Amos James, spinner, Geisendorff, r. 408 W. Washington.

Amos Thomas D., court house bailiff, r. 218 N. Davidson.

Amos Thomas B. (Amos & Co.) r. 218 N. Davidson.

Amos & Co. (J. Amos & T. B. Amos) plumbers and gas fitters, 21 Massachusetts av.

Amsler Fred., trunk maker, 39 S. Illinois, bds. Globe House.

Anawalt James P., tinner, with Munson & Johnston, bds. 17½ Virginia av.

Anderegg John A., conductor I. C. & L. R. R., bds. Ray House.

Anderson Archibald, (col'd) porter, 127 Meridian, r. Fatout's block.

Anderson Bell Miss, r. 186½ W. Washington.

ANDERSON, BULLOCK AND SCHOFIELD, (J. T. Anderson, J. B. Bullock, and M. N. Schofield) importers and wholesale dealers in hardware, 62 S. Meridian.

Anderson Caroline,(wid.) r. 226 E. North.

Anderson Charlotte Miss, servant, Palmer House.

Anderson Charles, carpenter, r. 28 N. New Jersey.

Anderson Chris. (col'd) cook, Sherman House.

Anderson Cynthia, (wid.) r. 177 E. Market.

Anderson David, salesman, New York store, bd's Macy House.

Anderson David S., operator P. & A. Tel., r. 333 N. Illinois.

Anderson Edward, lab., r. 16 Chadwick.

Anderson Edward, brakeman C. C. & I. C. R. R., bds. 58 Benton.

Anderson George P., real estate agent, 2 W. Washington, r. 279 E. South.

Anderson Harry, (col'd) lab, r. Huron.

Anderson Henry, clk., 102 E. Washington, bds 177 E. Market.

Anderson James, speculator, r. 177 E. Market.

Anderson James D., plasterer, r. 138 W Sixth.

Anderson James T., (A., Bullock & Schofield) r. 367 N. New Jersey.

Anderson Joseph N., clk., Browning & Sloan, bds. Pyle House.

Anderson Julia Mrs., deputy clerk U. S. Courts, r. 324 N. Alabama.

Anderson Lewis, brakeman, I. C. & L. R. R., bds. Ray House.

Anderson Martin, plasterer, r. 140 S. East.

Anderson Mrs., r. 324 N. Alabama.

Anderson Nettie, r. 191½ W. Washington.

Anderson Randolph W., carpenter, r. 435 E. Georgia.

Anderson R. J., bricklayer, r. 305 E. Washington.

Anderson Robert, saloon keeper, 191 E. Washington, r. same.

Anderson Thomas, carpenter, r. 413 N. Mississippi.

Anderson William, clk., bds. 177 E. Market.

Anderson William, clk., Western House, bds. same.

Anderson William, teamster, r. 139 W. Second.

Anderson William, conductor, C. C. & I. ' C. R. R., bds. 58 Benton.

Anderson William D., lab., bds. 366 W. Washington.

Andra John, saddle and harness maker, 178 E. Washington, r. same.

Andrew John B., eating house, 32 W. Louisiana, r. same.

Andrews Alfred A., cigar maker, bds. Illinois House.

Andrews Bub, lab., rolling mill, r. 236 S. Missouri.

Andrews James, lab., r. New York, bet. Blake and Minerva.

Andrews L. N., general freight agent I., P. & C. R. R., r. 444 N. Tennessee.

Andrew Samuel B., photograph gallery, 162½ Indiana av., r 82 Fort Wayne av.

Angle Abraham R., R. R. conductor, r. 115 Massachusetts av.

Angus Walter W., teacher, Indiana Institution for Deaf and Dumb.

Anhorn E., house and sign painter, cor. Spring and St. Clair, r. same.

Anker Aristides, (Haebl & A.) r. 182 E. Washington.

Annan Charles, book keeper, J. W. Copeland & Co., bds. Pyle House.

Ante Jacob, blacksmith, r. 426 S. Illinois.

Anthes Jacob, lab., r. 470 S. New Jersey.

Anthon William, bar tender, Washington Hall, r. 120 N. Noble.

Anthony Jacob, janitor Academy of Music, r. nr. Schmidt's brewery.

Anthony Joshua, carpenter, r. 256 Blake.

Anthony T. W., traveling salesman, Rickard & Talbott, bds. 36 W. Maryland.

Antibus John B., lab., r. 312 W. Merrill.

Antlees Hettie, (wid.) r. 373 E. Georgia.

Antrim James, draymen, E. Over & Co., r. 70 Plum.

BENHAM BRO'S,

36 East Washington St.,

AGENTS FOR THE

BURDETT ORGAN.

Antrim W. H., clk., Am. W. U. Express Co., r. 70 Plum.

Apperson Isaac H., traveling agent, r. 256 Chestnut.

Appleby Rob't, dealer in new and second hand furniture, 189 W. Washington, r. same.

Applegate A. W., traveling agent, J. C. Green, r. 175 E. Washington.

Applegate Berg., (Severin, Schnull & Co.) r. 194 E. Maryland.

Applegate Miss Eliza, seamstress, r. 18 Bates.

Arbuckle Matthew, (Witt & A.) r. N. Delaware, bet. Fourth and Tinker.

Archer Wm. R., clk. Trade Palace, bds. 285 W. Michigan.

ARDEN J., manufacturer of boots and shoes, 65 S. Meridian, r. same

ARMBRUSTER FRANK. E., saloon, 439 W. Washington, r. same.

Armbruster J. J., saloon, 215 W. Maryland, r. 79 S. West.

Arms —— Mrs. (wid.) r. 126 N. Mississippi.

Armsted James, teamster, r. 316 E. New York.

Armstrong A. R., farmer, r. Tinker, nr. canal.

Armstrong Alma H., clk., 40 S. Illinois, bds. Pyle House

Armstrong Geo., clk. Kingan's pork house, r. 162 S. Illinois.

Armstrong Henry, teamster, 24 W. Maryland, bds. 79 S. West.

Armstrong Minnie Miss, press feeder, bds. 6 N. Liberty.

Armstrong W. S. (Vinnedge, Jones & Co.) r. 180 N. Illinois.

Arnholder Henry, (A. & Brother) r. 25 S. New Jersey.

Arnholder Henry & Brother, (Henry A. & Wm. A.) saddles and harness, 225 E. Washington.

Arnholder Wm. (A. & Bro.) r. 25 S. New Jersey.

Arnold Jane, (wid.) r. 60 Michigan rd.

Arnold James W., clk., r. 143 Delaware.

Arnold Peter, lab., r. 17 N. New Jersey.

Aron Adolphus, book store, r. 54 W. New York.

Aron Chas. (Spellman & Co.) r. 189 Virginia av.

Arthur Richard, heater, rolling mill, bds. 225 S. West.

Arthur Thos., moulder, rolling mill, r. 75 Norwood.

Arthur Wm. watchman, rolling mill, r. 225 S. West.

Arthur Wm., w'ks rolling mill, r. 75 Norwood.

Artis Wm. H. (col'd) barber shop, 193 W. Washington, r. same.

Asa S., brick mason, r. 448 N. New Jersey.

Ash Frank, lab., r. 35 Bates.

Ash Mary, (wid.) r. 5 Spring.

Ash Wm., varnisher, Spiegle, Thoms & Co., r. 113 Spring.

Ashley Geo. T., foreman, stave factory, r. 402 E. Michigan.

Ashley Thos., foreman, Butsch & Dickson, r. 402 E. Michigan.

Ashmead Jacob N., miller, r. 240 N. Noble.

Ashmead John S., carpenter, r. 240 N. Noble.

Ashmead Seely W., engineer, C. C. C. & I. Rw., r. 240 N. Noble.

Ashmead Wash. S., wood and tie agent, I. & St. L. R. R., bds. 240 N. Noble.

Asmus Chas., bar keeper, 199 Indiana av., bds. same.

Asmus Fredrick, lab., r. cor. West and First.

Asmus Louis, saloon and billiard hall, 199 Indiana av., r. same.

Astan John, lab., r. 26 John.

Astley Jesse, harness maker, bds. 9 S. Mississippi.

Astley Sam'l C., drug clk, Campbell & Green, bds. 9 S. Mississippi.

Ashton Dudley, lab., bds. 9 Sharp.

ATHON JAMES S., physician and surgeon, office, McOuat's bl'k, 2d floor, r. 529 N. Meridian.

Atkins E. C. (E. C. & Co.) r. Idaho Territory.

ATKINS E. C. & CO. (E. C. A., J. H. Kappes & H. Knippenberg) props. Sheffield Saw Works, 210 to 216 S. Illinois.

Atkins Geo. R., machinist, r. 318 N. Alabama.

Atkinson Thos. J., r. 239 E. Louisiana.

Atridge Richard, carpenter, r. 333 N. Winston.

Auch Andrew, varnisher, C. C. C. & I. R. R. shops, r. 214 N. Liberty.

Aufderheide Godfrey, painter, r. 275 Davidson.

Aufderheide Henry, carpenter, r. 241 N. Davidson.

Aufderheide Jos., expressman, r. 432 E. Vermont.

Aufderheide Wm., turner, Cabinet Makers' Union, r. 235 N. Davidson.

Aughinbaugh Chas., traveling agent, bds. 28 W. Michigan.

Aughinbaugh E. L., clk., Browning & Sloan, r. 92 W. First.

Aughinbaugh Sarah, (wid.) r. 92 W. First.

Aughinbaugh Wm. M., clk., Stewart & Morgan, r. 92 W. First.

Augstein Chas., w'ks Cabinet Makers' Union, r. 344 Railroad.

Aukenbrook Henry, drayman, 38 S. Meridian, r. 351 S. Delaware.

Aukstein Chas., varnisher, r. 344 Railroad.

Ault Adam, railroader, r. 181 Meek.

Austin Albert T., with Frank A. Boyd.

Austin Berry, printer, Journal office.

Austin Geo., adjuster, Josslyn Bros. & Co., r. 129 E. Walnut.

Austin Geo. T., machinist, r. 160 E. St. Joseph.

Austin Sam'l, speculator, r. 166 N. Delaware.

Austin Lucius L., musician, bds. 137 E. St. Mary.

Austin Maggie, (wid.) r. 277 E. Georgia.

Austin Mrs., (wid.) r. 25 Gregg.

Avels Geo. driver, W. P. & E. P. Gallup.

Avels Jos., r. 75 N. Illinois.

Avels Maggie, (wid. Henry) r. 357 S. Delaware.

Averill Jos., checkman, T. H. & I. R. R. freight depot, r. 103 W. South.

Avery Jos., carpenter, r. 121 E. Ohio.

Avery I. L., treasurer Builders' and Manufacturers' Association, r. 356 N. East.

Avery J. P., physician, office, 1 Massachusetts av., r. 356 N. East.

Awalt Henry, blacksmith, r. 10 Arch.

Axum Wm., lab., r. 205 W. McCarty.

Ayres Alex. C., student at law, 24½ E. Washington, r. 2 miles e. city on Michigan road.

Ayres Annie, (wid.) r. 240 N. Meridian.

Ayers Geo. W., blacksmith, r. 139 N. Alabama.

Ayers Milton, wagon maker, r. 34 W. Ohio.

Ayers Scott, carriagesmith, bds. 34 W. Ohio.

BAAR BERNARD J., tailor, r. 170 E. Market.

Baas Christ, works T. H. & I. R. R. Depot, r. 170 Union.

Baas Henry, foreman Schmdt's brewery, r. 410 S. East.

Back Clemens, (B. & Wenken) r. 108 S. Noble.

Back John, eating house, 30 W. Louisiana, r. same.

Back & Wenken, (C. B. & E. W.) cigars and tobacco, 209 E. Washington.

Backmann Berhard, foreman at Weghorst's garden, r. same.

Backner A., book binder, bds. Globe House.

Backus J. W., clk. T. H. Freight Office, bds. Macy House.

Backstabler Charles, clk. Bryant's Drug Store, r. 72 W. South.

Backus Vick, carriage smith, Shaw, L. & Co., r. 35 W. Georgia.

Bacon E. H., physician, sw. cor. Washington and Meridian, res. room 6 Blackford's blk.

Bacon E. J. (wid.) r. 307 N. Alabama.

Bacon G., blower, glass works, bds. 164 W. Maryland.

Bacon George J., with B. F. Haugh & Co., r. 307 N. Alabama.

Bacon John L., blacksmith, 74 S. Pennsylvania, r. 307 N. Alabama.

Bacon R. B., with O. T. Porter, r. 75 N. Pennsylvania.

Bacon R. D., painter, bds. 75 N. Pennsylvania.

Bacon T. L., chief clk. U. S. Arsenal.

Bacon William, paper hanger, r. 174 E. North.

Bacon William, toll gate keeper, Fall Creek Bridge.

Bade Austin, lab., r. 209 S. Alabama.

Baggett Patrick, lab., r. 113 N. West.

Baggs Elizabeth, Mrs. (wid. William) r. 71 E. McCarty.

Baggs Frederick, book keeper, 108 S. Meridian, r. 125 E. Ohio.

Bagle Alex., cabinet maker, bde. Concordia House.

Babler Albert, salesman, r. 36 N. Pennsylvania.

Bailey Eveline, widow, r. 22 Bates.

Bailey Hamilton, lab., r. 348 W. Washington.

Bailey John, baggage master, P. C. & St. L. R. R.

Bailey Martha, domestic, Blind Institute.

Bailey Robert, lab., r. 50 Fletcher av.

Bainbridge Mahlon S., plasterer and boarding house, r. 248 E. Louisiana.

Bair George, shoe maker, 361 S. Delaware, r. same.

Baird John W., plasterer, bds. 112 N. Pennsylvania.

Baird William, cooper shop, cor. Maryland and Helen, r. 112 N. Pennsylvania.

BENHAM BRO'S,

35 East Washington St.,

SHEET MUSIC, VIOLINS,

GUITARS, STRINGS, &c.

Bakemeier Frederick, drayman, r. 235 Union.

Bakemeier Mrs. Mary, r. 419 Virginia av.

Baker Mrs. A., milliner, 194 E. Washington, r. same.

Baker A. H., r. 228 E. South.

Baker A. R., printer, H. C. Chandler, bds. 144 N. Tennessee.

Baker Abraham H., (B. & Surbey) r. 228 E. South.

Baker Alexander, book binder, W. & J. Braden.

BAKER BERTHA MRS., millinery, 244 E. Washington, r. same.

Baker Catharine, (wid.) r. cor. Illinois and Walnut.

Baker Charles, saloon and wholesale dealer in Madison Ale, 209 Massachusetts av., r. same.

BAKER CONRAD, Governor State of Indiana, office State House, r. 173 N. Tennessee.

Baker E., printer, H. C. Chandler, bds. 17½ Virginia av.

Baker Miss E. C., millinery and fancy goods, 194 E. Washington, r. same.

Baker Frederick, plasterer, r. cor. Walnut and Illinois.

Baker Henry, blacksmith, 74 S. Pennsylvania, r. 203 N. Illinois.

BAKER JAS. M., hats and caps, 194 E. Washington, r. same.

Baker James P., attorney at law, 45 E. Washington, bds. 343 N. Illinois.

BAKER JESSE A., musician, r. 244 E. Washington.

Baker J., machinist, r. 194 E. McCarty.

Baker Myra Miss, teacher, r. sw. cor. New York and East.

BAKER NATHAN S., manufacturer and dealer in mattresses, etc., 73 E. Washington, r. 203 N. Noble.

BAKER O. F. (Perkins B. & Perkins) attorneys, office 4 Ætna Bldg., r. 148 N. East.

Baker S. W., salesman Trade Palace, r. 67 W. New York.

Baker Mrs. Sarah E., boarding house, r. 392 N. Alabama.

Baker & Surbey, (Abraham H. Baker & Jacob S. Surbey) grocers, 199 Virginia av.

Baker Thomas M., tailor, r. 64 Oak.

THE CHINA TEA STORES

ARE LOCATED AT

No. 7 ODD FELLOWS HALL

AND

ACADEMY OF MUSIC CORNER.

SAME GOODS, SAME PRICES at BOTH.

Baker Winfield S., hose driver fire department.

Baldus John, saloon, 294 E. Washington, r. same.

Baldus John P., barkeeper, 294 E. Washington, r. same.

Baldwin Benjamin, engineer, C. C. & I. C. R. R., r. 301 E. Georgia.

Baldwin J. H. (J. H. B. & Co.) r. 400 N. Meridian.

Baldwin J. L., confectionery, 56 N. Illinois, r. same.

Baldwin J. P., fireman, I. C. & L. R. R., r. 323 Virginia av.

BALDWIN J. H. & CO. (J. H. B. & George S. Warren) Fancy Bazar, 6 E. Washington.

Baldwin Z. T., clk., 56 N. Illinois, bds. same.

Dalfe Vitelia Mrs., with Wm. Sumner & Co., r. 415 S. East.

Balke Charles, saloon and billiards, 231 E. Washington, r. same.

Ball William, carpenter, r. 135 W. Maryland.

Ballard A., seal engraver, 28 Circle, r. same.

Ballard G. M., Land Receiver, office in P. O. bldg., r. 356 N. Alabama.

Ballard Samuel, boarding house, 70 E. Market.

Ballard William, boot maker, bds. 18 S. Pennsylvania.

Ballard William, contractor and builder, r. 188 N. Tennessee.

Ballinger Elijah M., carpenter, r. 161 E. St. Mary.

Ballman J. H, grainer, 21 S. Meridian.

BALLS ANTHONY, bread and cracker bakery, and confectioner, wholesale and retail, 178 S. Illinois, r. same.

BALLWEG AMBROSE, manufacturer and dealer in guns and pistol, 129 W. Washington, r. 26 Ft. Wayne av.

Ballweg Frederick, saloon, 131 W. Washington, r. same.

Bals Charles H. G. (Hahn & B.) r. 110 E. St. Joseph.

Balser Miss Fannie, dress maker, 44 S. Illinois.

Balz Peter, (Sponsel & B.) Union Beer Brewery, r. Madison Road, S. of city.

Balz Philip, meat market, 427 N. Illinois, r. same.

Balzer George, machinist, r. 141 E. St. Mary.

Bamberger David, carpenter, r. 287 Indiana av.

BAMBERGER HERMAN, hats, caps, and furs, 16 E. Washington, r. 1 Ft. Wayne av.

Bamberger Isaac, salesman, H. Bamberger, bds. Circle Restaurant.

Bamberger Jacob E. (Rau & B.) r. 287 Indiana av.

Banen Mathew, blacksmith Eagle Foundry, bds. Illinois House.

Banghart Watson, welldigger and whitewasher, r. 779 N. Mississippi.

Bannworth Benjamin, boot and shoe maker, r. 36 Massachusetts av.

Banna Martin, blacksmith, Eagle Machine Works.

Barbee Robert B., policeman First District, r. 285 N. East.

Barbee Sampson, r. 291 N. Alabama.

Barbee Sampson, jr., moulder, r. 32 Dougherty.

Barber Edward H., carpenter, r. 75 Elizabeth.

Barber James H. (col'd) lab., r. 344 Indiana av.

Barber Walker, (col'd) lab., r. 344 Indiana av.

BARBOUR & JACOBS, (Lucien B. & Charles J.) attorneys at law, 14 N. Delaware.

Barbour Lucien, (B. & Jacobs) r. N. Meridian, cor. Fifth.

Barbour Samuel, r. 216 N. West.

Barclay James, stone cutter, r. 204 E. Market.

Bare Aldun, works Rolling Mill, bds. 77 W. McCarty.

Bare, Duncan, harness maker, bds. 52 N. Pennsylvania.

Barfugg G., watch maker, 79 S. Illinois, r. same.

Barker Catharine, dress maker, 17 Massachusetts av., r. same.

Parker Samuel, meat market, Pennsylvania, r. 210 E. St. Clair.

Barkes Sarah Mrs. (wid. William) boarding house, 9 S. Mississippi.

Barkley George B., student, bds. 75 N. California.

Barlow Abigal Mrs. (col'd) wash-woman, rear 141 W. Washington.

BARLOW THOMAS J., prop'r Opera saloon, 79 E. Washington, r. 84 S. Mississippi.

Barlow W. H., baggage master C. C. C. & I. R. R.

Barmfuehrer Chris., lab., r. Michigan rd.

Barmeir B., clk, C. Vonnegut, bds. Emmeneger's Hotel.

Barnard Eugene E., salesman, Murphy, Johnson & Co., r. 35 Cherry.

Barnard J., gen'l insurance agent, and sec'y Chamber of Commerce, r. 419 N. Illinois.

Barnard Mosee R., traveling agent, r. 35 Cherry.

Barneclo Henry H., railroader, r. 53 Bates.

Barneclo Lorenzo, machinist, r. 156 S. Noble.

Barneclo Rebecca, (wid.) r. 53 Bates.

Barneclo William, fireman C. C. & I. C. R. R., bds. 53 Bates.

Barnes A. A., (B. & Williams) r. 782 N. Illinois.

Barnes A. M., printer Journal office, bds. 98 N. East.

Barnes Daniel, blacksmith, r. 348 S. Meridian.

Barnes Edward, lab., r. cor. Grant and Eckert.

Barnes George H., carpenter, r. 328 N. Winston.

Barnes Jerome, cooper, r. 141 N. Blake.

BARNES R. H., M. D., office 62 Virginia av., r. same.

Barnes Mrs., (wid.) r. 52 S. Pennsylvania.

Barnes Wesley N., printer, News office, r. 142 N. Mississippi.

Barnes William, trav. ag't, r. cor. South and Virginia av.

Barnes & Williams, (A. A. B. & E. H. W.) produce and commission merchants, 26 N. Illinois.

Barnet Edward, lab., w'ks for Greenleaf & Co.

Barnet Francis, cooper, r. 19 S. Mississippi.

Barnett Thomas, sen., watchman city fire tower, r. 390 N. Mississippi.

Barnett Thomas, jr., railroader, r. 217 N. Mississippi.

Barney C., printer, Sentinel office, r. 26 Fletcher av.

Barney Ellen, r. 203 W. McCarty.

Barney Frederick, works with Jackson, Rider & Co.

Barney Jacob, physician, r. 245 N. Davidson.

Barnitz Charles, real estate, 115 E. Washington, r. 177 S. Noble.

Barnitz J. W., taxidermist, 115 E. Washington, r. 177 S. Noble.

Barr Jacob, carpenter, r. 424 N. Delaware.

Barr Lorenzo D., inspector, rolling mill, r. 233 S. Tennessee.

Barr William, lab., bds. 16 Oak.

Barrett E. G., solicitor, Evening News, r. 123 Huron.

Barrett James, laborer, r. 54 Bicking.

Barrett Joseph, (col'd) porter with L. Q. Sherwood, r. 156 Douglass alley.

Barrett Michael, r. 232 W. Georgia.

Barrett Solomon, wood turner, r. 270 S. Delaware.

Barrett Pat., lab., r. 174 Meek.

Barrett Patrick, lab., r. 31 Bradshaw.

Barrow Samuel, with G. W. Caldwell & Co., bds. 169 S. Tennessee.

Barrous H. W., foreman Chandler & Taylor, r. 293 W. Vermont.

Barry Edward H., grand sec'y I. O. O. F., office No. 2 Odd Fellows' Hall, r. 528 N. Tennessee.

Barry Charles L., clk, Stewart & Morgan, bds. 528 N. Tennessee.

Barry John, lab., r. 145 Huron.

Barry Thomas G., druggist, r. 197 N. Delaware.

Barth Charles, salesman, 29 W. Washington, r. 387 N. West.

Barth Jacob, with Bowen, Stewart & Co., r. 387 N. West.

Barth John W., salesman, 21 W. Washington, r. 387 N. West.

Barth L. A., prop'r Union Depot news stand, r. 233 Virginia av.

Barth Sebastian, Rev. pastor German Reformed Church, r. 387 N. West.

Bartholomew Eugene, boot maker, 65 S. Meridian, bds. Naegle House.

Bartholomew Thomas, cooper, r. 89 S. Liberty.

BARTHOLOMEW W. P., attorney, 20½ N. Delaware, room 1, bds. Bates House.

Bartlett Alice, (wid.) r. 335 N. New Jersey.

Bartlett Arthur, clk, 76 W. Washington.

Bartlett Bernard G., foreman cement pipe works, r. 277 Indiana av.

Bartlett Harrison, (col'd) porter, 399 N. Illinois.

Bartlett John A., carpenter, r. 777 N. Missouri.

Bartlett Joseph, w'ks at rolling mill, bds at Union House.

Bartlett Thornton, (col'd) lab., bds. at 158 Douglass alley.

Bartlett, Richard, (col'd) lab., r. 164 Douglass alley.

Barton Bridget Miss, servant, Spencer House.

Barton Kate Miss, waiter, Spencer House.

Basn A. H., engineer, 74 S. Pennsylvania, r. 76 E. Elm.

Basdoerfer George, groceries and produce, 546 E. Washington, r. same.

Base Christian, carpenter, r. 297 E. Georgia.

Base Henry, carpenter, r. 297 E. Georgia.

Base Henry, lab., r. Union.

Basey A. H., machinist, r. 79 Elm.

Basey Ellen Mrs., (wid. Gotleib) r. 267 N. Liberty.

Baskit John, (col' d, B. & Reed) 10 S. Pennsylvania.

Baskit & Reed, (John Baskit and J. Reed) barbers and hair dressers, 10 S. Pennsylvania.

Bass Geo. W., salesman, bds. 168 N. East.

Bass Geo. W. (col'd) barber, r. al. bet. West and canal.

Bass John, drayman, r. 146 Union.

Bass Josiah, (B. & Henderson) r 168 N. East.

Bass & Henderson (J. B. & J. W. H.), grocers, 143 and 145 N. Delaware.

Bassett H. A., clk, Frank Smith, r. 48 E. Ohio.

Bastor Edward, carpenter, r. 187 N. Davidson.

Bates Caroline, (col'd, wid. Atkins) r. 143 Bright.

Bates Chas., machinist, bds. 217 S. Illinois.

Bates Chas., machinist, w'ks rolling mill, bds. 169 S. Tennessee.

Bates David, moulder, Eagle Machine Works, r. 143 S. New Jersey.

Bates G. H., civil engineer, r. 232 E. Louisiana.

Bates Harvey, sr., r. 190 E. Market.

Bates Harvey, jr., ass't cashier, First National Bank, r. 185 N. Delaware.

BATES HOUSE, nw. cor. Washington and Illinois, C. W. Wesley & Son, props.

Batey Elizabeth Mrs. (wid. Abraham) r. 4 Catharine.

Batty Edwin, carpenter, r. 124 Broadway.

Batty John, slate roofer, bds. Illinois House.

Batty John A., deputy recorder, r. cor. Christian av. and Ash.

Batz Wm., blacksmith, r. 431 S. Meridian.

Baugher F. W., traveling salesman, 125 S. Meridian, bds. Ft. Wayne av.

Bauke John Henry, carpenter, r. 506 E. Georgia.

Baumass Henry, tailor, r. 237 N. Liberty.

Baumhofer Henry, carpenter and builder, r. 236 Chestnut.

Bauer Barbra Mrs., r. 300 W. Maryland.

Bauer Frank, lab., r. Lock.

Bauer Fredrick, w'ks paper mill, bds. 300 W. Maryland.

Bauer Geo., messenger Mansur's bank, r. 77 N. Illinois.

Bauer Gottleib, tailor, r. 30 Water.

Bauer Henry, cabinet maker, r. 68 E. Market.

Bauer Jacob, lab., r. 277 James.

BAUER JACOB, confectionery and eating house, 147 W. Washington, r. same.

Bauers John, engineer, r. 197 E. Washington, up stairs.

Baur Adolph, foreman Guttenberg Printing Co., r. 87 N. Noble.

Bauscher B. L., engineer, Spiegel & Thoms, r. 326 N. East.

Baxter & Davis, (Peter B. & A. E. D.) grocers and produce dealers, 250 W. Washington.

Baxter Geo., clk., 250 W. Washington, r. 197 W. Maryland.

Baxter Peter D. (B. & Davis) r. 250 W. Washington.

Baxter Wm. (col'd) r. Howard, bet. Third and Fourth.

Bayless G. B., printer, Sentinel office, bds. Little's Hotel.

Baylor Albert E., salesman Paris Store, r. 3 Odd Fellows' Hall.

Baylor Rachael M. (wid. James), r. 68 Plum.

Baymiller Parthena, (wid.) r. 77 Lockerbie.

Baz Jacob, shoemaker, r. 274 S. Delaware.

Beach Gaylor B., contractor, 331 N. Alabama.

Beal Joshua, paper hanger, r. 77 W. Walnut.

Beall John W., meat market, 306 W. Washington, r. same.

Beals Jerome, traveling agent, John Sweetser, r. 21 S. Pennsylvania.

Beam David, (Emerson B. & Thompson) r. 187 S. Tennessee.

Beam Dessie Miss, r. 187 S. Tennessee.

Beam J. F., agent Security Life Insurance Co., bds. 73 W. Maryland.

Beanbun Geo., salesman, Domestic Sewing Machine Co.

Beard Amos, wagon maker, w'ks Indianapolis Wagon and Agricultural Works, r. 443 S. Illinois.

Beard B. F., plow stocker, bds. 69 W. Market.

Beard David H., blacksmith, bds. 69 W. Market.

Beard House, 69 W. Market, Sol Beard, prop.

Beard S. (B. & Kimball) r. 69 W. Market.

Beard Wm., cooper shop, W. Maryland, r. 212 N. Pennsylvania.

Beard & Kimball, (S. F. & N. K.) plow manufactory, S. Tennessee, nr. N. Kentucky av.

Beardsley H. M, book keeper, R. E. Beardsley, bds. 125 E. North.

BEARDSLEY R. E., gen'l insurance agent, 11 N. Meridian, r. 125 E. North.

Beasley Thos., shoe maker, 137 N. Tenesssee, r. Benton.

Beatton Mrs. Mary, r. 773 Madison av.

Beaty David S., r. 194 E. Michigan.

Beaver E., teamster, r. 380 N. West.

Beaver Charlotte Mrs. (wid. Thos.) r. 217 Massachusetts av.

Beaver Catharine Miss, w'ks Capitol Tobacco Works, bds. 259 E. McCarty.

Beaver Geo., machinist, r. 114 W. Georgia.

Beaver Isaiah, book binder, bds. 380 N. West.

Beaver John, teamster, r. 259 E. McCarty.

Beaver Leon, draughtsman, Isaac Hodgeson, cor. Washington and Pennsylvania, bds. Pyle House.

Beaver Leonard, moulder, bds. 217 S. Illinois.

Beaver Maggie Miss, bds. 380 N. West.

Beck A. T., attorney, 20½ N. Delaware, room 6, r. 152 N. Mississippi.

Beck Christian, lab., bds. 122 S. Noble.

BECK CHRISTIAN, gunsmith, 12 S. Pennsylvania, r. 154 N. New Jersey.

Beck David, teamster, bds. 154 N. New Jersey.

BECK EDWARD, prop., Crystal Palace saloon and restaurant, r. 27 W. Maryland.

Beck Elizabeth Mrs., r. 294 Chestnut.

Beck Fredrick, meat market, cor. McCarty and Meridian, r. same.

Beck Henrietta Miss, r. 294 Chestnut.

Beck Harry, baker, r. 88 Ft. Wayne av.

Beck Hubert, lab., r. 126 Union.

Beck Isaac, express messenger, r. 293 Virginia av.

Beck Israel, attorney at law, r. 452 E. Market.

Beck James A., stone cutter, bds. 103 W. South.

Beck Jos. W., clk., 40 S. Meridian, r. 152 N. Mississippi.

Beck Miss Sarah, teacher, First Ward school, r. 154 N. New Jersey.

BECK SAMUEL, gunsmith, 63 E. Washington, r. 152 N. Mississippi.

BENHAM BRO'S,
36 East Washington St.,
STATE AGENTS
FOR THE
INDIANAPOLIS MANUFACTURING CO.'S
PIANOS.

Beck Wm., lab., r. 65 Dacota.

Becker August, tailor, bds. 65 S. East.

BECKER BROS. (F. P. B. & Jos. B.) confectioneries and ladies' restaurant, 17 N. Pennsylvania.

Becker F. P. (Becker F. P. & Bro.) 17 N. Pennsylvania.

BECKER & HUBER, (Jacob B. & Jacob H.) merchant tailors, 77 E. Washington.

Becker Jacob, (Becker & H.) r. 180 N. Jersey.

Becker Jas. cigar maker, 36 Virginia av., r. 176 S. Delaware.

Becker Jos. (Becker F. P. & Co.) 17 N. Pennsylvania, r. same.

Beckett Andrew, machinist, C. C. & I. C. R. R., r. 370 E. New York.

Beckett John, baggage master, I. P. & C. R. R., bds. Spencer House.

Beckett Theophilus M., engineer C. C. & I. C. R. R., r. 473 E. Georgia.

Beckler Jas. S., huckster, r. 554 S. Meridian.

Beckler Mollie C. Miss, dress maker, bds. 554 S. Meridian.

Beckler Sallie A. Miss, dress maker, bds. 554 S. Meridian.

Beckley John, lab., r. 516 S. Illinois.

Beckman Christina Mrs., r. 332 S. Alabama.

Beckman Hester, (wid. Wm.) r. 408 W. North.

Beckmann John W., die sinker and engraver, 29 S. Delaware, r. same.

Beckwith Frank, (col'd) lab., r. cor. Vine and Jackson.

Beckwith Jos, baggage master, I. P. & C. R. R.

Beeber Geo. P., carpenter and builder, r. 33 Meek.

Beeler John, dyer, Merritt & Coughlin, bds. 19 S. Meridian.

Beeler Josephine Miss, dress maker, r. 116 S. Meridian.

Beeler L. D., carpenter, r. 181 S. Tennessee.

Beerbouer E. J., upholsterer, r. 19 Biddel.

Beerman Henry, lab., r. 271 E. McCarty.

Beerman Trumen, carpenter, r. 262 N. East.

Behm C., cigar maker, 36 Virginia av., r. 246 Noble.

THE CHINA TEA STORES

Are very handsomely decorated with

Accurate Views and Scenes

or

CHINESE LIFE AND SCENERY.

Call and see them before leaving the City.

Behm Ferdinand, school teacher, 477 E. Market.

Behnear Mary Mrs. r. 211 E. Market

Behrens August, instructor of gymnastics, bds. at Emmenegger's Hotel.

BEHRINGER JOSEPH, saloon, 145 W. Washington, r. same.

Behymer Simeon, lumber dealer, r. 247, N. New Jersey.

Beiler J. L. (Fruaer B. & Co.) r. 264 E. McCarty.

Beilery Frederick, cabinet maker, bds. at 252 E. Washington.

Beiser Aug., r. E. Court, nr. East.

BEISER AUGUST, wholesale liquor dealer, 106 S. Illinois, r. Washington. bet. New Jersey and East.

Beiter Matthias, machinist, 71 S. Liberty.

Bell Alfred R., printer, w'ks News office, r. 384 W. North.

Bell Andrew, (col'd) shoe maker, r. 345 N. Alabama.

Bell C. H., r. 29 W. Georgia.

Bell Guido, physician, 19 N. East, r. same.

Bell James B., prop'r Pattison House, 53 N. Alabama.

Bell John, (B. & Webb) r. 14 Elizabeth.

Bell John, marble cutter, 66 Virginia av. bds. 17 Kentucky av.

Bell Miletus, druggist and apothecary, 261 Massachusetts av., r. 484 N. East.

Bell Samuel, P., C. & St. L. R. R., bds. at 426 S. Tennessee.

Bell Samuel, switcher C., C. & I. C. R. R., bds. 61 S. Noble.

Bell William, bricklayer, bds. 29 Chatham.

Bell William, expressman, r. 248 Blackford.

Bell William, (col'd) barber, Hill & Carter.

Bell & Webb, (J. B. & J. W. W.) flour and feed, 78 Mass av.

Bellis John R., fireman, engine house No. 3, bds. at Ray House.

Beltz Harry A., news dealer, cigars and tobacco, Spencer House, r. 175 Stevens.

Beltz Jacob, plasterer, r. 175 Stevenson.

Belzer George, machinist, Eagle Machine Works, r. 141 E. St. Mary.

Benagel Mary, (wid.) r. Wabash, bet. Liberty and Noble.

Bence Robert F., physician, r. 86 Ash.

Bender George A., Cabinet Makers' Union, r. 180 Massachusetts av.

Bender J. G., clk, 54 S. Meridian, bds. 180 N. Illinois.

Bender Tobias, (Bender T. & Co.,) r. 292 E. Market.

BENDER TOBIAS & CO., (Tobias Bender, John V. Cook, and John B. Stumph) wines and liquors, foreign and domestic, 189 E. Washington.

Beneker Frederick, lab., r. 496 S. East.

Benham Azel M., (Benham Bros.) r. 235 E. Vermont.

Benham H. L., (Benham Bros.) r. sw. cor. East and Vermont.

BENHAM BROTHERS, (A. M. B, & H. L. B.) wholesale and retail dealers in music, pianos, organs, and all musical instruments, 36 E. Washington.

Bennard Charles, expressman, r. 583 Maple.

Benner Arthur, porter, Wiles, Bro. & Co., r. 430 S. Tennessee.

Bennerscheidt August, machinist, r. 309 S. Pennsylvania.

Bennerschut Carle, machinist, r. 219 Alabama.

Bennett G. W., day police, r. 286 E. St. Clair.

Bennett Henry W., pattern maker, r. 23 Chatham.

BENNETT P. S., physician, office 33 Virginia av., r. 449 N. New Jersey.

Bennett William H., r. 431 N. Meridian.

Bensel George, lab., r. 282 N. Winston.

Benson David S., dealer in clothing and furniture, 206 S. Illinois, r. same.

Benson John A., toll collector, White river bridge, r. 391 W. Washington.

Benson John S., Sup't State Fair, r. 61 Fort Wayne av.

Benson Michael, dealer in rags and old iron, 412 S. Meridian, r. same.

Benson Richard, carriage wood workman, 181 St. Joseph.

Benster S. S., machinist, Josselyn Bros., bds. Pyle House.

Bently John H., peddler, Johnson & Co., r. 139 Huron.

Beohning William, lab., r. 168 S. Noble.

Bepley Frederick, lab., bds. 310 W. Washington.

Berauer Benedict, tailor, r. 50 Coburn.

Bercherd Amos, merchant, r. 75 E. Michigan.

Berendes Joseph, varnisher, 8 S. Tennessee, r. same.

Berg F. (wid.) r. 171 E. South.

Berg George L., gold penmaker, bds. at Little House.

Berg George F., pressman, Journal office, r. 171 E. South.

Berg Gustave, varnisher, piano factory, r. 171 E. South.

Berg Henry, (Berg & Waterman) r. 193 S. Tennessee.

Berg John, lab., bds. 112 Dakota.

Berg Martin, soap factory, r. 112 Dakota.

Berg William, hose reel driver, No. 3 Engine House, r. 22½ S. Alabama.

Berg & Waterman, (H. L. B. & Chris. W.) groceries and produce, 193 S. Tennessee.

Bergener Charles, cigar maker, r. 31 Chatham.

Bergener Gustave, clk, Fletcher & Sharpe.

Berger Frederick, book keeper, 29 W. Washington, bds. 285 N. Illinois.

Bergstein Carl, professor of music, 11 Martindale's block, r. 69 N. Alabama.

Bergundthal Charles, salesman, E. Over & Co., r. 267, S. New Jersey.

Bergundthal D. C., book keeper, E. Over & Co., r. 267 S. New Jersey.

Bering Albert, cigar maker, bds. Emennegger's Hotel.

Beringer John, expressman, r. 576 E. St. Clair.

Berkhofer George, show case maker, No. 5 Virginia av., r. 92 S. Liberty.

Berkhofer Louise Mrs., r. 92 S. Liberty.

Bernard Joseph, teamster, r. 132 Huron.

Berner Charles, lab., r. 248 Blake.

Berner Frederick, machinist, r. 373 S. Illinois.

Berner Henry, butcher, bds. 323 W. Washington.

Berner John, express wagon, r. 185 N. Davidson.

Bernet Andrew, peddler, r. 115 W. McCarty.

Bernhammer William, plasterer, r. 284 N. West.

Bernhard Ernst, clk, 397 S. Meridian, bds. same.

Bernhard John, teamster for Philip Dohn, 246 S. Meridian, bd. same.

Bernhard John, stone mason, r. 355 Spring.

Bernhard William, works Jackson, Rider & Co.

Bernhard William, porter, 52 S. Meridian.

Bernhardt William, r. 126 Hosbrook.

Bernhardt Zahm, engineer, C. C. & I. C. R. R., r. 113 S. Benton.

BERNHAMER WILL. F. A., (German) attorney and notary, over 83 E. Washington, bds. 174 W. New York.

Berring William, lab., r. 474 E. Washington.

BENHAM BRO'S,

36 East Washington St.,

PUBLISHERS OF

BENHAM'S MUSICAL REVIEW,

MONTHLY, $1.00 PER ANNUM.

Berry Casper B., bricklayer, r. 245 N. Liberty.

Berry Charles H., boot and shoe dealer, r 307 Indiana av.

Berry D. M. (Elliott & B.) r. 314 N. East.

Berry Daniel M., shoe shop, 199 Indiana av., r. same.

Berry Geo., lab., r. 320 E. Washington.

Berry John, w'ks Jackson, Rider & Co,

Berry Marion, (B. & Flathers) r. 337 Virginia av.

Berry Mary, (wid. Edward) r. E. St. Clair, cor. Peru R. R.

Berry Michael, stone cutter, r. 136 Spring.

Berry Thos., w'ks rolling mill, bds. 256 S. Tennessee.

Berry & Flathers, (M. Berry & J. D. Flathers) carpenters and builders, 36 S. Pennsylvania.

Berryman John, blacksmith and wagon maker, 88 S. Noble.

Berryman Wm. H., cooper, 308 E. Louisiana.

Bertelsman Frederick, watch maker, 93 E. Washington, bds. 108 E. Washington.

Bertelsman Lizzie, (wid. Henry) r. 264 Massachusetts av.

Bese Christian, carpenter, r. 279 E. Georgia.

BESE ERNST, boarding house, 65 S. East.

Bese Fred, R. R. lab., r. 334 E. Vermont.

Besemagel Chas., stone cutter, Smith, Ettenbach & Co., r. Wabash al., bet. Market and Ohio.

Besking Christian, r. 136 Huron.

Besking Chas., jr., lab., r. 150 Huron.

BESS WM. K., saloon, and liquor dealer, 284 W. Washington, r. same.

BESSONIES AUGUST, REV., pastor St. John's Catholic church, r. nr. church.

Best John F., basket maker, r. 46 Michigan road.

Betz Bernard, w'ks rolling mill, r. 232 S. Tennessee.

Betz Wm., blacksmith, r. 431 S. Meridian.

Beyschlag Carl, editor Daily Telegraph, and Zukunft, r. 227 S. Delaware.

Beyschlag Chas., jr., clk., H. H. Lee, bds. 227 S. Delaware.

Bickley Amos, blacksmith, r. 260 S. Missouri.

Biden E. E. (wid.) dressmaker, 30 N. East, r. same.

Biddle Stephen V., piano teacher, r. 38 S. Illinois.

Biddy Jas. M., w'ks rolling mill, r. 576 S. Illinois.

BIEDENMEISTER C. A., fire and life insurance agent, 139 E. Washington, r. 149 N. East.

Bieler Jas. L. (Frauer, B. & Co.) r. McCarty, e. of East.

Bieler John A., r. 145 W. Washington.

Bigelow Coal and Mining Co., cor. Tennessee and South.

Bigelow Herbert N., Deputy U. S. Marshal, r. 161 Massachusetts av.

Bigelow Isaac, plasterer, r. 141 N. New Jersey.

Bigelow J. K. (Todd & Bigelow) r. 123 W. New York.

Bigelow I. L., Deputy U. S. Marshal, r. 161 Massachusetts av.

Bigelow John, plasterer, r. Clinton, nr. New Jersey.

Bigger Samuel, clk., Trade Palace, r. 311 S. Delaware.

Bigham H. S., Wm. Love & Co., r. 510 E. Washington.

Bilger Jos., carpenter, r. 332 E. New York.

Billing Andrew, machinist, r. 136 S. East.

Billings, F. M., adjuster, Grover & Baker Sewing Machine Co., bds. 52 N. Pennsylvania.

BILLS J. M., attorney at law, Parker's bl'k, N. Delaware, r. 22 Lockerbie.

Brigham Chas. E., sup't, Braden & Co., r. 121 W. New York.

Dingham James, stone cutter, r. 44 Mud.

BINGHAM JOSEPH J., editor Indiana State Sentinel, r. 148 W. Maryland.

BINGHAM JOSEPH W., news editor, Sentinel, bds. 148 W. Maryland.

BINGHAM W. P., watches and jewelry, 50 E. Washington, r. 52 California.

Binkley Benjamin R., machinist, bds. 169 S. Tennessee.

Binkley Wm., butcher, bds. 210 E. St Clair.

Binsack Wm., painter, r. Wabash, bet. Liberty and Noble.

Birch Geo., lab., r. 197 E. Washington, up stairs.

Birch John, railroader, bds. 27 Hahn.

Birch Richard E., steamboat captain, r. 112 Broadway.

Birchard Alvin, r. 283 W. Michigan.

Birchwood Chas., broom maker, bds. cor. East and Cherry.

Bird Abram, r. 129 N. Illinois.

Bird Frank, clk, Evening News, bds. 129 N. Illinois.

Bird Frank, engineer, bds. 280 Chestnut.

Bird Henry, (col'd) barber, bds. 75 W. Georgia.

Bird Jas., spoke turner, r. 280 Chestnut.

Bird John C., carpenter, r. 72 Fayette.

Bird Mary, (wid. Patrick) r. 408 W. North.

Bird Wm. H., clk., auditor's office, I. & St. Louis R. R., r. 121 N. Illinois.

Birdsley R. A., insurance agent, r. 125 E. North.

Bisbee Thos. A., machinist, Central R. R., bds. 149 S. New Jersey.

Bisbing Jacob J., marshal, Union Depot., r. 212 N. West.

Bisbing Wm., carpenter, r. cor. St. Clair and Ft. Wayne av.

Bishop Geo. M., engineer. steam fire engine No. 1, r. 37 S. West.

BISHOP JAMES L, gen'l solicitor and compiler city directories, 16½ E. Washington, bds. 143 W. Washington.

Bishop J. W., engineer, r. 25½ Massachusetts av.

Bishop Maria, (wid. Mitchell) r. 291 Douglass al.

Bishop Sarah, (wid.) r. 393 N. New Jersey.

Bishop Wm. A Y., lab., rolling mill, r 395 S. Missouri.

Bisking Henry C., lab., w'ks Coburn & Jones, r. 140 Huron.

Bisplinghoff Herman, saloon keeper, r. 71 Wyoming.

Bixby Frank L., student, bds. 166 E. Market.

Bixler John, rope maker, r. Agnes, w. end New York.

Bjornholdt Frank, sheet iron works, r. 39 Bradshaw.

Black C. C., engineer, I. C. & L. R. R., r. 15 Lord.

Black Catharine, (wid. Geo.) bds. 217 S. Illinois.

Black Charles H., carriage smith, Shaw I. & C., r. 368 E. New York.

Black Elbridge G., w'ks Osgood, Smith & Co, bds. 390 N. West.

BLACK G. H., carpenter, r. 368 E. New York.

Black J. S., professor music, office 35½ E. Washington, r. 219 E. North.

BLACK JAMES B., reporter Supreme Court, office in State bld'g, bds. Palmer House.

Black Jerry, (col'd) lab., r. Blake, S. of Indiana av.

Black John H., Union express office, r. 168 N. Winston.

Black Lizzie Miss, servant, 217 S. Illinois.

Black R., shipping clerk 42 W. Louisiana, bds. California House.

Black Richard A., law student, bds. 126 E. Ohio.

Black Susan Miss, servant, 217 S. Illinois.

Black Thomas S, Union express office, r. 168 N. Winston.

Black William M., janitor, Masonic Hall, r. 168 N. Winston.

Blackburn George W., barber, r. 325 E. Washington.

Blackburn Reuben, (col'd) lab., r. 113 W. North.

Blackman Joseph, wood yard, cor. Pennsylvania and Maryland, r. 548 Virginia av.

Blackman Joseph, lab., 458 Virginia av.

Blackmer H. J., with Case & Parker, r. 600 N. Illinois.

Blackwell Thomas, works rolling mill, r. 129 Maple.

Blaegh William, r. 80 Elm.

Blaetner John, blacksmith, r. 284 E. Louisiana.

Blaich Gottlieb F, lab., r. 296 N. Noble.

Blain Thomas, machinist, bds. 175 W. New York.

Blain Thomas S. sen., moulder Eagle Machine Works, r. 175 W. New York.

Blain William, machinist, bds. 175 W. New York.

Blair James M., collar maker, r. 62 S. West.

Blair Joseph M., adv. agent Masonic Home Advocate, bds. 49 Indiana av.

Blair P. A. Mrs. (wid. F. M.) r. 49 Indiana av. cor. New York.

Blair Solomon, Judge Court Common Pleas, r. 254 N. East.

Blake Albert E., bus conductor Bates House, bds. same.

Blake Augustus, works rolling mill, bds. 15 Willard.

Blake F. R., watchman starch factory, r. 22½ N. Noble.

Blake Fred., bus driver, Bates House.

Blake Harrison, works rolling mill, r. 15 Willard.

Blake John G., clk. W. U. Telegraph Co., bds. 308 N. Tennessee.

BENHAM BRO'S,

36 East Washington St.,

Pianos, Organs and Melodeons Tuned, Moved and Repaired.

Blake J. R., clk. P. O., r. 87 W. North.

BLAKE JOHN W., attorney at law, 45 E. Washington, r. 500 N. West.

Blake J. W., hackman, r. 157 N. Mississippi.

Blake James, r. 308 N. Tennessee.

Blake Mathias, carpenter. r. 390 N. West.

Blake Samuel, r. 308 N. Tennessee.

Blake Walter A., r. 308 N. Tennessee.

Blake William M., r. 327 N. Tennessee.

Blakemore Jackson, (col'd) lab., r. cor. Second and Lafayette R. R.

Blalock Mattie, dress maker, r. 9 Massachusetts av.

Blanch Antonia, barber, bds. 328 E. Market.

Blanchard Henry, clergyman Unitarian church, r. 118 W. Vermont.

Bland Cora Mrs., publisher of Ladies' Own Magazine, 83 E. Market, r. 171 Ft. Wayne av.

Bland George, engineer, r. 336½ N. West.

Bland George W., engineer Aldrich & Gay, r. 310 Indiana av.

Blaud T. A. (Bland & Taylor) r. 171 Ft. Wayne av.

Bland & Taylor, publishers North Western Farmer, 83 E. Market.

Blank Anton, clk. C. Vonnegut, bds. 508 E. Market.

Blank August, machinist, bds. California House.

Blanker John, porter, Rink, bds. 23 Kentucky av.

Blankenship Louis S., lab., bds. 301 W. Maryland.

Blass Henry, lab., 167 Union.

Blattler Morris, lab., r. 22 John.

Blatz Kathrine, groceries and toys, 440 S. Illinois, r. same.

Blauvelt Abram G., woodhauler, 31 Mud.

Blauvelt Charles, lab., r. 53 Oriental.

Blauvelt David C., clk., r. 271 W. Vermont.

Blauvelt Henry, tailor, r. 237 N. Liberty.

Blauvelt James, fireman, C. C. & I. C. R. R., r. 427 E. Vermont.

Blauvelt James, cooper, r. 427 E. Vermont.

Blaybel Charles, shipping clk., 397 S. Missouri.

Blaymy Irwin, carriagesmith, Shaw, L. & Co., r. 35 W. Georgia.

H. H. LEE,
Dealer in
Teas, Coffees, Sugars & Spices,
No. 7 ODD FELLOWS HALL
AND
ACADEMY OF MUSIC CORNER.

Bleich Gotlieb, butcher, 170 S. Illinois, bds. same.

Bliebel Joseph, cabinet maker, r. 397 S. Missouri.

Bliss, carpenter, r. 346 N. New Jersey.

Blitner John, blacksmith, Eagle Machine Works.

Block Henry, painter, bds. 171 N. Davidson.

Block William, lab., 354 Virginia av.

Blodau J. H., clk. J. P. Meikel, r. same.

Blodau John, foreman Philip Dohn, r. 31 W. Market.

Bloomer Isaac L. (Parker & B.) r. 155 N. New Jersey.

Bloomingstock John, lab., r. 599 N. Tennessee.

Blue Chas. G., gas fitter, r. 365 N. East.

Blue Cyrus, carpenter, r. 365 N. East.

Blue Gerard, Farmer, r. 498 N. Illinois.

BLUME FRANCIS J., city contractor, r. over 308 E. Washington.

Bly Jacob, watchman, r. 77 N. Liberty.

Bly John, lab., r. 308 S. Illinois.

Bly John, teamster, r. 399 S. East.

Bly Oliver H. P., r. 34 N. New Jersey.

Blythe Samuel, driver, engine house No. 3., r. same.

Blythe William M., engineer, I. & St. L. R. R., r. 12 S. Mississippi.

Boardman Omer T., night police, r. 141 Union.

Boaz Charles G., asst. local mail agent, bds. 321 S. Pennsylvania.

Boaz E. (wid.) r. 34 W. North.

Boaz Fred., lab., C. C. & I. C. R. R.

Boaz William, local mail agent Union Depot, r. 321 S. Pennsylvania.

Bobbs Elizabeth Mrs., r. 195 N. Pennsylvania.

Bobbs J. S., physician and surgeon, 15 E. Washington, r. E. end Georgia.

Bobst Penuel, lab., r. 310 Indiana av.

Bode Anthony F., checkman, P. C. & St. L. freight depot, r. cor. South and Alabama.

Bode William, lab., P. C. & St. L. freight depot, r. 209 S. Alabama.

Bodenmiller Leonard, carriagesmith, r. 70 St. Mary.

Bodey Herman, baggage master, C. C. C. & I. R. R.

Boecher Henry, meat market, 122 S. Meridian, r. same.

Boedeker & Niemann, (H. B. & H. N.) carpenters and builders, 418 E. North.

Boedeker Henry, (B. & Nieman) bds. cor. Michigan and Noble.

Boehm John F., r. 398 N. West.

Boek C. C. Henry, carpenter, r. 576 E. Washington.

Boening William, lab., r. 168 S. Noble.

Boerich Emile, teacher in High School bds. 316 E. New York.

Boeruen Joseph S., carpenter, r. 414 N. Delaware.

BOETTICHER JULIUS, publisher Indiana Volksblatt, 164 E. Washington, r. same.

Boetticher Otto, printer, 164 E. Washington, r. same.

Bogardus William, carpenter, r. 170 Buchanan.

Bogart Anton, cabinet maker, r. 132 E. St. Joseph.

Bogart James, trunk manufacturer, 2 N. Meridian, r. 490 N. Mississippi.

Bogart Maggie, clk. Trade Palace, bds. 490 N. Mississippi.

Bogart W. J., trunk maker, bds. 490 N. Mississippi.

Bogen Mary Mrs., r. 235 Daugherty.

Bogert Caroline Mrs. (wid. Cornelius) r. 260 Patterson.

Bogert Charles C., lab. Chandler & Taylor, r. Minerva, nr. New York.

BOGGESS H. H., justice of the peace, 96 E. Washington, r. 612 N. Illinois.

BOHLEN D. A., architect, 19 Talbott & New's bl'k, r. 71 N. Noble.

Bohn Charles, joiner Union Factory, r. 295 E. Georgia.

Bohn Gustavus, machinist Eagle Machine Works, r. 326 S. Delaware.

Bohn William, carpenter, r. 506 S. New Jersey.

Bohnet Gotleib, blacksmith, bds. 68 S. Delaware.

BOHRMAN PETER, prop'r Gem Billiard Saloon, 9 W. Washington, r. same.

Boise A. R. Miss, teacher Indianapolis Young Ladies Institute, r. Chicago, Illinois.

Bokern Joseph, watch maker, r. 121 Spring.

Bolden James, clk., r. 323 Virginia av.

Bolen John, sawyer J. T. Presley, bds. 272 W. Maryland.

Bolen John, lab., r. 232 S. Missouri.

Bolen Peter, painter, r. 282 N. Winston.

Bolen Michael, lab., bds. Nagel House.

Bolen Michael, works rolling mill, r. 45 Henry.

Bolen William, day policeman, r. 176 N. Mississippi.

Bollinger James, (Dreher & B.) r. 119 North Liberty.

Bollman Charles, blacksmith, r. 479 E. Georgia.

Bollman Fred., bakery and confectionery, r. 107 E. Washington.

Bollman Herman, grocer, r. 349 S. Pennsylvania.

Bolser Frank, painter, r. 458 S. Meridian.

Bolser George, wagon maker, r. 471 S. Illinois.

Bolser George, painter, r. 425 S. Meridian.

Boltemiller John S., blacksmith, r. 134 E. St. Mary.

Boltemeyer William, lab., r. 339 E. McCarty.

Bolton Francis, clk., 13 W. Washington, bds. 141 S. New Jersey.

Bomming A., coal hauler, r. 472 S. West.

Bond A. V., (Bond & Smith) bds. 273 N. Tennessee.

Bond Edward, carpenter, C., C., C. & I. R. R., r. 146 N. Winston.

Bond Fred, lab., starch factory.

Bond Joel, r. 441 N. Mississippi.

Bond William, carpenter, r. 314 W. Merrill.

Bond & Smith, (A. B. Bond and J. Smith) boot and shoemakers, 16½ E. Washington.

Bone William, porter, r. 180 E. Vermont.

Bonebarger David, carpenter, r. 287 Indiana av.

Bonebarger J. E., r. 287 Indiana av.

Bonner C. S., conductor C. & I. R. R., r. 239 E. South.

Boochter George, grocery and produce, 52 California, r. same.

Book John, lab., r. Coburn.

Boone Daniel, (col'd) teamster, r. 508 N. Mississippi.

Boos William, baker, 264 E. Washington, r. same.

Boring Ephraim, plasterer, r. 345 N. West.

Borst Frederick, (Dietz & B.) r. Kansas, s. city limits.

Bosart Timothy L, clk., 151 W. Washington, bds. 12 S. Mississippi.

Bossert John, bakery, 112 S. Meridian, r. same.

Bostic Clara, (wid.) r. 8 N. Liberty.

Boston Ferrotype Co., 33 W. Washington.

Boston Jacob, works Osgood, Smith & Co., bds. 211 S. Illinois.

Boswell J. K., patentee wardrobe and fruit dryer, 16 S. Pennsylvania, r. Richmond, Indiana.

Boswell John, carpenter, r. 24 Wright.

Boswell Joseph, bailiff, r. 177 Massachusetts av.

Boswell William, turner, r. 521 Maple.

3

BENHAM BRO'S.

36 East Washington St.,

KEEP

THE VERY BEST

VIOLIN AND GUITAR STRINGS.

Bothwell Henry, dealer in groceries, etc., 530 N. Mississippi, r. 557 N. Mississippi.

Bott Mrs. (wid.) r. 308 N. Winston.

Bott Gottleib, baker, r. 376 E. New York.

Bouchet Sophia Mrs., cleaning and dying, 42 Kentucky av., r. same.

Bourgonne Stephen, cigar maker, r. 140 Union.

Bouvy Adrien, tinner, 308 Virginia av., r. 39 Forest av.

Bouvy Henry, cooper, r. 260 N. Noble.

Bowen Caroline, (wid.) r. 318 N. Winston.

Bowen Cornelius, engineer, C., C. & I. C. R. R., r. 141 Meek.

Bowen Curtis, fireman, C. C. & I. C. R. R., r. cor. Meek and Cady.

Bowen Edward, lab., C. C. & I. C. R. R., r. 141 Meek.

Bowen Frank, lab., r. Locke, opposite City Hospital.

Bowen John F., huckster, r. 456, Indiana av.

Bowen Mary Mrs., r. 77 N. Illinois.

Bowen Oliver, painter, r. sw. cor. Sixth and Mississippi.

Bowen Silas T. (B., Stewart & Co.) r. 82 W. Vermont.

BOWEN, STEWART & CO., (Silas T. Bowen, Mrs. S. W. and Chas. G. Stewart,) wholesale and retail booksellers, stationers, and paper dealers, 18 W. Washington.

Bowker Harrison, (B. & Co.) r. 227 S. New Jersey.

Bowker Willis L., book keeper, r. 227 S. New Jersey.

Bowker & Co. (Harrison Bowker, J. L. McFarland and C. A. McFarland) flour and feed, 146 Virgiana av.

BOWLES THOMAS H., attorney and counselor at law, 60 E. Washington, r. 493 N. Meridian.

Bowler John F., clk., r. 9 Bates.

Bowler William H., switchman, Cincinnati yard, r. 9 Bates.

Bowman Ernest, lab., P. C. & St. L. freight depot.

Bowman James, works Osgood, Smith & Co., bds. 211 S. Illinois.

Bowman L. F. (B. & Wakefield).

BOWMAN & WAKEFIELD, (L. F. B. & W. W.) great 25cts store, 61 N. Illinois.

THE CHINA TEA STORES

ARE AT

No. 7 ODD FELLOWS HALL

AND

ACADEMY OF MUSIC CORNER.

Bowser Levi, clk., r. 277 Virginia av.
Bowser William, wagon maker, r. 193 S. East.
Boyd David, r. 127 S. Alabama.
BOYD FRANK A., paints, oils, varnishes, etc., 22 S. Meridian, and 10 W. Pearl, r 230 N. Tennessee.
Boyd George W., clk., C. C. C. & I. R. R., r. 177, S. Alabama.
Boyd James, lab., r. James, nr. First.
Boyd James M., engineer, I. C. & L. R. R., r. 195 Harrison.
BOYD J. T., physician and Surgeon, 14½ S. Pennsylvania, r. 117 Massachusetts av.
Boyd Richard M., wagon maker, r. 6 N. California.
Boyd W. T., salesman, Trade Palace, bds. 230 N. Tennessee.
Boyd William H., telegraph operator T. H. & I. R. R., bds. Spencer House.
Boyer Lawrence, works Jackson, Rider & Co.
Boyle Mrs. Catharine, r. 101 S. New Jersey.
Boyle James J. (A. Reed & Co.) 276 W. Washington.
Boyle Bernhard, lab., r. 151 High.
Boyles Lyde, r. 101 S. New Jersey.
Boyles M. W., real estate and insurance agent, No. 6 Odd Fellows' Hall, r. 230 East Vermont.
Boyles Sallie, bookbinder, Journal office, r. 101 S. New Jersey.
Boynton John M., works Jackson, Rider & Co.
BRACKEBUSH C. J., r. 220 N. Tennessee.
Bracken Susie, (wid. James) r. nr. rolling mill, S. Mississippi.
Brackensick F., cigar maker, bds. Illinois House.
Brackenstone L., tinner, Munson & Johnston, bds. 17½ Virginia av.
Brackin T. R., (Isgrigg & B.) r. 403 W. New York.
Brackston Lewis, (col'd) Meridian Street Bath House.
Brademeyer Charles, driver, McCord & Wheatley, r. Clinton, nr. East.
Brademeyer Christian, lab., r. 279 N. Davidson.
Brademeyer Henry, lab., r. 279 Davidson.
Brademeyer John F., teamster, r. 315 E. New York.

BRADEN J., dealer in agricultural implements, seeds, etc., 75 and 77 W. Washington, r. 220 N. Tennessee.
Braden William, (B. & Burford) r. 473 N. Illinois.
BRADEN & BURFORD, (William Braden and William B. Burford) blank book manufacturers, and dealers in stationery, etc., 24 W. Washington.
Bradenhof Richard, expressman, r. 213 Virginia av.
Bradford George, (col'd) lab., bds. 130 Blackford.
Bradford John, fireman, Sherman House.
Bradford T. S., mail agent, P. C. & St. L. R. R.
Bradley J. H., r. 143 N. Pennsylvania.
Bradley Jeptha W., mill wright, r. 186 N. Mississippi.
Bradley Leland J., clk., 194 and 196 W. Washington, r. 377 North Mississippi.
Bradley William, lab., r. 46 Dougherty.
Bradley Wilhelmina, (wid.) r. end Dakota.
Brado Joseph, clk., Jones & Hess, r. 25 Fletcher av.
Bradshaw Etta Miss, teacher, Sixth Ward School House, bds 290 S. Meridian.
Bradshaw George, carpenter, r. 309 N. Winston.
Bradshaw George N., miller, works Ætna Mills, bds. 366 W. Washington.
Bradshaw John A., stock dealer, r. 26 E. Vermont.
Bradshaw James, r. 562 N. Pennsylvania.
Bradshaw Mary Miss, teacher, Fourth Ward School, bds. 264 N. Tennessee.
Bradshaw Margaret Mrs. (wid. William) r. 264 N. Tennessee.
Bradshaw W. A., business agent, office 14 New & Talbott's block, r. Western av.
Bradshaw William, broom maker, r. 23 W. St. Clair.
Bradshort Isaac, piano maker, r. 174 Stevenson.
Bradtmiller Henry, miller, works Hoosier State Mills, bds. 366 W. Washington.
Brady John, (col'd) cook 51 Douglass al.
Brady John, works Street R. R. Co., r. 128 S. Tennessee.
Brady Michael, bricklayer, r. 673 N. Illinois.
Bragg Eliza, (wid.) r. 68 S. Noble.
Brahm Otto, barber, r. 329 W. Market.
Brake John, fireman C. C. & I. C. R. R., r. 424 E. Maryland.
Bramberg ——, (wid.) r. 306½ E. Washington.

Bramble Hamilton, bricklayer, r. 128 N. East.

Brame Auther, barber, r. 329 W. Market.

Bramer William F., pattern maker, r. 324 S. Delaware.

BRAMWELL JOHN M., Grand Secretary F. & A. Masons, office Masonic Hall, r. 68 S. Mississippi.

Brmwell Zenas F., engineer, r. 98 Fletcher av.

Branan James, laborer, r. 487 Virginia av.

Branan John, porter, r. 439 Virginia av.

Branan John, cooper, r. 362 W. New York.

Branan John, lab. rolling mill, r. 356 S. Tennessee.

Brand J. G. (B. & Kreis) r. 62 W. South.

Brand & Kreis, (J. G. B. & S. K.) cider manufacturers, 198 E. Washington.

Brandt August, machinest, Eagle Machine Works.

Brandt Henry, works glass works, r. 127 St. Joseph.

Brandt Hermann, draughtsman, 19 Talbott & New's blk., r. 194½ E. Washington.

Brandt Hubbard, cook House of Lords, r. same.

Brandt J. B., city missionary, r. 230 S. Alabama.

Branham Edward, (Mahew & B.) r. 240 N. Tennessee.

Branham G. F., Assistant Superintendent Indianapolis & Vincennes R. R., cor. Virginia av. and Delaware, r. 216 E. South.

Branham Jennings, railroader, r. 313 S. East.

Brankamp Elizabeth, (wid. Henry) r. cor. Douglass and Vermont.

Brannon William, lab., r. 204 Buchanan.

Branson David A., salesman, bds. 94 N. East.

Branyan Sarah Mrs. (wid. Andrew) r. 278 S. Mississippi.

Brathers Elizabeth, (wid.) r. 560 E. Washington.

Brattain John, express driver, r. 178 N. Missipi.

Brattain W. J., produce dealer, r. 70 N. Delaware.

Brattmeirs James, machinest, r. 31 Douglass.

Bratton Henry I., letter carrier, r. 200 Buchanan.

Braun John, Cabinet Makers' Union, bds. 65 S. East.

Braxton Lewis J. (col'd) bds. Sixth nr. Lafayette R. R.

Bray John S., deputy assessor, r. 240 N. East.

Bray Peter L., plasterer, r. 176 Massachusetts av.

Bray William H., clk. Parrott, Nickum & Co., bds. 249 N. East.

Breckhill H. A., painter, r. cor. Illinois and Louisiana.

Breedlove E. M. (J. M. Todd & Co.) r. 366 N. West.

Breedlove Thomas J. (John M. Todd & Co.) r. 35 Bright.

Breedlove Sarah, (wid.) r. 143 N. Davidson.

Breen James, railroader, r. 389 N. Winston.

Brees Isaac, carpenter, r. 436 E. St. Clair.

Brenen Patrick, night-watchman Sherman House, r. cor. Merrill and Missouri.

Bremerman Benjamin, wagon maker, works at Indianapolis Agricultural Works.

Bremerman Cass, (Lowe G. & Co.) r. 783 N. Illinois.

Bremerman Frederick, Superintendent of Agricultural Works, r. 295 N. Alabama.

Brenker William, cooper, r. 343 N. New Jersey.

Brennan Daniel, hostler, bds. 26 W. Georgia.

Brennan Daniel, porter Hume, Adams & Co., r. 27 Plum.

Brennan Patrick, lab., r. Tinker nr. Canal.

Brennan Thomas, painter, Shaw, Lippencott & Conner, r. 204 Buchanan.

Brennener William, patternmaker, r. 324 S. Delaware.

Bretny Eugene, carder woolen mill, bds. 366 W. Washington.

Brett M. L., r. 2 E. Michigan.

Bretz Adam, grocery and produce dealer, 44 W. Louisiana, r. 118 S. Illinois.

Breunig George, sr., clk., r. 205 Jackson.

Breunig George A., fire insurance agent, r. 202 Jackson.

Brewer Robert, moulder, bds. Ray House.

Brewster Sarah J. (wid. John H.) bds. Spencer House.

Brice Frank, printer, Journal office, bds. 79 Massachusetts av.

Brick Fred, teamster, r. Madison rd.

Brickley John, lab., bds. 551 S. Meridian.

Brickley Patrick, lab., r. 551 S. Meridian.

Bridges C. W., salesman 42 S. Meridian, bds. 23 W. Maryland.

Brierly W. H., moulder, bds. 196 S. Tennessee.

Briggs ——, r. 127 W. First.

H. H. LEE

MAKES A SPECIALTY OF

Choice Green, Black & Japan Teas.

Briggs Alford, r. 456 S. New Jersey.
Briggs C. H., clk. Indianapolis & Vincennes R. R., cor. Virginia av. and Delaware, r. 93 S. Noble.
BRIGGS & BRO. (E. W. & W. Briggs) contractors and builders, 98 Indiana av.
Briggs W. W., freight conductor C. R. R., bds. 58 Benton.
Brigham Charles E., clk. W. & J. Braden.
Bright Charles A. moulder, Eagle Machine Works.
Bright David L., teamster, r. 319 N. East.
Bright George A., moulder, Eagle Machine Works, r. 118 S. Meridian.
BRIGHT MICHAEL G., r. 292 N. Meridian.
BRIGHT, R. J., proprietor Daily and Weekly Sentinel, Sentinel bldg., sw. cor. Circle and Meridian, r 172 N. Meridian.
Brill John, carpenter, r. 473 S. Illinois.
Brink T., teamster, starch factory.
Brink William, tailor, r. 393 E. Michigan.
Brinker August, dealer in groceries and provisions, 174 W. New York, r. same.
Brinkler Henry, machinest, Eagle Machine Works, r. 174 W. New York.
Brinkman Charles, glass factory, r. 131 N. New Jersy.
Brinkman Frank, carpenter, r. 512 E. Ohio.
Brinkman Fred, lab., r. 234 N. Davidson.
Brinkman George, lab., r. 238 N. Davidson.
Brinkman Harry, carpenter, r. 647 E. Washington.
Brinkman John, lab., r. 238 N. Davidson.
Brinkman Joseph, lab., Bunte & Dickson.
Brinkmeyer Fred (Butch, Dickson & Co.), r. 234 N. Davidson.
Brinkmeyer George (Butch, Dickson Co.), r. 238 N. Davidson.
Brinkmeyer John C. (Butch, Dickson & Co.), r. 288 N. Liberty.
Brison Dallis, r. 261 W. Merril.
Brison Hugh, lab., r. 281 W. Merril.
Bristle Adam, tailor, 170 E. Washington.
Bristol A. J., traveling agent, Browning & Sloan, bds. 59 W. Maryland.
Bristor Lizzie Miss, clk., R. Sedgwick's, r. 135 N. Delaware.
Bristor Samuel M., carriage maker, r. 135 N. Delaware.

Bristor William, carpenter, r. 426 E. South.
Bristor William A., dealer in boots, shoes, etc., 75 E. Washington, bds. 135 N. Delaware.
Brit Thomas, r. 103 S. West.
Britt Thomas J. (Carroll & B.) r. 86 S. Illinois.
Brittain H. J., letter carrier.
Brittain John G. (col'd) barber, shop 181 W. Washington, r. same.
Brittingham Frank, bell boy, Bates House.
Brittingham Mary S. Miss, saleslady, Trade Palace, bds. 16 S. Mississippi.
Broadbelt James, traveling agent, r. 121 N. Illinois.
Broadhurst Isaac, pianomaker, r, 174 Stevens.
Brochert Frederick, coppersmith, r. 282 E. Washington.
Brock James, blacksmith, bds. 217 S. Illinois.
Brock Robert, cabinetmaker, r. 352 Virginia av.
Brock Thomas, clk., 322 Virginia av., bds. 352 Virginia av.
Broden James, moulder, r. 271 E. New York.
Broden John, moulder, works Chandler & Taylor's, bds. 2 Henry.
Broden Mary Mrs., (wid. John) r. 142 Indiana av.
Broden Michael, printer, Sentinel Job Office, r. 269 E. New York.
Broden Patrick, moulder, r. 2 Henry.
Broderick John, machinest, C. C. & I. C. R. R., r. 421 E. Georgia.
Broeking Richard, works Transfer Co., r. 77 E. McCarty.
Brommer Frederick, painter, r. 570 E. Washington.
Bronson Andrew W., r. 126 E. Ohio.
Bronson E. A. (J. W. Lines & Co.) r. 94 N. East.
Bronson Mary, (wid. Ely M.) r. cor. Broadway and Butler.
BRONSON & JONES, (A. W. Bronson and B. F. Jones) manufacturers and whol. and retail dealers in boots and shoes, 17 West Washington.
Brooker Thomas, dealer in grocerie, feed, etc., r. same.
Brooks Bennet, carpenter, r. 178 Massachusetts av.
Brooks George C., money order clk. P. O., r. S. New Jersey nr. Merrill.
Brooks Nancy Miss, weaver, works woolen mill, bds. 416 W. Washington.
Brooks Newton, works Jackson, Rider & Co.
Brooksmith Henry, blacksmith, Eagle Machine Works, r. 122 Huron.
Brooksmith Lewis, machinest, Eagle Machine Works, bds. 122 Huron.

Brower George, printer, r. 126 E. Michigan.

Brower J. W., printer, Journal office.

Brown ——, (col'd) r. 370 N. Mississippi.

Brown Albert, grocery and saloon, 387 S. Delaware, r. same.

Brown Albert, baggage master, T. H. & I. R. R.

Brown Austin, (col'd) lab., r. 350 W. North.

Brown August, porter, 74 S. Meridian, r. 238 Union.

Brown Austin H., with Woollen, Webb & Co., r. 290 S. Meridian.

Brown Benjamin F. (Logan & B.) r. 294 W. St. Clair.

Brown C., telegraph operator, I. C. & L. shop, r. 106 Bates.

Brown Christ. (col'd) lab., bds. 160 Douglass al.

Brown E., sawyer, r. 243 E. South.

Brown G. A., salesman, 75 S. Meridian, r. 172 E. South.

Brown Eliza, r. 337 N. New Jersey.

Brown Elizabeth, (wid.) r. Douglass nr. New York.

Brown Elizabeth, (wid.) r. 383 N. Alabama.

Brown D. D. Mrs., boarding house, 54 S. Pennsylvania.

Brown D. R. (Fortner, Floyd & Co.) r. Noblesville, Ind.

Brown Frank, fireman, Vincennes R. R., bds. 61 S. Noble.

Brown Frank, cabinetmaker, r. 17 Kentucky av.

BROWN F. M., groceries and provisions, 59 W. Washington, r. 163 N. Illinois.

Brown George, carpenter, r. 392 N. Alabama.

Brown George, works Jackson, Rider & Co.

Brown George H., tinner, Tutewiler Bro.

Browning Gordon, clk. P. O., bds. 29 W. Ohio.

Brown Henry, lab., r. Nebraska bet. East.

Brown Henry, (col'd) lab., r. African al. bet. 6th and 7th.

Brown Henry P., clk., Hume, Adams & Co., bds. Pyle House.

Brown Henry P., porter, I. L. Frankem, r. 253 N. Liberty.

Brown J. J., grocer, 202 E. Washington, r. same.

Brown Ignatius, attorney at law, 8 E. Washington, r. 243 E. South.

Brown J. Burgess, passenger agent, Panhandle R. R., r. cor. Cherry and Plum.

Brown J. C., works rolling mill, bds. 576 S. Illinois.

Brown J. S. (col'd) domestic, Bates House.

Brown J. H., druggist, Keifer & Vinton, r. 181 Massachusetts av.

Brown Jacob, (col'd) barber, r. 129 Bright.

Brown James D., paper hanger, r. 352 N. Alabama.

Brown James J., carpenter, r. 274 Chestnut.

Brown James W., civil engineer, r. 115 N. Meridian.

Brown Jerry, express driver, r. 349 N. Alabama.

Brown John, works rolling mill, bds. 77 W. McCarty.

Brown John, bootmaker, 25 W. Washington, r. 61 Indiana av.

Brown John, shoemaker, r. 61 Indiana av.

Brown John, cabinetmaker, bds. 65 S. East.

Brown John, works rolling mill, r. 567 S. Illinois.

Brown John G., grocery and produce dealer, 300 N. New Jersey, r. same.

Brown John H. F., tinner, Tutewiler Bros., r. 366 N. Alabama.

Brown John M., janitor, North Western Christian University, bds. same.

Brown John W. (Goth, B. & Co.) r. 401 N. New Jersey.

Brown John W., sr., r. 302 N. New Jersey.

Brown Joseph, bootmaker, bds. Little's Hotel.

Brown Joseph H., cooper, r. 124 Meek.

Brown Joseph M., clk., 18 W. Pearl, r. 19 N. New Jersey.

Brown Joseph L., Plasterer, r. 327 N. New Jersey.

Brown Julia, (wid. Philip) r. 351 Massachusetts av.

Brown Lizzie Miss, r room 6, 186½ W. Washington.

Brown Mrs. M. J., seamstress, r. 46½ Massachusetts av.

Brown M. J. Miss, seamstress, r. 46½ Massachusetts av.

Brown M. O., clk. McGilliard & B., bds. 280 N. Mississippi.

Browning Mary Mrs. (wid. Wood) bds. 300 S. Meridian.

Brown Mary J. (wid) r. 124 N. East.

Brown Michael, marble polisher, cor. First and James.

Brown Nancy A., r. 30 W. Maryland.

Brown Rev. O., r. 208 N. Alabama.

THE CHINA TEA STORES

ARE AMONG THE

Attractions of Indianapolis.

Call and See Them before leaving the City.

Brown Patrick, Root's Foundry, r. 341 S. Delaware.

Brown R. H., assistant librarian, r. 30 W. Maryland.

Brown R. T., professor, North Western Christian University, r. 7 Western av.

Brown Samuel, clk., 251 N. Illinois, r. 366 W. Vermont.

Brown Samuel, cook, r. 291 E. New York.

Brown Susan Mrs. (wid. William J.) r. 300 S. Meridian.

Brown Thomas, traveling agent, bds. 15 S. Mississippi.

Brown Thomas, pressman, Sentinel Office, bds. 128 S. Illinois.

Brown T. B., saloonkeeper, r. Wabash bet. New Jersey and East.

Brown W. C., drug clk., r. 337 N. New Jersey.

Brown William, clk., P. C. & St. L. Freight Office, r. 352 N. Alabama.

Brown William H., bill clk. express office, r. Madison rd.

Brown William J., boss plasterer, cor. Ash and Christian av.

Brown William J., treasurer Geo. A. Huff & Co.'s Circus, r. out city limits.

Brown William P., lithographer, W. & J. Braden, r. 78 S. Delaware.

Brown Willis, (col'd) lab., r. 172 W. Georgia.

Brown Zecharia, (col'd) lab., bds. 154 Huron.

Browne T. M., United States Attorney's Office, P. O. bldg., r. Winchester, Ind.

Browning Edward, Register of Land Office, P. O. bldg., r. 109 Virginia av.

Browning Frank, clk., Browning & Sloan, bds. Depot Dining Hall.

Browning Robert, (B. & Sloan) r. 172 N. Illinois.

BROWNING & SLOAN, (Robert Browning and Geo. W. Sloan) whol. and retail druggists, 7 and 9 E. Washington.

Brough George, butcher, r. 215 N. Winston.

BROUGH JOHN W., Reporter Daily Sentinel, r. 333 S. Alabama.

Brouse Andrew, carpenter, r. 130 E. New York.

BROUSE C. W., Pension Agent, 87½ E. Market, rooms 10 and 11, r. 126 E. New York.

Brouse David W., Township Assessor, r. 130 E. New York.

Brouse J. A. Rev., r. 92 E. Market.

Broyles Rev. Moses, (col'd) pastor African Baptist Church, r. 297 Minerva.

Brubaker H. W. Dr., clk., Browning & Sloan, r. 43 Kentucky av.

Bruce Robert, moulder, works Greenleaf & Co., r. 298 Chestnut.

Brueggemann William, teacher, German Lutheran School, r. 67 N. Noble.

Bruening Edward, (E. & J. B.) r. 180 E. Washington.

BRUENING E. & J., photographers, over 6 E. Washington.

Bruening Frid, carpenter, r. 379 S. Delaware.

Bruening Fredrick, drayman, r. 439 S. Meridian.

Bruening Joseph, (E. & J. B.) r. 180 E. Washington.

Bruin Nathan, lab., bds. Bright, 2d house from New York.

BRUNDAGE EDWARD C., livery and feed stable, 223 E. Washington, r. 339 E. Market.

Bruner Augustus, Street Commissioner, r. 402 N. New Jersey.

Bruner Jacob, carpenter, r. 402 E. Michigan.

Bruner Martha, (wid.) r. 26 West McCarty.

BRUNNER JNO., dealer in groceries and produce, 684 N. Mississippi, r. same.

Brunnemer William, night police, r. 22 Douglass.

Bruman Patrick, porter, Sherman House.

Bryan Albert H. Dr., office 122 S. Illinois, r. 420 N. Delaware.

Bryan F. A., Capital Drug Store, cor. Massachusetts av. and Vermont, r. same.

Bryan J. M., clk., r. 420 N. Delaware.

BRYAN JAMES W., retail druggist, cor. Illinois and Louisiana, r. 420 N. Delaware.

Bryan Joseph, lab., r. 320 W. Washington.

Bryant John H., R. R. conductor, r. 138 N. New Jersey.

Bryant Mary, (col'd) r. cor. Michigan and Douglass al.

Bryant R. T., clk., Bee Hive Store, r. 420 N. Delaware.

Buchanan Andy, blacksmith, r. 314 E. Washington.

Buchanan Catherine, (wid) r. 314 E. Washington.

Buchanan George W., carpenter, r. 131 S. East.

BUCHANAN JAMES M., Union Plow Manufacturer, 27 S. East, r. 314 E. Washington.

Buchanan John, papermaker, r. 299 S. Missouri.

Buchanan John A., carpenter, r. 125 Duncan.

Buchanan Oliver, bricklayer, bds. 236 E. Market.

Buchner Aug, gasfitter, bds. Globe House.

Buchhorn Christian, wagonmaker, r. 104 South Noble.

Buchhorn Fred., teamster, r. cor. Vermont and Winston.

Buck Charles, road master, I. & C. J. R. R., r. 30 Biddle.

Buck Christian C., carpenter, r. 166 E. Michigan.

Buck John, lab., r. 246 N. East.

Buckingham W. S., baggage master, C. C. C. & I. R. R.

Buckler George, butcher, bds. 139 S. Illinois.

Buckley Dennis, cooper, r. 67 California.

Buckley John, switchman, I. C. & L. R. R., r. 32 Lord.

Buckley Margret, washerwoman, r. 303 Indiana av.

Buckley Tim., lab., r. 5 Benton.

Bucknell S. S., civil engineer, room 7 Ætua bldg., bds. 283 N. Pennsylvania.

Buckner John, (col'd) barber, works 193 West Washington, bds. same.

Bucksot George, helper, glass works, r. 381 N. Illinois.

Bucksot William, boarding and sale stable, Pearl, rear of Palmer House, r. 381 N. Illinois.

Buckstahler Charles, clk., J. W. Bryans, r. 72 W. South.

Buckstahler Martin, hotel runner, r. 342 Virginia av.

BUDD & HINSLEY, (Jno. R. Budd and A. J. Hinsley) poultry, butter, eggs, etc., 18 W. Pearl.

Budd John R. (B. & Hinsley) r. 250 N. East.

Buddenbaum H. C. (Prange & Co.) r. 396 E. Ohio.

Buddenbaum John A. (Krug & B.) r. 296 E. Georgia.

Budenz John, clk., Trade Palace, r. 266 S. Pennsylvania.

Budenz Henry, tailor, r. 266 S. Pennsylvania.

Budenz Louis, merchant tailor, Mozart Hall, r. 229 Union.

Buehler John, works Cabinet Maker's Union, r. 22 Wyoming.

Buehrig Henry, jr., r. 37 E. South.

Buehrig Rebecca Mrs. (wid. Henry) Vaux Hall Garden, 37 E. South.

Buehrig William, r. 37 E. South.

BUELL C. H., proprietor and manufacturer of Buell's Family Medicines, 75 East Market, r. 269 E. Market.

Buell J. R., r. 15 Madison av.

Buersdoerfer George, proprietor Great Western Saloon, cor. Indiana av. and Illinois, r. 314 E. Ohio.

Buennagel Fred., baker, 191 N. Noble.

Bugby Mrs. P. A. (wid. Lyman) r. 262 N. Noble.

Bugby Parker E., engineer, C. C. C. & I. R. W., r. 262 N. Noble.

Bugg Samuel, (col'd) lab., r. 451 E. Georgia.

Buhier John, brewer, Schmidt's Brewry, r. 22 Wyoming.

BUILDERS' AND MANUFACTURERS' ASSOCIATION, 225 N. Delaware; C. Eden, Pres't; James Husson, Sec'y; J. S. Avery, Treas.

Buisking Henry, machinest, works Greenleaf & Co.

Buist M. E. Mrs. (wid. Thomas) r. 60 N. California.

Bulach John, superintendent of Mozart Hall, r. Wabash, bet. Market and Ohio.

Bulk F., lab., bds. 563 E. St. Clair.

Bull George W., clk. Star Union Line Office, 85 Virginia av.

Bullard Emly, (wid. Charles) r. room 6 Fatout's blk.

Bullard Kate, (wid. Talbot) r. 175 E. Ohio.

Bullard W. R. physician, 72 E. Market, r. 175 E. Ohio.

Bullock James B (Anderson, B. & Schofield) r. 417 N. Tennessee.

Bulhman Charles, blacksmith, r. 479 E. Georgia.

Bumpas Sallie Miss, r. 172 Eddy.

Bundy J. B., carpenter, r. 44 Massachusetts av.

Bunte John B. (B. & Dickson) r. 415 E. Washington.

BUNTE & DICKSON, (John B. Bunte and Wm. B Dickson) lumber yard, black and white walnut, cherry, ash and staves, office and yard, 387 E. Market.

Burbank Water F., with G. W. Caldwell & Co., r. 111 Coburn.

Burbridge John, runner for Calforna House, bds. same.

Burch L. B., fish market, r. 227 Virginia av.

Burdensall David, clk., r. 267 S. New Jersey.

H. H. LEE

Makes a Specialty of

CHOICE GOLDEN RIO,

AND

OLD GOVERNMENT JAVA COFFEES.

Burford Wm. B. (Braden & B.) bds. Palmer House.

Burge A. J., baggagemaster, I. & V. R. R.

Burgan Eliza Miss, servant, 334 W. Washington.

Burger Barbara, (wid. John) r. 15 Arch.

Burger Charles, lab., r. over 475 E. Market.

Burgess C. C., dentist, 1 Odd Fellows Hall, second floor, r. 478 N. Pennsylvania.

Burges Cornelius N. (boarding house) 98 N. East.

Burgess O. A., Professor of Bible Department N. W. C. University, bds. cor. Alabama and Michigan.

Burk Amanda, (wid.) r. 94 N. East.

Burk, Earnshaw & Co. (W. C. B., J. E. & J. Turner) furniture dealers, 67 W. Washington.

Burk George, saloon keeper, r. 141 S. New Jersey.

Burk George, (col'd) lab., r. Fifth, bet. Mississippi & L. R. R.

Burk H. L., telegraph operator, bds. 264 E. Ohio.

Burk John, dealer in coal, 23 Virginia av., r. 254 N. Tennessee.

Burk Lemuel, cattle drover, r. 165 E. St. Joseph.

Burk Mary, (wid. Louis) r. 5 Vine.

Burk Rankin H., coal dealer, r. 163 W. South.

Burk S. M., carpenter, r. 5 Vine.

Burk Thomas L., lab., r. 286 W. Market.

Burk W. C. (B., Earnshaw & Co.) r. 235 N. Mississippi.

Burke Anna, (wid.) r. 454 E. Market.

Burke Henry, stonemason, r. 344 S. Delaware.

Burke Walter, railroader C. C. & I. C. R. R., bds. 283 E. Georgia.

Burkert C. M., baggagemaster P. C. & St. L. R. R.

Burkert Ed. A., bookkeeper, Wm. Simmons & Co., r. 157 W. Maryland.

Burkert E. J., assistant bookkeeper, 127 S. Meridian, r. 170 E. Walnut.

Burkert W. S, bookkeeper, 127 S. Meridian, r. 157 W. Maryland.

BURKHART GEO. P., ice dealer, cor. Mississippi and Michigan, r. same.

Burkhart Eve, (wid. Valentine) r. 152 Madison av.

Burkhart John, chairmaker, r. 152 Madison av.

Burkhart Susan, (wid. Andrew J. J.) ice dealer, r. 248 N. Mississippi.

Burmand Henry, lab., r. 122 S. Noble.

BURNAM S. W., real estate agent and broker, 19 N. Illinois, r. W. Second, bet. Tennessee and Mississippi.

Burnd Daniel, carriagesmith, Shaw L. & C., r. 348 S. Meridian.

BURNETT J. C., Deputy Auditor of State, r. 284 N. Tennessee.

Burnett James, brickmason, r. 126 Meek.

Burnett John J., bricklayer, r. 129 W. Maryland.

Burnham N. G. (B. & Tisdale) r. 38 W. Market.

Burnham & Tisdale, (N. G. B. & T. P. T.) physicians and surgeons, 38 W. Market.

Burns Christopher, peddler, r. 117 Oak.

Burns Daniel V., attorney, 62 E. Washington, r. 178 E. Walnut.

Burns George, conductor J. M. & I. R. R., r. 313 S. Delaware.

Burns F., clk., 62 E. Market, bds. 78 E. Market.

Burns J. F., blacksmith, r. 347 S. Pennsylvania.

Burns James, engineer with Hill & Wingate, r. 274 E. Louisiana.

Burns James, beltmaker Mooney & Co., r. 13 Henry.

Burns Jerry, lab., r. 28 Wyoming.

Burns John B., engineer C. C. & I. C. R. R., r. 466 E. Georgia.

Burns John, helper Bellefontaine R. R. shops.

Burns Mary Miss, milliner, 64 N. Illinois, r. 252 S. West.

Burns Michael, lab. T. H. & I. R. R. Depot, r. 252 S. West.

Burns Owen, lab., r. 251 S. Tennessee.

Burns Patrick, r. 1 Willard.

Burns Patrick, lab., bds. 199 W. Maryland.

Burns Sarah, (wid. James) r. 81 N. Missouri.

Burns Thos. E., millwright, bds. 18 S. Pennsylvania.

Burns William, lab., r. 259 S. West.

Burns William, (col'd) Bates House.

Burnside H. M., railroad man, r. 68 W. Michigan.

Burnsworth Mary Mrs., (wid. George) r. 22 Elm.

Burnsworth Ziba, blacksmith, bds. 22 Elm.

Burst Frederick, butcher, nr. Underhill's Mill, r. same.

Burst George, tanner, r. Maple, cor. Morris.

Burt Alphonso S., traveling agent, r. 264 E. Ohio.

Burt Harry L., telegraph operator, bds 264 E. Ohio.

Burt J. L., bds. 555 N. Illinois.

Burt Nellie Miss, bds. 139 W. Market.

Burtch O. B., salesman New York Store, bds. 158 N. New Jersey.

Burton ——, r. 170 E. Walnut.

Burton Daniel, cooper, shop cor. Agnes and New York, r. 427 W. New York.

Burton G. II., cooper, r. 138 N. Mississippi.

Burton J. C. (J. C. B. & Co.) r. 445 N. New Jersey.

BURTON JOHN C. & CO. (J. C. Burton, W. A. Pfaff, and J. W. Pfaff) wholesale dealers in boots and shoes, 114 S. Meridian.

Burton Martin, manufacturer and dealer in trunks, valises, etc., 39 S. Illinois, r. 202 N. Illinois.

Burr A. II., salesman Boston Store, bds. 35 E. Market.

Burris Luke, (col'd) porter, 277 Massachusetts av. r. 29 Charles.

Burroughs G. W., cigarmaker, 11 N. Pennsylvania, bds. Union Hall.

Burrows Asa W., clk. W. W. Northrop, r. Beachtree Cottage, nr. Deaf and Dumb Asylum.

Burrows Geo. G., salesman J. A. Baldwin, bds. Pyle House.

Burrows George W., agent, r. E. Washington, nr. Asylum.

Burrows Thompson, (col'd) porter Trade Palace, r. 446 N. West.

Burt William N., teacher Indiana Institution for Deaf and Dumb.

Busch Christian, boot and shoe manufacturer, 248 W. Washington, r. same.

Busch Jacob, saloon, 251 W. Washington.

Buscher Herman, switchman, r. 432 S. East.

Buschmann William, (Goth, Brow & Co.) r. 469 N. New Jersey.

Buschmer Fred., blacksmith, 547 Virginia av., r. same.

Buser A. M., salesman Rickard & Talbott, bds. 36 W. Maryland.

Buser George, night police, r. 60 W. Market.

Buser Jacob, r. 74 W. Louisiana.

Buser John, policeman, bds. 74 W. Louisiana.

Buser Samuel, night policeman 5th Ward, r. 163 W. Maryland.

Bush Adam, carpenter, r. 342 S. Delaware.

Bush David, lab., r. E. Benton.

Bush Hannah, (wid. Jacob) r. 163 N. Davidson.

Bush Jeremiah, railroader, r. 150 Meek.

Bush Michael, railroader, bds. 150 Meek.

BENHAM BRO'S,

36 East Washington St.,

AGENTS FOR THE

BURDETT ORGAN.

Busher Sophia, (wid. Henry) r. 270 S. Alabama.

Bushkel William, soldier, r. 44 Mud.

Buskirk John, woodworker, r. 133 S. Meridian.

Bussell E. T. Dr., r. 239 N. New Jersey.

Bussell Rue, printer, bds. 239 N. New Jersey.

Bussell W. M., salesman Bowen, Stewart & Co., bds. 239 N. New Jersey.

Bussey Harry, clk., National Hotel billiard rooms, bds. 19 Henry.

BUSSEY JOHN, proprietor National Hotel saloon and billiard rooms, 29 and 31 W. McNabb, r. 19 Henry.

Buster Edward, machinist, r. 187 Davidson.

Butcher Henry, capitalist, r. 26 S. Alabama.

Butler Charles C., printer, r. 107 N. Noble.

Butler George, general passenger agent, I. C. & L. R. R., r. 243 W. New York.

Butler James O., printer, Journal office, r. 107 N. Noble.

Butler Oakley, bookkeeper, r. 287 N. East.

Butler Ovid, president, Indianapolis Printing and Publishing House, r. Forest Home av.

Butler Ovid D., r. 257 N. East.

Butler Pallace, (col'd) porter 39 S. Illinois, r. n. city limits.

Butler William, nurse, city hospital.

BUTSCH, DICKSON & CO. (V. B., James D., James B. D., J. C. Brinkmeyer, George Brinkmeyer, Charles Kempker, Fred P. Rush and William Sims) Capital City Iron Works, office and warehouse, 96 and 98 S. Meridian.

BUTSCH, DICKSON & DELL, (V. B., J. D. and Wm. D.) dealers in coal, lime, cement, lath, plaster of paris, hair, etc., 27 E. Georgia.

Butsch George M., saloon, 247 S. Delaware, r. same.

Butsch John, salesman, Holweg & Reese, bds. 393 S. East.

BUTSCH JOSEPH, ice dealer, r. 68 W. South.

Butsch Valentine, (V. Butsch & Dickson) r. 553 N. Meridian.

Butterfield C. S., printer, Sentinel office, bds. 54 W. Market.

THE CHINA TEA STORES

Have the NAME of being the

MOST ATTRACTIVE STORES IN THE WEST.

No. 7 Odd Fellows Hall

AND

ACADEMY OF MUSIC CORNER.

Butterfield Jeremiah A., agent, American and M. U. Express, r. 475 N. Pennsylvania.

Butterfield Newton, sewing machine ag't, r. 473 N. East.

Butterfield S. A., physician, 366 N. East, r. same.

Butterfield W. W., drugs and medicines, 521 N. Illinois, r. same.

Byers George W., salesman, 5 E. Washington, bds. Circle Restaurant.

Byomholt Carl, blacksmith, r. 30 Bradshaw.

Byram Augusta Miss, teacher, city academy, bds. 462 N. Meridian.

Byram N. S. (Byram, Cornelius & Co.) r. 466 N. Meridian.

BYRAM, CORNELIUS & CO. (N. S. Byram, E. G. Cornelius, Oliver Tousey) wholesale dry goods and notions, 104 S. Meridian.

Byrkit Charles, tailor, r. 408 Virginia av.

Byrkit D. Y., bookkeeper, M. Byrkit & Sons, bds. 82 S. Tennessee.

Byrkit Edward M. (M. B. & Sons) r. 118 W. Georgia.

Byrkit H., candymaker, 26 S. Meridian, r. 143 Fort Wayne av.

Byrkit John W. (M., B. & Sons) r. 71 Norwood.

Byrkit Martin, (M., B. & Sons) r. 82 S. Tennessee.

BYRKIT M. & SONS, (M. B., W. B. and E. M. B.) manufacturers sash, doors and blinds, cor. Tennessee and Georgia.

Byron Will O., printer, Journal office, bds. 79 Massachusetts av.

Bywaters John, carpenter, bds. 199 W. Maryland.

CABINET MAKERS' UNION, (John Herrman, pres't, Gustav Stark, sec'y, Valentine Schlotzhauer, Treas.) 426 to 450 E. Market.

Cady A. A. Mrs., r. 24 Circle.

Cady David, r. 174 W. Ohio.

Cady Elmah, (C. & Hendricks) r. 25 W. First.

Cady & Hendricks, (E. C. & John H.) grocers and produce dealers, 523 N. Illinois.

Caffey Emma Miss, r. 57 Douglas al.

Caffey Jennie Miss, bds. 57 Douglas al.

Caffey John, moulder, bds. 169 S. Tennessee.

Caffey John H., feed and sale stable, Wabash, bet. Pennsylvania and Delaware, bds. Pyle House.

Caffe Mary, laundrymaid, Sherman House.

Caffey Michael, lab., bds. 256 S. Tennessee.

Caholone Patrick, lab., r. 130 S. Noble.

Cahill Alfred, blacksmith, cor. Plum and Massachusetts av. r. 114 Massachusetts av.

Cahill John, weaver, Merritt & Coughlin, bds. 347 W. Washington.

Cahill John, janitor at postoffice, r. 72 E. Ohio.

Cahill John S., r. 519 S. Illinois.

Cahill Joseph, spinner, Geisendorff & Co., bds. 347 W. Washington.

Cahill Mary Mrs. (wid. Hugh) r. 347 W. Washington.

Cahoe Michael, lab., r. over 98 Railroad.

Cain Eliza A. (wid.) r. 245 N. Illinois.

Cain George W., bookbinder, bds. Neiman House.

Cain Hattie Miss, saleslady, Trade Palace, bds. 245 N. Illinois.

Cain Joseph, barkeeper, bds. 84 S. Mississippi.

Cain James, teamster, r. 304 Walnut.

Cain Michael, barkeeper, Opera saloon, bds. 84 S. Mississippi.

Calder J. C., clk., New York Store, bds. Macy House.

Caldwell Andrew, (G. W. C. & Co.) r. 817 Madison av.

Caldwell Andrew H., carpenter, r. Tinker, bet. Pennsylvania and Delaware.

Caldwell Edward S., engineer, cotton mill, r. 338 N. Blake.

CALDWELL & FRANCIS, (J. W. C. & W. F.) produce and commission merchants, 61 S. Illinois.

Caldwell G. W. (G. W. C. & Co.) r. 253 N. Illinois.

CALDWELL G. W. & CO. (G. W. C. & Andrew C.) manufacturers of ærated bread, 14 and 16 E. South.

CALDWELL H. W., dealer in flour, feed and groceries, 149 Indiana av., cor. Michigan, r. 180 W. Michigan.

Caldwell J. B., clk., 4½ W. Washington, bds. Sherman House.

Caldwell J. M. (Crossland, Hauna & Co.) r. 54 N. Mississippi.

Caldwell J. W. (Caldwell & Francis) r. same.

Caldwell Parker D., G. W. Caldwell & Co., r. 178 Madison av.

Caldwell Thomas G., tailor, r. 292 E. Michigan.

Caldwell Victor M. (G.W. Caldwell & Co.) r. 178 Madison av.

Caldwell W. W., general insurance agent, 42 W. Washington.

CALEDONIA PAPER MILL, Field, Locke & Co., proprietors, office, 265 W. Washington.

Call Dominic, peddler, r. 116 Oak.

Call Hugh, peddler, r. 116 Oak.

Callahan Daniel, lab., r. 423 W. Washington.

Calahan Daniel, w'ks Vater & King, bds. 146 W. Maryland.

Callahan James, carpenter, r. 58 Fayette.

Callahan Jerry, machinist, bds. cor. Walnut and Missouri.

Callahan John P., scroll sawyer, Indianapolis piano manufactory, r. 167 E. South.

Callahan ——, r. 165 E. South.

Callahan Josephine, domestic, Bates House.

Callahan Margaret Mrs. (wid) r. 119 W. Washington.

Callahan Michael, lab. r. 36 Lord.

Callahan Michael, checkman, I. C. & L. R. R. r. 202 cor. Walnut and Missouri.

Callan James, driver Fire Engine No. 2, r. 120 E. New York.

Cullinan David J. clk. r. 300 Massachusetts av.

Calthoff Frederick, sr. lab. r. 83 Union.

Calthoff Frederick, jr., lab. r. 83 Union.

CALVERT CHARLES L. restaurant and confectioner, 143 W. Washington, r. same.

Calvert Jane Mrs., weaver, Geisendorff & Co., r. cor. Mississippi and New York.

Calvert James, r. 375 N. West.

Calvert John H. book agt. bds. 375 N. West.

Calvin ——, fireman, Junction R. R. bds. 61 S. Noble.

Cameron William D. printer, 8 E. Pearl, bds. 278 N. Alabama.

Cameron William S. steam job printer, 8 E. Pearl, r. 278 N. Alabama.

Campbell Andrew F. tailor, r. 334 W. Washington.

Campbell Charles C. r. 2 W. North.

Campbell Daniel lab. bds. 16 Willard.

Campbell F. C. sadler, bds. 220 E. Market.

CAMPBELL GEORGE H. notary public, 3 Odd Fellows Hall, r. cor. North and Meridian.

Campbell H. carpenter, r. 51 Wyoming.

Campbell Harrison, (col'd) teamster, r. 115 Ash.

Campbell James, dealer in lightning rods, r. 323 E. Ohio.

Campbell Jerry, carpenter, r. 51 Dougherty.

BENHAM BRO'S,

36 East Washington St.,

SHEET MUSIC, VIOLINS,

GUITARS, STRINGS, &c.

Campbell John, harnessmaker, bds. 131 S. Illinois.

Campbell John, traveling agent, r. 361 Massachusetts av.

Campbell John A. tailor, bds. 334 W. Washington.

Campbell John S. clk. P. O. bds. Pyle House.

Campbell John S. r. 128 N. Pennsylvania.

Campbell John T. (C. & Green), r. 128 N. Pennsylvania.

Campbell Maggie Miss, tailoress, bds. 134 W. Washington.

Campbell Maria, (col'd wid. Sanford,) r. 115 Ash.

Campbell Morris, works, Street R. R. Co. r. 16 Willard.

Campbell Owen, bridgebuilder, r. Dunlap, bet. New Jersey and S. East.

Campbell Richard C. sexton Third Presbyterian Church, r. 34 Union.

Campbell Robert, night policeman, r. 44 Harrison.

Campbell Stockton C. clk. for A. D. Streight, bds. 132 N. Alabama.

Campbell S. L. bookbinder, Journal Office, bds. 246 N. Illinois.

Campbell Thomas S. bookbinder Sentinel Office, r. 246 N. Illinois.

Campbell William, with McCord & Wheatley, r. 206 E. Ohio.

Campbell William, works Rolling Mill, r. 295 S. Tennessee.

Campbell Wm. W. teamster, r. 206 E. Ohio.

CAMPBELL & GREEN, (J. T. Campbell and Perry M. Green) drugs, medicines, paints, oils, etc., 149 W. Washington.

Canan John W. bds. Spencer House.

Canan William S. clk. Spencer House.

Canan Martin, lab. bds. 256 S. Tennessee.

Cander John B. clk. A. G. Willard & Co.

Canine Pedro, walker, Browning & Sloan, bds. 172 N. Illinois.

Canner Mary Miss, second cook, Spencer House.

Cannon LeGrand, clk. Peru R. R. office, r. 24 W. Washington.

Cantlon Thomas, drayman, r. 94 Fayette.

Cantrill D. M., printer, Wright & Holman, r. 132 W. Vermont.

Cantwell Michael, patternmaker, r. 132 N. Winston.

CAPITAL CITY VARNISH WORKS, cor. Mississippi and Kentucky av. Mears & Lilly, proprietors.

CAPITAL TOBACCO WORKS, 175 Cumberland, Thomas Madden, proprietor.

Cardan John, porter, Spencer House.

Carey Beverly Rev., (cold) r. 58 Oak.

Carey H. G., (J. S. Carey & Co.) r. 284 N. Meridian.

Carey Elizabeth A. Mrs., (wid. Samuel) r. N. Tennessee, bet. Fifth and Sixth.

Carey Jessen, dealer in staves, r. 187 N. Deleware.

Carey J. S., (J. S. Cary & Co.) r. 191 N. Deleware.

Carey J. S. & Co., (J. S. Carey and H. G. Carey) machine cooperage, terminus W. Georgia.

Carey Patrick, lab., Sinker & Davis, r, 365 S. Missouri.

Cargett J., bricklayer, r. 369 N. Alabama

Carl Michael, lab., r. 269 S. Missouri.

Carleton Andrew, lab., r. 47 Rose.

Carleton G. T. clk. W. & J. Braden, bds. 174 E. New York.

Carleton Philip J., clk. American and M. U. Express, Co., r. 174 E. New York.

Carlisle A. M. Mrs., (wid. Daniel) r. 117 N. Mississippi.

Carlisle Frank, miller, bds. 260 W. Washington.

Carlisle H. T., printer, Journal Office, r. 77 W. Ohio.

Carlisle H. D., proprietor Home Mills, W. Maryland, r. 77 W. Ohio.

Carlisle John, proprietor Carlisle Mills, Market and Canal, r. 260 W. Washington.

Carlisle Wm., clk. John Carlisle, bds. 260 W. Washington.

Carlon John, foreman press room, I. P. & P. House, r. 65 N. New Jersey.

Carmichael Andrew M., r. 763 N. Mississippi.

Carmichael Jesse D., (Todd, C. & Williams) r. 456 N. Meridian.

Carmichael John, (col'd) whitewasher, r. 255 N. Liberty.

Carnahan A. M., clk. C. C. C. & I. R. R. r. nw. cor. Delaware and Michigan.

Carney Squire, Black Smith Works, Greenleaf & Co. bds. 266 S. Tennessee.

Carney Thomas, carriage smith, r. Cumberland al. bet. Washington and Maryland.

Carpenter B. O. marble worker, 36 E. Market, r. 216 N. Blackford.

Carpenter C. F., painter, bds. 88 S. Noble.

Carpenter Ira, entry clerk, at Landers, Conduitt & Co., bds. Union Depot.

Carpenter Hattie A. Miss, teacher Institute for the Blind.

Carpenter I. John, deputy marshal Union Depot.

Carpenter, M. A. Mrs., (wid. David) r. 133 N. Mississippi.

Carr Charles, pianomaker, bds. 30½ N. Pennsylvania.

Carr Christian F., teamster, r. 37 Oriental.

Carr Geo. W., machinist, r. 420 E. Maryland.

Carr James, expressman, r. 96 Oak.

Carr Omer B., salesman, Carr & Alvey, bds. 490 N. Meridian.

Carr Richard, street contractor, r. 14 Water.

Carr Roland S., (Carr & Alvey) r. 490 N. Meridian.

CARR THOMAS, grocery and produce dealer, 276 S. Missouri, r. same.

CARR & ALVEY, (R. S. Carr & J. H. Alvey) wholesale dealers in hats, caps, etc., 6 W. Louisiana, opposite Union Depot.

Carroll Adolph, clothier, r. 75 Kentucky av.

Carroll James E., clk, John Simpson, r. 67 W. Georgia.

Carroll James E., carpenter, r. 213 N. Liberty.

Carroll John, lab. T. H. & I. Depot.

Carroll Michael, lab. T. H. & I. Depot, r. 369 S. Missouri.

Carroll William, lab. T. H. & I. Depot, bds. 391 S. Missouri.

Carroll & Britt, (T. B. C., and T. J. B.) saloon and billiards, 132 S. Illinois.

Carroll & Collier, (T. B. C., and J. C.) dealers in fruit dryers, 86 S. Illinois.

Carson H. L., r. 37 Forest av.

Carson Peter, lab., r. 199 W. Maryland.

Carson L. A. Mrs., r. 152 E. St. Clair.

Carter Albert, (col'd) barbershop 63 S. Illinois, r. same.

Carter B. M., carpenter, r. 540 N. Mississippi.

Carter C. C., candy mannfactory, 59 N. Illinois, r. same.

Carter Edward, (col'd, Hill and Carter) r. 780 N. Tennessee.

Carter Eliza, (col'd) chambermaid, City Hospital.

CARTER GEORGE, attorney at law, 96 E. Washington, r. 544 N. Tennessee.

Carter G. H., saw mill, r. 167 N. Illinois.
Carter George W., r. 169 N. Illinois.
Carter Harlin, r. 23 N. West.
Carter James F., sawyer, r. 254 N. Mississippi.
Carter John, (Carter J. & Co.) r. 490 N. Alabama.
Carter J. B., miller, r. 199 S. New Jersey.
Carter John E., watchmaker, 125 W. Washington, r. 213 W. Market.
Carter John W., wheat weigher at White Rose mill, r. 299 S. New Jersey.
CARTER JOHN & CO., real estate agents, nw. cor. Washington and Delaware.
Carter Joshua, carpenter, r. 412 N. East.
Carter L. S. Miss, teacher, Indianapolis Young Ladies' Institute, r. Elyria, O.
Carter Robert, lab. r. 67 Howard.
Carter Robert, (col'd) lab., r. 310 N. East.
Carter Sanford A., engineer J. M. & I. R. R., r. 31 Madison av.
Carter Vinson, attorney at law, 74 E. Washington, r. 21 E. St. Joseph.
Carter William, (col'd) barber, Hill and Carter.
Carter William E., saloon 87 S. Illinois, r. same.
Carty Charles C., r. 560 N. Illinois.
Carrin James M., physician, r. 438 S. Meridian.
Case David B., w'ks rolling mill, bds. 217 S. Illinois.
Case David H., engineer, r. 338 E. Ohio.
Case Ella Miss, instructress Grover & Baker Sewing Machine Co., bds. 251 N. Mississippi.
Case E. E., (C. and Parker), r. 94 N. Mississippi.
Case Harvy, lab., r. ne. cor. Ohio and Noble.
Case H. G., book keeper, Little's Hotel, r. same.
Case John B., engineer F. P. Rush, r. 338 E. Ohio.
Case John I., engineer C. C. & I. C. R. R., r. 128 Bates.
Case Lyman, traveling salesman, r. 251 N. Mississippi.
CASE & PARKER, (E. E. Case and J. F. Parker), dealers in agricultural implements, iron, etc., 84 W. Washington.
Casey James, wheelmaker, w'ks Osgood, Smith & Co., bds. 38 S. Tennessee.
Casey Jerry, lab., w'ks gas house, bds. 217 S. Illinois.
Casey Johanna Miss, w'ks Globe House.
Casey John, lab, w'ks paper mill, r. 438 S. West.
Casey Michael, harnessmaker, r. Sinker.
Casey Patrick, lab., r. 107 Hosbrook.
Casey Patrick, lab., r. 432 E Georgia.

Casey Patrick, lab., r. 354 S. West.
Casey Patrick, blower, gas works.
Casey Patrick, lab., bds. 69 Ann.
Casey Patrick, w'ks rolling mill, bds. 300 S Tennessee.
Casey Patrick, lab., works T. H. & I. Depot.
Casey Thomas A., lab., r. 253 N. West.
Cassey Catherine, (wid.) r. 19 Chadwick.
Cassibum Casper, lab., r. 592 E. St. Clair.
Cassidy Joseph, bricklayer, r. 362 E. New York.
Cassin John, engineer, Bates House, r. 91 S. West.
Cassion Michael, lab., r. 63 Wyoming.
Cassman Michael, lab., r. 19 Hosbrook.
Casteel Charles, w'ks Osgood, Smith & Co., r. 69 E. McCarty.
Casteel Hamen, cigarmaker, r. 252 S. Mississippi.
Castello William G., confectioner, r. cor. East and Cherry.
Castello Elizabeth, confectioner, 105 Massachusetts av, r. 31 Cherry.
Castello John, boilermaker, r. 114 Meek.
Castello John J., machinist, w'ks Sinker & Davis, r. 276 W. Maryland.
Castelters H. D., (Sailors & Co.) bds. Depot Dining Hall.
Castelton Hiram D., clk. Stewart & Morgans, bds. U. Depot dining hall.
Castle Hamen, cigar maker, r. 253 S. Mississippi.
Castor E. A., carpenter, r. N. Peru.
Caswell E., piano tuner, bds. Spencer House.
Cathcart Andrew, r. 258 S. New Jersey.
Cathcart Robert W., clk. r. 258 S. New Jersey.
Catherwood J., (Gapen &. Catherwood) bds. Bates House.
CATLIN M. J. MRS., milliner and millinery goods, 46 W. Washington, r. 44 N. Mississippi.
Catlin Wallace, r. 44 W. Mississippi.
Catterson Abel E., policeman, r. 276 E. South.
Catterson Elizabeth Mrs., (wid Robert W.) r. 57 Maple.
Catterson Horace, clk. W. D. Wyatt, r. 276 E. South.
Catterson Robert, mail agent, bds. 80 S. Mississippi.
Catterson William T., works Osgood, Smith & Co., r. 57 Maple.

THE CHINA TEA STORES

ARE LOCATED AT

No. 7 ODD FELLOWS HALL

AND

ACADEMY OF MUSIC CORNER.

SAME GOODS, SAME PRICES at BOTH.

Cavanaugh Edward, lab., r. 239 S. Tennessee.

Cavannaugh Michael, lab., r. 502 E. Georgia.

Cayle James, moulder, works Greenleaf & Co.

Caylor Allen, (C. & Wheatley) r. 183 Indiana av.

Caylor Frank, with Wm. Spootts, r. 136 N. Noble.

Caylor Henry, works cement pipe works, r. 227 N. West.

Caylor Otho, expressman, r. 272 Railroad.

Caylor Susan, (wid Jacob) r. 336 N. West.

Caylor & Co. (Allen Caylor and Martin Wheatley) flour and feed, 185 Indiana av.

Chadwick John, lab., r. 281 Indiana av.

Chadwick Mary J. Miss, operator Weed Sewing machine, r. 144 Stevens street.

Chamberlin William D. Rev., r. 336 W. Vermont.

Chambers Andrew, (col'd) barber, Hill & Carter.

Chambers Charles, baggagemaster, J. M. & I. R. R.

Chambers Mathew, bds. 35 W. Georgia.

Chambers William, (col'd) barber, Hill & Carter.

Champee Joseph, salesman, r. 130 N. Illinois.

Champion William, pressman Sentinel Office, r. 351 S. Meridian.

Chandler George R., printer, r. 119 Indiana av.

Chandler H. C., (H. C. & Co.) r. 278 W. Vermont.

CHANDLER H. C. & CO., (H. C. Chandler and George Merritt) engravers & printers, se. cor. Pearl and Meridian.

Chandler Thomas E., (Chandler & Taylor) r. 34 N. California.

Chandler William, (C. & Co.,) r. 278 W. Vermont.

Chandler William G., pattern maker, r. 278 W. Vermont.

CHANDLER & CO., (Wm. Chandler & ——) wholesale paper house, 24 S. Meridian Street.

Chandler & Taylor, (T. E. C. & F. T.) machinist and iron founders, 370 W. Washington.

Chapman David C., (Osgood & C.) r. 33 Ellsworth street.

Chapman George H., judge criminal court, r. 617 N. Meridian.

Chapman G. Vail, clk. Bates House.

Chapman Mrs. C., dress making, r. 164 N. Delaware.

Chapman Thomas S., carpenter, r. 75 James.

Charles Caroline (col'd, wid) r. 141 Bright.

Charles Fletcher, carriage painter, r. 224 N. Missouri.

Charles Thomas, hack driver, r. 109 S. Noble.

Charter William, works rolling mill, bds. 300 S. Tennessee.

Charter William, lab. rolling mill, r. 21 Rose.

Chase A. Sidney, pianofort maker, r. 304 E. New York.

Chase Arther, with E. B. Martindale, bds. 209 N. Pennsylvania.

Chase Benj. V., bookkeeper, bds. ne. cor. Liberty and New York.

Chase Mary A., (wid) r. 304 E. New York.

Chasteen Charles, cooper, r. cor. Missouri and New York.

Chasteen Harry W., cooper, r. New York third door from Minerva.

Chasteen Jesse V., lab., r. New York bet. Blake and Minerva.

CHATTERTON HENRY R., foreman job room Sentinel Office.

Cheatham Washington, (col'd) brick mason, r. 553 N. Mississippi.

Cheek Evans, engineer I. C. & L. R. R., r. 165 Bates.

Cheek John W., brakeman I. C. & L. R. R., r. 198 Bates.

Cheeney W. G., printer Journal office, r. 14 E. Michigan.

Cheneth Annie Miss, bds. 172 Eddy.

Chenscher Frank, lab. P. C. & St. L. Ft. Depot.

Cherry Andrew, fireman No. 2 engine, bds. 130 E. New York.

Cherry J. L., messenger U. S. Ex. Co., bds. National Hotel.

Chesnichee Thomas, lab., r. 47 Wyoming.

Chetterter W. G., moulder, r. 465 S. New Jersey.

Chibnall Charles, cigarmaker, 35 W. Washington, bds. 113 E. Washington.

Child M. Jr., (J. S. Dunlap & Co.) r. 79 Massachusetts av.

Childers J. R., agent life and fire insurance, room 4 Blackford's blk., r. 60 Fletcher av.

Childers Joshua, lab., r. 70 Virginia av.

Childers Eliza J., (wid John P.) r. 235 S. Noble.

Chill Thomas, carpenter, r. 302 Chesnut.

Chill William, lab., bds. 302 Chesnut.

CHINA TEA STORE, H. H. Lee, proprietor, Academy of Music and No. 7 Odd Fellows Hall.

Chipman L., r. 384 N. Illinois.

Chisolm R. (col'd) lab., r. 350 W. North.

Chister Albert A., stair builder, r. 275 N. Winston.

Chitty S. C., salesman, 46 N. Pennsylvania.

Chivalier Alphonso, house and sign painter, 23 S. East, r. same.

Chiver E. B., shoemaker, 63 Indiana av., r. 123 N. Tennessee.

Chiver J. A. shoemaker, 63 Indiana av., bds. 123 N. Tennessee.

Cholette Louisa H., r. 28 N. Mississippi.

Christ John, boot and shoe manufacturer, 138 S. Meridian, r. same.

Christ Nancy Mrs., (wid William) r. 59 E. McCarty.

Christianson David, bricklayer, r. 103 Hosbrook.

CHRISTIAN WILMER F. (Shover & Christian) r. 146 E. Vermont·

Christy Albert, saloon, 26 W. Louisiana, r. 13 E. South.

Christy Israel, lab. r. 29 Harrison.

Christy John, porter, Surgical Institute, r. same

Christy Levi, (col'd) r. 255 N. Liberty.

Christy William, porter, Speigel, Thoms & Co., r. 344 N. Blake.

Church Benj. F., pressman, Oil Mill, r. 84 S. Liberty.

Church Fannie Mrs. (wid Richard) r. 121 N. West.

Church Henry E., route agent, Daily Journal, r. 121 N. West.

Church Joseph H., works American Saw Works, r. 164 N. Blake.

Church Richard H., works American Saw Works, bds. 225 E. Market.

Churchers Michael, lab., r. 130 Meek.

CHURCHMAN F. M., (H. A, Fletcher & Co.,) r. 130 N. Alabama.

CHURCHMAN WM. H. Superintendent, Institute for the Blind.

Citer Cass, cooper, r. 183 Madison av.

Citizens National Bank, 11 and 13 E. Washington, bet. Meridian and Pennsylvania.

City Assessor's office, Cottrell & Knight's bldg. E. Washington, William Hadley assessor.

City Cemetery, J. M. Hedges, sexton, entrance, ws. Kentucky av. bet. Louisiana and River.

City Clerk's office, Cottrell & Knight's bldg. E. Washington, D. M. Ransdell, clerk.

CITY COUNCIL ROOMS, Cottrell & Knight's bldg. E. Washington.

City Engineer's office, Cottrell & Knight's bldg. E. Washington, R. M. Patterson, engineer.

CITY HOSPITAL, terminus Indiana av. cor. Margaret and Lock.

City Library, room 5, Martindale's blk. N. Pennsylvania.

CITY OFFICES, Cottrell Knight's bldg. E. Washington.

City Treasurer's office, Cottrell & Knight's bldg. E. Washington, R. S. Foster, treasurer.

Claffey Conrad, drayman, r. 69 N. Noble.

Claffey Christian, drayman, 328 N. Noble.

Claffey Fred, mechanic, r. 38 Dougherty.

Claffey Wm. porter, John Woodbridge, bds. 69 Huron.

Claflin C. C., (Treat & C.) r. 489 N. Meridian.

CLAFLIN DAVID B. photographer, 32½ E. Washington, r. 27 W. Ohio.

CLARK A. E. general ticket agent, I. C. & L. R. R., r. Cincinnati, Ohio.

Clark Absalom, r. 19 S. West.

Clark Bessie Miss, r. 186½ W. Washington.

Clark D. L, operator, Boston Ferrotype Co. 33 W. Washington, r. 196 E. Washington.

Clark George, clk. 43 and 45 N. Tennessee.

Clark Hampton, r. 266 Indiana av.

Clark Henry, lab. works Greenleaf & Co., r. cor. McCarty and Tennessee.

Clark Hugh, carriage maker, r. 312 W. Washington.

Clark Levy, produce dealer, r. 133 S. New Jersey.

Clark J. F., clk. C. C. C. & I. R. R. bds. Pyle House.

Clark John, lab., r. 525 S. Meridian.

Clark John, miller, r. 222 W. Ohio.

Clark John T., horse shoeing shop, 27 N. Tennessee, r. 370 S. Illinois.

Clark Maria Mrs. (wid. James B.) r. 177 W. Vermont.

Clark Milton L., works Rolling Mill, r. 310 S. Illinois.

Clark Olive Miss, servant, 44 N. Mississippi.

Clark Patrick, lab. bds. 256 S. Tennessee.

H. H. LEE'S

WHOLESALE PRICES FOR

TEAS, COFFEES & SUGARS,

ARE THE SAME EACH DAY

As are quoted in the

CINCINNATI DAILY PAPERS.

Clark Patrick, moulder, Eagle Machine Works, r. 262 S. Tennessee.

Clark Reuben O., carpenter, r. 176 W. Michigan.

Clark Richard A., (col'd) lab., r. 183 Douglas al.

Clark Thomas, machinist, r. 80 Fayette.

Clark Thomas, works Novelty Works.

Clark Thomas F., traveler, Fairbanks Scales, 43 and 45 N. Tennessee.

Clark Wm. H., merchant tailor, 58 N. Illinois, r. 180 W. Ohio.

Clark William, railroad agent, r. Lockerbie.

Clark Wilson, lab., r. 276 E. North.

Clark Jasper, drayman, r. 63 E. McCarty.

Clarey Patrick, porter, Palmer House, r. 104 Douglass.

Clary Jasper, drayman, 63 E. McCarty.

CLAWSON JOHN C., proprietor, Western House.

Clay Benjamin, (col'd) lab. 126 N. California

Clay Henry, (col'd) lab. r. African al. bet. Sixth and Seventh.

Clay Hillary, secretary, Gatling Gun Co., r. 240 N. Meridian.

Clayton C. J., carpenter, r. 278 S. East.

Clayton L. W., agent for Deloss Root, r. 131 E. New York.

Clear Jerry, lab., r. 241 S. Tennessee.

Clearwater C. H., express messenger, r. Dunlap, nr. Michigan rd.

Cleary Daniel, lab., r. 23 Hahn.

Cleary James, works, Rolling Mill, r. 127 Maple.

Cleary John W., machinist, works Greenleaf & Co. bds. 458 E. Georgia.

Cleaver Jefferson, bricklayer, r. 318 E. New York.

CLEM AARON, grocer and produce dealer, cor. Delaware and Masschusette av., r. 173 Massachusetts av.

Clem Frank, grocer, r. 266 N. Alabama.

Clem Wm. F., bookkeeper, A. Clem, r. 266 N. Alabama.

Clemens Levi, lab., r. 245 W. South.

Clements A. R., engineer C. C. C. & I. R. R., r. 138 N. Davidson.

Cletch Frederick, dyer at Geisendorff's woolen mills. bds. 408 W. Washington.

Cleveland John B. (John S. Spann & Co.) r. Christian av., nr. Plum.

Clifford Ellis, student, bds. 268 E. St. Clair.

Cline Peter, planer, r. 116 S. East.

Clinton James, (col'd) porter C. C. C. & I. R. R. office, r. 228 N. Noble.

Clinton John R., deputy city clerk, r. 284 N. New Jersey.

Close Eliza, (col'd, wid. John) washerwoman, r. 175 W. Washington.

Close W. H. (W. H. C. & Co.) r. 213 N. Pennsylvania.

Close W. H. & Co., proprietors Boston Store, 10 E. Washington.

Closkey David, cigarmaker, r. 296 S. East.

Cloud Caroline Mrs., (wid. James) r. 310 W. Washington.

Cluck William, well digger, r. 314 W. Merrill.

Clune Mary Mrs., (wid. John) mattressmaker, r. 3 72 S. Tennessee.

Clune Michael, mattress manufacturer, r. 474 S. Meridian.

Cooney Thomas, lab., r. 23 Douglass.

Cobb Edward, (Hay & Co.) r. 369 W. Vermont.

Cobb S. H, treasurer Indianapolis & Vincennes R. R., cor. Virginia av. and Delaware, bds. Depot Dining Hall.

Coble Daniel, teamster, r. 99 Hosbrook.

Coble David, (D. & G. Coble) r. 48 Fayette.

Coble George, traveling agent, r. 353 N Noble.

Coble George, (D. & G. C.) r. 386 N. Mississippi.

Coble D. & G., groceries and provisions, 152 W. Washington.

Cobleigh Henry M., works Jackson, Rider & Co.

Coburn Henry, (Coburn & Jones) r. 125 E. New York.

Coburn John, works Coburn & Jones, bds. 75 Oak.

Coburn John, Member of Congress, r. 121 N. Delaware.

Coburn Mary A. (wid. Augustus) r. 75 Oak.

Coburn Samuel, machinist, r. 716 W. Maryland.

Coburn & Jones, (Henry C. W. & H. J.) dealers in lumber, laths, shingles, etc., cor. Mississippi and Georgia.

Cochran Jesse H., bookkeeper White Rose Mill, bds. 322 W. New York.

Cochran Louisa Mrs. (col'd wid. Robert) r. 298 E. Michigan.

Cochran Michael, glassblower, bds. 231 W. South.

Cochran S. W., carpenter, r. 424 N. Mississippi.

Cochran William A., carpenter, r. 420 S. Illinois.

Coddington James, plasterer, r. 661 N. Illinois.

Coe Jacob brewerman, r. 259 W. Maryland.

Coe John, salesman New York store, bds. 228 E. Market.

Coe Willie A. (col'd) servant, 267 W. Vermont.

Coen Hattie Miss, dressmaker, bds. 169 S. Tennessee.

Coen John, boarding house, 169 S. Tennessee.

Coen Mary Miss, hairdresser, bds. 169 S. Tennessee.

Coen Susan Miss, bds. 169 S. Tennessee.

Coffield Elias, engineer, bds. 52 Fletcher av.

Coffield John, engineer I. C. & L. R. R., r. 29 Pine.

Coffield Lucy, (wid. Arthur) r. 52 Fletcher av.

Coffins Abraham, lab., r. 163 Stevenson.

Coffin B. (Wheat, Fletcher & Co.) r. 410 N. Pennsylvania.

Coffin C. E., bookkeeper L. R. Martin, bds. Pyle House.

Coffin Caroline, (wid.) r. 262 N. East.

Coffin D. W. (Wiles Bros. & Co.) r. 432 N. Pennsylvania.

Coffin Ella P. Miss, teacher Fourth Ward school, bds. 262 N. East.

Coffin J. V., traveling agent Wiles Bro. & Co., bds. Sherman House.

Coffin Katie Miss, teacher City Academy, bds. 410 N. Pennsylvania.

Coffin R. M., clk. R. R. Parker's, bds. cor. College and Christian av.

Coffman —— Mrs., millinery, 290 E. Washington, r. same.

Coffman C. W., traveler Vinnedge, Jones & Co., bds. 10 E Michigan.

Coffman John H., auctioneer, r. 290 E. Washington.

Coffman Henry, saddler, res. 65 N. Liberty.

Cogan James R., M. D., r. 460 Virginia av.

Cogel Mary E. Mrs. (wid. Stephen) r. 237 Huron.

Cogell William, contractor, r. 223 Virginia av.

Cohen Abraham, second-hand clothing store, 31 S. Illinois, r. Cincinnati, O.

Cohen Hyam, clk., 31 S. Illinois, r. same.

Colbus F. W., carpenter, r. 121 Forest av.

Colclazer J. H., salesman W. P. Bingham, bds. 179 N. Illinois.

Colden John E. (Colden & Johnson) r. 129 Union.

Colden & Johnson, real estate agents, Talbott & New's blk., N. Pennsylvania.

4

Cole Albert M., engineer, r. 608 E. Washington.

COLE BARTON W., Secretary N. W. C. University, bds. 171 Jackson.

Cole Burnam, stock dealer, r. Western av., nr. Butler.

Cole John, lab, bds 277 Indiana av.

Cole Oscar S., clk. general freight office T. H. & I. R. R.

Cole Samuel H., works Osgood, Smith & Co., r. 467 S. Illinois.

Cole William, (col'd) lab., r. African al., bet. Sixth and Seventh.

Cole W. M., traveler Hibben, Tarkington & Co., bds. Sherman House.

Coleman E. P., engineer, r. 37 Bates.

Coleman Herman, meat market, 300 N. West, cor. North, r. same.

Coleman Henry, works State House, r. Market, opposite State House.

Coleman Patrick, works Glass Works, r. 436 S. West.

Coleman Ruhanah, (wid. Henry) r. cor. Blake and Elizabeth.

Coleman Thomas, lab., r. 68 Bicking.

Coles Georgia, dressmaker, bds. 199 N. Illinois.

Coles Susan, dressmaker, 199 N. Illinois, r. same.

Colestock Ephriam, carpenter, r. 250 N. Illinois.

Colestock George N., bookbinder W. & J. Braden's, bds. 250 N. Illinois.

Coley Richard, (col'd) carpenter, r. W. Second, bet. Howard and Lafayette R. R.

Colgan Henrie Miss, principal Court House School, r. cor. of Christian and College av.

Colgan Henry G., farmer, r. Christian av., cor. College.

Colgan Miss Mary, teacher, school in Court House, r. cor. Christian and College av.

Colgrove S. W., mail agent C. C. C. & I. R. R.

Collett Moses, mercantile business, r. 413 N. New Jersey.

Colley Jane, (wid.) r. 338 N. New Jersey.

Collier William S., trader, r. 191 S. Alabama.

Collins Conrad, lab., r. 223 S. West.

Collins Dan, lab., American Saw Works, bds. 22 S. East.

THE CHINA TEA STORES

Are very handsomely decorated with

Accurate Views and Scenes

or

CHINESE LIFE AND S'ENERY.

Call and see them before leaving the City.

Collins Emanuel, (col'd) lab., bds. 231 W. Ohio.

Collins E.G, carpenter, r. 119 Buchanan.

Collins James, repairer Western Union Telegraph, bds. 34 W. Louisiana.

Collins Jeremiah, lithographer, r. 22 S. East.

Collins Jerry, machinist, r. 639 Buchanan.

Collins John, works rolling mill, bds. 272 S. Tennessee.

Collins John, carpenter, r. 239 Buchanan.

COLLINS JOSEPH G., proprietor Temperance House, 35 W. Georgia.

Collins L. (col'd) barber, bds. Bicking House.

Collins Martin, lab., r. 20 N. California.

Collins Thomas, works Street R. R. Co., bds. 20 N. Noble.

Collins William, lab., r. 187 Meek.

Colopy Patrick, turner, r. 136 W. Michigan.

Colwell Emma R. Mrs., teacher, Ninth Ward School, r. 67 N. Davidson.

Colwell Samuel, railroader, r. 67 N. Davidson.

Combs James W., peddler, r. 452 S. New Jersey.

Comegys Levi, r. N. Illinois, bet. Fifth and Sixth W.

COMER STEPHEN, groceries and produce, 668 N. Tennessee, r. same.

Comingore John A. Dr., office 1 Massachusetts av., r. 335 N. Liberty.

Comingore W. H. (Sherman & Co.) r. 320 N. Alabama.

Commander R. S, clk. Bee Hive store, bds. Macy House.

COMMONS JOHN M., Private Secretary, Gov. Baker, r. 863 N. Alabama.

Commons M C. Miss, teacher Fourth Ward bds. 363 N. Alabama.

COMMONWEALTH LIFE INSURANCE COMPANY, New York, V. T. Gibson & Brother, ag'ts, 5 Odd Fellows Hall.

Compton A. P., money broker, bds. Macy House.

Conant E P., engineer, C. C. & I. C. R. R.

CONATY JAMES B, dealer in millinery goods and notions and bleaching, 44 S. Illinois, r. same.

Conde Charles A. & Co., manufacturers of steam governors, 197 S. Meridian, cor. South, r. 13 Gas bldg.

Conde H. T., bookkeeper, C. Dickson & Co., bds. Pyle House.

Condit Alice A., manufacturer feather cloth, 10 S. Pennsylvania, r. same.

Condit Amza, engineer, r. 10 S. Pennsylvania.

Condit J. D., general agent, No. 1 Blackford's blk., r. 54 Circle.

Conduitt Alexander B. (Landers, C. & Co.) r. 256 N. Alabama.

Cone W. S., clk. J. M. & I. R. R., r. 211 W. Maryland.

Coney Cornelius, lab., r. 197 Meek.

Coney Thomas, lab., r. se. part of city.

Coney William J., carpenter, r. 71 Jackson.

Conipagne Andrew, carpenter, r. 118 Huron.

Conipagne Louis, carpenter, r. 118 Huron.

Conitott Allen, helper, glass works, bds. 88 S. Mississippi.

Conitott Jerome, blower, glass works, bds. 88 S. Mississippi.

CONKLIN H. N., Life Insurance Agent, 16½ E. Washington, r. 252 N. Mississippi.

Conklin Jenny Miss, dressmaker, bds. 148 Indiana av.

Conlen Michael, book agent, r. 323 Indiana av.

Conley Robert, dealer in coal, lime, etc., r. 296 N. Alabama.

Conley Thomas R. cooper, r. New York, bet. Blake and Minerva.

Connelly A. G., railroad engineer, r. 114 S. East.

Connelly Hugh, lab., r. 43 Henry.

Connelly Michael, lab., r. 16 Root.

Connelly Robert, (Fawkner & Co.) r. 296 N. Alabama.

Conner A. H. (Douglass & C.) r. 525 N. Pennsylvania.

Conner B. F., registry clk, P. O., bds. 425 N. Pennsylvania.

Conner Daniel, lab., r. 191 Meek.

Conner Elizabeth, (wid.) r. 425 N. Pennsylvania.

Conner Herbert J., clk. P. O., bds. 425 N. Pennsylvania.

Conner James, railroader, r. 485 E. Georgia.

Conner James H. (Shaw, Lippencott & C.) r. Greensburgh, Ind.

Conner John, lab., r. 288 S. Delaware.

Conner John T, clk. Pension Office, bds. Little Hotel.

Conner Mrs. (wid.) r. 124 S. Noble.

Conner Mary, servant, Sherman House.

Conner Mary E. Mrs., boarding house, 73 N. Illinois.

Conner Mark, lab., I. C. & L. depot, r. cor. Ellen and Elizabeth.
Conner Michael, horse shoer, John Hitchens, r. 113 Massachusetts av.
Conner Michael, lab , r. 237 Coburn.
Conner Michael, moulder, r. 50 W. South.
Conners Michael, lab., works Spencer House, r. Minerva, W. end Vermont.
Conner Minerva, domestic, Bates House.
Conner Patrick L., boot and shoemaker, 66 Massachusetts, av., r. same.
Conner Richard, (col'd) lab , r. 38 Bates.
Conner Robert, works Novelty Works.
Connor Michael, blacksmith, r. 113 Massachusetts av.
Conrad Charles P., livery stable, 19 S. Delaware.
Conrad Elder Rufus, r. 526 N. Mississippi.
Conrad Gabel, bds. California House.
Conroy Barnard, teamester, 24 W. Maryland, bds. 79 S. West.
Conroy P , tailor, r. 72 S. West.
Consins F. (wid. William) r. 182 W. Second.
Conti A., fruitstand, cor. Washington and Illinois, r. 113 E. Washington.
Converse Joel, carpenter, r. 166 S. East.
Conway Mag. Mrs , r. 334 S. Delaware.
Conwell Emma S. Miss, sewing operator, 18 N. Delaware, r. 12 S. New Jersey.
Conwell, I. S., sewing machine agent, r. 120 S. New Jersey.
Conzelmann George, clk., 27 W. Washington, bds. Emenegger's Hotel.
Conzlemann Michael, principal, German Lutheran School, r. 88 S. Liberty.
Cook A , baggagemaster, C. C. C. & I. R. R., bds. Sherman House.
Cook Charles, stovemoulder, bds. 14 Bates
Cook Charles, (C. and Weigman) r. 84 N. Liberty.
Cook Christian, baggageman, r. 26 Dicking.
Cook Christian, machinist, bds. 193 S. Tennessee.
Cook Cornelius C., w'ks Osgood, Smith & Co., bds. 169 S. Tennessee.
Cook Emma, domestic. Bates House.
Cook Frank, lab., r. 239 W. East.
Cook George W , painter, bds. James bet. Indiana av. and St. Clair.
Cook H., traveling agent, bds. Bates House.
Cook Hamilton, lab., r. 10 nr. Canal.
Cook Henry, clk., O. T. Porters, r. 22 John.
Cook Henry, bricklayer, r. 17 Morrison.
Cook Ignatz, machinist, w'ks Osgood, Smith & Co., r. 491 S. Illinois.
Cook Jane Mrs., r. 24 Indiana av.
Cook John, machinist, r. 38 Chatham.
Cook John, railroader, r. 342 N. Winston

BENHAM BRO'S,

36 East Washington St.,

Pianos, Organs and Melodeons Tuned, Moved and Repaired.

Cook John B., ag't for T. Bender & Co., r. 87 S. Benton.
Cook Lucinda, (wid. Jessie M.) r. James bet. Indiana av. and St. Clair.
Cook M. R., painter, r. 164 S. Noble.
Cook Robert, w'ks Osgood, Smith & Co., r. 169 S Tennessee.
Cook Samuel M., engineer, C. Glazier, r. 188 Virginia av.
Cook T. V., sign painter. 58 N. Pennsylvania, r. sc. city limits.
Cook Wm., grocer, r. 47 S. East.
Cook William, (Cook and Co.) r. 85 S. East.
Cook W. I., bookkeeper, r. 90 N. Delaware.
Cook William H., cooper, r. James bet. Indiana av. and St. Clair.
Cook W. & Co. (W. C. and C. Danmeyer) grocery and dry goods, r. 249 E. Washington.
COOK & WIEGMAN, dealers in flour, feed, grain, seeds, etc., r. 253 E. Washington.
Coole Christian, machinist, Eagle Machine Works, r. cor. South and Tennessee.
Cooney Bridget Mrs., clk., 46 W. Washington, bds. 27 N. East.
Cooney Dennis, lab., r. 27 N. East.
Cooney Patrick, moulder, Eagle Machine Works, bds. Ray House.
Cooney T. G., bds. 225 E. Market.
Cooney Thomas, lab., bds. 30 Douglass.
COONS JOHN W., deputy city treasurer, r. 405 N. New Jersey.
Cooper Amistral, lab., r. cor. Lafayette R. R. and Third.
Cooper Hamilton, tailor, r. 260 W. St. Clair.
Cooper I. I., feed stable, Court, r. 422 N. Illinois
Cooper Jane, (wid. Hamilton) r. 260 W. St. Clair.
Cooper John J., feed store, r. 422 N. Illinois.
Cooper Joseph M. Dr., r. 217 W. Michigan.
Cooper Job, bookkeeper, 132 S. Illinois, bds. same.
Cooper M. J., mail agent, T. H. & I. R. R., r. 409 N. New Jersey.
Cooper R. M., trunkmaker, 39 S. Illinois, bds. Stanridge House.
Cooper Rebecca, r. 257 E. McCarty.
Cooper William H., w'ks glass works, bds. 155 W. Maryland.

H. H. LEE,

Dealer in

Teas, Coffees, Sugars & Spices,

No. 7 ODD FELLOWS HALL

AND

ACADEMY OF MUSIC CORNER.

COORS AUGUST F., groceries and provisions, 151 W. Washington, r. 12 S. Mississippi.

Copeland J. W. & Co. (J. W. C. and C. Annan) jobbers of millinery and straw goods, 116 S. Meridian and 8 E. Washington.

Copeland J. W. (J. W. C. and Co.) r. 382 N. Meridian.

Copeland W. J., real estate and insurance agent, 14 S. Pennsylvania, r. 73 N. Liberty.

Coppard Harry, porter, surgical institute, r. same.

CORBALEY & COSSEL, (S. B. C. and W. C.) grocers and provisions, 414 W. Washington.

Corbaley Robert, clk. county clerk's office, bds. 80 S. Mississippi.

Corbaley Samuel B. (C. and Cossel) r. 414 W. Washington.

Corbaley Will H., notary public with B. F. Witt, r. 15 Fayette.

Corcoran Michael, blower, glass works, bds. 231 W. South.

Corey Leander H., machinist, Greenleaf & Co., r. 392 S. Tennessee.

Coridan Maggie Miss, waiter, Spencer House.

Coridan Thomas, saloon, 350 S. West, r. same.

Corley Dan., lab., r. 271 Merrill.

CORLISS C. T. DR., office, room No. 5 Miller's blk., up stairs, cor. Illinois and Market, r. 169 N. Illinois.

Cornelius Caskins, plasterer, r. 254 S. Alabama.

Cornelius E. G. (Byron C. and Co.) r. 138 E. Pratt.

Cornelius Wilbur F. (C. and Mellville) r. 112 Huron.

Cornelius & Melville, (W. F. C. and R. M.) house and sign painters, 31 Kentucky av.

Corrigan John, teamster, r. 311 W. Market.

Cornwell Chas. engineer, C. C. C. & I. R. R., r. 289 Winston.

Cormine William E., student, bds. 116 Broadway.

Cosly R. M., carpenter and builder, 317 Massachusetts av., r. 32 Christian av.

Cosler David W., carpenter, r. 195 N. Davidson.

Cosler William H., r. 801 N. Tennessee.

Coslon John, shoemaker, r. 347 S. Missouri.

Costello John, boilermaker, bds. 214 Meek.

Costello I. L., machinist, r. 276 W. Maryland.

Costello Martin, fireman, I. C. & L. R. R., r. 72 S. Benton.

Coster Mary Mrs., confectionery and restaurant, 22 N. Delaware, r. same.

COSTIGAN FRANK, r. 30 W. Pratt.

Costigan T. G., bds. Palmer House.

COTTRELL THOMAS, tin-plate, copper, sheet brass, sheet iron, etc., etc., 177 E. Washington, r. 160 S. New Jersey.

Coughlen Frank, clk. Merritt & Coughlen, bds. 282 W. New York.

Coughlen William, (Merritt & Coughlen) r. 282 W. New York.

Coughren Silas, lab. Rolling Mill, r. 27 Rose.

Coulon Charles, (C. G. Coulon & Co.) r. Arsenal Road.

Coulon Charles G. (C. G. C. & Co.) r. 168 E. Washington.

Coulon Charles G. & Co. (C. G. Coulon & C. Coulon) dealers in glass and queensware, 168 E. Washington.

Coulon James, railroader, r. Louisiana, bet. Alabama and New Jersey.

Coulter Arch. C., r. 256 S. Delaware.

Coulter James, lab., r. 376 S. Alabama.

Coulter John, works Rolling Mill, r. 213 S. Tennessee.

Coulter Margaret E Mrs. (wid. Charles) r. 191½ W. Washington.

Coulter William, blacksmith, 256 S. Delaware.

Council John F. (Reed, C. & Co.) r. sw. cor. Cherry and Jackson.

Courtney John, lab., r. 502 E. Georgia.

Couzzins Lizzie, domestic, Bates House.

Coval Alexander, cooper, r. 192 Virginia av.

Covault E. J., salesman Rickard & Talbott, bds. Sherman House.

Coverdale George, clk., bds. 149 S. East.

Coverdill Geo. W., lab., bds. 149 S. East.

Coverdill Thomas, lab., r. S. Mississippi, nr. Rolling Mill.

Covert Isaac, butcher, r. 80 Huron.

Covert William T., carpenter, r. 759 N. Mississippi.

Covey Benj. F., cooper, bds 314 E. Georgia.

Covington Emily, bookbinder, r. 12 N. California.

Covington Susan Mrs., chair repairer, r. 12 N. California.

Covour Catherine Mrs. (wid. Daniel) r. 50 Huron.

COWEN M. V. B., publisher of directories and general agent for popular subscription books, etc., r. 50 S. Illinois.

Cowen Robert B., clk., 30 Kentucky av., bds. Palmer House.

Cox A. J., salesman Dessar Bros. & Co. r. 76 N. Noble.

Cox Albert W., patent right agent, r. 174 E. Walnut.

Cox Ann, (wid.) r. 252 W. Market.

Cox Amy, (wid. Daniel) r. 18 Chatham.

Cox Charles, dealer in stoves and tinware, 57 W. Washington, r. 71 S. Meridian.

Cox Critt A., sleeping car conductor, r. 18 Chatham.

Cox David, tinsmith, r. 71 S. Meridian.

COX E. T., State Geologist, office in State House, r. 356 N. Illinois.

Cox Henry C., carpenter, r. 224 W. Washington.

Cox Edwin, works Merritt & Coughlin, r. S. Douglass.

Cox John A. M., sheet iron worker, 24 E. Georgia, r. 264 S. Alabama.

Cox John F., sawmill, r. 105 Bradshaw.

Cox Milton L. (Landers, Conduitt & Co.) r. 333 N. Illinois.

Cox Sarah L. Miss, seamstress, r. 18 Chatham.

Cox Sophia Mrs. (wid. Nathaniel) r. 252 W. Market.

COX THOMAS J., boiler and sheet iron works, 24 E. Georgia, r. 264 S. Alabama.

Cox Thomas T. (S. & C.) r. Louisiana, bet. Noble and East.

Cox Wm. A., foreman J. W. Adams, r. 395 N. West.

Cox William C. (Tomlinson & Cox) r. 30 W. St. Clair.

Coy Daniel C., trimmer, Shaw L. & Co., r. N. Alabama.

Coy Joseph, cooper, r. 52 California.

Coy Simeon, carriage painter, r. Gregg, nr. East.

Coyle Hannah Mrs. (wid. Michael) r. 126 W. Ohio.

Coyner J. S., carpenter, r. 598 N. Illinois.

Coyner Martin L., contractor, r. 449 E. St. Clair.

Coyner Martin L., jr., assistant engineer, bds. 31 W. Ohio.

Cozad Justus L., chief engineer, I. & St. L. R. R. Co., office, 142 Maryland, r. 195 Jackson.

Crabtree Abram, (col'd) lab., r. W. First, nr. Howard.

Craft Amelia G. (wid. William E.) r. 496 N. Tennessee.

Craft Frost, student, r. 496 N. Tennessee.

BENHAM BRO'S,

36 East Washington St.,

AGENTS FOR THE

BURDETT ORGAN.

Craft Hiram J., chief clk. U. S. Assessor Internal Revenue, bds. 17 S. Pennsylvania.

Craft John P., bookkeeper Sinker & Co., r. 496 N. Tennessee.

Craft R. P., machinist, r. 496 N. Tennessee.

Craft Smith, blacksmith, r. 286 Indiana av.

Craft Wm. H. (C. & Cutter) r. 163 N. Alabama.

Craft W. P., salesman Dury & Hawk, r. 496 N. Tennessee.

CRAFT & CUTTER, (W. H. Craft and H. P Cutter) watchmakers and jewelers, 24 E. Washington.

Craig Alex., salesman 123 S. Meridian r. 218 Huron.

Craig David P., carpenter, r. 183 Indiana av.

Craig J. C. (Francis & Co.) r. Lawrenceburg, Ind.

Craig James C., whisky gauger 6th district, bds Palmer House.

Craig William, miller, N. Delaware, nr. Tinker.

Craighan Henry, (col'd) messenger Fletcher's bank, r. 181 Elm.

Craighan Patrick, lab., r. 60 S. Alabama.

Craighead R., student, bds. 230 N. Tennessee.

Crail S. V., expressman, r. Wabash, bet East and New Jersey.

Crain Charles, engineer C. C. C. & I. R. R.

Crain Henry, salesman, bds. 30½ N. Pennsylvania.

CRAIN W. N., merchant tailor, 32 W. Washington, bds. Bates House.

Cramer Caroline, (wid.) r. nw. cor. of East and Ohio.

Cramer Francis Miss, bds. 366 N. West.

Cramer George H., steward Bates House, r. cor. New York and Blake.

Crane Dennis, porter depot dining hall, r. 6 Henry.

Crane E. G., machinist, bds. 378 N. Delaware.

Crane George W., blacksmith, r. 378 N. Delaware.

Crane H. A., salesman New York store, r. 30 N. Pennsylvania.

Crane J. D., photographer, 279 E. Washington, r. 254 S. Mississippi.

Crane Jacob, driver Meikel's brewery wagon, r. 239 W. Maryland.

Crane James F., potographer, r. 256 S. Mississippi.

Crane William, blacksmith, bds. 88 S. Noble.

Crans I. T., bookkeeper, 14 Talbott & New's blk., bds. Palmer house.

Crapo R. P., manager, S. Hudson, 196 E. Washington, r. same.

Craulley Thomas, moulder Eagle Machine Works, r. 64 Bicking.

Craven Annie Miss, dressmaker, works 34 S. Illinois.

Craven John, works rolling mill, r. 273 W. Merrill.

Cravin John, lab. T. H. & I. Depot, r. 85 McCarty.

Cravin Timothy, lab. T. H. & I. Depot, r. 229 S. West.

Crawford Belle Miss, teacher, r. 256 S. Pennsylvania.

Crawford C. C., bookkeeper, bds. 21 S. Pennsylvania.

Crawford Eli, moulder, r. 256 S. Pennsylvania.

Crawford George W., street car driver, r. se. cor. 6th and Tennessee.

Crawford James M. Rev., r. 330 N. East.

Crawford John T., fireman T. H. & I. R. R., r. 259 S. Mississippi.

Crawson Abner, (col'd) lab., r. 185 Elm.

Creeden Jerry, works Gas Works, bds. 217 S. Illinois.

Criley W. W., pastor, First English Lutheran Church, r. 409 N. Pennsylvania.

Crillman David, machinist, C. C. & I. C. shops, bds. Ray house.

Crone Henry, (col'd) porter Fletcher's bank, r. 181 Elm street.

Crone Jacob, driver J. L. Meikel, r. 259 N. Maryland.

Croney Timothy, lab. T. H. & I. R. R., r. 229 S. West.

Cronin John, lab., works T. H. & I. R. R. depot, r. 85 W. McCarty.

Cropper James, engineer C. C. C. & I. R. R., r. 219 N. Winston.

Cropper Joseph W., carpenter, r. 126 N. Noble.

Cropsey Mrs. A. M., r. 359 N. Alabama.

Cropsey Miss Mary, teacher first ward school, r. 359 N. Alabama.

Crosby John, lab., r. 69 E. Maryland.

Crosby Kate Miss, servent, 85 W. Maryland.

Crosby Mary Mrs., boarding house, r. 452 E Georgia.

Crosby Michael, clk. cor. Illinois and Georgia, bds. 67 W. Georgia

Crosby Toliver, (col'd) lab., r. Rhode Island near Blake.

Crosgrove Michael, works rolling mill, r. 29 Henry.

Crosgrove Patrick, blacksmith, r. 29 Henry.

Crosgrove Rose Mrs., (wid Dominick), r. 29 Henry.

Cross Frederick, lab. C. C. & I. C. R. R.

Crothston James, salesman New York store, bds. 31 W. Ohio.

Crouch John, huckster, r. 82 Green.

Crow Hannah (wid) r. over 280 E. Washington

Crowley John, works rolling mill, r. 372 S. Tennessee.

Crowley Patrick, lab., r. 64 S. Alabama.

Crowley Timothy, teamster, r. 40 Elizabeth.

Crowley William, lab. r. 237 N. Missouri.

Crozier George, night watchman New York store, r. 350 N. Meridian.

Crull Jacob, horse trader, r. 327 E Washington.

Crull Jacob, r. 85 Davidson.

Crullman David, machinest, C. C. & I. C. R. R.

Crum Jacob, tailor, 50 N. Illinois, bds. 64 W. Maryland.

Crum John, insurance agent, r. 228 E. Lousiana.

Crump George, yard man, Bates house.

Crusa Susan, (wid Christ) r. 165 N. Winston.

Cruse Bridget Mrs., (wid Micheal) r. 126 S. Tennessee.

Cruse John, lab., bds. 126 S. Tennessee.

Cruse John P., builder and contractor, r. 530 E. Washington.

Cruse Michael, boiler maker, bds. 126 S. Tennessee.

Cruse Solomon, farmer, r. 122 E. Pratt.

Crutchfield Stephen, lab., r. African al. bet. Sixth and Seventh.

Culbert Patrick, lab., r. 436 S. West.

CULLEY DANIEL B., bookkeeper, r. 486 N. Pennsylvania.

Culligan John, works Street R. R. Co., r. 28 Willard.

CULLINY'S EMPORIUM, 72 W. Washington.

CULLINY P. M., dry goods importer, 72 W. Washington, r. 54 Massachusetts av.

Cullum E., printer, Braden & Burferd, r. 41 Huron.

Culver E., groceries and produce, 240 Indiana av. r. same.

Cummins Charles, lab., r. 372 S. West.

Cummings Lewis, (col'd) butler, r. 175 Douglass al.

Cunningham Frank, bds. 350 N. Tennessee.

Cunningham John, bar keeper 52 S. Illinois, bds. 16 Willard.

Cunningham J. B., civil engineer, room 7 Ætna building, r. 286 N. Pennsylvania.

Cunningham James, drayman, 143 S. Meridian.

Cunningham John, moulder, r. sw. cor. Ray and Tennessee.

Cunningham Walker, machinest, C. C. & I. C. shops, bds. Ray House.

Curley John, lab., r. 4 Stevens.

Curly John R., lab., r. 159 Stevens.

Curran Bridget, chambermaid, Sherman House.

Curran Bridget, (wid.) r. 354. Winston.

Curran John, lab., r. 163 Dougherty.

Curran Michael, lab., r. 194 Bates.

Curran Michael, railroader, r. 489 E. Georgia.

Curran Patrick, blacksmith, C. C. & I. C. R. R.

Curran Patrick H. (Lawless & C.) r. 56 Huron.

Currans Barbary, domestic, Bates House.

Currans Catherine, domestic, Bates House.

Currans Mary, domestic, Bates House.

Currlen Fredrick, cabinetmaker, r. 142 S. Meridian.

Curry Joseph W., lumber dealer, bds. 24 Blake.

Curry Robert, lumber and log dealer, r. 24 Blake.

Curson J. E, carpenter, bds. 139 N. Alabama.

Curtin Christ, lab., bds., 199 W. Maryland.

Curtis Andrew, Justice of the Peace, r. 27 Ft. Wayne av.

Curtis David M., lab., r. 128 N. East.

Curtis Truman, engineer, r. 65 California.

Curtis H. K., general agent Atlas Life Insurance Co., 4½ West Washington, r. 106 Broadway.

Curtis J. P., conductor C. C. & I. C. R. R., bds. Spencer House.

Curtis Joseph, (col'd) cook, r. 203 W. North.

Cuny Hamilton, lab., r. 588 N. Mississippi.

Curzon Joseph, architect, room 4 Blackford's blk. r. 376 N. Illinois.

Cushing H., harnessmaker, bds. Illinois House.

Cussick Joseph, grocer and produce dealer, 75 S. West, r. same.

Custar Theodore, lab., r. 265 Union.

Cussen Garrett, dry goods and notions, 158 Indiana av., r. same.

Cute Jennie Miss., bds. 249 N Winston.

Cutter H. B. (Craft & C.) bds. Macy House.

Cutts Jeffry O., student, bds. 116 Broadway.

Cuts Milton, hatter. r. 239 S. Alabama.

Cutsinger John, railroader, r. 128 E. Merrill.

Cutsinger William, lab., r. 1 Rockwood.

Cuykendall Warren A., engineer, 350 E. Louisiana.

DACY PATRICK, lab., r. 17 Maple.

Dade Townsand, (col'd) lab., r. 232 N. Missouri.

Daffield Louis, r. 259 N. Liberty.

Daggett R. P. (D. & Roth) r. 280 N. New Jersey.

Daggett William, (D. & Co) r. 280 N. New Jersey.

DAGGETT & CO. (Wm. D., Geo. C. Webster and J. W. Smithers) confectionery and fruits, 26 S. Meridian.

DAGGETT & ROTH, (R. P. D. and Matthew Roth) architects, Vinton's blk.

Daglish John, clk., Bee Hive, r. 504 N. Mississippi.

Daily Bridget, servant, Palmer House.

Daily Edward, blacksmith, bds. 225 S. Tennessee.

Daily Hezikiah, (Sphar & D.) bds. 82 E. St. Clair.

Daily Jennie, r. 36 S. New Jersey.

Daily John, painter, Shaw, Lippencott & Conner, r. 343 Vincent.

Daily Joe Miss, servant, Sherman House.

Daily Julia, servant, Palmer House.

Daily Nellie Miss, weaver at Geisendorff. & Co., bds. 192 Virginia av.

Daily Mickee H. (wid. Hugh) r. 24 Center.

Daily Samuel, mechanic, bds. 354 E. Ohio.

Daily Thomas, conductor J. M. & I. R. R. bds. Depot Dining Hall.

Daily William, lab., r. 345 N. Winston.

Daily and Weekly Telegraph Office, se. cor. Meridian and Circle.

THE CHINA TEA STORES

ARE AT

No. 7 ODD FELLOWS HALL

AND

ACADEMY OF MUSIC CORNER.

Dain Robert C., paperhanger, r. 33 W. St. Clair.

Dain Thomas, night policeman, r. 114 E. St. Mary.

Dale Alfred, Carpenter, cor. Patterson and Vermont.

Dale Peter, lab., r. 31 McCarty.

Dall E. J., shoemaker, bds. California House.

Dallas Bell Miss, clk. R. Sedgwick, r. 190 N. Blackford.

Dallas Wm., edge tool maker, N. Kellog, r. 190 N. Blackford.

Dallas John, works rolling mill.

Dallas ——, (wid.) r. 190 N. Blackford.

Dalon John, lab., r. 360 S. Delaware.

Dalton Michael, lab., T. H. & I. Depot, r. 391 S. Minerva.

Dalton William, lab., bds. 551 S. Meridian.

Daly David M., varnisher, r. 326 E. New York.

Daly Eugene, carpenter, r. 343 Massachusetts, av.

DAME JASON, marble worker, 69 E. Washington, r. 287 S. New Jersey.

Dammeier Anthony, grocer, r. 683 E. Washington.

Dammeier Charles, (Cook & Co.) r. 310 E. Georgia.

Dammeier Fred, draymen, r. 266 E. Ohio.

Dame Mrs. P., r. 114 E. St. Mary.

Danforth Albert J., contractor, r. 178 E. Walnut.

Daniel Adam, engineer, r. 187 S. Anlabama.

Daniel Leopold, salesman H. Bamberger, r. 1 Ft. Wayne av.

Daniels Elliott, carpenter, r. 3 and 9 S. East.

Daniels George, machinist, works Greenleaf &c., r. 131 S. Meridian.

Daniels George T., boarding house, 131 S. Illinois.

Daniels Henry, (col'd) lab., r. 170 Douglass al.

Daniels L. H., carpenter, bds. 187 S. Tennessee.

Daniels S. P., tailor, r. 109 S. New Jersey.

Danihy Peter, lab., r. 374 S. Tennessee.

Danner John, lab., r. 218 S. New Jersey.

Danner Mahola, (wid. Andrew) r. 21 Center.

Danninberg Mrs. M., r. 175 E. South.

Danninberg William, tailor, r. 719 N. Mississippi.

Danridge Elias, (col'd) lab., r. 172 W. Georgia.

Darby John H. & Co., r. 227 W. New York.

Darby Samuel, sawmaker, r. 476 Alabama.

Darby Samuel F., sawfiler, r. 476 N. Alabama.

Dare William, brickmason, r. 532 E. Georgia.

Dark Charles E., clk., Fletcher & Sharp, bds. 348 N. Tennessee.

Dark Jonathan, (Lamis & Dark) r. 393 N. West.

Darmody Thomas, porter, 26 S. Meridian, r. Sinker, bet. Alabama and New Jersey.

Darnall Calvin, carpenter, r. 738 N. Illinois.

Darnell William W., carpenter, r. 342 E. New York.

Darr William, fireman, C. C. & I. C. R. R.

Darrow Benjamin, clk. J. C. Burton & Co., r. 545 N. Illinois.

Darrow George, teamster and contractor, r. 297 N. Winston.

Darrow M. W., printer, Sentinel office, r. 58 Massachusetts av.

Dasher M. A. (wid) r. 339 N. Illinois.

Daubenspeck Nelson, real estate, r. 121 N. Delaware.

Daugherty E. Miss, dress maker, room 12 Martindale's blk.

Daugherty James, lab., r. 14 Willard.

Daumont Henry, (H. D. & Co.) r. 439 N. Pennsylvania.

Daumont H. & Co. (Henry Daumont & ——) dealers in clocks, paintings, pictures, picture frames, etc., 15 W. Washington.

Dausch Catharine Miss, cook, Emeneger's hotel.

Davenport Malinda, (wid. John) r. Minerva, nr. New York.

Davenport Thomas, lab., r. 115 Huron.

Davenport Thomas, lab., r. 229 S. Alabama.

Davenport William, printer, bds. 24 W. Minerva.

David Daniel, machinist, r. 209 S. Illinois.

David Edward, wks. rolling mill, bds. 272 S. Tennessee.

David George, checkman, C. C. C. & I. depot, r. 273 E. Market.

David Thomas, butcher, r. 210 Union.

David William C., Deputy U. S. Marshal, r. 253 E. Market.

DAVIDSON C. B., pastor Grace church, r. 104 Massachusetts av.

Davidson George, capenter, r. 188 Daugherty.

Davidson James, printer, Journal office.

Davidson John, agent, Indianapolis Journal, r. 170 N. Davidson.

Davidson I. E., auditor, I. & St. Louis R. R., bds. Bates House.

Davidson Rufus, millwright, 132 S. Pennsylvania, r. 148 Blackford.

Davis A., machinist, Surgical Institute, r. same.

Davis Amos, (col'd) lab., r. 747 N. Tennessee.

Davis Abel E. (Baxter & D.) r. 325 N. West.

Davis A. W., physician, office, 130 N. Pennsylvania, bds. Palmer House.

Davis Benjamin, railroader, T. H. & I. R. R., r. 249 E. Louisiana.

Davis Benjamin & Co. (B. D. and John Weaver) coal dealers, office, 108 S. West.

Davis Charles B., gen'l agent, Imperial Fire Insurance Co., 6 Odd Fellows' Hall, r. 139 Indiana av.

Davis Charles S., butcher, bds. 234 N. East.

Davis Clinton, r. 21 Fletcher av.

Davis David, wk's rolling mill, r. 281 S. Tennessee.

Davis Edwin A. (Voss & Davis) bds. Bates House.

Davis Edward W., meat market, 155 W. Washington, bds. 234 N. East.

Davis F. A. W., cashier, Indiana Banking Co.

Davis George, watchmaker and jeweler, 39 W. Washington, r. 40 N. California.

Davis George, (col'd) porter, B. G. Stout & Bro.

Davis Greer W., painter, wks Indianapolis Agricultural Works, r. 172 S. Tennessee.

Davis Giles M., (col'd) blacksmith, shop 252 Indiana av.

Davis G. M., bds. 18 S. Pennsylvania.

Davis G. W., traveling agent, 27 N. Pennsylvania, r. 123 N. Illinois.

Davis Harvey, r. 8 Lord.

Davis Hattie J. Miss, wks city laundry, bds. 30 Ann.

Davis Henry, machinist, r. 188 Virginia av.

Davis Horace H., finisher, Howe Sewing Machine rooms, r. 257 E. New York.

Davis H. A. Mrs., principal Sixth ward school, bds. 290 S. Meridian.

DAVIS HARVEY D., butcher, 155 W. Washington, r. 234 N. East.

Davis Ira, bds. 164 W. Maryland.

Davis Isaac, (Isaac Davis & Co.) r. 426 N. Pennsylvania.

DAVIS ISAAC & CO. (I. D. & Berry Self) dealers in hats, caps and furs, 12 E. Washington.

5

Davis J., M. D., Indiana Surgical Institute, r. same.

Davis J. E., boots and shoes, 239 E. Washington, r. 299 N. Liberty.

Davis J. W., steam and gas fitter, and brass founder, 110 S. Delaware, r. 154 S. New Jersey.

Davis James, machinist, Sinker & Co., r. cor. Minerva and New York.

Davis Jacob, carpenter, r. 90 James.

Davis John L., pumpmaker, r. cor. West and First.

Davis John M., traveling agent, r. 75 S. Noble.

Davis Levi L., r. 234 N. East.

Davis M. C. Mrs., boarding house, r. 60 S. Pennsylvania.

Davis Maggie M., carpetmaker, r. 30 Ann.

Davis Mark Dr., office, 197 Indiana av., r. 305 W. North.

Davis Mary J. (col'd) milliner, 252 Indiana av.

Davis Mattie F. Miss, dressmaker, bds. 30 Ann.

Davis Nathan M., wagonmaker, r. 54 Oriental.

Davis Nathaniel, blacksmith, r. 128 W. First.

Davis Patsey, (col'd) lab., r. 490 S. Illinois.

Davis Richard A., teamster, Coburn & Jones, r. 48 W. North.

Davis Robert, lab., r. 273 S. Tennessee.

Davis Robert F., engineer, E. C. Atkins & Co., r. 305 S. Illinois.

Davis Rufus P., carpenter, r. 213 Massachusetts av.

Davis Samuel, well digger, r. 46 Thomas.

Davis Sarah C. (wid. P. L.) r. 92 Broadway.

Davis T. J. (Adams & D.) r. 150 W. New York.

Davis Thomas, (Sinker & D.) bds. 84 W. Vermont.

Davis Thomas, (col'd) barber, 267 W. Washington, bds. same.

Davis Wells, engineer, C., C. & I. C. R. R., r. 37 Bates.

Davis Wesley, trimmer, Shaw, L. & C., r. outside city limits.

Davis, William, carpenter, r. 45 E. McCarty.

Davis Wm. E. brickmason, r. 120 N. Davidson.

H. H. LEE

MAKES A SPECIALTY OF

Choice Green, Black & Japan Teas

Davis William H. pumpmaker, 133 N. Tennessee, r. 128 W. First.

Davis William H. student, bds. 92 Broadway.

Davis William M. (Davis & Jones) r. 430 N. New Jersey.

Davis & Jones, auctioneers, 88 E. Washington.

Davison ——, bds. Bates House.

Davlien Timothy, lab., r 209 Buchanan.

Davy Daniel, machinist, bds. 209 S. Illinois.

Davy John, porter, 30 S. Meridian, bds. Illinois House.

Davy Walter W. printer, News Office, r. 37 Fletcher av.

Dawson Geo. carriage painter, with S. W. Drew.

Dawson Louisa, (wid. Daniel) r. 113 Forest av.

Dawson Lewis A. commercial traveler, r. 28 Rose.

Dawson L. C. fireman, r. 273 S. West.

Dawson T. E. auctioneer, r. 121 Ft. Wayne av.

Dawson Thomas B. works Rolling Mill, r. 161 Maple.

Dawson W. P., r. 62 Fletcher av.

Day Benj. F. student, r. 73 Davidson.

Day Elisa, lab., r. 9 Elizabeth.

Day John, lab., r. 182 Elizabeth.

Day John, (col'd) cook, Little Hotel, r. same.

Day K. L. insurance agent, r. 547 N. Illinois.

Day Henry C. Rev. pastor, First Baptist Church, r. 122 N Pennsylvania.

Deal August, traveling agent, r. 196 E McCarty.

Dean Albert W. student, bds. 116 Broadway.

Dean Charles, bricklayer, r. 64 Bates.

Dean Charles H. moulder, bds. 154 S. Noble.

Dean Harrison, (col'd) saloon, r. 142 Elm.

Dean Isaac V. cigar maker, 39 W. Washington, bds. 74 N. Pennsylvania.

Dean Kate, servant, Palmer House.

Dean Joseph C. miller, r. 6 Geisendorff.

Dean Patrick, yardman, P., C. & St. L. R. R.

Dean Mary, servant, Palmer House.

Denne Thomas, pressman, r. 154 S. Noble.

Deans Fielding, (col'd) lab. r. 295 E. New York.

Dearinger Simeon, plasterer, r. 312 E. Georgia.

Dears Margaret, (wid.) r. 53 Dacota.

Death James C. traveling salesman, Scott, West & Co., r. Knightstown, Ind.

Deaver Mary, (wid.) r. cor. Missouri and Walnut.

DeBoss John, works Rolling Mill, bds. 256 S. Tennessee.

Decatur House, 328 E. Washington, E. McCutcheon, proprietor.

Decker Belle, servant, Palmer House.

Decker Conrad, blacksmith, r. 248 N. Winston.

Decker Eliza, pastry cook, Palmer House.

Decker S. H. clk., r. 309 E. Merrill.

Deder William, lab., r. Michigan rd. outside city limits.

Dedert Wm. lab. C., C. C. & I. R. R., r. 64 Michigan rd.

Dedueen James M. tailor, r. 27 Vine.

Dedrick George, clk. P. O. bds. 194 N. Illinois.

Deer John, lab., r. 584 E. St. Clair.

Deer Lewis, lab. 45 E. St. Clair.

Deerberg Frederica Mrs., r. 418 S. East.

Deery Bridget, (wid. Edward) r. Jackson, nr. Christian av.

Deery John, lab., r. Jackson, nr. Christian av.

Deffenback Jacob, carpenter, r. W. First, car. Howard.

Defrieeg M. M. asst. engineer, I. & St. L. R. R. Co., r. 10 Louisiana.

Degenring Christian, salesman, r. 143 E. Washington.

Dehart Austin, teamster, r. 27 Fayette.

Dellhaven A. J. clk. Hune, Adams & Co., r. N. Pennsylvania, nr. Fourth.

Dellhaven Jesse, plasterer, r. 330 S. Alabama.

Dehne Charles, (D. & Bros.) r. 65 S. East.

Dehne Wm. (D. & Bros.) r. 215 N. Davidson.

Dehner & Bros. (Wm. and Charles) flour and feed, 300 E. Washington.

Dehoff Samuel, machinist, at Osgood, Smith & Co., r. 309 E New York.

Deierling Jacob, barber and razor grinder, 223 Massachusetts av., r. same.

Deitch Charles, clk. bds. 173 E. Market.

Deitch Felix, merchant, r. 173 E. Market.

Deitch Joseph, dealer in horses, buggies, etc.. r. 85 N. Alabama.

Deiter Hans, bootmaker, r. 25 Biddle.

Deitrichs Chas jeweler, 66 N. Pennsylvania, r. 131 N. Pennsylvania.

Deitrick Charles H., clk. 38 S. Illinois, bds. 362 W. Vermont.

Deitrick Charles W., fur dealer, 33 S. Illinois, r. 362 W. Vermont.

Deitrich Louisa E. Miss, clk. Trade Palace, bds. 134 N. Pennsylvania.

DeKnight David C., printer Sentinel office, bds. 17 Kentucky av.

Delaney John, lab., r. 384 S. Delaware.

Delaney Michael, lab., r. 293 W. Merrill.

Delaney Michael, railroader, r. 135 N. Noble.

Delaney Peter, works rolling mill, r. 511 S. Tennessee.

Delaney William, lab., r. 169 High.

Delano Joel, constable, bds. 164 W. Maryland.

Delbrock William, shoemaker, r. 238 E. Washington.

Delks Frank N., teamster, r. 495 S. Illinois.

Dell Edward, clk. 27 E. Georgia, r. 135 E. Washington.

DELL WILLIAM, (Batsch, Dickson & D.) r. 135 E. Washington.

Dell William H. A., bookkeeper, with McKernan, bds. Union hall.

Dellefield Myer, with Rothchild & Co., r. 258 S. Delaware.

Deller Frederick, house and sign painter, r. 184 N. Noble.

Dellert John Charles, saddler, bds. 65 S. East.

DeLong E. L. Mrs., works Novelty works

Deloug J. M., cooper, r. 314 E Georgia.

Deloo Eugene, stone cutter, r. 442 Virginia av.

Delon John, machinist Eagle Machine Works r. Virginia av. near Cedar.

Delzell Samuel, capitalist, r. 276 N. Delaware.

Deming Wm H., harness maker, r. over 346 E. Washington.

Demmy Frank, pattern maker, r. 327 S. East.

DeMoss Leander, checkman T. H. & I. R. R., r. 123 W. South.

Demott John, carriage maker, r. 282 E. Ohio.

DeMunn George T. railroader, r. 111 Meek.

Denehan Patrick, railroader, r. 501 E. Georgia.

DeNight Clara Mrs., r. 17 Kentucky av.

Deniu Catherine Mrs., r. 201 E. Market.

Denk Andrew, vinegar maker, r. 326 N. West.

Denniger Daniel, carpenter, r. 437 N. Mississippi.

Denning O. H., foreman paint shop, Shaw, Lippencott & Conner, r. 17½ Virginia av.

Dennett C. I., foreman press room Sentinel office, r. 186 N. Tennessee.

Dennett John, carriage maker, r. 282 E. St. Clair.

Dennis Charles C., (Swing & D) 4 Martindale's blk.

Dennis Charles C., bookkeeper, Hume & Adams, r. 70 W. New York.

Dennis Francis M., saleslady Josselyn Bros. & Co., bds. 52 N. Pennsylvania.

Dennis Israel L., r. 372 N. East.

Dennis James M., artist, r. 140 N. East.

Dennis Joseph, chief engineer I. & V. R. R., bds Spencer house.

Dennis M. P., (J. W. Lines & Co.) bds. Sherman house.

Dennis Peter, bricklayer, r. 26 Buchanan.

Denniston Sarah, domestic Blind Institute.

DENNY A. F., attorney, 94 E Washington, r. same.

Denny James A, carpenter, bds. 189 N. Noble

Denny Joseph, mill wright, r. 58 Fayette.

Denny Robert, claim agent, 98 E. Washington, r. 76 E. Cumberland.

Denton Ansel, (Ransford & D.) bds. 87 Union.

Denselman Henry, pianomaker, r. 185 E Washington.

Densmore Samuel, brakeman C. C. C. & I. R. R, r. 247 N. Davidson.

Dersner William, carriagemaker, bds. 225 E. Market.

Denwiddie Hugh painter, r. 342 N. West.

Depple Henry, grainer, r. 499 S. New Jersey.

Deppell L, grocery and saloon, 557 Virginia av., r. same.

DePugh Henry, pastor, Broadway M. E. C., r. 325 N. Liberty.

Derby Adrian, lab, r. 444 W. North.

Derfield Myer, auctioneer, r. 258 S. Delaware.

Dergan John, lab., r. 37 Dougherty.

Derham Henry E, cigar manufacturer, r. 299 N. East.

DeRUITER D, wholesale oyster dealer, 65 S. Illinois, r. same.

DeRuiter Ralph, with D. DeRuiter, 65 S. Illinois.

Dersch John, lab, r. 157 N. Winston.

Dervey W. H., bricklayer, r. 385 S. East.

Deschler John, western furniture Co., r. 132 E. St Joseph.

DESCHLER JOSEPH F., Saloonkeeper, 15 N. Pennsylvania, r. 26 Cherry.

Deshong Jemima, (wid) dressmaker, r. 461 E. Georgia.

Desjardins Joseph, stairbuilder, r. 464 Virginia av.

THE CHINA TEA STORES

ARE AMONG THE

Attractions of Indianapolis.

Call and See Them before leaving the City.

DeSoto Mutual Life Insurance Company, Wilcox & Means State agents, No's 3 and 4 Wiley's blk. opposite Odd Fellows Hall.

Despa Ernst, painter, r. 50 Lockerbie.

Despa Wilhelmina, midwife, r. 50 Lockerbie.

Dessar Joseph B. (Dessar Bros. & Co.) r. 213 N. Illinois.

Dessar Lewis, (Dessar, Bro. & Co.) r. 165 N. Alabama.

Dessar, Bros & Co. (Joseph B., Lewis Adolwbers and David) wholesale clothiers, 60 S. Meridian

Detroit Insurance Co., Detroit Michigan, R. E. Beardsley agent.

Dever Charles, express driver, r. 248 S. Alabama.

Dever George, clk. Adams express Co.

Devine William, tailor, r. 160 S. Noble.

DeVinnish Collin T., gass fitter, r. 219 E. South.

DeVinnish S., r. 219 E. South.

Devoss Daniel, carpenter, r. 638 N. Mississippi.

Dewald Frank, clk. 45 E. Washington, r. 113 E. Washington.

Dewald Joseph, shoemaker, r. 236 Railroad.

Dewald Mathias, drayman, 27 E. Maryland, r. 236 Railroad.

Dewitt Henry, printer Sentinel office, r. 37½ S. Pennsylvania.

Dial Frank A. conveyancer, 8 E. Washington, r. 376 N. Tennessee.

Dick A. E. with Josselyn Bros. & Co. bds. Bates house.

Dicker Harriet, (wid James) r. 70 N. California.

Dickerson John, r. Ninth near canal.

Dickert Jacob, cabinetmaker, r. 220 N. West.

Dickey James B., watchman, r. 47 Dougherty,

Dickinson Alice, clk., Paris Store, r. 115 E. South.

Dickinson Harry, works Schneider & Co., r. 33 S. Liberty.

Dickinson Harry W., brass finisher, r. 66 S. Liberty.

Dickinson James L., physician, r. 460 S. New Jersey.

Dickinson John C., r. 235 E. South.

Dickinson Frank, (col'd) lab., works 117 W. Maryland.

Dickman Carl, saloon 208 E. Washington, r. same.

Dickman Charles, engineer T. H. & I. R. R., r. 42 N. New Jersey.

Dickman Fredrick, Jr., carpenter, r. 91 N. East.

Dickman Wm., carpenter, r. 91 N. East.

Dickson A., (Pettis, D. & Co.,) bds. Bates house.

Dickson C. (C. D. & Co.) r. 279 W. Vermont.

Dickson C. & Co. (C. D., W. E. and I. C. Dickson) dealers in woolen factory findings, 49 N. Tennessee.

Dickson George, hostler J. Landis, bds. 106 E. Ohio.

Dickson George, clk., 27 E. Georgia, r. 554 N. Pensylvania.

Dickson Geo. F., wagonmaker, bds. Decatur House.

Dickson George W. (col'd) carpenter, r. 225 W. Ohio.

Dickson James (V. Butsch & D.) r. 554 N. Pennsylvania.

Dickson James B. (Butch, D. & Co.) treasurer Academy of Music, r. 554 N. Pennsylvania.

Dickson James C. (C. D. & Co.) r. 262 S. Missouri.

Dickson James W., lab., r. 362 S. Missouri.

Dickson John T., clk., rolling mill, bds. 554 N. Pennsylvania.

Dickson J. W., yard master Bunte & Dickson, r. 196 N. Tennessee.

Dickson Thomas M., bookkeeper with Bunte & Dickson, r. 29 Grant.

Dickson Wallace E. (C. D. & Co.) r. 110 Indiana av.

Dickson Wm. B., lumber yard, r. 196 N. Tennessee.

Difenbach Jacob, carpenter, r. — First.

Diehl August, traveling agent T. F. Ryan.

Dieter Ernest, shoemaker, r. 25 Biddel.

Dietrichs Charles, jeweler, 66 N. Pennsylvania, r. 184 N. Pennsylvania.

Dietrichs Charles W., r. 34 N. Pennsylvania.

Dietrich Christian G., cabinetmaker, r. 464 E. Market.

Dietrichs M. Mrs., millinery, 68 E. Washington, r. 34 N. Pennsylvania.

Dietrichs William, sr., r. 34 N. Pennsylvania.

Dietrichs William, salesman, 33 E. Washington, r. 34 N. Pennsylvania.

Dietz Adam, grocer, 114 Ft. Wayne av., r. same.

Dietz August, baker, r. 107 E. Market.

Dietz Berhard, draughtsman, 19 Talbott & New's blk., r 171 N. Noble.

Dietz Ferdinand, (D. & Reissner) r. N. Noble.

Dietz Frederick, (D. & Haug) r. E. city limits.

Dietz J. (J. & L. D.) r. cor. Ft. Wayne av. and Delaware.

Dietz L. (J. & L. D.) r. cor. Ft. Wayne av. and Alabama.

Dietz J. & L., proprietors, Star Grocery, cor. Ft. Wayne av. and Alabama.

Dietz Sarah, (wid. H. W.) r. 7 Massachusetts av.

Dietz Theodore, butcher, works 17 S. Illinois, bds. same.

Dietz Peter, proprietor Washington House, cor. West and Maryland.

Dietz & Borst, (F. D. & F. B.) meat market, 104 S. Illinois.

Dietz Fred & Co., Wine and Beer Hall, 133 E. Washington.

Dietz & Haug, (F. D. & J. H.) saloon, 255 E. Washington.

DEITZ & REISNER, (F. D. & A. R.) leather, hides, oil and shoe finding, 17 S. Delaware.

Diggs John, bricklayer, r. 35 S. West.

Dill Anna, (wid.) r. 227 S. West.

Dill E. B., blacksmith, 197 S. Meridian, r. 121 Broadway.

Dill G. (wid. Alexander H.) r. 328 N. Illinois.

Dill James, r. 328 N. Illinois.

Dill Jasper W., clk. 187 W. Washington, bds. 60 S. Pennsylvania.

Dill John P., compositor, Sentinel office, r. 328 N. Illinois.

Dill Josiah B. W., student, bds. 121 Broadway.

Dill Mary, (wid.) r. 753 N. Tennessee.

Dillan Bridget Miss, r. 30 Willard.

Dillman George, lab., r. 11 Dacota.

Dillman James, lab., r. 11 Dacota.

Dillman Milton, carpenter, r. 755 N. Mississippi.

Dillon Daniel, lab., r. 61 Maple.

Dillon Levi, canvasser, r. Virginia av., nearly opposite St. Peters Church.

Dillon Mary, servant, Palmer House.

Dillon Sarah, (wid. Patrick.) r. 30 Willard.

Dillon Thomas, bricklayer, r. 29 Chatham

Dinn Charles, wiper, C. C. C. & I. R. R. shops.

Dingelday Theodore, German and English teacher, bds. 124 N. Alabama.

Dippel Henry, works Jackson, Rider & Co.

Dippel Henry, clk. J. Deschler's, r. 425 E. Vermont.

Dippel John, carpenter, r. 365 E. New York.

Dippel Joseph, lab., r. 195 North Noble.

Dirk Charles, blacksmith, r. 315 Virginia av.

DISHON JAMES M., City Bill Poster, office Journal bldg., r. 222 S. Noble.

Dishon William, with J. M. Dishon, Journal bldg.

Dishong Amos, fur trader, r. 676 N. Mississippi.

Ditto Edward, works M. Mason, bds. 207 W. North.

Diunzlman Henry, pianomaker, bds. California House.

Diver James, travelling merchant, r. 139 N. Davidson.

Dixon Emily C., (wid.) r. 298 E. Georgia.

Dixon George, wagonmaker, bds. cor. Washington and Noble.

Dixon John, bookkeeper, Trade Palace, bds. 306 N. Delaware.

Dixon Prophet, (col'd) porter, 5 E. Washington.

Dixon William, (col'd) cook, Sherman House.

Dobbins Martin, meat market, 751 N. Illinois, r. same.

Dobbs C. J., Sheriff Supreme Court, bds. Palmer House.

Dobson James, helper, Roots Foundry, bds. Illinois House.

Doehert Goodhart, stonemason, r. 175 Minerva.

Dockweiler Jacob, engineer, C. C. C. & I. R. R., r. 501 E. Market.

Dodd John W. Secretary and Treasurer Indiana Cement Pipe Co., r. 214 N. Illinois.

Dodd W. S., r. 214 N. Illinois.

Dodds Elihu, patternmaker, works Chandler & Taylor, bds. 146 Blake.

Dodge Harry, railroader, bds. Bates House.

Dodge Rufus, Messenger American M. U. Express, bds. Spencer House.

Dodson James, engineer, T. H. & I. R. R., bds. 151 W. South.

Doenges Casper, lab., bds., Emmenegger's Hotel.

Doepfner Chas., justice of the peace, office, 68 E. Washington, r. 62 S. Alabama.

Doerffel Mary Mrs, saloon and boarding house, cor. South and Illinois.

Doerr George, boarding house, 267 E. Washington.

Doharty Andrew, farmer and trader, Bluff road, outside city limits.

H. H. LEE

Makes a Specialty of

CHOICE GOLDEN RIO,

AND

OLD GOVERNMENT JAVA COFFEES.

Doherty Morris, lab., r. cor. Benton and Maryland.

Dohn Peter, engineer, Philip Dohn, 246 S. Meridian.

Dohn Peter, lab., r. 153 High.

DOHN PHILIP, manufacturer and dealer in all kinds of household furniture, 246 S. Meridan, r. same.

Dokes Mary, (wid. Jackson) r. 182 Douglass al.

Dold Ferd, blacksmith, Eagle Machine Works, r. 275 E. New York.

Dolmiish Eugene, salesman, 29 W. Washington, bds. 26 and 28 W. Georgia.

Dalton Thomas, lab., r. 214 Buchanan.

Dolus John, lab., r. 54 Hosbrook.

Domeyer Charles. (Cook and D.) grocer, r. 312 E. Georgia.

Domon Jacob, lab., r. 414 S. Illinois.

Domon Peter Emil, clk., California House, r. same.

Domon Sport, hunter, bds. California House.

Donahue Catherine, domestic, Bates House.

Donahue Daniel, brakeman, C. C. & I. C., R. R., bds 58 Benton.

Donahue Honora, domestic. Bates House.

Donahue Mary, domestic, Bates House.

Donahue Patrick, w'ks Street R. R. Co., r. 26 Willard.

Donahue Timothy, lab., r. 480 E. Georgia.

Donaldson C. S. (C. S. D. and D. E. Stout) r. 180 N. Illinois.

Donaldson Edward, clk. 54 S. Meridian, bds. 180 N. Illinois.

Donaldson J., machinist, Indiana Surgical Institute, r. same.

Donaldson Joshua, lab., r. 72 W. Maryland.

Donaldson & Stout, (C. S. Donaldson and D. E. Stout) wholesale dealers in hats, caps, furs and straw goods, 54 S. Meridian.

Donelly John, lab., r. 64 S. West.

Donelly Joseph, blacksmith, bds. 265 S. Delaware.

Donelly Michael, lab., r. 2 Rockwood.

Donelly Michael, lab., r. 246 S. West.

Doney Robert, r. 92 E. Market.

Donicker Paul, cabinetmaker, r. 192 Coburn.

Donnan Barbara, (wid. David) boarding house, 126 N. Tennessee.

Donnan Theodore, salesman 79 S. Meridian, r. 126 N. Tennessee.

Donnel John, lab., r. 553 E. St. Clair.

Donnellan Charles, lumber dealer, office room 6 Blake's row, r. 89 N. Delaware.

Donnelly Francis, groceries and provisions, 347 S. Delaware, r. same.

Donnon Wallace, tinner Munson & Johnston's, r. 126 N. Tennessee.

Donough Daniel R., ticket clk. Union Depot, r. 335 S. Meridian.

Donovan E., cabinetmaker, bds. Ray House.

Donovan James, drayman, r. 360 W. North.

Donovan John, engineer, r. 13 Meek.

Donovan Robert, bee culture, r. sw. cor. Tennessee and St. Clair.

Donovan William, fireman C. C. C. & I. R. W.

Donovan ——, (col'd) lab., r. 187 Elm.

Dooley William, cooper, r. 43 Hellen.

Doran George, turner, r. 21 Forrest av.

Doran Henry, tinner D. Root & Co., r. 21 Pine cor. Forrest av.

Doran John, importer and wholesale dealer in linen, 56 S. Illinois, r. same.

Doran M. W. E., cabinetmaker, r. 21 Forrest av.

Dorbecker Jacob, barber, r. 77 N. New Jersey.

Dorbecker John, barber, r. 77 N. New Jersey.

Dorland Mrs., dressmaker, 9 E. New York, r. same.

Darlton Michael, lab., r. 391 S. Missouri.

Doremus G. C., carriagemaker Shaw L. & C., r. 217 Massachusetts av.

Dorsey John W., miller, works Home Mills, bds. 147 W. Maryland.

Dorsey William, (Harden & D.) r. Douglass, nr. New York.

Dorsey Robert S., clk. J. T. Layman & Co., r. 1½ miles se. of city.

Dorsey Thomas, contractor, r. 516 S. Meridian.

Doty Harriet Mrs. r. S. Mississippi, nr. Rolling Mill.

Dougherty Bernard, (M. & B. D.) r. nr. Underhill Mill.

Dougherty Frank L., spinner, Merritt & Coughlen, bds. 272 W. Maryland.

Dougherty John, r. 226 E South.

Dougherty Michael, (M. & B. D.) r. nr. Underhill Mill.

DOUGHERTY M. & CO. (M. D. & Bernard D) tanners, w. of Canal, opposite Underhill Mill, ss. city.

Doughty George, wholesale liquor agent, r. 457 E. Georgia.

Doughty John G., printer, r. 27 Indiana av.

Doughty Lafayette, lab., r. 55 Colifernia.

Douglass Andrew, lab., r. 323 S. East.

Douglass Benj. W., sexton St. Paul's Cathedral, r. 40 Hosbrook.

Douglass George, bookbinder, bds. 129 W. New York.

Douglass James G. (Douglass & Conner) r. 129 W. New York.

Douglass Jacob L. (col'd) lab., r. 12 Ash.

Douglass Lizzie Mrs., 139 W. Market.

Douglass R. L, State agent Ætna Insurance Company, office Ætna building. N. Pennsylvania, r. 182 S. New Jersey.

Douglass Samuel M. (Douglass & Conner) r. 129 W. New York.

Douglass Satyre Miss, (col'd) teacher, bds. 79 Kentucky av.

DOUGLASS & CONNER, (J. G. and S. M. Douglass and A. H. Conner) proprietors Daily and Weekly Journal, New Journal Bldg.

Dow D., mailagent C. C. C. & I. R. R.

Dowd John, lab., r. 178 Meek.

Dowell William H., agent Wheeler & Wilson Sewing Machine, r. 268 W. Vermont.

Dowling James, lab., r. 313 W. Merrill.

DOWLING W. W., editor and publisher, office in Journal bldg., r. 488 N. Mississippi.

Downey Bridget, (wid.) r. 277 E. Georgia.

Downey John, lab., r. 22 Hahn.

Downey John, stonecutter, r. 277 E. Georgia.

Downey J E. publisher, r. 13 W. North.

Downey J. T. (Nickering & D.) r. cor. West and Michigan.

Downey Mrs. M. G. r. 241 Virginia av.

Downey W. B. letter carrier, bds. 52 N. Pennsylvania.

Downs Thomas, works, Rolling Mill, r. 39 Maple.

Downs Wm. (col'd) barber, 26 N. Pennsylvania.

Dox Jacob, confectioner, 107 E. Washington.

Dox William, salesman, 108 S. Meridian, bds. Spencer House.

Doxey Ed. O. salesman, Mayhew & Branham, bds. Sherman House.

Doyle John, clk., r. 133 N. East.

Doyle Mary Miss, clk. Trade Palace, bds. 112 N. Meridian.

Doyle T. R. clk. 33 N. Pennsylvania, bds. Pattison House.

Drake E. B. traveler, A. W. Sharpe, r. 148 Mississippi.

Draper J. H. grocer, 213 E. Washington, r. 299 E. Ohio.

Draper Minerva Mrs. (wid. J. M) r. 65 N. Missouri.

Draper Thomas, porter, Wiles, Bro. & Co., r. 31 Market.

Drapier W. H. verbatim reporter, office 21 N. Meridian, r. 236 N Mississippi.

Dreansfield Ezra, works, Cotton Mill, r. 236 Blake.

Dreher August, butcher, bds. 323 W. Washington.

Dreher Mathias, (D. & Bollinger,) r. 82 N. Liberty.

DREHER & BOLLINGER, [M. Dreher and Jos. Bollinger), dealers in dry goods and notions, 250 E. Washington.

Drew Harry, clk. Terre Haute Depot, bds. 88 Massachusetts av.

Drew J. A. (Sullivan & D) r. 88 Massachnse ts av.

DREW SAMUEL W. manufacturer of carriages, buggies, etc. E. Market Square, r. same.

Dreythaler William, saloon and boardinghouse, 123 S. Illinois.

Driftmeyer Henry, porter, 59 S. Meridian, bds 176 S. Noble.

Driggs N. S. clk. Browning & Sloan, bds. Union Depot Dining Hall.

Drinkout Wm. lab. CC. .C & I. R. R. r. 609 E. Washington.

Driscall A. E. Mrs. (wid. Wm. J.) r. 127 Huron.

Driscall Jerry, works, Rolling Mill, r. 272 S. Tennessee.

Driscall Wm. W fireman, I., C. & L. R. R., r. 63 Harrison.

Droege Charles J. salesman, C. P. Wilder, bds. 23 S. Pennsylvania.

Drotz E. (D. & Stienhauer) r. 258 S. Pennsylvania.

Drotz & Steinhauer, (E. D. and M. S.) Indianapolis Tile Works, 136 S. Pennsylvania.

Drout John, lab., r. 109 Elm.

Drum Robert, railroader, r. 22 S. East.

Drummond Hugh J. baker, r. 257 Henry.

Drummond Thomas, Judge United States Circuit Court, r. Chicago Ill.

DRUMMOND W. W. Attorney at Law, bds. Bates House.

Drummonds Joseph. dealer in wood, r. 212 S. New Jersey.

Dryer George W. ferotypist, 16½ E. Washington, r. same.

Dryer James W. druggist, 343 E. Washington, r. 244 N. East.

Dryer Peter, blacksmith, r. 70 Elm.

THE CHINA TEA STORES

Have the NAME of being the

MOST ATTRACTIVE STORES IN THE WEST.

No. 7 Odd Fellows Hall
AND
ACADEMY OF MUSIC CORNER.

Dubach John, striker, Eagle Machine Works, bds. 64 South East.

Dudley William, (col'd) lab., r. 184 N. Missouri.

Duecker Laura, (wid. John B.) r. 181 N. Noble.

Duel S. mail agent, C. C. C. & I. R. R.

Duff Alex. W. painter, r. 207 Union.

Duff E. W. painter, 197 and 199 S. Meridian, r. 207 Union.

Duffaulx Louis F. pianomaker, bds. 259 N. Liberty.

Duffey James, lab., r. St. Clair, bet. Missouri and Fayette.

Duffey James, lab. bds. 27 W. Maryland.

Duffey James, sawyer, bds. Nagle House.

Duffey John, tailor, r. 57 California.

Duffey Michael, tailor, r. Clinton, bet. East and New Jersey.

Duffey Patrick, lab. bds. Nagle House.

Duffey Thomas, moulder, r. 87 Ann.

Dugan Neal, saloon, 52 S. Illinois, r. 60 Oak.

DUGAN THOMAS, boot and shoe manufacturer, 136 S. Illinois, r. 305 S. Pennsylvania.

Dumont Richard S. (D. & Roberts) r. 125 E. Vermont.

Dumont & Roberts, (R. S. D. & E. Roberts) boiler makers, cor. Mississippi and Louisiana.

Dunbar M. dealer in boots and shoes, No. 2 Palmer House, bds. 254 S. Pennsylvania.

Dunbar Sarah Miss, r. 254 S. Pennsylvania.

Duncan David, lab., r. 249 W. Michigan.

Duncan John, bricklayer, r. 426 E. North.

Duncan John S. (J. S. & R. B. D.) r. North of city, on Fall Creek Gravel rd.

Duncan R. B. (J. S. & R. B. D.) r. North of city, on Fall Creek Gravel rd.

Duncan Thomas, shoemaker, r. 205 S. Pennsylvania.

DUNCAN R. B. & J. S. Attorneys at Law, 3 Brown's blk. N. Pennsylvania.

Duningberg James, saloon keeper, 89 E. South, r. same.

Duningberg George, speculator, r. 89 E. South.

Dunlap John, lab. bds. 30½ N. Pennsylvania.

Dunlap J. M. physician and surgeon, room 2 McOuat's blk. Kentucky av.

Dunlay L. M. D., r. 25 Virginia av.

Dunley Charles, driver, American Express Co., r. 35 Ellen.

Dunlop John S., (John S. D. & Co.) r. 286 N. Pennsylvania.

Dunlop Joshua, Rev. (col'd) r. 190 N. Missouri.

Dunlop S. H. clk. J. S. Dunlap & Co. bds. 288 N. Pennsylvania.

DUNLOP J. S. & CO. general insurance agents, 2 W. Washington.

Dunmeyer Christian, ice dealer, r. 217 S. Illinois.

Dunmeyer Fred. drayman, r. 266 E. Ohio.

Dunmeyer Sarah Mrs., Boarding house, 217 S. Illinois.

Dunn C. H., clk., 16 W. Pearl, bds. S. Illinois.

Dunn George T. (D. and W.) r. 410 N. Tennessee.

Dunn Jacob P. (Love and Co.) r. 410 N. Tennessee.

Dunn John, clk., Bee Hive store, bds. n. N. W. C. University.

Dunn John C., plumber and gas fitter, r. 544 N. Mississippi.

Dunn R. G. & Co., mercantile agency, room 4 Blackford's blk.

Dunn William, teamster, 24 W. Maryland, bds. 79 S. West.

Dunn William A., r. 77 S. Mississippi.

DUNN & WIGGINS, (George F. D. and Percival S. Wiggins) dealers in groceries, provisions, etc., cor. Indiana av. and New York.

Dunning James H., pressman, w'ks Journal, bds. 104 N. California.

Dunning Perry, contractor, r. 104 N. California.

Dunning Thomas, carpenter, r. 104 N. California.

Dunirgton William, (col'd) plasterer, r. W. Fourth, bet. Tennessee and Mission ss.

Dunzelman Henry, pianomaker, bds. California House.

Dupee Josephine Mrs. (col'd) r. 247 N. West.

Duphorne Sade J. Miss, school teacher, r. 77 W. Second.

Durant William S., cigarmaker, bds. 89 Delaware.

Durbon Aurelia Miss, bds. 577 S. Meridian.

Durbon C. R., pumpmaker, 197 and 199 S. Meridian, r. 320 S. Meridian.

Durbon J. H., pumpmaker, 197 and 199 S. Meridian, bds. South, nr. factory.

Durbon K. L., traveling agent, R. A. Durbon, r. 577 S. Meridian.

DURBON R. A., proprietor, pump factory, 197 and 199 S. Meridian, cor. South, r. South, nr. factory.

Durbon W. F., bookkeeper, Murphy, Johnson & Co., r. 346 N. Meridian.

Durgin Lyman W., foreman, C. C. C. & I. R. R. shop, r. 45 Winston.

Durham H. D. (Uhl and D.) r. 299 S. East.

Durfield John F. (Shoemaker and D.) real estate agent, 16½ E. Washington.

Dury John, (D. and Hawk) r. 184 Massachusetts av.

DURY & HAWK, (John D. and W. V. H.) dealers in boots and shoes, 3 E. Washington.

Dusner William, carriage wood workman, bds. 225 E. Market.

Duvall David C., salesman, 38 S. Illinois, r. 159 N. Illinois.

Duvall J. P., traveler, r. 260 Chestnut.

Duwall E., lab., r. 337 S. Alabama.

Duzan W. N. Dr., r. 418 N. Tennessee.

Dwyer Michael W., cupola tender, Greenleaf & Co.

Dwyer Thomas, lab., r. 36 Bicking.

Dwyer William, lab., r. 74 Bicking.

Dwyre Edward, lab., r. 24 Rose.

Dwyre Thomas, lab., r. Chesapeake, nr. canal.

Dye John F. (D. and Harris) 8 and 9 Talbott & New's blk., r. country.

Dye & Harris, (J. T. D. and A. C. Harris) attorneys and counselors, 8 and 9 Talbott & New's blk., N. Pennsylvania.

Dyer Frank P., salesman, E. C. Case, r. 605 N. Illinois.

Dynes Joseph A., printer, r. 364 N. Mississippi.

Dynes L. G., printer, r. 364 N. Mississippi.

EADES James M., clk., post office, r. 82 W. Market.

Eagan Daniel, lab., bds. 55 Fayette.

Eagan Patrick, lab., r. 52 Fayette.

Eagle John, express messenger, r. 205 Union.

Eagle John D., letter carrier, bds. 336 N. Alabama.

Eagle John H., grocery, sw. cor. Delaware and Fort Wayne av., r. 336 N. Alabama.

Eagle W. O., clk., J. H. Eagle, bds 336 N. Alabama.

EAGLE BRASS WORKS, 94 S. Delaware, Stierle and Loeper, proprietors.

EAGLE MACHINE WORKS, cor. Louisiana and Meridian, opp. e. end Union depot.

Eaglen Isaac, lab., r. 113 N. West.

Eaglen Lemuel, lab., r. 164 Patterson.

Eaglen Nannie Miss, w'ks Indianapolis Cotton Mill, bds. 164 Patterson.

Earl Simeon, shipping clk., Osgood, Smith & Co., bds. 370 N. West.

Earley William A., traveling agent, r. 213 N. Mississippi.

Early Peter, lab., r. 161 Stevens.

Early James, peddler, r. over 280 E. Washington.

Early Thomas, lab., bds. 34 Union.

Early W. A., salesman, r. 220 S. East.

Earnshaw Francis, cabinetmaker, bds. Ray House.

Earnshaw Joseph, (Burk E. and Co.) r. 257 S. Pennsylvania.

East Baptist Church, Noble, cor. South.

Eastridge Elizabeth, (wid. George) r. 58 Cherry.

Eastridge Lotty Miss, dressmaker, r. 58 Cherry.

Eberhardt George, cabinetmaker, r. 322 E. Market.

Eberline George, barber, 37 S. Illinois, bds. 23 Kentucky av.

Ebert John, (E. and Owens) r. 209 W. South.

Ebert & Owens, (John E. and B. F. O.) whol. dealers in walnut lumber, 44 Kentucky av.

Ebertine George W., cabinetmaker, r. 117 S. Illinois.

EBERTS JOHN, collector Joseph Butsch, r. 62 W. South.

Eberts Orpheus, M. D., sup't. Indiana Hospital for the Insane, r. same.

Ebner John, varnishmaker, r. 310 S East.

Eccles, William, prop., Hoosier Store, 22 W. Washington, r. 241 N. Alabama.

Echols H. H., carpenter, cor. South and Delaware, bds. 314 E. Georgia.

Echols William, conductor, C. & I. J. R. R., r. 177 Meek.

Eck Joseph, moulder, Spiegl, Thoms & Co., r. 502 E. Ohio.

Eckels Edward, gunsmith, Samuel Beck, r. 278 E. Washington.

Eddy Harrison, fireman T. H. & I. R. R., r. 250 S. Missouri.

Eddy Morris R., bookkeeper Ind. Nat. Bank, bds. Bates House.

Eddy M. W., brakeman T. H. & I. R. R., r. Cumberland, bet. Missouri and West.

6

THE CHINA TEA STORES

ARE LOCATED AT

No. 7 ODD FELLOWS HALL

AND

ACADEMY OF MUSIC CORNER.

SAME GOODS, SAME PRICES at BOTH.

Eden Charlton, pres't Builders and Manufacturers Association, r. 203 N. Pennsylvania.

Eden Samuel C., superintendent Builders' and Manufacturers, Association, r. cor. East and Gregg.

Edie Lorina, (wid. James) r. ne. cor. Mississippi and Sixth.

Edinger Fred., switchman, r. 13 Sharp.

Edmunds William, (Hendricks, Edmunds & Co.) r. 222 N. Illinois.

Edson H. A. Rev. pastor Second Presbyterian Church, r. 157 N. Tennessee.

Edwards David, bricklayer, r. 211 W. Michigan.

Edwards Edward, harnessmaker, 22 W. Maryland, r. 122 N. Illinois.

Edwards Edward, lab., r. 400 S. Tennessee.

Edwards J. V., clk., 49 N. Illinois, bds. Macy House.

Edwards John, (col'd) plasterer, r. 31 Harrison.

Edwards Louisa Miss, works Indianapolis Cotton Mill, bds. 572 Patterson.

Edwards Martha Mrs. (wid. John) boarding house, 122 N. Illinois.

Edwards Richard, painter, r. 398 S. West.

Egan E. C., cutter Treat & Claflin, bds. Pyle House.

Egerton Charles, proprietor Lafayette House, 179 S. Meridian, r. same.

Egger John, (E. & Muecke) r. 54 S. Alabama.

Egger & Muecke, (J. E. and Wm. M.) house and sign painters, 152 E. Washington.

Egger Annie Miss, servant Emenegger's Hotel.

Eggert William Dr., 75 E. Ohio, r. same.

Eggleston D. W., varnisher, r. 317 Wabash av.

Eglus Frederick, cabinetmaker, r. 130 N. Noble.

Ehrensperger Frank, salesman Vinnedge, Jones & Co., r. 266 N. East.

Ehrick Wm., tinner, r 41 S. Illinois.

Ehrisman Jacob, miller, bds. Union Hall.

Ehrmann Louis, brewer Schmidt's Brewery, r. same.

Eickoff Henry, clk. 172 S. Illinois, bds. same.

Eighth Ward School House. cor. Virginia av. and Huron, Miss Maria Jones, principal.

Einhouse Charles, moulder Eagle Machine Works, bds. 369 S. Illinois.

Eisman William, wiper, C., C. C. & I. R. R. shops.

Eix Henry. salesman 228 E. Washington, r. 84 Michigan Road.

Elbert Samuel A. (col'd) medical student, r. 229 N. Tennessee.

Elder Benjamin, sales stable, Court St., r. Knightstown, Ind.

Elder E. A , retail grocer, 52 N. Illinois, Miller's blk., r. 133 W. New York.

Elder J., wagonmaker, r. 87 S. Liberty.

ELDER JOHN R., pres't Carbon Block Coal Co., office 21 S. Pennsylvania, r. 150 N. New Jersey.

Elder Maggie Miss, teacher First Ward school, r. 150 N. New Jersey.

Elder Robert, wagonmaker, r. 87 S. Liberty.

Elder Samuel, lab., r. 313 W. Merrill.

Elder William G , boarding house, 58 S. Pennsylvania, r. same.

Eldridge Jacob, real estate agent, r. 71 S. Mississippi.

Elff Frank, barber, 135 S. Illinois, r. 273 S. New Jersey.

Elgin William Rev., r. 180 E. South.

Elias William, (C. C. Hutchinson & Co.) r. New York City.

Elias Henry, r. 26 Cherry.

Elick Lucy, (wid. Jacob) r. 293 Winston.

Elius C. H., engineer C. C. C. & I. R. R.

Elkins Nancy, (wid.) r. 62 Bates.

Ellett Wilber, (col'd) porter Browning & Sloan, r. 172 N. Illinois.

Ellingwood Emily Mrs., seamstress, r. 295 Huron.

Elliott Byron K. (E. & Holstein) r. 22 California.

Elliott Calvin A., r. 180 N. West.

Elliott Elizabeth, (wid. William) dressmaker, r. 225 W. Vermont.

Elliott J. T. Judge, bds. Bates House.

Elliott Jott, deputy sheriff, r. 77 N. Noble.

Elliott John M., with T. F. Ryan, bds. Sherman House.

Elliott Joseph T., clk. Recorder's office, r. 22 Chatham.

Elliott J. Perry, photographer, 8 E. Washington, r. 293 N. Delaware.

Elliott M. M., with Wm. Sumner & Co., r. 268 W. Vermont.

Elliott Russell A., assist. treas. I & St. L. R. R., r. 38 W. St. Clair.

Elliott Sarah P. (wid. James S.) r. 268 W. Vermont.

Elliott T. B. (E. & Berry) r. west end Michigan.

Elliott Wm. D., deputy county recorder, bds. 426 N. Pennsylvania.

Elliott Wm. J., county recorder, r. N. Tennessee, N. of corporation line.

Elliott W. S., city distributing clk. P. O., r. 98 N. East.

Elliott & Berry (T. B. Elliott and D. M. Berry) commericial brokers, 21 Circle.

Elliott & Holstein (B. K. E. and C. T. H.) attorneys at law, 24½ E. Washington.

Ellis James, (col'd) lab., r. 8 Rhode Island.

Ellis John S., clk. Millner & Sherwood, r. 258 S. Meridian.

Ellis Mary Miss, weaver at Geisendorff's, bds. Blake, bet. New York and Washington.

Ellis Oscar, clk., 5 W. Washington, r. 623 N. Illinois.

Ellis Thomas, commercial traveler, r. 406 S. West.

Ellis Thomas, cupolo tender, r. 35 Bradshaw.

Ellison Fred., assist. paymaster I. & St. L. R. R., r. 682 N. Illinois.

Ellmer John W., clk., r. 192 E. McCarty.

Ellms Cornelius H., engineer, r. 171 N. Davidson.

Elstun W. J., M. D., second assist. supt. Indiana Hospital for Insane, r. same.

Eltzroth John, candymaker, bds. 149 N. Delaware.

Elvin Gardener W. (E. & Fox) r. 500 S. East.

Elvin Thomas, lab., r. 337 S. Missouri.

ELVIN & FOX, (G. W. E. and J. H. F.) house and sign painters, 58 N. Pennsylvania.

Ely J. W., coustable, r. 130 E. St. Joseph.

Elyea Thomas, painter, r. 553 S. Meridian.

Embers Thomas. (col'd) lab., r. N. Mississippi, bet. Sixth and Seventh.

Embery Thomas, (col'd) barber, r. N. Mississippi, 3d house from Sixth.

Emda Wm., bartender, r. 120 N. Noble.

Emelle Stephen, watchmaker, bds. Emenegger's Hotel.

Emenegger M., saloon and hotel, 111 and 113 E. Washington.

Emerich Henry, cabisetmaker, r. 109 N. Davidson.

Emerich Henry, Secretary Glass Works, r. 224 W. Maryland.

Emerson, John B., bookkeeper, bds. 259 W. Market.

Emerson Roswell B. (E., Beam & Thompson) r. 259 W. Market.

EMERSON, BEAM & THOMPSON, (R. B. E., David B. and Eli T.) manufacture doors, sash, blinds, etc., 225 and 229 W. Market.

BENHAM BRO'S,

36 East Washington St.,

SHEET MUSIC, VIOLINS,

GUITARS, STRINGS, &c.

Emiel Christian, servant, 169 S. Tennessee.

Emmens Araminte, (wid. William) r. 51 Maple.

Emmons John B., sawmaker, bds. 51 Maple.

Ender Anna Mrs. r. 327 S. Pennsylvania.

Endleman Chris., machinest, r. 312 N. Noble.

Endleman Fred, machinest, r. 312 N. Noble.

Engine House, No. 1, (steam fire) ss. Washington, bet. West and California.

Engine House No. 2, (steam fire) cor. Massachusetts av. and New York.

Engine House No. 3, (steam fire) ss. South bet. Delaware and Alabama.

Engass H., tailor, 113 S. Illinois, r. same.

Engelhardt F. M., boot and shoe dealer, r. 286 E. Washington, r. same.

Engelke John, salesman, r. — S. Meridian.

Engle George B., jr., agent T. H. & I. R. R., r. 80 S. Tennessee.

Engle J. W. (E. & Hunt) r. Plainfield, Indiana.

Engle John, moulder, bds. 458 E. Georgia.

Engle S. S., traveling agent, Ward's Portable Gas Light, bds. 80 S. Tennessee.

Engle Theresa, (wid.) r. 97 Bates.

Engle Willis D., cashier T. H. & I. R. R., bds. 80 S. Tennessee.

Engle & Hunt, (J. W. E. and D.H.) dealers in stoves and tinware, r. 405 N. Alabama.

English Benjamin, works Aldrich & Gay, r. 38 Center.

English D. W., printer, Commercial Office, r. 35 N. Blake.

English Dora I. Miss, bds. 35 N. Blake.

English Orlando F., printer, works Journal office, bds. 35 Blake.

English W. H., clk. Empire saloon, r. 21 E. North.

English W. H., President First National Bank, r. 48 Circle.

Eniuger J. J., machinest, Surgical Institute, r. same.

Euler Anna Miss, house servant, r. 232 Railroad.

Euler Margaret, (wid. Philip) r. 232 Railroad.

H. H. LEE'S

WHOLESALE PRICES FOR

TEAS, COFFEES & SUGARS,

ARE THE SAME EACH DAY

As are quoted in the

CINCINNATI DAILY PAPERS.

Enners Henery, bricklayer, r. 287 Massachusetts av.

Enners Mena, (wid. Philip) r. 287 Massachusetts av.

Ennis Lewis, teamster, bds. 297 N. Winston.

Ennis Lewis, r. 367 N. Noble.

Ennis William, saloon, r. 369 N. Noble.

Enos B. H., draughtsman, r. 397 N. Alabama.

Enos B. V. (E. & Hubner) r. 397 N. Alabama.

Enos T. H. K., bookkeeper, Browning & Sloan, r. 236 S. Alabama.

ENOS & HUBNER, (B. U. E. and H. R. H.) architects, rooms 1 and 2 Eden's blk. E. Market.

Ensey John, engineer, C. C. C. & I. R. W.

Ensey Samuel, fireman, C. C. C. & I. R. R.

Entwistle George W., works cotton mill, r. 33 Blake.

Eoff S. A., commercial traveler, r. 42 W. Second.

Epler John, manufacturer of varnish, r. 310 S. East.

Eppert Frank, teamster, r. 297 N. Alabama.

Erbacher John, wagonmaker, bds. Globe House.

ERDLEMEYER FRANK, dealer in drugs, medicines, etc., 91 E. Washington, r. same.

ERHART FRANK, bakery and confectionery, 112 S. Illinois, r. same.

Erickson John, cabinetmaker, r. 117 S. Illinois.

Ernsberger Frank, salesman, r. 266 N. East.

Ernst Fred, varnisher, bds. 173 Union.

Ervine Oliver, medical student, bds. 139 N. Alabama.

Esamann Joseph, milk man, r. 310 Chestnut.

Escher William, varnisher, r. 111 Spring.

Eschmeier J. H. Rev., r. 41 N. Alabama.

Essigke August, meat market, 295 E. Washington, r. same.

ESSIGKE RICHARD, Meat Market, 170 S. Illinois, r. same.

Essmann Louis, clk. 183 S. Illinois, bds. same.

ESSMANN WILLIAM, proprietor Illinois House, 183 S. Illinois.

Etherton Samuel, carpenter, r. 23 Center.

Estler Theodore, bricklayer, r. 360 E. St. Clair.

Eurich Adam, lab., r. 204 E. Court.

EURICH JOHN L., proprietor St. Nicholals Saloon, 17 N. Illinois, r. Madison av., beyond city limits.

Eubank Rowland R., carriagepainter, r. cor. Tinker and Pennsylvania.

Euwic J. H., real estate agent, r. 120 Massachusetts av.

Evans Able, r. 169 Jackson.

Evans Andrew, machinest, r. 239 Massachusetts av.

Evans A. S., salesman, 112 S. Meridian, bds. Sherman House.

Evans B. F., physician, 20½ N. Delaware.

Evans David, works rolling mill, bds. 169 S. Tennessee.

Evans G. T., (J. E. Robertson & Co.) r. 548 N. Meridian.

Evans George A., bookkeeper, 75 S. Meridian, r. 259 Virginia av.

Evans H. C., lettercarrier, r. 78 Huron.

Evans Henry, W., w'ks I. C & L. car shops, r. 25 Lord.

Evans Isaac P. (Evans & Co.) r. Richmond, Ind.

Evans John J., shoemaker, r. 243 S. Mississippi.

EVANS JOHN D., Auditor of State's office in State building, r. 49 School.

Evans Joseph R. (I. P. Evans & Co.) r. 360 N. Alabama.

Evans I. P. & Co. (I. P. E., J. R. E. and W. R. E.) manufacturers of linseed oil, 124 S. Delaware.

Evans Lucinda, (wid Edward) seamstress, r. 203 N. Noble.

Evans Maria, (col'd, wid. James) r. 311 Massachusetts av.

Evans Rob., bricklayer, r. 476 N. Meridian.

Evans Thomas, circuit minister, United Brethern church, r. 166 N. Liberty.

Evans Thomas, brickmason, r. 496 N. Mississippi.

Evans William R. (Evans & Co.) r. 23 Ft. Wayne av.

EVENING COMMERCIAL, published by the Commercial Company, ne. cor. Washington and Illinois.

Everts Evert, blacksmith, glass works, r. nr. glass works.

Everett Edward, gasfitter, 70 N. Illinois, r. 524 N. Mississippi.

Everett P. E., gas and steamfitter, w'ks 70 N. Illinois, r. 340 N. Delaware.

Everett S. A., carpenter, bds. Pattison House.

Everling Amos, teamster, r. 38 Center.

Everling Mary Mrs. (wid. John) r. 228 W. Ohio.

Ewald William, blacksmith and wagonmaker, cor. Noble and Massachusetts av., r. 10 Arch.

Ewing Albert, railroader, r. 131 E. South.

Ewing Clayton, (col'd) lab., bds. 135 Bright.

EWING DAVID, physician, 33 Virginia av., r. same.

Ewing Henry, 39 S. Illinois, bds. 215 N. Mississippi.

Ewing William, carpenter, r. 215 N. Mississippi.

Ewing William M., trunkfinisher, 39 S. Illinois, r. 215 N. Mississippi.

Ewinger J. R., insurance agent, r. 177 N. Tennessee.

Exbert J. W., mailagent, C. & I. J. R. R.

EXCHANGE STABLES, William Hinesley, proprietor, 35 N. Illinois.

Exler —— lab., r. N. Pennsylvania bet. Fourth and Fifth.

Extoleen Thomas, lab., rolling mill, r. 424 S. West.

Eyman J. H., manufacturer of boots and shoes, 11½ N. Illinois, r. Cumberland bet. Canal and West.

FACKER JOHN, lab., r. 315 S. Pennsylvania.

Fagan B. B.(F. Ross & Co.) agent Buttonhole Sewing Machine, bds. Macy House.

Fagan Charles, stonecutter, r. 26 Center.

FAGAN, ROSS & CO., (B. B. F. and J. H. Ross) general agents Buttonhole over-seaming Sewing Machines, 18 N. Delaware.

Fahla Henry, machinist, Eagle Machine Works, r. 127 E. Merrill.

Fabler Henry, lab., r. 313 N. Noble.

Fahnley Fred., r. 86 N. Illinois.

FAHNLEY & McCREA, (F. F. and R. H. McCrea) importers and jobbers of millinery, straw and fancy goods, 131 S. Meridian.

FAHRBACH PHILIPP, proprietor Washington Hall and Academy of Music Saloons, r. Washington Hall.

Fahrion Christian, cabinetmaker, r. 363 N. Noble.

Fahrion J. George, dealer in wheat, rye, buckwheat, flour, baled hay, etc., etc., 90 and 92 E. South, r. same.

Fahy E. (C. C. Hutchinson & Co.) bds. Bates House.

Fairbanks J. J. (F. & Co.) r. 153 N. Tennessee.

Fairbanks S. E. (F. & Co.) r. 153 N. Tennessee.

Fairbank Philip, plasterer, r. 9 Coburn.

Fairbanks & Co., ladies' furnishing goods, 22 W. Washington.

Faley James, waiter, Depot Dining Hall, r. 223 W. Washington.

Falkenbach John, carriagesmith, r. 187 N. Liberty.

Falkenbach Wm., blacksmith, r. Washington, cor. East.

Faloud Valantine, carpenter, r. 299 E. Merrill.

FALLON J. J., delivery clerk, Dawson & Scribner, r. 374 S. Illinois.

Fancis S. Z., brakeman, C. C. & I. C. R. R., r. 585 E. Washington.

Faries Sallie Miss, teacher, r. 226 Merrill.

Faring Fred., machinist, bds. E. Washington.

Farley Michael, w'ks rolling mill, r. 6 Willard.

Farley Richard, lab., r. W. Second bet. Howard and Lafayette Railroad.

Farman Francis, stonecutter, r. 149 W. South.

Farmer A. B, grocer and produce dealer, 251 N. Illinois, r. 81 W. Walnut.

Farmer Albert, fireman, C. C. C. & I. R. R., r. 212 N. Noble.

Farmer Jerome B., w'ks C. C. C. & I. R. R. car shops, r. 212 N. Noble.

FARMERS' & DROVERS' HOTEL, West Indianapolis, Robert Turbeyville, proprietor.

Farnsworth Thomas, r. 431 N. Tennessee.

FARNSWORTH, T. W., physician, 21½ W. Maryland, r. same.

Farr Henry L., foreman, moulder, Greenleaf & Co., bds. 310 S. Illinois.

Farra John J., sergeant, U. S. Arsenal.

Farrall Mary, (wid. John) r. 169 N. Davidson.

Farrar John, boot and shoe manufacturer, 191 W. Washington, r. same.

Farreli C. J. Miss, dressmaker, r. 79 N. Pennsylvania.

Farrell O. Fergus, porter, r. 77 W. St. Clair.

Farres Milton, carpenter, r. 179 N. Noble.

Farrow James F. (col'd) painter, r. 122 S. Benton.

Fatout J. L. (J. L. & M. K.) bds. Palmer House.

Fatout M. K. (J. L. & M. K.) r. 238 N. West.

FATOUT J. L. & M. K., contractors and builders, shop, Wood, nr. old Lafayette freight depot.

Faucett A. H., shipping clk., Singer Sewing Machine Co., r. 230 W. Ohio.

Faulkner Eugene H., drives steam fire engine, r. w. end Washington.

H. H. LEE

PURCHASES HIS

Teas, Coffees, Sugars & Spices

DIRECT FROM THE

Importers and Refineries,

THUS SAVING

HIS CUSTOMERS TWO OR THREE PROFITS.

Faulkner Joseph H., sup't, Howe, Converse & Co., r. w. end Washington.

Faut Fred., glass factory, r. 222 N. East.

Fawkner John E. (F. & Co.) r. 328 W. Washington.

Fawkner & Connely, (J. E. F. and Robert C.) whol. and retail dealers in coal, coke, lime, plaster, cement, etc., 24 W. Maryland.

Fast E. E., bookkeeper, J. H. Vagen & Co., bds. Palmer House.

Fay Amos F., with G. F. Adams & Co., r. 255 N. East.

Fay John J., bookkeeper, Mears & Lilly, r. 26 S. Mississippi.

Feary Charles, bds. 318 E. North.

Feary Henry J., printer, Sentinel job rooms, r. 129 Stevens.

Feary Jeremiah E., carpenter and builder, r. 318 E. North.

Feary John J., cigarmaker, w'ks 39 W. Washington, r 182 N. Missouri.

Featherston James G., grocery cl'k., r. 386 N. New Jersey.

Featherston William E., auction and commission, 194 W. Washington, r. 165 Massachusetts av.

Feeser J C., saddler, bds. 23 California.

Fehr Christian, carpenter, r. W. Seventh, bet. Tennessee and Illinois.

Fehring Ernst, w'ks Cabinet Makers' Union, bds. E. Washington.

Fei Conrad, lab., bds. 473 S. Illinois.

Fei Henry, lab., r. 485 S. Illinois.

Feibelman Charles R. L., clk., r. 17 Lockerbie.

Feibleman C. B., traveling agent, John Sweetser, r. 229 S. Delaware.

Feibleman Leopold, salesman, Hays, Rosenthal & Co., r. 17 Lockerbie.

Feiel August, w'ks American Express Co., r. 43 Madison av.

Feihr Henry, tailor, bds. California House.

Feiner Julius, lab., r. 235 N. Winston.

Felbaum William, engineer I. C. & L. R. R., r. 200 W. North.

Feldkamp R. W., bookkeeper, r . 806 E. Washington.

Feller George Jr., fireman Depot Dining Hall, r. 226 E. Washington.

FELLER GEORGE, watchmaker, 226 E. Washington, r. same.

Feller John, bell boy, Palmer House.

Feiterner Henry, bootmaker, r. 396 S. Delaware.

Feltman Herman, shoemaker, r. 396 S. Delaware.

Feltpusch Conrad, lab., r. 426 E. Vermont.

Feltpusch John, lab., r. 168 W. Davidson.

Femile Andrew, moulder, r. 428 S. Missouri.

Fendrick Jacob, tinner, bds. 179 S. Meridian.

Fenley Theodore A., bricklayer, r. 36 Orion.

Fennesy John, lab., r. 128 S. Tennessee.

Fenton Bridget, servant, Palmer House.

Fenton Franklin, sawmaker, r. 131 E. St. Joseph.

Fenton John, proprietor Fenton house, 124 S. Meridian.

Fenton John, machinist, works Greenleaf & Co., r. 124 S. Meridian.

Fenton Kate, servant, Palmer house.

Ferber August, grocery, 419 S. West.

Ferchvacht Ernst, cabinetmaker, r. 338 Virginia av.

Ferger Charles, bakery and confectioner, 98 E. South, r. same.

Ferguson A. V. (wid) r. 122 N. Delaware.

Ferguson Clements A., dealer in watches Jewelry &c., 7 W. Washington, r. cor. seventh and Meridian.

Ferguson E. H., bricklayer, r. 463 N. Meridian.

Ferguson George, carpenter, bds. Nagel house.

Ferguson Kilby, lumber dealer, r. 251 E. McCarty.

Ferguson John A. (W. J. Holiday & Co.) r. 270 N. Tennessee.

Ferguson J. C. (J. C. F. & Co.) r. 139 N. Meridian.

Ferguson James, E., bookbinder Sentinel office, bds. Macey house.

Ferguson J. F., bricklayer, bds. 463 N. Meridian.

Ferguson J. C. & Co. (J. C. F., E. B. Howard and N. M. Neeld) pork packers and commission merchants, Georgia Western terminus.

Ferguson N. W. (White & F.) r. 155 N. Illinois.

Ferguson Rezin, clk. Trade Palace, r. 155 N. Illinois.

Ferguson Robert, plasterer and cistern builder, r. 27 W. Pratt.

Ferguson Thomas, lab., r. 61 Dacota.

Ferguson John A. (J. W. Holliday & Co.) r. 270 N. Tennessee.

Ferguson William, clk., 61 N. Illinois, bds. 270 N. Tennessee.

Ferl John, wagonmaker, r. 396 S. Illinois.

Ferling George, barber, shop cor. Meridian and Washington, r. 124 E. Maryland.

Fern Frank, machinest, works Chandler & Taylor, bds. 126 N. Mississippi.

Fernessy John, helper C. C. & I. C. R. R. shops.

Ferning William, r. 53 Harrison.

Fernon Henry, lab. rolling mill, r. 458 S. West.

Fernon James, lab., r. 399 S. West.

Ferrall Joseph, grocer. r. 241 Indiana av.

Ferrall Patrick, lab., r. 241 Indiana av.

Ferree F. M. & Co., manufacturers of medicines, 81 E. Market.

Ferree Louis, lab., r. 296 Blake.

FERREE F. M., physician, proprietor and manufacturer Ferree Quick Cures, 81 E. Market, r. 369 N. New Jersey.

Ferrell E. J., Tailor, r. 25½ Massachusetts av.

Ferretter James, lab., Benton, nr. Meek.

Ferris Henry E., engineer, r. 226 E. Merrill.

Ferry Jane, (wid) r. 26 Gregg.

Fertig Francis, painter, bds. California House.

Fertig Frank, house and sign painting, 21 S. Meridian, r. 65 W. South.

Fesler James M, carpenter, cor. South and Delaware, r. 216 S. East.

Fesler William B., carpenter, r. 512 S. Meridian.

Fesse Earnst, works glass works, bds. Union Hall.

Fetherling William, lab., r. 199 N. East.

Fette Arnold H., harnessmaker, r. E. Court bet. New Jersey and East.

Fettee Charles, machinist, r. 25 S. A'abama.

Fette George, repairer and scourer, 38 Virginia av., r. 123 Duncan.

Feyh Henry, (wid E. Miners) r. 484 S. Illinois.

Fibleman C. B., travelling agent J. Sweetser, r. S. Delaware.

Fidel Simon, saloon 211 W. Washington, r. same.

Fieber William, bookkeeper, Schmidt's brewery. r. 359 S. Alabama.

Fiel Augustus clk. Am. M. U. Exp. Co., r. 43 Madison av.

Field David, street car driver, r. 336 E. Washington.

Field Dexter, railroader, r. 336 E. Washington.

Field E. S. (Merrill & F.) r. 613 N. Illinois.

FIELD, LOCKE & CO., (E. S. Field, E. Locke and B. Scanlon) proprietors Caledonia Paper Mill, office 265 W. Washington.

Fields William, lab. r. over 343 E. Washington.

Fieldig David, lab. bds. 27 S. New Jersey.

Fielding George, helper, bds. 147 S. Mississippi.

Fifer Jemima Miss, dressmaker, r. 21 Douglass.

Fifer William, bootmaker, bds. Globe House.

Filbeck Sena Mrs., r. 11 Buchanan.

Filer Samuel J., salesman, Bowen, Stewart & Co., r. 117 N. Illinois.

Finby R., bds. Bates House.

Finch Flora Miss, teacher Ninth Ward school, bds. 286 E. Ohio.

Finch Tobias M. attorney, 6 and 7 Talbott and New's blk., r. 286 E. Ohio.

Finch John A., attorney, 6 and 7 Talbott and New's blk., r. 286 E. Ohio.

Fink Mary Mrs. (wid.) r. 51 E. McCarty.

Finley Bartlett, (col'd) lab., r. 263 N. West.

Finley J. J., r. 748 N. Pennsylvania.

Finn Bridget Mrs., (wid) r. 80 Maple.

Finn John, lab., r. 33 Dougherty.

Finnegan Daniel, works Am. Ex. Co., bds. 217 S. Illinois.

Finnegan William J., messenger, Am. Ex. Co., bds. Spencer house.

Finnel John W., clk. 144 S. Alabama, bds. Cumberland bet. Alabama and New Jersey.

Finney Jasper, salesman, Murphy, Johnston & Co., r. 430 Virginia av.

Finter Franklin, sawmaker, r. 131 St. Joseph.

Finter F. R., baker, 117 Ft. Wayne av. r. same.

First English Lutheran Church, cor. Alabama and New York.

Fischer Charles, G., cooper, r. 123 Spring.

Fiscus Andrew J., brickmason, r. 339 N. East.

Fiscus Frank, bricklayer, r. 415 N. East.

Fiscus J. R., brickmason, r. cor. Christian av. and Plum.

Fiscus Thomas W. brickmason, r. 280 E. St. Clair.

Fiscus William, bricklayer, r. 1 Vine.

Fish Edith, (wid. Samuel P.) r. 367 N. East.

Fish Frank O. collector, J. S. Spann & Co, r. 367 N. East.

Fish J. G. messenger, United States Express Co. bds. National Hotel.

Fish John L. bookkeeper, 129 S. Meridian, r. 78 E. Pratt.

THE CHINA TEA STORES

Are very handsomely decorated with

Accurate Views and Scenes
or
CHINESE LIFE AND SCENERY.

Call and see them before leaving the City.

Fish Wm. S. printer, News Office, r. 367 N. East.

Fishback Charles H. salesman, 125 S. Meridian, bds. cor. Illinois and Walnut.

FISHBACK JOHN, dealer in hides, leather, oil and belting, 125 S. Meridian, r. 351 N. Illinois.

Fishback W. O. bookkeeper, 125 S. Meridian, bds. cor. Illinois and Walnut.

Fishback William P. (Porter, Harrison & F.) r. E. Washington, nr. city limits.

Fisher Wm. A. r. 255½ E. Washington.

Fisher Andrew, salesman, 67 and 69 W. Washington, r. 406 N. East.

Fisher Benedict, barber, Union Depot, r. 189 S. Illinois.

Fisher Charles, clk. Moody Bros. bds. 21 Indiana av.

FISHER CHARLES, Justice of the Peace, room 4 Yohn's blk., r. 26 W. North.

Fisher Franklin, stonemason, r. 166 Buchanan.

Fisher George, boot and shoemaker, 119 Ft. Wayne av., r. same.

Fisher Henry, machinist, r. 72 E. Maryland.

Fisher Henry, blacksmith, bds. California House.

Fisher Jacob, painter, Shaw, L. & Co. bds. Fenton House.

Fisher John, bartender, Palmer House saloon.

Fisher John, barber, 366 Virginia av., r. same.

Fisher Louis, clk. 56 S. Meridian, r. 184 Virginia av.

Fisher Louis, miller, w'ks White Rose mill, r. 40 W. Louisiana.

Fisher Sarah Mrs., dressmaker, 114 S. Meridian, r. same.

Fisher William, r. 26 W. North.

Fisher William, butcher, bds. 257 E. Washington.

Fisler James, carpenter, r. 216 S. East.

Fistner William, machinist, Vater & King's, bds. 146 W. Maryland.

FITCH D. H., prop. Empire saloon and restaurant, 23 N. Illinois, r. same.

Fitch Ienllius D., carriage trimmer, S. W. Drew.

Fitchey Michael G., carpenter and builder, r. 79 N. California.

Fitzgerald Emanuel, lab., r. 156 Meek.

Fitzgerald Isaac, stone cutter, r. 158 Blackford.

Fitzgerald John, turner, r. 399 S. Delaware.

Fitzgerald Joseph, chairmaker, r. 158 Blackford.

Fitzgerald Mary, domestic, Bates House.

Fitzgerald Maggie Miss, domestic, Spencer House.

Fitzgerald Patrick, lab., r. 71 Fayette.

Fitzgerald Philander, clk., 62 E. Washington, up stairs, bds. 103 S. New Jersey.

Fitzgerald William, lab., r. 228 W. Merrill.

Fitzgerald William, lab., r. S. Maple, s. city limits.

Fitzgibbon John, lab., bds. 426 S. Tennessee.

Fitzhugh Lee M., clk., Murphy, Johnston & Co., r. ne. cor. Illinois and Pratt.

Fitzpatrick Joseph, carpenter, r. 240 W. New York.

Fitzpatrick Rev., r. Dougherty.

Flack Samuel, carpenter, r. 20 Thomas.

Flagan Joshua, lab., r. 18 Vinton.

Flaherty James, printer, Journal office, bds. 329 W. Maryland.

Flaherty John, lab., r. 690 N. Illinois.

Flaherty William, w'ks rolling mill, r. 12 Willard.

Flaig D., joiner, r. 503 S. Tennessee.

Flaig H., w'ks Jackson, Rider & Co., bds. 503 S. Tennessee.

Flaig M. V., carpenter, r. 136 N. New Jersey.

Flanigan W. L., baggage master, C. & I. J. R. R.

Flanner Orpha A. (wid. Henry B.) r. 17 Vine.

Flannery Kate, servant, Ray House, r. same.

Flatley Patrick B., lab., r. 39 Bright.

Flathers J. D. (Berry & F.) r. 151 Maple.

Fleger Jacob, carpenter, r. 181 N. Davidson.

Fleischman L., moulder, r. 246 Massachusetts av.

Fleitz Charles, blacksmith shop, 487 S Meridian, r. same.

Fleming L. W., salesman, New York Store.

FLEMING GEORGE H., city gas inspector, room 9, Miller's blk., bds. 24 W. New York.

Fleming John, press feeder, r. 199 W. Maryland.

Flenner M. B., conductor, C. & I. J. R. R., bds. Spencer House.

Fleper John, bookpeddler, r. 295 Coburn.

Fleshman Laurence, w'ks Vater & King, r. 264 Massachusetts av.

Fletcher Albert E. (Fletcher & Sharpe) r. 429 N. Pennsylvania.

FLETCHER'S BANK, 30 E. Washington, S. A. Fletcher, sr., and F. M. Churchman, proprietors.

Fletcher Bishop, lab., rolling mill, bds. 231 W. South.

Fletcher Calvin, w'ks rolling mill, bds. 308 Chestnut.

Fletcher Charles W., lab., r. 72 N. Liberty.

Fletcher Cornelius, (col'd) lab., r. rear 86 Broadway.

Fletcher Elizabeth, (wid. John) tailoress, r. 308 Chestnut.

Fletcher E. T. Rev., r. 250 N. Delaware.

Fletcher H. T., bookkeeper, 32 S. Meridian, r. 189 E. Market.

Fletcher Ingram, (Fletcher & Sharpe) r. cor. Pratt and Pennsylvania.

Fletcher James J. bookkeeper, 22 S. Meridian, bds. 35 Virginia av.

Fletcher John, teamster, r. 291 E. Ohio.

Fletcher Lucinda, (wid.) r. 72 N. Liberty.

Fletcher L. W. (Wheat, Fletcher & Co.) r. Franklin, Ind.

Fletcher Mary (wid.) dressmaker, r. 129 N. Liberty.

Fletcher Mason, engineer, C. C. & I. C. R. R., bds. 58 Benton.

Fleming Peter, drayman, r. 480 E. Georgia.

FLETCHER R. F. (D. E. Snyder & Co.) gen'l insurance agent, r. 477 N. Tennessee.

FLETCHER S. A., Sr. (S. A. Fletcher & Co.) r. 180 E. Ohio.

Fletcher S. A., jr., pres't, Indianapolis Gaslight and Coke Co., r. College av., nr. Forest Home.

Fletcher S. J., clk., Fletcher's Bank, bds. 180 E. Ohio.

Fletcher Mrs. V. (wid.) r. 240 E. Ohio.

Fletcher Walker, w'ks rolling mill, bds. 308 Chestnut.

Fletcher William, r. 326 Virginia av.

Fletcher William B. (F. & Wright) r. 105 N. Alabama.

Fletcher Z., cabinetmaker, bds 189 E. Market.

FLETCHER & WRIGHT, (Wm. B. F. and G. E. W.) physicians and surgeons, 107 N. Alabama.

Fletcher & Sharpe, (I. Fletcher, A. E. Fletcher and Thos. H. Sharpe) bankers, sw. cor. Washington and Pennsylvania.

Flike Andrew, carpenter, r. cor. North and West.

Flinn Corn, teamster, r. 21 Dougherty.

Flinn B. P., painter, Munson & Johnston.

Fling Davis, expressman, r. 95 Bradshaw.

Flinn J. M. Capt., traveling agent, T. F. Ryan, r. Shelbyville, Ind.

7

BENHAM BRO'S,

36 East Washington St.,

Pianos, Organs and Melodeons Tuned, Moved and Repaired.

Flinn Thomas, gas fitter, 336 S. Delaware.

Flockner Jacob, barber, r. 273 S. New Jersey.

Flood John, shoemaker, r. 232 W. Georgia.

Flood Wm. H., printer, Sentinel Office, r. 70 Indiana av.

Flowers Naomi, (wid. Washington) r. 248 W. Market.

Floyd Lottie, (wid.) r. 75 Lockerbie.

Floyd M. H. (Fortner F. & Co.) r. 269 E. South.

Floyd Thomas, (col'd) barber, r. 190 W. Washington.

Flynn D', works gas works, r. 227 Union.

Flynn Dennis, plasterer and bricklayer, r. 69 Maple.

Fogarty John, lab., r. 498 E. Georgia.

Fogle Frederick, r. 260 N. Winston.

Foland Valentine, cabinetmakee, r. 299 E. Merrill.

Foley Henry, engineer Eagle Machine Works, r. 127 E. Merrill.

Foley J. W. (M. & F.) bds. Plye House.

Foley Michael, works Novelty Works.

Foley Patrick, works Novelty Works.

Foley Patrick, lab., r. 128 N. Winston.

Foley Patrick, yard master, C. C. & I. C. R. R., r. 264 E. Louisiana.

Foley Patrick, lab., r. 93 Fayette.

Foley Thomas, works Novelty Works.

Foley Timothy, blacksmith, r. 39 Mud.

Foley W. W., physician and surgeon, office 53 Indiana av., bds. Pyle House.

Folkennig C. H., with McCord & Wheatley, r. 21 Coburn.

Folkenning Henry, with McCord & Wheatley, r. 21 Coburn.

Folkert Melchior, dealer in groceries, provisions, etc., 674 N. Mississippi, r. same.

Folley Tim., helper C. C. & I. C. R. R.

Folsom E. S., general agent Phœnix Life Insurance Co., 14 Talbott & New's blk., r. 134 Broadway.

Fo'som J. J., roadmaster I. B. & W. Railway, r. 171 Madison av.

Foltz Eliza Mrs., r. 231 W. South.

Foltz H. M. (Olin & F.) r. 279 N. Alabama.

Foncannon Rose Miss, seamstress, bds. 439 S. Illinois.

Foos Angeline Mrs., r. room 10 Fatout's blk.

H. H. LEE,

Dealer in

Teas, Coffees, Sugars & Spices,

No. 7 ODD FELLOWS HALL

AND

ACADEMY OF MUSIC CORNER.

Foot Charles, machinist, bds. Macy House.

Foot Maria, (wid.) r. 18 E. Michigan.

Forbes Joseph R., watchmaker and jeweler, 34 Virginia av., r. 244 Virginia av.

Forby C. H., manufacturer of trunks and valises, 109 S. Illinois, r. 34 S. Illinois.

Ford Alonzo, bds 78 S. Illinois.

Ford Eliza T. Miss, teacher Fifth Ward School, r. 188 W. Ohio.

Ford Henry, clk., r. 225 N. Mississippi.

Ford Ivin, carpenter, r. 149 N. Winston.

Ford John, grain dealer, r. 188 W. Ohio.

Ford Lews, lab., works City Hospital.

Ford Michael, shoemaker, r. cor. Camp and Pratt.

Ford Phebe, (wid. James) r. 73 S. Illinois.

Ford P. D. Miss, bds. 28 S. Illinois.

Ford Stephen, bootmaker, r. cor. Prat and Camp.

Ford Will N., clk. G. P. Tuttle, Tea Store, bds. 188 W. Ohio.

Fargus Wellington, clk. Trade Palace, bds. Sherman House.

Farley Sarah L., dress and cloakmaker, 34 S. Illinois, r. same.

Forsithes E. J., painter, r. 499 S. New Jersey.

Fortenbough James M., telegraph operator, r. 71 S. California.

Fortner A. J. (F., Floyd & Co.) bds. 405 N. Pennsylvania.

FORTNER, FLOYD & CO. (A. J. Fortner, W. H. Floyd, J. D. Evans and D. R. Brown) whol. notions, 75 S. Meridian.

Forwald John, wiper I. C. & L. Shops, r. 314 N. Noble.

Foster A. S., foreman boiler shop Eagle Machine Works, r. 38 S. Illinois.

Foster Chapin C., steward Indiana Institute for Deaf and Dumb.

Foster Dietrich, lab., 220 Union.

Foster F. J. (Hume, Adams & Co.) r. 339 N. Pennsylvania.

Foster George, carpenter, r. 367 S. Missouri.

Foster John B., railroader, r. 76 S. Benton.

Foster R., baker, 12 S. Meridian, r. same.

Foster Robert S., City Treasurer, also, F., Wiggins & Co., r. 352 N. New Jersey.

Foster T. H., photographer, A. R. Miller, r. 172 S. Illinois.

Foster Wallace, (Smith & F.) r. 20 E. Pratt.

Foster William N., mechanic, r. 71 Jackson.

FOSTER & WIGGINS, (R. S. F. and J. P. W.) whol. grocers and commission merchants, 68 and 70 S. Delaware.

Foudray John E. (Wood & F.) r. in country.

Foudray John, jr., harnessmaker, r. 215 N. New Jersey.

Fourth Ward School House, cor. Michigan and Blackford.

Foust C. J., salesman, bds. 352 N. New Jersey.

Fout Henry, teamster, r. 349 N. Winston.

Fowler Benjamin, railroader, r. 77 Davidson.

Fowler Harry, photographer at A. R. Miller, r. 17½ Virginia av.

Fowler James P., hardware, 203 Massachusetts, r. same.

Fox Arthur B., bookkeeper, J. G. Hanning, r. 584 N. Mississippi.

Fox Bernard, r. 70 Hosbrook.

Fox Ellen, (wid. Michael) boarding house, 199 W. Maryland.

Fox James, engineer rolling mill, r. 140 E. McCarty.

Fox J. H. (Elvin & F.) bds. 103 S. New Jersey.

Fox John, bartender Louis Lang, r. 70 Hosbrook.

Fox Judson, lab., bds. 30½ S. Pennsylvania.

Fox Martin, barkeeper Spencer House saloon, r. 318 N. East.

Fox S. R., assistant secretary Surgical Institute, r. same.

Foxcroft Francis, carriage painter, r. 86 Eddy.

Foxworthy John, merchant, r. 456 E. Market.

FOY OWEN, Agent Milick's Patent Vapor Burner, 74 Virginia av., r. 88 S. Benton.

Frailey Joseph, conductor T. H. & I. R. R., r. 10 Henry.

Francis Bros. (H. N. G. and A. E. F.) fruit and oyster dealers, 67 S. Illinois, r. same.

Francis George W., clerk Francis & Co., bds. 138 E. New York.

Francis Hillman, lab., r. Howard bet. Third and Fourth

Francis James, (Francis & Co.) r. 138 E. New York.

Francis James B., tinsmith, r. 271 Indiana av.

Francis William, (Caldwell & F.) r. 61 S. Illinois.

Francis & Co. (James F. and J. H. Craig) coal dealers, cor. Market and Canal.

Frank Adam, cabinetmaker, bds. 276 E. Washington.

Frank Amos J., works rolling mill, bds. 11 Willard.

Frank Andy, baggageman, r. 176 Union.

Frank Dietrich, varnisher, r. 112 Benton.

Frank Francis, sleeping car conductor, I. P. & C. R. R., bds. Sherman House.

Frank George II., engineer, C. C. & I. C. R. R.

FRANK JAMES, Real Estate Agent, 35½ E. Washington, r. 461 N. Tennessee.

Frankem I. L. (I. L. & Co.) bds. 235 N. Illinois.

Frankem Jonathan, r. 249 N Illinois.

Frankem I. L. & Co. (I. L. F. and Joseph Kline) dealers in stoves and house furnishing goods, 34 E. Washington.

Frankensteiner Jacob, delivery clk., 326 S. Delaware.

Franklin B. Rev., rector Christ Church, r. 65 Circle.

Franklin Benjamin, student, bds. 268 E. St. Clair.

Franklin G. E., notary public, office, No. 3 Ætna bldg., r. ne. cor. Tinker and Illinois.

Franklin William, (col'd) whitewasher, r. 161 Indiana av.

Franks Jessie J., lab., r. 127 Indiana av.

Franks John, w'ks Byrkit & Sons, bds. 73 Kentucky av.

Frantz Jacob, porter, 26 S. Meridian, r. Clinton nr. Vermont.

Franzman Amelia, (wid.) r. 292 E. Market.

Frash Walter E., printer, Commercial office, bds. 95 N. Meridian.

Frauer Albert, speculator, r. 28 N. East.

Frauer Herman E., drug clk., 246 E. Washington, r. 224 E. Ohio.

FRAUER I. C., druggist, 246 E. Washington, r. 224 E. Ohio.

Frauer Rudolph, (F., Beiler & Co.) r. 265 E. New York.

FRAUER, BEILER & CO. (R. F., J. S. B., and F. Rottler) saddles, harness and saddlery hardware, 109 E. Washington.

Frazee John W., lab., r. 303 N. Delaware.

Frazee Samuel E., paymaster Indianapolis & St. Louis R. R., r. 167 N. Illinois.

Frazell Agusta, welldigger, r. 34 Thomas.

Frazier Henry, engineer C. & I. J. R. R., bds. 52 Fletcher av.

Frazier John, carpenter, r. 271 E. Market.

Frazier Thomas, plumber J. G. Hanning, bds. Richmond House.

BENHAM BRO'S,

36 East Washignton St.,

AGENTS FOR THE

BURDETT ORGAN.

Frazier William, carpenter, 38 Center.

Fredrick John, fireman C. C. & I. C. R. R., bds. 113 Benton.

Frederick John, shoemaker, r. 2 Geisendorff.

Fredericks George, brickmoulder, r. 14 Bates.

Fredricks Godfrey, lab., r. 9 Willard.

Free Frederick, mechanic, r. E. Cumberland.

Free Herman, cabinetmakers Union, bds. 125 E. Washington.

Free John M., cabinetmakers Union, r. 25 Cook.

Freeman George W., clk. 40 S. Meridian, r. 350 N. Alabama.

Freeman Henry, machinest, Eagle Machine Works, r. 137 Union.

Freeman H. C, travelling agent, bds. Spencer House.

Freeman Joseph, moulder Eagle Machine Works, bds. 344 S. Pennsylvania.

Freeman Joseph W., carpenter, C. C. & I. C. R. R., r. 56 S. Noble.

Freeman Laura C., scamstress, Indiana Institution for Deaf and Dumb.

Freeman Lesh R., operator W. U. Tel., r. 104 Massachusetts av.

Freeman Madison, (col'd) cook, Bates House.

Freeman Mary Mrs., r. 320 N. Delaware.

Freeman Michael, pattern maker, Eagle Machine Works, r. 343 S. Pennsylvania.

Frees Mary Mrs., r. 27 S. New Jersey.

Freidman Joseph, peddler, r. 117 W. McCarty.

Fresdorff Frederick, cooper, r. 400 W. North.

Fremont Henry, machinist, r. 137 Union.

FRENCH C. C., watchmaker, 13 N. Meridian, r. 594 E. Washington.

Frendleman Christian, wiper C. C. C. & I. R. R. shops.

Frendleman Frederick, wiper, C., C. C. & I. R. R. Shops.

Frentz John Peter, carpenter, r. 222 N. Noble.

Frenzel John P. city tannery, cor. Washington and Davidson, r. 48 N. East.

Frenzel J. P. jr. bookkeeper, Merchants' National Band, bds. 48 N. East.

Frenzel O. N. messenger, Merchants' National Bank, bds. 48 N. East.

Frese Charles, (Charles Frese & Co.) bds. 27 W. Georgia.

Frese Charles & Co. (C. F. and C. F. Hahn) wholesale and retail dealers in hardware, cutlery, etc., 27 W. Washington.

Frese Paul, works, Fishback's Tannery, r. Fourth, bet. L. R. R. and Canal.

Frey Adolph, superintendent Gutenberg Publishing Co., r. 87 N. Noble.

Frey Frank, salesman, Over & Co. bds. 79 N. Alabama.

Freye William, brass finisher, r. 385 S. Delaware.

FRICK JOHN, groceries, provisions, dry goods, etc. cor. Massachusetts av. and St. Clair.

Frick Peter, clk. cor. Massachusetts av. and St. Clair, bds. same.

Frick Phillip L., tinner, r. 15 S. Alabama.

Fricke Henry, clk. 27 W. Washington, bds. California House.

Fricker Jacob, (Schmedel & F.) r. 300 Morris.

Fridley S. J. (wid.) r. 103 E. Michigan.

Frieeh Henry, saloon, W. Indianapolis.

Friedag John M. carpenter, r. 264 N. R. R.

Friedgen Cornelius, boot and shoe dealer, 36 W. Washington, r. 36 N. East.

Freidgen C. H. dyeing and cleaning, 41 N. Illinois, r. 123 W. Market.

Frink E O assistant superintendent, Union Novelty Works Manufacturing Co., r. 437 N. Tennessee.

Frink H. S. machinist, 27 N. Pennsylvania, r. 353 S. Delaware.

Frink J. H., r. 353 S. Delaware.

FRINK S. C. President Union Novelty Works Manufacturing Co, r. 476 N Illinois.

Fritche Louis, cabinet maker, r. 271 Massachusetts av.

Fritche Charles, clk. C. Vonegut, bds. 467 N Delaware.

Fritz Charles L. salesman, 21 W. Washington, r. 137 Massachusetts av.

Frizzell Allen, carpenter, r. 751 N. West

Froalking Frederick, bds. 469 N. New Jersey.

Frohlich William, bricklayer, r. 163 High.

Fromeyer Henry, salesman, 32 S. Meridian, r. 134 N. Mississippi.

Fromholte Peter, works, Schneider & Co., r. 467 S. Meridian.

Fromlet Peter, chair maker, bds. Court Street Boarding House.

Froschauer Adam, lab., r. 518 E. Washington.

Froschauer Casper, stonemason, r. 228 S. New Jersey.

Frost B. clk. 59 W. Washington, r. 72 E. Market.

Frost Homer M, conductor, J., M. & I. R. R. bds. Depot Dining Hall.

Frost Taylor B. commercial traveler, bds. 72 E. Market.

Fruichtriehte H. school teacher, bds. 82 James.

Fry Albert, works, 21 and 23 E. Pearl, r. 77 W. South.

Fry Frank, salesman, (E. Over & Co.) r. 79 N. Alabama.

Fry Monroe, barber, r. 79 W. South.

Fry Mrs. boarding house, 204 N. Illinois, r. same.

Fry W. H. (Maxwell, F. & Thurston) r. 721 N. Meridian.

Fuchs Phi ip, lab., r. 219 Coburn.

Fuerchenicht Albert, works, Cabinet Maker's Union, r. 330 Virginia av.

Fuerchenicht Ernst, works, Cabinet Maker's Union, r. 338 Virginia av.

Fuerst Charles, bootmaker, 861 S. Delaware, bds. same

Fugate J. L. (J. H. Vagen & Co.) r. 163 W. New York.

Fuger August, bookkeeper, 111 E. Washington.

Fuller Emma, (wid. William) r. 133 W. Fifth.

Fullmer Charles H., machinist, C. C. & I. C. R. R., r. 116 Bates.

Fulmer D. S., silverplater, r. 227 E. Market.

FULMER FREDERICK, silverplater, 30 Virginia av., r. 127 E. Market.

Fulton Harman H., clk., T. H. & I. R. R., bds. 152 N. Meridian.

Fulton Homer, works American M. U. Express Co., r. 214 Union.

Fulton F. L., cabinetmaker, r. 214 Union.

Fulton W. H., pianomaker, r. 151 N. Winston.

Fultz J. W., lab., r. 11 Willard.

Fuuke F. W., stocking manufacturer, 90 E. Washington, r. same.

FUNKHOUSER D. (Jameson & F.) physician, r. 40 N. Mississippi.

Funnelle A. F., r. 60 N. California.

Furgason Albert L., Superintendent, cooper shops, 123 S. Noble

Furgason Chas., fireman, C. C. & I. C. R. R., r. 325 E. Georgia.

Furman J. Byron, with M. O. Tracy & Co., r. 225 E. Market.

Furnas John, proprietor Quaker Store, r. 518 N. Delaware.

Furnich W. W., carpenter, r. 173 E. Washington.

Furrell Annie, domestic, Bates House.

Fussler ——, cooper, r. 66 California.

GABEL CONRAD, works Osgood & Smith's, r. 196 N. Noble.

Gabel Henry J., works Western Furniture Co., r. 21 Morrison.

Gabel Jacob, tinplate worker, bds. 75 N. Illinois.

Gaden Armsted, (col'd) lab., r. W. First, nr. Howard.

Gage Mary, (wid. James) r. N. Tennessee, bet. Fourth and Fifth.

GAHM JOHN, groceries and saloon, 196 Indiana av., r. same.

Gaither George, (col'd) lab., r. 9 Athon.

Garlick E. C. (G. & Collins) r. 673 N. Meridian.

Garlick & Collins, (E. C. G. and — Collins) manufacturers pig iron, office McKernan's blk.

Gaines P. O, clk., bds. Neiman House.

Gaither Thomas, (col'd) waiter Macy House.

Galbraith Arthur, salesman New York Store, r. 47 N. East.

GALE C. C., supt. Indianapolis Division C. C. C. & I. R. R., r. 370 Massachusetts av.

Gale John, lab., r. 81 N. Liberty.

Galeven Hanora, (wid. of M. A.) r. 169 N. Davidson.

Galehouse James E., traveling agent L. Q. Sherwood, bds. 556 N. Illinois.

Galivan Michael, lab., r. 148 S. Noble.

Gall Albert, (G. & Rush) r. 217 E. Ohio.

Gall E. F., clk. F. P. Rush, bds. 67 N. New Jersey.

Gall Elizabeth, (wid. John) r. 19 Russell.

Gail Caroline, (wid. A. D.) r. 67 New Jersey.

Gall & Rush, (C. Rush and A. Gall) carpets, wall paper, etc., 101 E. Washington.

Gallagher Frank, lab. rolling mill, bds. 231 W. South.

Gallagher Michael, wiper I. C. & L. Shops.

Gallagher P., salesman New York Store, bds. 31 W. Ohio.

Gallagher Patrick, pedler, r. 330 Railroad.

Gallagher Patrick, lab., r. 279 S. West.

Gallagher John, lab., r. 236 Massachusetts av.

Gallagher P. M., salesman, r. 261 Virginia av.

Gallatan John, (col'd) lab., r. 171 Blake.

Gallatan Sarah, (col'd, wid. Albert) r. 73 Bright.

Gallmeyer Conrad, carpenter, r. 170 Stevens.

Gallup E P. (W. P. & E. P. Gallup) r. 78 N. Tennessee.

Gallup W. P., (W. P. & E. P. Gallup) r. 78 North Tennessee.

Gallup W. P. & E. P., commission merchants, agents Fairbank's Scale, 43 and 45 N. Tennessee.

Gambold Thomas, with Wm. Spotts, r. 433 S. Meridian.

Gamerdinger Jacob, blacksmith, r. 630 E. Washington.

Gamilinger Jacob, blacksmith, C. C. C. & I. R. R., shops.

Gammonds M. (col'd) lab., r. Tennessee, N. of Seventh.

Gankle Jacob, beltmaker, r. 125 S. Meridian.

Ganeberg Fred, baggage master, Union depot, r. S. Liberty.

Gansehold Frederick, cabinetmaker, r. 164 S. Noble.

Ganter Cassean, confectionery and bakery 233 E. Washington, r. same.

Ganter Daniel, machinest, r. 311 E. Washington.

Ganter John, painter, r. 311 E. Washington.

Ganter Sarah Mrs., news depot, 311 E. Washington.

Gapin Philip M. (G. & Catherwood) r. Bluff rd. S. city limits.

GAPEN & CATHERWOOD, (P. M. Gapen and J. Catherwood) wholesale dealers in wines and liquors 118 S. Meridian.

Garahn Daniel, lab., r. 70 Railroad.

Garber Henry, boarding house, 80 S. Delaware.

Garbison James, lab., r. 29 Jones.

Garing Frank, lab, r 19 Willard.

Gardner Perry, (col'd) lab., r. W. Second near Laf. R R.

Gardner Joseph, foreman at R. L. & A. W. McOuat, r. 118 Indiana av.

Gardner Lotta, (wid) samstress, r. 357 E. Market.

Gardner Wendal, carpenter, r. 31 James.

Garey G. W. (col'd) bds. 29 N. Illinois.

Garlick E. C, Sec'y rolling mill, r. 673 N. Meridian.

THE CHINA TEA STORES

ARE AT

No. 7 ODD FELLOWS HALL

AND

ACADEMY OF MUSIC CORNER.

Garner Charles, House of Lords, bds. same.

Garner H. S., printer Sentinel Job rooms, bds. Palmer House.

Garner Lewellyn W., salesman 15 W. Washington, bds Palmer House.

Garner Perin, carpenter, r. 202 Huron.

Garratt A., second hand store, 257 E. Washington.

Garratt Jacob, (Solomon & G.) r. 257 E Washington

Garrett Benjamin D., carpenter, r. 308 Indiana av.

Garrett David, carpenter, r. 47 N. Noble.

Garrett William, painter, 18 S. Meridian, bds. 368 Indiana av.

Garriety John, lab., bds. 256 S. Tennessee.

Garrison Edward W., carpenter, r. 395 Massachusetts av.

Garshmiler William J. clk. 187 W. Washington r. 30 S. West.

Garter Frank, bookbinder, bds. 276 S. Illinois.

Garvison Louis, cooper, bds. Nagel house.

Garver Matthew, ice dealer, bds. 217 S. Illinois.

Gaslighter John, r. 310 Railroad.

Gass Andrew, butcher, r. 116 E. St. Joseph.

Gassner Oscar, steward, Emenegger's Hotel, bds. same.

Gaston Delilah, (wid. Hiram R.) r. se. cor. Indiana av. and Vermont.

Gaston Edward, musician, bds. 49 Kentucky av.

Gaston Edward V. carriage maker, r. 49 Kentucky av.

Gaston John M. physician, 66 E. Market, r. 147 N. New Jersey.

Gaston Sim. B. bartender, Bates House Saloon, r. 35 N. Alabama.

Gatch Candace B. salesman, 125 S. Meridian, bds. Sherman House.

Gates A. B. (G. & Brag) r. 91 N. Delaware.

Gates Abel B. (Ripley & G.) r. 289 W. Vermont.

Gates Herman, bartender, bds. 13 E. South.

Gates John, wiper, C. C. C. & I. R. R. Shops.

Gates John, lab., r. 172 Stevenson.

Gates John G. blacksmith, 26 S. New Jersey, r. 223 E. Market.

Gates Rufus, expressman, r. 256 S. Delaware.

GATES & PRAY, (A. B. Gates and Wm. Pray) livery and sale stables, East Market Square.

GATLING GUN CO., office, 24½ E. Washington, W. H. Talbott, prest. H. Clay, secy.

Gattenby John, lab. J. C. Ferguson & Co.

Gattenby Sallie J. (wid.)r. 183 N. Liberty.

Gaughan Luckey, teamster, r. 356 S. Tennessee.

Gaus Caroline. (wid. Charles) r. 65 W. McCarty.

Gaus Eugene, salesman, 29 W. Washington, r. 343 N. West.

Gaus William, patent agent, bds. 174 E. Walnut.

Gausepohl Frederich, cabinetmaker, r. 164 S. Noble.

Gaves James, (col'd) lab., r. 79 S. Missouri.

Gay Alfred, (Aldrich & G.) r. 38 N. West.

Gay Henrie E., engineer, r. 38 N. West.

Gay Leonard A., stationary engineer, bds. 38 N. West.

Gaynor Henry, porter, Ray House, r. same.

GEBHARD AUGUST, upholsterer and furniture dealer, 123 E. Washington.

Gebhard Henry, cigarmaker, r. 152 Greer.

Gedker Rudolph, tailor. r. 128 N. Noble.

Gehring Bernhardt, r. 287 Liberty.

GEHRING CONRAD, German Book Store, 147 E. Washington, r. same.

Gehring Fred., local editor, Guttenberg Publishing Company, r. 119 E. St. Joseph.

Geiger Adam, carpenter, bds. 313 E. Market.

Geiger G. W., salesman, Landers, Conduitt & Co., r. 434 N. Tennessee.

Geiger J. W., with W. Sumner & Co., r. 219 E. Market.

Geiger William, shoemaker, r. 347 S. Missouri.

Geir David, tailor, r. cor. Illinois and Kansas.

Geis John. saloon keeper, 62 S. Delaware.

Geis Joseph, brewer, w'ks Leiber's Brewery, r. 238 Chestnut.

Geis Lawrence, saloon, 99 E. Washington, r. same.

Geisel Christian, carpenter, r. 222 N. Davidson.

Geisendorff Abner, clk., C. E. Geisendorff, bds 328 W. New York.

Geisendorff C. E. (C. E. G. & Co.) r. 328 W. New York.

Geisendorff George, (M. E. G. & Co.) r. cor. Ohio and Mississippi.

Geisennorff J. C. (G. & Co.) r. 191 N. New Jersey.

Geisendorff Lewis, clk. Geisendorff & Co., bds. 328 W. New York.

Geisendorff C. E. & Co. (C. E. G. and D. A Richardson) proprietors Hoosier State Flour Mills, w. end Washington.

Geisendorff & Co. (C. E. G. and Isaac Thalman) proprietors Hoosier Woolen Mill, 402 W. Washington.

Geising Fred, machinist Eagle Machine Works, r. 233 S. East.

Gelzenleuchter Peter, clk., bds 188 N. Noble.

Geological Room and Chemical Laboratory and Cabinet of Natural History, State House bldg.

George Austin R., clk. 184 W. Washington, bds 24 N. Mississippi.

George James O., painter, r. 16 S. Mississippi.

George Robert, groceries, produce and liquors, 184 W. Washington, r. 24 N. Mississippi.

George Wesley, works Novelty Works, bds. 173 W. Maryland.

Gerau Jerry, lab., works Paper Mill, r. 24 S. Ray.

Gerard Charles, lab., r. 280 N. Winston.

Gerardy Nicholas, tailor, r. 313 E. Washington.

Geratts Henry, packer, 127 S. Meridian, r. 16 Buchanan.

German M. E. Church, Rev. G. Trefz, pastor, cor. New York and New Jersey.

German and English School, 122 E. Maryland.

GERSTNER A. J., merchant tailor, 171 E. Washington, r. same.

Gety Charles, barkeeper Circle Saloon, r. over 240 E. Market.

Getzendanner William, (O. H. & Co.) r. 150 W. Vermont.

Geutig Charles, clk., r. 252 E. Washington.

Geyer David, (M. Geyer & Co.) r. 161 Huron.

Gibberd Fred, lab., r. 228 Union.

Gibbons John, lab., r. 305 E. Market.

Gibbons Theodore, dentist, r. 243 W. McCarty.

Gibbs R. W., (col'd) barber, r. 181 W. Washington.

Gibbs William P., furniture and matress repairer, 78 E. Market, r. 234 E. Vermont.

Giblin David, lab., I. C. & L. Depot, r. 60 Bates.

Giblin James, lab., I. C. & L. Depot, r. 60 Bates.

Gibson Adam, baker 12 S. Meridian, r. same.

Gibson David, (Sohl, Gibson & Co.) r. 322 W. New York.

Gibson James, (Gibson & Terry) r. 36 Fayette.

Gibson Jasper, blacksmith, r. 10 Willard.

Gibson John, stonecutter, bds 72 Louisiana.

Gibson William, carpenter, bds. 44 S. Tennessee.

GIBSON WILLIAM T., Secretary Indiana Fire Insurance Company, Old Fellows Hall, r. 140 N. Alabama.

Gibson & Terry, (James Gibson and Joel Terry) marble dealers, 199 Indiana av.

Gieger William W., shoemaker, r. 317 S. Missouri.

Gies Frank J., bookbinder Journal office, r 163 Union.

Giesking Christian, carpenter, 83 Davidson.

Giesking Gottleib, organ maker, r. 321 N. Davidson.

Giesking Henry, lab., C. C. & I. C. R. R.

Giger John W., agent Wheeler & Wilson Sewing Machine, r. 219 E. Market.

Gilbert E. A., barber Union Depot, bds. same.

Gilbert Edward Gen'l Insurance agent, room four Blackford blk, r. 30 Indiana av.

Gilbert Jacob, shoemaker, r. 5 Elm.

Gilchrist David, lab., r. 273 N. Liberty.

Gilcrist David, lab., r. 193 N Tennessee.

Gilderman Frederick, lab, r. E McCarty.

Gilriber John, cooper, r. 77 S. East.

Gilkey O. B. (G. & Jones) r. 32 W. Maryland.

GILKEY & JONES, (O. B G and J. J.) carpenters and builders, 48 Kentucky av.

Gilkison W. F., printer, sentinel office, r. 127 Meek.

Gillespie Jane, (wid.) r. 116 N. Delaware.

Gillespie Wm. J. (J., M. & Co) r. 124 N. Delaware.

Gillet H. Smith, professor Deaf and Dumb Institute, r. 203 N. Noble.

Gilmore Dan, bricklayer, r. 242 Coburn.

Gilmann Fred, butcher, r. 311 E. McCarty.

Gilmore Samuel H., shoemaker, r. 91 Douglass.

H. H. LEE

MAKES A SPECIALTY OF

Choice Green, Black & Japan Teas.

Gilmore T. H., feeder, Sentinel office, bds. 242 Coburn.
Gimbel Mrs. B., r. 109 E. Stevenson.
Gimbel Henry K., salesman Hollweg & Reese, bds. 321 S. East.
Gimbel Michael, grocer, 329 S. East, r. same.
Gimber Henry, teamster, r. 432 S. Meridian.
Ginkle George, courier, Mooney & Co., r. 454 S. Illinois.
GINZ MICHAEL, saloon keeper, 185 E. Washington. r. same.
Gipe Wm., fireman, C. C. & I. C. R. R., bds. 58 Benton.
Gipps William, furniture repair shop, r. 234 East Vermont.
Girton Frank, teamster, bds. 291 E. Ohio.
Githens G. D., cabinetmaker, r. 211 E. Ohio.
Githens John C., engineer, r. 457 S. Missouri.
Githens L. M., engineer, J. T. Presley, r. 170 S. Tennessee.
Gitzindiner, (wid) r. 319 N. Noble.
Givens George, machinist, r. 21 Peru.
Glanmeyer William, mechanic, bds Canal street boarding house.
Glass Henry, watchman, Caledonia paper mill, r. 321 W. Market.
Glassby Will, grocer, r. N. Delaware.
Glasscock Wm., carpenter, r. 54 Bright.
Glavin Edward, moulder, Sinker & Co., r. 141 E. McCarty.
Glazier Catherine, (wid.) r. 178 S. New Jersey.
GLAZIER CHARLES, commission house, 146 S. Pennsylvania, r. 129 Virginia av.
Glazier Daniel, engineer, steam fire engine No. 4, r. 185 S. New Jersey.
Glazier Frank, r. 273 W. Washington.
Gleason John, messenger, Indianapolis Insurance Co., r. cor. Virginia av. and Pennsylvania.
Gleason Thomas, bartender, Circle restaurant, r. same.
Gleason Thomas, employe, T. H. & I. R. R., r. 396 S. Missouri.
Gleason Wm., salesman, New York Store, bds 31 W. Ohio.
Gleason William, w'ks gas works, bds. 217 S. Illinois.
Gledhill Ruth, (wid. George) r. cor. East and Cherry.

Glenn Amanda Miss, domestic, r. over 47 N. Liberty.
Glenn George, porter, Ray House, r. same.
Glenn Michael, lab., r. 17 Willard.
Glessing Thomas B., artist, r. 237 W. New York.
Glick Hermann, (G. & Schwartz) r. Evansville, Ind.
Glick & Schwartz, (Hermann Glick and Joseph Schwartz) hoop skirt manufactory and notion store, 54 N. Illinois.
Globe Mutual Life Insurance Co. of New York, R. E. Beardsley, agent.
Glassbrenner W. J. mail agent, J., M. & I. R. R.
Goddard Sarah, (wid.) r. 49 Jones.
Goddard Samuel, stone yard, r. cor. Georgia and Mississippi.
Goddard Samuel, jr. stone cutter, bds. 100 S. Mississippi.
Goddard Thomas, stone cutter, bds. 100 S. Mississippi.
Godfrey William, printer, Indianapolis Printing and Publishing House, bds. Pyle House.
Goe H. N. clk. bds. 352 W. New York.
Goe Henry, works, Osgood, Smith & Co., r. 15 Henry.
Goe Hezekiah M. groceries and provisions, 352 W. New York, r. same.
Goe John C. lab. Osgood, Smith & Co., r. 374 S. West.
Goebel Jacob, tinner, r. 75 N. Illinois.
Goebel John G. cabinetmaker, works, 246 S. Meridian, r. 221 S. Meridian.
Goebel R. editor Daily Telegraph, (German) r. 172 N. New Jersey.
Goebelt Wm. tailor, r. 22 Buchanan.
Goeken William, foreman, Marsee & Son's saw mill r. 43. S. New Jersey.
Goelting John, engineer, Western Furniture Co.
Goetz Charles, bartender, 15 N. Meridian r. cor. Noble and Market.
Goepper Francis, (Francis Goepper & Co.) r. 573 N. Meridian.
GOEPPER F. & CO. (Frederick G. & George Mannfeld) clothiers and merchant tailors, 17 E. Washington.
Goff Eliza, (col'd, wid. Samuel) r. 213 N. West.
Goff George, lab. bds. 276 W. Maryland.
Goff John, blacksmith, C. C. C. & I R. R. shops.
Goff William, (col'd) painter, r. 213 N. West.
Gogen Michael, lab., r. 460 S. East.
Goheen George, millwright, bds. 68 Indiana av.
Goins Lafe, (col'd) lab., r. cor. West and Ohio.

Gold Adam, grocer, 405 W. Washington, r. same.

Gold Christian, butcher, works 153 W. Washington, bds. same.

Gold John J., carpenter, r. 161 High.

Golden Dennis, blacksmith, r. 473 Virginia av.

Golden John, lab., bds. 9 Sharp.

Golden Pat. lab., r. 68 Davidson.

Goldhauser Frank, shoemaker, r. 198 E Washington.

Golding Andrew J., painter, r. 42 Ann.

Golding James, painter, r. 102 S. Tennessee.

Golding William G , carriage painter, r. 12 Ann.

Goldman Jacob, second hand store and rag dealer, 277 S. Delaware, r. same.

Goldsberry Bayles S., r. cor. Indiana av. and New York.

Goldsberry John, carpenter, r. 138 E. McCarty.

Goldsberry L. D., r. cor. Indiana av. and New York.

Goldsberry S. S., watchmaker, (McLene & Herron) r. 323 N. Illinois.

Gool Joseph, dyer, bds. 415 W. Washington.

Goodale Henry, wagonmaker, r. 253 N. West.

Goodall John, (G. & Grove) bds. 150 N. Davidson.

GOODALL & GROVE, manufacturers R. R. handles, rear of 329 E. New York.

Goode Joseph, dyer Indianapolis Cotton Mill, bds. 26 Blake.

Goodhart B. F., bookkeeper Wm. Spots, r. 223 E. Vermont.

Goodman Geo. K., furniture dealer, r. 23 Massachusetts av.

Goodman Mary J., millinery and dress making, 23 Massachusetts av., r. same.

Goodman Philip, works Osgood, Smith & Co., r. 184 Madison av.

Goodnoe J. D., lab., r. 81 E. McCarty.

Goodperle Peter, salesman Spiegle, Thoms & Co., r. 204 N. Noble.

Goodwin A., printer, r. 278 Railroad.

Goodwin Elijah Rev., bds. 171 Jackson.

Goodwin R. M., attorney at law, 6 Vinton blk., r. 282 N. Pennsylvania.

GOODWIN T. A., real estate agent and broker, 79 E. Market, r. Washington, es. of Deaf and Dumb Asylum.

Goodwiller Frank G , varnisher, r. 251 Virginia av.

Gooth Edward, machinist Eagle Machine Works, r. 364 S. Illinois.

Gordon B. G., conductor I. C. & J. R. R., r. 350 Spring.

8

GORDON GEORGE E., attorney at law, No. 6 Odd Fellows Hall, r. 215 N. Delaware.

Gordon James, r. 83 Indiana av.

Gordon Joseph C., teacher Indiana Institution for Deaf and Dumb.

Gordon J. W., attorney, 4 Talbott & New's blk., r. 433 N. New Jersey.

Gordon Robert, artist, r. cor. Vine and Broadway.

GORDON & HESS, (G. E. G. and J. W. H.) Paris Store, 3 Odd Fellows Hall.

Gordon Michael, sawyer, 470 S. East.

Gorham William H., awningmaker, r. 297 N. Mississippi.

Gorman Daniel, teamster, r. 266 Union.

Gorman John, lab. Rolling Mill, r. 382 S. West.

Gorman Robert, salesman New York Store, bds. 158 N. New Jersey.

Gorman Thomas, blacksmith, works Street R. R. Co.

Gorman Thomas, lab., r. Chespeak nr. Canal.

Gorrell A. W. (West, Morris & G.) r. 91 Fletcher av.

Gosney Newton, salesman, r. 127 S. New Jersey.

Goss George, r. 8 Fletcher av.

Gossett F. F., salesman, 79 S. Meridian.

Goth George, porter 123 S. Meridian, r. 443 N. New Jersey.

Goth Jacob, turner, D. Root & Co., r. 173 N. New Jersey.

Goth John L., turner, r. 153 N. New Jersey.

Goth John, tailor, r. 184 Liberty.

Goth Peter, (G., Brown & Co.) r. 456 N. New Jersey.

Goth Valentine, cooper, r. 95 S. Penton.

GOTH, BROWN & Co., (P. G., J. W. Brown and Wm. Bushman) grocers and dealers in flour and feed, 449 N. New Jersey.

Gott Frederick, works T. H. & I. R. R. depot, r. 170 Huron.

Gott Thomas, lab., r. 219 S. Tennessee.

Gottehall John, charge car department, P. C. & St. L. R. R., r. 165 Meek.

Gould Wm. salesman New York Store, bds. 72 E. Maryland.

Goweus Melinda, (wid.) r. 130 N. East.

Gowens Seminel, (col'd) cook, r. cor. Ohio and West.

H. H. LEE

.

MAKES A SPECIALTY OF

Choice Green, Black & Japan Teas.

Grab Charles, lab., r. 16 Lockerbie.

Graber Fred, lab., r. — Douglass.

Graber John, lab., r. 31 N. East.

Grace Church, Methodist Episcopal, ne. cor. East and Market.

Grace Samuel, w'ks glass works, bds. 231 W. South.

Grady Annie Mrs., cook, Ray House, r. same.

Grady Martin, lab., r. 28 Helen.

Grady Michael, lab., T. H. & I. Depot, r. 345 S. Meridian.

Grafenstein Frederick, meat market, 660 N. Tennessee, r. same.

Graff David B., patent right agent, r. 223 E. Ohio.

GRAFTON JOHN J., publisher of Indianapolis Railroad Guide, cor. Circle and Meridian, r. 273 E. South.

Graham George, lab., U. S. Arsenal.

Graham James, (col'd) railroader, r. 153 Huron.

Graham John, merchant, r. 244 E. New Jersey.

Graham Michael, patternmaker, r. 159 S. Alabama.

Graham Samuel, railroader, r. nw. cor. North and Mississippi.

Graifker Henry, r. 53 Harrison.

Gramling John, (J. & P. G.) r. 500 N. Delaware.

Gramling John A. (J. & P. G.) r. 41 Union.

Gramling Peter, (J. & P. G.) r. 502 N. Delaware.

GRAMLING J. & P., merchant tailors, and dealers in ready made clothing, 35 E. Washington.

Granney John, clk., bds. 190 Virginia av.

Grany Mary, (wid.) r. 175 Meek.

Granis Joseph, lab., bds. Nagle House.

Grannis Mary Mrs., dressmaker, r. 76 Massachusetts av.

Grannis S., salesman, M. O. Tracy, r. 281 N. East.

Granstien William, butcher, r. 491 N. Alabama.

Grant Floyd F., lab., r. 54 Oriental.

Grant William, lab., r. 46 Holbrook.

Grasson William, salesman, Keifer & Vinton, bds. 26 W. Georgia.

Graub Carl, works Jackson, Rider & Co.

Grauman J., variety store, 262 E. Washington, r. same.

Graver C. E., freight agent B. & O. R. R., r. 23 N. California.

Graves H., carpenter, r. 38 Forest av.

Graves H Jr., carpenter, r. 42 Forest av.

Graves James P., (col'd) lab., r. 79 S. Missouri.

Graves Richard, confectioner, cor. Kentucky av. and Tennessee, r. same.

Gravis Charles M., medical student, r. 47 Coburn.

Gravis Sebastian, brickmason, r. 47 Coburn.

Gray Alice Miss, teacher, r. 335 N. Illinois.

Gray Columbus V., moulder, r. 482 S. New Jersey.

Gray George, r. 105 Holbrook.

GRAY GEORGE, gold and silversmith and spectacle manufacturer, 498 E. Washington, r. same.

GRAY GEORGE W., custom tailor, 27 Kentucky av., r. same.

Gray Henry, ice dealer, bds. 217 S. Illinois.

Gray James W., proprietor, Spencer House

Gray Jessee, railroader, r. 801 N. Illinois.

Gray Jonathan, bricklayer, r. 224 N. Winston.

Gray Robert, engineer Bates City Mills, r. 28 Lord.

Gray Robert, traveling agent, Kimble Aikman & Co., bds. 23 W. Maryland.

Gray R. P. agent Sewing Machine, r. 52 Greer.

GRAY STEVEN F., agent Star Union Line, office 85 Virginia av.

GRAY STEPHEN & CO. (S. G. & ——) merchant tailors, 14 N. Pennsylvania.

Gray Thomas, bookkeeper, 33 E. Washington, r. 235 N. Illinois.

Gray William, engineer, r. 120 S. Noble.

Gray William, clk. H. H. Lee, r. 235 N. Illinois.

Gray William, conductor, I. C. & L. R. R. bds. Ray House.

Gray W. J. baggage master, P. C. & St. L. R. R.

Graydon Andrew, clk. P. C. & St. L. R. R. Freight Office, r. 332 E. Ohio.

Graydon Jane, (wid) r. 332 E. Ohio.

Graydon W. M., Freight Agent P. C. & St. L. R. R. cor. Virginia av. and Union Track, r. South of city limits.

Greany John, lab. r. 276 S. Tennessee.

Greaschopper Sebastian, boiler maker, r. 349 S. Alabama.

Green Allen T. painter, r. 199 Huron.

Green Davis M., clk. 17 W. Washington, bds. 364 N. Meridian.

Green E. S. agent Hartford Mutual Life Insurance Co. office, Citizens' Bank bldg., r. 708 N. Tennessee.

Green George, merchant tailor, 32 N. Pennsylvania, r. cor. Mississippi and Fifth.

Green Henry F. bookkeeper, Hoosier State Flour Mills, bds. Palmer House.

Green Hugh M. clk. Bee Hive Store, bds. 77 Kentucky av.

Green John, railroader, r. 203 Huron

Green John, (col'd) lab. r. 23 Maria.

Green J. C. (J. C. G. & Co.) r. 370 N. East.

Green John L. general agent, Berkshire Life Insurance Co. r. 84 Plum.

Green Lot, clk. 38 S. Meridian, bds. 74 N. Pennsylvania.

Green Martha J. (wid. Burgess) r. 37 Maple.

Green P. M. (Campbell & G.) r. 128 N. Pennsylvania.

Green Richard student, bds. 268 E. St. Clair.

Green Sallie, (wid.) r. 216 E. Washington.

Green W. H., carpenter, r. 102 N. Mississippi.

GREEN J. C. & CO. (J. C. Green and J. T. Houston) whol. dealers in cigars and tobacco, 38 S. Meridian.

Greene James, (G. & Royse) r. 364 N. Meridian.

GREENE THOMAS C., with Greene & Royse, 10 Blackford's blk.

GREENE & ROYSE, (James Greene and W. T. Royse) general insurance agents, 10 Blackford's blk.

GREENWALT JOHN G., Adjutant General of Indiana, r. 29 W. Michigan.

Greenwalt William, r. 29 W. Michigan.

Greene N. Scott, bookkeeper First National Bank, bds. 364 N. Meridian.

Greenen Joseph, freight conductor, bds. 58 Benton.

Greenen Michael, fireman C. C. & I. C. R. R, bds 58 Benton.

Greenwald Henry, cigar box maker, rear 174 E. Washington.

Greenfield Daniel C., deputy county clk., r. 328 W. Washington.

Greenfield Robert, r. 332 W. Washington.

Greenleaf Allen, (C. A. G. & Co.) r. 240 E. Vermont.

Greenleaf Clements A. (Greenleaf & Co.) r. 240 E. Vermont.

Greenleaf Timothy P., machinist, works Greenleaf & Co.

Greenleaf Wm. A., machinist, 74 S. Pennsylvania, r. 416 S. Tennessee.

GREENLEAF & CO. (C. A. G, E. J. Peck and J. S. Mothershead) founders and machinists, 319 S. Tennessee.

GREENLEE E. A., marble dealer, r. 572 N. Tennessee.

BENHAM BRO'S,

36 East Washington St.,

INDIANAPOLIS MANUFACTURING CO.'S

PIANOS,

ELEGANT IN TONE AND FINISH

Durable in Construction.

Greenrod Timothy, stonecutter, r. 76 S. Missouri.

Greenstreet J. H., bookkeeper Wheat, Fletcher & Co., r. 110 Broadway.

Greenwald Joseph, rag dealer, r. 642 S. Meridian.

Greenway ——, shoemaker, r. rear of 64 S. Alabama.

Greenway Thomas, clk. 29 S. Meridian, bds. same.

Greenwoldt Albert W., salesman Rikoff & Bro, r. 448 S. Illinois.

Greenwood Foster, baggage master P. C. & St. L. R. R.

Greenwood Joseph, r. 441 E. St. Clair.

Greenwood Marcellus, bookkeeper John Carlisle, bds. 260 W. Washington.

Greer Elisha, teamster, r. 82 Green.

Greer H. F., clk. 51 S. Illinois, bds. 266 S. Mississippi.

Greer James, cabinetmaker, 249 S. Mississippi, r. 242 S. Mississippi.

Greger Charles F., carpenter, r. 93 James.

Greger George, teamster, r. 23 James.

Gregg James, wagonmaker, 189 Indiana av.

Gregg Fred, machinist, r. 54 S. Pennsylvania.

Gregor Alexander, baker, 285 E. Washington.

Gregor J. W., checkman, I. C. & L. R. R., r. 76 Bates.

Gregory Dennis, fur dealer, 33 S. Illinois.

Gregory R. C., Judge Supreme Court, r. Lafayette, Ind.

Grein John, baker and confectioner, 246 E. Washington, r. same.

Greisel Michael, lab., r. 34 Cherry.

Grely Mich., lab., r. 187 High.

Gresh B. F., musician, r. 281 N. Liberty.

Gresh John, sr., r. 350 N. Noble.

Gresh John, carpenter, r. 360 N. Noble.

Gresh Samuel, carpenter, r. 360 N. Noble.

Gresham Walker O., Judge District Court U. S., r. New Albany, Ind.

Grenlich John, cabinetmaker, bds. 223 N. Noble.

Greuzard Louis, artist, r. 454 Virginia av.

Grieb John, stonemason, r. 334 Railroad.

Grieb John, lab., r. 110 N. Noble.

Griesheimer Lipman, clk. No. 1 W. Washington, bds. Circle Restaurant.

THE CHINA TEA STORES

ARE AMONG THE

Attractions of Indianapolis.

Call and See Them before leaving the City.

GRIESHEIMER M., dealer in clothing and gentlemen's furnishing goods, No. 1 W. Washington cor. Meridian, bds. Circle Restaurant.

Grieshopper Sebastian, moulder Eagle Machine Works, r. 319 S. Alabama.

Grieves Mary A. Miss, milliner, bds. 252 S. West.

Griffin George W., bartender, bds 376 S. Delaware.

Griffin James, lab., r. 2 Water.

Griffin John sr., lab., r. 75 Fayette.

Griffin John jr., lab., bds. 75 Fayette.

Griffin Martin, lab., r. cor. First and Camp.

Griffin Martin, lab., r. 115 Elm.

Griffin Mary, (wid) r. 149 S. Noble.

Griffin Mary A. Miss, piano teacher, bds. 370 S. Tennessee.

Griffin Micheal, drayman, r. 95 Fayette.

Griffin Michael, works coffee and spice mill, r. 115 Elm.

Griffin Michael J., drayman r. 90 Fayette.

Griffin Nellie Miss, r. 8 N. Mississippi.

Griffin Patrick, lab., r. 376 S. Delaware.

Griffin Patrick, lab., r. 39 Benton near Meek.

Griffin Patrick, porter, Bowen, Stewart & Co.

Griffin Sarah Mrs. r. 362 S. Delaware.

Griffin Timothy, lab., r. 133 W. Maryland.

Griffin Timothy, saloon, 48 S. Pennsylvania, r. 376 S. Delaware.

Griffins Dennis, lab., r. 252 S. Missouri.

Griffins John, lab., r. 29 Winston.

Griffith Allie Miss, music teacher, bds. 42 S. Mississippi.

Griffith Jerome, carpenter, r. 23 Short.

Griffith Edward, wks rolling mill, bds 256 S. Tennessee.

Griffith Edward Dr., r. 474 N. Pennsylvania.

Griffith C. J. (wid Josiah R.) r. 42 S. Mississippi.

Griffith George W., plasterer, r. 645 N. Tennessee.

Griffith Gordan, r. 42 S. Mississippi.

Griffith H., r. 78 N. Illinois.

Griffith J. F., bds. Bates House.

Griffith J. F. T., bookkeeper, 123 S. Meridian, bds. 125 E. Ohio.

Griffith John F., train dispatcher, C. C. & I. C. R. R., bds. 61 S. Noble.

Griffith James, engineer, I. C. & L. R. R., r. 47 Bates.

Griffith John, wks rolling mill, bds. 217 S. Illinois.

Grifhorn Henry, miller, John Carlisle, bds. Tully House.

Grigsby James, gardener, r. 114 Michigan road.

Grimes Elmore, cooper, r. 316 W. Merrill.

Grimm Casper, carriagepainter, bds. 174 E. St. Joseph.

Grimm Jacob jr., carriagemaker, bds. 174 E. St. Joseph.

Grimm Jacob cistern builder, r. 174 E. St. Joseph.

Grinsteiner George, undertaker, 276 E. Market.

Grissom James, shoemaker, r. W. Sixth bet. Mississippi and Tennessee.

Griswald Molinda, (wid James) r. 19 Douglass.

Grobe Charles, saloon, 12 W. Louisana, r. same.

Grogan G. W., saddler, r. 166 Indiana av.

Grooms A. C., bookkeeper Journal office, r. 412 N. New Jersey.

Grosman William, carpenter, r. 123 W. Fourth.

Gross Charles, baker, 264 E. Washington, r. same.

Grove Benjamin, with Wm. Sumner & Co., r. 329 E. New York.

Grove Samuel A., (Goodale & G.) r. 329 E. New York.

GROVER & BAKER SEWING MACHINE Co., 21 E. Washington, Wiley & VanBuren General agents for Indiana.

Groves Henry, machinist, r. 500 E. Washington.

Grubbs D. W., (Hammond & G.) r. 282 N. Illinois.

Grube Jacob, carpenter, r. 351 S. Illinois.

Gruener George, barkeeper, 33 S. Meridian, bds. same.

Gruener F., tinner, r. 141 W. Fourth.

GRUENERT JOHN, proprietor Jefferson House, 67 E. South, r. same.

GRUENERT HERMAN, proprietor Globe House, 164 S. Illinois, r. same.

Grunt George, blacksmith, Eagle Machine Works, r. 447 S. Meridian.

Gudelhofer John, wagonmaker, works Indianapolis Agricultural Works, r. 264 S. Alabama.

Guenther C., carriagemaker, bds. California House.

GUETIG HENRY, barber, shop ne. cor. Washington and Pennsylvania, r. 26 E. Market.

Guetig Mathias, gardner, r. S. East, city limits.

Guezet A., painter, r. 297 S. Delaware.

Guflin Henry C., (G. & Parker) r. Norwood.

Guflin Lewis, bds. 40 Christian av.

Guflin & Parker, Attorneys, 10 and 11 Talbott & New's blk.

Guigrich John, wood worker, Shaw, L. & C., r. 72½ S. Delaware.

Guion Jeremiah, stone sawyer, Smith, Ittenbach & Co., r. 148 S. Delaware.

Gulick John F. (G. & Kahn) r. 89 N. Delaware.

Gullian James, (col'd) wood sawyer, bds. 292 Massachusetts av.

Gulliver William, (Russell & G.) r. 79 Kentucky av.

Gundlefinger B., proprietor, Arcade, 6 W. Washington, r. 260 E. Ohio.

Gundlefinger M., clk. Arcade, bds. Bates House.

Gunkler Hermann, works, lumber yard, r. ne. cor. Elm and Cedar.

Gunlock August, blower, glass works, bds. 23 Kentucky av.

Gunlock Charles, blower, glass works, bds. 23 Kentucky av.

Gurst Nicholas, lab. bds. 200 S. Missouri.

Gurtey Joseph, carriage maker, r. Martinsville, Ind.

Gustarter Frederick, expressmen, r. 435 N. New Jersey.

Gustin Frank, lab. J. C. Ferguson & Co.

Gustin George M., telegraph operator, I., P. & C. R. R., bds. 275 N. New Jersey.

Gustin John, auctioneer, r. 27 E. North.

Gustin L. Dr., office, cor. Illinois and Louisina, r. 275 N. New Jersey.

Gustin Quinn, engineer, bds. 275 N. New Jersey.

Gustin Robert H., clk. G. Harlan, r. 344 N. Winston.

GUTENBERG PRINTING & PUBLISHING CO., se. cor. Meridian and Circle.

Guth Edward, machinist, works Eagle Machine Works, r. 364 S. Illinois.

Guthridge J. W., agent Baltimore & Ohio R. R., r. 81 W. Second.

Guthrie E. A., printer, Journal office, r. 124 N. Missouri.

Gutking Henry, railroader, r. Harrison.

Gutman Charles, r. E. Court, bet. New Jersey and East.

Gutrecht John, painter, r. 157 Fort Wayne av.

Gutterle Peter, clk. 71 and 73 W. Washington, r. 204 North Noble.

Gutwecht Rudolph, shoemaker, r. N. Mississippi, bet. First and Second.

BENHAM BRO'S,
36 E. Washington St,
AGENTS FOR THE
INDIANAPOLIS MANUFACTURING CO.'S
PIANOS.

Gutwiller Franz Joseph, lab., r. 251 Virginia av.

Guyer Anthony, jeweler, 43 S. Illinois, bds. Palmer House.

Gwinn Eliza J. (wid. Seth) r. 32 Henry.

Gwinn L. T., horse dealer, r. 83 N. Meridian.

Gwinn James, lab., r. 300 S. East.

Gwinn John, liveryman, r. 303 S. Pennsylvania.

Gwym Eri, brakesman, bds. 58 Benton.

Gymnasium Billiard Hall, Emanuel Hoefgen, proprietor, 48 S. Meridian.

HAAG CHARLES, lab., r. 274 Massachusetts av.

Haag Michael, clk., bds. 323 W. Washington.

Haagland A., lab., r. 373 W. Washington.

Haagland John B., messenger, American & M. U. Express Co., r. 389 N. West.

Habiney Henry, lab., r. 185 W. New York.

Hack John, gardner, Indiana Institution for Deaf and Dumb.

Hacker A. P., traveling agent, J. C. Green & Co., r. 425 E. Georgia.

Hacker James V., fireman, J. T. Pressels, r. 275 W. Merrill.

Hacker Wm., carpenter, r. 131 N. New Jersey.

Hackett Wm., lab., r. 64 S. Liberty.

Hackney Josephine Mrs., r. 162 S. Illinois.

Hackstein Christian, works rolling mill, r. 166 Union.

Haden John (col'd) lab., r. 47 Charles.

Haden William, (col'd) lab., r. 47 Charles.

Hadley Evan Dr., assistant Superintendent, City Hospital.

Hadley William, city assessor, r. 381 N. Delaware.

Haehl John, (H. & Auker) r. 178 E. Washington.

Haehl & Auker, State agents, Great Western Mutual Life Insurance Co., New York, 20 S. Delaware.

HAERLE WILLIAM, ladies' dress trimmings and laces, and furnishing goods, 4 W. Washington, r. 342 N. Illinois.

Haffield Uriah, woodhauler, r. 176 N. Davidson.

Haffield R. A., teamster, r. 164 S. East.

H. H. LEE

Makes a Specialty of

CHOICE GOLDEN RIO,

AND

OLD GOVERNMENT JAVA COFFEES.

Hafner August, boot and shoe manufacturer, 127 W. Washington, r. same.

Hafner John, butcher, works 153 W. Washington, bds. same.

Hagar E. C., bookkeeper, Fletcher's bank, bds Mrs. Reed.

Hagedorn William cigarmaker boards Union Hotel.

Hagerhorst C. F. (C. F. H. & Co.) r. 223 W. Ohio.

HAGERHORST C. F. & CO., (C. F. H. and Lew Nicoli,) grocers and produce dealers, 223 W. Ohio.

Hagg John R., agent Osgood & Smith, r. 287 S. East.

Haggerty James, currier, 125 S. Meridian, r. S. Delaware.

Haggerty Patrick, teamster, r. 251 S. Tennessee.

Haggerty Timothy, Maple, outside city limits.

Hahn Anthony, shoemaker, bds. 78 W. McCarty.

Hahn C. F. (C. F. H. & Co.) r. 79 N. Alabama.

Hahn Charles H. S. (H. & Bals) bds. Circle Restaurant.

Hahn Henry, musician, 69 S. East.

Hahn Jacob, meat market, 95 W. South, bds. 227 S. Tennessee.

Hahn John F., butcher, 92 N. Illinois, r. 115 N. Tennessee.

Hahn J. H., traveler, Milliner & Sherwood, bds Sherman House.

Hahn Louis, butcher, r. 227 S. Tennessee.

Hahn Theodore, musician, r. 71 S. East.

Hahn & Bals, (C. H. and C. Bals) whol. liquor dealers, 25 S. Meridian.

Hahnstein Sefrodis, Western Furniture Co., r. 21 Morrison.

Hainebach Herman, with Guttenberg Publishing Co., r. 19 Russell.

Hainebach S. Rev., r. cor. South and Alabama.

Haineger Michael, machinist, r. 295 S. East.

Haines Charles, salesman, r. 129 E. Walnut.

Haines Henry W. V. B., lab., bds. 291 W. Michigan.

Haines Mattie Miss, r. 252 W. Second.

Halbert Joseph, r. 139 Fort Wayne av.

Halbert J. D., lettercarrier, r. 445 N. New Jersey.

Hale A. C., r. 590 Virginia av.

Hale Henry, switchman C. C. & I. C. R. R., r. 281 E Georgia.

Hale Henry J., machinist, r. cor. College and Christian av.

Hale H. J., cabinetmaker, r. 196 W. Vermont.

HALE JUDSON, physician for diseases of the throat and lungs, office No. 1 Miller's blk., Illinois., nw. cor. Market, r. 163 N. Tennessee.

Haley Olliver, engineer, r. 180 Dougherty.

Haley James, carpenter, r. 268 Blake.

Haley Morris, lab., r. 233 Dougherty.

Haley W. D., special agent Empire Mutual Life Insurance Co., 75 E. Market, r. 218 E. Market.

Halford A. J., city editor News, bds. 363 N. New Jersey.

Halford E. W., editor Journal, r. 116 E. St. Mary.

Hall Adam, porter Institute for the Blind.

Hall Alford, ferreotypist, 16½ E. Washington, r. Chicago.

Hall Allen G., watchman, r. 278 Railroad.

Hall Andrew W., miller, r. 302 W. Washington.

HALL CHARLES E., bookkeeper Indianapolis National. Bank, r. 242 N. Pennsylvania.

HALL E. A., merchant tailor, 31 N. Pennsylvania, r. N. Illinois, outside city limits.

Hall E. K. (Lawyer & H.) r. Noblesville, Ind.

Hall Frank, gardner, r. 272 S. West.

Hall Franklin, lab., r. 283 Patterson.

Hall Franklin, farmer, r. 129 W. Fifth.

Hall Georgiana Mrs. (col'd) r. 129 Bright.

HALL H. L., assistant Superintendent I. C. & L. R. R., office Cincinnati Depot, bds. Bates House.

Hall Leonard, bds 193 S. Tennessee.

Hall Mrs., (wid) r. 255½ E. Washington.

Hall Nathan, (col'd) barber, 16 S. Meridian, bds. Pyle House.

Hall Reginald H. (Rand & H.) r. 210 N. Meridian.

Hall Robert, boss carpenter for Street R. R. Co., r. 63 W. Georgia.

Hall Thomas Q., salesman, Mitchell & Rammelsburg, r. 125 E. Walnut.

Hall William, machinist C. C. & I. C. R. R., r. 197 Bates.

Hall William, r. 423 E. St. Clair.

Hall William, (col'd) carpenter, r. 129 Bright.

Hall William H., lab., r. Wabash near New Jersey.

Halla William, stonecutter, r. 330 Madison av.

Hallahan Jerry, lab., r. 44 Elizabeth.

Hallam John, at American Saw Works.
bds. 89 S. Pennsylvania.

Halle Charles, works rolling mill, r. 452
S. East.

Hall Fred, stonemason, r. 400 S. East.

Haller George, plasterer, r. 277 James.

Haller Lon, clk., Trade Palace, bds. 25
S. Deleware.

Haller Mary Miss, r. 277 James.

Haller Philip H., stonemason, r. 349 N.
Noble.

Halmet John, porter post office, r. 347 N.
New Jersey.

Halpin M. H., printer, Journal office, r.
265 N. Liberty.

Haleker Benjamin, porter, Stewart &
Morgan, r. 505 S. Tennessee.

Halter Charles, shoemaker, r. 302 S. Illinois.

Halter Gustavus, butcher, r. 265 N. West.

Hamburg Henry, pastry cook, Spencer
House, r. 45 Union.

Hamil Charles, works, glass works, bds.
239 W. South.

Hamil Peter, carriage maker, r. 813 N.
Tennessee.

Hamill Machael, lab. Rolling Mill, r. 263
W. McCarty.

Hamilton Augustus, medical student, r.
20 Oriental.

Hamilton A. C., clk. A. G. Willard & Co.,
r. 305 E. New York.

Hamilton Charlotte, (wid.) boarding
house, 305 E. New York.

Hamilton David P., engineer, C. C. & I.
C. R. R., r. 377 E. Georgia.

Hamilton T. W., deputy County Auditor,
r. 191 S. New Jersey.

Hamilton James, moulder, r. 119 Maple.

Hamilton James B., fireman, Junction
R. R., r. 45 Mud.

Hamilton James F., clk. bds. Pattison
House.

Hamilton James W., carpenter, r. 321 S.
Missouri.

Hamilton Jennie Miss, dress maker, r.
186½ W. Washington.

Hamilton John, machinist, C. C. C. & I.
R. R. Shops.

Hamilton John F., lab. C. C. C. & I. R.
R., r. 45 Mud.

Hamilton Maggie Miss, teacher, Fourth
Ward School, bds. 74 S. Noble.

Hamilton M. D., letter carrier, r. 712 N.
Tennessee.

Hamilton Robert, wood chopper, r. 199
Harrison.

Hamilton Patrick, teamster, r. cor. Market and Blackford.

Hamilton Ruth A., housekeeper, Spencer
House.

Hamilton Samuel, machinist, C. C. C. &
I. R. R., r. 41 Grant, nr. Michigan
rt.

Hamilton Sarah Mrs., housekeeper, Sherman House.

Hamilton Sarah, (wid.) r. 45 Mud.

Hamilton S. A., moulder Eagle Machine
Works, bds. Ray House.

Hamilton Thomas D, salesman, bds. 166
E. Market.

Hamilton Thomas J., machinist Tate's
Factory, r. Oriental.

Hamilton Wm. S., machinist, r. 74 S
Noble.

Hamilton W. H. H., bookbinder, r. 248 N.
Illinois.

Hamlin Arthur, fireman I. C. & I. R. R.

Hamlin Carlin, (H. & Wright) bds. 23
S. Pennsylvania.

Hamlin Henry, (col'd) lab., r. 21 Marin.

Hamlin Richard, works Ozgood, Smith &
Co., r. 420 S. Illinois.

Hamlin W. A., train dispatcher, r. 274 S.
East.

Hamlin W. H., telegraph operator Indi-
anapolis & Vincennes R. R., cor.
Virginia av. and Delaware, r. 274 S.
East.

Hamlin & Wright, (Carlin, Hamlin and
Jacob T. Wright) military claim
agents, 62 E. Washington, up
stairs.

Hammel Bernard, clk., 34 South Meri-
din, r. 498 N. Mississippi.

Hammell George, cigarmaker, bds. 193
S. New Jersey.

Hammerle George, watchman, r. 461 S.
New Jersey.

Hammond Charles, glassblower, bds. 239
W. South.

Hammond S. W. (H. & Grubbs) r. 279 W.
Michigan.

Hammond Upton J. (H. & Judah) r. 569
N. Pennsylvania.

Hammond Wm. H., carpenter, bds. 142 S.
East.

HAMMOND & GRUBBS, (Sebra
W. Hammond and D. W. Grubbs)
general agents Continental Insurance Company of New York, room
No. 1 Citizens' Bank bldg.

Hammond & Judah, (W. J. H. and J. M.
J.) attorneys at law, 64 E. Washington.

Hamott Frederick, drayman, bds. 3
Charles.

Hampton Frank, clk. W. H. Hay. bds. ne.
cor. Blackford and Vermont.

THE CHINA TEA STORES

Have the NAME of being the

MOST ATTRACTIVE STORES IN THE WEST.

No. 7 Odd Fellows Hall

AND

ACADEMY OF MUSIC CORNER.

Hampton J. B., carriagemaker, r. 340 W. Vermont.

Hampton Stephen L., salesman, 36 S. Meridian, r. 88 E. Pratt.

Hampton Ezekiel B., carriagemaker, r. Vermont cor. Blackford.

Han Eliza, housekeeper, Bates House.

Hanaway Christian, wagonmaker, r. 2 Arch.

Hanaway Samuel, street contractor, r. 435 N. East.

Hand Adolphus C., bricklayer, r. Madison road, s. of city.

Hand William, brickmaker, r. Nebraska nr. Madison road.

Handrome L. P., cabinetmaker, bds. Madison av.

Handthorne Nancy, (wid.) tailoress, 188 E. Washington.

Handeyshell John L., teacher, Indiana Institution for Deaf and Dumb.

Hancaster William, carpenter, bds. 169 S. Tennessee.

Haneman John, (J. & T. H. H.) r. 135 Massachusetts av.

Haneman T. H., (J. & T. H. H.) r. 135 Massachusetts av.

Haneman J. & T. (John and Theodore H.) dealers in groceries and produce 135 Massachusetts av.

Haney John W., lab., r. 75 James.

Haney Mary Mrs., 354 S. Delaware.

Harf Valentine, expressman, r. 140 N. Davidson.

Hauger Andrew, lab., r. 77 S. East.

Hauger Henry, with C. Munn, r. 77 S. East.

Hank Nicholas, moulder, r. 404 S. Illinois.

Hann Albert, route carrier for Evening Mirror, bds. 156 W. Washington.

Hann Elizabeth, (wid.) tailoress, works 156 W. Washington, r. same.

HANN J. B., publisher popular subscription books, office, Journal bldg., r. 85 Ash.

Hann W. H., moulder, r. 257 Coburn.

Hanna David, cooper, r. 111 Forest av.

Hanna Geo. W., cooper, r. 111 Forest av.

Hanna John, (H. & Knefler) r. Greencastle, Ind.

Hanna John L., deputy Sheriff, r. 427 E. St. Clair.

Hanna M. E. Miss, teacher, Institute for blind.

Hanna O. J. R., M. D, Sec'ry and Treas. Indiana Surgical Institute, r. same.

Hanna S. C., (Crossland, H. & Co.) r. 388 N. Illinois.

HANNA & KNEFLER, (John Hanna and Fred Knefler) attorneys at law, Parker's blk. cor. Delaware and Court.

Hannah David, cooper, r. 111 Forest av.

Hannah J. Mrs., clk. Trade Palace, bds. 245 N. Illinois.

Hannaman H. G., druggist, (H. & Co.) r. 219 S. New Jersey.

Hannaman William, (H. & Co.) r. E. National Road.

Hannaman & Co. (Wm. & H. G. H.) druggist, 100 E. Washington.

Hannan Edward, lab., r. 183 High.

Hanneman Jacob, traveling agent, r. 321 Wabash bet. Liberty and Noble.

Hanner Emanuel, turner, r. 298 N. West.

Hanney Patrick, works rolling mill, bds. 78 W. McCarty.

HANNING JOHN G., plumbing, gas and steam fitting, 82 W. Washington, r. 135 E. St. Joseph.

Hanover Christ, blacksmith, r. Jackson.

Hanrahan Cathrine Mrs., (wid John) r. 225 S. Tennessee.

Hanrahan Frank, blacksmith, works Chandler & Taylor, r. 225 W. Merrill.

Hanrahan Kate Miss, bds. 225 S. Tennesse.

Hanrahan Mary, bds 225 S. Tennessee.

Hanrahan Michael, switchman T. H. & I. R. R., bds. 225 S. Tennessee.

Hanrahan Michael, works Novelty Works.

Hanrahan Patrick G., r. 263 S. Tennessee.

Hansacker Charles, conductor C. & I. J. R. R., bds. Spencer House.

Hansing Aaron, porter Ingram Fletcher.

Hanson Henry, works Gall & Bush, b. b. cor. Market and Illinois.

Hanson M., dealer in boots, shoes etc., 361 S. Delaware, r. same.

Hanson Mathias, shoemaker, r. 348 S. Delaware.

Hanson Peter, lab., bds. sw. cor. East and McCarty.

Hanyman M. V., baggage master J. M. & I. R. R.

Hapenny T. S., r. 32 W. St. Clair.

Harbin Thomas M. Dr., r. 124 W. Michigan.

Harbison Alexander, engineer Journal bldg., bds. 136 W. Vermont.

Harbison Robert, with American M. U. Express Co., r. 136 W. Vermont.

Harcourt Nancy, (wid.) boarding house, r. 287 East Georgia.

Harden Albert G., Jailor Marion county, r. 18 N. Alabama.

Harden R. E., carpenter, 237 E. Washington, r. same.

Harden Michael, lab., r. over 338 E. Washington.

Harden & Dorsey, (col'd, R. H. & W. D.) barbers, 180 W. Washington.

Hardesty E. J., train master J. M. & I. R. R., r. 335 S. Pennsylvania.

Hardin E. C., carpenter, r. 231 E. Market.

Hardin Maggie Mrs., (col'd, wid.) r. 251 N Liberty.

Hardin Richard, (col'd, H. & Dorsay) r. 39 Center.

HARDING GEORGE C., (H. & Vickers) editor Saturday Evening Mirror, r. 111 Broadway.

Harding J. O., printer, Mirror office, bds. Pyle House.

Harding Thomas W., carriage trimmer, r. 168 S. Illinois.

HARDING W. P., Book and Job Printer, se. cor. Meridian and Circle, r. 191 E. Market.

Hardwick John M, carpenter, r. 197 N. Illinois.

Hare M. L, stock dealer, r. 128 E. Maryland.

Harenberg Christ, carpenter, r. Gregg, bet. Jackson and East.

Harenberger William, shoemaker, bds. California House.

Hargon John, printer, Journal Office, bds. 213 N. Pennsylvania.

Hargus William F., carpenter, r. 299 Indiana av.

Harkness Angeline, (wid) r. 346 N. Meridian.

Harkness John, printer, r. 179 N. Pennsylvania.

HARLAN GEORGE W., grocer and produce dealer, cor. Massachusetts av. and New Jersey, r. 191 Massachusetts av.

Harlan L. D. Dr., office and residence, 178 Virginia av.

Harlan William A, machinist, works 244 S. Pennsylvania, bds. Ray House.

Harlin Susan, (wid. George W.) r. 136 N. Tennessee.

Harmon Charles, r. 432 W. Washington.

Harmonia Hermann, drayman, r. 76 Railroad.

Harmoning C., groceries and provisions, 283 S. Delaware, r. same.

Harmoning Christian, drayman, r. 508 E. Ohio.

Harmoning William, express driver, r. 141 Huron.

Harmoth August, cabinetmaker, r. 431 S. Meridian.

Harney Robert F., works, Schneider & Co., r. 127 S. Tennessee.

9

Harold Isaac, salesman Boston Store, bds. 68 E. Market.

Harper Edward, bds. 34 W. Louisiana.

Harper George, baggage master P. C. & St. Louis R. R.

Harper James, eating house, 34 W. Louisiana.

Harper James P., chief engineer C. & V. R. R., r. 434 N. Delaware.

Harper John F., clk. Trade Palace, bds. 209 N. Pennsylvania.

Harper John L., engineer, r. 359 N. Pennsylvania.

Harper R. D. Rev, r. 209 N. Pennsylvania.

Harper William, cooper, r. 462 S. Meridian.

Harper Henry, cooper, r. 462 S. Meridian.

Harrington Dennis, lab., works Greenleaf & Co., r. 224 Eddy.

Harrington John, lab., r. Tinker, bet. Canal and Lafayette R. R.

Harris Adam, carpenter, r. 474 N. Alabama.

Harris Addison C. (Dye & H.) r. 728 N. Meridian.

Harris Benj., (col'd) whitewasher, r. 231 Minerva.

Harris Charles E., constable, r. 140 E. North.

Harris David, lab., r. 42 Helen.

Harris Henry L. (col'd) barber, 19 S. Delaware, r. 23 S. New Jersey.

Harris John T, plasterer, bds. Bicking House.

Harris Lewis, hackdriver, r. Court, bet. New Jersey and East.

Harris Mary, (col'd) dressmaker, 252 Indiana av.

Harris Mary, M. D., Indiana Surgical Institute, r. same.

Harris Solomon, lab., r. 39 E. McCarty.

Harris William, (col'd) whitewasher, r. 252 Indiana av.

Harrison Alfred, (A. & J. C. S. Harrison) r. 252 N. Meridian.

Harrison Anna, (col'd) cook, Palmer House.

HARRISON A. & J. C. S., (Alfred and John C. S. Harrison) Bankers, 15 E. Washington.

Harrison Benjamin, (Porter, H. & Fishback) r. 299 W. Alabama.

THE CHINA TEA STORES

ARE LOCATED AT

No. 7 ODD FELLOWS HALL

AND

ACADEMY OF MUSIC CORNER.

SAME GOODS. SAME PRICES at BOTH.

Harrison F. P., engineer I. C. & L. R. R., bds. Ray House.

Harrison John C. S. (A. & J. C. S. Harrison) r. 262 N. Meridian.

Harrison Reuben E., attorney at law and notary public, 17½ W. Washington, room 3, r. 86 Broadway.

Harrison Sarah Jane, Mrs., r. 9 Morrison.

Harrison Thomas, works Novelty Works.

Harrison Thomas, lab., r. Missouri, nr. First.

HARRISON TEMPLE C., Attorney at Law and Notary Public, 17½ W. Washington, room 3, r. 23 Cherry.

Harrison T. W., bds. 23 Cherry.

Harrison U. C., agent Evening Commercial, r. Dunlop, bet. East and New Jersey.

Harrison William, works novelty Works.

Harrison Wm. H. (col'd) cook, Palmer House.

Harrison Chas. B., carpenter, bds. cor. Tennessee and Kentucky av.

Hart Abram, pedler, r. 320 Railroad.

Hart A. F., tinsmith, Tutewiler Bros., bds. Macy House.

Hart Ed. F., with Bowen, Stewart & Co., r. 52 S. West.

Hart Edward K., jr., Registry Clerk P. O., bds. 563 N. Mississippi.

Hart George blacksmith, r. 90 S. East.

Hart Michael, lab., r. 57 Dougherty.

Hart Robert M., broommaker, r. 272 Railroad.

Hart F. J., r. 799 N. Tennessee.

Hart Thomas, porter, Murphy, Johnson & Co., r. 54 S. Pennsylvania.

Hart Thomas (col'd) lab., r. 456 Indiana av.

Hart Thomas H., messenger, American & M. U. Express Co., r. 52 S. West.

Harter Mahala, (wid. Daniel) r. room 24 Fatout's blk.

Harter John A., r. se. cor. East and Market.

Harting & Bros. (F. and H. H.) brewers, 7 Norwood.

Harting Frederick, (H. & Bro.) r. 62 Russell.

Harting Henry, (H. & Bro.) r. 363 S. Illinois.

Hartline George, cabinetmaker, r. 381 E. Georgia.

HARTMAN CHARLES F., dairyman, three miles se. Brookville road.

Hartman Charles L., clk., r. 116 N. New Jersey.

Hartman Christian, lab., r. 275 E. Ohio.

Hartman Christian, lab., r. 150 Madison av.

Hartman Christian, jr., lab., r. 279 E. Ohio.

Hartman C. F., foreman, F. P. Rush.

Hartman Ellen (wid.) r. 119 N. New Jersey.

Hartman Fred., wagonmaker, r. 479 E. Georgia.

Hartman Herman, clk., 55 S. Meridian, bds. 119 N. New Jersey.

Hartman Henry, packer, Keifer & Vinton, r. 263 Vermont.

Hartman M., plasterer, r. 262 N. Alabama.

Hartman Phillipina,(wid.) r. 80 Railroad.

Hartnett P. E., saloon, 101 S. Illinois, r. same.

Hartpence Walter r. 17 S. Mississippi.

Hartstein Marks, clk, 25 S. Illinois, bds. 18 S. Mississippi.

Harttrodt Herman, saloon, 249 Kentucky av., r. same.

Hartwell E., bds. National Hotel.

Hartwell William, (col'd) fireman Bates House.

Hartwieg Adam, printer, bds. 65 S. East.

Harvey Alonzo D., route agent I. C. & R. R., r. 315 E. Ohio.

HARVEY JOHN S., attorney at law, 101 E. Washington, r. 236 E. Market.

Harvey Michael, lab., works Root's foundry, r. 76 Maple.

Harvey Silas L., deputy county clk. bds. 236 E. Market.

Harvey T. B. Dr., 58 E. Market, r. 302 N. Delaware.

Harwood Irvin W., cabinetmaker, r. 67 Madison av.

Haselden Charles, shoemaker, r. over 325 E. Washington.

Haskell Sallie Mrs., (wid) dressmaker, r. 109 Massachusetts av.

Haskit Cartney, lab., bds 68 W. South.

Haskit W. I., (H., Morris & Co.) r. 647 N. Meridian.

HASKIT, MORRIS & CO., (W. I. H., Cha's M. & —) wholesale and retail druggist, 14 W. Washington.

Haslep Maria Miss, teacher, r. 255 Virginia av.

Haslup I. D., machinist, r. 255 Virginia av.

Hasselberg Christian, lab., r. S. Tennessee.

Hasselman Lewis W., President Indianapolis Agricultural, Mechanical and Horticultural Association, r. cor. Meridian and Vermont.

Hasselman Otto H. (J. & H.) r. cor. Meridian and Vermont.

Hassingler Leonard, machinist, r, 578 E. Washington.

Hassmann Henry, lab. r. 55 Morris.

Hassold Ernst, varnisher, r. 97 Bates.

Hasson Charles, works plaining mill, r. 423 N. N. Jersey.

Hasson Edward, salesman, Isaac Davis & Co. bds. 423 N. New Jersey.

Hasson James, Secretary Builders and Manufacturers Association, r. 423 N. New Jersey.

Hasson William, r. 444 N. Meridian.

Hastings E. L., superintendent Journal Othce, r. 550 N. Illinois.

Hasty John A., repairer, Western Union Telegraph, r. 89 S. Liberty.

Hatfield Frederick, lab., r. Eighth, nr. Canal.

Hatfield James, clk. T. Broker, r. 774 N. Tennessee.

Hatfield John J. B, foreman, U. S. Arsenal.

HATHAWAY H., boarding house and saloon, W. Indianapolis.

Hathaway Perry C., clk. Neiman House, 130 S. Illinois.

Hathaway S. P., traveling agent, r. 776 N. Illinois.

Hattendorf Henry, cutter, J. & P. Granling, r. 314 E. Georgia.

Hatton J. S., works Aldrich & Gay, r. 213 N. Mississippi.

Hauck John, (H. & Co.) r. 373 N. East.

Hauck Philip, helper, C. C. C. & I. R. R. Shops.

Hauck John & Co. (John Hauck and John Darby) farmers grocery, 11 W. Washington.

Haufter John, works Jackson, Rider & Co.

Haufter John, lab. r. 452 Indiana av.

Haug John, (Dietz, F. & Co.) r. 255 E. Washington.

Haug Michael, saloon, 138 S. Pennsylvania, r. same.

Haugh Alex. W., finisher, 74 S. Pennsylvania, r. 244 E. Vermont.

Haugh B. F. (B. F. H. & Co.) r. 504 N. Pennsylvania.

Haugh Emanuel, traveling agent, B. F. Haugh & Co, r. 244 E. Vermont.

Haugh J. R., cashier Citizens' National Bank, r. 175 N. New Jersey.

Haugh William A., finisher, B. F. Haugh & Co., r. 186 N. Davidson.

HAUGH B. F. & CO. (B. F. and Joseph R. Haugh) manufacturers of wrought and cast iron railing, jails, etc., 74 S. Pennsylvania.

HAUGHEY T. P., pres't Indianapolis National Bank, r. 242 N. Pennsylvania.

BENHAM BRO'S,

36 East Washington St.,

SHEET MUSIC, VIOLINS,

GUITARS, STRINGS, &c.

Hauiesen Robert, salesman 29 W. Washington, bds. 113 E. Washington.

Hauiesen William, (C. Mayer & Co.) r. 32 N. Mississippi.

Hauk John, foreman Meikel's brewery, r. same.

Hauk Thomas A., carpenter, r. 170 N. Winston.

Hauley John, dealer in groceries, etc., 340 Virginia av., bds. 352 Virginia av.

Haupt Robert, notions, etc., 151 E. Washington, r. 17 Chatham.

Hauschild C, bookbinder, r. 60 Hosbrook.

Hauschild Max, printer Daily Telegraph, r. 60 Hosbrook.

Hauser James, boxmaker, bds. Illinois House.

Havens Annie, (wid. Churchill) r. 191½ W. Washington.

Havens Thomas, mail ag't C. & I. J. R. R., bds. 18 S. Pennsylvania.

Hawey A. C., lab. P. C. & St. L. freight depot.

Hawk William V. (Dury & H.) r. cor. College av. and Butler.

Hawkey Nathan B., brickmason, r. 138 N. Winston.

Hawkins A. A., clk. Sherman House, bds. same.

Hawkins Eliza Miss, boarding house, r. 171 Jackson.

Hawkins Ira, (col'd) lab., r. 116 Ash.

Hawkins James, engineer Sentinel office, bds. 192 Virginia av.

Hawkins John S., carpenter, r. 186 Meek.

Hawkins Mary, (col'd, wid. Pryor) r. 116 Ash.

HAWKINS WM. M., prop'r Sherman House, Louisiana, bet. Meridian and Illinois, opp. Union Depot.

Hawley Miss S. D., matron Indianapolis Young Ladies' Institute.

Hawley Miss S. W., teacher of mu. ic Institute for the Blind.

Hawthorn Charles E., bds. 113 S. New Jersey.

Hay Campbell, formerly Hay & Co., r. 326 N. Illinois.

Hay John C., with Wm. Sumner & Co., bds. 152 N. Meridian.

Hay Lawrence G., receiver of Sinking Fund, office in State bldg., r. 128 S. Meridian.

H. H. LEE'S

WHOLESALE PRICES FOR

TEAS, COFFEES & SUGARS,

ARE THE SAME EACH DAY

As are quoted in the

CINCINNATI DAILY PAPERS.

Hay William H., gen'l agt. Charter Oak Life Insurance Co., room 6 Blackford's blk., r. 222 N. Tennessee.

Hayden L. Rev., superintendent Indianapolis Young Ladies' Institute.

Hayden M. I P. Mrs., principal Indianapolis Young Ladies' Institute.

Hayden W. H, bds. 18 N. Pennsylvania.

Hayes B. S., portrait painter, 24 Talbott & New's blk. N. Pennsylvania, r. 41 Madison av.

Hayes E. M., clothing dealer, r. 223 E. Ohio.

Hayes Thomas, with T. F. Ryan, r. 83 W. St. Clair.

Hayes Walter, carpenter, r. 94 N. California.

Hayle Jerry, lab., r. 68 Coburn.

Haynes Charles, salesman Landers, Conduitt & Co., r. 129 E. Walnut.

Haynes Edward, sheet iron worker, 24 E. Georgia, r. 39 Elm.

Haynes Henry M., works Cement Pipe Co., r. se. cor. Michigan and California.

Haynes James, with McCord & Wheatly, r. 39 Elm.

Haynes J. R. physician, r. 81 Massachusetts av.,

Haynes Lewis, traveler for Fairbanks' Scales, 43 and 45 N. Tennessee.

Haynes Martha, (wid. James) r. 39 Elm.

HAYNES PHILIP, wholesale and retail confectioner, 40 W. Washington, r. 169 N. Illinois.

Haynes W. H., printer, Braden & Burford, bds. cor. Mississippi and Maryland.

Hays Barton S., artist, r. 41 Madison av.

Hays Emanuel M., (H., Rosenthal & Co.) r. 233 E. Ohio.

Hays Frank H., with Snyder & Hays, bds 340 N. Alabama.

Hays Isaac C., (Snyder & H.) r. 340 N. Alabama.

Hays John, engineer, C. C. & I. C. R. R., bds 61 S. Noble.

Hays Lizzie E Miss, bds. 41 Madison av.

Hays Maggie Miss, servant Spencer House.

Hays Mattie Mrs., bds 41 Madison av.

Hays Sarah, (wid) r. 177 E. Maryland.

HAYS, ROSENTHAL & CO., (E. M. Hays, H. Rosenthal and M. Rosenthal) wholesale clothiers, 64 S. Meridian.

Haywood Alfred, (H. & Rooner) r. 261 E. Market.

Haywood & Rooner, (Alfred H. and H. C. R.) American leg and arm Co., 172 E. Washington.

Hayworth Ira, roofing, r. 166 N. Delaware.

Hazelton W. H., attorney, 4 Ætna bldg., r. 348 N. Alabama.

Hazzard Samuel P., Western freight agent, B. & O. R. R., r. 166 N. West.

Heaf August, scourer and dyer, 65 N. Illinois, r. same.

Healey Dennis, works rolling mill, r. 85 Ann.

Healey John, lab, r 247 Missouri.

Healey Patrick, grocer, 225 S. Tennessee, r. same.

Hearn Thomas Dr., r. 165 N. Mississippi.

Heath A. G., salesman, Carr & Alvey, bds. 518 N. Tennessee.

Heath C. A., traveling agent, J. C. Green & Co., r. 71 N. East.

Heath Caroline Miss, r. 35 Chatham.

Heath John, farmer, r. 35 Chatham.

Heath Sylvester, student, r. 35 Chatham.

Heatline George, cabinetmaker, r. 381 E. Georgia.

HEBBLE J. W. & SON, prop'rs

Bicking House, 89 S. illinois.

Heber ——, clk. Boston store, r. 408 N. New Jersey.

Heck Israel, lab. r. cor. Massachusetts av. and St. Clair.

Heckert William, works glass works, r. 131 Chestnut.

Heckman Christopher, (H. & Sheesley) r. 413 E. Washington.

HECKMAN & SHEESLEY,

(Christoph H. and Eli S.) prop'rs City Mills, 354 E. Washington.

Hedge A., baggage master, I. B. & W. R. R.

Hedderich Peter, cabinetmaker, r. 231 N. Noble.

Hedgepeth Jane, (col'd wid. John) r. Indiana av.

Hedges Elijah, (Weaver & Hedges), r. 39 N. Illinois.

Hedges Francis M., lab., r. 474 S. Tennessee.

Hedges I. L., bookkeeper Thos. Madden, r. S. city limits.

Hedges James H., city sexton, r. 140 N. Tennessee.

Hedges Vinton, tinner Munson & Johnsons, r. 132 N. Tennessee.

Hegelorn Henry, lab, r. 5 Buchanan.

Hegeharth Christina Mrs., r. 221 S. Alabama.

Heid Fred., butcher, 342 E. Market, r. 2 miles E. on National road.

Heid John T., butcher, r. 2 miles E. on National road,

Heid Louis, meat market, nw. cor. Michigan and Noble, r. same.

Heid Ludwig, butcher, r. 2 miles east on National road.

Heider Paulina, (wid.) r. over 200 E. Washington.

Heidlinger John A., r. 14 N. Mississippi.

Heidnurich Christ, tailor, r. 128 Huron

Heier Frank, railroader, r. 60 Railroad.

Heiler Henry, blacksmith, bds. Globe House.

Heim Jacob F., butcher, r. 553 E. Washington.

Heim John R., butcher, r. 553 E. Washington.

Heimbuch George, Cabinetmakers' Union, r. 287 N. Noble.

Hein Charles, mechanic, r. 160 N. Liberty.

Heine Henry, shoemaker, r. 304 Virginia av.

Heiner Andrew, watchman C. C. & I. C. R. R., 60 S. Noble.

Heiner Ann. (wid.) r. 157 Buchanan.

Heiner Frederick, night watchman Bellefontaine R. R. Shops.

Heiner Henry, r. 304 Virginia av.

Heiner John, carriagesmith, Shaw L. & C., bds. 98 S. Pennsylvania.

Heiner John, works C. Glazier, r. 157 Buchanan.

Heinrich Charles, clk. 55 and 57 S. Meridian.

Heinrich Christian, butcher, 170 S. Illinois, r. same.

Heir Charles, works Rolling Mill, r. 317 S. Pennsylvania.

Heiser Casper, lab. U. S. Arsenal.

Heiser Charles, saloonkeeper, 76 S. Delaware, r. 73 Spring.

Heiser Wm., painter Eagle Machine Works, r. 478 E. Georgia.

Heiskel W. L., dentist, 76 E. Market, r. 80 E. Market.

Heisler Chris, wiper I. C. & L. R. R. shops.

Heisler Jacob, works I. C. & L. R. R. shops, r. 122 S. Noble.

Heisser J. H., clk. 34 S. Meridian, r. 503 N. Mississippi.

Heit Henry, cooper, r. 116 South Noble.

Heit Louis L., butcher, 41 S. Noble, r. 322 Hermann.

Heitchew T. G., bookkeeper, 146 S. Pennsylvania, r. 251 S. Alabama.

Heite George, cooper, r. 498 E. Georgia.

HEITKAM GEO. H., merchant tailor, 8 W. Washington, r. 154 N. Winston.

Heitkam Henry, barber, r. 30 S. Delaware.

Heitkam John, Cabinetmakers Union, r. 112 North Winston.

Heitz George, gardener, r. 131 N. East.

Heitz Louis, works Sinker & Co., r. 62 Hosbrook.

HEIZER C. C., Township Trustee, 14 N. Delaware, 3d floor, r. 78 Lockerbie.

Heizer Henry, plasterer, r. 356 N. Noble.

Heizer John, r. 350 Railroad.

Heizer Wm. L., painter Eagle Machine Works.

Heizer ——, (wid.) r. 477 N. New Jersey.

Heizman Mathias, sawfiler 63 S. Pennsylvania, bds. California House.

Helcher Charles, lab. r. 76 Coburn.

Held Louis, machinist, Eagle Machine Works, r. 467 S. Meridian.

Helker Henry, florist, 124 E. St. Joseph, r. same.

Helle Louis, house and sign painter, 248 S. Pennsylvania, r. same.

Heller Jacob, lab. r. 40 Douglass.

HELLER JAMES E., attorney at law, 20½ N. Delaware, r. 221 N. New Jersey.

Helm Adam, carpenter, r. 296 Liberty.

Helm Charles C., painter, r. in Blackford blk.

Helm Henry, stonemason, r. 651 E. Washington.

HELM JOHN, groceries and saloon, 272 Winston, r. same.

Helmish George, baker, works 178 S. Illinois, bds. same.

Helmich John, porter, P. O., r. 317 N. New Jersey.

Helms Thomas M., chairmaker, r. 107 N. Noble.

Helwig Charles, carpenter, Eagle Machine Works.

Helwig Charles, dealer in furniture, 115 and 117 E. Washington, r. 224 W. New York.

Helwig John, cabinetmaker, bds. California House.

Hely Mary, (wid. Joseph) r. 172 Eddy.

Henderson James, fireman I. C. & L. R. R., bds. Ray House.

Henderson James, clk. Bee Hive Store, r. 77 Kentucky av.

Henderson John W. (B. & Henderson) r. 168 N. East.

HENDERSON WM., prest. Indianapolis Insurance Co. and attorney at law, r. 134 N. Meridian.

Henderson William, lab., Osgood, Smith & Co., r. 404 S. Missouri.

H. H. LEE

PURCHASES HIS

Teas, Coffees, Sugars & Spices

DIRECT FROM THE

Importers and Refineries,

THUS SAVING

HIS CUSTOMERS TWO OR THREE PROFITS.

Henderson W. H., tinner, r. 329 Virginia av.

Hendricks A. W. (H., Hord & Hendricks) r. 296 N. Meridian.

Hendricks James T., carpenter, r. 196 Blake.

Hendricks John, (Cady & H.) r. 19 W. Pratt.

Hendricks John E., cigarmaker, r. 33 W. McCarty.

Hendricks Thomas A., (H., Hord & H.) r. South of city on Madison rd.

Hendricks V. K. (H., Edmunds & Co.) r. 455 N. Meridian.

HENDRICKS, EDMUNDS & CO. (V. K. H. and Wm. Edmunds) whol. dealers in boots and shoes, 79 S. Meridian.

HENDRICKS, HORD & HENDRICKS, (T. A. H., O. B. H. and A. W. H.) attorneys at law, 24½ E. Washington.

Hennesey Ambrose, cooper, bds. 271 S. Alabama.

Hennesey David, lab., r. 271 S. Alabama.

Hennesey John, switchman, T. H. & I. R. R., bds. 217 S. Illinois.

Hennesey Patrick, lab., r. 260 Union.

Henning Fred. A., barber, r. 337 E. Market.

Henning Gottlieb A., tailor, r. 307 Wabash.

Henning G. F., porter, 28 Kentucky av., r. 307 Wabash.

Henning Henry, carpenter, r. 357 E. Market.

Henning Joseph, lab., rolling mill, bds. 239 W. South.

Henninger G. & E., dealers in toys and fancy goods, 115 S. Illinois, r. same.

Henry Charles W., bookkeeper, Josselyn Bro. & Co., bds. Bates House.

Henry John, teamster, bds. 286 S. East.

Henry Joseph, lab., r. 128 E. St. Joseph.

Henry Lawrence, lab., r. 286 S. East.

Henry Mary A. Miss, bds. 139 W. Market.

Henry Michael, teamster, bds. 586 S. East.

Henry Peter lab., r. 282 S. East.

Henschen Joseph, r. 75 Harrison.

Henschen Wm. H., carpenter, r. 252 E. South.

Henshaw Jerry, (col'd) lab., r. 75 S. Missouri.

Hensley John, carpenter, r. 333 N. Illinois.

Hensley William, clk., 110 S. Meridian, bds. 333 N. Illinois.

Henson Sarah, (wid) r. 8 N. Liberty.

Henthorn W. O., night clk., National Hotel, r. same.

Hepp John K., carpenter, r. 325 E. Michigan.

Herburg Charles, inspector I. C. & L. R. R. depot.

Herd John, currier, r. 122 E. Michigan Road.

Herden Michael lab., r. over 238 E. Washington.

Hereth Ad., saddles and harness, 24 N. Delaware, bds. 268 N. Delaware.

Hereth J. C., (Hereth J. C. & Co.) r. 268 N. Alabama.

Hereth John G., carpenter, r. 263 N. East.

Hereth Lewis, lab., 155 Spring.

Hereth Peter P., joiner, works cor. Tennessee and Georgia, r. 64 Bates.

Hereth Phillip, saddler, r. 127 N. Liberty.

Hergd Fred, butcher, 234 E. Washington, r. 405 E. Washington.

Herington Ellen, servant Sherman house.

Herington Ellen Mrs., r. 228 W. Georgia.

Herington Mary, domestic Bates house.

Herit William F., tinner, r. 174 E. Washington.

Hermsey John, lab., r. 82 Bradshaw.

Herne Elizabeth Mrs., (wid John) r. 32 Ann.

Herne Joshua, lab., r. 32 Ann.

Herue Mollie Miss, seamstress, bds. 32 Ann.

Horner Ermill, sawyer, r. 398 N. West.

Herr John, carpenter, r. 462 E. Georgia.

Herring Philip, pianotuner C. Soehner, r. 279 N. East.

Herrmann Catherine, (wid.) r. Arsenal road.

Herrmann Charles, machinist, r. 66 Railroad.

Herrmann Echitz, lab., r. 328 S. Delaware.

Herrmann F. J., undertaker 26 S. Delaware, r. 272 E. Market.

Herrmann Gabriel, undertaker, 26 S. Delaware, r. same.

Herrmann George, cabinetmaker, r. 220 N. Winston.

Herrmann Gustave, cabinetmaker, r. cor. Ohio and Harvey.

Herrmann Jacob, carpenter, r. 277 N. Winston.

Herrmann John, pres't Cabinetmakers' Union, r. 472 E. Market.

Herron F. M. (McLene & H.) r. 416 N. Illinois.

Hersey George, bootmaker, bds. 18 S. Pennsylvania.

Hershey John W., varnisher, r. 55 Maple.
Hert William, engineer C. C. C. & I. R. R.
    r. 383 E. Michigan.
Hertwig Henry, drayman, r. 128 N. Da-
    vidson.
Hesey Allen, carpenter, bds. California
    House.
Hespelt Charles, (C. H. & Co.) r. 219 N.
    Mississippi.
Hespelt Charles & Co., (Charles Hespelt
    and Wm. Geitzendcen) prop'rs Na-
    tional bakery, 150 W. Vermont.
Hess Caspar, lab., r. Madison road.
Hess George, varnisher, r. 376 Virginia
    av.
Hess Gottfried, lab., r. 198 N. Missis-
    sippi, up stairs.
Hess Gustave, baker, r. 406 S. East.
Hess Hannass, carpenter, r. S. Delaware,
    nr. corporation line.
Hess J. N., confectioner, r. 267 N. Noble.
Hess J. W. (Gordon & H.) r. 385 N. Illi-
    nois.
Hess Sebastian, wood sawyer, r. 505 N.
    Illinois.
Hessling Bernhardt, tailor, r. 225 N.
    Winston.
Hester W. W., M. D., first assist. supt.
    Indiana Hospital for Insane. r. same.
Henton Thomas, (col'd) lab., r. 179 Eddy.
Hethrington B. F. (B. T. H. & Co.) r. 45
    Madison av.
Hetherington Charles, works I. C. & L.
    R. R. Shops, r. 101 Bates.
Hetherington Christopher, machinist, r.
    101 Bates.
Hetherington John S., bookkeeper, r. 101
    Bates.
Hetherington Mary Miss, teacher, r. 101
    Bates.
Hetherington B. F. & Co. (B. F. H., F.
    Berner and J. Kindel) foundry and
    machine works, 214 S. Pennsyl-
    vania.
Hetselgesser L. W. (H. & Son.) r. 595 E.
    Washington.
Hetselgesser Samuel, (H. & Son) r. 595
    E. Washington.
Hetselgesser & Son, livery and sale sta-
    bles, cor South and Illinois.
Heustas Edward L., engineer T. H. & I.
    R. R., r. 223 W. South.
Heusten Joseph, works Novelty Works.
Hewitt Robert, bookkeeper Mitchell &
    Rammelsburg, bds. 25 Fort Wayne
    av.
Hiatt Francis, (wid. Samuel) r. cor.
    Smith and Maria.
Hiatt Naomi S., teacher Indiana Institu-
    tion for Deaf and Dumb.
Hibbard Horace W., general freight agent
    T. H. & I. R. R., bds. Bates House.
Hibbard L. D., baggageman T. H. & I.
    R. R.

Hibben E. C., attorney at law, r. 176 N.
    East.
Hibben James S. (Hibben, Tarkington &
    Co.) r. 435 N. Tennessee.
Hibben W. W., correspondent State Sent-
    inel. r. 195 N. East.
HIBBEN, TARKINGTON &
    CO., (J. S. Hibben, W. C. Tarking-
    ton, C. B. Pattison, W. S. Webb and
    A. E. Pattison) jobbers of dry goods
    and notions, 112 S. Meridian.
Hice Samuel, railroader, r. 395 S. West.
Hickey John, lab., r. 23 Willard.
Hickey Joseph, stonecutter, r. 30 Grant.
Hickey Mary, (wid) r. over 338 E. Wash-
    ington.
Hickman John, clk, 173 W. Washing-
    ton.
Hicks ——, lab., r. 164 W. Michigan up
    stairs.
Hick Dan C., carpenter, r. 119 Broadway.
Hicks Joseph M. patentwright dealer, r.
    175 Eddy.
Hicks Walter G., fruit tree trimmer, r. 315
    Wabash.
Hied George, cooper, r. 498 E. Georgia.
Hied Henry, cooper, r. 114 S. Noble.
Higdon William C., lab., r. 181 S. Ten-
    nessee.
Higgins Charles, engineer C. C. C. & I.
    R. R.
Higgins Mary, domestic Institute for the
    Blind.
Higgins Monroe, (col'd) lab., r. 289 E.
    New York.
Higgins William B., silverplater, 75 E.
    Washington, r. 78 Plum.
Higgins W. H., upholstering, r. 426 N.
    Meridian.
High School, cor. Meridian and Circle.
Highland Connelly, cabinetmaker, r. 105
    Buchanan.
Highland Michael, contractor, r. 673 N.
    Illinois.
Hilcher Christian, tailor, r. 42 S. Noble.
Hildebrand Amelia Mrs., r. 373 E. New
    York.
Hilderbrand C. L., watchmaker, C. G.
    French, r. 51 Madison av.
Hildebrand H. W. (H. & Kepple) r. 308
    N. Delaware.
Hildebrand J. F., bds. 321 N. Pennsylva-
    nia.
Hildebrand J. S. (J. H. Vagen & Co.) r.
    51 Madison av.

THE CHINA TEA STORES

Are very handsomely decorated with

Accurate Views and Scenes

or

CHINESE LIFE AND SCENERY.

Call and see them before leaving the City.

Hildebrand Philip N., conductor T. H. & I. R. R., bds. 51 Madison av.

HILDEBRAND & KEPPLE. (H. W. H. and John K.) Saw Mill office and Lumber Yard, cor. Indiana av. and Canal.

Hilgimeir Christinia, grocer, se. cor. Delaware and McCarty, r. 43 Wyoming.

Hilkenbach William, porter Wiles Bros. & Co., r. 494 N. Mississippi.

Hill Albert, (col'd) lab., r. 37 Vine.

Hill Augustus, lab., r. 287 Davidson.

Hill Augustus, (col'd) lab., r. 37 Vine.

Hill Benjamin F., stock dealer, r. 50 Cherry.

HILL E. C., dealer in Boots and Shoes, 3 W. Washington, r. 577 N. Tennessee.

Hill Ettie, (wid. Jerome) bds. 188 W. Georgia.

HILL GEO. W., manufacturer of doors, blinds, sash, mouldings, and dealer in all kinds of lumber, cor. East and Georgia, r. 110 S. East.

Hill James, groceries and provisions, 314 W. New York.

Hill James, farmer, r. 252 N. Noble.

Hill James, (col'd) barber, r. 190 N. Missouri.

Hill James B., Beach Wood Nursery, r. same.

Hill James D. (col'd) barber, H. & Carter.

Hill John B., artist, studio 84 N. Alabama, r. same.

Hill Joshua, (col'd) carpenter, r. 132 Bright.

Hill J. F., proprietor of Beach Wood Nursery, r. 84 N. Alabama.

Hill J. F. (col'd, H. & Carter) r. 756 N. Tennessee.

Hill Nathan, lab., r. 47 Geisendorff.

Hill R. M., Captain and Brevet Major, U. S. Arsenal, r. same.

Hill S. H., printer, Journal Office, r. 193 W. Vermont.

Hill William A., lab., r. 112 Jackson.

Hill & Carter, (col'd, J. F. H and E. C.) barbers and hair dressers, 14 N. Illinois.

Hillard Lucy Mrs. (col'd) r. 75 W. Georgia.

Hillix Kate Mrs., bds. 300 W. Maryland.

Hillman Charles, carpenter, r. 32 Water.

Hillman Fred., lab., r. 36 Water.

Hillman John, drayman Wiles, Bro. & Co., r. 238 Union.

Hillman Mary, cook, se. cor. New York and New Jersey.

Hillman Michael, carpenter, 27 S. New Jersey.

Hillman William, porter 74 S. Meridian, r. 425 S. Meridian.

Hillman William, blacksmith, nr. cor. Virginia av. and East, r. 38 Water.

Hilth August, machinist, r. 287 Davidson.

Hilt Charles W., clk. bds. cor. Madison av. and S. Meridian.

Hilt Frank L., with B. F. Haugh & Co., r. 159 Spring.

Hiltebrand Jacob M. (Rankin & H.) r. 317 Indiana av.

Hilton Henry, spinner Geisendorff & Co., r. 5 Geisendorff.

Hime William H., moulder, r. 257 Coburn.

Himes J. L., (Klingensmith & Co.) r. 160 N. Meridian.

Hindman Robert D., news stand, Palmer House.

Hindman Wm., bell boy, Palmer House.

Hinds Charles, teamster, bds. 297 N. Winston.

Hinds Frank M., with P. G. C. Hunt, r. 83 E. St. Clair.

Hines Andrew, lab., r. 321 N. Davidson.

Hines Cyrus C., Judge, Civil Circuit Court, r. 428 N. Tennessee.

Hines Henry, (col'd) lab., r. cor. Michigan and Minerva.

Hines Jesse, brickmason, r. 452 N. Delaware.

Hines R. M., clk., 405 N. Alabama, r. 452 N. Delaware.

Hinsley Andrew J. (Budd & H.) r. 491 N. Tennessee.

Hinesley John T., carpenter, r. 230 E. Merrill.

HINESLEY WILLIAM, proprietor Exchange Stables, 35 N. Illinois, r. 469 N. Tennessee.

Hinkel Henry, blacksmith, r. 511 N. Mississippi.

Hinkle Christian, spinner, Merritt & Coughlen.

Hinkley O. W., clk., Fletcher & Sharpe, bds. Depot Dining Hall.

Hinsdale D. C., chief operator, W. U. Telegraph, bds. Pyle House.

Hinton James S. (col'd) barber, r. 229 N. West.

Hippard Geo. F., salesman, Bowen, Stewart & Co., r. 31 W. North.

Hirneger Michael, machinist, r. 295 S. East.

Hirsch Herman, tailor, r. 317 S. Pennsylvania.

Hirt Albert, lab., r. 383 S. Illinois.

Hitchcock Alex., r. 186 E. St. Joseph.

HITCHENS JOHN, horseshoer, 44 E. Maryland, r. 126 N. Broadway.

Hite Charles W., machinist, r. 193 W. South.

Hite Wm. (col'd) teamster, r. Blake nr. Indiana av.

Hoaf Henry, moulder Eagle Machine Works.

Hoagland Thos, engineer Insane Hospital.

Hoagland John A., carpenter, r. 723 N. Illinois.

Hobbs Barnabas C., Superintendent Public Instruction, r. 187 E. Ohio.

Hobbs Solomon, lab., r. 384 N. West.

Hobbs Walter, clk., bds. 126 E. Ohio.

Hobbs Wm. H., Assistant Superintendent Public Instruction, r. 187 E. Ohio.

Hoch Joseph, carpenter, Eagle Machine Works, r. 212 Madison av.

Hockersmith Judiah, lab., r. 493 E. Georgia.

Hockersmith Thomas, freight conductor I. C. & L. R. R., r. 156 S. Noble.

Hockstetter Christian, pastor German Lutheran Chuch, r. 251 E. Ohio.

Hodaff William, pianomaker, r. 182 E. Washington.

Hodapp William, pianomaker, r. 185 E. Washington.

Hodgson Isaac, architect Brown's blk, r. 433 N. Illinois.

Hodler Gottlieb, clk. Keifer & Vinton, r. 133 E. McCarty.

Hodson Edward, paperhanger, bds. 283 N. Alabama.

Hodson Thomas, paperhanger, r. 283 N. Alabama.

Hoefgen Emanuel, proprietor billiard hall, r. 64 Indiana av.

Hoefgen Samuel, lawyer, r. over 46 S. Meridian.

Hoefler Gustave A., varnisher, r. 42 Elm.

Hoefler George A., varnisher, bds. California House.

Hofacker Charles, bakery, 277 N. Noble, r. same.

Hofacker Gottlieb, boot and shoemaker, 16 S. Delaware, r. same.

Hofacker John, baker, works 257 Massachusetts av., bds. same.

Hofet George, shoemaker, r. 400 S. Missouri.

Hoff John C., (Todd & Hoff) r. 119 S. New Jersey.

Hoff Louis, works rolling mill, r. 270 Chesnut.

Hofferbergh Kate Miss, works Indianapolis cotton mill, bds. 175 Minerva.

Hoffington M. A., teamster, r. 31 Dougherty.

Hoffman Casper, blacksmith, r. 534 N. Alabama.

Hoffman Eph, wagonmaker, r. 383 S. Delaware.

BENHAM BRO'S,

36 East Washington St.,

Pianos, Organs and Melodeons Tuned, Moved and Repaired.

Hoffman George W., clk. with Frank Erdlemyer, bds. 263 E. Washington.

Hoffman Gustave, cigarmaker, 35 W. Washington.

Hoffman Henry, tinner, r. 236 E. Washington.

Hoffman John, cook, r. 288 S. East.

Hoffman John J., carpenter, r. 305 Virginia av.

Hoffman Henry, shoemaker, 173 S. Meridian.

HOFFMAN MAX. F. A., Secretary of State, office State building, r. 80 N. New Jersey.

Hoffman Philip, dealer in groceries &c., se. cor. Sixth and Tennessee. r. same.

Hoffman Valentine, lab., r. 110 S. Noble.

Hoffman William T., weaver, r. 58 Massachusetts av.

Hoffmeister Nicholas, grocery and feedstore, 150 N. Noble, r. same.

Hoffmeyer Fred. W., drayman, r. 224 N. Davidson.

Hoffmeyer Henry, tailor, r. 195 N. Liberty.

Hoffmeyer William, driver at Lieber's brewery, r. 376 E. New York.

Hoffner Samuel, lab., C. C. & I. C. R. R., r. 13 Grant near Michigan road.

Hoffner Seth, yardman, P. C. & St. L. R. R.

Hoffner Luke, flagman, T. H. & I. R. R., r. Michigan.

Hoffrogge Joseph, finisher, 74 S. Pennsylvania, r. 339 Virginia av.

Hogan John, railroader, r. 41 Mud.

Hogan M. A. Mrs., dressmaker, 64 N. Illinois, r. same.

Hogan Phillip, tobacconist, r. 2 Douglass.

Hogan Samuel, wagonmaker, bds. 23 S. Pennsylvania.

Hogan Sarah J. (wid. Thomas) r. cor. Illinois and Louisiana.

Hogarty Michael stonecutter, r. 225 Virginia av.

Hogate Charles F., U. S. Internal Revenue Collector, office, P. O. bldg., r. Danville, Ind.

Hogle S. M., furniture dealer, bds. 18 S. Pennsylvania.

Hogshire Wm. R. (Reid, C. & Co.) r. 287 N. Meridian.

Hohl Christopher, bookkeeper, Hahn & Bals, r. 265 Massachusetts, av.

H. H. LEE,

Dealer in

Teas, Coffees, Sugars & Spices,

No. 7 ODD FELLOWS HALL

AND

ACADEMY OF MUSIC CORNER.

Hohler Phillip, watchman, C. C. & I. C. R. R. Depot, r. N. Noble.

Hoke Lewis A., salesman 21 W. Washington, bds Palmer House.

Holbrook H. C. (Ryan & H.) bds. 157 N. Alabama.

Holbrook Preston, (P. H. & Co.) r. 293 S. New Jersey.

Holbrook Thomas E·, bookkeeper, 19 S. Meridian, r. 157 N. Alabama.

Holbrook P. & Co., boots and shoes, 9 Odd Fellows Hall.

Holcomb Wm. L., special agent, Continental Life Insurance Co., bds Macy House.

Holdzkam Charles, harnessmaker, 182 W. Washington.

Holerman Thomas, watchman, P. C. & St. L. freight depot.

Holford J. F., freight clk., American & M. U. Express Company bds. Pyle House.

Holland Charles A., fireman C. C. C. & I. R. R., r. 293 Massachusetts av.

Holland C. R., harnessmaker, r. 126 W. Sixth.

Holland G. G., gardener and sodder, r. 126 W. Sixth.

Holland John, carpenter, r. 303 S. Delaware.

Holland J. W. (H. Ostermeyer & Co) r. nw. cor. Tennessee and Walnut.

Holland Thomas, lab., r. 160 Meek.

Holland T. F. (H. O. & Co.) r. 383 N. Illinois.

HOLLAND, OSTERMEYER & CO. (J. W. H., F. O., T. F. H. and W. A. Krag) whol. grocers, 27 and 29 E. Maryland.

Holle Henry, clk. Stewart & Morgan, 428 S. East.

Holle Herman C., stonemason, r. 343 E. Market.

Hollen John, lab., 293 S. East.

Hollen Emma, (wid. George) r. cor. Ray and Maple.

Hollenbeck John, express messenger, bds. 73 W. Maryland.

Holler Phillip, day watchman C. C. & I. C. R. R., r. 205 N. Noble.

Hollett Mattie Miss, student, 24½ S. Pennsylvania, r. 43 Chatham.

Holliday C. F. (W. & C. F. Holliday) r. 131 N. Meridian.

Holliday Eliza J. Mrs., milliner and dressmaker, 46 S. Illinois, r. same.

Holliday F. C. Rev., pastor Robert's Chapel, r. 131 N. Meridian.

Holliday J. D., salesman 59 S. Meridian, r. 398 N. Delaware.

HOLLIDAY JOHN H., managing editor Daily News, r. 242 N. Alabama.

Holliday Julius, clk., 49 N. Illinois, r. 46 S. Illinois.

Holliday Samuel, clk., 49 N. Illinois, bds. 46 S. Illinois.

Holliday William Mrs., r. 242 N. Alabama.

Holliday William D., r. 398 N. Delaware.

Holliday W. (W. & C. F. Holliday) r. 131 N. Meridian.

Holliday W. J. (W. J. H. & Co) r. 241 N. Meridian.

HOLLIDAY W. & C. F., wholesale dealers in lamps, chmineys, chandeliers, etc., 15 S. Meridian.

HOLLIDAY W. J. & CO., (W. J. H., J M. Murphy, J. H. Furnas and H. W. Voight) whol. dealers in iron, steel, nails, etc., 59 S. Meridian.

Hollingsworth D., r. 286 E. St. Clair.

Hollingsworth W. W., mail agent I. & V R R.

Hollingsworth B. (Mills & H.) r. 24 N. West.

Hollins George, sawmaker, r. 171 E. South.

Hollis Edwin, works Novelty Works.

Holloway H. C., Superintendent P. O., r. 432 N. Delaware.

Holloway James M., clk. P. O., r. 43 Fletcher av.

HOLLOWAY WM. R., Postmaster, office, se. cor. P. O. bldg., bds. 125 E. Ohio.

Holloway Amos, bookkeeper, 110 S. Meridian, bds. Pyle House.

Hollowell Calvin, r. 404 W. New York.

Hollowell Edwin, r. 404 W. New York.

Hollweg Louis, (H. & Reese) bds. 213 N. Pennsylvania.

HOLLWEG & REESE, (L. H. and C. E. R.) wholesale dealers in queensware, stone and yellow ware, 90 and 92 S. Meridian.

Holly Theodore, shoemaker, works 83 W. Washington, r. 35 N. Blake.

Hollywood Richard, r. 77 S. Illinois.

Holman B. M., printer, bds. 30½ N. Pennsylvania.

HOLMAN G. G., commission and produce dealer, 6 Bates House blk., r. Western av., nr. College.

Holman James R., bookkeeper G. G. Holman, r. 82 Huron.

HOLMAN JOHN A., attorney at law, 12 Talbott & New's blk. r. Western av.

Holman John H., teamster, bds. Eighth, nr. Canal.

Holman M. C., broommaker, r. nw. cor. North and Mississippi.

Holmes Chris., porter, Sherman house.

Holmes Henry, plasterer, r. 64 California.

Holmes James, carpenter, r. 181 N. Liberty.

Holmes W. C., President citizens national bank, r. out city limits.

Holstien Charles L., (Elliott & H.) r. 155 N. Tennessee.

Holster Richard, bds. Union House.

Holt Alexander, bookkeeper, r. 45 Elizabeth.

Holt Charles A., machinist, Eagle Machine Works, bds. 22 W. Georgia.

Holt Frank, clk., r. ne. cor. East and Vermont.

Holt Louisa M. (Wid) r. ne. cor. Vermont and East.

Holt W. L., clk., 85 Virginia av., r. 197 N. Liberty.

Holtman Herman, lab., r. 149 N. Noble.

Holtman John, lab., r. 38 Oriental.

Holtman John H., lab., 335 N. Noble.

Holtz August, lab., r. 451 S. Meridian.

Holtz George & Co. (G. H. and Wm. Pope) merchant tailors and clothiers, 124 S. Illinois.

Holtz John, lab., r. 338 Chesnut.

Homan Jerry, builder and cementer, r. 130 E. South.

Homburg R., physician, 194 E. Washington, r. same.

Homburg W. T., lettercarrier, bds. 194½ E. Washington.

Home of the Friendless, N. Tennessee nr. Tinker, James Smith Superintendent.

Homeyer Fredrick, painter, bds 65 S. East.

Homeyer William, slateroofer, bds. 65 S. East.

Homier William, tinner, Munson & Johnston.

Hood H. P., modelmaker Novelty Works.

Hood William, shoemaker, r. 177 N. Delaware.

Hook Francis M., physician, r. 75 N. East.

Hook Jacob, butcher, bds. 424 S. Illinois.

Hook Jesse, (col'd) lab., r. 276 E. North.

Hook and Ladder Company, Fire Department, es. New Jersey, nr. Washington.

Hooker E. M. B., printer, r. 215 W. Michigan.

Hooker John, route agent I. C. & L. R. R.,

BENHAM BRO'S,

36 East Washignton St.,

AGENTS FOR THE

BURDETT ORGAN.

Hoover Daniel, groceries and produce dealer, 149 Blake, r. same.

Hoover Jacob, teamster, r. 311 W. Washington.

Hoover Jacob B., huckster, r. W. Sixth, bet. Mississippi and Tennessee.

Hoover John, lab., bds. 355 W. Washington.

Hoover John W., boilermaker, r. 231 N. Liberty.

Hoover J. N., telegraph operator, bds. Pyle House.

Hoover Wm. H., plowmaker, 29 S. East, r. 171 E. Christian av.

Hope Christina Miss, weaver Merritt & Coughlen, bds. 8. Henry.

Hope Jennie Miss, bds. 51 Douglass al.

Hope Jesse, (col'd) porter Tutewiler Bros., r. 300 E. Walnut.

Hopkins Henry, bookbinder, bds. 28 N. Mississippi.

Hopkins H. C. (Martin & H.) bds. 218 N. Alabama.

Hopkins J. H., bookbinder, bds. 28 N. Mississippi.

Hopkins P. (wid. Moses) r. 274 W. Market.

Hopp Aaron, peddler, r. 318 Wabash, bet. Liberty and Noble.

Hoppe John W., tinner, r. 58 Hosbrook.

Hopper Louis M., carpenter, r. 110 Jackson.

Horan Daniel, fireman C. C. & I. R. R.

Horan James, wagonmaker, r. 128 Blackford.

Hord Oscar B. (Hendricks, H. & Hendricks) r. cor. New York and California.

HORN HENRY J., Sr., whol. and retail dealer in groceries, wines and liquors, 174 W. Washington, r. 72 N. Mississippi.

Horn Henry J., jr., clk. 174 W. Washington, bds. 72 N. Mississippi.

Hornaday John E., carpenter, r. 365 N. Alabama.

Hornaday T. B., night watchman State House, bds. 143 W. Washington.

Hornberger Christian, carpenter, r. 70 Jackson.

Horning John, brewer, r. 383 S. Delaware.

Hosbrook Daniel D., civil engineer, r. 437 N. Illinois.

H. H. LEE
HAS BUT
ONE PRICE, SELLS FOR CASH,
And Guarantees all Goods
Sold at the China Tea Stores,
To be as Represented.

Hose James, lab., r. 433 Virginia av.

Hoshour S. K., professor North Western Christian University, r. 172 N. East.

Hoskins Robert S. (Sims & H.) r. 159 Meek.

Hoss John C., real estate agent, r. 139 E. St. Mary.

Hoss John T. (Wood & H.) r. 56 Massachusetts av.

Hoss Nelson, city assessor, r. N. Delaware, nr. city limits.

Hossman Henry, drayman, r. 186 Harrison.

Hotchkiss Z. P., operator Western Union Telegraph, bds. 188 S. Mississippi.

Hotze Eugene, printer Daily Telegraph, bds. Emenegger's Hotel.

Hough Charles, r. 94 N. East.

Hough Charles A., carriage painter, r. 394 N. Delaware.

Hough Joseph, carpenter, r. 210 Madison av.

Houghtaling Hiram, freight conductor C. C. & I. C. R. R., bds. 58 Benton.

Houghtaling Hiram, sr., bds. 58 Benton.

House Ben D., notary public, 62 E. Washington up stairs, bds. 193 S. New Jersey.

House George, baggagemaster, T. H. & I. R. R.

Houser Annie Miss, milliner, (N. & G. Ohmer) r. Dayton, Ohio.

Houston C. B., salesman, r. 77 E. St. Joseph.

Houston J. T., (J. C. G. & Co.) r. sw. cor. East and St. Clair.

Houzen Peter, bootmaker, 255 S. Delaware, bds. 259 S. Delaware.

Howard Alice Miss, (col'd) cook Neiman house.

Howard Bridget, laundrymaid, Sherman house.

Howard Edward, cancer doctor, 92 S. Illinois, r. same.

Howard Edwin, telegraph operator, bds. 310 N. Illinois.

Howard Edward, railroad conductor, bds. 321 S. Missouri.

Howard E. B. (J. Ferguson & Co.) r. 141 N. Meridian.

Howard Hattie Miss, r. 322 E. Washington.

Howard Henry, (col'd) porter, 29 S. Illinois.

Howard James, (col'd) lab., bds. 116 Ash.

Howard Frank, tinsmith, r. 386 W. New York.

Howard Frank, tinner, Munson & Johnston, r. 162 N. Mississippi.

Howard Frank, bartender, r. over 322 E. Washington.

Howard Liberty, operator W. U. Telegraph, r. 364 S. Pennsylvania.

Howard Stephen, (col'd) lab., r. 153 Huron.

Howard William, works Street R. R. Co., r. 240 W. Market.

Howard William O., r. 92 S. Illinois.

Howden Jacob, currier, 125 S. Meridian bds. Union house.

Howden William, fireman C. C. & I. C. R. R., bds 58 Benton.

Howe Mrs. ——, r. 128 S. East.

Howe E. P., Secretary Franklin Life Insurance Co., r. 420 N. Pennsylvania.

Howe J. W., clk. Bee Hive Store, r. 36 Forest av.

Howe Robert, r. 175 W. Ohio.

Howe Thomas, works Aldrich & Gay, r. 6 James.

Howe Wm. H., carpenter, r. 33 Forest av.

Howe & Converse, (P. H. & E. A. C.) manufacturers and dealers in the Stafford Loom, 372 W. Washington.

Howell John W., traveling agent Foster & Wiggins, r. 96 W. First.

Howell Thomas, clk. 399 N. Illinois, r. 508 N. Mississippi.

Howes Charles, butcher, r. 76 Huron.

Howes Henry, carpenter, r. 342 E. McCarty.

Howie James, r. 453 E. Market.

Howie Wm. W., machinist C. C. C. & I. R. R., r. 453 E. Market.

Honk Philip, works C. C. C. & I. Shops, r. cor. North and Davidson.

Howland Arsa, boxmaker, r. 239 S. Mississippi.

Howland John D., clk. U. S. District Court, r. 98 W. Vermont.

Howlett Charles, telegraph operator, bds. 333 N. Illinois.

HOWLETT E. C., manager Pacific and Atlantic Telegraph Co., 22 E. Meridian, r. 310 N. Illinois.

Howlett G. N., operator Western Union telegraph, bds 333 N. Illinois.

Howson William, filemaker American Saw Works, bds. 89 S. Pennsylvania.

Hoyl Clinton D., railroader, r. 314 E. Louisiana.

Hoyt D. Walter, musician, bds. 84 Massachusetts av.

Hoyt Mrs. Harriet, boardinghouse, r. 84 Massachusetts av.

Hubbard George M., salesman J. R. Marot, r. 228 Huron.

Hubbard Wm. H., bookkeeper, 74 S. Pennsylvania, r. 616 N. Meridian.

Hubbard Wm. S., treasurer, Franklin Life Insurance Co., r. 616 N. Meridian.

Huber Jacob, (Becker & H.) r. 77 E. Washington, up stairs.

Hubert Harry, tinner, r. Huron.

Hubert John, woodworker, L. Shaw & Co, r. 79 S. Meridian.

Huckaba Alfred, lab., 278 S. Tennessee.

Huckaba A. C., machinist, Surgical Institute, r. same.

Huey M. D., jeweler, r. 289 Virginia av.

Hudson Annie Miss, r. room 5 Fatout blk.

Hudson James W., r. 74 Jones.

Hudson Richard, confectioner, bds. cor. East and Cherry.

Hudson S., photograph material, 196 E. Washington, r. same.

Hudson Thomas, blacksmith, Eagle Machine Works, r. Georgia, nr. Illinois.

Huebner Henry R. (Enos & H) r. 440 E. Washington.

HUEGELE JOHN, proprietor National Billiard Saloon, 39 E. Washington r. 40 N. New Jersey.

Huelpuesch William, watchmaker, r. 44 Coburn.

Huey D. N., varnisher, r. 19 S. Mississippi.

Huey Milton S., varnisher, Spiegel, Thoms & Co., r. 293 Winston.

Huff ——, railroader, r. 331 N. Noble.

Huff A. H., varnisher, bds. Court Street boarding house.

Huff John, confectioner, r. 119 S. New Jersey.

Huff J. T., grocer and produce dealer, 298 N. Pennsylvania, r. same.

Huffer Jas., harnessmaker, r. 69 Fletcher av.

HUFFER JAMES M., dealer in saddlery and harness, 23 S. Meridian, r. 69 Fletcher av.

Huffman John H., tannery, 25 S. East, r. 263 E. Washington.

Huffman Wm., clk., r. 236 E. Washington.

Hufmann William P., lithographer, bds. cor. Sixth and Tennessee.

Hugg Christina, (wid. Martin) r. 81 N. New Jersey.

Hughes James L., law student, bds. Pattison House.

Hughes John, engineer C C. C. & I. R. R., r. cor. North and Davidson.

Hughes R. Miss, teacher, bds. 244 S. New Jersey.

Hughes S. A., conductor C. C. & I. C. R. R., bds. Bates House.

Hughes William, r. 181 S. Tennessee.

Hughey Temperance, (wid.) r. 310 E. Louisiana.

Hugins Mattie Miss, r. room 8 Fatout's blk.

Hugle Samuel, (col'd) lab., r. 130 Massachusetts av.

Hugo Charles, carpenter, r. 79 N. Noble.

Hugo Charlotte, (wid.) r. 79 N. Noble.

Hugo H. A., plasterer, r. 359 S. East.

Huicher Charles, mechanic, r. 72 Coburn.

Hull Armstrong, teamster, r. 776 N. Tennessee.

Hull Jane, (wid. William) r. 725 N. Tennessee.

Hulsker Bernhard, clk. Stewart & Morgan, r. 595 S. Tennessee.

Hulsker Henry, lab. P. C. & St. L. freight depot.

Human John, piano tuner, bds. 94 N. East.

Hume, Adams & Co., (J. M. Hume, W. L. Adams, E. J. Foster and A. L. Wright) whol. and retail dealers in carpets, wall paper, and house furnishing goods, 26 and 28 W. Washington.

Hume James M. (H., Adams & Co.) r. 25 E. Ohio.

Hume Judson, railroader, r. 673 N. Pennsylvania.

Hume N., lettercarrier, r. 556 N. Tennessee.

Humes Thomas, lab., r. 303 Indiana av.

Humphrey John, bussrunner, Palmer House.

Humphrey S. D., printer, bds. 41 Huron.

Humphreys W. W., deputy clk. U. S. Court, bds. Pyle house.

Hunt Albert, machinist, r. 119 W. South.

Hunt A. C., tanner, r. 390 N. Delaware.

Hunt A. L., auctioneer, r. 320 N. Illinois.

Hunt Charles, engineer, Capital Tobacco Works, bds 119 W. South.

HUNT CHARLES C., dealer in cigars and tobacco, wholesale and retail, 61 E. Washington, r. 366 S. Alabama.

Hunt D. (Engle & H.) r. 68 S. Noble.

Hunt D. B., Insurance agent, r. 96 Fletcher av.

Hunt Fred, clk., Crystal Palace, bds. same.

Hunt Gideon P., clk., r. 394 N. Pennsylvania.

Hunt Harry, operator W. U. Telegraph, bds. 320 N. Illinois.

THE CHINA TEA STORES

ARE AT

No. 7 ODD FELLOWS HALL

AND

ACADEMY OF MUSIC CORNER.

Hunt Henry C., works paper mill, r. 324 W. Washington.

Hunt Lemuel C., compositor, r. 488 W. North.

Hunt Mary Mrs., (wid John) r. 520 S. Illinois.

Hunt Mrs , (wid) r. 52 S. Pennsylvania.

Hunt Patrick, works rolling mill, r. 7 Willard.

Hunt P. G. C. Dr., dentist rooms 76½ E. Market, r. 172 N. Delaware.

Hunt Walter, H., bookkeeper, r. 320 N. Illinois.

Hunter James, salesman New York store, bds. 158 N. New Jersey.

Hunter James, (col'd) lab., r. 233 N. West.

Hunter Thomas, cooper r. 71 California.

Hunter Tyra, student, bds. 128 Ft. Wayne av.

Huntington James N., carpenter, r. 476 N. Mississippi.

Huntley J. M. sleeping car conductor, r. 19 E. North.

Hupp A. C., grainer, r. over 336 E. Washington.

Hupp William, works Jackson, Rider & Co.

Huppertegraft Daniel, saloonkeeper, cor. Massachusetts av. and St. Clair, r. same.

Hurd Clarissa L., boarding house, 44 N. Tennessee, r. same.

Huron Kate Miss, teacher Fourth Ward School, bds. 89 Indiana av.

Hurley Frank, hack and expressman, r. 132 Maple.

Hurley John, expressman, r. 22 N. California.

Hurley Michael, lab., r. 23 Ellen.

Hurley Richard, hackman, r. 101 S. Illinois.

HURRLE IGNATZ, merchant tailor, 170 E. Washington, r. 63 N. Noble.

Hurst Frederick J., works Osgood, Smith & Co., r. 120 S. Meridian.

Hurt Albert, sawmaker, works E. C. Atkins & Co., r. 383 S. Illinois.

Hurt James R., railroader, r. 111 N. Davidson.

Hurt T. J., carpenter, se. cor. Pennsylvania and Maryland, r. 799 N. Tennessee.

Hurtt David, bellboy, Bates House.

Husban Linsey, (col'd) lab., r. 165 Indiana av.

Huskinson John, with A. Clem, bds. 145 N. New Jersey.

Huskinson Thomas, carpenter, r. 145 N. New Jersey.

Hussey Edmond, lab., r. 356 S. West.

Hust George C., butcher, 564 E. Washington, r. same.

Husted H.C., tanner and currier, r. 255 E. McCarty.

Huston C. B., salesman D. Root, r. 77 E. St. Joseph.

Huston Felden, (col'd) carpenter, r. 75 Bright.

Huston George, general stock agent, C. C. & I. C. R. R., r. 274 N. Mississippi.

Huston George W., teamster, r. 384 S. West.

Huston John, engineer, r. 552 N. Mississippi.

Huston J. T. (J. C. Green & Co.) r. 370 N. East.

Huston Mrs., r. over 579 E. Washington.

Huston Robert, r. 370 N. East.

Hutchins B. D. W., broommaker, bds. Neiman House.

Hutchins H. H., bookkeeper, r. East Market, city limits.

Hutchins E. S., grocer and produce dealer, 407 N. Alabama, r. 115 E. St. Clair.

Hutchins Thomas, lab., r. Ash, nr. Christian av.

Hutchinson B., conductor C. C. & I. C. R. R., bds. Spencer House.

HUTCHINSON C. P., publisher Indianapolis City Directory, 16½ E. Washington, r. 93 W. First.

Hutchinson C. C. & Co., (C. C. H., E. Fahy and Wm. Elias) proprietors Dollar Store, 16 W. Washington.

Hutchinson C. C. (C. C. H. & Co.) r. Louisville, Ky.

Hutchinson David, engineer, J. M. & I. R. R., r. 202 E. McCarty.

Hutchinson E. B., general agent P. C. & St. L. R. R., cor. Virginia av. and Delaware, bds. 86 N. Mississippi.

Hutchison Anna Miss, dressmaker, 281 N. East, r. same.

Hutchison John, cooper, bds. 314 E. Georgia.

Hutchison William, machinist, r. 383 Massachusetts av.

Huth Anton, Cabinet Maker's Union, r. 474 E. Market.

Hutton Eliza J. (wid. William) r. 652 N. Tennessee.

Hutton George, carpenter, r. 187 Doughtery.

Hutz Louis, grinder, r. 62 Osborn.

Hyatt John, bartender, Bates House Saloon, r. 30 circle.

Hyde Nathaniel Rev., agent, American Home Missionary Society, r. 116 N. Alabama.

Hyland J. brick and stonemason, r. N. Illinois, bet. Fifth and Sixth.

IDLER CLINTON, foreman, T. H. & I. R. R. shops, r. 171 W. Somb.

Igan Thomas P., cutter, 31 N. Pennsylvania, bds. Pyle House.

Igoe M., attorney at law, r. 54 Lockerbie.

Igou Alfred, bds 44 S. Tennessee.

Ihrzohn Ernest, brewer, C. F. Schmidt, r. same.

ILG GEORGE, Saloon and Boarding House, 323 W. Washington.

Iliff Charles E., salesman, H. Bamberger, bds. 73 N. Alabama.

Iliff Lewis S., salesman, Bowen, Stewart & Co., r. 73 N. Alabama.

Iliff Mary M. (wid.) r. 73 N. Alabama.

Imelli Max., painter, 213 E. Washington, r. over 198 E. Washington.

Imelli Stephen, watchmaker, bds. over 198 E. Washington.

Imes Mary A. (wid.) r. cor. Merrill and Kentucky av.

Ince Thomas, soldier, U. S. arsenal, r. 228 Massachusetts av.

Inders John, carpenter, r. 427 N. East.

INDIANA BANKING CO., 28 E. Washington, W. H. Morrison, President, F. A. W. Davis, Cashier.

Indiana Cement Pipe Co., manufactory, bet. North and Walnut, nr. Canal.

INDIANA FIRE INSURANCE CO., 5 Odd Fellows Hall, I. S. Hursey, President, W. F. Gibson, Secretary.

INDIANA HOSPITAL FOR THE INSANE, Orpheus Evarts, M.D., Superintendent, W. Indianapolis, outside city limits.

INDIANA INSTITUTE FOR THE EDUCATION OF THE BLIND, W. H. Curchman, Superintendent, ns. North, bet. Meridian and Pennsylvania.

INDIANA INSTITUTE FOR THE EDUCATION OF THE DEAF AND DUMB, Thomas McIntire, Superintendent, E. Washington, outside city limits.

INDIANA JOURNAL OF COMMERCE, Morton & Ricker, proprietors, office ne. cor. Meridian and Circle, old Journal bldg., 2d floor.

INDIANA NATIONAL BANK, ne. cor. Washington and Meridian, Geo. Tousey, President, D. M. Taylor, Cashier.

Indiana State Board of Agriculture, J. D. Williams, President; J. Poole, Secretary; office in State House.

Indiana State Offices, cor. Washington and Tennessee.

Indiana Transfer Co., 42 E. Maryland.

INDIANA VOLKSBLAT, (German,) Julius Boeticher, editor and proprietor, 164 E. Washington.

Indianapolis, Bloomington & Western R. R., office cor. Virginia av. and Delaware, W. Slater, Superintendent.

IND'POLIS BRANCH BANKING Co., (Fletcher & Sharpe) sw. cor. Washington and Pennsylvania.

Indianapolis Brewery, 399 W. Washington, J. P. Meikel, proprietor.

IND'POLIS CINCINNATI & LAFAYETTE R. R., offices cor. Delaware and Louisiana.

Indianapolis, Cincinnati & Lafayette Machine Shop, Louisian E. of city limits.

Indianapolis City Academy, ss. New York bet. Meridian and Pennsylvania.

Indianapolis Cotton Manufactory, W. end Washington, N. of bridge.

Indianapolis Female Bible Society, 33 E. Washington.

IND'POLIS GAS LIGHT AND COKE Co., cor. Pennsylvania and Maryland, S. A. Fletcher, President.

Indianapolis Glass Works, Kentucky av. nr. river.

INDIANAPOLIS INSURANCE Co., Bank of Discount and Deposit, cor. Virginia av. and Pennsylvania, Wm. Henderson, President; Alex. C. Jameson, Secretary.

INDIANAPOLIS JOURNAL, daily and weekly, Douglass & Conner, publishers, cor. Circle and Market.

INDIANAPOLIS NATIONAL BANK, ne. cor. E. Washington and Pennsylvania, T. P. Haughey, President.

Indianapolis Patent Agency, 87 E. Market, G. H. Zeigler, business manager.

Indianapolis, Peru & Chicago R. R., offices 101 E. Washington, D. Macy, President.

IND'POLIS PIANO MANUFACTURING Co., 159 and 161 E. Washington, C. Ingersol, Superintendent.

H. H. LEE

MAKES A SPECIALTY OF

Choice Green, Black & Japan Teas.

INDIANAPOLIS PRINTING & PUBLISHING HOUSE, se. cor. Circle and Meridian, J. M. Tilford, Superintendent.

Indianapolis Rolling Mill Co., office citizens bank building, John M. Lord President.

Indianapolis Skating Rink, sw. cor. Georgia and Tennessee.

IDIANAPOLIS STEAM LAUNDRY, J. L. Spaulding, proprietor, r. 22 and 24 S. New Jersey.

Indianapolis & St. Louis R. R., T. A. Morris Pres't, office 53 S. Alabama.

Indianapolis & Vincennes R. R., D. C. Branham Superintendent, cor. Virginia av. and Delaware.

IND'PODIS WAGON AND AGRICULTURAL WORKS, 172 S. Tennessee.

Ingall Jacob, lab., r. 191½ W. Washington.

Ingersoll Charles, Superintendent Indianapolis Piano Manufacturing Co., r. 163 E. Washington.

Ingersoll Frank, turner, r. 255 S. Alabama.

Ingersoll Mary Miss, principal Seventh ward school, r. 333 S. Alabama.

Ingersoll Selmah Miss, teacher Fourth ward school, r. 333 S. Alabama.

Ingle Alexander, r. 70 E. Market.

INGLE MARK W., dealer in all kinds coal, also salt agency, 36 E. Market.

Inglecash John, lab., r. 437 S. Missouri.

Ingles John, coppersmith, C. C. & I. C. R. R.

INGRAHAM C. B., art gallery, 32½ E. Washington, r. 27 W. Ohio.

Ingram Thomas, sawyer, r. 47 Helen.

Insprucker John A., shoemaker, r. 173 West Washington.

Inwalle Benjamin J., proprietor Inwalle's garden, 367 Virginia av., r. same.

Inwalle J. H., painter, r. 339 Virginia av.

Ireland William H., stairbuilder, bds. 38 Forest av.

Irish Adam, woodsawyer, r. 204 E. Court.

Irick Morris C., carriagepainter, r. 133 Ft. Wayne av.

Irick William H., bricklayer, r. 326 N. New Jersey.

Irons Catherine, (wid. Stephen) r. 193 W. Maryland.

Irvin Isaac W., r. ne. cor. First and Mississippi.

Irvin R. C., printer Journal Office, r. 32½ N. Pennsylvania.

Irvin William, (Ritter & I.) r. 30 W. Maryland.

Irving A. B., music dealer, r. 98 E. New York.

Irving C. L., patent agent, bds. 18 E. Michigan.

Irving David, salesman New York Store, bds. 158 N. New Jersey.

Irving H. B., carpenter, r. 213 N. Pennsylvania.

Irving James, machinist, Eagle Machine Works, bds. 86 S. Mississippi.

Irving J. R., agent for William Sumner & Co., r. 360 N. East.

Isensee Albert, locksmith and bellhanger, 28 N. Illinois, r. same.

Isgrigg James A. (I. & B) r. 413 W. New York.

ISGRIGG & BRACKEN, (J. A. I. and T. E. B.) dealers in lumber, lath and shingles, 180 W. Market.

Ishmael Joshua, lab., r. 23 Kingan.

Iske Caroline, domestic, Blind Institute.

Iske Christian, lab., r. 427 Virginia av.

Iske William, machinist, r. 81 Huron.

Ittenbach Frank, (S. I. & Co.) r. 272 E. South.

Ittenbach Gerhard, (S. I. & Co.) r. 272 E. South.

Ivery Peter, teamster, r. 329 N. Noble.

JACHMAN A. MRS., r. 312 E. Washington.

Jachman Herman, merchant tailor, 257 E. Washington, r. 312 E. Washington.

Jack Charles, papermaker, 24 E. Georgia, r. Louisiana, bet. Noble and East.

Jack George, custom tailor, 250 Indiana av., r. same.

Jack Matthew, jr., clk. North Western Farmer Office, r. 62 S. Pennsylvania.

Jack Matthew W., tailor, r. 62 S. Tennessee.

Jacks Isaac N., clk. 156 W. Washington, r. cor. New York and Tennessee.

Jackson Andrew, clk. 18 W. Pearl, r. Minerva, nr. Union.

Jackson Elizabeth N. (wid.) r. 56 Bates.

Jackson John, (col'd) pastry cook Palmer House.

Jackson John, lab., r. 72 Bicking.

Jackson Rachel, (col'd) r. 397 Howard.

Jackson Thomas, currier Moony & Co., r. 191 W. Maryland.

Jackson Thomas, (L. R. Martin & Co.) bds. Pyle House.

Jackson T. B. (VanCamp & J.) bds. cor. Mississippi and Maryland.

Jackson T. M. (J. Rider & Co.) r. 71 Indiana av.

JACKSON W. N., Secretary and Treasurer Union Railway Co., r. 82 W. North.

Jackson William, slate roofer, r. 186 N. Davidson.

Jackson Willis, (col'd) lab., r. 177 Indiana av.

Jackson, Rider & Co. (T. M. J. and T. H. R.) furniture and cane seat chairs, factory and wareroom, cor. New York and Canal.

Jacob Joseph, notions and wool goods, 115 E. Washington, r. 156 N. East.

Jacobi A., butcher, 387 S. Delaware, r. 67 Wyoming.

Jacobs Adel, (wid.) r. 156 N. East.

Jacob Charles P. (Barbour & J.) r. 166 Christian av.

Jacobs Frank, receiver, bds. 145 S. New Jersey.

Jacobs John, carpenter, bds. 256 Blake.

Jacobs Milton, blacksmith, r. 145 S. New Jersey.

Jacobs Richard, boxmaker, r. 58 Bright.

Jacobs Stephen, boxmaker, 39 S. Illinois.

Jacobs Valentine, r. 145 S. New Jersey.

Jacobs William B., agent Babcock's Fire Extinguisher, 24 N. Pennsylvania.

Jacoby Jerome, candymaker, 26 S. Meridian, bds. 78 S. Pennsylvania.

Jacoby David R., fish store, Pearl, r. 73 S. Pennsylvania.

Jacquenin Frank foreman P. Lieber & Co.

Jacquise J., cigar manufacturer, 196 N. Mississippi, up stairs, r. same.

Jager Otto, brewer Meikel's Brewery, bds. 323 W. Washington.

James Elizabeth, servant, Ray House, r. same.

James Frank, (col'd) lab., r. 410 S. Tennessee.

James John, (col'd) lab., bds. 410 S. Tennessee.

James M. C., clk., r. 66 W. New York.

James Mary, (wid. John) r. 24 W. McCarty.

James Oliver H., plasterer, r. 299 W. Vermont.

James Seth C., marblecutter, r. 46 Fletcher av.

James T. S. (J. T. S. & Co.) bds. Ray House.

James T. S. & Co. (T. S. James and ——) marble dealers, 136 S. Meridian.

Jameson Alex. C., secretary Indianapolis Insurance Company, r. 21 S. Pennsylvania.

Jameson L. H., assistant U. S. Internal Revenue Assessor, r. 159 W. South.

BENHAM BRO'S,
36 East Washington St.,
Pianos, Organs and Melodeons
FOR
CASH OR ON TIME.

Jameson Ovid, clk., 249 N. Alabama.

Jameson Patrick H. (J. & Funkhouser) r. 249 N. Alabama.

JAMESON & FUNKHOUSER, (P. H. Jameson and D. Funkhouser) physicians and surgeons, office, 35 E. Market.

Janeway John, works Novelty Works.

Jarrell Francis Miss, dress and cloak maker, 36 N. Illinois, r. 148 Indiana av.

Jasper Aldrich, (col'd) lab., r. 201 W. Second.

Jasper Fred. W., grocer, 333 and 335 Virginia av. r. same.

Jasper Herman, lab., r. 487 E. New Jersey.

Jasper Hermann, works Jackson, Rider & Co.

Jeffers James, soldier, U. S. arsenal, r. 472 E. Washington.

Jefferson Robert, (col'd) carpenter, r. 247 Minerva.

Jeffery Thomas, carriagepainter, r. 69 Ann.

Jeffrey William, lab., r. Chespeake nr. West.

Jeffries Robert, works glass works, r. Madison rd., South of city limits.

Jeffries Thomas, works glass works, r. 69 Canal bet. McCarty and Railroad.

Jehrling John P., repairer and cleaner 3 Virginia av., r. 125 E. McCarty.

Jenison Alexander F., gold and silver plater, 22 Talbott & New's blk., r. 19 W. Ohio.

Jenison George, traveler, bds. 346 N. Meridian.

Jenison George M., watch materials and tools, 22 Talbott & New's blk.

Jemison John, saddle and harness manufacturer, 128 S. Meridian, r. 147 Union.

Jenkins A. W., r. 119 Massachusetts av.

Jenkins C. W., checkman, P. C. & St. L. freight depot, r. 223 E. Market.

Jenkins D. H., messenger, American & M. U. express Co., r. 232 S. Alabama.

Jenkins Ebenezer, painter, r. 74 Ft. Wayne av.

Jenkins Jennie Miss, r. 166 E. Market.

Jenkins John, works Frink & Moore, r. 304 N. Mississippi.

Jenkins John, works novelty works.

11

H. H. LEE

MAKES A SPECIALTY OF

Choice Green, Black & Japan Teas.

Jenkins J. W., telegraph operator, bds. 74 Ft. Wayne av.

Jenkins Peter, painter, bds. 152 Blake.

Jenkins Robert, (col'd) barber, r. 228 W. Vermont.

Jenkins William, confectioner, works Daggett & Co., r. 270 N. West.

Jenkins W. F., stock dealer, r. 512 N. Illinois.

Jenks George W., engineer, r. 536 E. Georgia.

Jenks W. R. C., foreman Journal of Commerce, r. 26 N. Mississippi.

Jennings C. F. (wid. Henry C.) dressmaker, r. 181 N. Tennessee.

Jennings Charles T., physician, r. 65 Lockerbie.

Jennings George R., works Osgood, Smith & Co., r. 312 Chesnut.

Jennings P.' teacher, r. 248 N. Davidson.

Jennings W. T., tin and sheetiron worker, 60 E. Market, r. 277 W. Michigan.

Jenson H. C., cabinetmaker, r. 275 S. West.

Jerrion Nicholas, carpenter, r. 317 N. Davidson.

Jillson J. M., clk., C. C. C. & I. R. R., bds. Pyle house.

Jines William, carpenter, r. 30 Circle.

Joachim Joseph C., butcher, 88 Fort Wayne av., r. same.

Joeke Adolph, lab., r. se. cor. Elm and Cedar.

Johannas Charles, wagonmaker, r. 60 S. Delaware.

Johautgen George, blacksmith, r. 290 E. Lousiana.

Johautgen Joseph, blacksmith, r. 404 S. Illinois.

John Charles, r. 273 N. Mississippi.

Johns Joel, lumber merchant, bds. 151 N. Davidson.

Johns James H., soldier U. S. Arsenal.

Johnson Albert, clk. 173 W. Washington, r. 167 W. Maryland.

Johnson Annie, (wid.) r. 26 W. Second.

Johnson Andy, fireman Sherman House.

Johnson A. H., wholesale dealer in liquors, 197 W. Washington, r. 140 E. St. Clair.

Johnson A. W., carpenter, r. 57 Huron, cor. Noble.

Johnson Benjamin, hackman, r. 253 N. West.

Johnson Benjamin, (col'd) waiter 29 S. Illinois, r. same.

Johnson Benjamin, (col'd) porter J. T. Huff, r. 217 W. Second.

Johnson Benjamin F., miller, r. 231 Massachusetts av.

Johnson B. F., carpenter, r. ne. cor. Mississippi and Ohio.

Johnson B. N., salesman 112 S. Meridian, bds. Sherman House.

Johnson Charles, expressman, r. 327 S. Alabama.

Johnson Cynthia, (wid.) r. 438 W. North.

Johnson C. L. F., cl'k McLene & Heron, bds. 68 E. Market.

Johnson E. (E. Johnson & Co.) 170 E. Michigan.

Johnson E. F. (wid. George) r. 21 Fletcher av.

JOHNSON EDWARD T., attorney at law, room 9 Blackford's blk., r. 474 N. Pennsylvania.

Johnson Edward C., r. 34 S. Meridian.

Johnson Elizabeth, (wid. John B.) r. 167 W. Maryland.

Johnson E. & Co. (E. J. and J. J. Smith) manufacturers of brass and copper ware, 108 S. Delaware.

Johnson Frederick, works rolling mill, r. 462 S. Illinois.

Johnson George H., salesman J. T. Layman & Co., r. 370 S. Alabama.

Johnson George W., bookkeeper Citizen's National Bank, r. 26 W. Second.

Johnson Green C., (col'd) barbershop, 267 W. Washington, r. same.

Johnson H. A., grocer and produce dealer, 399 N. New Jersey, bds. cor. Plum and Christian av.

Johnson Harriet, (col'd, wid. Charles) r. 356 W. North.

Johnson James, (Colden & J.) r. 129 Union.

Johnson James, (col'd) lab., r. 175 Elm.

Johnson James, real estate agent, bds. 129 Union.

Johnson James, carpenter, r. 394 N. West.

Johnson James A., carpenter, r. 57 Huron.

Johnson James A., carpenter, bds. 64 W. Maryland.

Johnson James A., carpenter, r. 312 S. East.

Johnson James E., florist, r. Michigan rd. nr. Washington.

Johnson John, (col'd) barber, Hill & Carter.

Johnson John, lab., r. 223 N West.

Johnson John, barber, 303 E. Washington.

Johnson Johnson, clk. Dunn & Wiggins, bds. 328 E. New York.

Johnson John W., bookkeeper 26 S. Meridian, r. 491 N. Mississippi.

Johnson Joel M., bookkeeper with A. H. Johnson, r. 197 W. Washington.

Johnson Lewis, (col'd) hostler Sullivan & Drew, r. 225 N. Tennessee.

Johnson Lewis, (col'd) lab., r. Second, bet. Howard and Lafayette R. R.

Johnson Mary Miss, r. room 2 over 188 W. Washington.

Johnson Mary F. (wid. Dr. T. E.) r. 81 S. Illinois.

Johnson M. L., agent Continental Life Insurance Co., Citizens' Bank bldg., r. 546 N. Illinois.

Johnson N., blacksmith, bds. 25 Dacota.

Johnson Oregon, servant, 248 S. Meridian.

Johnson P. W. H. (col'd) lab., r. 7 Athon.

Johnson Philip A., carpenter, r. 256 N. East.

Johnson P. DuBois, law student, 21 E. Washington, bds. Pyle House.

Johnson Richard, (col'd) lab., r. Tennessee, North of Seventh.

Johnson R. J. (R. J. J. & Co.) r. 399 N. Illinois.

Johnson R. J. & Co. (R. J. J. and Russell Elliott) grocers and produce dealers, 399 N. Illinois.

Johnson Serena Miss, bds. 394 N. West.

Johnson Sarah Miss, bds. 139 W. Market.

Johnson Sarah, (col'd, wid. William) r. 356 W. North.

Johns S. E., paperbox maker, bds. 444 N. New Jersey.

Johnson S. L., printer, Sentinel Office, r. 28 Fletcher av.

Johnson S. S. r. 208 E. St. Joseph.

JOHNSON THOMAS E., attorney at law, 42 E. Washington, r. 355 N. East.

Johnson Wesley S., moulder, r. 320 S. Delaware.

Johnson Warren, (col'd) lab., r. 51 Hosbrook.

Johnson William, lab. 328 Blake.

Johnson William, lab., r. 81 S. Missouri.

Johnson William, soldier U. S. Arsenal.

Johnson William, (col'd) lab., r. W Second, nr. Lafayette R. R.

Johnson William, (col'd) lab., r. 176 Douglass al.

Johnson William H. (col'd) lab., r. 196 Missouri.

Johnson William H. H., r. 155 Union.

Johnson Wm. W., printer, Journal Office, r. 236 E. Vermont.

Johnson W. P., M. D., Indiana Surgical Institute, r. 74 W. Vermont.

Johnston George W., bookkeeper Citizen's National Bank, r. 2 W. Second.

Johnston John C., clk., r. 328 E. New York.

Johnston John F., dentist, 19 W. Maryland, r. same.

Johnston John M., attorney at law, r. 328 E. New York.

Johnston Reed, lab., r. 156 Stevenson.

Johnson Robert, (col'd) barber, 26 N. Pennsylvania.

Johnston R. J., druggist, bds. 158 N. New Jersey.

Johnston Samuel A., clk. Munson & Johnston, r. 220 N. New Jersey.

Johnston Thomas, lab., r. 126 Stevenson.

Johnston Wm. J. (Munson & J.) r. 86 E. Vermont.

Johnston W. W. (Murphy, J. & Co.) r. 546 N. Meridian.

Joilet Samuel Rev., r. 249 S. New Jersey.

Jolly James, watchman I. C. & L. R. R. shops, r. 86 Bates.

Jolly John, lab., r. 14 Lord.

Jones A., jr. (Vinnedge, J. & Co) r. 467 N. Pennsylvania.

Jones Aquilla, treasurer Rolling Mill, r. 187 N. Pennsylvania.

Jones Alexander, (col'd) r. 824 N. Illinois.

Jones B. D., r. 188 N. Delaware.

Jones Ben. F. (Bronson & J.) bds. 187 N, Pennsylvania.

Jones Braton, (col'd) lab., r. Dunlop, nr. Madison rd.

Jones Charles, (John Woodbridge & Co.) r. 187 N. Pennsylvania.

Jones Charles, (col'd) r. 558 N. Mississippi.

Janes Charles B., clk., Trade Palace, bds. 64 W. Maryland.

Jones Charles E., clk., Hume, Adams & Co., r. 64 W. Maryland.

Jones C. M. Dr., clk., 188 E. Washington.

Jones Curtis, baggagemaster, P. C. & St. Louis R. R.

Jones Edward, (col'd) expressman, r. 205 N. West.

Jones Emma M. Miss, r. 419 N. East.

Jones Evan J., lab., r. 398 S. Tennessee.

Jones E. B., day watchman, C. C. C. & I. R. R. shops.

Jones E. B., engineer, r. 104 E. Second.

Jones E. C., expressman, r. 339 S. Pennsylvania.

Jones E. F., engineer, r. 22 Lord.

Jones F. J., broom manufacturer, r. 805 N. Illinois.

Jones George W., r. 793 N. Illinois.

Jones Hester, (wid) r. 35 Dacota.

THE CHINA TEA STORES

ARE AMONG THE

Attractions of Indianapolis.

Call and See Them before leaving the City.

Jones Jessee, real estate agent, 17½ W. Washington, r. 488 N. Illinois.

Jones Jesse, druggist, bds. 310 Indiana av.

Jones Jesse M., clk., 180 Indiana av., bds. 310 Indiana av.

Jones John, watchman, bds. 228 E. Louisiana.

Jones John, (col'd) barber, r. 289 N. Missouri.

Jones John L. (Davis & J.) bds. 430 N. New Jersey.

Jones John S., carpenter, r. 158 Huron.

Jones J. W., night clk., Spencer house.

Jones J. W., yardmaster T. H. & I. R. R., r. 30 S. Mississippi.

Jones John W., (J. & Hess) bds. 432 N. Delaware.

Jones John W., teamster, r. 412 S. West.

Jones John W. (col'd) barbershop, 16 S. Meridian, r. same.

Jones Julius, (Gilkey & J.) bds. Palmer House.

Jones L., mail agent, I. C. & L. R. R., r. 295 Massachusetts av.

Jones Lewis, druggist, 48 N. Pennsylvania, r. 231 N. East.

Jones L. W., traveler, Kimble, Aikman & Co., bds. Sherman House.

Jones Marshall, (col'd) teamster, r. 454 S. Tennessee.

Jones Richardson, lab., r. 57 S. Pennsylvania.

Jones Robert A., stairbuilder, 232 N. Winston, r. 299 N. Winston.

Jones R. L. (col'd, J. & Stewart) r. North, bet. California and West.

Jones Sillivan, (col'd) lab., r. 170 W. Georgia.

Jones Spicer, farmer, r. 126 N. Tennessee.

Jones Thomas, cooper, r. 45 Hellen.

Jones Thomas, (col'd) lab., bds. 198 S. Illinois.

Jones Thomas E. (J. & Pickerill) r. 77 Jackson.

Jones Wm. (col'd) barber, r. 141 W. Washington.

Jones Wm. (col'd) lab., r. cor. Blake and Rhode Island.

Jones Willis D. (Davis & J.) r. 74 Plum.

Jones Wm. H. (Coburn & J.) r. 278 N. Illinois.

Jones Wm. M., grain merchant, r. 199 Jackson.

Jones Wm. T., clk., r. 310 Blake.

Jones W. W. (Davis & J.) r. 70 N. East.

Jones W. T., works Osgood, Smith & Co., r. 35 Fletcher av.

Jones & Hasselman, (John W. Jones and Otto H. Hasselman) merchandise brokers, 30 S. Meridian.

JONES & PICKERILL, (T. E. J. & S. J. P.) grocery and produce dealers, cor. Cherry and Broadway.

Jones & Stewart, (col'd B. L. Jones and George Stewart) barbers and hair dressers, 29 N. Illinois.

JORDAN ELLA Miss, dressmaker, r. 186½ W. Washington.

Jordan Emma Miss, teacher Fourth Ward School, bds. 186 N. Tennessee.

Jordan Gilbert, r. 186 N. Tennessee.

Jordan Harry, clk. r. 308 E. New York.

Jordan John, groceries and provisions, 158 W. Washington, r. 172 N. Mississippi.

JORDAN LEWIS, attorney, 1 and 2 Talbott & New's blk., r. 352 N. Meridian.

Jordan Phineas, clk., r. 308 E. New York.

Jordan P. G., clk. 76 W. Washington.

Jordan William, barber, r. Indiana av. bet. North and California.

Jordan William, barber, N. E. cor. E. Washington and Pennsylvania, r. 202 Indiana av.

Jose Albert, picture framemaker, r. 413 Virginia av.

Jose Nicholas, new and second hand furniture, 8 S. Pennsylvania, r. S. city limits.

Joselan Thomas, contracting agent C. & I. J. R. R., office 110 and 112 Virginia av.

Joseph George W. (Long & Joseph) r. 29 N. California.

Joseph Richard C., insurance agent, r. 29 N. California.

JOSSELYN A. K., (J. Bros. & Co.) r. 16 Indiana av.

Josselyn J. B., traveler Josselyn Bros. & Co., bds. 16 Indiana av.

Josselyn William, with Josselyn Bros. & Co., bds. 16 Indiana av.

JOSSELYN BROS. & CO. (A. K. Josselyn, & ——) dealers in the Singer Manufacturing Co.'s sewing machines, 74 W. Washington.

Joyce John, marbleworker, r. 333 James.

Joyce M., lab, r. cor. First and James.

Joyce Robert, foreman C. C. C. & I. R. R. yard, r. 121 N. Winston.

Jozlynn Charles D., carpenter, r. 21 Wright.

Judah J. M. (Hammond & J.) r. 203 N. Illinois.

Judd Frederick, carder Merritt & Coughlen, r. 253 N. Blake.

Judge James, lab., r. 47 Wyoming.

Judge Thomas, works rolling mill, r. 508 S. Illinois.

Judkins Lorenzo D., ferrotypist 16½ E. Washington, r. same.

Judson C. E., traveling salesman 27 and 29 E Maryland, r. 135 N. Illinois.

Judson Henry, r. 80 S. Mississippi.

Judson William, (J., Maguire & Co.) r. 152 N. Meridian.

JUDSON, MAGUIRE & CO., (Wm. Judson, Doug. Maguire and Wm. Gillespie) Indianapolis Coffee and Spice Mills, 51 E. Maryland.

Justice James, lab., r. rear 77 W. New York.

KADER JOHN, saloon, W. Indianapolis.

Kafader Joseph, stonecutter, r. 461 S. Illinois.

Kahn Abram, r. 282 S. Delaware.

Kahn Adolphus, (K. & Kaufman) r. 75 Kentucky av.

Kahn Casper, cabinetmaker, r. 392 E. Michigan.

Kahn Emille, clk. 174 E. Washington, r. 283 E. Market.

Kahn Isaac, (S. Kahn & Bros.) r. 139 N. Delaware.

Kahn Jacob, clk. No. 3 Palmer House, r. 193 N. East.

Kahn Leon, (Kahn & Bros.) r. 133 N. East.

Kahn Leon, with S. Kahn & Bros., r. 164 N. East.

Kahn Lyon, Sherman House clothing store, 24 W. Louisiana, bds. Oriental House.

Kahn S. (S. Kahn & Bros.) r. 139 E. Ohio.

Kahn S. (K. & Bros.) r. 283 E. Market.

Kahn S. & Bros. (S. Kahn and I. Kahn) dealers in dry goods and notions, 45 and 47 E Washington.

Kahn S. & Bros. (S. K. and L. K.) dry goods and notions, 174 E. Washington.

KAHN & KAUFMAN, (Adolpous Kahn and Bernhard Kaufman) clothiers, 71 and 133 S. Illinois.

Kaiser Jacob, miller, r. 327 S. Pennsylvania.

Kalb Frederick, grocer, 310 N. Winston, r. same.

Kalb Henry, lamplighter, r. 164 E. St. Joseph.

Kalb John, tinsmith, 164 E. St. Joseph.

Kallmeier Henry, lab. r. 249 S. Alabama.

Kanam Gottlieb, teamster, r. 505 S. New Jersey.

Kane Dennis, blacksmith, r. 400 E. Georgia.

Kane Samuel, carpenter, r. 142 Stevenson.

BENHAM BRO'S,

36 E. Washington St,

AGENTS FOR THE

INDIANAPOLIS MANUFACTURING CO.'S

PIANOS.

Kantman Mathias, well digger, r. 236 Massachusetts av.

Kapper Frederick, carpenter, r. 23 Hahn.

Kappes J. H. & Co., pianomakers, 210 to 216 S. Illinois.

Kappes J. H. (E. C. Atkins & Co.) r. 123 E. North.

Kappes Anthoney, shoemaker, bds. Emmenegger's Hotel.

Kares Joseph, carpenter, r. 113 N. Davidson.

Karle Christian, dealer in boots and shoes, 83 E. Washington, r. 72 S. Delaware.

Karle Christian J., blacksmith, bds. cor. East and Ohio.

Karle J. J., shoemaker, 301 E. Washington, r. same.

Karney John, plumber, gas and steam fitter, 78 Virginia av., r. 307 S. Delaware.

Karras Joseph, carpenter, I. C. & L. R. R. Shops, r. 113 Davidson.

Kasser John, shoemaker, bds. 578 E. Market.

Kasberg Peter, moulder, r. 71 Hosbrook.

Kassabaum Casper, ale bottler V. Meir & Bros., r. 592 E. St. Clair.

Kassabaum Frederick, lab., r. 592 E. St. Clair.

Kassell Margret, (wid. Nicholas) r. Michigan road N. First.

Kassel Nichols, lab., r. West, N. of First.

Kassler Frederick, groceries and provisions, cor. Massachusetts av. and Plum, r. same.

Kastle, Rose, (wid. Jacob) bakery and confectionary, 170 West Washington, r. same.

Kaufman Aaron, (A. & S. K.) r. 389 N. Pennsylvania.

Kaufman A. F., collarmaker, 76 S. Delaware, r. same.

Kaufman A. & S., whol. liquor dealers, 116 S. Delaware.

Kaufman B., (Kahn & K.) r. 23 Madison av.

KUAFMAN CHARLES, whol. liquor dealer, 23 W. Maryland, r. 355 N. Pennsylvania.

KAUFMAN CHARLES, manufacturer and dealer in showcases &c., 11 N. Delaware, r. same.

Kaufman Caroline Mrs., r. 261 E. Market.

H. H. LEE

Makes a Specialty of

CHOICE GOLDEN RIO,

AND

OLD GOVERNMENT JAVA COFFEES.

Kaufman John, pastor Evangelical Church (German) r. Wabash bet. E. and New Jersey.

Kaufman Louis, meatmarket, 82 Virginia av., r. 160 High.

KAUFMAN MORITZ, meat market, cor. North and West, r. same.

Kaufman Moses, whol. liquor dealer, 42 W. Lousiana, v. 119 N. Illinois.

Kaufman S., r. N. Pennsylvania cor. Fifth.

Kaufman S. (wid) r. 261 E. Market.

Kaufman Simon, clk. Charles Haufman, r. 201 N. Liberty.

Kaufman Solomon, (A. & S. K.) r. N. Pennsylvania near city limits.

Kaum Gotleib, clk. William Smith, r. 505 S. New Jersey.

Kavanah Mathews works Osgood, Smith & Co., r. 55 Eddy.

Kay Hannah, (wid. Joseph) r. cor. Missouri and Walnut.

Kay Robert, stonecutter, r. 376 N. East.

Kayler Frank, teamster, r. 136 N. Noble.

Kayler Louisa, (wid.) r. 156 E. St. Joseph.

Kearsting Robert, barkeeper, 15 N. Pennsylvania, r. 16 S. Pennsylvania.

Keating Jeffery, lab., r. 207 High.

Keating John, teamster, 24 W. Maryland, r. 79 S. West.

Keating Joseph J., organist St. John's Cathedral, r. 90 S. Illinis.

Keating L. W. Mrs., teacher, r. 250 Dougherty.

Keating Thomas, lab., r. 77 W. McCarty.

Keay George, clk., W. C. Newcomb, r. 378 N. East.

Keay William F., clk., U. S. Arsenal.

Keef John, railroader, r. 43 Harrison.

Keef Mary, domestic, Bates House.

Keefe Arthur, lab., r. 308 S. Tennessee.

Keehn Mary Miss, teacher Fourth Ward School, bds. 204 N. Illinois.

Keely Henry S., brickmason, r. 308 E. Ohio.

Keely Lou Mrs., r. 322 E. Washington.

Keely Oliver, brickmason, r. 501 E. Ohio.

Keely William, r. 158 E. Michigan.

Keely Wm. H., bricklayer, r. 163 E. Ohio.

Keen Lawrence, shoemaker, 167 Virginia av., r. 175 S. New Jersey.

Keenan James, clk., r. 100 S. Noble.

Keenan John, lab., r. 108 S. Noble.

Keenan Margaret, (wid.) r. 105 S. Noble.

Keers Samuel, lab., works Hoosier State mills, r. 25 Blake.

Keers Wm. J., cooper, r. Minerva west end St. Clair.

Kees Hiram W., engineer, I. C. & L. R. Rz, r. 167 S. Noble.

Keesee George, lab., r. New York bet. Blake and Minerva.

Kegan Hubert, plasterer, r. 49 Bradshaw

Kehr Charles, baker, bds. 191 N. Noble

Keifer A. (K. & Vinton) r. 483 N. Illinois.

Keifer Jacob, machinist, works Sinker & Co., r. 177 Union.

Keifer Peter, bakery, 255 Indiana av., r. same.

Keifer Philip, jr., baker, r. 255 Indiana av.

Keifer & Vinton, (A. K. and A. E. V.) wholesale druggists, 68 S. Meridian.

Keis H. W., engineer, I. C. & L. R, R.

Keiser Catherine Mrs. r. 73 Massachusetts av.

Keiser Charles, cigarmaker, r. 61 Russell.

Keiser Charles, meat market, W. Fourth bet. Tennessee and Mississippi, r. same.

Keiser Geo., plumber, bds. 152 N. Blake.

Keiser John, machinist, r. 23 Kentucky av.

Keker John, carpenter, r. Morris, S. city limits.

Kelcher James, boot and shoemaker, r 20 Douglass.

Kelemjer Henry, lab., P. C. & St. L. freight depot, r. 249 S. Alabama.

Keller Daniel, stonemason, r. 466 S. East.

Keller Henry, lab., r. 110 E. St. Mary.

Keller P., cabinetmaker, 62 N. Pennsylvania, r. same.

Keller Robert F. H., salesman 29 W. Washington, r. 50 N. East.

Keller Zac. P., engineer C. C. & I. C. R. R., r. 202 Meek.

KELLISCH MARTIN, proprietor Bates House Meat Market, r. 110 Madison av.

Kellemeyer Henry, lab., r. 249 S. Alabama.

Kelley Andrew, printer, News office, bds. 24 Buchanan.

Kelley Anthony, tailor, r. 84 W. South.

Kelley B. G. (Gates, Prey & Co.) r. Morgan county.

Kelley Cornelius, switchman T. H. & I. R. R., r. 240 S. Missouri.

Kelley Elijah, (col'd) carpenter, r. 387 Elizabeth.

Kelley Hugh, porter at New York Store, r. 20 N. Cahfornia.

Kelley Jenette, (wid. James) r. 153 W. South.

Kelley John I., works pork house, r. 290 W. Washington.

Kelley Katie, servant Sherman House.

Kelley Michael, lab., r. 280 S. Missouri.

Kelley Patrick, lab., r. 243 Kentucky av.

Kelley Theresa Miss, servant Spencer House.

Kellogg Amos V., engineer C. C. & I. C. R. R., r. 377 E. Georgia.

Kellogg Newton, edge tool manufacturer, 411 W. Washington, r. 47 N. West.

Kelly ——, lab., r. 2 Dougherty.

Kelly Catherin Mrs., r. 24 Buchanan.

Kelly Cornelius, carriage painter, r. 140 Massachusetts av.

Kelly Daniel, fireman C. C. C. & I. R. W.

Kelly Hugh, clk. 18 W. Pearl, r. 216 E. Washington.

Kelly John B., painter, r. 19 Cherry.

Kelly John R., machinist Eagle Machine Works, bds. Ray House.

Kelly M. Mrs., dressmaker, 41 N. Tennessee, r. same.

KELLY P., merchant tailor, 46 S. Illinois, r. same.

Kelly P. H., drug clk. W. W. Butterfield, bds. 437 N. Tennessee.

Kelly R. H., Evening News, r. 483 N. Meridian.

Kelly William R., works Osgood, Smith & Co., r. 13 Willard.

Kelsey J. M., student, bds. 64 S. Illinois.

Kemp Armsted, (col'd) lab. r. 179 Indiana av.

Kemper John, carpenter, r. 192 S. New Jersey.

Kempker Charles, (Brinkmeyer & Co.) r. 190 N. East.

Kendall John McD., printer, r. 41 Grant.

Kendrick Ellen, (wid. Edward) r. 123 Maple.

KENDRICK WM. H., physician and surgeon, 73 N. East, r. same.

Keneally Dennis, carpenter, r. 85 W. McCarty.

Keneaster N. D., r. 560 N. Illinois.

Kenedy Michael, baggageman T. H. & I. R. R.

Kenkler Henry, baggageman, bds. California House.

Kennedy Dan, moulder, r. 163 High.

Kennedy Daniel, blacksmith, r. 163 High.

Kennedy Frank, (K., Byram & Co.) r. 247 N. Meridian.

Kennedy James, helper C. C. C. & I. R. R.

Kennedy John, boilermaker, r. 235 W. South.

Kennedy John M., street contractor, r. 292 S. Illinois.

Kennedy Maggie Miss, bds.292 S. Illinois.

Kennedy Patrick, lab., r. 151 S. Alabama,

Kennedy Samuel, carpenter, r. 172 Buchanan.

Kennedy Sarah, (wid.) r. 235 W. South.

Kennedy Thomas, lab., r. 179 E. South.

Kennedy Wm. T., signpainter, 18 S. Meridian, bds. 30 N. New Jersey.

Kenney Cornelius, lab., r. 270 W. St. Clair.

Kenny Michael, lab., r. 47 Elizabeth.

Kenney Thomas, cutter, G. H. Heitkam, r. 58 S. West.

Kennington John, r. 272 S. Alabama.

Kennington Robert, blacksmith, r. 325 S. Pennsylvania.

Kens Jacob, lab., r. 483 S. New Jersey.

Kensal George, grocery and produce, cor. McCarty and West, r. same.

Kensler Maria Mrs. (wid. William) r. Michigan rd., cor. Tinker.

Kensler Patrick, railroader, r. 86 Indiana av.

Kentemeir Charles, carpenter, r. 317 E. Market.

Kenton James, blacksmith, r. 41 Ellen.

Kentzel Joseph, printer, Commercial Office, r. 50 Elsworth.

Kepper, Christian, lab., r. 176 N. Winston.

Kepple Henry, heater, Rolling Mill, r. 272 S. Illinois.

Kepple John, (Hildebrand & K.) r. Morgantown, Ind.

Kepple Josiah, works Rolling Mill, r. 270 S. Tennessee.

Kepple Martin, eating house, 36 W. Louisiana, r. same.

Kercheval Wm. J., bookkeeper, Jas. T. Layman & Co., bds. 289 N. New Jersey.

Kerfoot John B., clk. 17 W. Washington, bds. 202 N. West.

Kerfoot L. B., salesman G. H. Heitkam, r. 164 S. New Jersey.

Kerfoot R. A., clk. Smith & Foster's, r. 216 N. Delaware.

Kerk D. A., turner, r. 131 Meek.

Kerkhoff Anton, lab., r. 143 N. Davidson.

Kern ——, tailor, r. 328 S. Delaware.

Kern Casper, cabinetmaker, r. 392 E. Michigan.

Kern Jacob, porter Post Office, r. 288 E. Michigan.

Kern Louis, clk. Post Office, r. 27 S. Delaware.

THE CHINA TEA STORES

Have the NAME of being the

MOST ATTRACTIVE STORES IN THE WEST.

No. 7 Odd Fellows Hall

AND

ACADEMY OF MUSIC CORNER.

Kerns Mary, (wid. James) r. 32 Douglass.

Kerper Charles, r. 73 W. Maryland.

Kerper Elizabeth Mrs. boarding house, 73 W. Maryland.

Kerper James, checkman P. C. & St. L. Freight Depot, bds. 73 W. Maryland

Kerper James B., works C. C. & I. C. Depot, bds. 73 W. Maryland.

Kerr George, painter, Shaw, Lippencott & Conner, r. 35 W. Georgia.

Kerr H. A., pastor Third Christian Church, r. 268 N. Blake.

Kersch John, works Osgood, Smith & Co., r. 144 Union.

Kersey Precilla Miss, dressmaker at Boston Store, r. 372 E. New York.

Kershaw Joshua, bookkeeper, 42 W. Louisiana, bds. Sherman House.

Kerz Nicholas, works A. Wiegand, bds. same.

Ketcham Jane, (wid. John L.) r. 165 Merrill.

Ketcham William A. (Newcomb, Mitchell & K.) r. se. cor. Alabama and Merrill.

Kettenbach Edward, (K., Newmeyer & Co.) r. 279 Massachusetts av.

Kettenbach Elizabeth, (wid. Henry) r 279 Massachusetts av.

Kettenbach Henry C., traveling agent, bds. 279 Massachusetts av.

Kettenbach William F., (K., Newmeyer & Co.) r. 279 Massachusetts av.

KETTENBACH, NEWMYER & CO., (Edward K., J. A. N. and W. S. Kettenbach) groceries, provisions and dry goods, 273 and 277 Massachusetts av.

Kettinghorn John T., salesman, r. 241 Virginia av.

Kettler G. H., varnisher, 286 E. Louisiana.

Kettler John H., varnisher, r. 286 E. Lousiana.

Kevere John H., dealer in groceries and provisions 525 N. Mississippi, r. same.

Kiasel John, baker, works 178 S. Illinois, bds. same.

Kiefer Jacob, machinist, r. 177 Union.

Kiefer L. A (Kiefer & Son) r. 463 N. Delaware.

Kiefer L. F. (Kiefer & Son) r. 463 N. Delaware.

Kiefer L. F. & Son, clock and watchmakers, 2 Odd Fellows Hall.

Kiel Caroline Miss, clk. A. Ball, 178 S. Illinois, bds. same.

Kiel Conrad, lab., r. 353 E. New York.

Kiel Henry, carpenter, r. 275 N. Noble.

Kiemeyer William, cigarmaker, 35 W. Washington, bds. 113 E. Washington.

Kiley Daniel, engineer, r. 106 Spring.

Kiley James T., picture dealer, 124 N. East, r. same.

Killay Mat., lab., r. 155 Meek.

Kilgore J. D., dentist, 70 N. Illinois, Miller's blk. r. same.

Kilgore J. W., shoemaker, 64 S. Delaware.

Killinger, John G., carpenter, 328 E. Market, r. same.

KIMBALL EBEN W., attorney at law, notary public, U. S. commissioner, office 46 E. Washington, r. 387 N. Meridian.

Kimball George H., flaskmaker, r. 61 Russell.

Kimball James N., deputy treasurer of State, r. 475 N. Illinois.

KIMBALL NATHAN, Treasurer of State, office in State bldg., r. 475 N. Illinois.

KIMBLE, AIKMAN & CO. (T. V. K., J. B. A. and D. J. Still) whol. dealers in hardware, cutlery, etc., 110 S. Meridian.

Kimble Thomas V. (K., Aikman & Co.) r. 275 Indiana av.

Kimble Wm., lab., r. se. cor. Sixth and Tennessee.

Kinan Augustus, car inspector, Junction Depot, r. 130 N. East.

Kinchen Amanda, (wid. Sinco) r. 44 Harrison.

Kindel Jos., cabinetmaker, r. 150 Winston.

Kindel Joseph, with B. F. Hetherington & Co., r. 19 Madison av.

Kindel Joseph, cabinetmaker, r. 150 E. New York.

Kinder C., locksmith and bellhanger, 60 N. Pennsylvania, r. 215 N. Noble.

Kinder M. W. (wid.) r. 27 Lockerbie.

Kindler Charles, locksmith, r. 215 N. Noble.

King Christian, carpenter Eagle Machine Works, r. 123 E. McCarty.

King Cornelius, lumber yard E. St. Clair, nr. Pern railroad, r. Western av. nr. Butler.

King David, lab., bds. 9 Sharp.

King David, ice dealer, r. 261 N. Mississippi.

King E., blacksmith, 73 Huron.

King Edward, sec'y and treas. I. & St. L. R. R., r. National road.

King Ernest, night watchman, r. 503 N. Illinois.

King George, carpenter, r. 272 E. St. Clair.

King Ham, lab. rolling mill, bds. Illinois House.

King Ira S. Dr., office 13 S. Mississippi, r. same.

King Isaac, blacksmith, r. 73 Huron.

King Jacob, machinist, r. 18 W. Georgia.

KING JACOB, (Vater & K.) r. 493 S. Tennessee.

King James, shoemaker, 105 Indiana av., r. 111 Indiana av.

King James M., deputy U. S. Revenue Collector, r. 214 Davidson.

King Johanna, servant Palmer House.

King John, boarding house, 35 Circle.

King John, salesman, bds. 510 E. Washington.

King John W., traveling agent Geisendorff & Co., bds. 35 Circle.

King Lavina Miss, dressmaker, bds. 250 S. Meridian.

King Lillie, teacher Fifth Ward School, bds. 296 S. Meridian.

King Mary Miss, clk. W. Haerle, bds. 111 Indiana av.

King Ottie, teacher Fourth Ward School, bds. 296 S. Meridian.

King Rose Miss, teacher, bds. cor. Alabama and Merrill.

King Thomas, lab., bds. 9 Sharpe.

King Thomas, lab., bds. 172 S. Mississippi.

King Vina, dressmaker, bds. 296 S. Meridian.

Kingan T. D. (Kingan & Co.) bds. Bates House.

KINGAN & Co., (T. D. Kingan and Samuel Kingan) Pork Packers and Commission Merchants, W. terminus Maryland.

Kingan Joseph, broommaker, r. 253 Massachusetts av.

Kingan John A., student, r. 253 Massachusetts av.

Kingman Frank, clk. J. Layman & Co., r. 510 N. Delaware.

Kingman Nelson, bookkeeper D. Root & Co., r. 510 N. Delaware.

Kingsbery John E., clockmaker, r. 227 Massachusetts av.

Kingsbury A. M. (K. & Co.) r. 14 Indiana av.

Kingsbury G. M., clk. 47 S. Illinois, bds. 14 Indiana av.

KINGSBURY & Co., manufacturers and commission dealers in boots and shoes, 47 S. Illinois.

Kingston Samuel, painter, r. 231 S. Mississippi.

Kinister Henry W., cigar maker, works 138 S. Illinois.

12

Kinkler Henry, works baggage room depot, bds. California House.

Kinley Samuel, lab., 380 S. Missouri.

Kinney Michael, lab., bds. 174 Meek.

Kinney Walter, lab., r. 486 E. Georgia.

Kinsey Martha Miss, seamstress, r. 311 W. Market.

Kinsley William, carriage liner, Shaw, Lippencott & Conner, bds. 85 W. Georgia.

Kinston Paul, clk., bds. Pyle House.

Kipp Albert, salesman, 29 W. Washington, bds. 113 E. Washington.

Kirby James H., plasterer, r. 635 N. Illinois.

Kirby H. W., salesman, 62 S. Meridian, bds. Sherman House.

Kirby William L., salesman, 131 S. Meridian, bds. Sherman House.

Kirch Jacob, brakesman, bds. Decatur House.

Kirchner, Fred., farmer, r. 311 S. Pennsylvania.

Kirchof Herman, lab., r. 33 Oriental.

Kirk Daniel, turner, Speigel, Thoms & Co., r. 181 Meek.

Kirk E. Mrs., millinery, 73 N. Pennsylvania, r. same.

Kirk N., r. 73 N. Pennsylvania.

Kirkhoff Andrew, lab., Bunte & Dickson, r. E. New York.

Kirkhoff Charles, drayman, r. 25 Coburn.

KIRKPATRIC JOHN, physician, 35 W. Market, r. 204 N. Illinois.

Kirkpatrick Samuel, lab. r. 223 W. Washington.

Kirland Patrick, r. 900 N. Tennessee.

Kirlin James, grocer at Traders Point, r. 526 N. Illinois.

Kirsey Oliver, carpenter, r. 240 Union.

Kirshner Fred., salesman, 125 S. Meridian, r. 311 S. Pennsylvania.

Kise John W., works, Aldrich & Gay, r. 336 N. West.

Kiser George, plumber, bds. 152 Blake.

KISSEL FREDERICK, saloon, cor. McCarty and Russell, r. same.

Kissel Harriet Mrs, (wid.) r. 400 S. Tennessee.

Kissell Jacob W., barkeeper, r. 22 S. West.

Kissinger Charles M., house and sign painter, r. 112 S. Meridian.

KISTNER ADAM, proprietor California House, 184 S. Illinois.

THE CHINA TEA STORES
ARE LOCATED AT
No. 7 ODD FELLOWS HALL
AND
ACADEMY OF MUSIC CORNER.

SAME GOODS, SAME PRICES at BOTH.

Kistner F., painter, bds. 336 S. Meridian.
Kistner John, boot and shoe manufacturer, 83 S. Illinois, r. 336 S. Meridian.
KITCHEN J. M., physician, Vinton's blk., r. 145 N. Pennsylvania.
Kitzmiller William, carpenter, r. 244 W. Washington.
Klafter Henry, tailor, with Becker & Huber, bds. 52 E. Harrison.
Klanke Wilhelm, painter, r. 292 S. East.
Klare F. (K. & Schroeder) r. 576 S. Meridian.
KLARE & SCHROEDER, (Fred K. & Wm. S.) saloon and bowling alley, 588 S. Meridian.
Klass John, tailor, bds California house.
Kleiber John, cooper, r. 77 S. East.
Kleiber Louis, confectioner, r. 143 E. Washington.
Klein Charles, cigarmaker, 35 W. Washington, bds. 113 E. Washington.
Klein Frederick, engineer I. C. & L. R. R., r. 360 E. Georgia.
Klein Joseph, stove and tin merchant, r. 295 S. New Jersey.
KLEIN J. G., barber and hair dresser, 2 Martindale's blk. N. Pennsylvania, r. cor. Third and Missouri.
Kleins Peter, planer, r. S. East.
Kleinsmidt Christian, street sprinkler, r. 284 E. Market.
Kleis Fritz, lab., r. 483 E. Georgia.
Klepfer Andrew J., meat market, 313 Massachusetts av., r. same.
Kletsch Mary A. Miss, weaver at Glesendorff's, bds 408 W. Washinhton.
Klies Henry, fireman Peru R. R., r. 526 E. Georgia.
Kline ——, painter, r. 234 S. Missouri.
Kline Frederick, engineer I. C. & L. R. R.
Kline Frederick, glassblower, r. 522 S. Meridian.
Kline George W., machinist, r. 405 S. Meridian.
Kline Henry, shoemaker, r. 361 Spring.
Kline Henry, (col'd) woodsawyer, r. 434 N. East.
Kline Joseph, (I. L. Franken & Co.) r. 295 S. New Jersey.
Kline Nicholas, boot and shoe manufacturer, 283 Massachusetts av., r. 361 Spring.

Kline W. W., lawyer, bds. 179 S. Meridians.
Klines William, cooper, r. 49 Hellen.
Kling C. Mrs., r. 283 S. East.
Klingensmith Israel, (K. & Hines) r. 478 N. Tennessee.
Klingensmith Jacob, patentright agent, r. 478 N. Tennessee.
KLINGENSMITH & HINES, (Israel K. and J. L. H.) attorneys at law, 115½ E. Washington.
Klodle Dora, (wid. Sebastian) r. 264 Massachusetts av.
Klug G. A., machinist, bds. California House.
Klumpp Frederick, brewer, r. 202 W. Maryland.
Klusmann Fred., carriagesmith Shaw, Lippincott & C., r. 123 St. Mary.
Knapp Albert, printer, bds. 50 Ellsworth.
Knapp Carrie Miss, bds. 19 Henry.
Knapp F. C., job printer 30 S. Meridian, r. 182 Peru railroad.
Knapp Gardner, r. 50 Ellsworth, cor. Vermont.
Knarzer George, saloon keeper 60 S. Delaware, r. same.
Knarzer Phillip, barkeeper, bds. 60 S. Delaware.
Knass Wm. J., lab., r. 297 E. New York.
Knauf Adam, bakery, 257 Massachusetts av., r. same.
Knearim Henry, painter, 272 Winston.
Kneffer Charles, bookkeeper Hays, Rosenthal & Co., bds. 18 W. Circle.
Kneffer Fred, (Hanna & K.) r. 466 N. Pennsylvania.
Kneip Jno., cabinetmaker, r. 294 N. Liberty.
Knifen Nicholas, lab., r. 688 N. Illinois.
Knight C. W., brickmason, r. 107 Forest av.
Knight E., r. 107 Forest av.
Knight John, painter, r. 294 N. Liberty.
Knight John, engineer Vincennes R. R., bds. 61 S. Noble.
Knight John, coppersmith, r. 304 N. Delaware.
Knight Newton J., painter, r. 666 N. Tennessee.
Knighton Charles J., mechanic, r. 781 N. Illinois.
Knippenberg H. (E. C. Atkins & Co.) r. 497 N. Meridian.
Knippenberg Jacob, salesman New York Store, bds. 158 N. New Jersey.
KNODLE ADAM, r. 8 Indiana av.
Knodle George, r. 80 W. Ohio.
Knoll Samuel, (col'd) lab., r. 43 Douglass al.
Knotts Nim. K., house, sign and wagon painter, 32 S. New Jersey, r. 143 Michigan rd.

Knowles Harvey, messenger American Express Company, bds. Spencer House.

Knowlton George, clk., r. 240 S. Alabama.

Knox Francis (col'd., wid. George) r. 311 E. St. Clair.

Knox Joseph A., works Paper Mill, r. 7 Geisendorff.

Knox Thomas, (col'd) barber, r. Howard, bet. Second and Third.

Koble Elizabeth, (wid. Jacob) r. Minerva, west end St. Clair.

Koch George, shoemaker, 271 Massachusetts av., bds. same.

Koch H. H., groceries, provisions, etc., 192 S. Noble. r. same.

Koch Simeon, wiper I. C. & L. R. R. shop.

Koch Thomas, works Jackson, Rider & Co.

Koch Thomas, lab., r. 16 Lockerbie.

Koch William, works Jackson, Rider & Co.

Koch William, clk., bds. cor. South and Noble.

Koehl Peter, groceries and produce, 188 S. Illinois, bds. 189 S. Illinois.

Koehler August, patent right dealer, bds. Globe House.

KOEHLER JOHN, groceries, feed store and saloon, 247 N. Noble, r. 244 N. Noble.

Koehler William, coffee stand, E. Market, r. 106 N. Davidson.

Koehne Charles, (H. Lieber & Co.) r. 467 N. Delaware.

Koehnen Peter, moulder, r. 238 Chestnut.

Koehring Charles, teamster, r. 93 Elm.

Koelblin Gottlieb, watchmaker, 7 W. Washington. bds. 23 Kentucky av.

Koenig M. C. F., r. 123 McCarty.

KOENIGER GEORGE, saloon and beer hall, 338 S. Meridian, r. same.

Koepper H. W., lab., starch factory.

Koepper John, lab., r. 278 Union.

Koerner Conrad, (C. K. & Co.) bds. Emeneger's Hotel.

Koerner Michael, saloon, 18 S. Delaware, r. same.

KOERNER C. & CO., commercial college and institute of modern languages, room 5 Ætna bldg., N. Pennsylvania.

Kohley John, blacksmith, r. 98 E. New York.

Kohlman Christina, (wid. Henry) r. 105 S. Meridian.

Kohner Acedreas, brewer Schmidt's brewery, r. Schmidt's brewery.

Kohnel John, carriagesmith, Shaw, Lippencott & Conner, r. cor. New York and Delaware.

Kohrar John, lab., r. 89 Elm.

Kolb Adam, huckster, bds. 177 Union.

KOLB LOUIS, plain and ornamental turner, 23 E. South, r. 17 E. South.

Kolb Phillipp, r. 127 E. St. Mary.

Kolb William, clk., 10 Louisiana, r. same.

KOLB WILLIAM, boarding house, 23 Kentucky av.

Kolitzer Fred., lab., P. C. & St. L. freight depot.

Koller Charles, lab., r. Arsenal rd.

Kolthop Fred, machinist, r. 56 Union.

Koluschke George, brewer, r. 370 S. Delaware.

Konitzer Henry, drayman, r. 197 Harrison.

Koontz George W., dealer in patent beehives and bees, bds. 52 N. Pennsylvania.

Kopper Christopher, porter, 23 S. Meridian, r. 176 N. Winston.

Korn Martin, painter, r. 32 S. Alabama.

Kort Frederick, lab., cotton mill, r. 373 W. Michigan.

Kortletzky Henrich, cabinetmaker, r. 181 Madison av.

Kortpeter Henry, salesman, r. 162 Buchanan.

Kortpeter William, tailor, r. 400 S. East.

Koser A. M. Mrs., midwife, r. 255 S. Pennsylvania.

Koser John, locksmith, 18 Virginia av., r. 255 S. Pennsylvania.

Koser Michael, r. 255 S. Pennsylvania.

Koshe Henry, cigarbox manufacturer, 187 E. Washington, r. same.

Koss Charles, salesman, 108 S. Meridian, bds. 23 W. Georgia.

Koss Louis, stonemason, r. 329 N. Davidson.

Koss W, stonemason, r. 329 N. Davidson.

Koster C. J. M., dealer in cigars and tobacco, 14 Indiana av., r. 181 Blake.

Koster Joseph, confectioner, r. 435 S. Illinois.

Kothe William, grocer, 130 N. Davidson, r. same.

Kowan Alexander, r. 300 E. St. Clair.

Kown Newton, teamster, r. 169 N. East.

Kown Wm., teamster, r. 169 N. East.

Krabber John, lab. r. 502 S. New Jersey.

Krabben John, lab. r. 402 S. New Jersey.

Kraft Henry, lab., r. Madison rd. South of city limits.

Kraft Louis, brewer, r. 417 S. East.

H. H. LEE'S

WHOLESALE PRICES FOR

TEAS, COFFEES & SUGARS,
ARE THE SAME EACH DAY

As are quoted in the

CINCINNATI DAILY PAPERS.

Kragg A., salesman, J. H. Baldwin & Co., bds 36 N. Pennsylvania.

Kragg Wm. A., (Holland, Ostermeyer & Co.) bds. 204 N. Illinois.

Kramer A., clk. Rosenthal & Co., r. 48 N. East.

Kramer Andrew, shoemaker, r. 199 N. Liberty.

Kramer Gottlieb, corporal United States Arsenal.

Kramer Henry, butcher, 80 Fort Wayne av., r. same.

Kramer Jacob, carriagesmith, r. 199 N. Liberty.

Kramer William, cabinetmaker, r. 333 S. East.

Kramer Wm., butcher, 319 Virginia av., r. same.

Kraus Frederick, lab., bds. 203½ E. Washington.

Kraus Christ., lab., r. 450 Indiana av.

Kraus Christian, lab., r. 514 E. Ohio.

Kraus William, machinist, r. Lock, opp. City Hospital.

Krause George, upholster, 71 and 73 W. Washington, bds. 456 Michigan.

Krause Reinhold, (K. & Riemenschneider) r. 456 E. Michigan.

Krause & Riemenschneider, stocking manufactory, 84 E. Washingnon.

Krauss Charles, assistant bookkeeper citizens bank, bds. 259 E. New York.

Krauss Christopher, works Jackson, Rider & Co.

Krauss Paul, messenger, Indianapolis National Bank, bds 259 E. New York.

Krauss William G., with Benham Bros., bds 259 E. New York.

Krautter John, lab., r. 377 E. Michigan.

Kregels Charles, agent Weed sewing machines, r. cor. Indiana av. and New York up stairs.

Kregelo David, undertaker, r. 223 N. West.

Kregelo Jacob, carpenter, 82 E. St. Clair.

Kreger Henry, foreman, Mooney & Co. r. 331 E. Georgia.

Kreger William, porter Mooney & Co.

Kreider Ruben G., traveling agent, r. 218 E. South.

Kreis Phillip, (Brand & K.) r. 327 S. Delaware.

Kreitzer ——, r. N. Tennessee bet. Fourth and Fifth.

Krentler Frederick, clk., Dessar Bro. & Co., r. 349 E. McCarty.

Krentler F. C., bds. California house.

KRETSCH PETER, dealer in cigars and tobacco, 141 S. Illinois, r. 325 S. Meridian.

Krieg Frederick, soldier U. S. Arsenal.

Krieger, Henry, lab., r. 331 E. Grorgia.

Krieger Wilham, porter, Mooney & Co., r. 454 S. Illinois.

Kriger Henry, brewer, works Harting & Bro., r. cor. S. Illinois and Norwood.

Krindle Samuel, conductor T. H. & I. R. R., r. 419 W. New York.

Kring John L., foreman, Byrkitt, r. 378 S. West.

Kring John L., joiner and stair builder, works cor. Tennessee and Georgia, r. 378 N. West.

Krome Augustus, teacher German Lutheran school, r. 280 E. Georgia.

Kronenberger John, musician, r. 269 W. Merrill.

Kronenberger William, musician, r. 143 E. Washington.

Kronia Fred., lab., r. 148 Huron.

Krouch George W., plasterer, r. 218 S. East.

Krug G. C. (K. & Buddenbaum) r. 67 S. Noble.

KRUG G. C. & CO., (Gottlieb C. K. and John A. Buddenbaum) grocers, 296 E. Georgia.

Kruger Chas., r. 276 E. Market.

Kruger Chas. H., tailor, r. 221 N. Noble.

Kruger Christ, grocer, r. 343 E. McCarty.

Kruger Fred., lab., r. 389 S. East.

Kruger Joseph, contractor, r. 267 E. Market.

Kruger Joseph E., gasfitter, r. 267 E. Market.

Krumholtz Lambert, carpenter Eagle Machine Works, r. 527 S. Illinois.

Kruse Christian, carpenter, r. 15 E. McCarty.

Kruse John, lab., r. 149 E. Washington.

Kuerst Henry, carpenter, r. 182 Madison av.

Kugalman William, r. 134 W. Maryland.

Kuhlenberg Barney, butcher, works 122 S. Meridian, r. same.

Kuhlman Ernest, grocer, 1 Buchanan, r. same.

Kuhlman Charles, piano finisher, r. 118 N. Noble.

Kuhlmann Conrad, Cabinetmakers' Union, bds. 386 N. Tennessee.

Kuhn A. M., salesman 131 S. Meridian, bds. Emenegger's Hotel.

Kuhn Charles, meatmarket, 207 W. Michigan, r. same.

Kuhn Ernst, watchman, Eagle Machine Works.

Kuhn Frederick, blacksmith, bds. 160 Ft.
Wayne av.
Kuhn John, blacksmith, 74 S. Pennsylvania, r. cor. New Jersey and Ft.
Wayne av.
Kuhn Philip, blacksmith, r. 160 Ft.
Wayne av.
Kuhn Phillip J., grocer and produce
dealer, cor. Ft. Wayne and St. Joseph,
r. same.
Kuhn Wm., proprietor Indiana bakery, r.
150 N. East.
Kuichler Louis, brewer, bds. 323 W.
Washington.
Kullsmann Louis, tailor, r. 123 E. St.
Mary.
Kumline George, lab., r. 18 Hosbrook.
Kun John, bartender, Sherman House.
Kune Thomas, lab., r. Nebraska nr. Madison rd.
Kunkel Charles, works city mills, r. 434
Virginia av.
Kunkle Henry, works Osgood, Smith &
Co., r. 289 S. Illinois.
Kunsman George, blower, glass works.
Kunz Herman, cabinetmaker, r. 276 E.
Washington.
Kunz Jacob, carpenter, r. 27 Lord.
Kunz M. A. Miss, millinery, 9 S. Delaware, r. same.
Kunz N. H. (K. & Richmond) bds. 9 S.
Alabama.
KUNZ & RICHMOND, (N. H. K.
and W. R.) stoves and tinware, 229
E. Washington.
Kurtz Lewis, clk., P. C. & St. L. freight
office, r. 396 N. Alabama.
Kuser Daniel, lab., r. 44 Dougherty.
Kyler John, engineer, I. B. & W. R. R.,
bds. 61 S. Noble.

L AATZ HENRY, blacksmith, Chandler
& Taylor.
LaBarre Louis moulder, r. 79 Elm.
Lack Henry, confectioner, bds. 81 E.
Washington.
Lack Rudolph, clk. Harrison's Bank, r.
22 W. St. Clair.
Lacy A. C., printer Journal Office, r. 117
N. West.
Laden Michael, lab., bds. 199 W. Maryland.
Ladow Abbie, (wid. Boswell) r. 35 Ellsworth.
Laduque Adolphus, painter, Bates House,
bds. same.
Lager William, deck hand, r. 556 N.
Alabama.
Lagg Daniel D., blower Glass Works,
bds. 164 W. Maryland.
Lagg Henry, blower Glass Works, bds.
164 W. Maryland.
Lagg William, blower Glass Works, bds.
164 W. Maryland.

Lake Ellis R., r. 565 S. Meridian.
Lahey Michael, shoemaker, r. 72 W.
Louisiana.
Lahla Ulrich, cigarmaker, 108 S. Illinois, bds. same.
Lahman Charles, carpenter, r. 555 E. St.
Clair.
Lahmann William, drayman Kuhn &
Bals, r. 541 S. Illinois.
Lahning Henry, lab., r. 85 Maple.
Lahr Martin, works South Side Livery
Stable, bds. 198 S. Illinois.
Lair Jacob, cooper, r. 140 S. Meridian.
Laird Charles P., insurance solicitor, r.
174 Virginia av.
Laird Emma W. Miss, teacher Fourth
Ward School, bds. 174 Virginia
av.
Laird Robert, r. 554 N. Illinois.
Laird Wm. H., bookkeeper Keifer &
Vinton, r. 554 N. Illinois.
Lake Ellis R., r. 565 S. Meridian.
Lake John, butcher, 22 N. Illinois, r. S.
city limits.
Lake Joseph P., carpenter, r. 131 Ind. av.
Lakin Edward, carpenter, bds. 432 E. St.
Clair.
Lakin Joseph, railroader, C. C. & I. C. R.
R., r. 68 S. Noble.
Lakin M. L., baggage master C. & I. J.
R. R., bds. 18 S. Pennsylvania.
Lally Thomas, tailor, r. 225 W. South.
Lamb Amos, salesman 75 S. Meridian,
r. 102 E. Pratt.
Lamb Margaret Miss chamber maid, California House.
Lamb Peter, lab., r. 253 S. Tennessee.
Lamb Samuel, State detective, r. 102 E.
Pratt.
Lamb William C., Librarian Supreme
Court, bds. 201 N. Illinois.
LAMBERT JAMES M., proprietor
Ray House, cor. South and Delaware,
r. same.
Lambert Joseph, lab. r. 373 W. Washington.
Lamme Edwin, student, bds. 335 N. East.
Lamotte Joseph, stoves and tinware, 102
Massachusetts av. r. same.
Lampman Frank D., clk. Bates House.
Lampman T. P., clk. Bates House.
Lampolt M. J., sawyer, Osgood, Smith &
Co., r. 35 Vinton.
Lanahan Thomas, lab., freight house, C.
& I. J. R. R., r. 2 Meek.

H. H. LEE

PURCHASES HIS

Teas, Coffees, Sugars & Spices
DIRECT FROM THE
Importers and Refineries,
THUS SAVING

HIS CUSTOMERS TWO OR THREE PROFITS.

Landauer N. J., general agent Seymour Woolen Mills, office 164 W. Washington, r. 11 Ft. Wayne av.

Landers, Conduit & Co. (F. L., B. C. and Milton Cox) whol. dealers in dry goods and notions, 95 and 97 S. Meridian.

Landers C. M. Rev., pastor Mayflower Church, r. 300 E. St. Clair.

Landers Franklin, (L., Conduit & Co.) r. 402 N. Pennsylvania.

Landers John, farmer, r. 382 N. East.

Landers John, messenger, Am. M. U. Express Co., r. 209 S. Illinois.

Landers June, (col'd) r. 141 W. Washington.

Landers Thomas, lab., r. 200 E. McCarty.

Landgrof Jacob, cutter, Moritz Bros., r. 44 Douglass.

Landis A. C. Mrs., matron, Institute for the Blind.

Landis Jacob, livery and boarding stables, 30 S. Pennsylvania, r. 310 N. Illinois.

Landis James, engineer, r. 153 N. Winston.

Landis C. C. Miss, teacher, Institute for the Blind.

Landis M. M., agent, White Line Transportation Co., r. 506 N. Meridian.

Landis William, (col'd) hostler, J. H. Caffey, r. 114 W. Washington.

Landman Joseph, upholsterer, bds. 89 S. Delaware.

Landon L. Mrs., seamstress, r. 42 Kentucky av.

Landrigan Michael, fireman, I. & V. R. R., r. 136 S. Noble.

Lane David H., medical student, bds. 139 N. Alabama.

Lane Edith, (col'd, wid. David) r. 23 Vine.

Lane Euriah, carpenter, r. 428 N. East.

Lane John, lab., r. 211 W. Maryland.

Lane John A., bailiff, bds. 428 N. East.

Lane Laure Miss, teacher, Fourth Ward School, bds. 216 N. West.

Lane William, conductor, I. B. & W. R. R., bds. Spencer House.

Lang C. F., lab. r. 77 W. Third.

Lang Daniel, (L. & Black) r. 543 N. Illinois.

Lang David, clk. St. Nicholas Saloon, r. 23 Bright.

Lang Frederick, r. 75 California.

Lang James, carpenter, r. 378 N. West.

Lang Joseph, shoemaker, r. Western av. cor. Butler.

LANG LOUIS, whol. and retail dealer in wines and bottled goods, 29 S. Meridian, r. 221 E. Ohio.

Lang Peter, lab., T. H. & I. R. R., r. 203 W. South.

Lang Samuel, tinner, Munson & Johnston, r. 23 N. Bright.

Lang Thomas F., r. 268 S. Illinois.

LANG & BLACK, (David L. and G. H. B.) carpenters and stair builders, shop 61 W. Pratt.

Langbein Joseph, variety store, 200 E. Washington, r. same.

Langdon Caroline Mrs., (wid. Lemuel C.) r. 235 Minerva.

Lange August, works Cabinet Maker's Union, bds. 292 S. East.

Langenberg H. H. & Co., (H. H. L, Aaron Rozier and F. Voight) groceries and provisions, 244 and 246 W. Washington.

Langenberg Henry, (H. H. L. & Co.) r. Bluff road outside city limits.

Langenberg W., clk. 3 E. Washington, bds. Bluff road S. of city.

Langford W. S. Rev., (col'd) r. 115 N. Davidson.

Langhorn T. A., telegrapher, P. C. & St. L. R. R., bds. National Hotel.

Langhorn W. A., telegrapher, P. C. & St. L. R. R., bds. National Hotel.

Langley S. D. C., clk. Ætna Insurance office, bds. Sherman house.

Langsdale Geo., bds. 225 E. Ohio.

Langsdale J. M. W., r. 225 E. Ohio.

Langsdale Thos contractor, r. 214 Huron.

LANGSENKAMP WILLIAM, coppersmith, 96 S. Delaware, r. 184 S. Delaware.

Lankford Annie M., (wid. Robert F.) r. 364 E. St. Clair.

Lannes David G., clk., r. 27 Chatham.

Lannis Mattie A. Miss, teacher, Ninth Ward School, r. 27 Chatham.

Lansmann Henry, clk., r. 382 E. Michigan.

Lappert Leopold, teacher, r. 170 E. South.

Laird Samuel P., works rolling mil bds. 77 W. McCarty.

Large Michael, pumpmaker, r. 332 Indiana av.

Larger Eugene, clk., Trade Palack, bds. Macy House.

Larger Jerome, brakeman, I. C. & L. R. R., bds. 58 Benton.

Larkin John, lab., r. 25 Ellen.

Larned Charles, patent right agent, r. 630 N. Illinois.

Larnerd J. A., asst. sup't, C. & I. J. R. R., office, 110 and 112 Virginia av. r. Connersville, Ind.

Larnerd James, lab., r. 32 Hellen.

Larry John, lab., r. 35 Wyoming.

Larsen Andrews, tailor, r. 173 E. Washington, up stairs.

Larsen Jens., tailor, r. 173 E. Washington.

LaRue J. S., painter, r. 429 E. St. Clair.

LaRue Willis, lab., r. 429 E. St. Clair.

LaRuff T. D., painter, Shaw, L. & C., r. 20 W. Georgia.

Lasley Catherine, (wid.) seamstress, r. over 325 E. Washington.

Latham Charles, teller Fletcher's Bank, bds. 614 E. Washington.

Latham G. A., clk., 52 N. Illinois, bds. 76 N. Mississippi.

LATHAM HENRY, Cashier, Indianapolis National Bank, r. 614 E. Washington.

Latham William H., teacher, Indiana Institution for Deaf and Dumb, r. 614 E. Washington.

Latshaw John F., real estate trader, r. 92 S. Mississippi.

Lauck William, filler, r. 391 S. Delaware.

Lauer Charles, saloonkeeper, r. 15 Russell.

LAUER CHARLES, prop'r Empire saloon and restaurant, 202 E. Washington, r. same.

Lauer Daniel, stonemason, r. 15 Russell.

Laughlin Albert, lab. Gates, Pray & Co., E. Market Square.

Laughlin Andrew, helper, C. C. C. & I railroad shops.

Laughlin Andrew, machinist, r. 306 N. Noble.

Laughlin Dennis, lab., r. 40 Ellen.

Laughlin Elizabeth, (wid. Timothy) r. 256 S. Tennessee.

Laughlin James, machinist, r. 306 N. Noble.

Laughlin James, helper C. C. C. & I. R. R. shops.

Laughlin John, moulder, bds. 256 S. Tennessee.

Laughlin Mary E. Miss, teacher Fourth Ward School, bds. 264 N. Tennessee.

Laughlin Sarah, (wid.) r. 306 N. Noble.

Laupheimer August, saloon, 139 S. Illinois, r. 472 N. Alabama.

Laute Henry, cabinetmaker, bds. 182 N. Noble.

Law Charles J., salesman Spiegel, Thoms & Co., r. 318 N. Liberty.

Law Stephen, carpenter, r. Fifth, bet. Mississippi and Lafayette railroad.

Lawbron Oliver P., lab., bds. 216 N. Winston.

Lawhorn Reuben, (col'd) r. 167 Indiana av.

Lawler Denis, servant Dr. Allen's.

Lawless & Curran, (M. L. and P. H. C.) grocers, 138 S. Noble.

BENHAM BRO'S,

36 East Washington St.,

PUBLISHERS OF

BENHAM'S MUSICAL REVIEW,

MONTHLY, $1.00 PER ANNUM.

Lawless Michael, (L. & Curran) r. 138 S. Noble.

Lawless Thomas, lab., r. 319 W. Merrill.

Lawrence Arthur V., groceries and produce, 173 W. Washington, r. 211 W. Ohio.

Lawrence James, (col'd) barber, Hill & Carter's.

Lawrence James H. (col'd) barber, bds. 441 S. Illinois.

Lawrence John, (col'd) barber, Hill & Carter's.

Lawrence John L., chairmaker, r. 297 W. Vermont.

Lawrence John W. (col'd) barber, bds. 441 S. Illinois.

Lawrence Malinda E. (col'd, wid. Thomas) r. 441 S. Illinois.

Lawrence M. L., sup't Central Transportation Sleeping Coach Co., bds. Depot Dining Hall.

Lawrence Thomas, clk., r. 39 Maple.

Laurie Wm., salesman New York Store, bds. 204 E. Market.

Lawson Milton T., lab., r. 216 N. Winston.

Lawton Charles A., traveling agent Erie Transportation Company, bds. Palmer House.

Lawton Henry W., clk. C. C. C. & I. R. R. Depot, bds. 201 N. Davidson.

Lawyer P. C. (L. & Hall) bds. Little Hotel.

Lawyer & Hall, (P. C. L. and E. R. H.) dealers in groceries, flour, flaxseed, etc., 49 S. New Jersey.

Lay William N., watchmaker, works 190 W. Washington, bds. same.

Laycock Charles, carpenter, r. 167 Eddy.

Layers Martin, watchman, r. 269 S. Pennsylvania.

Layman James T. (J. T. L. & —) r. 289 N. New Jersey.

Layman John, brewer, 326 S. Delaware.

Layman J. T. & Co. (J. T. L. & —) hardware and cutlery, 64 E. Washington.

Layton T. M., railroad conductor, r. 45 Virginia av.

Leach Eliza, (wid.) servant, 300 S. Meridian.

Leach James, salesman, r. Louisiana, bet. Alabama and New Jersey.

Leach Joshua, lab., T. H. & I. R. R., r. 279 W. Merrill.

THE CHINA TEA STORES

Are very handsomely decorated with

Accurate Views and Scenes

or

CHINESE LIFE AND SCENERY.

Call and see them before leaving the City.

Leady John, lab., r. 51 Wayoming.

Leahey Michael, shoemaker, works 135 S. Illinois, r. 272 W. Louisiana.

Leake W. H. (L. & Dickson) r. 75 N. Illinois.

Leake & Dickson, (W. H. Leake and Jas. B. Dickson) lessees Academy of Music and Metropolitan Hall.

Leaman Maggie Miss, bds. 139 W. Market.

Learkamp John, clk. 272 Winston, bds. same.

Leary Edward, lab., r. 42 Bicking.

Leary James, clk. 23 E. Washington.

Leary James, railroad lab., r. 82 Bates.

Leary P. C., attorney, 87½ E. Market.

LEATHERS W. W. attorney at law, 3 Odd Fellows Hall, r. 273 N. New Jersey.

Leauty Gustavus, gunsmith, 129 W. Washington, bds. Union Hall.

LeBarre Louis, moulder, r. 79 Elm.

Leck Rob. M., salesman, r. 480 N. Mississippi.

Lee Charles N., solicitor Indianapolis Insurance Co., r. 261 N. Davidson.

Lee George, (col'd) lab., r. 215 W. Ohio.

Lee Henry, wood turner, r. 88 Indiana av.

LEE H. H., druggist, 18 and 20 Bates House, r. 198 N. Illinois.

Lee James, (L. & Replogle) r. 190 Davidson.

Lee Kate Miss, bds. 51 Douglass al.

LEE M. G., editor Evening Commercial, r. 39 Ellsworth.

Lee William E., superintendent I. & St. L. Sleeping Coach Co., r. 173 S. Tennessee.

Lee & Replogle, (J. L. and J. R.) saloon, 346 E. Washington.

Leeds George, salesman, r. 256 N. Mississippi.

Lefever Samuel, street contractor, r. 145 W. South.

Legg George, farmer, r. 374 S. West.

Lehey Timothy, lab., r. 498 E. Goergia.

Lehr Ferdinand A., real estate agent, 83 E. Washington, r. 419 N. New Jersey.

Lehr Henry, carpenter, r. 347 E. New York.

Lehr Philip, grocer, cor. Noble and Massachusetts av., r. same.

Lehr Philip, blacksmith, r. 421 E. Vermont.

LEHRRITTER CONRAD, saloon keeper, 92 E. Washington, r. same.

LEHRRITTER GEORGE, saloon keeper, 143 E. Washington, r. same.

Lehrritter Henry C., bds. 172 N. New Jersey.

Lehrritter John A., clk. C. Sbroeder, r. 61 N. New Jersey.

Lehrritter Mathias, r. 172 N. New Jersey.

Leibhardt Joseph, dyer, Merritt & Coughler.

Leible Andrew, meat market, cor. Cherry and Plum, r. same.

Leible George, shoemaker, 204 E. Washington, r. 134 Spring.

Leibrick Louis, porter, Browning & Sloan, r. 330 W. North.

Leininger George, farmer, r. 129 N. Noble.

Leishman William, lab., r. 9 Peru.

Leistner William, machinist, bds. 223 W. Washington.

Lelewer David, (D. Lelewer & Bros.) r. 140 Virginia av.

Lelewer Isador, (D. Lelewer & Bros.) r. 184 Virginia av.

Lelewer D. & Bros., New York fur manufacturers and dealers in cloth caps and ladies' furs 56 S. Meridian.

Lemar ——, painter, r. N. Mississippi, bet. Second and Third.

Lemon A. E., clk. Indianapolis Fire Insurance Co., r. 68 N. Liberty.

Lemon Charles, fireman, r. 68 N. Liberty.

Lemon D. A., groceries and produce, 188 W. Washington, r. 46 N. Mississippi.

Lemon Peter H., attorney at Law, r. 68 N. Liberty.

Lemons William, bricklayer, r. 158 N. Winston.

Lenardy Michael, lab. r. 277 S. West.

Lendormi Desiree, (wid.) r. 434 E. North.

Lendormi Ernest, fireman, bds. 434 E. North.

Lendormi Joseph, fireman, C. C. C. & I. R. R, bds. 434 E. North.

Lendormi, P., policeman, r. 434 E. North.

Lennort S. E. Mrs., stamping and embroidery, 96 N. Pennsylvania, r. 34 S. Illinois.

Lenox E., merchant tailor, 20 N. Pennsylvania.

Lenox William, tailor, 68 E. Market, r. same.

Lentz J. G., varnishmaker, r. 110 Stevens.

Lentz William, porter, 78 S. Meridian, r. S. East.

Leonard Abbigail, (wid.) r. 183 N. Liberty.

Leonard E. Miss, waiter, Spencer House.

Leonard James D. (L. & Victor) bds. 229 S. Illinois.

Leonard John, machinist, Eagle Machine
Works, r. 118 W. Vermont.
Leonard Michael, groomsman, Gates, Pray
& Co., East Market square.
LEONARD & VICTOR, (J. D. L.
and J. V.) saloon, 65 W. Washington.
Leonhardt Herman, cooper, bds. 90 Union.
Leons T., lab., r. 370 S. Delaware.
Leppers Henry, plasterer, r. 55 Charles.
Leopard Enos B., engineer, C. C. & I. C.
R. R., r. 33 Meek.
Lepperd Leopold, tailor, 17 E. Washing-
ton, r. 161 E. South.
Leppert Nicholas, switchman, I. C. & L.
R. R. shops, r. 23 Lord.
Leser John, tailor, Treat & Claflin, r. 114
W. Georgia.
Lesh A. B., (S. Tousey & Co.) bds. 62 S.
Pennsylvania.
LESH, TOUSEY & CO. (A. B.
L. and M. J. T.) pork packers, pro-
duce and commission merchants 72
and 74 S. Delaware.
Lesman Simon, lab., r. 141 Huron.
Lestman August, stonemason, r. 75 Co-
burn.
Levell Anna Mrs., r. Dunlop E. of Madi-
son road.
Levette G. M., assistant State Geologist,
bds. 154 W. Maryland.
Levi Racheal Mrs., r. 83 W. South.
Levy Henry, second hand clothing, 199
E. Washington, r. same.
Lewark Joseph, fur dealer, 16 W. Pearl,
bds. Ballard house.
Lewelen Frank, tailor, 249 W. Michigan.
Lewey Edward, lab., r. 8 Willard.
Lewis A. M. Dr., cashier G. W. Despatch,
80 Virginia av., r. 526 N. Meridian.
Lewis Albert, (col'd) hostler county jail,
r. bet. First and Second, nr. Lafay-
ette Railroad.
Lewis Anderson, (col'd., Lewis & Dark)
r. 151 North.
Lewis Anson, (col'd) blacksmith, r. cor.
North and Minerva.
Lewis Belle Miss, servant, 172 N. West.
Lewis Charles, lab., r. African al. bet.
Sixth and Seventh.
Lewis Cyrus, (col'd) lab., r. 94 S. Mis-
souri.
Lewis C. S., clk., T. A. Lewis, bds 526 N.
Meridian.
Lewis Edward, r. 85 N. Missouri.
Lewis Edward, works rolling mill, bds.
272 S. Tennessee.
Lewis George H., physician, office cor.
Liberty and Washington, r. 359 E.
Market.
Lewis James, lab., r. 106 Spring.
Lewis James F., lab., r. 104 Spring.
Lewis John, (col'd) cook Bates House.
Lewis John H., teamster and lumber
dealer, r. 485 S. Meridian.

13

BENHAM BRO'S,

36 East Washington St.,

Pianos, Organs and Melodeons Tuned,
Moved and Repaired.

Lewis J. R., moulder, 71 S. Pennsylva-
nia, bds. Stanridge House.
Lewis Minnie, (wid.) r. 83 W. South.
Lewis T. A., sup't Erie Transportation
Company, 80 Virginia av., r. 526 N.
Meridian.
Lewis Thomas, teamster, bds. 485 S. Me-
ridian.
Lewis Walter, moulder Eagle Machine
Works, r. 75 Norwood.
Lewis Wesley, (col'd) lab., r. Ash, third
house south of Christian av.
Lewis William, (col'd) lab., r. 157 Maple.
Lewis Wm. B., upholsterer, r. 433 E. Ver-
mont.
Lewis W. H., City Marble Works, 50
Kentucky av., r. 27 Kentucky av.
Lewis W. H. H., printer, r. 50 N. East.
Lewis & Dark, (col'd, Anderson L. and
Jonathan D.) blacksmiths, 189 In-
diana av.
Lex Elizabeth, (wid.) r. 191 N. East.
Lex Jacob, printer, bds. 191 N. East.
Lianty John B., shoemaker, bds. Union
Hall.
Lick Robert M., bookkeeper Gall & Rush,
r. 480 N. Mississippi.
Licker George, railroader, r. 393 S. Dela-
ware.
Lickert John, r. 269 S. West.
Lickert S., expressman, r. 393 S. East.
Lidel Thos., railroader, r. 388 S. Missouri.
Lieber Herman, (H. L. & Co.) r. 404 N.
Delaware.
LIEBER H. & CO., (H. L. and
Chas. Koehne) Art Emporium, 60 E.
Washington.
Lieber Peter, (P. L. & Co.) r. 246 S. Penn-
sylvania.
LIEBER PETER & CO. (P. L.
& ——) brewers, 213 and 215 S.
Pennsylvania.
Liebel Elizabeth, (wid.) r. 222 Railroad.
Liestner William, moulder, works Chand-
ler & Taylor.
Lietz Arthur, musician, r. 316 E. New
York.
Lietz Theobald, portrait painter, r. 316
E. New York.
Lightfoot Thomas, (col'd) lab., r. African
al., bet. Sixth and Seventh.
LIGHTFORD J. G., consulting
mechanical engineer, room 1 Fitz-
gibbons' blk., up stairs, r. 61 E.
Maryland.

H. H. LEE,

Dealer in

Teas, Coffees, Sugars & Spices,

No. 7 ODD FELLOWS HALL

AND

ACADEMY OF MUSIC CORNER.

Lightford James G., jr., foreman Western Machine Works, r. 61 E. Maryland.

Lilienkamp Ernst, tailor, r. 249 N. Winston.

Lilley Samuel, (col'd) lab., r. 154 Douglass al.

Lilly J. O. D. (Mears & L.) r. N. Tennessee, bet. Second and Third.

Lilly Mary, (wid. James) bds. 73 W Maryland.

Linas Daniel, conductor C. C. & I. C. R. R., bds. 75 Davidson.

Linas Daniel, stonecutter, r. 203 Kentucky av.

Linas Mary, domestic, Bates House.

Linas Rachel, domestic, Bates House.

Linch James, lab., r. 2 Orient.

Linch Michael, bds. 143 S. East.

Linch Owen, lab., r. 16 Central.

Lincoln Charles, clk. Arcade, 6 W. Washington.

Lindenbower William, r. 682 N. Mississippi.

LINDERMAN FRANK, grocer, 206 E. Washington, r. 15 N. New Jersey.

Linderman L. (wid) r. 293 E. Washington.

Linderman William, moulder, r. 109 S. Benton.

Lindley A. P. (wid. H. J.) r. 74 State.

Lindley Hiram, (Lindley & Co.) r. 91 E. Michigan.

Lindley L. G., conductor, C. C. C. & I. R. R., r. 22 Fletcher av.

LINDLEY & CO. (H. L. and ——) real estate agents, 8 E. Washington.

Lindner Fred., printer, Journal office, bds. Circle Restaurant.

Lindsay A., cooper, bds. 9 S. Mississippi.

Lindsay Jonathan, salesman, New York Store, bds. Macy House.

Line Isaac, bricklayer, r. 291 Liberty.

Linehan John, lab., works Gas Works, r. 374 S. Illinois.

Lines J. W. (J. W. L. & Co.) r. 176 W. Ohio.

Lines J. W. & Co. (J. W. L., E. A. Bronson and M. P. Dennis) whol. tobacco and cigars, 4 W. Louisiana opp. Union Depot.

Lingenfelter Archibald, carpenter, 74 S. Pennsylvania, r. outside city limits.

Lingenfelter Ashford jr., carpenter, bds. 271 Davidson.

Lingenfelter Ashford, carpenter, r. 271 Davidson.

Lingenfelter John J., plasterer, r. 267 N. Mississippi.

Lingenfelter Wm., bds. 35 Circle.

Link Gralando, city scavenger, r. 314 S. Illinois.

Linn Jossie Miss, bds. 75 W. South.

Linnes Daniel, conductor, C. C. & I. C. R. R., bds. 75 Davidson.

Linter Abraham, clk., C. H. Linter, bds. 269 N. West.

Linter Amos H., groceries, 182 Indiana av., res. same.

Linter Christ. H., dry goods and notions, 184 Indiana av., r. 285 Indiana av.

Linton James W., cattle drover, r. 270 N. Liberty.

Lintz Benjamin, clk., Stewart & Morgan.

Lintz John, lab., r. 110 Stevens.

Lintz J. H., bds. Palmer House.

Lintz William F., packer, r. 319 S. East.

Lipp Henry, carpenter, r. se. cor. Tennessee and Third.

Lipp Henry, tailor, shop 13 Massachusetts av.

Lippencott Samuel, (Shaw L. and Conner) r. Richmond.

Lipperd W. H., clk. W. N. Crain, bds. 314 N. Pennsylvania.

Lippert Kate Miss, servant 174 Madison av.

Lippert Nicholas, blacksmith, r. 23 Lord.

Lippuns William, stonemason, r. 416 N. East.

Liscomb E. A, Mrs., r. 137 N. Illinois.

Lister Rolla, baggage master I. C. & L. R. R., bds. 442 N. Pennsylvania.

Little Casper, cigarmaker, bds. 287 E. Georgia.

Little Chief, office, Indianapolis Book Publishing House, A. C. Shortridge, editor.

Little Joseph C., works rolling mill, r. 225 S. Tennessee.

Little Sallie Mrs. dressmaker, r. 74 N. Liberty.

Little Sower, Sunday school weekly, office, Journal bldg., W. W. Dowling, publisher.

Little Watchman, semi-monthly, office, Journal bldg., W. W. Dowling, publisher.

LITTLE'S HOTEL, cor. Washington and New Jersey, Geo. Longfellow, proprietor.

Litton ——, bricklayer, r. Vine, nr. Broadway.

Livingston H. B., clk. No. 2 Bates House, r. 194 Virginia av.

Livingston William, grainer, 18 S. Meridian, bds. Mrs. Reeds.

Lloyd Spencer, clk. Hildebrand & Kepple r. E. of city.

Locie Samuel, engineer, bds. 58 Benton.

Locke Josiah, manufacturer of lightning rods, r. 463 N. Pennsylvania.

Locke William M., r. 211 S. Illinois.

Locke Erie, (Locke, Field & Scanlin) r. 76 N. California.

Lockner Auther, (col'd) teamster, r. 126 N. California.

Lockwood Henry, cooper, r. cor. New York and Minerva.

Lockwood I., cooper, r. clinton nr. East.

Lockwood James, cooper, r. 36 Douglass.

Lockwood Matthew, with Wm. Sumner & Co., bds. 11 S. Mississippi.

Lockwood Nelson, cooper, r. 36 Douglass.

Lodge James, bookkeeper, Landers, Conduitt & Co., bds. 15 Virginia av.

Lodge R. P., traveling agent Indiana State Sentinel, bds. 172 N. Meridian.

Loeneauer C., dealer in groceries, provisions &c., 380 Virginia av. r. same.

Loeper Frank Wm., physician, 192 E. Washington, r. same.

Loeper Jacob W., (Stierle & L.) r. 69 Davidson.

Logan John, works Osgood, Smith & Co. bds 55 Eddy.

Logan Mathew, works Josselyn Bros. & Co. r. 23 Fayette.

Logan Patrick, lab., r. 27 Grant.

Logan R. D. (L. & Brown) r. 422 N. East.

Logan Thomas J., carpenter, r. 171 Meek.

Logan & Brown, (R. D. Logan and B. T. Brown) attorneys at law, 4½ W. Washington.

LOGSDON LAWRENCE, proprietor brick yard, end Virginia av.

Lonergan John, groceries &c., 151 cor. Pine and Noble, r. same.

Loney Wesley, student, r. 79 Broadway.

Long David, D., agent for Munday & Snyder, r. 222 E. South.

Long E. C., grainer, r. 176 E. South.

Long Frederick, porter, Browning & Sloan, r. N. Illinois.

Long Gabriel, r. 37 rose.

Long George Rev., r. 202 E. Market.

Long G. G., shoemaker Dury & Hawk, r. 476 N. East.

Long Henry C., clk., r. 202 E. Market.

Long I. S., (L. & Joseph) r. 264 Blake.

LONG JOSEPH T., Supervisor Internal Revenue, room 4, Vinton's blk., bds. Palmer House.

Long & Joseph, (J. S. L. and G. W. J.) saw mill and lumber dealers, cor. Walnut and Lafayette railroad.

LONG MATHEW, undertaker, 15 Circle, bds. se. cor. Market and Circle.

Long Robert, undertaker, with Mathew Long, r. 15 Circle.

BENHAM BRO'S,

36 East Washington St.,

AGENTS FOR THE

BURDETT ORGAN.

Long Thomas F., dealer in produce, 188 W. Washington, r. 268 S. Illinois.

Longreich Edward, tailor, r. 282 E. North.

LONGFELLOW GEO., proprietor Little's Hotel, cor. Washington and New Jersey.

Longsdorff Henry, lab. r. 251 N. West.

Longsdorff William, carpenter, r. 234 N. Mississippi.

Longtree George, lab., r. 37 Dacota.

Loomis G. B., music teacher, r. 312 E. North.

Loomis William H., assistant Secretary Indianapolis Agricultural, Mechanical and Horticultural Association, r. 237 S. New Jersey.

Looney Edward, works G. F. Adam's lumber yard, r. 107 Huron.

Looney James, plasterer, r. 159 High.

Looney M., night policeman, r. 111 Huron.

Looney Mill Mrs., r. 101 West.

Looney William, lab., r. 111 Huron.

Lord John M., pres't Indianapolis Rolling Mill Co., office Citizens' Bank bldg., r. 297 N. Pennsylvania.

LOSEE CHARLES E., timekeeper P. C. & St. L. R. R., r. 326 E. Georgia.

LOSEE THOMAS V., master mechanic P. C. & St. L. R. R. shops at Indianapolis, r. 326 E. Georgia.

Losey M. D., (M. O. Tracey & Co.) r. 112 S. East.

Loucks Christ B., carpenter, r. 186 Bates.

Loucks George W., carriagepainter, r. 85 N. Delaware.

Loucks James, r. 175 Ash, nr. Forest Home av.

Loucks John, corporal, U. S. Arsenal.

Loucks John, railroader, r. 82 S. Benton.

Loucks Joseph W., moulder, r. 186 Bates.

Loucks Mary Mrs., r. 391 S. Delaware.

Loucks W. W., railroader, r. 341 N. Alabama.

Louden A. M., bookbinder, bds. 76 N. New Jersey.

Louden Henry A., assistant bookkeeper Journal Office, r. 76 N. New Jersey.

Louis Burrows, whitewasher, r. 172 E. Market.

Louis Hiram, teamster, r. 407 S. East.

Louney Michael policeman, r. 111 Huron.

Lout Reinhart, lab., r. 168, S. Noble.

Love John, r. 81 N. Tennessee.

Love J. W., artist, r. 509 E. Washington.

H. H. LEE
HAS BUT
ONE PRICE, SELLS FOR CASH,
And Guarantees all Goods
Sold at the China Tea Stores,
To be as Represented.

Love Samuel, railroader, r. 163 S. East.

Love William, (L. & Co.) r. 506 E. Washington.

LOVE WM. & CO. (W. Love, J. P. Dunn and H. S. Bigham) real estate agents, room 1 Talbott & New's blk.

Lovecraft Joseph, r. 500 N. Mississippi.

Lovecraft Joshua E., r. 132 W. First.

Lovejoy John, printer, r. 81 W. Michigan.

Lowe Albert, (col'd) lab., r. 16 Rhode Island.

Lowe Geo. (Lowe G. & Co.) r. 321 N. Pennsylvania.

Lowe George, attorney at law, r. 321 N. Pennsylvania.

LOWE GEO. & CO., carriage manufacturers, No. 26 and 28 S. Tennessee.

Lowe N. H., sr. (Lowe N. H. & Son) r. 308 E. North.

Lowe N. H., jr. (Lowe N. H. & Son) r. 303 E. North.

Lowe N. H. & Son, carpenters and builders, 30 S. New Jersey.

LOWE WILLIAM A., attorney at law, 16½ E. Washington, r. 44 Christian av. cor. Jackson.

Lowe William, coal cart driver, r. 48 Bicking.

Lowe Wingate R., student N. W. Christian University, r. 267 N. East.

Lowes John, carpenter, r. 386 N. Delaware.

Lowes John W., salesman, Coburn & Jones, bds. 366 N. Alabama.

Lowman James M., clk., 18 W. Pearl, r. 112 E. St. Clair.

Lowman Nancy Mrs., r. 112 E. St. Clair.

Lowman Nelson D., works Budd & Hendesley, r. 118 Fort Wayne.

LOWRY WILEY M., druggist 65 Massachusetts av. r. 73 Massachusetts av.

Loy David M., foreman D. Root & Co. r. 419 N. East.

Lucas Charles H. Dr., (col'd) office 167 Indiana av., r. 66 N. Missouri.

Lucas James, (col'd) whitewasher, 66 N. Missouri.

Lucas John G., millright, 132 S. Pennsylvania.

Lucas Walter A., bookkeeper W. P. & E. P. Gallup, bds. 78 N. Tennessee.

Lucett Bridget, servant, Sherman House.

Lucid John, lab., r. 358 S. West.

Lucid Morris, lab., r. 336 S. West.

Lucid Morris, lab., r. 339 S. Missouri.

Lucky G. W., bricklayer and paver, office 75 E. Washington.

Ludington William H., publisher, r. 37 Kentucky av.

Ludlow ——, tailor, r. 368 S. New Jersey.

Ludlow George, carpenter, r. 46 N. New Jersey.

Ludlow George S., carpenter, r. 500 Virginia av.

Ludlow J. C., foreman at Warren Tate's, r. 136 N. New Jersey.

Ludlow Jason, carpenter, r. 136 N. New Jersey.

Ludlow Silas, traveling agent, r. 91 Broadway.

Ludlum Joseph E., r. 49 Chatham.

Ludorff L., (L. & Co.) r. 304 S. Meridian.

Ludorff L. & Co., (L. Ludorff and B. E. Thonnsen) wholesale notions and furnishing goods, 42 S. Meridian.

Ludwick Francis, r. 253 Union.

Ludwig James, engineer Geisendorff's, r. 27 Blake.

Ludwig Louis, carter, r. 269 E. Washington.

Ludwig Otto, importer of wines, 115 E. Washington, r. 178 E. Washington.

Ludwig Pauline Mrs., millinery, 269 E. Washington, r. same.

Lueders Elizabeth, (wid. Thomas) r. 484 N. Mississippi.

Lueders L. Misses, (Catherine, Eliza, Louisa and Caroline) milliners and dressmakers, 71½ E. Market, r. 484 N. Mississippi.

Lueisser Frank, butcher, bds. 336 Virginia av.

Lueisser Julius, meat market, 131 Massachusetts av., bds. 336 Virginia av.

Luellen James, (col'd) lab., r. 289 Douglass al.

Lukens Thomas G., moulder, r. 318 S. Delaware.

Lukens Frederick, teamster, r. 462 S. Illinois.

Lukens R. L., agricultural implements, 81 W. Washington r. 281 Virginia av.

Luker Kate Miss, dressmaker, r. 68 S. Illinois.

Luker R. A. Mrs., (wid. R. A.) r. in rear of 440 Virginia av.

Lucky Christ. F., lab., r. 474 E. Washington.

Lulbing Earl, lab., r. 176 S. Illinois.

Lumpkins H. (col'd) porter, C. Dickson & Co.

Lupton Albert, entry clk., Hibben, Tarkington & Co., bds. 24 Indiana av.

Lupton G. Dr., dentist, r. 24 Indiana av.

Lupton Elizabeth, (wid.) r. cor. Pennsylvania and First.

Lupton Wm. C. jr., bds. 402 N. East.
Lupton W. C., house and sign painter, 71 N. Pennsylvania, r. 402 N. East.
Lutcher Jesse, (col'd) cook, r. ne. part city.
Luther Calvin, blacksmith, r. 224 E. Washington.
Luther Carrie Mrs., r. 59 Indiana av.
LUTHER ROBERT D., carriage maker, 224 E. Washington, r. same.
Lutz George, shoemaker, r. 400 Virginia av.
Lutz George F., bellboy Spencer House.
Lutz John J., soldier, United States Arsenal.
Luzingler George, lab., r. 81 S. Missouri.
Lybrand C. C., works Rolling Mill, r. 223 S. Tennessee.
Lynch Bridget, laundry maid, Sherman House.
Lynch C., r. 74 W. Louisiana.
Lynch Charles, clk., ticket office, C. & I. J. R. R., r. 83 S. Liberty.
Lynch Dennis, machinist, r. 109 Harrison.
Lynch Jacob, cooper, r. 53 Hellen.
Lynch James, lab. r. 175 E. Louisiana.
Lynch John, lab., T. H. & I. Depot, r. 249 S. Missouri.
Lynch John, lab., r. 349 S. Missouri.
Lynch John S., grain buyer, bds. 18 S. Pennsylvania.
Lynch Mary Miss, waiter, Spencer House.
Lynch Michael, works rolling mill, r. 452 S. Tennessee.
Lynch Michael, bricklayer, r. 669 N. Illinois.
Lynch M. P., traveler, Keifer & Vinton, bds. Palmer House.
Lynch Patrick, engineer Sinker & Davis r. 109 Harrison.
Lynch Patrick, works Express Co., bds. 74 W. Louisiana.
Lynch Timothy, works Street Railroad Co., bds. 74 W. Louisiana.
Lynn Adam, teamster, r. 43 Chatham.
Lynn P. A., clk., Star Union Line, office, 85 Virginia av., r. se. cor. Second and Tennessee.
LYNN W. C., freight agent, C. & I. J. R. R., office, 110 and 112 Virginia av.
Lynn Winfield S., clk., Brewing & Sloan. bds. 172 Virginia av.
Lyon Annie, servant, Palmer House.
Lyons Chas., engineer, C. C. C. & I. R. R.
Lyons Daniel, lab., bds. 217 S. Illinois.
Lyons Geo. W., foreman, J. C. Furguson & Co.
Lyons John, lab., r. 243 Missouri.
Lyons Mary Miss, chambermaid, Spencer House.
Lyons M. A. (wid. A. E.) r. 509 N. Tennessee.

BENHAM BRO'S.

36 East Washington St.,

KEEP

THE VERY BEST

VIOLIN AND GUITAR STRINGS.

Lyons Patrick, lab., bds. 217 S. Illinois.
Lyons Richard, works rolling mill, bds. 217 S. Illinois.
Lyons Robert, carriagesmith, Shaw, Lippencott & C., bds. 218 S. New Jersey.
Lyons Wm. H., lab., r. 378 E. Georgia.
Lytle B. K., clk., J. A. McGaus, bds. 268 S. West.
Lytle Ezra W., lab., r. 268 S. West.
Lytle Robert J., carpenter, r. 268 S. West.

McABEE DANIEL H., lab., works Rolling Mill, r. 376 S. Illinois.
McAdams Belle Miss, r. Douglass al., nr. Ohio.
McAllen Kate Miss, weaver Geisendorff, bds. cor. West and Maryland.
McAlpin A. R., machinist C. C. C. & I. shops.
McAndrews Walter, saloon, 251 W. Washington, bds. same.
McAntle Patrick, works Rolling Mill, bds. 272 S. Tennessee.
McArthur James, salesman New York Store, bds. 158 N. New Jersey.
McArthur John B., r. 270 N. West.
McAvoy Thomas, clk., bds. 79 Massachusetts av.
McBeth M. B., salesman New York Store, bds. Macy House.
McBRIDE JOHN C., saloon, 195 West Washington, r. 137 W. Ohio.
McBride Michael, linen peddler, r. 274 N. Liberty.
McBride Riley, carpenter, r. 37 Ellen.
McCabe Mathew, saloon, 329 E. Washington, r. 9 Forest av.
McCabe John, lab., r. 164 Buchanan.
McCann Cloud, painter, r. Tinker, bet. Pennsylvania and Delaware.
McCain John, machinist, r. 228 S. Noble.
McCain William, carpenter, r. over 300 E. Washington.
McCain Wm. H., carpenter, r. 395 E. Michigan.
McCaslin Myron, blacksmith, bds. 164 W. Maryland.
McCALLIAN R. J., agent Cincinnati papers, 13 N. Pennsylvania, bds. 62 Huron.
McCallion John, machinist, r. 62 Huron.
McCann James, clk., J. H. V. Smith, bds. 69 N. East.

THE CHINA TEA STORES

ARE AT

No. 7 ODD FELLOWS HALL

AND

ACADEMY OF MUSIC CORNER.

McCann James A., student, bds. 236 N East.

McCann James D., painter, r. 18 S. Meridian.

McCann Mary, (wid.) r. 368 S. Tennessee.

McCann Mary Mrs., seamstress, 42 Kentucky av., r. same.

McCann Pat., lab., r. 100 S. East.

McCann Samuel D., physician and surgeon, office 236 N. East, r. same.

McCarty Dennis, cooper, bds. Blake bet. Washington and New York.

McCarty John, turner, bds. 27 Hahn.

McCarty John, turner, r. cor. Georgia and East.

McCarty Kate, servant Ray House, r. same.

McCarty Nicholas, real estate agent, office Hubbard's blk., r. 122 N. Pennsylvania.

McCARTHY SIMON, prop. Bates House Saloon, r. 81 W. St. Clair.

McCarty Stephen, lab., r. 393 E. Michi-

McCARTY THOMAS B. insurance agent, office, Odd Fellows Hall, r. 191 N. Illinois.

McCarty Timothy, lab. r. 57 Wyoming.

McCarty Wm., moulder, r. 137 N. Davidson.

McCarty Wm., lab., r. 533 E. Georgia,

McCauley Jacob, wagonmaker, r. 270 S. Illinois.

McCauley Thomas, bookbinder, bds. 148 Indiana av.

McChesney Edward, baggage master I. C. & St. L. R. R., r. 454 N. Tennessee.

McChesney Jacob B., bookkeeper Maxwell, Fry & Thurston, r. 454 N. Tennessee.

McChesney, William L., bookkeeper J. C. Ferguson & Co., r. 454 N. Tennessee.

McClain E. J., queensware and furniture, 212 E. Washington, r. same

McClain John S., (Peacock & McC.) r. Douglass near Ohio.

McClain Moses, clk., bds 452 E. Georgia.

McClellan ——, carpenter, r. 113 E. St. Joseph.

McClellan John, butcher, r. 52 S. West.

McClellan John G., clk., bds. 52 S. West.

McClellan Robert, carpenter, r. 378 E. Market.

McClintock Robert, lab., r. 24 Greer.

McClosky David, cigar maker, 36 Virginia av., r. 206 S. East.

McClosky John, moulder, r. 324 E. Lousiana.

McClosky John, carpenter, r. 88 S. Mississippi.

McClosky John H., baggage recorder Union Depot, r. 7 Ellsworth.

McCloud Edward, (col'd) barber, bds. 233 W. Ohio.

McCloud John, (col'd) lab., bds. 233 W. Ohio.

McCloud Mahla Mrs.,(col'd, wid. Thomas) r. 233 W. Ohio.

McCloud Sarah, (col'd) washerwoman, r. 233 W. Ohio.

McClure Alexander, boilermaker, r. 221 W. Merrill.

McClure Charles R., potographer, bds. 52 N. Pennsylvania.

McClure George W., carpenter, r. Eighth nr. Canal.

McClure J. E., clk., 75 E. Market, r. 61 Fort Wayne av.

McClure M. T., foreman, rolling mill yard, r. 351 E. McCarty.

McClure Nathaniel, r. 68 Athon.

McClure Theophilus, printer, works Chandler & Co., r. 272 W. Vermont.

McConaghy James, carpenter, r. Indiana av. cor. New York.

McConbiary Thomas, moulder, r. 343 S. East.

McCool William, carpenter, r. 307 S. East.

McCooney D., machinist, r. 302 E. North.

McCord B. R. (McC. & Wheatley) bds. 149 S. East.

McCord Mrs. S., r. 92 E. New York.

McCORD & WHEATLEY, (B. R. McC. and Wm. M. W.) planing mill and lumber yard, 186 and 198 S. Alabama.

McCormick Alice D. Miss, teacher City Academy, bds. 393 N. Pennsylvania.

McCormick Catharine, (wid. Patrick) r. 303 Indiana av.

McCormick George, r. 31 W. Ohio.

McCormick James A., works Osgood, Smith & Co., r. 191 Huron.

McCormick John L., carpenter, r. 726 N. Tennessee.

McCormick W. H., conductor I. C. & L. R. R., r. 181 S. New Jersey.

McCoulry Thomas, moulder, r. 343 S. East.

McCoy Charles D., night policeman, r. cor. California and Michigan.

McCoy J. C. Dr., r. 96 E. New York.

McCOY THEODORE W., clk. Supreme Court, office State bldg., r. 109 N. California.

McCrea R. H. (Fahnley & McC.) bds. Sherman House.

McCready Eliza Mrs., Librarian Indianapolis Library Association, Martindale's blk., r. same.

McCreedy James, bookkeeper Indianapolis National Bank.

McCullough J. S., bookkeeper Hibben, Tarkington & Co.

McCune T. J., machinist, r. 78 Forest av.

McCune Thomas, machinist, Chandler & Taylor, bds. 366 W. Washington.

McCURDY GEORGE W., auction and commission merchant, cor. Virginia av. and Washington, r. 214 N. Alabama.

McCutcheon ——, r. 620 N. Illinois.

McCutcheon Elizabeth, proprietor Decatur House, 328 E. Washington.

McCutcheon George E., yardmaster, Peru Railroad, r. 328 E. Washington.

McCutcheon John C., bookkeeper and cashier, Crossland, Hanna & Co., r. 226 N. Meridian.

McDaniel W. J., lab., bds. Nagle House.

McDaniel Mary, (wid.) bds. 17 Henry.

McDaniel Reason, teamster, r. 591 Maple.

McDaniels J. R., works Emerson, Bean & Co., bds. 23 N. West.

McDermed E. C., clk., N. & G. Ohmer, bds. Depot Dining Hall.

McDermot Joseph, stove mounter, r. 159 S. Alabama.

McDermott Thomas, works rolling mill, r. 43 Henry.

McDevitt Edward, machinist, bds. Ray House.

McDole Osa, conductor, T. H. & I. R. R. r. 79 W. Louisiana.

McDonald Currun E., patent agent, 87 E. Market, r. 300 E. Market.

McDonald Ezekiel M. (McD. & McDonald) r. 228 N. Meridian.

McDonald James, papermaker, r. 49 S. West.

McDonald Jas., pressman, Journal office, r. 329 W. Maryland.

McDonald Joseph E. (McDonald & McD.) r. 229 N. Pennsylvania.

McDonald Mary, (wid.) r. 79 E. St. Clair.

McDonald Mary, domestic, Bates House.

McDonald Patrick, produce dealer, r. 133 S. New Jersey.

McDonald Patrick, works rolling mill, r. 20 Willard.

McDonald Patrick, lab., r. 129 S. New Jersey.

McDonald Robert, works Street Railroad Co., r. 53 Maple.

McDonald & McDonald, (J. E. McD. and E. M. McD.) attorneys at law, room 5 Ætna bldg.

McDonough A. W., messenger, American M. U. Express Co., bds. Spencer House.

McDonough D. B., dealer in coal, lime, lath &c., 144 S. Alabama, r. 123 E. Vermont.

McDougall E. R., brickmaker, r. 165 Huron.

McDougall William, engineer C. C. C. & I. R. R., r. 291 N. Liberty.

McDowell Joseph, bookkeeper, Bowen, Stewart & Co., r. 238 S. Alabama.

McElroy Ann, (wid) r. 286 E. Louisiana.

McElroy Frank, porter, Journal office, bds. Macy house.

McElvane John, house and sign painter, 46 Kentucky av., r. Athon.

McElwee J., carpenter, r. 78 N. Liberty.

McFadden Lewis M., bailiff, bds. 195 N. Davidson.

McFarland C. A., (Bowker & Co.) r. 130 Virginia av.

McFarland Carey, r. 67 Virginia av.

McFarland Charlotte Miss, r. 26 E. St. Clair.

McFarland J. L., (Bowker & Co.) r. 130 Virginia av.

McFarland Laura Miss, r. 26 E. St. Clair.

McFarland Robert, flour and feed store, 155 W. Washington, r. 164 Dougherty.

McFarland Wm. K., bakery, No. 12 S. Meridian, r. same.

McGalliard Harry, machinist C. C. & I. C. R. R.

McGarahan Thomas, with Wm. Sumner & Co., r. 195 N. Tennessee.

McGaughey Charles, clk., Street R. R. Co., bds. Globe house.

McGaw J. A., cigars and tobacco, 16 N. Illinois, r. 182 N. Mississippi.

McGee Bruce, clk., with W. A. Bristor, bds. nw. cor. Pennsylvania and Market.

McGee Edward, porter 52 S. Meridian, r. 215 S. Alabama.

McGee Richard, physician, 56 Massachusetts av., r. same.

McGee William, engineer J. M. & I. R. R., r. 121 W. Duncan.

McGill Margaret, (wid. Robert) r. McGill, bet. South and Louisiana.

McGill Wm. C., r. 642 N. Mississippi.

McGilliard Martin V. (McG. & M. O. Brown) r. 280 N. Mississippi.

McGILLIARD & BROWN, (M. V. McG. and M. O. B.) general insurance agents, 11 S. Meridian.

H. H. LEE

MAKES A SPECIALTY OF

Choice Green, Black & Japan Teas.

McGinn G. T., teamster, r. 283 Virginia av.

McGinnis C. E., bookkeeper, Hollweg & Reese, bds. 41 Virginia av.

McGinnis Charles J., clk. County Auditor's office, bds. Pyle House.

McGinnis Eliza, (wid. William) r. 41 Blake.

McGinnis Francis Mrs., r. 41 Virginia av.

McGinnis Frank T., clk. Murphy, Johnston & Co., r. 41 Virginia av.

McGINNIS GEORGE F., Auditor Marion county, r. Perry township.

McGinnis Jasper N., bricklayer, r. 397 Massachusetts av.

McGinnis John, grocer, 280 E. Washington, r. same.

McGinnis Nicholas, tailor, r. 81 W. South.

McGinnis N. S., railroader, r. 103 Forest av.

McGinnis Thomas, tailor, Clinton, bet. East and New Jersey.

McGinnis Thomas, lumber dealer, r. 547 N. Mississippi.

McGinnis William, conductor I. C. & L. R. R., bds. Ray House.

McGinty Martin, flagman, r. 34 Chadwick.

McGlaughlin Frank, harnessmaker, bds. Little's Hotel.

McGlen Thomas, bookseller, r. 316 S. West.

McGlenn Michael, expressman, r. cor. North and Douglass.

McGowen Lunsford, grocer, r. 81 W. Walnut.

McGowen Thomas, works rolling mill, bds. 217 S. Illinois.

McGrarty John, saloon, 116 S. Illinois, r. same.

McGrarty Neal, clk. 116 S. Illinois, r. same.

McGrath Daniel, lab. r. 25 Maple.

McGrath Mary, domestic Bates House.

McGrath T. W., cabinetmaker, r. 329 S. Pennsylvania.

McGrathy Daniel, lab. r. 248 S. Delaware.

McGraw Dennis, teamster, r. 478 E. Georgia.

McGraw Michael, varnisher, bds. Court Street Boarding House.

McGrew Maggie A. Miss, servant, 360 E. St. Clair.

McGrimes, proprietor Concordia Saloon cor. South and Meridian, r. same.

McGruder Moses, (col'd) lab., r. cor. Michigan and Douglass al.

McGuff Thomas, bell boy Bates House.

McGuire Richard, gasfitter, bds. Palmer House.

McHugh Dennis, lab. 23 Maple.

McHugh J., letter carrier, bds. 252 S. West.

McHugh John, plasterer, bds. 104 Cherry.

McHugh Thomas, lab., r. 104 Cherry.

McHutcheon Thomas, clk. Trade Palace, bds. 620 N. Illinois.

McIntire James, auctioneer, r. 281 N. Noble.

McIntire Lucius, works rolling mill, r. 18 Henry.

McIntire William, lab., r. al. bet. West and Canal.

McIver John I., salesman New York Store, bds. 158 N. New Jersey.

McKannay William, baggage master J. M. & I. R. R.

McKay Horace, r. Broadway, cor. Forest av.

McKeeby Dyer S., conductor, C. C. C. & I. R. R., r. 277 N. East.

McKeeby Frank S., conductor, C. C. C. & I. R. R., r. 249 N. Davidson.

McKechan Benj., clk. P. O., bds. 333 S. Pennsylvania.

McKechan Benj., lab., r. 333 S. Pennsylvania.

McKechan James, clk., r. 333 S. Pennsylvania.

McKechan John, stock agent, C. C. & I. C. R. R., r. 61 S. Noble.

McKeever George, roadmaster, I. B. & W. R. R., r. 129 Bates.

McKeever John, engineer, T. H. & I. R. R., bds. Spencer House.

McKendry J., stave and heading manufacturer, Pratt, nr. Mississippi, r. sw. cor. Mississippi and St. Clair.

McKenley A. D., expressman, bds. 150 Ft. Wayne av.

McKenney William, boss carder at Cotton Mill, bds. 366 W. Washington.

McKenny John, carpenter, r. 167 E. St. Joseph.

McKeon M., engraver, H. C. Chandler, bds. 55 Bates.

McKernan Daniel S., with J. H. McKernan, r. 117 W. New York.

McKERNAN JAMES H, real estate agent, 2 Blake's blk., r. 117 W. New York.

McKernan Louis, clk. J. H. McKernan, r. 576 N. Mississippi.

McKernan Michael, expressman, r. 39 Jones.

McKinney Davis, lab., r. 4 Meek.

McKinney R., barber, r. 303 E. Washington.

McKinney William, overseer Cotton Mill, r. 366 W. Washington.

McKinney Rachael, (wid. Duncan) r. 206 Blake.

McKinsey William L., carpenter, r. 108 Blake.

McKnight Mattie Miss, r. 27 N. California.

McLaflin Myran, blacksmith, Chandler & Taylor, bds. 164 W. Maryland.

McLain Albert, painter, r. 12 W. North.

McLain L. C., physician, Indiana Surgical Institute, r. same.

McLAIN MOSES G., State Librarian office in State House, bds. 126 N. Tennessee.

McLaren John, printer Journal office, r. 350 N. Noble.

McLaughlin Debroe E. Miss, dressmaker, r. 217 Massachusetts av.

McLaughlin, Gridley H., minister, r. two miles se. on Michigan road.

McLaughlin William, saloon 344 S. West, r. same.

McLAUGHLIN WILLIAM H., farmer, r. two miles se. Michigan road.

McLene Jerry, (McL. & Herron) r. 139 N. Pennsylvania.

McLENE & HERRON, (J. McL. and F. M. H.) wholesale and retail jewelers, 1 Bates house blk.

McLeod Mary Mrs., saleswoman, 27 N. Pennsylvania, r. W. Maryland, Webb's boarding house.

McMahan Dennis, wiper, C. C. & I. C. R. R., shops.

McMahan Ellen, (wid) r. 203 Meek.

McMahan John M., conductor T. H. & I. R. R., r. 27 W. First.

McMahan J. W., lab., r. 334 S. Alabama.

McMahan T. C., cabinetmaker, r. 65 S. East.

McMahon Charles, carpenter, r. 273 McCarty.

McMamara Mary, domestic Blind Institute.

McManara Michael, lab., r. 165 E. South.

McManmen Bryon, lab., r. 122 Stevenson.

McMullen Henry, deputy clk. U. S. court, bds 126 E. Ohio.

McMullen James, r. 74 E. Vermont.

McMurray Robt., tobacconist, r. 56 Bright.

McMurray Robert, cigarmaker, r. 242½ E. Washington.

McNabb Stephen, baggagemaster, Union Depot, r. 227 S. Mississippi.

McNalley Barney, works rolling mill, 542 S. Meridian.

McNamee John, law student, r. Massachusetts av.

14

BENHAM BRO'S,
36 East Washington St.,
Pianos, Organs and Melodeons
FOR
CASH OR ON TIME.

McNead Mary, (wid.) r. 23 E. Ohio.

McNeeley E., cooper, r. 242 N. Illinois.

McNeeley John, carpenter, r. First bet. Illinois and Tennessee.

McNeeley John B., clk., P. C. & St. L. R. R. freight office, r. 185 W. Maryland.

McNulty P. A., bds. Macy House.

McNutt A. D., bricklayer, r. 177 Meek.

McOuat Andrew W. (R. L. & A. W. McOuat) r. ne. cor. New York and East.

McOuat David, works paper mill, r. cor. Patterson and Elizabeth.

McOuat George, speculator, r. ne. cor. New York and East.

McOuat Janet, (wid. Thomas) r. ne. cor. New York and East.

McOuat R. L. (R. L. McO. & A. W. McO.) r. 74 W. Market.

McOUAT R. L. & A. W., stoves and tinware, 61 and 63 W. Washington.

McPherson Cary, salesman, bds. 90 N. Delaware.

McQuaid Pat., expressman, r. 79 Fayette.

McSweeney Owen, railroader, r. 130 W. New York.

McVey D., blacksmith shop, W. Washington, r. 58 S. California.

McVey H. O., piano tuner, 159 E. Washington, r. 76 Kentucky av.

McVey Joseph, carpenter, r. 24 Coburn.

McVey William, tax collector, r. 76 Kentucky av.

McVey W. R., student, 171 E. Washington.

McVicker A. W., merchant tailor, r. 176 W. Ohio.

McWilliams James, r. 25 W. St. Clair.

McWorkman Henry, clk., P. O., bds. Macy House.

McWorkman J., clk., bds. National Hotel.

MAAS LOUIS, cigarmaker, 11 N. Pennsylvania, r. 278 E. Michigan.

Mabb Maria Mrs., r. 27 N. New Jersey.

Mac John, works Sentinel office, bds. 165 E. South.

Mac William, pressman Sentinel office, r. 165 E. South.

MACAULEY DANIEL, Mayor of City Indianapolis, office Cottrell & Knight's bldg., r. 18 W. North.

Macauley John T., bookkeeper paper mill, bds. 526 N. Illinois.

H. H. LEE

MAKES A SPECIALTY OF

Choice Green, Black & Japan Teas.

Macauley R. (col'd) bds. 190 N. Missouri.
Machett R. M., carpenter, r. 169 E. St. Joseph.
MacIntire H. N.,teacher Indiana Institution for Deaf and Dumb.
MacIntire John,salesman Butch, Dickson & Co., r. 25 S. West.
MacIntire M. E. Mrs.,matron Indiana Institution Deaf and Dumb.
MacINTIRE THOMAS, A. M.,superintendent Indiana Institution for Education Deaf and Dumb, r. same.
Mack George, (col'd) lab., bds. 116 Ash.
Mack John, lab., r. 193 High.
Mack Morris, lab. T. H. & I. R. R. depot, r. 322 S. West.
Mack Philip, lab. r. 300 W. Maryland.
Mack William, bds. Calafornia House.
Macy David, president I. P. & C. R. R., office 101 E. Washington, up stairs, r. 298 N. Delaware.
MACY HOUSE, se. cor. Market and Illinois, S. W. Melsheimer, proprietor.
Madden Elizabeth, (wid.) r. 181 Elizabeth.
Madden Joseph, plasterer, r. 387 S. Missouri.
Madden Thomas, bricklayer, r. 169 N. Davidson.
MADDEN THOMAS, proprietor Capital Tobacco Works, 172 W. Cumberland, r. 181 W. First.
Madison Charles, (col'd) lab., r. 156 Douglass al.
Mads Peter, (col'd) lab. starch factory, r. 91 Elm.
Magee George, harnessmaker, works 182 W. Washington.
MAGLEY JACOB, meat market, 186 W. Washington, r. Mount Jackson.
Maguire Charles, salesman New York Store. bds. 112 N. Pennsylvania.
Maguire Douglass, (Judson, M. & Co.) r. 78 E. Ohio.
Maguire Mary, (wid. David) r. 81 Ann.
Mahan James, peddlar, r. 117 Oak.
Mahan Wm. H., bookkeeper Rickhoff & Co., r. 74 Indiana av.
Mahoney Catherine Miss, servant, Spencer House.
Mahoney Charles, brakeman C. C. & I. C. R. R., bds. 58 Benton.
Mahoney John, flagman Union track, r. 10 Buchanan.

Mahoney Margaret, (wid. James) r. 58 S. Alabama.
Mahoney Michael, lab., r. 18 Buchanan.
Mahoney Pat., lab., r. 298 S. Delaware.
Mahoney Richard, works Street Railroad Co., bds. 72 W. Louisiana.
Mahoney William, works Street Railroad Co. Stables, r. 81 Maple.
Mahorney A. E., hairworker, 235 Blake, r. same.
Mahorney J T., hair dealer, r. 235 Blake.
Mahurin Matilda L., teacher Market Street Colored School, bds. 303 cor. North and New Jersey.
Mai August, carpenter and joiner, r. 264 Chestnut.
Maiden John, blacksmith, r. 66 S. West.
Maier Jacob, barber, 149 E. Washington.
MAJOR STEPHEN T., groceries, provisions and willow ware, 342 E. Washington. r. 218 W. Georgia.
Major S. F., r. 218 W. Georgia.
Majors William, cooper, r. 317 W. Market.
Maker Thomas, painter, r. 319 N. East.
Makepeace H. B. salesman, 26 S. Meridian, r. 201 E. St. Mary.
Malloh Mary, (wid. Adolph) r. 338 W. North.
Malone ——, (wid.) r. 128 Virginia av.
Malone Abner, machinist, r. 128 Virginia av.
Malone Isaac, blacksmith, r. 27 Wyoming.
Malone Lewis D. (col'd) carpenter, r. 141 Bright.
Malone William L., salesman, 25 W. Washington, r. 128 Virginia av.
Maloney James, carpenter, r. cor. McCarty and Tennessee.
Maloney John, shoemaker, r. 257 S. Mississippi.
Maloney John, blacksmith, r. 12 N. New Jersey.
Maloney John, printer, News Office, bds. cor. McCarty and Tennessee.
Malott V. T., cashier, Merchants' National Bank, r. 280 N. Delaware.
Maloy Hugh, lab., r. 80 John.
Maloy James, marble dealer, r. 67 W. McCarty.
Malpas Henry, (H. M. & Co.) r. 72 State.
Malpas H. & Co. (H. M. & ——) steam bleachery, 17 and 18 Miller's blk.
Manaham Mary, domestic, Bates House.
Manahan Timothy, boot and shoemaker, r. 474 E. Georgia.
Manchester Lewis, clk. J. W. Copeland & Co., bds. Pyle House.
Mansfield George, (F. Gepper & Co.) r. 336 N. East.
Mangold Fred, saw grinder, r. 180 E. St. Mary.
Manheimer D., r. 172 E. Ohio.

Manheimer Louis, clk. 3 Bates House blk. bds. 172 E. Ohio.

Manhenney Alex., carpenter, 127 E. Maryland, r. 314 E. Market.

MANKEDICK BROS., (Henry Mankedick and William Mankedick) dealers in hardware and cutlery, 123 E. Washington.

Mankedick Henry, (Mankedick Bros.) r. two miles se. of city.

Mankedick William, (Mankedick Bros.) r. 270 E. Washington.

Manlove W. R., attorney, 87½ E. Market, room 15 Thorp's blk., r. sw. cor. Forest av. and Broadway.

Manloy Charlotte, (wid) r. 310 W. Washington.

Mann A. C., lab., r. 1 Thomas.

Mann Alfred J., carpenter, cor. South and Delaware, r. 157 Davidson.

Mann Henry C., (col'd) barber shop, 10 S. Delaware, r. 361 E. New York.

Mann Jackson, carpenter, r. 157 N. Davidson.

Mann James B., grocer, r. 149 S. East.

Mann Losen, carriagemaker, works Miller's carriage shop.

Mann Samuel, works Indianapolis Agricultural Works, bds. 211 S. Illinois.

Mann William, (col'd) barber, r. 211 W. Ohio.

Mannan Julia, servant, J. W. Hess.

Mannfeld William, tailor, F. Gepper & Co., bds. 28 W. Georgia.

MANNING THOMAS S., carriage painter, 224 E. Washington, r. 76 W. Ohio.

Mansfield John L., r. 557 N. Alabama.

Mansfield Julius, tailor, r. 26 Chatham.

Mansfield Thomas, blacksmith, 31 S. Pennsylvania, r. 161 W. Maryland.

Manson John, salesman New York store, bds 158 N. New Jersey.

Mansur Charles W., salesman, 21 W. Washington, r. 19 E. Ohio.

Mansur Frank, (Wool & M.) r. 18 E. Vermont.

Mansur Isaih, banker 154 E. Washington, r. 10 E. Vermont.

Mansur Jeremiah, r. 18 E. Vermont.

Mansur William, r. 19 E. Ohio.

Many Adolph, carpenter, r. 125 N. Noble.

Many Chas., carpenter, r. 216 N. Noble.

Many C. J., carpenter, r. 125 N. Noble.

Many Carmel, carpenter, r. 214 Railroad.

Many John, dealer in groceries and provisions, cor. Noble and Virginia av., r. same.

Many John B., carpenter and contractor, r. 125 N. Noble.

Many Zerah, teacher of languages, r. 125 N. Noble.

Maraney Matthew, machinist, Greenleaf & Co., r. 142 E. McCarty.

Marchant Isaac, jr., book keeper, Merrit & Coughlen, r. west end Washington.

Mardick James Y., grocer, 399 E. Georgia r. same.

Marien John, stonecutter, r. 19 School.

Marien N., stonecutter, r. 19 School.

Mark Maggie Miss, works Globe House.

Markey Thos., fireman, Caledonia paper mill, bds. 30 Douglass.

Marklie Matthew, barkeeper, bds. Fattout's blk.

Marley David, lab., r. West nr. First.

Marlott Frank, moulder, 74 S. Pennsylvania, r. 165 Eddy.

Marlott Zara C., patternmaker, r. 177 S. New Jersey.

Marlow J., painter, r. 120 W. Maryland.

Marmont Hall, sw. cor. Illinois and Georgia, H. Marmont, prop'r.

Marmont Hugo, proprietor Marmont Hall, cor. Illinois and Georgia, r. same.

Marony Matthew, machinist, r. 142 E. McCarty.

Maroskey Henry, works Fishback's tannery, r. Fourth bet. L. R. R. and Canal.

Marot John R., dealer in second hand furniture, stoves, etc., 87 E. Washington, bds. 221 E. Market.

Marrow John, r. 145 W. Washington.

Marquis George, works Osgood, Smith & Co.

Marquis Joseph O., expressman, r. 528 S. Meridian.

Marrinen John, bell boy Bates House.

Marrs C. B. (wid.) r. 23 E. St. Joseph.

Marrs William, mail agent, I. & V. R. R.

Marsee Joseph W. Dr., r. cor. New Jersey and South.

Marsee John L., (M. & Son) r. cor. South and New Jersey.

Marsee J. & Son, (Joseph and John L. M.) saw mill, New Jersey bet. Washington and Railroad.

Marsh Alice Miss, teacher Fourth Ward School, bds. 185 W. Maryland.

Marsh D., mail agent I. C. & L. R. R.

Marsh David M., traveling agent, r. 370 N. West.

Marsh E. J., printer 8 E. Pearl, bds. 126 N. Pennsylvania.

Marsh H. B, (H. M. & Son) r. 515 N. Meridian.

Marsh Harrison, (H. M. & Son) r. 519 N. Meridian.

THE CHINA TEA STORES

ARE AMONG THE

Attractions of Indianapolis.

Call and See Them before leaving the City.

Marsh H. & Son, (Harrison Marsh and H.
  B. Marsh) oculists, room 2 Miller's
  blk., Illinois nw. cor. Market.
Marsh William J., saddle and harness
  manufacturer, 182 W. Washington, r.
  185 W. Maryland.
Marshall Benjamin, machinist, r. 150 N.
  Winston.
Marshall Charles C. Rev., r. 101 E. St.
  Mary.
Marshall Emly, (col'd, wid. Thomas) r.
  311 E. St. Clair.
Marshall Frederick, lab., bds. 518 E.
  Washington.
Marshall Henry, (D. Sellers & Co.) r. 90
  N. East.
Marshall Isaac A., r. 240 N. New Jer-
  sey.
Marshall James, brakeman, C. C. & I. C.
  R. R., bds. 58 Benton.
Marshall James, carpenter, r. 347 N.
  Noble.
Marshall James H. (Marshal & Sons) r.
  90 N. East.
Marshall James G. (Marshal & Sons) r.
  311 N. Alabama.
Marshall James P., wagonmaker, r. 175
  W. Washington.
Marshall James P., blacksmith, r. 72 N.
  California.
Marshall John, lab., r. 168 E. New York.
Marshall Joseph, student, bds. 38 S. Ten-
  nessee.
Marshall J. N., clk. Martin & Hopkins, r.
  398 N. New Jersey.
Marshall Levi S., carpenter, r. 344 N.
  Winston.
Marshall Mary, (wid.) r. 243 N. New
  Jersey.
Marshall N. F., paperhanger. r. 37 India-
  na av.
Marshall William B., trimmer, bds. 114
  N. Tennessee.
Marshall William W. (M. & Sons) r. 98
  Broadway.
Marshall & Sons, (J. G., J. H. and W. W.
  Marshall) grocers, cor. Cherry and
  Broadway.
Martin A. H., clk. Charles Mayer & Co.,
  bds. Macy House.
Martin Brother, teacher St. John School,
  bds. same.
Martin Caroline Mrs., confectionery and
  restaurant, 80 E. Washington, r.
  same.

Martin D., with L. R. Martin, r. 192 W.
  Ohio.
Martin Dennis, traveling agent, John
  Sweetzer, rooms over 30 S. Meridian.
Martin Edward P., salesman, Carr & Al-
  vey, bds. Pyle House.
MARTIN EMIL, druggist and
  apothecary, cor. Meridian and Mc-
  Carty. r. same.
Martin Gilbert, blacksmith, cor. Tenth
  and Michigan rd., r. same.
Martin Gottlieb, drayman, r. 233 Union.
Martin Gustave, clk , 27 Washington,
  bds. Emenegger's Hotel.
Martin H., upholsterer, Hume, Adams &
  Co., r. 113 Indiana av.
MARTIN H. C., (M. & Hopkins) r.
  203 N. Illinois.
Martin John, work Cabinet Maker's Un-
  ion, r. N. Tennessee near corpora-
  tion line.
Martin John, contractor, r. 133 N. Penn-
  sylvania.
Martin John, lab., r. 570 N. Mississippi.
Martin John, works cotton factory, r.
  415 W. Washington.
Martin John, carder, cotton mill, r. 32
  Blake.
Martin Joseph T. (M. & Myers) r. 31
  Kentucky av.
Martin Jesse, boarding house, 33 W.
  Maryland.
MARTIN J. O., Secretary Masonic
  Mutual Benefit Society of Indiana,
  30 Kentucky av., bds. Palmer house.
Martin J. O., bookkeeper, Martin & Hop-
  kins, bds. 218 N. Alabama.
Martin J. T., special agent for W. H.
  Hay, bds. Pyle House.
Martin Louis, salesman, H. Reese, 113
  West Washington, bds. same.
Martin Louisa, (wid. Enos) r. 27 Henry.
MARTIN LUTHER R., (M. &
  Brown) real estate broker 10 E. Wash-
  ington, r. 97 E. Michigan.
Martin Preston H., carpenter, r. 121 N.
  Tennessee.
Martin Robert, moulder, r. 221 N. New
  Jersey.
Martin R., gasfitter, J. G. Hanning.
Martin Wesley, (col'd) lab., r. 344 Indi-
  ana av.
Martin William, clk., r. sw. cor. South
  and Delaware.
Martin William, r. 220 S. Noble.
Martin William, general traveling agent,
  r. 496 N. Mississippi.
Martin William H., teamster, r. 755 N.
  Mississippi.
Martin William L., harnessmaker, r. 27
  W. Henry.
MARTIN & BROWN, (L. R. M. and
  I. B.) abstract of titles, 10 E. Wash-
  ington.

MARTIN & HOPKINS, (H. C. M. and H. C. H.) general insurance agents, fire and life, Journal bldg.

Martin & Myers, (J. T. M. and J. A. M.) dealers in stoves and tinware, 157 W. Washington.

Martindale E. B. (M. & Tarkington) r. N. Meridian bet. Fifth and Sixth.

Martindale Julia A. (wid. Austin) dress maker, r. 194 W. Georgia.

Martindale William, bookkeeper, r. 83 Bradshaw.

Martindale Zue Miss, dressmaker, bds. 194 W. Georgia.

Martindale & Tarkington, (E. B. M. and J. S. T.) attorneys at law, Martindale's blk.

Martius H., lab. r. 113 Indiana av.

Marty Henry K., carpenter, 23 N. Noble, r. 189 N. Noble.

Martz C. Miss, dressmaker, r. 90 S. East.

Marvin G. D., printer, Journal office, r. 79 Massachusetts av.

Masher Theodore, foreman, I. C. & L. R. R., r. 191 Bates.

Maskill Dennis, lab., r. N. Tennessee bet. First and Second.

Mason Benjamin, (M. & Son) Oriental House.

Mason Chas. S., r. 161 N. Davidson.

Mason Hamett, (wid. Stewart) r. 241 N. Tennessee.

Mason Hampton, (col'd) barber, works M. Mason, r. 207 W. North.

Mason James, r. 161 N. Davidson.

Mason John, (col'd) barber, works M. Mason, bds. 207 W. North.

Mason Johnson T., lab., r. 270 Patterson.

Mason Louisa Mrs., boarding house, 23 W. Georgia.

Mason Madison, (col'd) proprietor Palmer House barber shop, r. 207 W. North.

Mason Stewart, clk. C. Friedgen, r. 241 N. Tennessee.

Mason Tyler, (M. & Son) r. Oriental House.

MASON & SON, (B. M. & T. M.) proprietors Oriental House.

Mason Wm. C., stamp clk. Post Office, bds. 17½ Virginia av.

Masonic Home Advocate, 44 N. Pennsylvania, Martin H. Rice, editor.

Mass Lovell, (col'd) cook, r. 126 Benton.

Masson James P., salesman, 123 S. Meridian, r. 407 N. East.

Masson William, boarding house, 202 S. West.

Mast E. tinsmith, bds. 23 Kentucky av.

MASTERS JOHN H., dealer in furniture of all kinds, 141 W. Washington, r. same.

Masters John H., clk. Jones & Co., r. 359 E. Market.

Masters Thomas E., salesman, bds. Court, bet. East and New Jersey.

Matchet John, railroader, r. 128 W. Ohio.

Matelan Thomas A., boilermaker, r. 169 Davidson.

Mather John, engineer I. C. & L. R. R., r. 189 Bates.

Matlock J. M., salesman Murphy, Johnston & Co., r. 328 N. Alabama.

Matlock William, gasfitter, 70 N. Illinois, r. 210 W. Ohio.

Matlock W. W., clk., r. 210 W. Ohio.

Matson Edwin S., moulder D. Root & Co., r. 534 E. Georgia.

Mattern Jacob H., works Commercial office, r. cor. Missouri and Walnut.

Matz John, boot and shoe manufacturer, 176 W. Washington, r. same.

Matzke Julius, butcher, bds. 358 E. New York.

MATTLER STEPHEN, saloon and boarding house, sw. cor. Illinois and South.

Mattler Maria (wid) r. 314 E. Ohio.

Matthews A., pressfeeder, bds. 31 N. Douglass.

Matthews Clem, lab., r. 246 Chestnut.

Matthews David, lab. peg and last factory, bds. 272 S. Missouri.

Matthews Edward, candymaker, bds. 169 N. Illinois.

Matthews Elias E., carriage trimmer S. W. Drew's, bds. 31 Indiana av.

Matthews Frederick, engineer I. C. & L. R. R., r. 178 E. New Jersey.

Matthews George, pudler Rolling Mill, r. 235 W. Merrill.

Matthews James, lab. American Saw Works, r. 20 Douglass.

Matthews John, engineer I. C. & L. R. R. shops, bds. Ray House.

Matthews Joseph F., notary public, 62 E. Washington.

Matthews Joseph K., carpenter and builder, r. 20 Harrison.

Matthews J. C. (wid.) bds. 31 N. Douglass.

Matthews Margaret, (wid.) r. 292 E. Market.

Matthews Martha A. (wid. Granville M.) r. 237 N. Noble.

Matthias Jacob, plasterer, r. 515 N. Mississippi.

Mauber John, tailor W. F. Rupp, bds. 23 Kentucky av.

H. H. LEE

Makes a Specialty of

CHOICE GOLDEN RIO,

AND

OLD GOVERNMENT JAVA COFFEES.

Mauer Henry, clk. cor. Massachusetts av. and St. Clair, bds. same.

Mauer John, moulder, r. 48 Greer.

Mauer John P., lab., r. 71 Elizabeth.

Mauloy Michael, machinist, works Greenleaf & Co., bds. 126 S. Tennessee.

Maurice J. N. (M. & Spohr.) r. 5 Dougherty.

Maurice & Spohr, (J. N. M. and G. S.) boot and shoemakers, 69 N. Pennsylvania.

Maus Albert, brewer, works W. end New York, r. same.

Maus Casper, ale and beer brewer W. end New York, cor. Agnes, res. same.

Maus Frank, law student, bds. cor. Agnes and East.

Maus Joseph, brewer, works W. end New York, bds. same.

Maus Louis, cigarmaker, r. 278 E. Michigan.

MAY A. D., notary public and mailing clk. Sentinel Office.

MAY ANDREW, dealer in flour barrels and cooperage, 102 S. East, r. 125 S. East.

May August, carpenter, Eagle Machine Works, r. 264 Chestnut.

May Charles, carpenter, Eagle Machine Works, r. Madison av.

May Daniel B., clk. Hoosier Store, r. 378 W. New York.

May Edwin, architect, r. 173 N. Pennsylvania.

May Henry, drayman, bds 365 S. Delaware.

May Herman, soldier, United States Arsenal.

May John, (S—— & M.) r. 360 S. Alabama.

May William W., foreman cooper shop, 102 S. East, r. 125 S. East.

Mayer Charles, saloonkeeper, 133 E. Washington, r. same.

Mayer Charles, barkeeper, r. 198 E. Washington.

Mayer Charles, (C. M. & Co.) r. 285 N. Illinois.

MAYER CHARLES & CO., (Chas. M. and Wm. Haueisen) importers and wholesale and retail dealers in toys, notions and fancy goods, 29 W. Washington.

Mayer Christian, salesman, 29 W. Washington, bds. 29 Coburn.

Mayer Jacob, barber, 37 S. Illinois, r. 146 E. Washington.

Mayer John, butcher, works 220 S. Meridian, bds. Wisconsin, outside city limits.

Mayer John, dealer in umbrellas and parasols, 69 E. Washington, r. 123 E St. Joseph.

Mayer Joseph, (M. & Bros.) r. 32 N. East.

Mayer Leopold, (M. & Bros.) bds. 18 Circle.

Mayer Mathias, dealer in cigars and tobacco, 96 S. Illinois, r. same.

Mayer Melchoir, Elder Evangelical church, r. 180 N. Noble.

Mayer Micheal, meat market, 220 S. Meridian, r. Wisconsin, outside city limits.

MAYER & BRO., (Joseph Mayer, and Leopold Mayer) dealers in cigars and tobacco, whol. and retail, 33 W. Washington.

Mayers X., shoemaker, 322 S. Delaware.

Mayhew E. C. (M. & Branham) r. 199 N. Pennsylvania.

Mayhew Frank H., sign painter, bds. 113 W. Washington.

Mayhew James Nelson, optican, r. 25 Circle.

MAYHEW O. F., solicitor of American and foreign Patents, office State house.

Mayhew P. L. (Mayhew, Warne & Co.) r. 59 W. Maryland.

Mayhew R. H., entry clk., 103 S. Meridian, bds. 23 W. Georgia.

MAYHEW, WARNE & CO., (P. L. Mayhew, J. B. Warne, and ——) whol. dealers in boots and shoes, 8 W. Louisiana.

MAYHEW & BRANHAM, (E. C. Mayhew and Edward Branham,) whol. dealers in boots and shoes 129 S. Meridian.

Mays Alfred, (col'd) barber, shop 160 Indiana av., r. 245 Howard.

Mays Philip, (col'd) barber, bds. 245 Howard.

Maxwell, Fry & Thurston, whol. dealers in iron, nails &c., 34 S. Meridian.

MAXWELL G. W., marble works 66 Virginia av., bds. Stanridge House.

Maxwell John, agent I. C. & L. R. R., r. 31 W. First.

Maxwell John M., (M., Fry & Thurston) r. 330 N. Meridian.

Maxwell T. H., shipping clk., Wiles, Bro. & Co., bds. Spencer house.

Mazeuer Samuel, lab., r. 103 Hosbrook.

Mazzuchelli Archille, second hand and notion store, 35 S. Illinois, r. same.

Mead James, millwright, r. 50 Forest av.

Mead W. H., traveling salesman, Mayhew & Branham.

Mead William, lab., bds., 131 S. Illinois.

Meads Peter, (col'd) lab., r. 94 Elm.

Meadowcroft John, carpenter, r. 749 N. Illinois.

Meadowcroft J. E., tinsmith, r. 749 N. Illinois.

Means John, r. 199 W. Ohio.

Means Thomas A. (Wilcox & M.) r. 88 Michigan rd.

Means William, r. 238 Madison av.

Mears G. W. Dr., office 11 W. Vermont, r. 210 N. Meridian.

Mears Henry B. (Mears & Lilly) r. 210 N. Meridian.

MEARS & LILLY, (H. B. M. and J. O. D. L.)Capital City Varnish Works, cor. Mississippi and Kentucky av.

Measel N. T., brewer, r. 72 S. West.

Medaris Amanda, (wid.) seamstress, r. 251 E. Market.

Medaris Amanda, (wid.) dressmaker, r. 25½ Massachusetts av.

Medina F. J., hair goods, 34 W. Washington, r 165 N. Tennessee.

Medsker W. T., r. 162 N. New Jersey.

Meehan Edward, lab., r. 280 Railroad.

Meek Alonzo, engineer I. C. & L. R. R.

Meek N. B., letter carrier, P. O.

Mefford William M., clk., 164 Indiana av., r. same.

Megga John, grocer, sw. cor. Delaware and McCarty, r. 88 Wyoming.

Meigs C. D., bookkeeper, 5 E. Washington, bds. Pyle House.

Meikel J. M., r. 112 N. Mississippi.

MEIKEL JOHN P., proprietor Meikel's brewery, 297 W. Washington, r. 213 W. Maryland.

Meikel Philip, r. ne. cor. Mississippi and Ohio.

Meikels Philip, machinist, r. 429 S Missouri.

Meikel Elizabeth, (wid. John) r. 246 Chestnut.

Meiley James, lab., bds. 256 S. Tennessee.

Meiley Patrick, lab., bds. 256 S. Tennessee.

Meiners Cornelius, lumber merchant, r. 325 E. Ohio.

Meiners John B., student North Western Christian University, r. 325 E. Ohio.

Meier Henry, lab., bds. 47 Oriental.

Meier Henry, (Roeth & M.) r. 87 S. New Jersey.

Meier Joseph, (V. M. & Bro.) r. 225 W. Washington.

Meier Lewis, (L. M. & Co.) r. 457 N. New Jersey.

Meier Lewis & Co. (L. M. and William Buschmann) dry goods and notions, 151 Ft. Wayne av.

Meier V., (V. M. & Bro.) r. 225 W. Washington.

Meier V. & Bro. (V. M. and Joseph M.) dealers in bottled ale and porter, 225 W. Washington.

Melano Augustus, cook Louis Lang bds. same.

Melchar Joseph, works rolling mill, bds. 78 W. McCarty.

Meldone Andrew, lab., r. 292 S. Missouri.

MELSHEIMER A. W., proprietor Macy House, r. same.

Melville R. B., merchant tailor, 24 Kentucky av., r. 179 W. South.

Melville Robert J., (Cornelius & M.) bds. 179 W. South.

Melvin Edwin, clk. r. 37 Chatham.

Melvin T. E., clk. 75 and 77 W. Washington, bds. 168 N. Noble.

Menaugh George, moulder, bds. 310 S. Illinois.

Menaugh Silas, moulder, bds. 310 S. Illinois.

Menaugh William, moulder, bds. 310 S. Illinois.

Mendenhall M. H., pastor, Grace M. E. Church, r. 117 N. East.

Menger Christian, telegraph reporter, r. 266 S. Delaware.

Mengis Francis, cigars and tobacco, 182 S. Delaware, r. same.

Mercer William, cabinetmaker, bds. Ray House.

Merchant Alfred, agent, McCormick's reaper, r. 691 N. Tennessee.

Merchant Sylvina,(wid. William) r. 160½ Indiana av.

MERCHANTS' NATIONAL BANK, 48 E. Washington, J. S. Newman, Prest.

Meredith Edward, works American Saw Works, r. 235 S. Mississippi.

Meredith Frank, clk., lunch stand Union Depot.

Meredith Richard O., carpenter, r. 80 Oak.

Meredith S. C., mailing clerk, Journal office, r. 212 Blackford.

Meredith Wm. M., printer, Journal office, r. 178 Blackford.

MERIDIAN STREET BATH HOUSE, se. cor. Meridian and Circe, J. M. Tilford, proprietor.

Meridian Street Dining-Rooms, 48 S. Meridian.

THE CHINA TEA STORES

Have the NAME of being the

MOST ATTRACTIVE STORES IN THE WEST.

No. 7 Odd Fellows Hall

AND

ACADEMY OF MUSIC CORNER.

Merk Martin, engineer, r. 32 N. Douglass.

Merkle Jacob, tailor, r. 31 N. Douglass.

Merks Martin, works Jackson, Rider & Co.

Merl Nicholas, saloon, 286 W. Washington, r. same.

Merrifield C. E., bookkeeper, 75 W. Washington, bds. 60 California.

Merrill Catherine Miss, teacher, University, r. 83 Ash.

Merrill Dennis H., broom manufacturer, 290 N. East, r. same.

Merrill Lucinda, (wid. John H.) r. 244 W. New York.

Merrill Minerva Miss, r. 244 W. New York.

Merrill Samuel, (M. & Field) r. cor. Merrill and Alabama.

Merrill W. H. D., plumber, Conrad Neab, r. 244 W. New York.

MERRILL & FIELD, (S. M. and E. S. F.) whol. and retail dealers in books and stationery, 5 E. Washington.

Merritt George, (M. & Coughlen) r. 175 N. West.

Merritt William, hostler, bds. 169 S. Tennessee.

Merritt & Coughlen, (Geo. M. and Wm. C.) proprietors Ohio Woolen mills, W. End Washington.

Mort N. D., lab., rolling mill, r. 273 S. West.

Merz Christian, butcher, 153 W. Washington.

Merz Fred, editor Daily Telegraph, r. 170 E. Washington.

Mertz Jacob, butcher, r. 139 S. Illinois.

Meskamp William, lab., r. 43 Ellen.

Meskil James, baker, 178 S. Illinois, bds. same.

Meskil Lendry, baker 178 S. Illinois, bds. same.

Meskill William D., bookbinder, Sentinel office, r. N. Tennessee near First.

MESSICK THOMAS B., paper hanger, r. 194 W. Vermont.

Messing M., minister Hebrew Congregation, r. 229 E. Ohio.

Messinger Lyman, carpenter, r. 9 Vine.

Metcalf George W., traveler Fairbank's scales, bds. Palmer House.

Metcalf J. S., bds. Macy House.

METZGER ALEXANDER, general Insurance agent, room 6 Odd Fellow's Hall, r. 385 N. Pennsylvania.

Metzger Catherine, (wid. George) r. 382 E. Michigan.

Metzger Conrad, shoemaker, r. 475 E. Market.

Metzger Charles, tailor, r. 475 E. Market.

Metzger David, lab., r. 501 N. East.

Metzger Elizabeth, (wid) r. 475 E. Market.

Metzger Engelbert J., printer, r. 79 N. East.

Metzger Frank B., clk., and collector, 6 Odd Fellows Hall, r. 385 N. Pennsylvania.

Metzger Henry, brewer Schmidt's brewery, r. Buchanan.

Metzger Jacob, bookkeeper H. Leiber & Co., r. 404 N. Delaware.

Metzger W. F., attorney at law, bds. 162 N. New Jersey.

Metzler John, brewer, r. 497 S. New Jersey.

Metzler John, bartender, 33 N. Pennsylvania, r. 31 N. East.

METZNER ADOLPH, Eagle Pharmacy, 127 E. Washington, r. same.

Meurer F. M., shoemaker, r. 219 Virginia av.

Meyer Aug. B, clk., 35 W. Washington, bds. 180 N. Delaware.

Meyer Charles, clk., 250 E. Washington, r. 98 N. Davidson.

Meyer Charles F., clk., 11 N. Pennsylvania, r. 180 N. Delaware.

MEYER CHARLES F., dealer in cigars and tobacco, 11 N. Pennsylvania, r. Cincinnati, O.

Meyer Christian L., carpenter, r. 275 E. Ohio.

Meyer Cornelius, confectioner, 17 N. Pennsylvania, r. same.

Meyer C. F., dealer in pictures and looking glasses, 7 Martindale's blk., r. 227 N. Liberty.

Meyer Frederick, carpenter, r. 236 E. Vermont.

Meyer Geo. F. (G. F. M. & Co.) r. 180 N Delaware.

MEYER GEO. F. & CO. (George F. Meyer and ——.) manufacturers and whol. and retail dealers in cigars, tobaccos, pipes, etc, 35 W. Washington.

Meyer Henry, (Roelh & M.) r. 31 S. New Jersey.

Meyer Henry, lab., 219 Union.

Meyer Henry, clk. German dry goods store, r. 641 N. Tennessee.

Meyer Henry, painter, r. 55 Charles.

Meyer L, drayman, r. 98 N. Davidson.

Meyer Martin, turner in bone, ivory and horn, 19 S. Alabama, r. same.

Meyer William, blacksmith C. C. & I. C. R. R., r. 426 E. Georgia.

Meyer William, (H. Altman & Co.) r. 224 Union.

Meyer William, machinist, Eagle Machine Works, r. 98 N. Davidson.

Meyers Jacob, cigar dealer, cor. Maryland and Illinois, bds. Neiman House.

Meyers Jacob C., carpenter, r. 321 N Liberty.

Meyers John, carpenter, r. 327 N. Winston.

Meyers John G., lawyer, r. 485 N. Alabama.

Meyers J. W., school teacher, r. 802 N. Illinois.

Meyers Louisa Mrs., seamstress, r. 373 E. New York.

Michael Gustav, lab, r. 121 Spring.

Michales John G., carpenter, r. 656 N Tennessee.

Michelfelder John, Cabinet Maker's Union, r. 377 E. Michigan.

Michelfelder John G., Cabinet Maker's. Union, r. 375 E. Michigan.

MICK, GEYER & CO., (W. E. Mick, D. Geyer and D. H. Shoneberger) real estate agents and brokers, 16½ E. Washington.

Mick James F. (M. & Marshall) r. 170 Jackson.

Mick & Marshall, (J. F. M. and L. M.) proprietors Star Shoe Store, 13 W. Washington.

Mick Wm. E. (M., Geyer & Co.) r. 158 Christian av.

Middaugh Charles, painter, bds. 312 Virginia av.

Middaugh George, shoemaker, 148 Virginia av., r. 312 Virginia av.

Middaw James M., fireman, I. C. & L. R. R., r. 110 Bates.

Middleton Eliza, (col'd) r. cor. Ash and Christian av.

Miers Joseph T., works Rolling Mill, bds. 63 W. Georgia.

Miflin James H. (col'd) barber, 10 S. Delaware, bds. 6 W. Alley.

Milbourn Charles F., clk. N. & G. Ohmer, r. 244 S. Alabama.

Miles John C., clk. T. H. & I. R. R., bds. 152 N. Meridian.

Millard E., checkman, P. C. & St. L. freight depot, r. 9 Grant.

Millender Wm. B., painter, r. 132 N. Liberty.

Miller Albert A., check clerk, Trade Palace, bds. 339 N. Pennsylvania.

Miller Adam, watchmaker, r. 268 E. Washington.

Miller Alfred, (col'd) porter, Bates House.

BENHAM BRO'S,

36 East Washington St.,

Pianos, Organs and Melodeons Tuned, Moved and Repaired.

Miller Alfred E., clk., Browning & Sloan, bds. Pyle House.

Miller Anna, (wid.) dealer in pictures, r. over 570 E. Washington.

Miller Alfred J., lab., r. 397 N. West.

Miller Anthony, r. 244 S. Tennessee.

Miller Anthony F. W., carpenter, r. 237 E. Vermont.

Miller A. R., photographer, 45 E. Washington, r. 143 N. Delaware.

Miller B. W., bookkeeper, Strong, Smith & Co., bds. Lyttle Hotel.

Miller Cam, (col'd) lab., r. 350 W. North.

Miller Cary W., messenger, First National Bank, r. 373 N. Delaware.

Miller Charles, coppersmith, bds. 187 E. Washington.

Miller Charles, lab., r. 47 Oriental.

Miller Charles, conductor, C. C. & I. C. R. R, bds. 58 Benton.

Miller Charles, conductor, C. C. & I. C. R. R., bds. 210 N. Noble.

Miller Charles F., clk., Bryant, Cornelius & Co., r. 27 N. California.

Miller C. F., salesman, 108 S. Meridian, bds 27 N. California.

Miller Christian, lab., r. 219 Union.

Miller Christ'n F., carpenter and builder, 230 N. Davidson, r. same.

Miller Corwin, engineer, C. C. & I. C. R. R., r. cor. Louisiana and New Jersey.

Miller Dora Miss, teacher, r. 25 S. Delaware.

Miller Edward, engineer T. H. & I. R. R., bds. 111 W. South.

Miller Elizabeth, (wid.) r. 373 N. Delaware.

Miller Elizabeth, (wid.) r. 12 Indiana av.

Miller E. (wid. Aleck) r. 293 Indiana av.

Miller E. M., physician, r. 41 Bradshaw.

Miller E. T., druggist, 49 S. Illinois, r. 30 Indiana av.

Miller Frank, barber, 37 S. Illinois, bds. 23 Kentucky av.

Miller Frank, cooper, r. Douglass, third house E. side.

Miller Frederick, blacksmith, r. 172 S Noble.

Miller Frederick, carpenter, r. 21 Biddle.

MILLER GEORGE, carriage manufacturer, cor. Kentucky av. and Georgia, r. Kentucky av.

Miller Geo., blacksmith, r. 456 S. Meridian.

Miller George, lab, r. 124 Duncan.

H. H. LEE,
Dealer in
Teas, Coffees, Sugars & Spices,
No. 7 ODD FELLOWS HALL
AND
ACADEMY OF MUSIC CORNER.

Miller Geo. W., wagon and carriage maker, r. 666 N. Missouri.

Miller George F., butcher, 150 Virginia av., r. 213 S. Alabama.

Miller G. S., foreman, starch factory, r. 290 N. Winston.

Miller Gustin, fireman C. C. & I. C. R. R., r. cor. Louisiana and New Jersey.

Miller Harrison S., gasfitter, r. 372 E. New York.

Miller Henry, lab., r. 350 E. Michigan.

Miller Henry, lab., r. 206 W. Vermont.

Miller Henry, works C. Eden's, bds. 154 E. St. Clair.

Miller Henry, currier Mooney & Co., bds. 410 S. Illinois.

Miller Henry, lab., r. Coburn nr. Virginia av.

Miller J., shoemaker, bds. Globe House.

Miller James, brakeman, J. M. & I. R. R., r. 409 S. Illinois.

Miller James, conductor, C. C. & I. C. R. R., r. 210 N. Noble.

Miller James Frank, clk., G. F. Meyers, bds Palmer House.

Miller Jeremiah, lab., r. 46 Elm.

Miller Jerry, clk., B. Davis & Co., r. 46 Elm.

Miller Jesse, hackman, bds. 206 W. Vermont.

Miller John, lab., r. 376 S. West.

Miller John A., butcher, r. 235 S. Alabama.

Miller John H., machinist, r. 60 Fayette.

Miller John W., lab., r. 173 N. Winston.

Miller Joseph F., clk., r. 293 Indiana av.

Miller J., attorney, 94 E. Washington, bds. Little House.

Miller J. A., bookkeeper, Vinedge & Jones, bds. 10 E. Michigan.

MILLER J. F., Superintendent Western Division P. C. & St. L. R. R., r. Richmond, Ind.

Miller J. V., shoemaker, r. 63 Indiana av.

Miller Kate, (wid. William B.) r. 240 Blake.

Miller Louis, wagon and plowmaker, 478 E. Washington, r. 136 Michigan rd.

Miller Louisa, (wid.) r. 116 N. Noble.

Miller M. Mrs., r. 149 S. New Jersey.

Miller Margaret, (wid.) r. 314 E. New Jersey.

Miller Mark D., railroader, r. 372 N. New York.

Miller Milton R., foreman, C. C. & I. C. R. R. shops, r. 21 Grant, nr. Michigan rd.

Miller Mollie E. (wid. Charles) r. 133 N. Mississippi.

Miller Peter, lab., r. 272 Blake.

Miller R., upholsterer Hume, Adams & Co., r. 93 N. New Jersey.

Miller Reinold A., jeweler and watchmaker, 268 E. Washington, r. same.

Miller Robert, locksmith, bds. 23 Kentucky av.

Miller Robert E., machinist, bds. 217 S. Illinois.

Miller Lidney C., teamster, r. 102 Elm.

Miller Stephen, lab., r. 169 E Stevens.

Miller S. S., plasterer, r. 42 Rose.

Miller Thomas, watchman, I. P. & C. R. R., r. 23 Hahn.

Miller Thomas P., r. 372 E. New York.

Miller William, lab., r. 116 N. Noble.

Miller Wm., sawmaker, r. 124 Duncan.

Miller William, bds. 73 W. Maryland.

Miller William, engineer, C. C. C. & I. R. R.

Milligan Frank, (col'd, R. & M.) r. 164 Douglass al.

Millman Fred, lab., r. 349 E. McCarty.

Millner Davis, mailing clk. Journal office, r. 173 Dougherty.

Millner W. J. (M. & Sherwood) bds. 121 N. Illinois.

Millner & Sherwood, (W. J. M. & F. W. S.) whol. tea dealers, 27 McNabb, under National Hotel.

Mills David, (M. & Hollingsworth) r. 24 N. West.

Mills Julia A. Mrs., dressmaker, r. 793 N. Tennessee.

Mills Richard H., shoemaker, bds. Globe House.

Mills & Hollingsworth (David M. and Zeph H.) livery and feed stables, 277 W. Washington.

Millspaugh Oscar, painter, bds. 30½ N. Pennsylvania.

Milroy Frank, lab., r. 376 S. West.

Milroy Francis J., lab., r. 266 S. Illinois.

Milton Hiram T., carpenter, r. 338 Indiana av.

Minahon Thomas, lab., r. 197 Meek.

Miner Maggie, (wid. Milton) r. 32 S. Mississippi.

Miner Wilford H., carpenter, r. 257 N. West.

Miner Willis R., bookkeeper, 149 S. Meridian, r. 441 N. Mississippi.

Miney John, lab., r. 31 Maple.

Minick Hiram, proprietor Palmer House Saloon, r. 256 S. Meridian.

Minick D. C. (M. & Co.) r. 17½ W. Washington.

MINICK D. C. & CO., real estate brokers, 17½ W. Washington.

Minthorn John G., carpenter, bds. 268 E. St. Clair.

Miscall John, tailor, r. 233 S. West.

Miscall Joseph, lab., r. 30 John.

Mitnell Barnard F., lab., r. 44 Oriental.

Mitchell Catherine, (wid.) r. Wabash bet. East and New Jersey.

Mitchell James C., clk., 414 W. Washington, bds. 152 N. Blake.

Mitchell Jennie, servant, Palmer House.

Mitchell Joseph, mail agent, I. C. & L. R. R.

Mitchell Joseph, servant, Palmer House.

Mitchell J., prop. Oak Hall clothing store, 2 Bates House blk., r. 174 E. Ohio.

Mitchell J. L. (Newcomb, M. & Ketcham) r. E. Market, E. city limits.

Mitchell J. M. D., barber, 24 N. Delaware, r. same.

Mitchell Louise, servant, Palmer House.

Mitchell Mary, (col'd, wid.) r. 230 N. Missouri.

Mitchell Mary J. (wid. Henry B.) seamstress, r. 152 Blake.

Mitchell N. C., publisher Illustrated Bee Journal, r. Marion, Ohio.

Mitchell R. S., helper, C. C. & I. C. R. R. shops.

Mitchell Robert G., brickmason, r. 114 Michigan.

Mitchell Lawrel, engineer C. & I. J. R. R. bds. 61 S. Noble.

Mitchell S. J., r. 676 N. Mississippi.

Mitchell William, (M. & Rammelsberg) r. 25 Fort Wayne av.

MITCHELL & RAMMELSBERG, furniture company, manufacturers and dealers in furniture, sales-room 38 E. Washington, Wm. Mitchell Superintendent.

Mittay H. A., clk. 92 E. South, bds. same.

Mittay John C., Sr., saddler, r. 335 E. New York.

Mittay John C., Jr., shoemaker, r. 347 E. New York.

Mitty ——, lab., r. 233 Huron.

Mix Lemuel W., Insurance agent, bds. 218 E. Market.

Mock Martin, clk., J. Staub, r. 127 N. Davidson.

Moch William, r. 399 S. East.

Mode Michael, with C. Karle, r. 229 N. Noble.

Moffat Charles A., cabinetmaker, r. 115 N. Tennessee.

Moffitt Emma G. Miss, clk. Josslyn Bros., r. 675 E. Washington.

Moffit John, foreman Braden & Burford bds. 35 Virginia av.

Moffitt John, physician, r. 250 Minerva.

Moffitt Oliver I., printer, Sentinel office r. 35 Virginia av.

Moffatt William, clk., Browning & Sloan, r. 675 E. Washington.

Moghan Patrick, shoemaker, r. 353 E. McCarty.

Mohare Mary, servant, Palmer House.

Mohar John, machinist Eagle Machine Works, r. 172 W. Washington.

Mohr George, cabinetmaker, bds. 65 S. East.

Mohr George, bottler, at Gresch's, r. 191 N. Noble.

Molitor William, basketmaker, bds. 451 S. Meridian.

Monaghan Timothy, salesman, 41 E. Washington, r. 474 E. Georgia.

Monahan Catherine, (wid. John) r. 368 S. Tennessee.

Monahan John, works rolling mill, r. 390 S. Tennessee.

Monahan Thomas, lab., 290 S. Missouri.

Monfort C. B., coachmaker, r. 39 W. St. Joseph.

Monninger Conrad, saloon, 167 W. Washington, r. 292 W. Maryland.

MONNINGER DANIEL, saloon and wine house, 20 Kentucky av., r. 386 N. Tennessee.

Monroe Franz, cabinetmaker, r. 81 S. Liberty.

Monroe F. T., printer, Commercial office, r. 32 S. Mississippi.

Monroe Jacob, lab., r. 4 Geisendorff.

Monroe John, (Johnson & M.) r. 330 E. Vermont.

Monroe John L., carpenter, r. 331 E. St. Clair.

Monroe S. Mrs., (col'd) r. 10 Rhode Island.

Monroe Samuel, lab., r. 307 E. McCarty.

Monroe & Johnson, (J. M. and A. W. J.) carpenters and builders, 40 W. Market.

Montague Martha Mrs., r. 105 S. New Jersey.

Montague Mollie Miss, seamstress, bds. 105 S. New Jersey.

Monteith David, r. 333 N. Davidson.

Monteith John, carpenter, r. 127 E. South.

Monteith Taylor, carpenter, bds. 127 E. South.

Montgomery Ezra, shoemaker, r. 505 N. Meridian.

Montgomery Silas, (col'd) lab., r. 454 S. Tennessee.

Moorbach Charles, bootmaker, 301 S. Delaware, r. same.

Moorbach Peter, dealer in boots and shoes, 301 S. Delaware, r. same.

MOODY BROTHERS, (E. M. and C. W. M.) props Cincinnati Drug Store, junction of Tennessee, New York, and Indiana. av.

Moody C. W. (M. & Bro.) bds. Pyle House.

Moody Edward R. (M. & Bro.) r. 128 W. Vermont.

MOODY JOHN B., physician, Moodys' drug store, r. cor. Indiana av. and Tennessee.

Moodey L. D., agent, Home Insurance Co., r. Southport.

Mooney J. E. (M. & Co.) bds. 152 N. Mississippi.

Mooney Thomas, lab., r. 340 S. Alabama.

MOONEY & CO (J. E. M. and A. S. Mount) manufactures and dealers in shoe and saddlery leather, tanners' oil, etc., 147 S. Meridian.

Moore Aaron, (col'd) lab., r. 245 W. Ohio.

Moore Adam, (col'd) lab., r. 43 Charles.

Moore Charles, carpenter, r. 314 S. Illinois.

Moore Charles P., carpenter, r. 231 N. Noble.

Moore Chauncy, capitalist, r. 242 N. Pennsylvania.

Moore Clara, (wid. Thomas) notions and toys, 253 W. Washington. r. same.

MOORE C. G., clk., Indianapolis National Bank, r. 242 N. Pennsylvania.

Moore C. W., clk., r. 296 Virginia av.

Moore Edmond, (col'd) lab., r. cor. Oak and Vine.

Moore Emma Miss, seamstress, r. 47 N. Noble.

Moore Frank D., printer, bds. 30½ N. Pennsylvania.

Moore Frank M., tinner, r. 394 Virginia av.

Moore G. T., sec'y and treas'r, Indianapolis Wagon and Agricultural Works, r. 377 N. Illinois.

Moore Henry H., physician and surgeon, r. 298 E. Ohio.

Moore H. A., sec'y Union Novelty Works, r. 476 N. Illinois.

Moore H. Clay, clk., Browning & Sloan, r. 298 E Ohio.

Moore James, engineer, C. C. & I. C. R. R., bds. 61 S. Noble.

Moore James L., plasterer, bds. 314 E. Louisiana.

Moore James, lab., r. cor. Grant and Eckert.

Moore James, teamster, bds. 435 N. East.

Moore John, salesman, New York store, bds. Palmer House.

Moore John, clk., Kingan & Co., bds. 180 N. Tennessee.

Moore John O, notary public, 6 Talbott & New's blk., r. one half mile E. city.

Moore Jno. H., r. 231 N. Noble.

Moore Joseph, huckster, r. 319 E. North.

Moore Joseph A. (Altred, Talbott & Co.) r. 435 N. Pennsylvania.

Moore Joshua, broom peddler, r. 246 S. Missouri.

Moore Julia Mrs., r. 145 E. Merrill.

Moore J., clk., bds. 66 W. New York.

Moore J. L., bookkeeper, Kingan & Co., bds. 80 W. Washington.

Moore J. P., ra Ironder, bds. Bates House.

Moore J. R., expressman, Union Depot, bds. Bates House.

Moore Michael, lab., r. 394 S. West.

Moore Michael H., carriage trimmer, r. 211 N. Davidson.

Moore Montie Miss, teacher, Ninth Ward School, r. 298 E. Ohio.

Moore M. H., carriage trimmer, r. 211 N. Davidson.

Moore Nich., lab., r. 9 Dougherty.

Moore Philip H., pianomaker, bds. 121 N. West.

Moore Richard, tailor, r. 67 S. West.

Moore Samuel H., physician, 72 E. Market.

Moore Spencer, student, bds. 206 E. Ohio.

Moore Squire, (col'd) lab., r. 270 N. Noble.

Moore Thomas, blacksmith, r. 553 Virginia av.

Moore Thomas, cooper, r. 57 Hellen.

Moore Thomas C., bookkeeper Murphy, Johnston & Co., r. 28 E Michigan.

Moorhead T. W., clk. New York Store, r. 350 N. Meridian.

Moore Wm., cooper, r. 101 S. New Jersey.

Moore William, plasterer, r. 387 Massachusetts av.

Moore William, horse trader, r. 185 N. Noble.

Moore William, clk. C. Pottage, r. 25 Elsworth.

Moore William, cooper, r. 103 S. New Jersey.

Moore William G., physician, 262 Massachusetts av., r. same.

Moore W. A., clk., r. 25 Ellsworth.

Moran Ellen, (wid. Thomas) boarding house, 38 S. Tennessee.

Moran Ellen J. Miss, clk. Trade Palace, bds 38 S. Tennessee.

Moran John, engineer, C. & I. J. R. R.

Moran John, lab., r. 31 Idaho.

Moran Mary Miss, cook City Hospital.
Moran Mary T. Miss, bds. 38 S. Tennessee.
Moran Michael, lab., r. 24 Hahn.
Moran Nelly Miss, clk., Trade Palace, bds. 38 S. Tennessee.
Moran Patrick, lab., r. 294 S. East.
Moran Samuel, signpainter, r. 140 W. Vermont.
Moresn Jeremiah. works B. F. Haugh & Co., r. 156 N. Davidson.
Morgan Benj F., pastor first United Brethren Church, r. 105 N. Noble.
Morgan David E., heater rolling mill, r. 248 S. Missouri.
Morgan Daniel R., switchman. r. 131 E. Merrill
Morgan Elizabeth, (wid) r. 351 E. Market.
Morgan Griffith, clergyman, r. 186 W. Vermont.
Morgan John, works rolling mill, bds. 33 E. McCarty.
Morgan Laurence, cooper, r. 291 E. Georgia.
Morgan Margaret, (wid) r. 146 Stevenson.
Morgan Maria Mrs., (wid) bds. 73 W. Maryland.
Morgan Mary Jane Miss, dressmaker, r. 351 E. Market.
Morgan Pauline Mrs., (wid. John) r. 33 E. McCarty.
Morgan Samuel, traveling agent Grover & Baker sewing machines, r. 322 N. Alabama.
Morgan Sarah A. (wid. George) r. 167 W. Washington.
Morgan S. W., (Stewart & Morgan,) r. 502 N. Illinois.
Morgan William, fireman, C. C. C. & I. R. R.
Morgan William, painter, bds. 33 E. McCarty.
Morgan William H., works rolling mill, bds. 310 S. Illinois.
Morgenveck Valentine, groceries and saloon, 21 Chatham, r. same.
Moriarty Daniel, lab., r. 32 Bates.
Moriarty Daniel, lab., Union Depot, r. 248 S. Delaware.
Moriarty James B., brickmason, r. 403 S. East.
Moriarty John, lab., 40 Benton.
Moriarty Michael, plasterer, r. 11 Coburn.
Moriarty Morris, lab., T. H. & I. R. R.
Moriarty Pat., lab., r. 23 Bates.
Moriarty Thos., moulder Eagle Machine Works, r. 348 S. Delaware.
Moriarty William, flagman, r. 53 Maple
MORIARTY WM. C., bookkeeper, Sentinel Office, r. 255 N. Mississippi.

BENHAM BRO'S.

36 East Washington St.,

KEEP

THE VERY BEST

VIOLIN AND GUITAR STRINGS.

MORITZ BROTHERS, (Myer and Sol. Moritz) clothiers and merchant tailors, also, dealers in cloths, cassimeres and vestings, 19 W. Washington.
Moritz Myer, (M. Bros) r. New York City
Moritz Sol. (M. Bros.) r. 226 E. New York.
Marley Thomas, lab., r. 226 S. Missouri.
Morning Watch, monthly paper, W. W. Dowling, publisher
Morrell William, clk. New York Store, r. 130 W. New York.
Morrell W. B., clk. Bee Hive Store, r. 130 W. New York.
Morris Alfred W., painter, works 31 Kentucky av.
Morris Charles G. (Haskit, M. & C.) r. 112 Jackson.
Morris Emeline, (col'd, wid. John M.) r. 149 Bright.
Morris Grigsby, cook Spencer House.
Morris Harmony, clothes cleaner and repairer, r. 330 Indiana av.
Morris Jacob, boarding house, 18 Circle.
Morris James, clk., r. 112 Jackson.
Morris John, shoemaker, r. 5 Dougherty.
Morris John J. (West, M. & Gorrell) r. outside city limits.
Morris J. D, freight agent I. C. & L. R. R., r. 112 Jackson.
Morris J. W., clk. I. & V. R. R, bds. 112 Jackson.
Morris L. C. (col'd) barber, bds. cor. Bright and North.
Morris Mary C. (wid. Francis A.) r. 360 E. St. Clair.
Morris Samuel B., r. 79 Norwood.
Morris Sanford, clk. Trade Palace, r. 275 W. Vermont.
Morris William, painter, bds. 74 State.
Morris William J., plasterer, r. 290 Chestnut.
Morris W. B., carpenter, r. 210 Huron.
Morrison Charles, clk. C. C. C. & I. R. R., r. cor. St. Mary and Ft. Wayne av.
Morrison Hetty A. Mrs., clk. P. O., r. 344 N. Alabama.
Morrison Jacob, agent fruit drier, r. 85 E Pratt.
Morrison James, r. 108 Plum.
Morrison James A., carpenter, r. 137 N. Noble.
Morrison John I. (Wiles, Bro. & Co.) r. 298 N. Tennessee.

THE CHINA TEA STORES

ARE AT

No. 7 ODD FELLOWS HALL

AND

ACADEMY OF MUSIC CORNER.

Morrison Michael, r. 135 Union.

Morrison Robert J., Deputy Treasurer of State, r. 298 N. Tennessee.

Morrison Sarah Miss, r. 351 N. East.

Morrison Squire, lab., r. 449 S. Missouri.

Morrison S. L, bill clk. 123 S. Meridian, r. St. Mary, cor. Ft. Wayne av.

Morrison Thomas, Osgood & Smith, bds. 136 W. Vermont.

Morris Thomas A., r. Fall Creek rd. N. city limits.

Morrison William, teamster, r. 270 Railroad.

Morrison Willouby L., clk., Stewart & Morgan, r. cor. Ft. Wayne av. and St. Mary.

Morrison W. H., Prest. Indiana Banking Co.

Morrison W. H. (Alford, Talbott Co.) r. 63 Circle.

Morrison W. H., bookbinder, Journal office, r. 144 N. Tennessee.

Morrison W. Henry, civil engineer, r. 56½ N. Illinois.

Morrow George, cartman, bds. 164 W. Washington.

Morrow Robt., engineer, r. 164 W. Washington.

Morrow Thomas, lab., P. C. & St. L. freight depot, r. 327 W. Market.

Morrow Wilson, (M. & Trussler) r. 282 N. Pennsylvania.

MORROW & TRUSLER, (Wilson M. and Nelson T.) attorneys at law, 6 Vinton's blk.

Morse A C, roadmaster, I. C. & L. R. R., bds. 58 Benton.

Morse Charles A., machinist, r. 204 N. Winston.

Morse J. W., woodworker, Shaw, Lippencott & Conner, bds 26 W. Georgia.

Mortea William, filler, r. 32 Bicking.

Mortland A. M., r. 227 N. Illinois.

Morton E. B. carpenter, r. 325 N. Davidson.

Morton George T., attorney, Talbott & New's blk., N. Pennsylvania, bds. Pyle House.

Morton Isaac D., carpenter, bds. 195 N. Davidson.

Morton John, bricklayer, r. 67 Norwood.

Morton John R. (M. & Ricker) bds. Bates House.

MORTON O. P, U. S. Senator, r. 194 N. Pennsylvania.

Morton Thomas R., bookkeeper, r. 215 W. Ohio.

MORTON & RICKER, (J. R. M. and F. R.) props. Journal of Commerce, office, old Journal bldg.

Mosby Elizabeth, (wid. Dart) bds. 157 Indiana av.

Moser George, meat market, 295 S. Missouri, r. same.

Moses L. W., optician, 59 E. Washington, r. 87 E. Michigan.

Mosher Theodore, foreman I. C. & L. R. R. shop, r. 191 Bates.

Moss Alexander, (col'd) r. 1 Elizabeth.

Moss Jerry, works rolling mill, bds. 256 S. Tennessee.

Mossler A. L., hoopskirt manufacturer, 59 S. Illinois, bds. N. 35 East.

Mossler L. I. (L. I. M. & Bros.) r. 250 E. Vermont.

Mossler M. L., bookkeeper, 37 E. Washington, bds. 35 N. East.

Mossler S. (L. I. M. & Bro's) r. 35 N. East.

MOSSLER L. I. & BRO'S, merchant tailors and dealers in ready made clothing, 37 E Washington.

Mosser William, printer, r. 43 Dougherty.

Mothershead John L., Greenleaf & Co., bds. depot Dining Hall.

Motterg Ferdinand, proprietor Concordia House cor. South and Meridian, r. same.

Moulton D. S., bookkeeper, Olin & Foltz, 21 N. Pennsylvania, r. 219 E. South.

Moulton Levi H., lab., r. Michigan road bet. Eighth and Ninth.

Moulton Robert, lab., r. 32 Bicking.

Mount A. S., Mooney & Co., r. 455 N. Tennessee.

Mount G. A., boarding house, 143 Indiana av.

Mount John, r. 197 N. Illinois.

Mount William P., currier, Mooney & Co., r. 197 N. Illinois.

Mountain Michael, lab., r. 17 Willard.

Mowe Frank, cabinetmaker, r. 81 S. Liberty.

Mowe Henry, jr., machinist, r. 120 N. Noble.

Mowe Henry, machinist, r. 120 N. Noble.

Mowrer Joseph, lab., r. W. Washington.

Moyer E. R., with Wm. Sumner & Co., bds. 33 W. Maryland.

Moyer Joseph, carpenter, r. nw. cor. College and Home av.

Mozart Hall, John Grosh, proprietor, 37 and 39 S. Delaware.

Muchett Charles, carpenter, r. 116 Fort Wayne av.

Mucho William, cigarmaker, r. 41 Russell.

Muckenberger John, cigar box, manufacturer, r. 368 S. East.

Muecke Wm. (Egger & Co.) r. 235 E. Washington.

Mueller August, school teacher, r. 212 E. Ohio.

Mueller Carl, coppersmith, r. 155 E. Washington, up stairs.

Mueller Catharine, wid., r. 573 E. St. Clair.

Mueller Charles G., carpenter, r. 47 Oriental.

MUELLER CHARLES G., Singer's Hall, 25 S. Delaware, r. same.

Mueller Charles L. custom tailor, 53 S. Illinois, r. 412 S. Illinois.

Mueller Christian, lab., C. C. & I. C. R. R.

MUELLER EDWARD, groceries and produce, 141 E. Washington, r. 305 E. Market.

Mueller Ernst, cabinetmaker, bds. 65 E. East.

Mueller E, drayman, r. 170 Madison av.

Mueller Frederick, cabinetmaker, bds. 65 S. East.

MUELLER JOHN, wholesale liquor dealer, 300 E. Washington, r. Madison rd.

Mueller John A., stairbuilder, r. 486 N. East.

Mueller S. H., druggist, 187 E. Washington, r. same.

Mueller Martha, (wid.) r. 304 E. Ohio.

Mueller Peter, Cabinetmakers' Union, r. 135 North Noble.

Mueller Valentine, letter carrier, r. 142 N. Davidson.

Mueller Victoria, (wid.) r. over 568 E. Washington.

Muhlemann Charles, cabinetmaker, bds. 488 S. New Jersey.

Muhlemann Christian, cabinetmaker, r. 488 S. New Jersey.

Muier C., saw mill. cor. Alabama and Louisiana, r. 325 E. Ohio.

Muir James. r. 121 N. Mississippi.

Muir J. W. (M. & Foley) bds. Pyle House.

Muir Thomas, engraver, H. C. Chandler & Co., bds. 55 Bates.

Muir & Foley, (J. W. Muir and J. W. Foley) notions fancy goods and human hair, 60 N. Illinois.

Mulbarger William, carriagemaker, r. 575 Maple.

Mulchy Michael, lab., r. 87 S. Noble.

Mulky Jane B., bds. Bates House.

Mull J. H., works S. W. Drew, r. 273 N. Tennessee.

Mullaly Edward, drayman, r. 62 Huron.

Mullaney D. J, with T. F. Ryan, r. 355 N. Illinois.

Mullaney P. J., with T. F. Ryen, r. 355 N. Illinois.

Mullen Anna Mrs, r. 20 Dougherty.

Mullen Daniel, brakeman, C. C. & I. C. R. R., bds. 58 Benton.

BENHAM BRO'S,

36 East Washington St.,

AGENTS FOR THE

BURDETT ORGAN.

Mullen William, clk. 77 S. Meridian, r. 521 N. Tennessee.

Muller Christian, Carpenter, r. 489 S. East.

Muller Eearnest, cabinetmaker, r. 255 E. Washington.

Muller George F., butcher, r. 213 S. Alabama.

Mulligan T. D., stereotyper, Journal office, bds. Pyle House.

Mulliken John, agent, J. S. Cary & Co., r. 71 Davidson.

Mulliken Mary Mrs., dressmaker, r. 71 Davidson.

Mullin Bernard, lab., r. 73 W. McCarty.

Mullivan Patrick, brakeman, T. H. & I. R. R., bds. 228 W. Georgia.

Mundan Benjamin, teamster, r. 300 S. Illinois.

Mundan Jessie, clk.. r. 379 N. West.

Munday Madison, (M. & Snyder) r. Dayton, Ohio.

Munday & Snyder, (M M. and A. S) manufacturers of malt, etc , 214 and 216 S. Delaware.

Munhall C. A., clk, Macy House, bds. same.

Munhall L. W., dentist, 35½ E. Market, bds. Macy House.

Munro Alex., salesman, New York store, bds. 158 N. New Jersey.

Munro C. H., salesman, New York store, bds. Avenue House.

Munselt Exra. wagonmaker, r. 63 Charles.

Munsell F., fireman, C. C. C. & I. R. R.

Munsel H.. carriagemaker, r. 71 Charles.

Munson Chanles, (M. & Johnston) r. 286 N. Alabama.

Munson David, lightning rod office, 62 E. Washington, r. 228 E. Market.

Munson Wm. G., salesman, bds. 228 E. Market.

Munson Wm. L., grocer, 51 N. Alabama, r. 286 N. Alabama.

MUNSON & JOHNSTON, (C. H. M. and W. J. J.) dealers in stoves and hollow ware, 62 E. Washington.

Muniz James, plasterer, r. 404 Virginia av.

Muniz Thomas, plasterer, r. 111 Elm.

Muniz William, plasterer, r. rear of 442 Virginia av.

Murdock Joseph, moulder, r. 385 S. Illinois.

H. H. LEE

MAKES A SPECIALTY OF

Choice Green, Black & Japan Teas.

Murison J. B., Seventh Ward grocery, se. cor. New Jersey and Virginia av., r. 149 S. East.

Murphy Carrie Mrs., (wid) r. 70 E. Ohio.

Murphy Chloe A. Miss, teacher, bds. 244 S. New Jersey.

Murphy Daniel E., r. 396 W. North.

Murphy Dennis, hostler, bds. 18 S. Pennsylvania.

Murphy George W., salesman Murphy, Johnston & Co., bds. 54 S. Pennsylvania.

Murphy James, soldier U. S. Arsenal.

Murphy James, lab., r. 278 E. Lousiana.

Murphy James, conductor C. C. C. & I. R. R., r. 177 Meek.

Murphy Jesse T., day policeman, r. 331 E. Vermont.

Murphy John, expressman, r. 26 N. California.

Murphy John, lab., r. S. Maple outside city limits.

Murphy John, lab., r. Michigan road near Washington.

Murphy John, clk., 396 W. North, r. same.

Murphy John W., (M., J. & Co.) r. 166 N. Meridian.

MURPHY, JOHNSTON & CO., (Jno. W. M., W. W. J. and W. J. Holliday) whol. dealers in dry goods and notions. se cor. Meridian and Maryland.

Murphy Lenox, breaksman C. C. & I. C. R. R., bds. 177 Meek.

Murphy Lizzie, servant Palmer House.

Murphy Michael, r. 396 W. North.

Murphy Michael, lab., r. 244 S. Missouri.

Murphy Milton, machinist I. C. & L. R. R. shops, r. 24 Lord.

Murphy Morris, tarroofer, r. 146 Meek.

Murphy Patrick, railroader, r. 501 E. Georgia.

Murphy Patrick, lab., works T. H. & I. Depot.

Murphy P. H., clk. American M. U. Express Co.

Murphy Timothy, shoemaker, shop 15 Massachusetts av., r. same.

Murphy Timothy, grocery and saloon, 396 W. North, r. same.

Murphy Tobias M., agent Home Life Insurance Co, of New York, room 9 Martindale's blk, r. 321 E Georgia.

Murphy W. D., painter, bds. Illinois House.

Murray James A., agent, Empire Fast Line, 96 Virginia av., bds. Bates House.

Murray Charles W., lumber dealer, r. 440 N. East.

Musgrave J. L., works Merrit & Coughlin, r. 725 N. Tennessee.

Musgrave Moses, works Geisendorff's factory, r. 65 California.

Musgrave Philip D., physician, r. 725 N. Tennessee.

Mussmann Diedrich, lab. r. 544 S. Meridian.

Mussmann Diedrich, jr. (W & D. M.) r. 544 S. Meridian.

Mussmann Frederick, teamster, bds. 544 S. Meridian.

Mussmann William, (W. & D.) r. 544 S. Meridian.

MUSSMANN W. & D., groceries and provisions, 544 S. Meridian.

Muth Peter, saloon, 8 S. Delaware, r. E. Cumberland.

Mutual Life Insurance Co., of N. Y., A. Anker, general agent, 182 E. Washinton.

Mutz Anthony, barber, Union Depot, r. 315 S. Delaware.

Muzey Benjamin, machinist, r. 70 N. Delaware.

Myer Fred, Indiana Transfer Co., 42 E. Maryland, r. 141 Union.

Myer Frederick, lab., r. 219 Union.

Myer Henry, lab., r. 219 Union.

Myers Catherine, (wid.) r. 244 S. Delaware.

Myers Charles S., printer, works Sentinel news room, r. 138 Blackford.

Myers Christian, brassmoulder, r. 76 S. Liberty.

Myers Daniel M., pumpmaker, r. 369 S. Illinois.

Myers Irvin M., clk. H. W. Caldwell, r. 168 W. Michigan.

Myers George, (col'd) barber, works 128 S. Illinois.

Myers James, machinist, r. 31 Douglass.

Myers James M., patent agent, r. 228 N. Tennessee.

Myers John, works, Novelty Works.

Myers John, carpenter, r. 327 N. Winston.

Myers John A. (Martin & M.) r. 119 W. Washington.

Myers John G., real estate agent, 14 S. Pennsylvania, r. 485 N. Alabama.

Myers J. M., clk. H. W. Caldwell, r. 168 W. Michigan.

Myers Louis, machinist, Eagle Machine Works, r. 98 N. Davidson.

Myers Robert, student, bds. 70 Plum.

Myers S. H., clk., 3 W. Washington, r. 422 N. Illinois.

Myer Wm., blacksmith, r. 426 E. Georgia.

Myers Wm. H., assistant booekkeper Sentinel office. r. 322 N. New Jersey.

Myhan James H., works Vater & King, r. 4 Douglass.

NAEGELE JOSEPH, paper hanger, bds. 26 S. West.

Nagel August, r. 272 W. Maryland.

Nagle Fred, lab., bds. 30½ W. Pennsylvania.

Nagle George, (col'd) lab., r. 177 Indiana av.

Nahn William, shoemaker, r. 266 N. Noble.

Naltner A., (Seidensticker & N.) r. 186 E. McCarty.

Naltner Frederick, cooper, r. 263 S. West.

NALTNER JOSEPH, saloon, 134 S. Meridian, r. same.

NALTNER MARTIN, saloon keeper, 207 Virginia av., r. same.

Nale Mary Mrs., (wid. Isaac) r. 52 Maple.

Nan Valentine, packer, r. 472 S. East.

Nardin Ethan T., piano maker, r. 407 S. East.

Nash Martha Mrs. (wid.) bds. 186 N. New Jersey.

Nathan Joseph, (col'd) porter, Macy House, bds. same.

NATIONAL HOTEL BILLIARD ROOMS, John Bussey proprietor, 29 and 31 McNabb.

Naughton Jerry, works Street R. R. Co., bds. 72 Louisiana.

Naughton Patrick, grocer, 201 E. Washington, r. 190 Virginia av.

Navin John N., vetenary surgeon, r. 208 W. Washington.

Naylor David, boxmaker, works Pfaendler, & Zogg, bds. 181 S. Meridian.

Naylor William C., bookkeeper, Ray House, r. same.

NEAB CONRAD, plumber, steam and gas fitter, dealer in all kinds of gas fixtures, 70 N. Illinois, Miller's blk. bds. Palmer House

Neal A. C., printer Sentinel office, r. 286 Virginia av.

Neal Jonhnathan R., dealer in produce, r. 218 E. Market.

Neal William, (col'd) expressman, r. 165 Elizabeth.

Neeb Charles, saloonkeeper, 20 N Delaware, r. same.

Needding Louis, stove mounter, r. 322 S. Noble.

Needham N. W., eggpacker, G. G. Holman, bds. Little's Hotel.

Neeld N. M. (J. C. F. & Co.) r. 145 N. Meridian.

Neenan Annie Miss, chambermaid, Sherman House.

16

Neenan Bridget, chambermaid, Sherman House.

Neermann Christ, boot and shoemaker, 271 Massachusetts av., r. same.

Neermann Christ, shoemaker, r. 70 Lockerbie.

Neff Albert H., photograph gallery, 121 W. Washington, bds. 35 W. Georgia.

Neff Charles, cooper, r. 470 E. Georgia.

Neffler Fred, butcher, bds. 235 S. Alabama.

Neffler Frederick, lab. Union Depot, r. 275 S. West.

Negley P. L., lawyer, 24½ E. Washington.

Neibergall John, carpenter, r. 266 N. Winston.

Neidigh Catharine Mrs., boarding house, 416 W. Washington.

Neidling Louis, finisher, Root's Foundry, r. 352 Virginia av.

Neiger Jacob, driver, A. Reed & Co., r. Court, bet. Alabama and New Jersey.

Neighbors Charles, expressman, r. 241 S. Mississippi.

Neighbors Robert, drayman, r. 151 Union.

Neihaus Joseph L. (Zimmer & N.) r. 349 S. Delaware.

Neiman Daniel, bds. Neiman House.

Neiman House, 130 S. Illinois, Mrs. Lahae Neiman, proprietress.

Neiman Jacob S., miller, r. 260 N. Noble.

Neiman John S., delivery clk. Trade Palace, bds. 130 S. Illinois.

Neiman Joseph, lab., r. 42 Douglass.

Neiman Lahae Mrs., proprietor Neiman House, 130 S. Illinois.

Neiman Martin, night watchman Trade Palace, bds. 130 S. Illinois.

Neiman T. J., trunkmaker, r. 42 N. Douglass.

Neimeister A., shoemaker, r. 420 Virginia av.

Neimeyer Fred, bootmaker, bds. 396 N. Alabama.

Neimeyer Henry, boot and shoemaker, 126 Fort Wayne av.

Neison Rudolph, cigarmaker, bds. 23 Kentucky av.

Nell Emilie Mrs., 197 E. Washington.

Nelson Edwin, engineer, r. 500 E. Georgia.

Nelson Frank, telegraph operator, bds. 125 N. Mississippi.

Nelson George, works Pork House, r. 22 S. West.

THE CHINA TEA STORES

ARE LOCATED AT

No. 7 ODD FELLOWS HALL

AND

ACADEMY OF MUSIC CORNER.

SAME GOODS. SAME PRICES at BOTH.

Nelson Henry, carpenter, r. 125 N. Mississippi.

Nelson Horatio L., jeweler, r. 146 W. Vermont.

Nelson James, lab., r. 311 Massachusetts av.

Nelson John, conductor, C. C. C. & I. R. R., bds. Spencer House.

Nelson James, (col'd) woodsawyer, r. 292 Massachusetts av.

Nelson T. A., cashier New York Store, r. 158 N. New Jersey.

Nelter Frank, works Cabinet Maker's Union, r. 310 S. Illinois.

Neno Wm. J., moulder, Eagle Machine Works, r. 310 S. Illinois.

Nerney Alfred G., silver plater, r. 78 Plum.

Nessler Christine, (wid.) r. 426 S. East.

Nessler George, cabinetmaker, r. 253 N. Noble.

Nevill Althea C., dressmaker, r. 376 E. Market.

New Barney, chair painter, r. 361 S. Delaware.

New G. W., physician, room 15 Miller's blk., r. 426 N. Illinois.

New J. F., minister Fourth Christian church, r. 82 N. Illinois.

NEW JOHN C., cashier First National Bank, r. 243 N. Pennsylvania.

New Valentine, packer, 36 S. Meridian, r. 361 S. Delaware.

Newbacher Louis, brass finisher, r. 265 S. Alabama.

Newbery Leonhardt, brickmoulder, bds. California House.

Newby R. H., (col'd) engineer, r. W. First near Howard.

Newcomb E., salesman, Smith & Foster.

Newcomb H. C., watchmaker, Craft & Cutter, bds. 243 N. East.

Newcomb H. C. Jr., clk., r. 243 N. East.

Newcomb Horatio C. (N., Mitchel & Ketcham) r. 275 N. Tennessee.

Newcomb Richard H., clk. P. O., r. 320 N. Alabama.

Newcomb W. C., dealer in groceries, provisions &c. 302 N. Illinois, r. 446 N. New Jersey.

NEWCOMB MITCHELL & KETCHAM, (H. C. Newcomb, J. L. Mitchell and W. A. Ketcham) attorneys at law, 21 and 23 E. Washington.

Newcomer F. S., physician, office room 6 Blake's blk., r. 82 W. North.

Newell Alice Miss, music teacher, bds. 402 N. Pennsylvania.

Newell L. S., librarian, Vinton's blk., r. same.

Newell R. A., carpenter, r. 318 N. Delaware.

Newland Dallas, music teacher Institute for the Blind.

Newland R. A., music teacher Institute for the Blind.

Newman Charles, cooper, r. 25 Bright.

Newman Isaac L, broommaker, r. 425 W. New York.

NEWMAN JOHN S., President Merchant's National Bank, 48 E. Washington, r. 243 N. Pennsylvania.

Newman Michael C., cooper, r. 25 Bright.

Newman P. Mrs., hoop skirt manufactory, 95 E. Washington, r. 140 Virginia av.

Newman Peter, woodsawyer, r. 305 S. Missouri.

Newman William, teamster, r. 27 N. California.

Newmeyer Julius A. (Kettenbach, N. & Co.) r. 277 Massachusetts av.

Newton Delos, cooper, r. 19 Fayette.

Newton George, clk. P. C. & St. L. R. R. Freight office, r. 240 S. Alabama.

Newton Jennie Miss, teacher Market Colored School, bds. 240 S. Alabama.

Nenton M. S. (wid.) milliner, 307 E. Washington, r. same.

Newton S. E. Mrs., teacher of painting, etc., Indianapolis Young Ladies' Institute, r. Cleveland, Ohio.

Nicely W., bds. Macy House.

Niccum J. G., blacksmith, r. 53 Maple.

Nichol James M., teller Indianapolis National Bank, r. 357 N. Illinois.

NICHOL JOSEPH W., attorney and counselor at law, 16½ E. Washington, r. 292 N. Meridian.

Nicholas William, (col'd) lab., r. 390 W. North.

Nichols Catharine, (wid. William) r. 68 Indiana av.

Nichols Harry J, telegraph operator, bds. 68 Indiana av.

Nichols John S, bookkeeper, 30 S. Illinois, bds. Pyle House.

Nichols Nancy, (wid. Addison) r. 172 Virginia av.

Nichols Norman C., pumpmaker, 85 S. Liberty.

Nichols R. P., traveler, J. C. Burton & Co., bds. Depot Dining Hall.

Nichols T. M., dentist, 25 W. Washington, r. se. city.

Nichols Willard, printer, r. 73 E. St. Clair.

Nichols William, (col'd) porter 21 W. Washington, r. North near Bright.

Nichols William F., works Street R. R Co., r. 298 S. Illinois.

Nicholson David, (Scott & N.) r. 166 W. George.

Nicholson Jane, (wid.) r. cor. Broadway and Forest av.

Nicholson J. W., salesman C. Dickson & Co., r. 84 Union.

Nicholson P., clk., bds. 139 Virginia av.

Nicholson Walter, salesman J. Osterman & Co., bds. 74 State.

Nickerson J. B. (N. & Downey) r. 90 N. East.

NICKERSON & DOWNEY, (J. B. N. and J. L. D.) general agents Weed Sewing Machine, 12 N. Pennsylvania.

Nickum J. R., (Parrott & N.) r. 155 N. Tennessee.

Nicoli Arustine, (wid.) r. 109 W. Washington.

Nicoli Charley, saddles and harness, 326 E. Washington, r. same.

Nicoli Henry, butcher, 67 Massachusetts av., r. same.

Nicoli Lewis, (C. Hagerhorst & Co.) bds. 223 W. Ohio.

Nicoli L. C., saddler, r. 326 E. Market.

Niebacher Louis, machinest, r. 269 S. Alabama.

Niemann Christian, carpenter, r. 231 Davidson.

Niemann Henry, (Bœdeker & N.) r. 456 E. North.

Niemeyer Charles W., breaksman T. H. & I. R. R., r. 165 S. Tennessee.

Niemeyer Christian, (wid.) r. 104 S. Noble.

Niles Charles, (C. N. & Co.) r. Eddy nr. South.

Niles Charles & Co. (C. N. & G. Bauer) cleaning and repairing, 134 S. Illinois.

NOBLE A. F., dealer in Ward's portable gas light, 28 Kentucky av., bds. 80 S. Tennessee.

Noble James, sleeping car conductor.

Noble J. F., teamster, works Home Mill.

Noble Nannie Mrs., teamster, r. 85 S. Union.

Noble Sarah, (wid. Joseph) r. 126 Broadway.

Noble Thomas, Y., engineer I. W. & D. R. R., r. 129 Bates.

NOBLE WILLIAM J., boarding house, 18 and 20 S. Pennsylvania.

NOBLE WM. H. L., general agent. Indianapolis, Cincinnati & Lafayette Railroad, office, Cincinnati depot, cor. Louisiana and Delaware, r. Madison av., S. of city limits.

Noe A. J., painter, r. 21 N. East.

Noe Daniel M., carriagesmith, r. 121 S. New Jersey.

Noe M., carpenter, r. 280 N. Alabama.

Noe Martha, (wid.) r. 119 S. New Jersey.

Noe Mary, dressmaker, r. 21 N. East.

Noe Valintine, baker, works 173 S. Illinois, bds same.

Noel E. B. (N. & Son) bds. 234 W. New York.

Noel S. V. B. (N. & Son) r. 234 W. New York.

Noel Woodward, clk., bds. 234 W. New York.

NOEL & SON, (S. V. B. and E. B.) grain and produce dealers, 86 Virginia av.

Noelky F., works B. F. Haugh & Co., bds. California House.

Nofsinger Wm. R., physician, r. National rd. one mile E. of city.

Nolan Joseph, shoemaker, 10 Virginia av., r. nw. city limits.

Nolan Joseph, shoemaker, r. cor. First and James.

Nolan Michael, brakeman, C. C. & I. C. R. R., bds. 58 Benton.

Nolen Lavina, (wid. Samuel) boarding house, 188 S. Illinois.

Nolting Charles, porter, r. 127 E. St. Joseph.

Norden Eli, pianomaker, r. 407 S. East.

Norman Perry, butcher, bds. 554 S. Meridian.

Norman Seloma, (wid) r. 16 W. First.

Norr George, driver furniture wagon, r. 403 N. Alabama.

Norris James C., salesman, 131 S. Meridian, bds. Mrs. Mason.

Norris John, dealer in boots and shoes, 23 E. Washington, r. 56 S. Pennsylvania.

Norris John C., bds. 9 Cherry.

Norris Mary C. Miss, clk. 23 E. Washington, r. 56 S. Pennsylvania.

Norris Thomas Jr., tanner, bds. 518 E. Washington.

Norris Thomas, tanner, r. 518 E. Washington.

North Myron, depotmaster I.C. & L. Depot, r. 291 W. Michigan.

North Pinckney A., watchman, r. 488 E. Georgia.

North Western Christian University, cor. College and Forrest av.

H. H. LEE'S

WHOLESALE PRICES FOR

TEAS, COFFEES & SUGARS,
ARE THE SAME EACH DAY
As are quoted in the
CINCINNATI DAILY PAPERS.

Northam William, carpenter, W. Third bet. Tennessee and Mississippi.

Northway George, plasterer, r. 186 N. New Jersey.

Northway John, plasterer, r. 203 E North.

NORTHROP W. W., general agent for Indiana and Southern Illinois of Security Life Insurance Company, 2 Blake's Row, r. 77 W. North.

Norton Luther, carpenter, r. 417 E. St. Clair.

Norton William D. (col'd) lab., r. 271 Patterson.

Norton W. H., baggage master C. C. C. & I. R. R., r. 234 S. Alabama.

Norwood G., retired, r. 482 N. Illinois.

Norwood John, mail agent Union Depot, bds. Neiman House.

Norwood John L., assistant mail agent, bds. 126 N. Delaware.

Norwood Margaret, (wid) r. 126 N. Delaware.

Nothelfer Casper, lad., bds. 323 W. Washington.

Notter Steven, painter, r. Morris, bet. Alabama and New Jersey.

Nowland E. R., press feeder, bds. 283 E. South.

Nowland J. H. B., r. 283 E. South.

Nowland Lloyd, printer, Indianapolis Printing and Publishing House, r. 283 E. South.

Nuetzel John, butcher, 175 Madison av., r. same.

Nugen Catharine, domestic, Blind Institute.

Null Samuel, painter, r. 46 Indiana av., up stairs.

Nutman ——, cooper, r. 21 Sharp.

Nutmier Chris, carpenter, r. 293 E. Ohio.

Nutting A. F., clk 66 N. N. Illinois, bds. same.

Nutting Rufus, (N. & Wood) r. 368 N. East.

Nutting & Wood, (Rufus Nutting and D. L. Wood) Insurance agents, 17½ W. Washington, room 1.

Nutts Jacob, baker, r. 121 Massachusetts av.

Nye Benjamin, painter, bds. 94 N. East.

Nye Michael, tinner, r. 197 E. Washington.

Nye Michael, salesman, with Spellman & Co., r. 85 E. Washington.

O'BRIEN CHRISTOPHER H. O., route agent Daily Sentinel, r. 213 N. Liberty.

O'Brien George, baggage master, I. P. & C. R. R.

O'Brien Jerry, tinner, r. 28 Wyoming.

O'Brien John, r. 80 Bates.

O'Brien John, baggage master, I. P. & C R. R.

O'Brien John, lab., bds. 225 S. West.

O'Brien Joseph, lab., rolling mill, r. 280 S. Tennessee.

O'Brien Julia Miss, domestic Spencer House.

O'Brien Michael, lab. rolling mill, bds. 280 S. Tennessee.

O'Brien Michael, carpenter, r. 136 N, Winston.

O'Brien Richard, varnisher, r. 395 S. East.

O'Brien Thomas, lab., r. 59 California.

O'Brien Thomas, lab., r. 271 N. Liberty.

O'Bryan John, lab., r. 360 N. East.

O'Bryan John H., baggage master, C. & I. J. R. R.

O'Connell Daniel, lab., r. 385 E. Ohio.

O'Connell James, drayman, r. Lord.

O'Connell Massy, lab., r. 290 S. Delaware.

O Connor James, blacksmith, works Indianapolis Wagon and Agricultural Works.

O'Connor John, watchman, First National Bank.

O'Connor John, lab., r. 14 N. Noble.

O'Connor John, lab., r. 167 Meek.

O'Connor John, lab., r. 388 S. Delaware.

O'Connor Michael, foundryman, r. 124 Duncan.

O'Connor Michael, lab., bds. Illinois House.

O'Connor Michael, (Prennatt & O'C.) r. 28 W. Pratt.

O'Connor Michael, lab., Spencer House.

O'Connor Michael lab., r. rear 288 E. Ohio.

O'Connor Micheal J., saloon and agent for Toledo ale, 54 S. Illinois, bds 90 S. Illinois.

O'Connor Patrick, tailor, r. 309 Indiana av.

O'Connor Patrick T., lab., 150 Meek.

O'Connor Thomas, shoemaker, r. 294 S. Delaware.

O'Donan C., lab., r. 579 E. St. Clair.

O'Donnell Patrick, salesman, John Doran 56 S. Illinois, bds same.

O'Donnell Patrick, linen store, 69 S. Illinois, bds. Palmer House.

O'Driscoll John, stereotyper, Sentinel Office, bds 30½ N Pennsylvania.

O'Flaherty Thomas, clk., bds. Ray house.

O'Flaherty W. T., bar keeper, r. se. cor. Duncan and Delaware.

O'Hare John, shoemaker, r. 365 S. West.
O'Hare Matthew, tailor, r. 233 S. West.
O'Harra Michael, lab., r. 167 Madison av.
O'Haver Georgia Miss, bds. 416 W. Washington.
O'Haver Mary Miss, bds. 416 W. Washington.
O'Haver Patterson, lab., r. 38 W. North.
O'Horo Anthony, lab., r. 243 S. West.
O'Keane Patrick J., clk. 56 S. Illinois, bds. 325 S. Delaware.
O'Keiffe Timothy, lab., r. 18 Williard.
O'Keiffe Patrick, corporal, U. S. Arsenal.
O'Key Phillip, fence builder, r. 273 E. North.
O'Key Remus, cooper, bds. 114 S. Noble.
O'Leary Daniel, expressman Union Dept, r. 315 S. Meridian.
O'LEARY JEREMIAH, saloon, 103 S. Illinois, r. same.
O'Leary Jerry, works rolling mill, bds. 72 W. Louisiana.
O'Leary Mary, domestic. Bates House.
O'Leary William, boilermaker, r. 42 Dicking.
O'Loucklin John, moulder, r. 256 S. Tennessee.
O'Malia Patrick, porter, 26 S. Meridian, bds. Macy House.
O'Mara James, porter American M. U. Express Co., r. Minerva, W. end Vermont.
O'Mara Mary, servant, Palmer House.
O'Mara Patrick, boilermaker, r. Sinker bet. Alabama and Delaware.
O'Mara R., boarding house, 24 W. Georgia.
O'Neal Charlotte, Mrs., r. 130 Virginia av.
O'Neal James, flagman Union track, r. 83 W. Louisiana.
O'Neal John, lab. rolling mill, r. 301 Kentucky av.
O'Neal Joseph, miller, r. 31 Blake.
O'Neal Michael, cutter J. & P. Grauling, r. 43 E. McCarty.
O'Neal T. H., operator W. U. Telegraph, bds. 73 W. Maryland.
O'Neal W. H., blacksmith, r. 253 S. West.
O'Neal James H., switchman, T. H. & I. R. R., bds. 83 W. Louisiana.
O'Neill John, lab., r. 211 E. Market.
O'Neil Matthew, cutter, r. 143 E. McCarty.
O'Neil Michael, lab., r. 164 Meek.
O'Neil Robert, teamster, r. 155 Meek.
O'Neil Thomas, lab., r. 164 Meek.
O'Neil Thomas, teamster, r. 190 Meek.
O Neil Timothy, lab., r. 168 Meek.
O'Neil William, blacksmith, r. 253 S. West.
O'Reager Jerry, bricklayer, bds. 669 N. Illinois.
O'Reilly Michael, shoemaker, r. 414 S. Tennessee.

O'Shea Patrick, wiper I. C. & L. R. R. Shops, r. 109 Huron.
O'Towell Edward, moulder, Eagle Machine Works.

OAKY EDWARD H., carpenter, r. 395 N. New Jersey.
Obergfell Isador, lab., r. 392 S. Delaware.
Obergfell Joseph, checkman, P. C. & St. L. R. R. Freight Depot.
Obergfell Mathias, carpenter, r. Madison rd.
Oberly Amos, works Paper Mill, bds. 261 W. Washington.
Obermeyer M. A. Mrs., dressmaker, r. 79 W. Ohio.
Obermeyer W. M., dealer in hats and caps, 2 Palmer House, r. 79 W. Ohio.
Obrecht John, school teacher, bds. 134 N. Pennsylvania.
Obrey Clinton, painter, r. ne. cor. Mississippi and Ohio.
Ocher Louis, works, Osgood, Smith & Co., bds. 323 W. Washington.
Odd Fellows Hall and Building, ne. cor. Pennsylvania and Washington.
Odell James, lab. C. C. & I. C. R. R., r. 147 Huron.
Odell James T., r. 78 Meek.
Oechsle Kate Miss, teacher, Ninth Ward School, bds. 395 E. New York.
Oehler Andrew, watchmaker and jeweler, 20 S. Delaware, r. same.
Oehler David, saloon and beer garden, 48 Russell, r. same.
Oehler Roman, watchmaker and jeweler, 183 W. Washington, r. same.
Oehri Lewis, engineer, r. 526 E. Market.
Oelschlayer J. B., machinist, r. 424 E. St. Clair.
Off Christian, lumber dealer, r. 297 N. Noble.
Off Gottleib, lumber dealer, r. 305 N. Noble.
Off Jacob, miller and lumber dealer, r. 291 N. Noble.
Offett James, carpenter, r. 530 N. Alabama.
Ogden Mary Miss, weaver, bds. 416 W. Washington.
Ogden W. S., clk. T. H. & I. R. R. office, r. 522 N. Meridian.
Oglesby J. S., commission merchant, r. 294 N. Pennsylvania.

Obeler G. P., cabinet maker, r. 128 St. Joseph.

Ohr Andy, printer, S E. Pearl, bds. 278 N. Alabama.

Ohr Aaron D, ticket clk. Union Depot, r. 473 N. Tennessee.

Ohr Henry, r. 448 N. Meridian.

OHR JOHN H., agent Adams Express Co. in new Sentinal bldg., r. 448 N. Meridian.

Ohleyer George, basket manufacturer, 456 S. Meridian, r. same.

OHMER N. & G, proprietors Union Depot Dining Hall, r. Dayton Ohio.

Oiler Phillip H., works Osgood, Smith & Co., bds 424 Virginia av.

Okey Joseph, patent right agent, r. 474 S. Illinois.

Olin Chauncey C., general Insurance ag't, 2½ W. Washington, r. 183 E. Ohio.

Olin E. D. (Olin & Foltz) r. 183 E. Ohio.

Olin F. W., clk. 21 E Washington, r. 183 E. Ohio.

OLIN & FOLTZ, (E. D. O. and H. M. F.) general agents Howe Sewing Machine, 21 N. Pennsylvania.

Oliver Charles, tobacco manufacturer, 283 W. Washington, r. same.

Oliver D. H., physician, 582 E. Market r. 28 Gregg.

Oliver Theodore, butcher, r. 315 S. Missouri.

Olivet Presbyterian Church, cor. Union and McCarty.

Ollcott ——, professor in elocution N. W. C. University.

Olmstead ——, (wid.) r. 15 Willard.

Olsen Rasmus C., clk. 257 S. Delaware, bds. 259 S. Delaware.

Olson Peter, bricklayer, r. 55 Union.

Operman Henry, iron puddler, r. 314 W. Merrill.

Olstott Daniel, moulder, bds. 169 S. Tennessee.

Oren Sarah, (wid. Charles) r. 85 N. California.

Orf Peter, stonecutter, bds. 516 E. Washington.

Orm Sanford, miller, bds. 512 S. Meridian.

Ormsby Emma F., works Tobacco Works, bds. 19 S. Illinois.

Orphans' Home, 711 N. Tennessee, Anna M. Johnson Matron.

Osborn D. M., teacher, r. 150 Ft. Wayne av.

Osborn John H., traveling agent Wheeler & Wilson Sewing Machines, r. 225 N. Liberty.

Osgood Charles J., bookkeeper, r. 843 Michigan.

Osgood John B. (O. & Chapman) r. 46 N. New Jersey.

Osgood J. R. (O. & Smith) r. 84 E. Michigan.

Osgood, Smith & Co. (J. R. O., S. F. S. and J. H. Woolburn) manufacturers of hubs, wheels and spokes, 230 S. Illinois.

Osgood & Chapman, (J. B. O. and D. C. C.) house and sign painters, cor. Virginia av. and Washington.

Ossenforth Fred, porter, 48 S. Meridian, r. 315 N. Winston.

Osterman John, (J. O. & Co.) r. 74 State.

Osterman John & Co. (J. Osterman and J. Stuckmeyer) commission merchants, 86 W. Washington.

Ostermeyer Christian, (wid. Louis) r. 263 N. Liberty.

Ostermeyer Christian F., groceries and dry goods, 350 E Ohio, r. same.

Ostermeyer Frederick, (Holland, O. & Co.) r. 635 E. Washington.

Ostermeyer Henry, carpenter, r. 278 E. Louisiana.

Ostermeyer Louis, drayman, r. 9 Charles.

Oswald D., tinsmith, cor. Tennessee and Garden.

Otis Clark, photographer, r. 237 E. South.

Otis W. H., r. 421 N. Tennessee.

Out John, furniture manufacturer, r. terminus Dacota.

Otte William, carpenter, r. 190 N. Noble.

Otten Deitrich, cigarmaker, r. 127 Spring.

Otto August, lithographer, Braden & Burford, r. 71 Plum.

Otto Charles, bricklayer, r. 48 Oriental.

Otto Philip, lab., r. 429 S. East.

Otwell Francis, r. 236 N. Illinois.

Otwell Francis A., salesman, r. 109 S. New Jersey.

Otwell Will. S., clk. G. P. Tuttle's tea store, bds. 136 N. Illinois.

Ousler Lafayette, traveler, Vinnedge, Jones & Co.

Owsley William, carpenter, r. 24 Douglass.

Ovalman ——, bds. 74 N. Pensylvania.

Over Ewald, (E. Over & Co.) r. 79 N. Alabama.

OVER E. & CO. (E. Over and H. Schnull) wholesale dealers in iron, steel, window glass, etc., 82 and 84 S. Meridian.

Overholser Jacob, patent right agent, r. 47 N. Alabama.

Overman E. C., commercial traveler, r. 58 N. Pennsylvania.

Overman Joseph K., joiner, works, cor. Tennessee and Georgia, r. 86 Minerva.

Overman Rob, carpenter, r. 86 Minerva.

Overmyer Nelson, wagonmaker, r. cor. Jackson and Arch.

Overstreet J. B., r. 201 S. Pennsylvania.

Owens B. F. (Ebert & O.) r. 580 N. Mississippi.

Owens Henry, (col'd) cook, 29 S. Illinois, r. same.

Owens Jas., storefitter, r. 68 Virginia av.

Owens John, lab., r. 4 Rockwood

Owens Robert, (col'd) lab., r. cor. Lafayette R. R. and Third.

Owings James, brakeman, C. C. C. & I. R. R., bds. 139 E. South.

Owings Joseph, telegraph messenger, bds. 139 E. South.

Owings Nathaniel B., plasterer, r. 139 E. South.

PABST WILLIAM, tailor, bds. California House.

PACIFIC AND ATLANTIC TELEGRAPH CO , 22 S. Meridian, E. C. Howlett, Manager.

Paetz Oscar B., clk. W. W. Ingle, bds. 84 S. Illinois.

Paetz William, physician, r. 84 S. Illinois.

Paff Hugh, carpenter, r. 173 Stevenson.

Paff Samuel, carpenter, r. 405 S. East.

Page Joseph, shoemaker, r. cor. New York and Blake.

Page W. H , salesman, Scott, West & Co., r. 303 S. Meridian.

Paine Daniel L., salesman, China Tea Store, r. 71 E. St. Clair.

Paine Henry, lab., r. 548 N. Alabama.

Paine Thomas, (col'd) teamster, r. 351 W. North.

Painter Edward R., works, Saturday Evening Mirror, r. 370 W. Vermont.

Painter John, clk. B. G. Stout, r. 597 N. Illinois.

Painter Joseph R., carpenter r. 82 W. Market.

Paisley Samuel, carpenter, r. 191 W. Maryland.

Palmer Ben G., paper hanger, r. 178 E. South.

Palmer Charles C., r. 57 W. Maryland.

PALMER EDWARD L., Catholic book dealer and news agent, 60 S. Illinois, r. 56 S. Illinois.

Palmer Frank, painter, r 121 N. Noble.

PALMER HOUSE, se. cor. Washington and Illinois, Jeff K. Scott proprietor.

Palmer J. L., r. 493 N. Pennsylvania.

Palmer Marshall E, r. 57 W. Maryland.

Palmer Mary, (wid) r. 121 N. Noble.

Palmer Mary A.(col'd) r. 183 Douglass al.

Palmer Mary E., clerk, bds 121 N. Noble.

Palmer Nathan B., r. 57 W. Maryland.

PALMER T. G., deputy Auditor of State, r. 156 N. Illinois.

Pangburn J. G., bds. Bates House.

Paper Albert, lab., r. 320 W. Washington.

Parish Frank R., dealer in hot and cold air Furnaces, r. 67 N. Alabama.

Parker Andrew J. (col'd) lab., r. Howard bet. First and Second.

Parker Augustus A., piano tuner, r. 231 E. South.

Parker Columbus C., bds. 163 S. Tennessee.

Parker Daniel M., lab., r. 231 W. Vermont.

Parker Earl, lab., Gates, Pray & Co.

Parker Eben A. (P. & Bloomer) r. 75 N California.

Parker Elizabeth, (wid. Archey) boarding house, 73 Kentucky av.

Parker Geo. W., sheriff Marion County, r. 18 N. Alabama.

Parker James, saddler, 89 S. Pennsylvania.

Parker James F., (Case & P.) r. 600 N. Illinois.

Parker J. H., harnessmaker, r. 87 S. Pennsylvania.

Parker Lucas, student, bds. 128 Fort Wayne av.

Parker P. Robert, (Guffin & P.) r. nr. Shelbyville rd., South of city.

PARKER R. R., men's furnisher, 50 W. Washington, r. 90 N. Mississippi.

Parker Sarah J. Miss, dressmaker, r. 156 E. Market.

Parker Wilson, bricklayer, r. 163 S. Tennessee.

Parker W. Wallace, turnkey county jail, r. 18 N. Alabama.

PARKER & BLOOMER, (E. A. P. and J. L. B.) attorneys at law, 32½ E. Washington.

Parker's Block, Delaware, bet. Washington and Market.

Parkeson P., blacksmith, r. 21 Maple.

Parkman Charles B., secretary Indianapolis Rolling Mill Company, r. 230 N. West.

Parks Hiram J. (col'd) cook, r. 123 S. Benton.

Parlee Alex., painomaker, bds. Patterson House.

THE CHINA TEA STORES

Are very handsomely decorated with

Accurate Views and Scenes

or

CHINESE LIFE AND SCENERY.

Call and see them before leaving the City.

PARLOR SALOON, 179 E Washington, James McB. Shepperd, proprietor.

Parmelee J. R., traveler, Keifer & Vinton, bds. Palmer House.

Parmelee W. H., freight agent, Baltimore & Ohio R. R., cor. Virginia av. and Alabama, r. 29 W. Pratt.

Parr Henry, teamster, r. 354 E. Market.

Parrisette Joseph, confectioner and restaurant, 25 N. Illinois, r. same.

PARROT HORACE, (P. & Nickum) r. 349 N. Delaware.

PARROT, NICKUM & CO. (Horace Parrot and John R. Nickum) proprietors steam cracker bakery, 188 E. Washington.

Parry Roger, foreman blacksmith shop, T. H. & I. R. R., r. 12 Henry.

Parsley Asbury, teamster, r. 545 N. Mississippi.

Parsley James, carriagesmith Shaw, Lippencott & Connor, bds. 89 S. Pennsylvania.

Parvin Theophilus, physician, office, 135 N. Alabama, r. 113 N. Alabama.

Pascoe James, boilermaker, C. C. & I. C. R. R., r. 450 E. Georgia.

Pasquier John B., carpenter, r. 406 N. Michigan.

Patterson Andrew, (J. P., A. P. & Co.) r. 280 E. Ohio.

Patterson Augustus, lab., r. 206 E. Ohio.

Patterson A. W., physician, 135 N. Alabama, r. 126 E. Ohio.

Patterson Clemens Mrs., dress and cloakmaking, 25 Massachusetts av., r. same.

Patterson John, carpenter, r. 362 S. Illinois.

Patterson John, (J. P., A. P. & Co.) r. 52 Bright.

Patterson John, carpenter, r. 25 Massachusetts av.

Patterson John, machinist, C. C. & I. C. R. R. shops.

Patterson J. P. (Alford, Talbott & Co.) r. 163 N. New Jersey.

Patterson Robert, carpenter, r. 225 N. Noble.

Patterson R. M., city civil engineer, r. 272 N. Tennessee.

Patterson Samuel W., street contractor, r. 332 W. Washington.

Patterson Thomas, cattletrader, r. se. cor. Tinker and Pennsylvania.

Patterson William, attorney, 98 E. Washington, r. 280 E. Ohio.

Patterson William H., clk., German dry good store, r. 520 N. Mississippi.

Patterson Wm. O., clk., P. O., r. 140 Massachusetts av.

Patterson Wm. T., lab., r. 193 S. Tennessee.

Patterson J. & Co. (J. P., A. P. and Wm. P.) produce and provisions, 45 Virginia av.

PATTERSON, MOORE & TALBOTT, (J. P. P., J. A. M., R. L. T. and W. H. Morrison) whol. druggists, 123 S. Meridian.

Pattison ——, r. 741 N. Meridian.

Pattison A. E. (Hibben, Tarkington & Co.) r. 429 N. New Jersey.

Pattison Catherine M., r. 136 Massachusetts av.

Pattison C. B. (Hibben, Tarkington & Co.) r. 413 N. Illinois.

Pattison House, 63 N. Alabama, James B. Bell, proprietor.

Pattison J. D., r. 404 N. Illinois.

Pattison M. A. W. (wid.) r. 140 Massachusetts av.

Pattison Terrell, salesman, 112 S. Meridian, r. 416 N. Pennsylvania.

Pattison T. T. N., trader, r. 416 N. Pennsylvania.

Pattison W. O., bds. 136 Massachusetts av.

PAUL HENRY, Chief Police, r. 17 E. McCarty.

Paulding G. W., clk. Masonic Hall, bds. Macy House.

Pauli Henry, carpenter, r. 181 N. Davidson.

Paulini Otto, bookkeeper, 14 N. Delaware.

PAULMAN E. L., dealer in watches, clocks and jewelry, 114 S. Illinois, r. same.

Paver J. M, agent American M. U. Express Co., Union Depot, r. 229 E. Vermont.

Paxton Elizabeth, (wid.) r. 22 Circle.

Payne John, (col'd) lab., r. Sixth nr. Lafayette R. R.

Payne Richard, works rolling mill, bds. 217 S. Illinois.

Payton Elisha B., car inspector Crawfordsville R. R., r. 568 E. Washington.

Payntz Florence, (wid. John C.) bds. 147 W. Maryland.

Peabody John, stock trader, r. 524 N. Delaware.

Peacock James, bookkeeper L. Q. Sherwood, r. 196 W. Ohio.

Peacock Mary A. H. Mrs., r. 365 W. Vermont.

Peacock & McLain, (Wm. P. and J. S. Mc.) boot and shoe manufacturers, 298 Blake.

Peacock William, (Peacock & McLain) r. Elizabeth nr. Blake.

Peak David, carpenter, r. 302 W. Maryland.

Peak Moses, (col'd) porter Cady & Hendricks.

Peak Susan Mrs., washerwoman City Hospital.

Pearsall P. R. Prof., music teacher, r. 24 W. New York.

Pearson John, (P. & Co.) r. 135 E. St. Joseph.

Pearson John C., brickmason, r. 127 W. Second.

PEARSON JOHN & CO. (J. P. and ——) props. House of Lords saloon, 78 W. Washington.

Pearson Jno.O., foreman, Jno. McKendry, r. 487 N. Mississippi.

Pearson S. D., tailor, r. cor. Ohio and Massachusetts av.

Pease T. W., r. 163 Ft. Wayne av.

Pease Lewis P., carpenter, r. 141 N. Noble.

Pease Sidney, patent right man, r. 281 N. Noble.

Peauer Philip, (col'd) railroader, r. 168 Huron.

Peck Edwin J., (Greenleaf & Co.) Prest. Union Depot Co., r. 59 W. Maryland.

Peck T. S., Supt., D. Root's foundry, r. 488 N. Tennessee.

Peck Wm., butcher, r. 225 E. Market.

Peckham Caleb H., architect, 6 Blake bldg., r. 380 N. Delaware.

Peckham C. S., traveler, Fairbanks' Scales, 43 and 45 N. Tennessee.

Peden Jos. S., bartender, Spencer House, r. 168 N. Noble.

Pedlan Robert J., moulder, r. 29 Coburn.

Pee Emmett, salesman, Stoneman, Pee & Co., r. 78 N. Delaware.

Pee Geo. W. (Stoneman, P. & Co) r. 81 W. Ohio.

Peek Conrad, confectioner, 107 E. Washington.

Peele Thomas, salesman, New York store, bds. Pyle House.

Peelle S. J., attorney at law, 68 E. Washington, r. 361 E. Market.

Peil Wm. F. jr., bookkeeper, r. 665 E. Washington.

Peirce Converse, teamster, r. 307 W. Market.

Peirce Margaret, domestic, Bates House.

Peirce Morris, lab., r. 223 S. West.

Peirson C. C., commercial traveler, bds. 426 N. New Jersey.

Peirson Joseph, lab., r. room 11 Fatout's blk.

Pellett Wm. A., freight conductor, P. & I. R. R., r. Cady bet. Georgia and Bates.

Peltier Eugene, stonecutter, r. 55 Hosbrook.

Peltier Leon, stonecutter, r. 55 Hosbrook.

Pelton Theo., machinist, works Greenleaf & Co., bds. 134 S Meridian.

Pence Abijah, works Glass Works, r. S. Illinois, nr. South.

Pence Caroline, (wid. John) r. 151 Union.

Pence Louis, flour and feed, 243 E. Washington, r. same.

Pendergast J. G., foreman Adam & Osgood, r. 413 N. Tennessee.

Pendergast William, lab., r. 273 E. North.

Pendleton R. C. J., agent I. B. & W. R. R., r. 97 Buchanan.

Penn George W., secretary Eagle Machine Works, r. 352 S. Pennsylvania.

Penn J. W., bookkeeper, r. 331 S. Pennsylvania.

Pennicke Morris, with Wm. Sumner & Co., r. 191 W. South.

Peoples Nancy, (wid.) r 297 N. Alabama.

Peoples' Dispatch, office, 19 Virginia av.

Pepper Edward, machinist, 431 r. N. Missouri.

Percival A. K., salesman M. O. Tracey, bds. 237 E. South.

Perdue George W., fireman C. C. C. & I. R. R., r. 7 Peru.

Perdue Rebecca, (wid.) r. 7 Peru.

Perhanmus John T., clk 54 S. Meridian, bds. 398 Virginia av.

Perkins Amos G, machinist, r. 316 E. Georgia.

PERKINS, BAKER & PERKINS, (S. E. P., J. P. B. and S. E. P., jr.) attorneys at law, room 4 Ætna bldg.

Perkins C. E., adjuster, Wheeler & Wilson's sewing machine rooms, r. 337 N. Tennessee.

Perkins E. H., printer, r. 67 Dougherty.

Perkins H. W., clk. 24 S. Meridian, bds. Sherman House.

Perkins J. A., agent P. C. & St. L. R. R., r 373 N. Pennsylvania.

Perkins James A., boilermaker, Sinker & Co., r. 154 cor. Pine and Elm.

Perkins J. Wallace, printer, H. C. Chandler & Co., bds. 17½ Virginia av.

Perkins Samuel E. (P., Baker & Perkins) r. 276 W. New York.

Perkins Samuel E. jr. (P., Baker & Perkins) r. 276 W. New York.

H. H. LEE

MAKES A SPECIALTY OF

Choice Green, Black & Japan Teas.

PERKINSON GEORGE W., barber, shop, 552 S. Meridian, r. same.

Perkinson Patrick, blacksmith, r. 21 Maple.

Perrin George K., attorney at law, 45 E. Washington, r. 293 N. New Jersey.

Perrine F. C., with Shaw, Lippencott & Connor, r. 60 S. Pennsylvania.

Perrine Horace G., trunkmaker, 20 Virginia av. r. 293 N. Alabama.

Perrine Lindon L. R., clk. P. O., bds. 204 N. Illinois.

Perrine Peter R., ass't Assessor, r. 293 N. Alabama.

Perrine Truman B., engraver, 34 Virginia av., r. 169 N. Mississippi.

Perrott Jackson, works White Rose Mill, r. 34 S. West.

Perrott Mary E. Miss, principal Ninth Ward School, r. 34 S. West.

Perrott Samuel, lab., r. 34 S. West.

Perry Herbert, blacksmith, works Indianapolis Wagon and Agricultural Works, bds. 317 S. East.

Perry James H., carpenter, r. 427 N. Mississippi.

Perry J. E. (J. E. Robertson & Co.) r. 235 E. Michigan.

Perry Mary E. Miss, teacher, City Academy, bds. 410 N. Pennsylvania.

Perry Mathias moulder, r. 495 S. Delaware.

Perryman C., hostler, H. Allen, bds. 18 S. Pennsylvania.

Peters S. J., agent, Weed Sewing Machine Co., r. 82 N. Pennsylvania.

Peterson Brothers, (Nils and Jens Peterson) merchant tailors, 258 S. Delaware.

Peterson Erasmus, bootmaker, bds. 259 S. Delaware.

Peterson Hanz, confectionery, 257 S. Delaware, r. same.

Peterson James, cabinetmaker, r. 373 S. East.

Peterson James, engineer, r. 389 S. East.

Peterson Jesse P. (P. & Bro.) bds. 225 S. Delaware.

Peterson John, carpenter, Eagle Machine Works bds. California House.

Peterson John J., clk., Western House, bds. same.

Peterson Lawrence, boot and shoemaker, 16 W. Maryland, bds. California House.

Peterson Louis, shoemaker, bds. California House.

Peterson Niel, (P. & Bro.) bds. 255 S. Delaware.

Peterson Taylor, student, E. T. Johnson, rooms same.

Petny John, (col'd) lab., r. 170 Elm.

Pettibone A. H. (P. & Burke) rooms 20 and 21 Talbott & New's blk.

Pettibone Edward, house and signpainter, r. 124 Blackford.

Pettibone & Burke, (A. H. P. and J. H. B.) fine job printers, 20 and 21 Talbott & New's blk.

Petticor John, lab., r. 60 Beaty.

Pettis A. P. (P., Dickson & Co.) r. New York City.

PETTIS, DICKSON & CO. (A. P. P., A. D. and ——) whol. and retail dealers in dry goods and notions, Glenn's blk.

Pettit A. H. (P., Braden & Co.) r. N. Tennessee N. of Tinker.

PETTIT, BRADEN & CO., bankers, 3 Bates House blk.

Pettit Cornelius B., plasterer, r. 142 N. Winston.

Pettit Joseph, pastor, St. John's Catholic Church, r. 76 W. Georgia.

Pettit William, (P., Braden & Co.) r. cor. Tennessee and Tinker.

Pettit Willis H., teller, Citizens' National bank, r. same.

Petty James, teamster, r. 131 Bates.

Petty John, works Aldrich & Gay, r. 25 Bright.

Petty Julius, lab., r. 350 Indiana av.

Petty Mansur, lab., r. 350 Indiana av.

Petty Ransom, lab., bds. 350 Indiana av.

Peyton Wm. B. (col'd) r. 187 W. Second.

Pfaendler Nicholas, (P. & Zogg) r. 326 W. Washington.

PFAENDLER & ZOGG, (W. P. and F. Z.) box manufacturers, cor. Louisiana and Mississippi.

Pfaff John, salesman, r. 405 N. Pennsylvania.

Pfaff J. L., traveler, Landers, Conduitt & Co., bds. 153 N. West.

Pfaff John W. (J. C. Burton & Co.) r. 405 N. Pennsylvania.

Pfaff William A. (J. C. Burton & Co.) r. 153 N. West.

Pfafflin Theodore, clk., F. Smith, r. 25 W. North.

Pfafflin Wm. F., salesman, 29 W. Washington, bds 468 N. Tennessee.

Pfaifling Theodore, grocer, cor. Mississippi and Vermont, r. 25 W. North.

Pfau George, commercial traveler, r. 487 N. Illinois.

Pfeifer George, woodsawyer, r. 150 E. St. Joseph.

Pfeifer Wm., shoemaker, bds. Globe House.

Pfenning Wm., guilder, r. 131 n. East.

Pfent Michael, lab., r. al. bet. East and North.

Pfingst Charles, clk., W Haerle, bds. California House.

Pfingst George F., clk., W. Haerle, bds. 342 N. Illinoss.

Pfitzer John, lab., r. 58 Coburn.

Pfleger Jacob, tailor, r. 124 N. Davidson.

Pfleger Jacob K., carpenter, r. 121 N. Davidson.

Phelan Catherine Mrs. r. 361 Virginia av.

Phelen James, lab., r. 138 Maple.

Phelen Michael, lab., r. 138 Maple.

Phelen Wm., machinist, C. C. & I. C. R. R.

Phelps Allen C., carriagepainter, bds. 276 N. Mississippi.

Phelps Allen E, saddler, r. 276 N. Mississippi.

Phelps Joseph, lab., r. 222 S. Missouri.

Phelps Simon, engineer, C. C. C. & I. R. R., r. 332 E. Louisiana.

Pherson William, lab., r. 191½ W. Washington.

Philbin J. W., traveler Josselyn Bros. & Co., bds. cor. Market and Circle.

Phillips Edward, porter Tutewiler Bros.

Phillips James, boilermaker, r. White's boarding house.

Phillips James E., conductor J. M. & I. R. R., bds. Depot Dining Hall.

Phillips James, (col'd) lab., r. Lafayette R. R., bet. First and Second.

Phillips J. B., eating house, 75 S. Illinois, r. same.

Phillips Thomas H., tailor, r. 147 W. Maryland.

Phillips Warren, clk., r. 147 W. Maryland.

Pillips W. S., clk. Hoosier Store, bds. 147 W. Maryland.

Phipps Bros. (E. R. P. and C. R. P.) watches, clocks, jewelry, etc., 32 W. Washington.

Phipps C. R. (Phipps Bros.) r. cor. National rd. and Arsenal.

Phipps E. R. (Phipps Bros.) bds. 172 N. Delaware.

Phipps John M., physician and surgeon, r. 233 N. Noble.

Phipps Joseph, bookkeeper Braden & Burford, r. 224 E. Market.

Phipps L. M., Assistant U. S. Assessor Internal Revenue, r. 187 N. Alabama.

Phipps Rebeca, (wid. William) r. 154 N. West.

PHŒNIX BELL AND BRASS FOUNDRY, 26 Union Railroad track, Schneider & Co., proprietors.

Phole William H., clk. Browning & Sloan, bds. Pyle House.

Pholma Otto P., vetrinary surgeon, bds. California House.

PICKERILL GEO. W., physician and surgeon, 30½ N. Pennsylvania, r. 104 Plum.

Pickerill Samuel J. (Jones & P.) r. 104 Plum.

Pickett Michael, cooper, bds. 366 W. Washington.

Piel Henry, blacksmith; r. 122 N. Illinois.

Piel Richard, works rolling mill, bds. 78 N. McCarty.

Piel Sophia, (wid.) r. 51 Oriental.

Piel Will F., proprietor, Union Starch Fretory, r. 665 E. Washington.

Picle Herman, lab. P. C. & St. L. freight depot, r. 130 E. McCarty.

Pierce Albert, engineer, I. C. & L. R. R., bds. 47 Bates.

Pierce Charles, carpenter, bds. 64 W. Maryland.

Pierce Converse, works, John Carlisle, r. 307 W. Market.

Pierce Doe, (col'd) r. 189 Douglass al.

PIERCE D. J., agent, 16 N. Delaware, bds. Mrs. McCormick's.

Pierce Ephriam, (col'd) lab., r. cor. Christian av. and Ash.

Pierce Harrison, (col'd) r. Cherry, cor. Ash.

Pierce Henry D., lawyer, 24½ E. Washington, r. 570 N. Meridian.

Pierce James, teamster, r. 177 N. Liberty.

Pierce S. J., printer, News Office, bds. 60 Indiana av.

Pierce William, teamster, r. 292 Massachusetts av.

Pierce Winslow S., pres't North and South R. R. Co., r. 570 N. Meridian.

Piermont Annie, chambermaid, Ray House, r. same.

Pierson Charles, barbershop, r. 316 E. Washington.

Pierson C. C. (Strong, Smith & Co.) r. cor. Christian av. and Plum.

Pierson David, hackdriver, r. 109 Railroad.

Pierson E. W. physician, r. 340 N. Noble.

Pierson I. J., cutter, 37 E. Washington, bds. Palmer House.

Pierson James, carpenter, r. 432 E. St. Clair.

Pierson Lewis, barber, r. 325 E. Washington.

Pierson S. D., cutter, G. Green, r. 11 Massachusetts av.

Pigg Sarah Mrs., r. 231 E. Louisiana.

Pilbeam Sarah C. Miss, r. 279 Kentucky av.
Pinkston Andrew, (col'd) porter, 21 S. Meridian, bds. 131 Bright.
Pinney J., machinist, r. 18 W. Georgia
Piscator August, manufacturer of surgical instruments, 12 S. Delaware, r. same.
Pittman G. S., with McCord & Wheatly, r. 437 E. Georgia.
Pittman Robert C., engineer, r. 208 W. Ohio.
Pitts Geo. W., ice dealer, r. 370 N. Tennessee.
Pitts Henry, lab, r. 124 E. Merrill.
Pitts Thomas, lab., r. N. Missouri.
PITTSBURG, CINCINNATI & ST. LOUIS R. R., J. F. Miller, Superintendent, office cor. Virginia av. and Delaware, bds. Depot Dining Hall.
Pitzer Henry, clk., bds. 157 N. Alabama.
Pitzer W. H., clk., 48 S. Meridian, bds. 157 N. Alabama.
Place Daniel W., nursery agent, r. 22 Bates.
Placke J. Henry, cigarmaker, bds. Illinois House.
Plank Charles, harnessmaker, bds. California House.
Plank Isaac, switchman C. C. C. & I. R. R., r. 384 E. Market.
Plank James, conductor, C. C. & I. C. R. R., bds. 58 Benton.
Plant George, engineer, r. 310 E. Georgia.
Plant John, lab., 310 E. Georgia.
Platt Wm., engineer, r. 207 N. Winston.
Platt William, machinist, C. C. C. & I. R. R. shops.
Platz Valentine, mechanic, r. 455 E. Market.
Plimpton C. H., checkman P. C. & St. L. freight depot, r. 393 E. Georgia.
Plisten Charles F., pianomaker, bds Pattison House.
Ploch John, clk., bds. 518 E. Washington.
Plogsterth Victor, grocery and feed store, 207 N. Davidson, r. same.
Plumb H. H., salesman, J. H. Baldwin & Co., bds. 36 N. Pennsylvania.
Plummer Edward, painter, Shaw, Lippencott & Conner, r. 216 E. Market.
Plummer Eleanor, (wid.) r. 216 E. Market.
Plummer J. T., letter carrier, r. 58 Huron.

Plummer William M., railroader, r. 133 Harrison.
Plunket L. C., salesman, New York store, bds. Mozart Hall.
Plumpton C. H., checkman, P. C. & St. L. R. R. freight office, r. 29 Fletcher av.
Pœhler Fredrick, clk., cor. Meridian and Ray, bds. same.
Pœhler Louis, groceries and provisions, cor. Meridian and Ray, r. same.
Pohler Christian, drayman, r. 385 Virginia av.
Pohler William, lab., r. 397 Virginia av.
Phom R. Mrs, midwife, r. 203 E. South.
Pokemeier John, lab., r. 116 N. Winston.
Pollitt John, draughtsman, O. F, Mayhew.
Pollock James, telegraph operator, bds. Depot Dining Hall.
Pollock John C., r. 253 N. Mississippi.
Pollock J. E., telegraph operator, bds. cor. New York and Delaware.
Polsom Jas., brakeman, I. P. & C. R. R., bds. Spencer House.
POLSTER FREDERICK, saloon, 144 Indiana av., r. same.
Ponder Milton, stock agent, B. & O. R. R., r. 144 N. East
Poole Joseph, Sec'y, Indiana State Board of Agriculture, office, State House, r. Attica, Indiana.
Poole A. J., engineer, C. C. & I. C. R. R., r. 53 Bates.
Poore Mark, general agent, Amicable Life Insurance Co., 45½ E. Washington.
Poorman David S., express driver, r. 476 Virginia av.
Pope Abner, retired, r. 74 W. North.
Pope A. G., salesman, 59 S. Meridian, r. 179 Massachusetts av.
Pope Charles, actor, r. 14 W. North.
Pope Henry, chairmaker, r. 381 Virginia av.
Pope Henry, lab., r. 199 N. West.
Pope Henry F., carpenter, r. 199 N. West.
Pope James P., harnessmaker, r. 29 Meek.
Pope Mary Ann, (wid.) r. 29 Meek.
Pope William, r. 67 Harrison.
Pope William, (George Holtz & Co.) bds California House.
Popenhaus Henry, baggageman, Union Depot, r. 17 Meek.
Popp Albert, machinist, bds. Kolb Boarding house, Kentucky av.
Poppensicker Gottlieb, lab., r. 362 E. New York.
Porter Albert G. (P. Harrison & Fishback) r. 501 N. Tennessee.
Porter A., (wid.) r. 307 W. McCarty.
Porter Casper, bds. 429 E. St. Clair.
Porter Casper, woodworker, Shaw Lippencott & Conner, bds. 60 S. Pennsylvania.

PORTER, HARRISON & FISH-
BACK, (A. C. P., Ben. H. and W.
P. F.) attorneys at law, 5 Yohn's blk.

Porter Jacob, (col'd, Porter & Morris)
bds. cor. North and Bright.

Porter Omer T., dealer in canned foreign
fruits, 61 S. Meridian, r. 194 E. St.
Clair.

Porter S. P., bookkeeper, 40 S. Meridian,
r. 350 N. Meridian

PORTER THEO R., custom tailor,
over 24 W. Washington, bds. cor.
North and Blake.

Porter William, cooper, r. 270 W. Merrill.

Porter William, (col'd) saloon, cor. Kentucky av. and Mississippi, r. 149
Bright.

Porter W. H., yardman, J. M, & I. R. R.,
r. 361 S. Delaware.

Porter W. H., boardinghouse, 74 N. Pennsylvania.

Porter W. M. & J. F., barbers and hair
dressers, 129 S. Illinois, r. cor. Bright
and North.

Pott Charles jr., clk 74 N. Illinois, bds.
same.

Pottage Benjamin, r. 127 W. Market.

POTTAGE CHARLES E., hard-
ware merchant, 77½ W. Washington,
r. 9 Ellsworth.

Pottage Thomas, bds. 127 W. Market.

Potter George, (col'd) lab , r. Lafayette
Railroad bet. First and Second.

Potter N. C., bookkeeper, St. Louis Mutual
Life Insurance Co., bds 35 Circle.

Potter John L., carpenter, r. 169 N. Illinois.

Potter John L., sawfiler, r 77 Jones.

Potts John, cigarmaker, bds. Clinton nr.
New Jersey.

Pound William, associate editor, Evening
News, r. 222 N. Delaware.

Powell Charles, wiper, C. C. C. & I. R. R.
shops.

Powell David, railroader, r. 434 N. New
Jersey.

Powell Geo. W., bds. 434 N. New Jersey.

Powell James, (col'd) lab , r. African al.
bet. Sixth and Seventh.

Powell John, blacksmith, C. C. & I. C. R.
R.

Powell John M., salesman, r, 434 N. New
Jersey.

Powell M. M , clk., 19 W. Washington, r.
82 W. Market.

Powell Robert, lab., r. 48 Cherry.

Power John, machinist, r. 507 S. Tennessee.

Power Stephen, lab., r. 65 Maple.

Powers Margaret, (wid. Patrick) r. 55
Fayette.

Powers Michael, cigarmaker, 108 S. Illinois.

Powers Michael J., cigarmaker, bds. 26
W. Georgia.

Powers Pat'ck, machinist, r. 271 S. Pennsylvania.

Powers Thomas, lab , r. 273 S. Pennsylvania.

Powers Thomas, lab , r, 27 Hahn.

Prail Frederick J., bricklayer, r. 214 N.
Winston.

Prange Anthony F. (P. & Co.) r. 318 E.
Washington.

Prange Charles, (P. & Co.) r. 94 Michigan rd.

Prange Frederick, expressman, r. 103 N.
Davidson.

Prange Frederick, carpentershop, r. 289
S. Illinois.

Prange & Co. (C. P., A. F. P. and R. C.
Buddenbaum) dry goods and groceries, 318 E. Washington.

Prasse Henry, variety store, 446 Virginia
av., r. same.

Prather Austin R., assistant assessor, r.
82 N. Mississippi.

Pratt Julius F , bookkeeper Osgood &
Co., bds. 341 S. Meridian.

Pray Enos G., r 84 Christian av.

Pray William, (Gates & B.) r. 77 N. Alabama.

Pregor Henry, stonemason, r. 320 Railroad.

Prenatt F. J. (P. & O'Connor) r. Madison, Ind.

Prenatt & O'Connor, (F. J. Prenatt and
Michael O'Connor) whol. dealers in
foreign and domestic liquors, cigars,
etc., 141 S. Meridian.

Prentice Lena Miss, actress, bds. 73 W.
Maryland.

Prentzel August, lab., r. 207 Kentucky
av.

Pressel Albert, porter Butsch, Dickson &
Co., r. 110 Plum.

Pressel Anna, (wid. Augustus) r. 102
Oak.

Pressel Charlotte, (wid. Philip) r. 110
Plum.

Pressel George, bricklayer, bds. 102 Oak.

Pressel John H , carpenter, r. 110 Plum.

Pressel Mary, (wid.) r. 476 N. East.

Pressel Oliver H., teamster, bds. 110
Plum.

Pressel Thomas J., carpenter, r. 160 W.
Washington.

Pressel Wm. H., carpenter, r. 171 Spring.

H. H. LEE

Makes a Specialty of

CHOICE GOLDEN RIO,

AND

OLD GOVERNMENT JAVA COFFEES.

Pressly John T., saw mill and lumber dealer, cor. Louisiana and West, r. 119 S. East.

Preston Alfred, clk., r. 32 E. Court.

Preston Elliott, expressman Union Depot, r. 324 S. Meridian.

Preston Margaret, (wid.) r. 32 E. Court.

Preston S. N., printer, Sentinel Office, bds. Circle Restaurant.

Price Benjamin, mill wright, r. 115 W. South.

Price Carrie Mrs., seamstress, r. 47 Noble.

Price E. J. Mrs , teacher, N. W. C. University, r. 92 Broadway.

Price John P., bartender, 103 S. Illinois.

Price Joseph, (col'd) lab , r. 116 Ash.

Price William B., produce dealer, r. 379 N. West.

Priegnitz August, lab., bds. 112 S. Benton.

Priegnitz Wm., carpenter, r. 112 S. Benton.

PRIER HENRY J., agent reapers and mowers and dealer in agricultural implements, 203 E. Washington, bds. 691 N. Tennessee.

Primis Samuel, (col'd) lab., r. 233 N. West.

Princel Henry, (col'd) lab., r. 94 Elm.

Princel Henry, moulder, r. 125 E. Stevens.

Prindle Bruce, moulder, r. 298 Chestnut.

Prine Thomas, clk. Murphy, Johnston & Co., bds. Sherman House.

Pringle W. W., law student, r. 96 E. Washington.

Prinz John D., salesman, 123 S. Meridian, r. 83 N. Noble.

Prosser John, dyer and scourer, 50 N. Illinois, r. same.

Protzman Belle Miss, dress and cloak maker, 48 S. Illinois, bds. same.

Protzman Ferdinaud, publisher, r. 48 S. Illinois.

Protzman W. H., painter, r. 159 N. Mississippi.

Prunk D. H., physician, 30 N. Mississippi, r. 372 W. New York.

Pryor Lewis, (col'd) lab., r. 298 E. Michigan.

Pugh James, traveler, Kinble, Aikman & Co., bds. National Hotel.

Puller John, barkeeper, r. Wabash, bet. Liberty and Noble.

Purcell Michael D., picture dealer, r. 124 N. East.

Purcell Persey, watchman, Bunte & Dickson, r. 384 E. Market.

Purcell Pizarro, engineer, r. 376 E. Market.

Purcell Sarah, (col'd, wid. Daniel) r. W. Second nr. Howard.

Purcell T. W., salesman, 108 S. Meridian, bds. Sherman House.

Pursel Peter, foreman, Munson & Johnston, r. 26 Douglass.

Pursell A. E., dentist, 1 and 2 Martindale blk., r. 278 N. Mississippi.

Purton Henry, works rolling mill, r. 278 Chestnut.

Putins Louis, tailor, r. 229 Union.

Putnam L. R. Miss, editor, Little Chief, r. 16 Center.

Putnam Sarah, (wid. Silas) r. 16 Center.

Puttyman James, (col'd) lab., r. 266 W. North.

Pyburn Hahneman, gardener, bds. 79 N. Pennsylvania.

Pyburn Mrs. H., dealer in books, periodicals, etc., P. O. news stand, N. Pennsylvania.

Pyle House, 95 N. Meridian, John Pyle, prop'r.

Pyle John, prop'r, Pyle House, 95 N. Meridirn.

Quack Christian, lab., r. 37 Madison rd.

Quauck C., lab., starch factory.

Quanitance Daniel, grocer, 68 Virginia av., r. same.

Quarmby Joseph T., stonemason, r. 182 N. Missouri.

Quig Edwin, lab., r. 9 Sharpe.

Quigley Albert, works American saw works, bds. 54 S. Pennsylvania.

Quigley Bridget, (wid. Patrick) r. 22 Eddy.

Quill John, lab., U. S. arsenal.

Quillan William, roller, Thos. Madden.

Quinell Isaac, confectioner, 311 E. Washington, r. same.

Quinlan M., soldier, U.S. Arsenal.

Quinlan James, porter, Spencer House.

Quinn David, notion dealer, r. 312 S. Illinois.

Quinn Edward, shoemaker, r. 250 S. Mississippi.

Quinn James, works rolling mill, bds. 300 S. Tennessee.

Quinn John, saloon, 245 W. Maryland, r. same.

Quinn John, foreman, H. Allen, r. 303 S. Pennsylvania.

Quinn Martin, lab., r. 109 n. West.

Quinn William, lab, r. 810 Blake.

Quinnis John, clk., 33 E. Washington, r. 32 W. Ohio.

RAAB JOHN, wood dealer, r. 261 Massachusetts av.
Rabb Maggie Mrs., r. 149 N. California.
Rabb Mary, (wid.) bds. Macy House.
Rabb Sebastian, boot and shoemaker, 9 N. Illinois, r. 242 S. Delaware.
Raber Gottfred, stonecutter, r. 268 S. Delaware.
Raby William, works, Osgood, Smith & Co., r. 274 W. Market.
Racker Peter, saloon and grocery, 290 W. Maryland.
Radcliffe J. O., with Woollen, Webb & Co., bds. 167 N. Tennessee.
Raebley Lewis, cabinetmaker, r. 132 Spring.
Rachel R. C., seamstress, r. 44 Massachusetts av.
Rafert Anthony, carpenter, r. 74 E. North.
Rafert A. F., Builders Emporium, 75 E. Walnut, r. 74 E. North.
Rafert C. F., carpenter, r. 83 E. Pratt.
Rafert Henry, r. 119 E. St. Mary.
Rafferty Thomas, lab., r. 175 Meek.
Raffert Wm., drayman, r. 242 Chestnut.
Ragin Charles, railroader, C. C. & I. C. R. R., r. 283 E. Georgia.
Rahn Albert, lab., bds. 293½ E. Washington.
Rahrer & Bro. (S. B H. and H. R.) groceries and provisions, 162 Indiana av.
Raible Louis, cabinetmaker, r. Spring.
Raible John, tailor, r. 340 E. Market.
Rail John, lab., r. 393 S. Missouri.
Railsback Adaline C. Mrs., dressmaker, r. 186 Blake.
Raine Charles I., miller, r. 19 Douglass.
Rains H., sawmill, r. 23 E. North.
Rains Levi, bds. 28 E. North.
Rains Mary, (wid. George) r. 19 Douglass.
Ralph A. J., traveling agent, Scott, West & Co., r. 40 N. East.
Ramsey Alex., plumber, bds. 135 E. St. Joseph.
Ramsey Geo. B., trader, r. 99 S. Benton.
Ramsey J. F., r. 260 N. Illinois.
Ramsey Samuel, (col'd) lab., r. 38 Center
Ramsey Thomas, bricklayer, r. 336 E. Washington.
Ramsey Walter, plumber, bds. 135 E. St. Joseph.
Ramsey William, gas fitter, bds. 135 E. St. Joseph.
Ramsier Christian, gardner. r. 351 W. Pennsylvania.
Rand Frederick, (R. & Hall) r. 270 N. Illinois.
Rand W. M., clk., Martin & Hopkins, bds 398 N. Alabama.
Rand & Hall, (F. R. and R. H.) attorneys at law, 24½ E. Washington.

BENHAM BRO'S,

36 East Washington St.,

AGENTS FOR THE

BURDETT ORGAN.

Randall B., clk., 29 S. Illinois, r. same.
Randall George, carpenter, r. 784 N. Illinois.
Randall Henry, carpenter, r. 784 N. Illinois.
Randall H. P., assistant assessor, r. 19 E. St. Joseph.
Randall Nelson A., prop. New York oyster house, 29 S. Illinois, r. same.
Randalls Charles, clk., r. 323 N. Delaware.
Ranihan James, undertaker, r. Indiana av. bet. North and California.
Rankin Albert, plasterer, r. 754 N. Tennessee.
Rankin William, paper finisher, works Caledonia paper mill.
Rann Eve, (col'd, wid.) r. 269 Blake.
Rann Kate, (col'd, wid. Bryant) r. 171 Indiana av.
Rann Mary A. (col'd) bds. 167 Indiana av.
RANSDELL DANIEL M., city clerk, r. 346 N. Meridian.
Ransford William P. (R. & Denton) r. Laporte, Ind.
Ransford & Denton, (W. P. Ransford and A. B. Benton) general agents Continental Life Insurance Co., of Hartford, Conn, S. W. cor. Washington and Meridian.
Rapp Casper, farrier, r. 230 S. Pennsylvania.
Rapp Fritz, barkeeper, bds. 161 E. South.
Rapp Fred J., r. 240 E. Market.
Rapp Sebastian, shoemaker, r. 242 S. Delaware.
Rarig Alex., foreman Greenleaf & Co, bds. 52 Eddy.
Rasch Joseph, brewer, r. 328 S. Delaware.
RASCHIG CHARLES M., dealer in cigars, tobacco and snuff, 11 E. Washington, r. 200 N. Tennessee.
Raschig Edward, clk. American M. U. Express Co., r. 126 E. North.
Rasener Fred. Wm., grocer, 288 E. Washington, r. same.
Rasener William, tollman, r. 155 Union Pennsylvania.
Rasfeld Ferd., clk, with Henry Reese, 113 and 115 W. Washington, r. same.
Rassmann Carles, Arsenal Exchange, r. E. Washington, nr. Deaf and Dumb Asylum.
Ratti Francis A., r. 318 N. East.

THE CHINA TEA STORES

Have the NAME of being the

MOST ATTRACTIVE STORES IN THE WEST.

No. 7 Odd Fellows Hall

AND

ACADEMY OF MUSIC CORNER.

Ratti Francis A., jr., pressman, r. 313 N. East.

Ratti Joseph, printer, Journal office, r. 318 N. East.

Rau Benjamin, (R. & Bombarger) r. 283 Indiana av.

RAU & BOMBARGER, (B. Rau & J. E. Bombarger) dealer in groceries, provisions, etc., 46 Indiana av.

Rauh Bernhard, readymade clothing, No. 1 Palmer House. r. 16 E. Michigan.

Rauh Lip, (R. & Bro.) r. Cincinnati, O.

Rauh Brothers, (Sol. Rauh and Lip Rauh) dealers in clothing and gents furnishing goods, No. 1 Palmer House.

Rauh Sol. (R. & Bro.) r. Cincinnati, O.

Rawlings B. F. Rev., r. 80 Christian av.

Rauschenbach Caroline, Mrs., bds. 275 E. New York.

Rauser George, bakery, 68 S. West, r. same.

Ravencraft Francis M., cooper, r. cor. New York and Blake.

Ravendish Charles, shoemaker, r. 187 E. South.

Raver Charles, lab., Peru Depot, 139 E. Merrill.

Raver ——, r. 268 E. Merrill.

Rawzell Samuel, flagman, railroad crossing, r. 272 Union.

Ray A. S., produce dealer, r. 147 Buchanan.

Ray Charles A., Judge Supreme Court, r. 144 N. Illinois.

Ray H. C., attorney at law, r. N. Pennsylvania. cor. Seventh.

Ray H. J., billiard saloon, 274 E. Washington. r. same.

Ray Isaac, moulder, starch factory, r. 44 Forest av.

Ray James, pres't Bank of the State of Indiana, r. 112 N. Meridian.

Ray John, cabinetmaker, with N. S. Baker, r. 274 N. Noble.

Ray John W., attorney at law, 42½ E. Washington, r. National rd., outside city limits.

Ray Martin M., attorney, 12 Talbott & New's blk., r. nw. cor. Pennsylvania and Tinker.

Ray S. W., patentwright, r. 23 Bates.

Ray William, lab., r. 24 Bates.

Ray W. S., attorney, 12 Talbott & New's blk., r. nw. cor. Pennsylvania and Tinker.

Raymond Annie Miss, waiter, Spencer House.

Raymond Samuel, blacksmith, r. 49 S. Pennsylvania.

Rayser Jacob, (col'd) porter, Hume, Adams & Co., r. Third, bet. Tennessee and Mississippi.

Rayner L. A., 24 N. Pennsylvania, bds. 52 N. Pennsylvania.

Raynor C. A., traveling agent H. F. West & Co., r. 523 N. Tennessee.

Read George D., machinist, I. C. & L. R. R. shops, r. 185 Bates.

Read George H., lab., 185 Bates.

Reade E., marblecutter, 36 E. Market, bds. 419 N. East.

Reading T. C., sup't Shaw, Lippencott & Conner, r. 20 W. Georgia.

Reading W., works Shaw, Lippencott & Conner, bds. 20 W. Georgia.

Reagen D. J., bookkeeper, 54 S. Meridian, r. 623 N. Illinois.

Reagan Edward, boilermaker, r. 132 S. Tennessee.

Reagan Martha A. (wid.) r. 623 N. Illinois.

Ream Robert, shoemaker, bds. 44 S. Tennessee.

Ream Laura Miss, newspaper correspondent, r. 25 Virginia av.

Reasner Anthony, drayman, r. 23 E. McCarty.

Reasner Fred W., grocer, r. 68 Michigan rd.

Reasner Wm., lab., r. 286 N. Noble.

Reasner Wm. F. (R. & Schildmeyer) r. Michigan rd.

Reasner & Schildmeyer, (W. F. R. and A. S.) dry goods and groceries, 593 E. Washington.

Reaume Anthony, r. 2 McGill.

Reaume John A., clk., R. R. Parkers, r. 2 McGill.

Rech George, clk., 44 W. Louisiana, bds. 118 S. Illinois.

Rech William, telegraph operator, bds. Bluff rd., S. city limits.

Reck Mattie, (wid. George) r. 77 W. First.

Recker Alexander, cabinetmaker, r. 219 E. Ohio.

Recker George, cigarmaker, r. 135 E. Washington.

Recker Gossfield, clk., r. 238 S. New Jersey.

Recker Hubert, carpenter, r. 507 E. Market.

Recker Robert, musician, bds. 507 E. Market.

Rector N., inspector I. C. & L. freight depot.

Rerding Jeremiah, machinist, r. 71 S. Pennsylvania.

Redfield D. A., r. 71 W. Michigan.

Redford James, lab., r. 409 S. Delaware.

Redford J. E., r. 80 N. Pennsylvania.

Redman Dennis, lab. roofing mill, r. 301 W. Merrill.

Redman John, stovefitter, r. 243 W. Maryland.

Redman O. A., printer, Journal office, bds. 31 W. Ohio.

Redman Mrs., r. 243 W. Maryland.

Redmond Henry, lab., r. 31 W. St. Clair.

Redmond Harriet Mrs., r. 38 S. Illinois.

Redmond Laura Miss, bds. 38 S. Illinois.

Redmond Thomas, saloon and produce dealer, 346 W. Washington, r. same.

Redmond William, surveyor, r. 242 W. Market.

Redmond William, messenger, I. C. & L. R. R, r. 258 S. Tennessee.

Reece Clifford K., printer, Sentinel news room.

Reece Mary Miss, boarding house, 89 N. Delaware, r. same.

Reed A. (A. R. & Co.) bds, 143 W. Washington.

Reed A. & Co. (A. R. and J. J. Boyle) soda water manufacturers, 276 W. Washington.

Reed Benj. F., local editor, Commercial, r. 176 Virginia av.

Reed Edward, (col'd) lab., works Osgood, Smith & Co, r. 79 Ann.

Reed Elizabeth, (wid. William K.) r. 293 Indiana av.

Reed Enoch, marblecutter, bds. 419 N. East.

Reed Enos B., editor Indiana Journal of Commerce, r. 176 Virginia av.

Reed E. R., engraver, W. P. Bingham & Co., r. 21 S. Pennsylvania.

Reed Frank, bottler, A. Reed & Co., bds. 143 W. Washington.

Reed George, lab., bds. 355 W. Washington.

Reed George D., machinist, r. 185 Bates.

Reed George L., weaver, r. California ar. North.

Reed G. H., moulder, r. 185 Bates.

Reed Hattie, (wid.) seamstress, r. 433 S. Illinois.

Reed Howard, switchman, I. & C. J. R. R., bds. 176 Virginia av.

Reed Jerry, (col'd) barber, r. 266 W. North.

Reed John, (col'd) lab., r. 2 Ann.

Reed John, clk. E. Washington, bds. 134 N. East.

Reed John F., clk. r. 134 N. East.

Reed J. W., merchant, r. 231 Virginia av.

Reed James, cooper, bds. 114 S. Noble.

Reed Landy H., carriage painter, r. 134 S. East.

18

BENHAM BRO'S,

36 East Washington St.,

Pianos, Organs and Melodeons Tuned, Moved and Repaired.

Reed Louisiana, (wid. John R.) r. 291 Massachusetts av.

Reed Martha J., (wid.) r. 134 N. East.

Reed Michael, porter, Bates House, r. 87 S. West.

Reed Orlando H., coachmaker, r. 134 N. East.

Reed S. A. Mrs., boardinghouse, 301 N. Pennsylvania.

Reed S B., railroader, r. 185 Bates.

Reed Thaddeus, civil engineer, bds. 176 Virginia av.

Reed William E., clk. 3 W. Washington, bds. 80 S. Mississippi.

Rees Catharine, (wid.) r. 95 Oak.

Reese Charles, sr., cabinetmaker, r. 188 N. Noble.

Reese Charles, cabinetmaker, r. 188 N. Noble.

Reese Charles E. (Hellweg & Reese) r. 83 N. East.

Reese Henry, groceries and provisions, 113 and 115 W. Washington, r. same.

Rees H., physician, office 7 S. Alabama, r. 315 Virginia av.

REEVES FRANK J., compiler, J. D. Campbell's directories, r. 87 Union.

Reeves Sarah, (wid.) r. 469 N. Meridian.

Reeves Tomas, lab., r. 18 Dacota.

Regeela Conrad, clk. 49 W. Washington, bds. 23 Kentucky av.

Regan Edward, foreman Sinker & Davis' boiler shop, r. 132 S. Tennessee.

Regan John, bell boy, Sherman House.

Regenauer Casper, janitor City offices.

Regenauer Louis, lithographer, r. 273 S. New Jersey.

Reger Charles, cabinetmaker, r. 79 Davidson.

Reger Charles William, Cabinetmakers' Union, r. 79 Davidson.

Rehan Harry S., cooper, r. 30 N. New Jersey.

Rehe Harmann, carpenter, r. 241 Davidson.

Rehling William, dealer in boots and shoes, 255 S. Delaware, r. same.

Reible Charles, works Jackson, Rider & Co.

Reible Charles, r. 518 E. Washington.

Reich August, policeman, r. 49 Virginia av.

Reichel Edward, carpenter, Eagle Machine Works, r. 123 Spring.

H. H. LEE,
Dealer in

Teas, Coffees, Sugars & Spices,

No. 7 ODD FELLOWS HALL

AND

ACADEMY OF MUSIC CORNER.

Reichwein John P., lab., r. 199 N. Davidson.
Reichwein Philip, saloon, 50 N. Noble, r. same.
REID, COUNCIL & Co. (Earl Reid. John F. Council and W. R. Hogshire) whol. and retail dealers in boots and shoes, 25 W. Washington.
Reid Earl. (R.. Council & Co.) bds. 33 W. Maryland.
Reid George L., weaver at Geisendorff's Woolen Mill.
Reid Julia, (wid.) r. 171 Spring.
Reider E. C., grocer, 298 E. Washington, r. same.
Reidy Michael, lab., r. 315 S. Meridian.
Reiße Martin, file cutter, 136 S. Pennsylvania, r. 36 Union.
Reimenschneider Herman, (Krause & R.) r. 83 N. New Jersey.
Reinacher Jacob. clk., Mayhew, Warren & Co., bds. Sherman House.
Reiners Henrietta, (wid. Martin) r. room 9 Fatout's blk.
Reinert G., butcher, 153 W. Market, r. same.
Reinett George T., grocer, 70 E. Maryland.
Reinfelt Ezra, works cotton mill, r. 236 Blake.
Reinfelt Henry, lab., r. 272 Union.
Reinhart Joseph P., locksmith, 81 S. Illinois, r. same.
Reinhart Robert, blacksmith, 81 S. Illinois.
Reinhart Valantine, vinegar manufacturer, r. 577 S Meridian.
Reinheimer Augusta, (wid. Jacob) r. 193 Huron.
Reinheimer Lewis, lab., r. 109 Huron.
Reinheimer Nathan, Palmer House clothing store, r. 275 S. Delaware.
Reinicke Frederick, sr., moulder, Eagle Machine Works, r. 347 S. Alabama.
Reinicke Frederick, jr., moulder, Eagle Machine Works, bds. 347 S. Alabama.
Reinicke Julius, clk., P. Lehr, bds. same.
Reinkin Albert, cigarmaker, r. 753 N. Tennessee.
Reinkin Henry, cigars and tobacco, 266 E. Washington, r. same.
REINMAN REINHART, beer garden, 252 E. Washington, r. same.
Reis Isaac, cabinet maker, r. 169 Winston.

Reising Louis, gasfitter, r. 338 S. Delaware.
Reisner A., drayman, r. 23 E. McCarty.
Reisner Ellen, (wid.) r. 240 S. Tennessee.
Reisner George, salesman, 25 W. Washington, r. 240 N. Tennessee.
Reisner William, lab., r. 286 N. Noble.
Reissner Albert, (Deitz & R.) r. 184 N. Blake.
Reissner Frank, currier, r. 385 S. East.
Reitz Charles, agent sewing machine, 15 Virginia av, r 287 S. Pennsylvania.
REITZ FRANK R., city beer garden, 156 E. Washington, r. same.
Reitz Henry, piano teacher, room 8 Ætna bldg., r. 277 S. Pennsylvania.
Reitzel Christian, machinist r. 419 S. Illinois.
Rely Frederick, watchman, J. M. & I. R. R. engine house, r. 232 Madison av.
Remas Victor, gardener, r. 270 S. Noble.
Renahan Joseph, lab., r. 72 Fayette.
RENARD EUGENE, proprietor, People's Saloon, 299 E. Washington, r. same.
Renard John, stonecutter, r. 321 E. New York.
Renauer ——, r. 69 Hosbrook.
Rench Henry, boilermaker, C. C. C. & I. R. R. shops.
Renchler Adam, works Novelty Works.
Rennehan Joseph, porter, Bates House.
Renner Christian, blacksmith, shop 423 S. Meridian, r. 427 S. Meridian.
Renner John B., carriage trimmer, r. 34 S. Alabama.
Renner Louis, stonemason, r. 201 Huron.
Rennert George, salesman, 171 W. Washington, r. 70 E. Maryland.
Rensman Hermann, dyer and scourer, 23 Virginia av., r. same.
Rentsch Edward, groceries and provisions, 172 S. Illinois, r. same.
Rentsch Herman, grocer, r. 141 E. Washington.
Rentchler Adam, foreman, Union Novelty Works, bds. California House.
Rentchler Fred., salesman, r. E. Court.
Rentsch Ferdinand, clk. 55 and 57 S. Meridian, bds. Emennegger's Hotel.
Rentsch Robert, clk. 55 and 57 S. Meridian, bds. 132 N. New Jersey.
Renzelbrink William, lab., r. 94 Eddy.
Reader William, butcher, bds. 293½ E. Washington.
Replogle John, (Lee & R.) r. 190 Davidson.
Resch Joseph, brewer, Schmid's Brewery, r. 328 S. Delaware.
Reisener Anthony, (Reissner & Bro.) r. 320 E. Vermont.
Resener Christian F., boot and shoe manufacturer, St. Clair, nr. Massachusetts av., r. same.

Resener Chris H., chairmaker, r. 511 S. New Jersey.

Resener C. F., carpenter and builder, r. 161 N. New Jersey.

Resener Frank, currier, r. 337 S. East.

Resener Fred W., clk, r. 179 N. East.

Resener Henry, dealer in boots and shoes, 370 Virginia av., r. 368 Virginia av.

Resener Henry F., carpenter, r. 285 N. Winston.

Resener Hermann, porter, r. 246 N. Winston.

Resener John F., dry goods and groceries, r. 179 N. East.

Resener William F. (R. & Bro.) r. 331 E. Ohio.

RESENER & BRO., Union Star Mill, Cumberland, bet. Alabama and Delaware.

Ressler C. Henley, student, bds. cor. Broadway and Christian av.

Ressler Theodore, lab. Roots Foundry, r. 124 Hosbrook.

Reutter William, lab., r. 23 Ellsworth.

Revels Willis R. (col'd) r. 205 N. West.

Revel Wm. W., engineer I. & V. R R., r. 303 E. Georgia.

Rexford Eugene, express messenger, r. 244 N. Illinois.

Reyer Frederica, midwife, r. 78 N. Noble.

Reyer George, salesman J. K. Sharpe, r. 677 N. Meridian.

Reynolds Chas, cigar maker, r. 512 E. Washington.

Reynolds Charles E., clk., C. C. C. & I. Depot, r. 323 N. Delaware.

Reynolds Chesley, expressman, r. 79 Ash.

Reynolds C. H., locksmith, r. 512 E. Washington.

Reynolds David, cigarmaker, r. 512 E. Washington.

Reynolds Edward, manufacturer of medicines, r. 160 Virginia av.

Reynolds Frank, yardmaster C. C. C. & I. R. R. yard, r. 156 N. Liberty.

Reynolds Henry, lab., bds. 199 W. Maryland.

Reynolds Isaac, (Smith, R. & Thomas) bds. Ray House.

Reynolds James, lab., bds. 199 W. Maryland.

REYNOLDS J., township assessor, office, 35½ E. Washington, r. 287 N. Alabama.

Reynolds John, r. 92 W. Ohio.

Reynolds John, (col'd) lab., r. 177 W. Second.

Reynolds John R. manufacturer of medicine, r. 160 Virginia av.

Reynolds John M., expressman, bds. 79 Ash.

Reynolds John W., carpenter, r. 78 S. Benton.

BENHAM BRO'S,

36 East Washignton St.,

AGENTS FOR THE

BURDETT ORGAN.

Reynolds J. M., cigarmaker, r. 512 E. Washington.

Reynolds Miles M., lab., r. 119 Ash.

Reynolds M. W., cigar manufacturer, 244½ E. Washington, r. 512 E. Washington.

Reynolds Orin, traveling agent, r. 107 W. South.

Reynolds Samuel, works Osgood, Smith & Co., r. 456 Virginia av.

Reynolds S. Frank, agent for W. W. Reynolds, r. 512 E. Washington.

Reynolds Thomas E. (Wiles & R.) r. 16 Virginia av.

Reynolds William, clk., r. 323 North Delaware.

Rez Jacob, shoemaker, 9 N. Illinois.

Rheinheimer N., dealer in clothing and gents furnishing goods, 3 Palmer House, r. 275 S. Delaware.

Rheinschild John, boot and shoemaker, 395 N. New Jersey, r. 154 St. Joseph.

Rhinehold Jacob, carpenter, r. 373 W. Vermont.

Rhoads Charles W., watchman, fire tower, r. 231 W. New York.

Rhoads James, lab., r. 264 Indiana av.

Rhoads James F., traveler, Browning & Sloan, bds. 444 N. Meridian.

Rhoads John P., teamster, r. 380 S. Missouri.

Rhoads John W., r. 82 E. St. Clair.

Rhodes Milton, printer, Journal Office, bds. 79 Massachusetts av.

Rhodewalt Henry, porter, bds. 48 Oriental.

RHODIUS MRS. GEORGE, proprietress, Circle Saloon and Restaurant, 15 N. Meridian.

Rice Alex., clk. 164 W. Washington, bds. 184 W. Ohio.

Rice George H., pumpmaker, r. 69 W. New York.

Rice Gustavus, dry goods and notions, 164 W. Washington, r. 184 W. Ohio.

Rice Isaac, Cabinetmakers' Union, r. 107 N. Winston.

Rice John, lab, bds. 217 S. Illinois.

RICE MARTIN H., editor Masonic Home Advocate, bds. Palmer House.

Rice Patrick, lab., bds. 209 S. Illinois.

Rice William, clothier, r. 184 W. Ohio.

Rich Harriet, (wid.) r. 368 W. Washington.

H. H. LEE
HAS BUT
ONE PRICE, SELLS FOR CASH,
And Guarantees all Goods
Sold at the China Tea Stores,
To be as Represented.

Rich Jane Miss, r. 220 N. Missouri.

RICH T. C., physician, 58 E. Market, bds. 52 N. Pennsylvania.

Richard George, lab., bds. E. Court, nr. East.

Richard Wm. C., carpenter, r. 314 E. Market.

Richards Edward N., r. 30 W. Pratt.

Richards Frank, stonecutter, r. 485 E. Georgia.

Richhards George, compositor, r. 135 E. Washington.

Richards Harvey W., works rolling mill, r. 378 S. Illinois.

Richards J. H., manufacturer of cotton and woolen goods, r. 228 E. Louisiana.

Richards Kazie, (wid. Richard) r. 176 N. Missouri.

Richards William L., railroader, r. 106 Hosbrook.

Richardson Alfred, lab., r. Tenth, nr. Lafayette R. R.

Richardson B. A., bookkeeper, r. 49 S. Pennsylvania.

Richardson Charles, lab. Osgood, Smith & Co., r. 331 S. Missouri.

Richardson Daniel A., Geisendorf, R. & Co., bds. Bates House.

Richardson Daniel A., teamster, r. 277 Indiana av.

Richardson Frank, agent Singer Sewing Machine Co., r. 444 N. New Jersey.

Richardson Frank M., teamster, r. 9 Elizabeth.

Richardson Fredrick W., printer, works Journal office, r. 102 N. Missouri.

Richardson G. O., traveling agent L. Q. Sherwood, bds. 556 N. Illinois.

Richardson Jennie, (wid.) boarding house, 79 Massachusetts av.

Richardson John, teamster, r. 122 Maple.

Richardt John, carpenter, r. 425 N. East.

Richert William, brewer, works Frank Wright, bds. 323 W. Washington.

Richer William C., works Frank Wright's brewery, bds. Nagle House.

Richey Charlotte C. (wid.) r. 124 N. Missouri.

Richey Julius, tinner, 223 S. Delaware, r. 308 S. East.

Richmann Charles, r. 16 Fletcher av.

Richman William, carpenter, r. Howard, bet. Third and Fourth.

Richmond John, lab., r. 37 E. South.

RICHMOND TEMPERANCE HOUSE, 35 W. Georgia, J. G. Collins, proprietor.

Richter August, contractor, r. 310 Virginia av.

Richter Anton, lab. I. C. & L. Depot, r. Lord, sw. cor Benton.

Richter Henry, blacksmith, Eagle Machine Works, r. 261 S. Mississippi.

Richter Henry, machinist, r. 261 S. Mississippi.

Richter Hermann, cabinetmaker, Deaf and Dumb Assylum, r. 256 N. Winston.

Richter John F., painter, r. cor. Camp and First.

Richter Joseph, shoemaker, 217 E. Washington, r. same.

Richter Simeon, brakeman, C. C. & I. C. R. R.

Richter William, sr., saloon, 418 Virginia av., r. 414 Virginia av.

Richter William, jr., dealer in groceries, etc., 416 Virginia av., r. same.

Richter & Schrosluck, (T. B. R. and J. S.) groceries and provisions, cor. Illinois and Russell.

Richwren J., wiper, I. C. & L. R. R. shops.

Rickard Philip, r. 314 N. New Jersey.

Rickard Henry, (R. & Talbott) bds. Depot Dining Hall.

Rickard & Talbott, (H. R. and C. H. T.) wholesale dealers in hats, caps, and furs, 78 S. Meridian.

Rickards Thomas, carpenter and builder, 127 E. Maryland, r. 314 E. Market.

Rickards William C., carpenter, works Chandler & Taylor, r. 314 E. Market.

RICKER FRANK, (Morton & R.) bds. 144 N. Mississippi.

Ricker ——, (wid.) r. 269 E. Ohio.

Ricketts Dillard, Prest. J. M. & I. R. R., r. Madison rd.

Ridenour Jonathan M., Vice Prest. C. & I. J. R. R., r. Michigan rd.

Rider T. N. (Jackson, R. & Co.) r. 189 E. Ohio.

Rider ——, with Jackson, Rider & Co., r. 240 N. Mississippi.

Ridge Jonathan J., carriage trimmer, r. 317 E. Ohio.

Ridges Howard, bellboy, Sherman House.

Ridgeway J. F., physician, 88 E. Market, r. 191 N. New Jersey.

Ridgeway Ottis N., watchmaker, with G. Davis, bds. Circle Restaurant.

Riebel Fred., cigarmaker, 35 W. Washington, r. nr. Fishback's tannery.

Rieger George, machanic, bds. 300 E. Market.

Rienendish Henry, cigarmaker, r. 187 E. South.

Rifle Louis, butcher, works cor. McCarty and Meridian, bds. same.

Rifle Peter, lab., r. 36 Union.

Rigg Joseph, physician, r. 100 Holbrook.

Rihl Charles H., bricklayer, r. 30 N. New Jersey.

Rihl H. S., cooper, r. 30 N. New Jersey.

Rikhoff Bernhard, (Rickhoff & Bros.) bds. 351 N. Noble.

Rikhoff Herman, (R. & Bros.) r. 278 E. South.

Rikhoff J. G. (R. & Bros.) r. Cincinnati, Ohio.

Rikhoff & Brothers, wholesale liquor dealers, 80 S. Meridian.

Riley Cornelius, works Osgood, Smith & Co., bds. 169 S. Tennessee.

Riley Daniel, engineer, stave factory, r. 105 Spring.

Riley Frank, deputy County Treasurer, r. 37 Kentucky av.

Riley George W., soldier, U. S. Arsenal.

Riley Henry, lab., r. 43 Russell.

Riley Hugh, lab., r. Meek.

Riley H. H., with B. F. Haugh & Co., r. 34 Russell av.

Riley James, waiter, Union Depot dining hall, bds. same.

Riley Michael, lab., r. 286 S. Tennessee.

Riley Terrence, works, rolling mill, r. 26 Maple.

Riley Timothy, lab., r. 287 S. Tennessee.

Riley William, works, Osgood, Smith & Co., r. 66 Eddy.

Ring John, lab., r. 183 Dougherty.

Ringelsky A., pedlar, r. 406 S. Tennessee.

Ringer Eliza J. (wid. David F.) r. 72 Ash, cor. Vine.

Ringer John, upholsterer, 71 and 73 W. Washington, bds. 23 Kentucky av.

Rinkle David, barber, 94 E. South.

Ripley William, (R. & Gates) r. 225 W. New York.

Ripley & Gates, (William Ripley and A. B. Gates) grocers and produce dealers, 47 and 49 N. Illinois.

Rist John, works, 112 S. Meridian, bds. same.

Ritche Arnold, lab., r. 470 S. New Jersey.

Ritche E. Mrs., boarding house, 17½ Virginia av.

Ritche Julius, tinner, r. 308 S. East.

Ritchey Thomas J., cooper, r. cor. Washington and Noble.

Ritchey Sarah Miss, dressmaker, r. 22 Douglass.

Ritching Thomas, cooper, r. over 346 E. Washington.

Rittenhouse George, r. 479 N. Meridian.

Ritter August, teamster, r. 496 S. New Jersey.

Ritter Eli, attorney at law, r. 368 N. Alabama.

Ritter E. F. (R. & Irving) r. 368 N. Alabama.

Ritter Frederick, teamster, r. 63 Beatty.

RITTER & IRVING, (E. F. R and W. M. I.) attorneys at law, 24½ E. Washington.

Ritzinger A. W., bookkeeper Ritzinger's Bank, r. 226 E. Ohio.

RITZINGER'S BANK, 14 E. Washington, J. B. Ritzinger, proprietor.

Ritzing Frederick L., teller Ritzinger's Bank, bds. 226 E. Ohio.

RITZINGER FRED., Secretary G. M. Insurance Co., and agent Bremen and Hamburg steamers, 16 S. Delaware, r. 226 E. Ohio.

RITZINGER J. B., banker, 14 E. Washington, r. 240 E. Ohio.

River J. T., barber, ne. cor. E. Washington and Pennsylvania, bds. Pattison House.

Roach A. C., publisher Jolly Hoosier, r. 555 N. Illinois.

Roach Charles, engineer, r. 297 S. East.

Roach Milton E., lab., 297 S. East.

Roach Nicholas, works Frank Wright's Brewery.

Roache A. L., attorney, office No. 3 Ætna bldg., r. 613 N. Pennsylvania.

Roark Thomas, steward Union Depot, r. 66 California.

Roback Albert G., conductor T. H. & I. R. R., r. 26 S. West.

Roback Eli, bookbinder, Sentinel office, bds. 231 N Mississippi.

Roback Henry, lab., r. 242 N. West.

Roback Sarah, (wid. George) r. 231 N. Mississippi.

Robb I., saloon and hotel, Tenth bet. Lafayette Railroad and Canal.

Robbins James M., traveling agent, Moody Bros., r. 121 W. Vermont.

Roberts A. B. S., pumpmaker, 197 and 199 S. Meridian, r. 97 E. St. Clair.

ROBERTS PARK, (Methodist) F. C. Holliday, pastor, ne. cor. Vermont and Delaware.

Roberts Edward, (Dumont & R.) r. 3 Willard.

Roberts E. A. (wid.) r. 24 N. Noble.

Roberts H., bookbinder, Sentinel office.

Roberts Hezekiah W. (R. & Hildebrand) r. 124 Blackford.

Roberts Jeff. (col'd) lab., r. 811 Massachusetts av.

Roberts John, lab., r. 31 Blake.

Roberts John A. Rev., r. 15 Vine.

THE CHINA TEA STORES

ARE AT

No. 7 ODD FELLOWS HALL

AND

ACADEMY OF MUSIC CORNER.

Roberts John W., machinist, r. 454 E Michigan.

Roberts Joseph, tinner, r. 217 Virginia av.

Roberts Joseph, brakeman, bds. 58 Benton.

Roberts Joseph T., attorney at law, room 3 Kinder's blk., r. 272 E. North.

Roberts Joseph T. jr., hostler, r. 123 W. Market.

Roberts J. W., printer, Journal office, bds. Bates House.

Roberts Rebecca, (col'd, wid. William) r. 172 W. Georgia.

Roberts S. W., hostler, Sullivan & Drew, bds. 123 W. Market.

Roberts Thomas B., works 21 and 23 W. Pearl.

Roberts Wm., fireman, C. & I. J. R. R., bds. 61 S. Noble.

Roberts Wm. G., engineer, bds. 77 Davidson.

Roberts W. J., engineer, Cabinet Makers' Union, r. 77 Davidson.

Roberts William J. D., stock trader, r. 163 E. St. Joseph.

Roberts & Hillebrand, (H. W. R. and J. M. H.) marble workers, 46 Virginia av.

Robertson A. M. (Robertson A. M. and Bro.) r. 96 E. Washington.

Robertson A. M. & Bro., dry goods and notions, 96 E. Washington.

Robertson Benjamin, (col'd) lab. r. 287 Douglass al.

Robertson Charles B. superintendent of Union track, r. 381 S. Alabama.

Robertson Fount., (Robertson & Bro.) r. 96 E. Washington.

Robertson James H., clk. 96 E. Washington.

Robertson James W., plasterer, r. 339 S. Alabama.

Robertson John, lab., r. 280 W. Market.

Robertson Joseph, contractor, r. cor. North and Patterson.

Robertson Josie, jr, clk. 74 S. Meridian, bds. 177 N. Alabama.

Robertson J. E. (J. E. R. & Co.) r. 177 N. Alabama.

ROBERTSON J. E. & CO. (J. E. R., G. T. Evans and J. C. Perry) whol. grocers, 74 and 76 S Meridian.

Robertson Mary S., wid. (John M.) r. 149 N. California.

Robertson Melissa Mrs., (wid.) Joshua, r. 49 Ann.

Robertson Milton, (col'd) lab., r. 116 Ash.

Robertson Robert, (col'd) lab., r. 239 N. West.

Robertson William, machinist, r. 223 Union.

Robinius Francis, boot and shoe manufacturer, 223 W. Washington, r. 222 W. Maryland.

Robinius Francis, jr., shoemaker, bds. 222 W. Maryland.

Robins Charles J., butcher, 34 N. Pennsylvania, r. 393 W. New York.

Robins Charles J., jr., bds. 393 W. New York.

ROBINSON BROTHERS, (Lafe R. & Bruce R.) manufacturers and dealers in trunks and valises, wholesale and retail, 20 and 22 Virginia av.

Robinson Bruce, (R. Bros.) r. 318 Massachusetts av.

Robinson Charles H., conductor T. H. and I. R. R., bds. Spencer House.

Robinson D. D., bartender, 87 S. Illinois, r. same.

Robinson F. M., bookkeeper, r. 10 Water.

Robinson G., painter, r. 402 S. Illinois.

Robinson H. S, switchman, C. C. C. & I. R. R., r. 250 N. Davidson.

Robinson Jane, (wid. Robert W.) r. 110 N. Missouri.

Robinson Jerome, clk. 94 Virginia av., r. 339 S. Alabama.

Robinson John, map agent, r. 151 Davidson.

Robinson L. B. (Robinson & Bro.) r. 318 Massachusetts av.

Robinson Lafayette, (R. & Bro.) r. 318 Massachusetts av.

Robinson Martin S, clk. T. H. & I. freight office, r. 341 S. Meridian.

Robinson Mathew B., r. 318 Massachusetts av.

Robinson Wallace A., teacher, r. 400 N. East.

Robinson R. D. Rev., Presiding Elder, Southeastern Indiana Conference, r. N. New Jersey.

Robinson Sarah Mrs., r. 176 N. East.

ROBINSON WM. I. H., manager Indianapolis Piano Manufacturing Co., r. 143 E. Washington.

Robinson W. H., engineer, r. 182 E. McCarty.

Robinson W. L., driver, G. G. Holman, r. 126 N. Mississippi.

ROBISON ANTHONY W., flour, feed and wood dealer, 201 Indiana av., bds. cor. North and Patterson.

Robison A. M., gen'l agent, American overseaming and sewing machine, 18 N. Delaware, r. 6 Morrison.

Robison Henry, works, Paper Mill, bds. 261 W. Washington.

Robison Joseph H., contractor and teamster, r. cor. North and Patterson.

Robson Charlotte F. (wid. William) r. E. Michigan.

Robson George B., carriage trimmer, works Miller's carriage shop, r. 33 S. West.

Robson Kate Miss, teacher Fourth Ward School, bds. 236 N. West.

Rocny Francis B., carpenter, r. 201 N. Davidson.

Rockey Henry S., r. 202 E. Ohio.

Rockwell James, fireman, C. C. C. & I. R. R., bds. 345 N. Noble.

Rockwood Wm. O., r. 276 N. Illinois.

Rodden James, cooper, r. 109 N. Illinois.

Roddius ———, r. 169 N. Illinois.

Rodebaugh Adam, r. 685 N. Tennessee.

Rodebaugh Omer, clk. J. Tarlton, r. cor. Fourth and Tennessee.

Rodenbeck Gustave, drayman, r. 502 S. East.

Rodenberger F. E. Mrs., dressmaker, 221 E. North, r. same.

Rodenberger Samuel, carpenter, r. 221 E. North.

Rodes Susan Mrs., (col'd) r. rear 66 Missouri.

Rodewald Henry, grocer, 441 Virginia av., r. same.

Rodewalt Henry, porter, 27 and 29 E. Maryland.

Rodgers B., lab. Bunte & Dickson.

Rodgers Harvey, physician, r. 49 Ann.

Rodgers Levi, brickmason, r. Arsenal rd.

Rodius Andrew, barber, bds. 34 W. Georgia.

Rodman Charles, salesman, 74 S. Meridian, r. 75 S. Noble.

Rodney Cæsar, messenger, T. H. and I. R. R. freight office, bds. cor. Alabama and Virginia av.

Roe Alice, (wid.) r. terminus Rose.

Roehling John F., student, bds. 212 E. Ohio.

Roesener Charles, blacksmith, St. Clair nr. Massachusetts av., r. cor. Broadway and Arch.

Roesener Christian H., chairmaker, r. 511 S. New Jersey.

Roesener Henry, lab., bds. 292 W. Winston.

Roesener Henry, car inspector C. C. & L. C. R. R., r. 110 N. Noble.

Roeth Adam, tailor, bds. Little House.

Roeth John, (R. & Meier) r. 329 E. Michigan.

ROETH & MEIER, John Roeth and Henry Meier) merchant tailors, 198 E. Washington.

Rogan George W., puddler Rolling Mill, r. 62 Grant.

Rogan Henry, (col'd, Rogan & Milligan) 148 N. Tennessee.

Rogan & Milligan, (col'd, H. R. and F. M.) restaurant, 148 N. Tennessee.

Rogers Andrew, works Osgood, Smith & Co., bds. 217 S. Illinois.

Rogers George, sawmaker, r. 229 S. Alabama.

Rogers Isaac, lab., r. 38 Hellen.

Rogers James, lab., r. 2 Catherine.

Rogers John T., salesman New York Store, bds. Avenue House.

Rogers Newel J., bookkeeper Bee-Hive, bds. 35 Cherry.

Rogers Kate, (wid. James W.) r. 15 Madison av.

Rogers Levi, brickmaker, r. 337 N. Noble.

Rogers W. P., agent Harper Bros., bds. 160 N. Meridian.

Rogge Henry, tailor, bds. California House.

Rogge Rudolph, tailor, bds. California House.

Rogge Rudolph Mrs., merchant tailoress, 335 Virginia av., r. same.

Rohrer Henry, (R. & Bro.) bds. cor. West and North.

Rohrer Joseph, saloon, 293 Kentucky av., r. same.

Rohrer S. B. (R. & Bro.) bds. cor. West and North.

Rohrer & Bros., groceries, 162 Indiana av.

Roll Rebecca, (wid.) r. 351 N. New Jersey.

ROLL WILLIAM H., dealer in carpets, wall paper and shades, 35 S. Illinois, r. 117 W. Maryland.

Rollin Samuel, (col'd) cook.

Roman Matthias, turner, 216 S. Meridian, r. 24 W. McCarty.

Ronan John, lab., r. 327 W. Market.

Ronan L., conductor C. & I. J. R. R., bds. Spencer House.

Ronan Michael, lab., r. 131 S. Tennessee.

Ronerell G. H., chairmaker, r. 342 N. East.

Roney Cyrus S., street contractor, r. 173 N. East.

Roney Elias M., teamster, r. 676 N. Mississippi.

Roney Felix, works rolling mill, bds. 272 S. Tennessee.

H. H. LEE

MAKES A SPECIALTY OF

Choice Green, Black & Japan Teas.

Roney Henry, (Haywood & R.) r. 129 N.
East.

Ronon John, bricklayer, r. 334 S. Delaware.

Rooker Alfred, painter, r. 37 Douglass.

Rooker C. F., deputy county clerk, r. 778
N. Illinois.

Rooney H. C. (Haywood & Co.) r. 129 N.
East.

Rooney Kitty, domestic, Bates House.

Roop J. A., traveler, Dr. Buell, r. 48 N.
New Jersey.

Roos, Jacob, meat market, 137 S. Illinois,
r. same.

Roos Louie Miss, r. 301 W. Market.

Root Adolph, barkeeper, r. cor. Missouri
and Cumberland.

Root Deloss, (D. R. & Co.) r. 441 N. Meridian.

ROOT D. & CO. (D. R. and J. B. R.)
manufacturers of stoves, hollowware
and casting; factory, 183 S. Pennsylvania, salesroom, 66 E. Washington.

Root Jerome B. (D. R. & Co.) r. 511 N.
Illinois.

Root Julia Miss, r. 429 N. Meridian.

Root O. H., salesman, 62 S. Meridian,
bds. Pyle House.

Root Samuel, painter, r. 314 E. Georgia.

Ropka Helen, (wid. Frederick) groceries
and notions, cor. McCarty and Madison av.

Ropkey H. Fr., clk., r. 450 E. Georgia.

Rorison Brainard, general agent, Connec-
ticut Life Insurance Co., Citizens'
Bank bldg., bds. Bates House.

Rose Alonzo, fireman, C. C. C. & I. R. R.,
r. 138 N. Davidson.

Rose Annie E. Miss, r. 97 W. South.

Rose A. D., printer, Journal office, r. 127
W. First.

Rose Frank Miss, r. 127 W. First.

Rose Frank, printer Journal office, r. 48
W. New York.

Rose Frank B., agent Evening Commercial, r. 67 Madison av.

Rose J. H., coal dealer, r. 294 N. Tennessee.

Rose J. N., manufacturer ladies' and
gents' boots, 90 E. Market, r. 83
Jackson.

Rose Margaret, (wid.) r. Wabash, bet.
New Jersey and East.

Rose Robert, bootmaker, bds. 83 Jackson.

Rose Thomas, bootmaker, bds. 83 Jackson.

Rosebrock C. H., clk., 365 S. Delaware,
bds. same.

Rosebrook F. W., dealer in groceries, etc.,
178 Virginia av., r. same.

Rosemeyer Charles, lab., r. 105 Hosbrook.

Rosenbaum Christopher, teamster, r. 21
Elm.

Rosenbaum William, porter Institute for
the Blind.

Rosenberg John, cutter A. J. Gerstner, r.
77 S. Liberty.

Rosenberg Samuel, peddler, r. 83 Ann.

Rosener Solomon, bookkeeper, A. & S.
Kaufman, bds. Circle Restaurant.

Rosengarten A, bookkeeper and cashier
Paris Store, bds. 30½ S. Pennsylvania.

Rosengarten Chas. O, entry clk. 62 S.
Meridian, bds. Pyle House.

Rosengarten Louis, musician, r. 33 N.
Noble.

Rosenthall Henry, (Hays, R. & Co.) r.
160 N. East.

Rosenthall Moses, (Hays, Rosenthal &
Co.) r. 212 E. Market.

Rosex Mary, (wid. Martin A.) r. 81 W.
McCarty.

Rosier Adam, lab., bds. 435 N. East.

Roswinkel George, manufacturer and
dealer in cigars and tobacco, 183
Massachusetts av., r. same.

Ross Almira, (wid.) r. 41 Dacota.

Ross D. M., r. 316 N. Illinois.

Ross Elzer, lab., r. Ninth, nr. Canal.

Ross Fannie Miss, bds. room 1 Fatout's
blk.

Ross F. D., boxmaker, r. 36 Helen.

Ross Henry J., r. 65 Indiana av.

Ross Isaac, (col'd) lab., r. 227 Minerva.

Ross James, carriage painter, r. 62 Huron.

Ross John, (col'd) lab., r. Blake nr. Rhode
Island.

Ross John, (col'd) grave digger, r. Blake
nr. North.

ROSS J. H., dealer in all kinds of
coal, 24 E. Pearl, r. 294 N. Tennessee.

Ross J. J., cooper, r. 335 W. Maryland.

Ross Reuben, well digger, r. 109 Huron.

Ross Robert, lab., r. 89 Ann.

Ross Thomas, teamster, bds. 317 W. Market.

Ross William, lab., r. 29 Meek.

Rossman Belle Miss, saleslady Grover &
Baker Sewing Machine Co., bds. 294
E. Market.

Rossman Minnie W. Miss, waiter California House.

Rost August, cigarmaker, r. 99 N. Noble.

Roth Mathew, (Daggett & R.) r. 4 Buchanan.

Rothchild Joseph, (R. & Co.) r. Brazil, Ind.

Rothchild Moses, glazier, r. 390 E. Market.

Rothchild & Co., auction and commission house, 97 E. Washington.

Rother John, bookkeeper, bds. 333 Virginia av.

Rothrock Valetine, superintendent Smith, Osgood & Co, bds. Ray House.

Rothschild Henry, dealer in clothing. 125 W. Washington, r. 207 S. Illinois.

Rottler Frank M., (Frauer, Beiler & Co.) bds. Union Hall.

Rouhette Arthur, agent A. Seidensticker, r. 8 N. Liberty.

Rouse H. J., clk. 94 N. Illinois, bds. 31 Indiana av.

Rouser Charles H., clk. Union Depot dining hall, bds. same.

Rout Thomas, r. 218 E. Market.

Routier Anathal carpenter, r. 98 Fletcher av.

Routier Peter, carpenter and builder, cor. Hosbrook and Cedar, r. 394 Virginia av.

Row Jacob J., machinist, r. 28 Grant.

Rowe Austin, engineer, C. C. & I. C. R. R., r. 19 Davidson.

Rowe Eliza, (wid. Titus) r. 273 S. Tennessee.

Rowe Samuel P., clk. J. F. Layman, r. 284 E. Michigan.

Rowe William, bookkeeper, Rolling Mill, r. 5 Madison av.

Rowe Wm. E., yardmaster, P. C. & St. L. R. R., r. 230 N. East.

Rowe Wm. H. (Close & Co.) r. 5 Madison av.

Rowland Jno., engineer, C. E. Geisendorff, r. 30 Douglass.

Rowland Lewis, lab., bds. 30 Douglass.

Rowland Michael, r. 30 N. Douglass.

Rowland Thomas, cooper, r. 423 N. New York.

Rowland Timothy, works, Caledonia Paper Mill, r. 263 W. Washington.

Rowley Fayette R., traveling agent, L. Q. Sherwood, r. 242 N. Illinois.

Roy Otto, salesman, 29 W. Washington, r. sw. cor. East and Market.

Royer George, engineer, C. C. C. & I. R' R., r. 7 Charles.

Royer Buckner F., r. 266 Blake.

Royse William T. (Green & R.) r. 392 N. West.

Rozier Aaron, (H. H. Langenberg & Co.) r. 146 Blackford.

Rozier P., printer, H. C. Chandler & Co., bds. 146 Blackford.

Rubush Alexander, bricklayer, r. 75 S. Noble.

Rubush Willian, bricklayer, r. 73 Huron.

Ruckersfeldt Charles, with Gapen & Catherwood, r. 183½ W. New York.

19

Ruckersfeidt Leopold, porter Browning & Sloan, bds. 23 Kentucky av.

Rucklos Jacob, cigar dealer Bates House, r. over 342 E. Market.

Ruddell James H. (Woollen & Ruddell) bds. 34 W. Maryland.

Rudolph Jane Mrs., r. 75 N. Tennessee.

Rugenstein William, woodcutter, r. 96 Greer.

Ruiderknight Charles, machinist, r. 21 Wyoming.

Rumell John A., works Rolling Mill, r. 250 S. Tennessee.

Rumely Joseph, news stand, 26 Virginia av., r. same.

Rummert ——, plasterer, r. 342 N. East.

Runge Christ., butcher, 141 N. Delaware.

Runge Henry, painter, r. 50 Lockerbie.

Runyon Sout, painter, 18 S. Meridian.

Rupp John, grocery and produce dealer, 201 Kentucky av., r. same.

RUPP WILLIAM F., merchant tailor, 38 W. Washington, r. 131 E. Washington.

Ruschaupt August, (R. & Wands) r. 81 E. Washington.

Ruschaupt Frederick, president Eagle Machine Works, r. 270 N. Delaware.

Ruschaupt & Wands, (A. R. and A. W.) saloon, 81 E. Washington.

Ruse George, fireman C. C. C. & I. R. R.

Rush Casper, lab, r. 121 E. Merrill.

Rush Charles, (Gall & Rush) 115 N. New Jersey.

Rush Fred. P., dealer in flour, grain and seeds, 99 S. Delaware, r. 105 N. Meridian.

Rushton John, cigarmaker, r. 257 E. Washington.

Ruske Henry A., carpenter, r. 86 S. East.

Russe Charles, works Schneider & Co., r. 417 E. Washington.

Russe Conrad, stonemason, r. 417 E. Washington.

Russe Conrad, jr., brassfinisher, r. 417 E. Washington.

Russell Alexander W., clk. Thomas Madden, bds. 46 S. Tennessee.

Russell Annie E. (wid.) clk. P. O., bds. 204 N. Illinois.

Russell David, foundry, cor. Benton and Market, r. 396 E. Market.

Russell David, jr., bookkeeper, r. 396 E. Market.

THE CHINA TEA STORES
ARE LOCATED AT
No. 7 ODD FELLOWS HALL
AND
ACADEMY OF MUSIC CORNER.

SAME GOODS. SAME PRICES at BOTH.

Russell George, (col'd) barber, works 167 W. Washington, r. same.

Russell Henry, r. 377 N. Illinois.

Russell James, railroader, r. 77 Massachusetts av.

Russell John, cooper, r. 112 S. East.

Russell John M., wagonmaker, r. 3 Geisendorff.

Russell John S., carpenter, r. 351 S. Delaware.

Russell Laren M., day policeman, r. 82 S. Noble.

Russell Lotta Miss, r. 24 S. New Jersey.

Russell Nellie, servant, Sherman House.

Russell Samuel, lab. P. C. & St. L. freight depot, r. 190 Blackford.

Russell Thomas, lab., r. 299 S. Missouri.

Russell William, lab., r. cor. Market and Blackford.

Russell William, (col'd, R. & Gulliver) r. 212 W. Vermont.

Russell W. M., mail agent, P. C. & St. L. R. R.

Russell & Gulliver,(col'd,W. R. and W. G.) barbers, 26 N. Pennsylvania.

Ruth Adolph, bartender 39 E. Washington, r. cor. Canal and Cumberland.

Ruth Charles, bartender, r. 297 E. Ohio.

Ruth Louis, bartender Washington Hall, r. 224 N. East.

Ruth Robert, bartender, Academy of Music Saloon, bds. same.

Ruthard Charles, works Jackson, Rider & Co.

Ruyer John, glass blower, bds. 164 W. Maryland.

Ryan ——, railroader, r. 578 E. St. Clair.

RYAN BROTHERS, (G. W. R. and J. B. R.) painters, 18 S Meridian.

Ryan Ellen, (wid. John) r. 75 S. Mississippi.

Ryan Francis M., lab., r. 117 Indiana av.

Ryan F. D., decorator and paper hanger, Gall & Rush, r. 126 Indiana av.

Ryan G. W. (R. Brothers) r. 31 Coburn.

Ryan James, lab., r. 78 Eddy.

Ryan James B (R. & Holbrook) r. 158 N. Mississippi.

Ryan Johanna, (wid. Dennis) r. 35 Vine.

Ryan John, works, Sims & Hoskins.

Ryan John, teamster, 24 W. Maryland, lab, 79 S. West.

Ryan John, fireman, C. C. C. & I. R. R.

Ryan John, carriagesmith, Shaw, Lippencott & Connor, bds. 268 E. Washington.

Ryan John, lab., r. 278 S. Delaware.

Ryan John, machinist, C. C. & I. C. R. R.

Ryan John, lab., r. 276 S. Tennessee.

Ryan John B. (R. & Brothers) r. 72 Coburn.

Ryan Louis, tailor, r. 8 E. Washington.

Ryan Martin, fireman, C. C. C. & I. R. R.

Ryan Michael, lab., r. 155 High.

Ryan M. B. Mrs., dressmaking, r. 209 Virginia av.

Ryan Sarah, servant Palmer House.

Ryan Thomas, lab., r. over 280 E. Washington.

Ryan Thomas, jr., clk. 48 S. Meridian, bds. 75 S. Mississippi.

RYAN T. F., whol. dealer in foreign and domestic liquors, etc., 143 S. Meridian, r. 355 N. Illinois.

Ryan Walter, foreman cooper shop, r. 39 Blake.

Ryan Walter, jr., lab., r. 41 Blake.

Ryan William, carriagesmith, Shaw, Lippencott & Connor, r. 268 E. Washington.

Ryan William, lab., r. 34 Helen.

Ryan William J., clk., cor. Illinois and George, r. 75 S. Mississippi.

RYAN & HOLBROOK, (J. B. R. and H. C. H.) whol. dealers in foreign and domestic liquors, 48 S. Meridian.

Ryner Russel M., bricklayer, E. Washington, nr. Asylum.

SABEL HENRY, lab., r. 32 Ann.

Sachs John, cigar manufacturer, 348 S. Meridian, r. same.

Sage Charles, jr., attorney at law, 172 W. Washington, r. 327 W. Washington.

Sage Charles, sr., druggist, 172 W. Washington, r. 327 W. Washington.

Sage Wm. E., plasterer, bds. 75 S. Pennsylvania.

Sagehorn Jacob, grocer, 122 E. Washington, r. same.

Sahm Louis, carpenter, bds. 142 Fort Wayne av.

Sahm Roderick, grocery, 142 Ft. Wayne av., r. same.

Sailors H., bookkeeper Coburn & Jones, bds. Depot Dining Hall.

Sailors H. C., (Tracy & S.) bds. Depot Dining Hall.

Sailors James L., dry goods and merchant tailor, 156 W. Washington, r. 122 N. Mississippi.

Sailors Pratt, clk. J. L. Sailors, bds. 122 N. Mississippi.

Sain H. A. N., clk. T. A. Lewis, bds. Union Depot Dining Hall.

St. Clair Mission Sabbath School, cor. St.
Clair and East.

St. John's Catholic Church, Georgia, bet.
Illinois and Tennessee, Rev. August
Bessonies pastor.

St. John's Home for Invalids, 85 W. Maryland, Sisters of Providence, Sister
Henriette in charge.

St. John's School for Boys, Georgia, bet.
Illinois and Tennessee, Brother Aloy-
sius director.

St. John's School for Young Ladies, cor.
Georgia and Tennessee.

St. Louis Mutual Life Insurance Co., 4
Yohn's blk., E. A. Whitcomb State
agent.

St. Mary's Catholic Church, Maryland,
bet. Delaware and Pennsylvania.

St. Mary's School for Young Ladies, rear
St. Mary's Church.

St. Paul's Church, (Episcopal) cor. Illinois and New York.

St. Peter's Church, (Catholic) Dougherty
nr. Virginia av.

Salsbury Percival, carpenter, b ls. 80 Oak.

SALSBURY & CO., (Henry Salsbury, A. E. Vinton, J. McLene and
W. H. Talbott) manufacturers news
and book paper, W. end Maryland
on White river.

Satter Herman, butcher, works 207 W.
Michigan, r. same.

Salter William, photographer, r. 222 N.
New Jersey.

Sammons Allen, (J. Roberts & Co.) r. 75
E. Pratt.

Sample James C., constable, r. 52 Cherry.

Sampson Mathew T., barkeeper, 159 W.
Washington, bds. 143 W. Washington.

Sanburn A. G., painter, r. 176 Blackford.

Sanders Theodore, agent Western Fur
Co., r. 14 N. Delaware.

Sanders E. G., painter, 18 S. Meridian, r.
27 Vine.

Sanders John, carpenter, r. 282 N. Liberty.

Sanders John, (col'd) teamster, r. nr. 261
W. Washington.

Sanders John, (col'd) whitewasher, r. 66
N. Missouri.

Sanders William, works Novelty Works.

Sanders William, (col'd) blacksmith, r.
cor. Elizabeth and Blake.

Sanderson C. J., secretary and treasurer
I. & St. L. Sleeping Coach Co, bds.
98 W. Walnut.

Sanderson H. Q., president I. & St. L.
Sleeping Coach Co., r. 98 W. Walnut, cor. Tennessee.

Sandmann John, clk., r. 187 E. Washington.

Sandman Joseph, upholsterer, bds. Union
House.

Sands Mary, (wid.) r. 76 Maple.

BENHAM BRO'S,

36 East Washington St.,

SHEET MUSIC, VIOLINS,

GUITARS, STRINGS, &c.

Sanger Joseph, car recorder I. C. & L.
R. R., r. 113 S. New Jersey.

Sanson A, room 4 Blackford's blk, bds.
National Hotel.

Santo Edward, groceries and saloon, cor.
Indiana av. and North, r. same.

Santo Henry, r. 266 N. West.

Sapp George, pressman Sentinel office,
bds. 206 Winston.

Sapp W. D. (Winchester & S.) Nationa
Hotel.

Sargent Annie Mrs., r. 25½ Massachusetts av.

Sargent Frank, blacksksmith, r. 336 N.
West.

Sartain James, currier, r. 60 Oriental.

SATORIUS JOHN, barbershop, 37
S. Illinois. r. 321 E. Ohio.

SATURDAY EVENING MIR-
ROR, Harding & Vickers, publishers, 19 N. Meridian.

Sauceman Wm., porter, Pyle House.

Sauer John, harnessmaker, r. 27 W.
McCarty.

Sauley Charles, harnessmaker, r. 148 N.
Tennessee, up stairs.

Saunders Theodore, Western Furniture
Co.

Sawleor William, engineer, r. 289 S.
East.

Sawyer Charles, millwright, r. 65 Bright.

Sawyer J. S. (Crossland, Hanna & Co.)
r. 179 W. Market.

Sawyer Louis, lab, r. 23 Wyoming.

Sawyer R. A. Mrs., r. E. Court bet. New
Jersey and East.

Saxton Richard, r. 66 S. Alabama.

Sayers M., lab., works T. H. & I. depot,
r. 269 S. Pennsylvania.

Sayers Thomas. sr., flagman, P. C. & St.
L. freight depot, r. 118 Meek.

Sayles C. F. bookkeeper, J. H. Baldwin &
Co., bds. 35 Virginia av.

Saylor Jackson, foreman, rolling mill, r.
285 S. Illinois.

Saylor Wm. J., works rolling mill, bds.
285 S. Illinois.

Scanlon Bridget, (wid.) Locke, Field & S.
r. 261 W. Washington.

Scanlon Patrick, foreman, Caledonian
paper mill, r. 271 W. Washington.

Scanthir John M., policeman, r. 81 Elizabeth.

Schaaf Abel, filecutter, 136 S. Pennsylvania, r. 183 N. Noble.

Schaaf Conrad, Cabinet Makers' Union, r. E. Court.

Schaaf Valentine, carpenter, r. 313 E. Market.

Schaala Fred., blacksmith, r. 37 Henry.

Shad Christian, clk., bds. California House.

Schad George, varnisher, Hellwig's, r. 101 N. Davidson.

Schad Gottlieb, carriagemaker, at Drew's, r. 101 N. Davidson.

Schad George, works Jackson, Rider & Co.

Schad William, works Jackson, Rider & Co.

Schaefer August, bootmaker, 17 W. Washington, r. 204 E. Washington.

Schaefer James, carpenter, r. 318 N. Delaware.

Schafer Henry, night watchman Journal office, r. 271 N. Noble.

Schafer Peter, r. 567 E. St. Clair.

Schaffer Hiram, saddler, r. 387 S. Meridian.

Schaffer Jacob I., cooper, bds. 314 E. Georgia.

Schaffer William, porter, r. Smith, bet. Tennessee and Mississippi.

Schafner C. G., r. 361 N. Noble.

Schako Charles, machinist, r. 48 Bradshaw.

Schaler Henry, sr., lab., r. 225 S. Alabama.

Schaler Henry, moulder, Eagle Machine Works, r. 227 S. Alabama.

Schaler John, lab., r. 209 Kentucky av.

Schaler Joseph, boilermaker, r. 225 S. Alabama.

Schenabel Frederick, cook California House, bds. same.

Schannaman William, works Madison Depot, r. 448 S. Meridian.

Schanzbenbacher Otto, stonecutter, bds. California House.

Schaub Elizabeth, (wid. Peter) r. 217 N. Noble.

Schaub Henry, saloon, 168 W. Washington, r. same.

Schaub Henry, saloon and beer garden, 334 Virginia av., r. same.

Schaub John, sr., lab., r. 225 N. Noble.

Schaub Peter, teamster, r. 158 Huron.

Schegel Fritz, lab., r. 57 Coburn.

Scheigert Frederick, merchants' police, r. 264 S. Illinois.

Scheiter Henry, works Jackson, Rider & Co.

Schellenberg Fritz, chairmaker, r. 504 S. East.

Scheller Max, physician, r. 210 E. Ohio.

SCHELLSCHMIDT ADOLPH,
music teacher and dealer in all kinds of musical instruments, 173 E. Washington, r. 246 E. Ohio.

Schellschmidt Amelia, (wid.) r. 507 E. Market.

Schellschmidt Ferdinand, musician, r. 511 E. Market.

Schendel Fred., carpenter, r. 33 N. East.

Schering Chas. Henry, drayman, r. 41 Oriental.

Scherling Bernard, tailor, r. 356 S. Alabama.

Scherling Hermann, porter Post Office, bds. 292 N. Liberty.

Scherling Nicholas, porter Post Office, r. 292 N. Liberty.

Schesslesee John, lab., r. 14 Buchanan.

SCHETTER CRISTIAN, groceries, provisions, flour and feed, 99 E. South, r. same.

Schetter Lawrence, baker, r. 285 N. Noble.

Scheuer John, lab., r. 382 E. New York.

Scheuer Conrad, stonemason, r. 222 Railroad.

Schieffer Rudolph, cigarmaker, 35 W. Washington, bds. 89 N. Delaware.

Schields Kane, lab., r. 68 Bicking.

Schienelle Christian, lab., r. 15 Russell.

Schildmeyer A., boots and shoes, 313 E. Washington, r. 375 E. Michigan.

Schildmeyer Anthony, (Reasner & S.) r. Brookville rd, 12 miles east.

Schildmeyer Charles C., engineer C. C. & I. C. R. R., r. 195 Meek.

Schildmeyer C. L., clk., r. 310 E. Market.

Schildmeyer Fred., merchant tailor, 182 E. Washington, r. 310 E. Market.

Schildineger George, jr., porter, Tousy & Bryant's, r. 168 Spring.

Schiller Godfrey, butcher, bds. 207 W. Michigan.

Schilling Charles, lab., P. C. & St. L. freight depot.

Schilling Dudrich, (S. & Bro.) bds. 134 E. McCarty.

Schilling H. (S. & Bro.) r. 134 E. McCarty.

Schilling & Bro. (H. S and D. S.) chair manufacturers, 134 E. McCarty.

Schillinger George, sr., lab., r. 167 N. Spring.

Schindler Oscar, clk., C. Vonegut, bds. 191 E. Washington.

Schindler Robert, clk., r. 187 E. Washington.

Schine John, lab., r. 116 Stevens.

Schiner Bernard, moulder, Eagle Machine Works, bds. 307 S. Pennsylvania.

Schisler, Abel, moulder, Eagle Machine Works, r. 85 N. New Jersey.

Schisley Christian, works E. C. Atkins & Co., r. 15.Russell.

Schley George J., foreman, Journal of Commerce, bds. 26 S. Pennsylvania.

Schley John, foreman, Sentinel news room, r. 25 E. Ohio.

Schliebitz F. W., watchmaker, 147 E. Washington, r. nw. cor. Noble and Market.

Schlotzhauer Adam, grocer, 248 N. Liberty, r. same.

Schlotzhauer G., works Cabinet Makers' Union, r. 152 Davidson.

Schlotzhauer Valentine, treas'r and foreman, Cabinet Makers' Union, r. nw. cor. New York and Davidson.

Schmelz Casper, bar tender, r. 76 N. Noble.

Schmedei Fritz, carpenter, r. 33 N. East.

Schmedel H. (S. & Fricker) r. 176 E. Stevens.

Schmedel & Fricker, (H. S. and J. F.) manufacturers of brushes, 300 Morris.

Schmehl Henry, moulder, r. 109 Stevens.

Schmehl Henry, jr., moulder, r. 109 Stevens.

Schmelzer Jacob, cooper, bds. Minerva nr. New York.

Schmidt August, (A. & C.S.) r. 23 Charles.

Schmidt Charles, (A. & C.S.) r. 23 Charles.

Schmidt A. & C., meat market, 221 Massachusetts av.

Schmidt Charles, lab., wks. T. H. & I. R. R., r. 203 Union.

Schmidt Charles, agent soap factory, r. 215 Union.

Schmidt Christian, lab., r. 120 Dacota.

Schmidt Christian, stonecutter, r. 131 Stevens.

SCHMIDT C. F., brewer of lager beer, south end Alabama, cor. McCarty, r. same.

Schmidt Elizabeth Mrs., midwife, r. 131 N. East.

Schmidt Frederick, butcher, r. 131 N. East.

Schmidt Fred. jr., clk., r. 131 N. East.

Schmidt Harold, (S. & Son) r. over 308 E. Washington.

Schmidt Hermann, packer W. & C. F. Holliday, r. 31 N. Liberty.

Schmidt Herman, clk., r. 3 N. Noble.

Schmidt Lorenz, 14 S. Delaware, r. 106 . E. Washington

Schmidt Louis, works, Jackson, Rider & Co.

Schmidt Ludwig, lab., r. 111 E. Washington.

Schmidt Nicoli, lab., r. 186 S. Illinois.

Schmidt Rob, tanner, 96 S. East, r. same.

Schmidt Rudolph, (S. & Son) r. over 308 E. Washington.

Schmidt R & Son, cigar manufacturers, 308 E. Washington.

Schmith Leonard, brewer, works Harting & Bro, r. 29 McCarty.

Schmith Louis, butcher, bds. 300 N. West.

Schmitt Adolph, painter, r. 230 S. Pennsylvania.

Schmitt George, lab., r. 220 Railroad.

Schmitt John A., machinist, Eagle Machine Works.

Schmitt Joseph, carpenter, r. 204 N. Noble.

Schmitt L., turner, r. cor. North and West.

Schmucker Louis, cabinetmaker, r. 253 N. Noble.

Schnavel C. A., bookbinder, bds. 507 N. Mississippi.

Schneider Adam, lab., r. 106 E. St. Mary.

Schneider Cany, lab., r. 61 Wyoming.

Schneider Christ., lab., r. 138 E. St. Mary.

Schneider Christian, saw filer, wks. E. C. Atkins & Co.

Schneider Conrad P., carpenter, r. 217 N. Liberty.

Schneider S., (S. & Co.) r. 195 S. East.

Schneider John A., porter D. Root & Co., r. 106 St. Mary.

Schneider Louis, moulder, r. 125 Stevens.

Schneider Matthew, wks. Schneider & Co., bds. 195 S. East.

Schneider Nicholas, stonemason, r. 31 Buchanan.

Schneider Valentine, Cabinet Maker's Union, r. 263 E. New York.

Schneider John, lab., r. 507 N. Mississippi.

SCHNEIDER & CO., (John S., Louis Neubacher and C. Karle) proprietors Phoenix Bell and Brass Foundry, 26 Union.

Schnull Henry, (Severin & S. also E. Over & Co.) r. 124 N. Alabama.

Schnull's Block, sw. cor. Meridian and Georgia.

Schoen Andrew, finisher, 3 Martinsdale's blk.

Schoen Geo., porter, A. E.Vinton, r. same.

Schoettle Christian, barkeeper, Marmont Hall, cor. Illinois and George, r. same.

Schofield James B., salesman, 62 S. Meridian, bds. Sherman House.

H. H. LEE

PURCHASES HIS

Teas, Coffees, Sugars & Spices

DIRECT FROM THE

Importers and Refineries,

THUS SAVING

HIS CUSTOMERS TWO OR THREE PROFITS.

Schofield Nathan, jr. (Anderson, Bullock & S.) r. Franklin, Indiana.

Scholer John, works, Schneider & Co., bds. LaFayette House.

Schomberg Wm., boots and shoes, 218 E. Washington, r. 131 Davidson.

Schomeir William, cooper, r. 311 N. Noble.

Schonacker Clara, hair braider, r. 134 N. Illinois.

Schonacker Louis, ticket clk. Union Depot, r. 134 N. Illinois.

Schonager Christian, carpenter, r. 307 E. Washington.

Schooby Thomas, r. 520 N. Illinois.

Schoppe William, tanner, r. 359 S. Delaware.

Schoppenhorst W., (wid.) r. 42 Lockerbie.

Schortz Joseph, with McCord & Wheatley, r. 30 E. Coburn.

Schowe Frederic, blacksmith, r. 1 Water.

Schowe F. W., carpenter, r. 338 S. Alabama.

Schowe Henry J., machinist, r. 9 Water.

Schowe William, carpenter, r. 338 S. Alabama.

Schowe Wm., machinist, Eagle Machine Works, bds. 350 Virginia av.

Schrader Anthony, lab., r. 276 N. Liberty.

Schrader Charles, (S. & Harting) r. 133 E. Merrill.

Schrader Christian, grocer, 389 Virginia av. r. 355 E. McCarty.

SCHRADER CHRISTIAN, glass and queensware, 94 E. Washington, r. 126 N. Mississippi.

Schrader Frederick, cooper, r. 322 N. Noble.

Schrader John A., r. rear of 126 N. Mississippi.

Schrader Rudolph, machinist, r. 332 E. Market.

Schrader William, (Klare & S.) r. 574 S. Meridian.

Schrader & Harting, (Charles S. and John Harting) dealers in groceries and provisions, 299 S. Delaware.

Schrake Henrietta Miss, teacher Fourth Ward School, bds. 253 N. Noble.

Schrake Mary, (wid. Christopher) r. 253 N. Noble.

Schramm Charles, bookkeeper, r. 78 E. St. Joseph.

Schramm J. C. A., bookkeeper, 71 and 73 W. Washington, r. 78 E. St. Joseph.

Schrutz Joseph, lab., r. 30 Coburn.

Schreicher Barbara, (wid.) r. 167 Fort Wayne av.

Schreider Valentine, lab., r. 181 N. Noble.

Schreiner Wm., tanner, r. 307 S. Pennsylvania.

Schroeder Christian, grocer, 401 Virginia av, r. same.

Schroeder Christian, works Washington Foundry, r. 124 F. McCarty.

Schroer H. H., grocer, 269 S. Alabama, r. same.

Schroerlucke John, grocer, r. 165 Stevens.

Schruzer John, tailor, r. 77 Coburn.

Schubert George, lab., r. 328 N. West.

Schubert George J., plasterer, r. 328 N. West.

Schuck Frederick, cigarmaker, bds. Neiman House.

Schuck Michael, cigarmaker, bds. 287 E. Georgia.

Schuck Fred., cigarmaker, bds. 33 S. Illinois.

Schuerle Frederick, bartender Meridian Exchange.

Schuesser Able, r. 220 S. East.

Schuessler Abel, bricklayer, r. 85 N. New Jersey.

Schuessler Conrad, lab., r. 93 N. New Jersey.

Schulmeyer Frederick, gaslighter, r. 109 E. St. Joseph.

Schulmeyer Louis, butcher, r. 234 E. Washington.

Schuler Frydel, cabinetmaker, r. 301 Vincent.

Schuler Henry, boilermaker, r. 235 S. Alabama.

Schullenberg Fred., chairmaker, r. 555 S. East.

Schulmier Henry, butcher, 207 Virginia av., r. 252 S. Delaware.

Schulmier Lewis, with Stewart & Morgan, r. 449 N. New Jersey.

Schultz Frank, currier, r. Court.

Schultz Christine Miss, r. Court, nr Alabama.

Schultz John, blacksmith, r. 7 Morrison.

Schultz William, plasterer, bds. 422 N. New Jersey.

Schultheis John, carpenter, r. 410 S. Illinois.

Schultheis Michael, carpenter, r. 468 S. Illinois.

Schultzheis John, machinist, r. Louisville, Ky.

Schultz August, finisher, r. 360 S. Alabama.

Schultz Henry, cigars and tobacco, 26 Virginia av. r. 175 S. Delaware.

Schunk Peter, clk, r. nw. cor. Tennessee and Market.

Schur Charles, salesman, r. Court, bet.
East and New Jersey.

SCHURICH FREDERICK, groceries and saloon, W. Indianapolis, r. same.

Schurich Peter, clk. C. Ludwig, r. cor. Market and Tennessee.

Schurr Leonard, sr., clock repairer, 78 Indiana av., r. same.

Schurr Leonard, jr., watchmaker and jeweler, 78 Indiana av. r. same.

Schuster Joseph, tailor, r. 521 E. Market.

SCHUTTER CHRISTIAN, groceries and provisions, 239 S. Meridian, r. same.

Schutz August, machinist, r. 361 S. Alabama.

Schutz Herman, flagman, r. 436 S. East.

Schuyler C. H., printer, News office, r. 142 N. Mississippi.

Schuyler William, printer, r. 142 N. Mississippi.

Schwabacher Joseph, (S. & Selig) r. 249 N. Illinois.

Schwabacher & Selig, (Joseph S. and Abram S.) wines and liquors, 41 S. Delaware.

Schwabb Henry, printer, Journal office, r. 26 Kentucky av.

Schwabb Leonard, miller White Rose Mill.

Schwauenberger Leonard, teamster, r. W. end Washington.

Schwartz Andrew, r. 19 Lord.

Schwartz Charles, cabinetmaker, r. 19 Lord rd.

Schwartz Charles, salesman, Paris Store, bds. 28 W. Georgia.

Schwartz Henry, tailor, r. 189 E. Ohio.

Schwartz Joseph, (Glick & S.) r. ne. cor. Market and Illinois.

Schwartz Joseph, peddler, r. Mississippi bet. Second and Third.

Schwartz Peter, teamster, r. cor. Vermont and Winston.

Schwarther Joseph, capmaker, 151 E. Washington, r. Coburn.

Schwear C. H. (S. & Spear) r. 576 E. Washington.

Schwear Mary, (wid.) r. 576 E. St. Clair.

Schwear & Spear. (C. H. S. and F. S.) groceries and dry goods, 576 E. Washington.

Schweitzer Adam, varnisher, r. 283 S. East.

Schwegel Daniel, collarmaker, r. 261 S. Pennsylvania.

Schweinleger Wm., meat market, 329 S. Delaware, r. same.

Schweinhart E., bootmaker, r. 68 E. St. Clair.

Schweizer, Adam, works Cabinet Makers' Union, r. 77 S. East.

Schwicho Charles, grocer and produce 524 S. Meridian.

Schwcho Charles, jr., clk., bds. 524 S. Meridian.

Schwomeyer Charles, dealer in groceries and provisions, 397 S. Meridian, r. same.

Schwinge Henry, clk., r. 174 W. Ohio.

Schwomeyer Christian, drayman, r. E. Michigan bet. Noble and Railroad.

Scofield S. A. Miss, teacher, Institute for the Blind.

Scott Adam, (S. & Nicholson) r. 118 N. East.

Scott Amos, teamster, r. 229 N. Winton.

Scott A. E., clk., G. Holman, r. 172 N. East.

Scott Albin A., salesman, 5 Bates House blk., r. 472 N. East.

Scott Charles, carriagesmith, r. 472 N. East.

Scott Charles, lab., r. 525 S. Illinois.

Scott E. E. Mrs., matron, City Hospital.

Scott George W., lab., r. 574 N. Mississippi.

Scott Harvey, carpenter, r. 122 S. East.

Scott H. B., salesman, Trade Palace, bds. 203 N. Illinois.

Scott James W. (S., West & Co.) r. Richmond, Ind.

Scott James W. (col'd) porter, W. H. Roll's carpet house, r. 77 Ann.

SCOTT JEFF. K., proprietor Palmer House, se. cor. Washington and Illinois, r. same.

Scott Jennie Miss, milliner, works Copeland's, r. 415 S. Tennessee.

Scott John, baker, 12 S. Meridian, bds. same.

Scott John, bookkeeper, r. 57 Fayette.

Scott John, (col'd) lab., r. 592 N. Mississippi.

SCOTT JOHN N, attorney at law, 321 E. Washington, r. 170 N. Alabama.

Scott John, Rev., r. cor. Jackson and Butler.

Scott Joseph, lab., r. Patterson, nr. North.

Scott Lou F., salesman, Hollweg & Reese.

Scott Mary Mrs., printer, r. 6 N. Liberty.

SCOTT S. T., agent Peoples' and Merchant's Despatch, 19 Virginia av., r. 217 E. Ohio.

Scott Thomas, carpenter, r. 222 S. East.

THE CHINA TEA STORES

Are very handsomely decorated with

Accurate Views and Scenes

or

CHINESE LIFE AND SCENERY.

Call and see them before leaving the City.

Scott William, carpenter and joiner, r. 415 S. Tennessee.

Scott W. H., clk. C. C. C. & I. R. R., r. 271 E. Ohio.

SCOTT, WEST & CO. (James W. S., John C. W. and John A. Burbank) whol. dealers in china, glass and queensware, 127 S. Meridian.

Scott & Nicholson, (Adam S. and David N.) stone cutters, cor. Canal and Kentucky av.

Scribner George B. (Dawson & S.) bds. 257 Indiana av.

Scribner James, works, Glass Works, bds. 217 S. Illinois.

Scudder Edward D., honey dealer, r. 158 W. Washington.

Scudder Helen, (wid.) notions and trimmings, 85 N. New Jersey, r. same.

Scudder Henry, teamster, r. 1 Geisendorff.

Scudder John, foreman Exchange Stables, r. 29 E. Ohio.

Scudder M. H., sleeping coach conductor.

Scully Michael, lab., r. 39 S. West.

Seag Jerry, lab., bds. Illinois House.

Seaman Edwin, (S. & Strickland) bds. Ohio House.

SEAMAN E. & Co., (Edwin S. and David H. Strickland) dealers in wrapping papers, bags, twine, etc., 79 Masonic Hall bldg.

Seamer Conrad, upholsterer Philip Dohn, r. 10 Lord.

Seapp Samuel, checker I. & V. R. R., bds. 65 S. East.

Search John, brassmoulder, r. Cincinnati, Ohio.

Sears John, telegraph operator, bds. 426 S. Tennessee.

Sears Thomas, switchman T. H. & I. R. R, r. 426 S. Tennessee.

Seaton E. A., dealer in hats, caps and furs, 25 N. Pennsylvania, r. 233 E. Michigan.

Seaton William D., salesman 25 N. Pennsylvania, bds. Pyle House.

Seatt John, bookkeeper Geisendorff & Co., r. 57 N. Fayette.

Second Universalists Church, meets Masonic Hall.

Second Presbyterian Church, nw. cor. Pennsylvania and New York.

Secor S. B., printer Journal office, r. 137 E. St. Marys.

Secrest Charles, justice of the peace, 45½ E. Washington, r. 317 S. Alabama.

Secrest Alice Miss, teacher Ninth Ward School, r. 317 S. Alabama.

Secrest Henry, candymaker, r. 3 Hosbrook.

Secrest John, watchman, J. M. & I. R. R. depot. r.408 E. Ohio.

Secrest Nathan, r. 317 S. Alabama.

Secrest S. Rev., pastor St. John's Church, r. 75 E. Maryland.

Sedam Charles, (col d) lab., r. 101 E. St. Joseph.

Seddelmeyer, M. L., salesman Paris Store, bds. 489 N. Alabama.

Sedgwick R., dealer in fancy dry goods, 68 N. Illinois, r. 129 N. Mississippi.

Seeber S. S., floor walker, Trade Palace, bds. Union Dining Hall.

Seeberger Louise Miss, teacher, bds. 203 S. Illinois.

Seemann Christian, grocer, 615 E. Washington.

Seele Henry, works Mansur's pork house, r. 303 N. Liberty.

Sees Mary, (wid. William P.) r. 136 N. Tennessee.

Seger William, clk. 29 W. Washington, bds. 26 W. Georgia.

Seger Jonathan M., carriage and wagon maker, 173 Indiana av., r. 267 N. West.

Seger Levy, clothing, 227 E. Washington, r. same.

Segrue Abbie Miss, servant, 290 W. Vermont.

Sehad Mathias, groceries, notions, etc., 300 Blake, r. same.

Schaffer Fannie Miss, servant, 336 N. West.

Schell Christian. lab., r. 575 S Illinois.

Seibert Cicero, engineer fire department, bds. 130 E. New York.

Seibert David, r. 205 E. Market.

Seibert Geo. W., grocer, 51 Noble, r. same.

Seibert R. S., blacksmith, r. 11 N. Liberty.

Seibert S. M., blacksmith, shop 302 E. Washington, r. 11 N. Liberty.

Seibert T. B., painter, r. 11 North Liberty.

Seidensticker A. (A. S. & Co.) r. 174 Madison av.

SEIDENSTICKER A. & CO. (A. S. and A. Naltner) real estate and law office, 14 S. Delaware.

Seidensticker Frederick, saloon, 248 N. Noble, r. same.

Seider C., cooper, bds. California House.

Seiders William H., insurance agent, r. 374 N. West.

Seifert Augustus, clk. 13 N. Illinois, bds. same.

Seig J. H., Mrs. r. 91 E. Michigan.

Seiger Robert, machinist, bds. Emeneger's Hotel.

Seimon C., lab., 253 N. Noble.

Seimon Fidels, saloon, 211 W. Washington, r. same.

Seirs H. Mrs., washerwoman, I. C. & L. R. R. shops.

Seise Annie, servant, G. P. Tuttle.

Seisselle Christian, lab., r. 15 Russell.

Seiter Christ, cooper, bds. California House.

Seiter K., cask and tub manufacturer, 92 Union, r. same.

Seitz Charles, saloon, 110 S. Illinois, r. same.

SEITZ FRED., proprietor Chicago House, 117 S. Illinois, r. same.

Selig Abram, (Schwabacher & S.) r. 142 Virginia av.

Self Berry, (I. Davis & Co.) r. 169 Massachusetts av.

SELKING WILLIAM, saloon and billiards, 33 N. Pennsylvania, r. 26 S. Alabama.

Selking William, sen., superintendent 33 N. Pennsylvania, r. same.

Selking Louis, clk. H. Lieber & Co., r. 467 N. Delaware.

Sellers John H., blacksmith, bds. 69 W. Market.

Sellers Daniel, (S. & Lee) rooms Wiley's blk.

Sellers John, with D. Sellers & Co., bds. 90 N. East.

Sellers Richard, wood yard, r. 163 N. Noble.

Sellers & Co. (Daniel S. and Henry Marshall) dealers in harness and saddlery, 11 S. Meridian.

Sells Michael, cattle dealer, r. 176 S. New Jersey.

Selman A. G., physician, 21 Virginia av., r. 29 School.

Semeus E. C., Boston Store, r. 213 N. Pennsylvania.

SEMPLE J. A., general ticket and freight agent C. & I. J. R. R., office 110 and 112 Virginia av.

Senecal A., printer, Sentinel office, bds. Circle Restaurant.

Senour John, (S. & Co.) r. 24 W. Michigan.

SENOUR J. & CO. (J. S., W. S. and ——) dealers in boots and shoes, 5 W. Washington.

Senour W., pianomaker, r. 104 Vermont.

Senour Wm. (S. & Co.) bds. Pyle House.

Senour Zachariah, bootfitter, 20 W. Maryland, r. same.

Sentence John, lab., 33 Mud.

Sephus Josephus, lab., r. W. Pennsylvania nr. Fourth.

Serginson Joseph, works rolling mill, r. 441 S. Illinois.

20

Server Gramulle, clk., Layman & Fletcher, r. 322 N. Winston.

Serviss Wm., bookkeeper, J. S. Carey & Co., bds. 191 N. Delaware.

Seventh Presbyterian Church, Elm nr. cor. Cedar; John B. Brandt, pastor.

Seventh Street School, Seventh bet. Tennessee and Illinois.

Severin Henry, (S., Schnull & Co.) r. 132 N. New Jersey.

SEVERIN, SCHNULL & CO. (H. S., H. S. and B. Applegate) whol. grocers, 55 and 57 S. Meridian.

Sewall Elmer C., salesman, 129 S. Meridian, bds. Sherman House.

Seward Annie Miss, seamstress, r. 15 Madison av.

Sexauer Edward, grocer, 125 E. Washington, r. same.

Sexton J., printer, Journal office, bds. 79 Massachusetts av.

Sextron William, clk., Louis Lang, 29 S. Meridian, bds. same.

Seybold James H., marble dealer, r. 233 E. Ohio.

Seymour Conrad, upholsterer, r. 10 Lord.

Shaddock D. J., engineer, C. C. C. & I. R. R.

Shade Gottlieb, carriagemaker, r. 101 Davidson.

Shade R. W., clk., Trade Palace, r. nw. cor. Blackford and Vermont.

Shafer A. C., shoemaker, cor. Indiana av. and Illinois.

Shafer John, meatmarket, 92 N. Illinois, r. Bluff rd. outside city limits.

Shafer John, shoemaker, cor. Indiana av. and Canal, r. 65 N. California.

Shafer Simon, woodsawyer, r. 7 Osage.

Shaffer George W., painter, r. 83 James.

Shaffer James, bootmaker, 65 S. Meridian, bds. 35 Kentucky av.

Shaffer John, shoemaker, r. 65 James.

Shaffer I. J., miller, r. cor. Christian av. and Plum.

Shaffer Mollie, (wid.) r. 84 S. Benton.

Shaffer Mary Mrs., seamstress, r. 188 E. Washington.

Shaffer Weller, painter, Shaw, Lippencott & Connor, r. 186 E. Washington.

Shaler Henry, helper, C. C. C. & I. R. R. shops.

Sceneberger David H. (Mick, Geyer & Co.) r. 346 N. Meridian.

H. H. LEE

MAKES A SPECIALTY OF

Choice Green, Black & Japan Teas.

Shank Benjamin S., teamster, r. 219 N. Davidson.

Shank John M., farmer, r. 219 N. Davidson.

Shank Wm. R., butcher, r. 219 N. Davidson.

Shannon Sallie Y. (wid.)boarding house, 126 E. Ohio.

Shannon Thomas A., watchmaker, Craft & Cutter, bds Pyle House.

Share George, saddlery and harness, r. 332 N. Alabama.

SHARE GEORGE K., saddlery hardware and carriage goods, 40 S. Meridian.

Share George K. (G. K. S. & Co.) r. 314 W. New York.

Sharff Nathan, clk. Raub & Bros., r. 153 W. Maryland.

Sharp A. L., mail agent, Peru R. R.

Sharp George, cigarmaker, r. 121 E. Meek.

Sharp John S., bookkeeper, r. 493 S. New Jersey.

Sharp R. J. (S. & Long) r. 119 S. Illinois.

Sharp Stephen, engineer, r. 257 S. Alabama.

Sharp & Long, (R. J. S. and Thomas L.) fish and oysters, 119 S. Illinois.

Sharpe A. W., wholesale and retail dealer in tobacco and cigars, 28 N. Pennsylvania, r. 193 S. New Jersey.

Sharpe Calvin L., with A. W. Sharpe, bds. 193 S. New Jersey.

Sharpe David, (col'd) lab., r. Ash, near Christian av.

Sharpe Ebenezer, clk. Fletcher & Sharpe, r. cor. First and Pennsylvania.

Sharpe James, fish market, r. 107 S. New Jersey.

Sharpe John, painter, r. 497 N. Alabama.

Sharpe J. K., boots, shoes, and leather, 47 and 49 S. Delaware, r. N. Pennsylvania, outside city limits.

Sharpe Leander, assistant mailing clk. Sentinel Office.

Sharpe N. K., banker, r. N. Pennsylvania.

Sharpe Thomas H., (Fletcher & S.) r. 239 N. Pennsylvania.

Sharpless Pennell, clk. H. H. Lee, r. 71 California.

Shattuck David L., engineer, r. 393 Massachusetts av.

Shaughnessey John, bar tender, 23 W. Washington, r. 46 S. Bicking.

Shaughnessey Thomas, lab., r. 235 Minerva.

Shaw Augustus D., R. R. checkman, r. 222 N. Winston.

Shaw B. C., (S., Lippincott & Conner) r. 22 Gregg.

Shaw E., mail agent, I., B. & W. R. R.

Shaw Frank T., fireman, Central R. R., bds. 377 E. Georgia.

Shaw George W., policeman, bds. National Hotel.

Shaw Henry, trimmer, Shaw, Lippincott & Conner, r. Gregg, between East and New Jersey.

Shaw James, boiler maker, works Eagle Machine Works, bds. 41 Russell.

Shaw James, carriage maker, r. 219 Buchanan.

Shaw James C., wood worker, Shaw, Lippincott & Conner, r. 219 Buchanan.

Shaw Jennie Miss, shirt maker, bds. 41 Russell.

Shaw J. C., carriage maker, r. 219 Buchanan.

SHAW, LIPPINCOTT & CONNER, (Benjamin C. S., Samuel R. L., James H. C.) proprietors Indianapolis Coach Works, 26, 28 and 30 E. Georgia.

Shaw Malinda Mrs., r. 41 Russell.

Shawver Arnas P., saddler James Sulgrove, r. 297 Indiana av.

Shawver Christ. J., saddlemaker, r. 297 Indiana av.

Shay Margaret Mrs., (wid. Patrick) r. 307 W. Market.

Shay Robert, works rolling mill, bds. 310 S. Illinois.

Shea Catherine, domestic Bates House.

Shea Cornelius, lab., r. nw. cor. New York and Missouri.

Shea Dennis, lab., r. 72 Railroad.

Shea Jane, (wid.) r. 96 Railroad.

Shea Jerry, lab., bds. 199 W. Maryland.

Shea Johanna, domestic Bates House.

Shea John, lab., U. S. Arsenal.

Shea John, lab., r. 356 N. Winston.

Shea Josie, domestic Bates House.

Shea Mary, domestic Bates House.

Shea Mary, (wid.) r. 162 Meek.

Shea Michael, contractor, r. 520 N. Delaware.

Shea Patrick, lab., r. 145 Huron.

Shea Thomas, lab., r. 356 N. Winston.

Shea Thomas R., lab., r. 114 Plum.

Shea Tim, railroader, r. 497 E. Georgia.

Shea Timothy W., railroader, r. 503 E. Georgia.

Sheahy John, stonemason, bds. 199 W. Maryland.

Sheakle Fred., with McCord & Wheatley, r. 49 Coburn.

Shear James, lab., r. 345 S. Missouri.

Shearer Charles J., painter, r. 180 N. Missouri.

Shearer Daniel, lab., r. 577 E. St. Clair.

Shearer Frederick, teamster, r. 123 Maple.

Shearer John W., carpenter, r. 149 N. Winston.

Shearer Louisa Miss, dressmaker, r. 167 W. Washington.

Shearer Mary, (wid. George) dressmake r. 167 W. Washington.

Shearer William, teamster, r. 577 E. St. Clair.

Shean Thomas, lab., r. 98 Railroad.

Sheau Jolly, lab., r. 90 Railroad.

Sheay John, engineer T. H. & I. R. R., bds. Globe House.

Sheek George, lab., r. 149 N. Noble.

Shekell Edward, trimmer Shaw L. & C., bds. 60 S. Pennsylvania.

Sheesley Eli, (Heckman & S.) r. 317 E. Washington.

Sheets David, grocery and meat market, 241 W. McCarty, r. same.

Sheets William, blank books and stationery, 79 W. Washington.

SHEFFIELD SAW WORKS, 210 to 216 S. Illinois, E. C. Atkins & Co., proprietors.

Shehan Daniel, lab., r. 237 S. West.

Shehan Maggie, servant Palmer House.

Sheinder Chas', grocer, r. 85 Bradshaw.

Shelbert Peter, (col'd) lab., r. ne. cor. Second and Howard.

SHELDON J. H., general superintendent C. & I. J. R. R., office 110 and 112 Virginia av., r. Cincinnati, Ohio.

Shellansen Mary, (wid.) r. 301 W. Market.

Shellenberger Alexander, carpenter, r. 486 N. Delaware.

Shellman Harry J., reporter Journal of Commerce, r. 174 E. New York.

Shelly Fred, saloon keeper, r. bet. New Jersey and East.

Shelly Thornton, (col'd) lab., Palmer House.

Shepard Abner H., carpenter, 127 E. Maryland, bds. 314 E. Market.

Shepard Jonathan, carpenter, 127 E. Maryland, r. 314 E. Market.

Shepard M. Mrs., dressmaker, 331 N. New Jersey, r. same.

SHEPHERD JAMES McB., Parlor Billiard Rooms, 179 E. Washington, r. 215 W. Maryland.

Shepherd McB. H. V., conductor I. B. & W. R. R., r. 32 S. West.

Shepherd Sophia Miss, servant, 23 Madison av.

Shera William, carpenter, r. 22 W. Georgia.

Sherer Adam, boot and shoemaker, 34 N. Illinois, r. 23 Grant.

Sheridan Barney, works Novelty Works.

Sheridan Bridget Mrs., domestic, Bates House.

Sheridan John, lab., r. 20 Merrill.

Sheridan John, bell boy Bates House.

Sheridan John, works Novelty Works.

Sheridan P., salesman New York Store, bds. Palmer House.

Sherling Fred, teamster, r. 485 S. New Jersey.

Sherman Charles H., salesman Trade Palace, bds. 203 N. Illinois.

Sherman Gustavus, capitalist, r. 258 N. Pennsylvania.

Sherman Leroy, (S. & Comingore) r. 239 W. McCarty.

Sherman Paul, harnessmaker, r. 62 Indiana av.

Sherman & Comingore, (L. S. and W. D. C.) whol. dealers in feathers, produce, etc., 21 W. Maryland.

Sherwood F. W. (Millner & S.) bds. National Hotel.

SHERWOOD L. Q., whol. dealer in reapers, mowers and threshers, 79 and 81 N. Illinois, r. 556 N. Illinois.

Sherwood Newton, railroader, bds. 395 S. West.

Sherwood William O., carpenter Chandler & Taylor, r. 152 Blake.

Shide Charles, cooper, r. 337 W. Maryland.

Shidaler Th. J., carriagesmith, bds. 74 N. Pennsylvania.

Shidmyer Chris, works Novelty Works.

Shieds J. D., agent Bellefontaine Stock Yard, r. 26 Biddle.

Shields ———, (col'd) lab., r. Tennessee N. of Seventh.

Shifler John, blower glass works.

Shiffler Richard, carriagesmith, bds. 68 E. Market.

SHILLING R. L., dealer and manufacturer of trunks and valises 55 W. Washington, r. 259 N. New Jersey.

Shilling R. W., trunkmaker, r. 120 N. Tennessee.

Shilling William, trunkmaker, r. 169 N. Illinois.

Shillinger George, porter 108 S. Meridian, r. 167 Spring.

THE CHINA TEA STORES

ARE AMONG THE

Attractions of Indianapolis.

Call and See Them before leaving the City.

Shindle Rebecca V., Mrs., (wid.) r. 121 W. Vermont.

Shinner Burns, machinist, bds. 88 S. Mississippi.

Shipp J. P., salesman Landers, Conduit & Co., bds. 26 W. Maryland.

Shipp S. M., bookkeeper Rickard & Talbott, bds. National Hotel.

Shippy John, works rolling mill, r. 71 Maple.

Shlott Sarah A. Mrs., (wid. William H.) r. 88 N. California.

Shmalsigang Mary, (wid. Mathew) r. 76 Garden.

Shoe Samuel, moulder, bds. 19 Madison av.

Shoemaker Amanda J. Miss, teacher 9th Ward School, bds. 305 E. New York.

Shoemaker Charles, trunkmaker 39 S. Illinois, bds. 45 Fletcher av.

Shoemaker Fredolin, (S. & Durfield) r. 45 Fletcher av.

Shoemaker George, lab., r. 127 Stevens.

Shoemaker John F., pianomaker, r. 347 N. Noble.

Shoemaker O., pumpmaker, r. 57 Massachusetts av.

SHOEMAKER & DURFIELD, (E. S. and J. F. D.) real estate brokers and patent solicitors, 16½ E. Washington.

Shoen Andrew, tailor, r. E. Court, bet. New Jersey and East.

Shonaker Alfred E., car recorder, T. H. & I. R. R., bds. 134 N. Illinois.

Shonies William, currier, 125 S. Meridian, r. 307 S. Pennsylvania.

Shook Michael, cigarmaker, bds. 287 E. Georgia.

Shopp George, boot and shoemaker, 121 S. Illinois, r. 140 Union.

Shortall Christ., brakeman, C. C. C. & I. R. R., bds. 197 Meek.

SHORTRIDGE A. C., superintendent Public Schools, r. 161 Jackson.

Shortridge A. F., r. 123 W. Vermont.

SHORTRIDGE W. C, agent John Hancock Mutual Life Insurance Co., 4 Citizens' National Bank bldg., bds. Pyle House.

Shotts Susie, (wid. Charles) r. 24 Center.

Shotwell Mahala Mrs., r. 133 Harrison.

Shoughensby Patrick, lab., r. 305 W. Merrill.

Shoup Calvin, fireman, C. C. & I. C. R. R. bds. 61 S. Noble.

Shove Fred, finisher, 74 S. Pennsylvania, bds. California House.

Shove Fred E., blacksmith, 74 S. Pennsylvania, r. 41 Water.

Shover James E. (Shover & Christian) r. 318 N. Delaware.

SHOVER & CHRISTIAN, (J. E. S. and W. F. C.) carpenters and builders, 124 E. Vermont.

Shovie Frederick, works, I. C. & L. R. R. shops, r. 350 Virginia av.

Shovie Jacob, wiper, I. C. & L. R. R., r. 9 Water.

Shwalter Samuel, groceries and provisions, 257 Indiana av., r. same.

Shrader Fred, boots and shoes 85 W. Washington, r. same.

Shoerer Harman H., piano manufacturer, rear 141 W. Washington, r. 260 S. Alabama.

Shoerer William H., pianomaker, bds. 260 S. Alabama.

Shubert Lena Miss, teacher Ninth Ward School, bds. 328 N. West.

Shue Wolfgang, works Novelty Works.

Shughrue Patrick, lab., works T. H. R. R., r. 579 Maple.

Shuh John, dealer in groceries, provisions, etc., 322 Virginia av., r. same.

Shuir John, porter, 52 S. Meridian, r. S. Illinois.

Shultz John, lab., r. 471 E. Georgia.

Shute Alfred, proprietor Little Hotel Saloon, r. 249 N. Mississippi.

Shute Mary Miss, bds. 249 N. Mississippi.

Shuth James, r. 251 S. Meridian.

Shutter Christopher, grocer, r. 283 S. Pennsylvania.

Shutts Charles P., cooper, bds. 335 W. Maryland.

Shutts John W., cooper, bds. 335 W. Maryland.

Sickels Alma, (wid. William) r. 351 N. East.

Sickels William W. Rev., r. 351 N. East.

Siddall J. P., physician, 166 Virginia av., r. 227 E. Louisiana.

Siddel Nathan, lab., bds. 272 S. Missouri.

Sides David T., agent Franklin Life Insurance Co., cor. Illinois and Kentucky av., r. 50 W. New York.

Sidey Thomas, salesman New York Store, bds. Avenue House.

Sidney J. Vail, teacher Indiana Institution for Deaf and Dumb.

Siebert Ferdinand, painter, r. 211 N. Winston.

Siebert Hiram, street contractor, r. 143 S. East.

Siebold John, cabinetmaker, r. 213 N. Noble.

Siegel Ferdinand, stonemason, r. 25 Biddel.

Siene Christian, cigarmaker, r. 553 E. St. Clair.

SIERSDORFER L., manufacturer and dealer in boots and shoes, 41 E. Washington, r. 187 Virginia av.

SIETZ FRED., proprietor Chicago House, 117 S. Illinois, r. same.

Sikes Joseph, (col'd) porter 18 W. Pearl.

Silverman A., shoemaker, bds. Globe House.

Silvers Wm., coachmaker, r. 29 Massachusetts av.

Simcox Samuel, machinist, r. 35 Elm.

Simmermann George, r. 248 N. East.

Simmilink Mary, (wid) r. 299 E. Ohio.

Simmons Hermann, optician, 43 S. Illinois.

Simms Addison, works Sims & Hoskins, r. 423 N. Mississippi.

Simms August, baker, 178 S. Illinois, bds. same.

Simms John, lab., r. 217 W. South.

Simms John, carpenter, r. 25 W. St. Clair.

Simms John W. (S. & Hoskins) r. 423 N. Mississippi.

Simms Wm., sup't new rolling mill, r. cor. South and McGill.

Simms Wm., teamster, bds. 272 Winston.

SIMS & HOSKINS, (J. M. S. and R. S. H.) gravel and tar roofers, cor. Georgia and Canal.

Simon Andrew, with Holland & Ostermeyer, r. 581 E. Washington.

Simon A. F., porter, 27 E. Maryland, r. 185 E. Washington.

Simon Charles, carpenter, r. 12 Arch.

Simon Christian, works lumber yard, r. 263 N. Noble.

Simon Frederick, grocer, 188 N. Noble, r. same.

Simon John P., currier and tanner. r. 344 E. Market.

Simon Peter, currier, 125 S. Meridian.

Simons G. B., r. 552 N. Meridian.

Simons Hiram T., carpenter, bds. 26 S. West.

Simpson Charles, stonecutter. r. 31 Grant.

Simpson Charles E., T. H. & I. engineer corps, bds. Spencer House.

Simpson James P., carpenter, r. 183 Meek.

SIMPSON JOHN, groceries and provisions, cor. Illinois and Georgia, bds. Spencer House.

Simpson John E., assistant superintendent, T. H. & I. R. R., bds. cor. Virginia av. and Alabama.

Simpson J. L., works Jackson, Rider & Co.

Simpson Nicholas, retail grocery, 235 S. Delaware, r. 263 S. Delaware.

Simpson Oliver, teamster, r. 129 N. Liberty.

Simpson R., flour and feed, 43 S. Delaware. r. 355 S. Delaware.

Simpson Richard, groceries and provisions, 56 S. Illinois, r. 325 S. Delaware.

Sincoe William, (col'd) lab., r. 43 Ellen.

Sindlinger Godfrey, meat market, 194 S. Illinois, r. same.

Sindlinger Peter, clk. 194 S. Illinois.

SINGLE ABDEN, saloon and bowling alley, 176 E. Washington, r. same.

Sirk Frank, teamster, r. 121 E. Ohio.

SINKER ALFRED T., proprietor American Saw Works, cor. Pennsylvania and Georgia, r. N. city limits, on Western av.

Sinker E. T., (S. & Davis) r. 84 W. Vermont.

SINKER & DAVIS, (E. T. S. and T. D.) proprietors Western Machine Works, 125 S. Pennsylvania.

Sinkes James M., carpenter, r. nw. cor. Vermont and Bright.

Sinks Laura, (wid.) George, r. 75 W. First.

Sipf Emma, domestic, Institute for the Blind.

Sipf Minnie, cook, Institute for the Blind.

Sipp Charles, machinist, r. 512 N. Mississippi.

Sisco H. C., works Osgood, Smith & Co.

Sisco Joseph, lab., Osgood, Smith & Co.

Sixth Ward School House, Union, between Merrill and McCarty, Ellen A. Davis, Principal.

Skillen James, sr., proprietor Ætna Mills, 354 W. Washington, r. 48 N. West.

Skillen James, works Ætna Mills, bds. 48 N. West.

Skillen William M., bookkeeper Ætna Mills, bds. 366 W. Washington.

Skinner Ellison E. (S. & Braddock) r. 124 W. Sixth.

Skinner John, clk. O. F. Mayhew.

Skinner Mary Mrs., r. 22 S. East.

Skinner & Braddock, (E. E. S. and Joseph B.) dyers and scourers, 62 S. Illinois.

Slahlhut Charles, carpenter, Murphy, Johnston & Co.

Slate Benjamin F., teamster McCord & Wheatley, r. 215 Coburn.

H. H. LEE

Makes a Specialty of

CHOICE GOLDEN RIO,

AND

OLD GOVERNMENT JAVA COFFEES.

Slate H., clk. McCord & Wheatley, r. 215 Coburn.

Slattery William, lab., r. 3 Bates.

Slaton Thomas, (col'd) lab., r. Huron.

Slaughter J. L., teller First National Bank, bds. Palmer House.

Slaughter Milton A., carpenter, r. 203 Meek.

Slaven Mary M., pastry cook Bates House.

Slavin Maria, (wid. James) dressmaker, r. 264 S. Tennessee.

Sleeth James, harnessmaker, bds. 315 S. Missouri.

Sleight Robert, machinist, bds. Washington House.

Slein Herman J., clk. Trade Palace, r. 231 E. Washington.

Sliebitez Fred, jeweler, r. over 350 E. Market.

Slife John, lab., r. Minerva, nr. Frank Wright's brewry.

Sloam E. W., r. 451 N. Pennsylvania.

Sloan George W. (Browning & S.) r. 350 N. Illinois.

Sloan James K., stairbuilder, r. 549 N. Mississippi.

Sloan John, works Jackson, Rider & Co.

Sloan John, r. 230 N. Tennessee.

Sloss Robert, minister, r. 198 N. Illinois.

Sloan Robert, clk. Stoneman, Pee & Co., r. 230 N. Tennessee.

Sloan Samuel, carpenter, r. 134 W. Maryland.

Sloan William G., r. 142 Bates.

Sloniger Christian, teamster, r. 303 E. Washington.

Sloss George, (col'd) expressman, r. 12 Center.

Slotzhauer Valentine, foreman Cabinet Maker's Union, r. 152 N. Davidson.

Slusher Henry, dealer in watches, clocks and jewelry 190 W. Washington, r. same.

Slusser Henry M., lab., r. 432 S. West.

Smalhorse Simons, cigarmaker 166 N. Noble.

Small Charles A., lab., r. 88 Michigan rd.

Small David, carpenter, r. 89 Jackson.

Small Henry, tailor, r. 144 W. New York.

Small Jerome N., engineer I, C. & L. R. R., r. 111 Meek.

Small Luella Miss, with William Sumner & Co., r. E. Washington beyond city limits.

Small William, salesman New York Store, bds. Pyle House.

Smallholz Casper, saloonkeeper, r. 64 N. Noble.

Smallholz John, lab., r. 64 N. Noble.

Smelser Olive P., (wid. Jacob) r. 38 Christian av.

Smiley Michael, works Osgood, Smith & Co., r. 59 Eddy.

Smith Abraham, lab., r. 3 Rockwood.

Smith Adaline, (wid. John) r. 168 Spring.

Smith Albert, brakeman C. C. & L. C. R. R., bds. 58 Benton.

Smith Albert, lab., r. 352 Indiana av.

Smith Alice Mrs., boarding house, r. 171 S. Alabama.

Smith Amos D., carpenter, 86 W. Market, bds. 340 W. Vermont.

Smith Andrew, engineer Peru R. R., r. 96 Bates.

Smith Andy, bar tender, H. Schaub, bds. 334 Virginia av.

Smith Arthur H., sleeping car conductor.

Smith Athlic, professor of music, r. 146 Buchanan.

Smith Aurelius, printer, r. 70 N. Mississippi.

Smith Belle Miss, bds. 75 W. South.

SMITH BUTTLER K., jr., retail grocer, 94 N. Illinois, r. same.

Smith B. W., R. R. engineer, r. 301 S. East.

Smith Charles W., attorney at law, r. College av, 3d house N. of Christian av.

Smith Christian, (S., Ittenbach & Co.) r. 131 Stevens.

Smith Christina, r. 84 Michigan Road.

Smith Clara Miss, teacher Sixth Ward school house, bds. 144 N. Tennessee.

Smith Collins H., carpenter, r. 163 Spring.

Smith Columbus, (col'd) lab., r. African al., between Sixth and Seventh.

Smith Cornelius J., blacksmith, r. 526 S. Illinois.

Smith C. M., traveling agent, Josselyn Bros. & Co., bds. 112 N. Pennsylvania.

Smith C. W., jr., lawyer, 5 Yohn's blk.

Smith David, lab., r. 446 Indiana av.

Smith Eben, (Strong & S.) r. 150 Christian av.

Smith Edward D., painter, bds. 176 Blackford.

Smith Elizabeth B., (wid. Caleb B.) r. 296 W. New York.

Smith Enoch, driver, r. 11 S. Alabama.

Smith E. J., (wid.) Isaac, r. 70 N. Mississippi.

Smith E. M., physician, office 40 N. Pennsylvania, r. same.

Smith F, puddler, r. 350 S. Delaware.

Smith Frank, printer, Sentinel office, r. 70 N. Mississippi.

Smith Frank, real estate and money broker, 31 W. Washington, r. nw. cor. Tennessee and Third.

Smith Frank E., dealer in groceries, provisions, etc., 164 W. Michigan, r 371 W. New York.

Smith Fred, blacksmith, r. 46 Water.

Smith Frederick, blacksmith C. C. C. & I. shops.

Smith Frederick, dealer in groceries and provisions, cor. Vermont and Mississippi, r. 468 N. Tennessee.

SMITH FULLER, Citizens' Carriage and Wagon Manufactory, se. cor. Liberty and Washington, r. 318 E. Market.

Smith F. A., bookkeeper Sentinel office, bds. National Hotel.

Smith F. P., r. 336 N. Noble.

Smith George, cartman, 144 S. Alabama.

Smith George, painter, r. 191 N. Liberty.

Smith George, works Novelty Works.

Smith George, r. 347 N. Tennessee.

Smith George, second-hand furniture, 78 S. Delaware, r. same.

Smith George B., student, bds. 116 Broadway.

Smith G. T., salesman, 25 N. Pennsylvania, r. 229 N. New Jersey.

Smith G. W. B., printer, r. 60 S. Pennsylvania.

Smith Henry Rev., r. 400 N. New Jersey.

Smith Harriet, (wid. William) r. 467 S. Illinois.

SMITH HENRY, saloon, 129 W. Washington, r. same.

Smith Henry, wiper C. C. C. & I. R. R. shops.

Smith Henry C., railroader, bds. 62 Bates.

Smith Herold, clk., r. over 306 E. Washington.

Smith Hiram, (col'd) barber, works M. Mason, r. W. Vermont.

Smith Horace W., r. 296 W. New York.

Smith H., clk., r. 116 N. Alabama.

Smith H. B., freight agent, bds. Pyle House.

Smith Isaac, peddler, r. 414 S. Tennessee.

SMITH, ITTENBACH & CO. (C. S., G. I. and F. I.) marble works, two squares E. of Noble, bet. Harrison and Lord.

Smith Jacob, cigar manufacturer, 32 Jones, r. same.

Smith Jacob, (col'd) lab., r. 102 Howard.

Smith Jacob, (col'd) lab., r. 126 N. California.

Smith Jacob, barber, bds. 144 N. Pennsylvania.

Smith Jacob W., foreman, Braden & Burford's bookbindery, bds. 86 N. California.

BENHAM BRO'S,

36 East Washington St.,

AGENTS FOR THE

BURDETT ORGAN.

Smith James, supt. Home Travelers Insurance Co., r. cor. Pennsylvania and Fourth.

Smith James, clk., Warren Tate, r. 45 Fletcher av.

Smith James, railroad conductor, r. 326 E. Michigan.

Smith James, r. 33 S. West.

Smith James, painter, r. 228 Massachusetts av.

Smith James, brickmaker, r. 285 Massachusetts av.

SMITH JAMES H. V., dealer in books and stationery, 4 E. Washington, r. 225 S. New Jersey.

Smith Jennie Miss, servent, 124 S. Meridian.

Smith John, lab., r. 397 W. New York.

Smith John, bds. California House.

Smith John, lab., r. 72 Fayette.

Smith John, (B. & S.) r. 69 Bright.

Smith John, with W. Smith, r. 222 E. Washington.

Smith John, shoemaker, r. 69 Bright.

Smith John B., dyer and scourer, 3 Martindale's Block, r. 266 N. West.

Smith John C., carpenter, r. 86 James.

Smith John W., teamster Frank Wright's Ale House, bds. Pyle House.

Smith John W., porter 22 S. Meridian, r. 62 E. Bates.

Smith Jonathan, printer, Sentinel job rooms, bds. 60 S. Pennsylvania.

Smith Jos., lithographer, bds. 147 N. Noble.

Smith Joseph, dealer in books, newspapers, etc., 13 N. Illinois, bds. same.

Smith J. C., conductor I. C. & L. R. R., r. 171 S. New Jersey.

Smith J. C., insurance agent, r. 229 N. New Jersey.

Smith J. C., carpenter, r. 394 S. Delaware.

Smith J. G., blacksmith, r. 162 N. New Jersey.

Smith J. H., commission merchant 322 E. Washington, r. 19 Short.

Smith J. J., (E. Johnson & Co.) r. Waterloo, N. Y.

Smith J. L., insurance agent, r. 218 N. Alabama.

SMITH J. W., agent Florence Sewing Machine, 27 N. Pennsylvania, also Smith & Foster, r. 123 N. Illinois.

Smith J. W., cigarmaker, r. 244½ E. Washington.

THE CHINA TEA STORES

Smith J. W., shipping clk. 52 S. Meridian, bds. Sherman House.

Smith J. H. C., bookbinder, r. 329 N. Illinois.

Smith Lavinia, (wid. William J.) r. 371 W. New York.

Smith Lawrence, porter, r. 72 Davidson.

Smith Lizzie D., milliner and dressmaker 40 S. Illinois, bds. Pyle House.

Smith Louis, lab., r. African al., bet. Sixth and Seventh.

Smith Maggie Miss, servant, 19 Henry.

Smith Mary Mrs., r. 51 N. Tennessee.

Smith Mary E., (wid.) r. over 383 E. Market.

Smith Mathew, carpenter, works Chandler & Taylor, r. Douglass, bet. New York and Ohio.

Smith M. W., traveling agent, r. 227 Virginia av.

Smith Nannie A. Mrs., r. 149 N. California.

SMITH N. R. & CO., importers and dealers in dry goods, 26 and 28 W. Washington, r. 442 N. Illinois.

Smith Peter G., cabinetmaker, r. 394 E. Market.

Smith Richard, (col'd) lab., r. 170 W. Georgia.

Smith Robert, cigar maker, r. over 306 E. Washington.

SMITH, REYNOLDS & THOMAS, (S. S. S., I. R., and R. B. T.) manufacturers of all kinds of tobaccos, 85 and 87 E. South.

Smith Samuel, agent Gutenberg Printing Co., r. 120. E. Merrill.

Smith Samuel, shoemaker, bds. Globe House.

Smith Samuel, (col'd) lab., r. 184 N. Missouri.

Smith Sarah, assistant superintendent, Home of the Friendless.

Smith Sarah A., tailoress, works 156 W. Washington, bds. 208 W. Ohio.

Smith Sarah A., (wid.) Harrison, r. 423 W. Washington.

Smith Sophia, (wid.) r. 196 Bates.

Smith Sophia, (wid.) r. 148 E. Pratt.

Smith Squire, salesman, bds. 208 W. Ohio.

Smith S. A. Miss, school teacher, r. 45 N. Alabama.

Smith S. F., (Osgood, S. & Co.) r. 28 Fort Wayne av.

Smith S. S., (S., Reynolds & Thomas) r. 62 Greer.

Smith Theodore, r. 184 N. Tennessee.

Smith Thomas, lab., r. 298 W. Market.

Smith Thomas, lab., r. 11 Dacota.

Smith Thomas, baggagemaster C. C. C. & I. R. R.

Smith Thomas, (col'd) lab., r. 131 Bright.

Smith Thomas A., clk. Hoosier Store, bds. Macy House.

Smith Washington, carpenter, bds. Chicago House.

SMITH WILLIAM, manufacturer soda water, 222 E. Washington, r. same.

Smith William, lab., r. 24 Jones.

Smith William, salesman, bds. Deiler's, S. Tennessee.

Smith William, wagonmaker, r. 131 Bates.

Smith William, fireman I. C. & L. R. R., r. 196 Bates.

Smith William, tobacconist, r. 312 S. Delaware.

Smith William S., fruit dealer, r. 31 W. Michigan.

Smith William Q., wheelwright, r. 20 W. Georgia.

Smith William W., railroad agent, r. 203 W. South.

Smith W. (Tucker & S.) r. 97 N. Delaware.

Smith W. A., saloon, 40 W. Louisiana, r. same.

Smith W. H., bookkeeper Mooney & Co., bds. 162 N. New Jersey.

Smith W. P., surveyor, 248 N. East.

Smith Wm. Q., r. 180 N. East.

SMITH & FOSTER, (J. W. S. & Wallace F.) prize medal shirts and men's furnishing goods, 22 E. Washington.

Smithers Henry, r. 368 N. Mississippi.

Smithers James W. (Daggett & Co.) r. Jackson, cor. Christina av.

Smithers John, sr., r. 184 N. Tennessee.

Smithers John W., bookkeeper Chandler & Taylor, bds. 184 N. Tennessee.

Smithert Annie E. Mrs., r. 97 W. South.

Smock George W., auctioneer for Spellman & Co., r. 14 S. Mississippi.

Smock John, lab., r. 302 W. Maryland.

Smock Mattie Miss, 24 S. New Jersey.

Smock Newton, express messenger, r. 256 Virginia av.

Smock Peter, clk., r. 229 Virginia av.

Smock Richard M, deputy county clerk, r. Western av., bet. Butler and Forest av.

Smock R. T., lab., r. 317 W. Washington.

Smock Samuel, jr. (S. & Cox) r. 36 N. New Jersey.

Smock Samuel J. (S. & Cox) r. 36 N. New Jersey.

Smock William, lab., r. 302 W. Earyland.

Smock Wm. C., clk. Marion County r. 410 N. Delaware.

Smock William H., car deliverer, T. H. & I. R. R., r. 493 S. Tennessee.

Smock & Cox, (S. J. S. and T. T. C.) boiler and sheet iron works, 24 E. Georgia.

Snell Ellen, (wid.) r. 172 W. Georgia.

Snell Louis, lab., r. 339 S. East.

Snider C., works Jackson, Rider & Co.

Snider G. W., bookkeeper, Anderson, Bullock & Schofield, bds. Pyle House.

Snider W. H., dealer in drugs, medicines, etc., cor. Virginia av. East and South, r. same.

Snow Wm. S., machinist, r. 282 N. Alabama.

Snowden Mary, (wid. James) r. 348 Indiana av.

Snyder Adam, (Munday & S.) r. Dayton, Ohio.

Snyder Charles D. (S. & Wolf) r. 85 Bradshaw.

Snyder David C. (S. & Hays) r. 454 N. Tennessee.

SNYDER D. E. & CO. (D. E. S. and R. F. Fletcher) general insurance agents, 13 E. Washington.

Snyder D. W., farmer, r. Virginia av., outside city limits.

Snyder Frederick M., machinist, works Greenleaf & Co., r 375 S. Illinois.

Snyder Hattie Miss, bds. 15 S. Mississippi.

Snyder John F., carpenter, r. 508 N. Mississippi.

Snyder Peter, porter 123 S. Meridian, r. ws. Spring, nr. Michigan.

Snyder Stephen, works Osgood, Smith & Co., r. 437 S. Illinois.

SNYDER & HAYS, (D. E. S. and J. C. H.) general insurance agents, 13 E. Washington.

Snyder & Wolfe, (C. D. S. and W. A. W.) dealers in groceries and provisions, 200 Virginia av.

Sobbe Charles, carpenter, r. 247 N. Winston.

Sobbe Christian F., teamster, works 397 S. Meridian, bds. same.

Sobbe Henry, carpenter, bds. 231 N. Davidson.

Sobbe Henry, clk. 193 S. Tennessee, bds. same.

Socks Philip, cooper, r. 77 N. Illinois.

Soewell H. M., grocer, 232 E. Washington, r. 266 E. Market.

Soewell Samuel H., clk., r. 266 E. Market.

Soewell Wm. P., clk., bds. 266 E. Market.

SOEHNER CHARLES, ag't Steinway Pianos, and dealer in organs, melodions, etc., 85 N. Illinois, r. 86 N. Illinois.

21

Soehner Charles, jr., salesman Meridian, r. 86 N. Illinois.

Sogemeier Wm. (H. Altman & C Ray and Meridian.

Sogen John, machinist, r. Sin New Jersey and Alabama.

Sohl Alfred J. (S. Gibson & Co W. New York.

SOHL, GIBSON & CO. (G. and A. J. S.) proprieto Rose Flouring Mill, 352 W ington.

Sohl Levi, (Sohl, Gibson & Co.) ville, Ky.

Sohl Nathan, miller, r. 295 Indi

Solomon Charles, dealer in sec clothing, 200 S. Illinois, r.

Solomon Henry, (S. & Garrett) S. Illinois.

Solomon Joseph, (J. & M. S.) East.

Solomon Morris, (J. & M. S.) Mississippi.

SOLOMON J. & M., (Jos Morris S.) Central Loan O Illinois.

SOLOMON & GARRET and J. G.) proprietors Capi Store, 42 W. Washington.

Sommerlad C., varnisher and po and 73 W. Washington.

Sonderegger Frank, painter, r. 1

Sonnefield William, teamster, r. ble.

Soper Solon R., clk. 18 W. Pe Henry.

Soule Charles E., printer Senti r. 138 Blake.

Soule Eliza M., (wid. Joshua) Blake.

Soule James, lab. P. C. & St. L.

Soule James, carpenter, bds. 65

Southard A. B., general ticket a & C. R. W., r. 80 W. St. Cl

Southard George, telegraph op 274 E. St. Clair.

Southard James M., carpenter Meek.

Southard J. P., bookkeeper, r. 3 bama.

Southard Mathew K., r. 49 Chat

Southerland James W., machin Greer.

Sowders J. M., (S. & Jacob) Blake.

JOHN SENOUR.   WILL SENOUR.

J. SENOUR & CO.,

CITY SHOE STORE,

No. 5 West Washington St.,

Indianapolis, Ind.

Sowders & Jacoby, (J. N. S. & D. K. J.) fish dealers 26 W. Pearl.

SPADES M. H., dealer in dry goods, notions, human hair, etc., 20 E. Washington.

Spahr F. L., bookkeeper 131 S. Meridian, bds. Sherman House.

Spahr George W., (Spahr & Daily) r. 21 Lockerbie.

Spahr Peter, works Jackson Rider & Co.

SPAHR & DAILY, (Geo. S. and Hez. D.) attorneys, 20½ N. Delaware, room 2.

Spann John M., student, r. 163 N. Pennsylvania.

Spann John S., (J. S. S. & Co.) r. 163 N. Pennsylvania.

SPANN JOHN S. & CO., (J. S. S., T. H. S., and J. B. Cleveland) real estate agents, Brown's blk.

Spann Thomas H., (J. S. S. & Co.) r. 163 N. Pennsylvania.

Spaps Kate Miss, clk. Trade Palace, bds. 344 N. East.

Sparks John C., lab., r. 223 W. Washington.

Sparks R. A., cigar maker, bds. Neiman House.

Spaulding J., baggage master, J., M. & I. R. R.

SPAULDING J. L., proprietor Steam Laundry, office 74 E. Market, bds. Pattison House.

Spaulding Ralph, (col'd) teamster, r. 360 W. Market.

Speer Fred, (Schwear & S.) r. 548 E. Washington.

Speckman Henry, cigar manufacturer and dealer in tobacco, 108 S. Illinois, r. same.

Speed L. Hawkins, clk. Harrison's bank, bds. 252 N. Meridian.

Speers Sarah, (col'd wid. John.) r. 142 Douglass.

Spellman Fred, lab., Starch Factory.

Spellman John, merchant police, r. 340 Railroad.

Spellman Samuel, (S. & Aron) r. 180 Virginia av.

SPELLMAN & CO., (S. S. and C. A.) auction and commission, 111 S. Illinois, and 85 E. Washington.

Spencer Andrew, fireman C. C. & I. C. R. R., bds. 61 S. Noble.

SPENCER CHARLES N., traveling agent, West, Morris & Co., r. 85 N. Noble.

Spencer Eli, brickmason, r. 695 E. Washington.

Spencer Charles F., clk. Bee Hive, bds. 89 Indiana av.

Spencer James, (col'd) proprietor eating saloon, r. 225 N. Tennessee.

SPENCER MILTON, grocer, 132 E. Washington, bds. same.

Spice Adolph, (col'd) lab., r. cor. North and Blake.

Spicer A., bds. 67 N. Davidson.

Spicer Bloomfield, r. 67 N. Davidson.

Spicer E. M., letter carrier, r. Pyle House.

Spicer Wm., lab., Bunte & Dickson.

Spiegel Augustus, (S., Thoms & Co.) r. 219 N. Liberty.

Spiegel Christian, (S., Thoms & Co.) r. 310 N. East.

Spiegel Edward, cabinetmaker, r. 215 Massachusetts av.

Spiegel F. H., turner, r. 310 N. East.

SPIEGEL, THOMS & CO. (Aug. Spiegel, Fred Thoms and H. Frank) whol. and retail dealers in all kinds of furniture, 71 and 73 W. Washington.

Spiegel William, cabinetmaker, r. 310 N. East.

Spiegel William C., cabinetmaker, r. 219 N. Liberty.

Spilker Charles, teamster, bds. 37 Oriental.

Spittel Joseph, machinist, r. 203 N. Davidson.

Spitzelweiner Jack, watchman, r. 79 N. Noble.

SPITZFADEN PETER, meat market, 71 E. Washington and 152 Virginia av., r. 252 S. Delaware.

Spitznagel Leopold, barber, r. 454 S. Meridian.

Splain Timothy, lab., r. 365 E. Market.

Splann James, teamster, 24 W. Maryland, r. 89 S. West.

Splann Nicholas, coalheaver, r. 95 S. West.

Splann Timothy, boss teamster, 24 W. Maryland, r. 79 S. West.

Spohr J. G. (Maurice & S.) bds. 113 E. Washington.

Sponable M. J. (wid. Philip) r. 175 N. Tennessee.

Sponsel Conrad, (S. & Balz) Union Beer Brewery, r. Madison rd., S. of city.

SPONSEL HENRY, dealer in groceries and provisions, 355 S. Delaware, r. same.

Sponsel George, saloon, 231 S. Delaware, r. same.

Sponsel George, night policeman, r. 240 S. Delaware.

SPONSEL & BALZ, (Conrad S. and Peter B.) Union Beer Brewery, Madison rd., south of city.

Spooner B. J., U. S. Marshall, bds. Bates House.

Spooner John C., Deputy U. S. Marshall, r. Lawrenceberg, Ind.

Spotts William, commission house and feed store, cor. Delaware and Virginia av., r. 329 E. Market.

Spothegel Sweedey Paper, published by the Gutenberg Printing and Publishing Co.

Spratt John E., bookkeeper, 24 W. Maryland, bds. 126 N. Tennessee.

Spratt S. D., trunkmaker, bds. 126 N. Tennessee.

Spratt T. B., superintendent Union Depot Dining Hall, bds. same.

Spray Jessie, brakeman, C. & I. J. R. R., r. 326 W. Maryland.

Spray Jennie Miss, seamstress, r. 326 W. Maryland.

Spray Joseph, lab., bds. 326 W. Maryland.

Spray Lizzie Miss, with W. H. Valentine, r. 326 W. Maryland.

Spreng Adam, stonecutter, r. 128 N. Liberty.

Sprengpfeil Henry, (S. & Co.) r. 42 S. Liberty.

SPRENGPFEIL & CO., (H. S. and C. Wagner) boot and shoe manufacturers, 122 S. Illinois.

Springer David, carpenter and stair builder, 260 Massachusetts av., r. 13 Chatham.

Springer J. E., sup't agencies, Security Life Insurance Co., 2 Blake's row, r. 115 Meek.

Springer J., patternmaker, r. 305 Bates.

Springer Martin B., moulder, r. 103 Meek.

Springle Mrs., boarding house, r. 103 S. New Jersey.

Springsteen Abram, brickmason, r. 268 E. Market.

Springsteen Abraham F., bricklayer, r. 117 Spring.

Springsteen Charley, clk. lunch stand Union Depot, bds. 117 Spring.

Springsteen Jefferson, deputy marshall Union Depot, r. 117 Spring.

Springsteen John, signpainter, bds. 117 Spring.

Sproudle George, saw mill, r. 11 Ellsworth.

SPROULE, CONKLIN & LEE, (Frank S., John P. C. and D D. L.,) manufacturers patent steam bent chair backs and seats, nw. cor. New York and Canal,

BENHAM BRO'S,

36 East Washington St.,

Pianos, Organs and Melodeons Tuned, Moved and Repaired.

Sproule J. E., clk., bds. 132 N. Alabama

Sproule Robert S., r. 132 N. Alabama.

Sproule William K., bookkeeper, r. 92 S. Mississippi.

Sprord Louise Mrs., washerwoman, r. 464 S. East.

Spurier J B., lab., r. 322 W. Washington.

Staats G. D., janitor Odd Fellows Hall, r. 10 E. Michigan.

Staats Mattie Mrs., seamstress, r. 48½ Massachusetts av.

Staats W. K., bds. 10 E. Michigan.

Stabler Michael, teamster, r. 133 Spring.

Stacy Mahlon D., watchmaker, 34 Virginia av., r. 269 Virginia av.

Stacy M. H., finisher Merritt & Coughlin, r. 331 N. Blake.

Stacy Sanford, works Merritt & Coughlin, bds. 331 N. Blake.

Stafford Dan, fireman Sherman House.

Stagg Charles W., attorney at law, r. 267 W. Vermont.

Stagg Eliza P. (wid.) r. 146 W. New York.

Stahnhaut Frederick, saddler, r. 664 N. Tennessee.

Stake Charles, engineer C. C. & I. C. R. R., bds. 21 Meek.

Stake John, fireman C. C. & I. C. R. R.

Stake Joseph, chair ornamenter, r. 21 Meek.

Staley F. J., r. W. North, nr. Lafayete, Depot.

Stalker Martha, (wid.) r. 87 S. Liberty.

Stalker Malinda, housekeeper, r. 87 S. Liberty.

Stanbaker George, teamster, r. 32 W. Market.

Stanley Ellen, (wid.) r. 358 N. Winston.

Stanley Cleopatre Miss, actress, r. 358 N. Winston.

STANRIDGE HENRY J., prop. Stanridge House, 41 W. Maryland.

Stanton Anna, (wid) bds. 157 High.

Stanton A. P., lawyer, r. 357 N. East.

Stanton John, moulder D. Root & Co.

Staples Joshua, civil engineer, r. 368 N. New Jersey.

Staples Fleetwood, (col'd) lab., r. cor. Tinker and Lafayette R. R.

Staples Eliza, (wid.) r. 368 N. New Jersey.

Stapley Samuel, cigarmaker, bds. Decatur House

L. H. LEE,
Dealer in
Coffees, Sugars & Spices,
7 ODD FELLOWS HALL
AND
MY OF MUSIC CORNER.
___

JAMES H., real estate agt.
attorney at law 10 S. Pennsyl-
ia, r. 721 N. Mississippi.

B., letter carrier, r. 110 N. Mis-
i.

UNION LINE — FAST
FIGHT — S. F. GRAY,
ENT, 85 Virginia av., r. 70 E.
Clair.

Richard, works Indianapolis
on and Agricultural Works, bds.
S. East.

ristian, carriagemaker, r. 38 S.
ama.

J., (wid.) r. 140 Massachusetts

stav G., secretary Cabinet Mak-
Union, r. E. end Ohio.

rmann, boot and shoemaker, r.
New Jersey.

lliam, lab., r. 14 N. California.

LING S. S. MRS., artist 77½
arket, r. same.

orge W., medical student, bds.
N. Alabama.

n, carpenter, r. 253 S. Missouri.

C., works Novelty Works.

u., merchant policeman, r. 164
Washington.

nd of Agricultural, office, State
se.

use, bet. Mississippi and Ten-
ce, and Washington and Mar-

ices in State Building, cor. Ten-
re and Washington.

SENTINEL, (Daily and
kly) R. J. Bright, prop'r; office,
or. Meridian and Circle.

exander, tinner, r. 200 N. Noble.

s., tinner, Tutewiler Bros., r. 200
oble.

JOSEPH, merchant tailor,
ld Fellows Hall, r. 200 N. Noble.

William, clk., Concordia House,
same.

——, r. 28 W. First.

1. D., watchmaker, 24 Virginia
r. 244 Virginia av.

n Henry S., chief clerk, Ben
Bros., r. 174 Jackson.

nel, physician, r. 78 S. Illinois.

I CRACKER BAKERY,
ott & Nickum, propr's, 188 E.
hington.

Stearns John. fireman, C. C. & I. C. R. R.,
bds. 58 Benton.
Stebbins Sarah (wid. John) r. 33 Henry.
Stebbs W. (wid.) dressmaker, r. 46½
Massachusetts av.
Stebzel John. barber, r. 376 E. Ohio.
Steckhon Louis, upholsterer, r. 17 S. Mis-
sissippi.
Stedman E. P., clk., I. C. & L. freight
office, r. 52 Bates.
Stedman Percival, asst. freight agent, r.
cor. Jackson and Ruth.
Stedwick Catherine, (wid.) r. 144 Ste-
vens.
Steel E. R., bookkeeper, r. 218 E. Mar-
ket.
Steel T. J., printer, News office, r. 304 E.
Georgia.
Steel William H., carpenter, r. 304 E.
Georgia.
Steele Oliver, cooper, r. 127 N. Liberty.
Steelsmith Simon, r. 512 N. Mississippi.
Steffens Charles, saloon and beer gar-
den, 192 N. Mississippi, r. same.
Steffens E. F, r. 183 Blake.
Stiffins George, butcher, bds. 207 W.
Michigan.
Stegall Jerry, blacksmith, r. 120 W.
Maryland.
Steiert Leopold, laborer, r. 64 Railroad.
Stein Abraham, butcher, r. 177 Virginia
av.
Stein Ameil, clk., 24 W. Louisiana.
Stein Ferd, barber, 276 E. Washington,
r. same.
Stein H. J., salesman Trade Palace, bds.
231 E. Washington.
Stein Joseph, boot and shoe manufac-
turer, 106 S. Meridian, r. same.
Stein William, baker, r. 107 E. Wash-
ington.
Steinacker Ernst, drayman, r. 481 S.
New Jersey.
Steinbauer Leonard, watchman Leiber's
Brewery, r. 152 Madison av.
Steiner John, upholsterer, with N. S.
Baker, r. 62 W. South.
Steinhauser B. F., bookbinder, 164 E.
Washington, r. 171 E. Washington.
Steinhauer Fred F., tilecutter, 136 S.
Pennsylvania, r. 323 S. Pennsyl-
vania.
Steinhauer M. (D. & S.) r. 260 S. Penn-
sylvania.
Steinhilber Annie, (wid.) r. 316 Rail-
road.
Steinmann George, tailor, bds. 139 Vir-
ginia av.
Steinmann John, merchant tailor, 32
Virginia av., r. 139 Virginia av.
Steinmeyer William, porter, 59 S. Meri-
dian.
Steinmitz John, blacksmith, r. 50 Hos-
brook.

Steinwinter Catherine, (wid.) 128 E. St.
    Joseph.
Steitley John, works Sentinel office, r.
    341 N. Liberty.
Stelbrick Henry, lab., r. 625 N. Missis-
    sippi.
Stellham Christ, framemaker, H. Lieber
    & Co., r. 306 N. Noble.
Stellhorn Frederick, carpenter, r. 175 N.
    Davidson.
Senmyer William, porter, Holliday &
    Co., r. 141 Union.
Stephens A. D., printer, Journal office, r.
    213 N. Pennsylvania.
Stephens Brother, teacher St. John's
    School, bds. same.
Stephens Hattie M., Exchange Store, 32
    S. Illinois, r. same.
Stephens James, boilermaker, r. 118
    Benton.
Stephens James V., boilermaker, r. 93 S.
    Benton.
Stephens Samuel, boilermaker, C. C. & I.
    C R. R., r. 118 Benton.
Stephens Thoms D., r. 233 W. McCarty.
Stephens Thomas D., confectioner, 164
    Indiana av., r. same.
Stephenson John, cooper, r. 213 N. Mis-
    souri.
Stephenson John W., engineer, r. 552 S.
    Meridian.
Sterling George, carpenter, r. rear 31
    Indiana av.
Stern M. G. J. Rev., r. 30 Chatham.
Stern R., clk , 54 N. Illinois, bds. ne. cor.
    Market and Illinois.
Sterne Sham, peddler, r. 123 W. McCarty.
Sterr Wm , rheumatic doctor, r. Bates.
Stetser John, barber, r. 376 E. Ohio.
Steubing Philip, lab., C. C. & I. C. R. R.,
    r 211 N. Noble.
Steubing Wm., engineer C. C. & I. C. R. R.
Stevens A. G., r. 241 Virginia av.
Stevens Albert E., conductor, C. C. & I.
    C. R. R., r. 318 E. Georgia.
Stevens B. F., tinner, 32 S. Meridian,
    r. 358 N. Winston.
Stevens Edward, (col'd) lab., bds. 170 W.
    Georgia.
Stevens H. C., paperhanger, r. 516 N.
    Mississippi.
Stevens James N., Lieutenant of police,
    r. First, bet. Tennessee and Missis-
    sippi.
Stevens Levi B., brickmaker, r. 87 Union.
Stevens M. Mrs., boarding house, r. 213
    N. Pennsylvania.
Stevens Sarah Mrs., r. 348 N. Alabama.
STEVENS THAD M., physician,
    over 15 E. Washington, r. 255 S. New
    Jersey.
Stevenson D., bds. Bates House.
Stevenson David, cooper, r. 213 N. Mis-
    souri.

Stevenson Samuel, boilermaker, r. 118 S.
    Benton.
Steward Robert, clk. pension office, r. 77½
    E. Market.
Steward Madison, (col'd) bds. 58 Oak.
Stewart Annie, (wid.) r. 226 N. Meri-
    dian.
Stewart Axim, (col'd) cook, r. 229 N.
    Tennessee.
Stewart A J., turner, r. 129 E. Merrill.
Stewart Charles, machinist, r. 332 S. Del-
    aware.
Stewart Charles G. (Bowen, S. & Co.) r.
    469 N. Illinois.
Stewart Daniel, (S. & Morgan) r. 265 N.
    Illinois.
Stewart Elizabeth, (wid. Andrew) r. 311
    Indiana av.
Stewart George, (col'd, James & S.) r.
    Missouri, bet. Market and Ohio.
Stewart G. H. W. (col'd) school teacher,
    r. 173 Blake.
Stewart Harriett, (wid.) r. 158 Douglass.
Stewart H. J., tinner, bds. 6 W. Market.
Stewart James, (col'd) porter, 40 S. Meri-
    dian.
Stewart John, flagman, r. 379 S. East.
Stewart John, salesman bds. 74 S. Dela-
    ware.
Stewart John, traveling agent, American
    M. U. Express Co., r. 194 N. Noble.
Stewart John, night watchman, C. C. C.
    & I. R. R. shops.
Stewart John W., porter, bds. 66 N. Mis-
    souri.
Stewart Joseph, switchman, T. H. & I. R.
    R., r. 169 Eddy.
Stewart Martin, lab., rolling mill, bds.
    231 W. South.
Stewart Sophia W. Mrs. (Bowen, S. & Co.)
    r. 78 W. North.
Stewart William, teamster, bds. 311 Indi-
    ana av.
Stewart & Morgan, (D. S. and S. W. M.)
    druggist, 40 E. Washington.
Stick Floraberger, carpenter, r. 281 S.
    New Jersey.
Stiedel George, filecutter, 216 N. Noble.
Stieger Frederick, painter, r. 144 N. Win-
    ston.
Stiegmann Charles, groceries, dry goods
    and notions, 150 Madison av., r.
    same.
Stierle Charles, (S. & Loeper) bds. Em-
    enegger's Hotel.

H. H. LEE
HAS BUT
ONE PRICE, SELLS FOR CASH,
And Guarantees all Goods
Sold at the China Tea Stores,
To be as Represented.

STIERLE & LOEPER, (C. S. and J. W. L.) brass foundry, 92 S. Delaware.

Stiles Elijah, works Aldrich & Gay.

Stiles D. J. (Kimball, Aikman & Co.) r. 335 N. East.

Still Henry, soldier, U. S. arsenal.

Stillhamn Christian, r. 306 N. Noble.

Stillinger John, fireman, I. B. & W. R. R., bds. Neiman House.

Stillwagon John, meatmarket, 442 S. Illinois. r. same.

Stilter Charles, baker, bds. 150 N. East.

Stiltz John, drug clk., r. 131 Ft. Wayne av.

Stiltz William, clk., bds 129 N. Noble.

Stilwell J. D. B., bookkeeper, bds. Little Hotel.

Stilwell W. M., steward Institute for the Blind.

Stilz Frederick, salesman J. H. Baldwin.

Stilz J. George, dealer in agricultural implements, seeds, &c., 78 E. Washington, r. S. city limits.

Stilz John G., clk. with F. Erdelmeyer, r. 131 Ft. Wayne av.

Stipp G. W., clk. D. E. Wilkinson, bds. Pyle House.

Stirk D. P., blacksmith 19 N. Alabama, r. 24 N. East.

Stirk Thomas, edge tool maker, r. 323 W. Market.

Stock Lawrence, porter Emenegger's Hotel, bds. same.

Stockman G. W., foreman, Kingan & Co., r. cor. Maryland and Hellen.

Stockmeyer August, butcher 397 Virginia av., r. same.

Stockwell James, works Jackson, Rider & Co.

Stoelting Charles, railroader, r. 86 Railroad.

Stofer Thomas, engineer C. C. & I. C. R. R., r. 19 N. East.

Stokely Benjamin, machinist, r. 164 N. Winston.

Stokes Charles, pumpmaker 33 N. Tennessee, r. Fatout's Block.

Stokes Harry S, cooper, r. 295 N. East.

Stokes James, (col'd) lab., r. 450 S. Tennessee.

Stolhut Frederick, carpenter, r. 228 Railroad.

Stoll John, tinner Munson & Johnstons.

Stoll Louis, tailor, bds. 23 Kentucky av.

Stolt John H., machinist Eagle Machine Works, r. cor. New York and Tennessee.

Stolte Henry, (S. & Cook) bds. 284 E. Market.

Stolte H. B., student Bryant & Stratton's College, bds. 365 S. Delaware.

Stolte William, (S. & May) r. 365 S. Delaware.

STOLTE & COOK, (H. S. and C. C.) flour and feed store, 253 E. Washington.

Stolte & May, (Wm. Stolte and John May) dealers in groceries and provisions, flour and feed, 365 S. Delaware.

Stoltz Charles, harnessmaker, r. 451 S. Illinois.

Stoltz Francis, basketmaker, r. 17 Henry.

Stoltz John, beltmaker Mooney & Co., r. 416 S. Illinois.

Stone Oscar, r. 113 N. Illinois.

Stone W. O., bookkeeper, 79 S. Meridian, r. 113 N. Illinois.

STONEMAN, PEE & CO. (W. H. Stoneman, G. W. Pee and S. Alward) whol. dealers in notions and fancy goods, cor. Meridian and Louisiana.

Stoneman Wm. H. (S., Pee & Co.) r. 330 N. New Jersey.

Stoner Abraham L., carpenter, r. 237 N. Noble.

Stonestreet G. H., conductor I. P. & C. R. R., r. 174 E. South.

Storer Emile, clk. C. Friedgen, bds. 36 N. East.

Stortz Christina Miss, servant Emenegger's Hotel.

Stortz Pauline Miss, servant Emenegger's Hotel.

Stott Isiah, works Rolling Mill, r. 516 S. Meridian.

Stough Charles, carriage painter, r. 394 N. Delaware.

Stough Jacob L., carriage painter, r. 394 N. Delaware.

Stout B. G. (B. G. S. & Bro.) r. 142 N. Mississippi.

STOUT BEN G. & BROS., whol. and retail grocers, 7 and 8 Bates House blk.

Stout Carhart, coal dealer, r. 133 W. South.

Stout David, (B. G. S. & Bros.) bds 142 N. Mississippi.

Stout David E. (Donaldson & S.) bds. 169 N. Illinois.

Stout Frank, lab., P., C. & St. L. freight depot.

Stout Ferman, (F. S. & Son) r. 331 W. Washington.

Stout George W., (F. S. & Son) r. 162 W. Washington.

Stout Harvey, bds. 115 Meek.

Stout Hiram W., engineer, T. H. R. R.,
bds. 9 S. Mississippi.
Stout Ira H., lab., r. 95 Hosbrook.
Stout John, lab., r. 272 Blake.
Stout J. B., printer, 79 W. Washington,
bds. 133 W. South.
Stout M., clk. E. S. Greer, r. 133 W.
South.
Stout Oliver B., clk. (B. G. S. & Bros.)
r. 173 W. New York.
Stout Remsen, engineer, rolling mill, r.
382 S. Illinois.
Stout Richard C., (B. G. S. & Bros.) r.
173 W. New York.
Stout & Son, (Ferman and George) whole-
sale liquor dealers, 160 W. Washing-
ton, livery and sale stables, 103 W.
Washington.
Stowe S. S., chief clk. Indianapolis and
Vincennes R. R., cor. Virginia av.
and Delaware, r. Union Depot Dining
Hall.
Stowe Augusta Miss, seamstress, bds. 281
Indiana av.
Stowe John, helper, Bellefontaine R. R.
shops.
Stowell M. A., music dealer, 46 N. Penn-
sylvania, r. 78 W. Michigan.
Strader Charles, filler, r. 263 N. Liberty.
Strahan George C., clk., r. 26 Fayette.
Strang Gabriel, shoemaker, r. 195 Harri-
son.
Strang G. L., foreman, shoe shop Indiana
Institution for Deaf and Dumb.
Strange Chapel, Rev. J. W. T. McMullen,
pastor, cor. Michigan and Tennes-
see.
Strangmeier Frederick, porter, Landers,
Conduitt & Co., r. S. Delaware.
Stratford J. W., physician, r. 426 N. Mis-
sissippi.
Stratton E. H., bookkeeper, 42 S. Meridi-
an, r. 13 Cherry.
Straub Vincent, boot fitter, over 38 S.
Illinois.
Strauss Leopold, clk. 1 W. Washington,
bds. Circle Restaurant.
Strauss Samuel, produce dealer, r. 79 E.
Michigan.
Strauss Sol., 19 W. Washington, bds.
Palmer House.
Straus Fred, cutter F. Goepper & Co., r.
r. 479 N. Alabama.
Straubridge Hanah, (wid.) r. 350 N.
Winston.
Straubridge Wm., clk., r. 350 N. Winston.
Street E. A., commercial traveler, bds.
Bates House.
Street Nathan, carpenter, r. 41 Charles,
cor. John.
Streeter Noble, clk. Hume, Adams & Co.,
bds. 268 E. St. Clair.
Strehle Frederick, cabinetmaker, r. 525
E. Market.

BENHAM BRO'S.

36 East Washington St.,

KEEP

THE VERY BEST

VIOLIN AND GUITAR STRINGS.

Streicher Gabriel, brewer, bds. Schmidt's
Brewery.
Streight A. D. (S. & Wood) book publisher,
Yohn's blk, r. E. city limits.
STREIGHT & WOOD, (A. D. S. &
W.) lumber merchants, office Yohn's
blk.
Stretcher Elmira F. (wid. Joseph J.) r.
421 N. Tennessee.
Stretcher Howard, r. 421 N. Tennessee.
Striback Charles, bakery, 319 N. West, r.
same.
Striblen M. E. B. Mrs., r. 596 N. Dela-
ware.
Striblings William, engineer C. C. & I.
C. R. R., r. 302 E. Georgia.
Strickland David H. (Seman & S.) bds.
213 W. Market.
Strickland Harry, bookbinder, bds. 252
W. Market.
Strickland R. J., publisher Odd Fellows
Talisman, 30 S. Meridian, r. Center-
ville, Ind.
Stringer W. H., candy dealer, r. 22 W.
North.
Strohel John, shoemaker, r. 554 E. Wash-
ington.
Stroble Mary, (wid.) r. cor. West and
Maryland.
Stroele Fred, Cabinetmakers' Union, r.
525 E. Market.
Strong A. M., surgeon, Empire Mutual
Life Ins. Co., 75 E. Market, r. 84
Massachusetts av.
Strong M. (S., Smith & Co.) r. 426 N.
New Jersey.
Strong, Smith & Co. (M. S., E. S. and C.
C. Pierson) wohl. dental goods, 48
N. Pennsylvania.
Strongmier Fred, porter, r. 412 S. Dela-
ware.
Strothman Henry, lumberman, r. Michi-
gan rd., nr. Washington.
Stroube J. A., carpenter, r. 23 Fletcher av.
Strow John, hostler, Sullivan & Drew,
bds. 18 S. Pennsylvania.
Struckman Frederick, baggageman, Un-
ion Depot, r. 173 Union
Stuck John, teamster, r. 327 W. Mary-
land.
Stuck John, lab., r. 348 Virginia av.
Stuck Mathias, boilermaker, Sinker &
Co., r. 24 Elm.
Stuck Robert, lab., r. cor. Noble and Vir-
ginia av.

THE CHINA TEA STORES

ARE AT

No. 7 ODD FELLOWS HALL

AND

ACADEMY OF MUSIC CORNER.

Stuck William, works, Osgood, Smith & Co., r. 266 S. Illinois.

Stuckey Charles, cooper, r. 111 Spring.

Stuckmeyer John, (J. Ostermeyer & Co.) r. 362 Virginia av.

Stuckmeyer John H., grocer, 362 Virginia av., r. 358 Virginia av.

Stump Catharine, (wid. J. H.) r. 344 N. East.

Stump John G., stonemason, r. 21 John.

Stumpf H. A., tin and sheet iron worker, shop 94 Indiana av., bds. 79 Indiana av.

Stumpf John G., carpenter, r. 91 Buchanan.

Stumph George, works, Rolling Mill, bds. 300 S. Tennessee.

Stumph Henry, helper, glass works, r. Morris, bet. East and Madison rd.

Stumph Henry, lab., r. Morris bet. Alabama and New Jersey.

Stumph John, contractor and builder, r. Michigan rd. outside city limits.

Stumph John B. (Tobias Bender & Co.) r. 459 E. Market.

Stundon Patrick, expressman, r. 367 N. West.

Stundon Thomas, works paper mill, r. Eighth nr, Canal.

Stundon Thomes, lab., r. 391 N. West.

Sturk David P., blacksmith, r. 124 N. East.

Sturgeon Alfred, speculator, bds. 226 E. Court.

Sturges Levick, shoemaker, r. cor. Blake and New York.

Sturm Herman, speculator, r. Arsenal rd.

Sturm George, tailor, bds. Globe House.

Sturm George, r. 111 S. Illinois.

Sturm John, teamster, bds. Nebraska nr. Madison rd.

Sturm F. C., farmer, r. Arsenal rd.

Sturr Wilbur, bell boy, Bates House.

Sturtz John, butcher, bds. Union House.

Styner Jacob, conductor, I. C. & L. R. R., bds. Sherman House.

Styner John H., locomotive fireman, r. 35 Forest av.

Smart John B., groceries and provisions, 219 Massachusetts av., r. same.

Sudbrock Frank, lab., r. 227 N. Davidson.

Sudbrock Henry, carpenter, r. 318 N. Noble.

Sudbrock Herman, clk., with Reasner & Sudbrook, bds. Michigan rd.

Suddith George, r. 239 S. Delaware.

Suess Charles A., merchant tailor, Mozart Hall, r. same.

Suess George, shoemaker, r. 320 E. Ohio.

Suess Martin, carpenter, Eagle Machine Works, r. 388 E. Market.

Suher Louis, saw filer, r. 23 Wyoming.

Suhr Albert, lab., works T. H. & I. R. R. Co., r. 531 S. Meridian.

Suhr Henry, works T. H. & I. engine house, r. 543 S. Illinois.

Suhre Frederick, express wagon, r. 178 N. Winston.

Suhre Henry C., carpenter, r. 178 N. Winston.

Suhre J. Henry, lab., r. 178 N. Winston.

Suitt James B., Superintendent Eagle Machine Works, bds. 251 S. Meridian.

Sulgrove Berry R., r. 125 W. South.

Sulgrove Eli L., harnessmaker, James Sulgrove, r. 25 W. Henry.

Sulgrove Geo. W., letter carrier, r. 126 Blackford.

Sulgrove James W., bookkeeper, James Sulgrove, r. 137 W. New York.

SULGROVE JAMES, wholesale and retail dealer in sadlery hardware, 20 W. Washington, r. S. of city.

Sulgrove Jerome B., with James Sulgrove, r. 190 N. Mississippi.

Sulgrove Joseph B., mail carrier, r. 235 W. Vermout.

Sulgrove John M., harnessmaker, r. 27 Henry.

Sulgrove Henry J., clk. James Sulgrove, bds. 190 N. Mississippi.

Sulgrove Milton M., with James Sulgrove, r. cor. Illinois and Indiana av.

Sullivan B. W., (Wells & S.) r. 160 N. Meridian.

Sullivan Catharine, domestic, Spencer House.

Sullivan Cornelius, lab., r. 142 Meek.

Sullivan Dan, lab., r. 36 Dougherty.

Sullivan Daniel, lab., r. Michigan rd., nr. Washington.

Sullivan Daniel, lab., r. 212 Meek.

Sullivan Daniel, lab., r. 130 Meck.

Sullivan Daniel D., lab., r. Michigan rd. nr. Washington.

Sullivan Ellen, servant, Palmer House.

Sullivan George J., lab., r. 72 S. Benton.

Sullivan George T., agent fast freight line, r. 321 S. Alabama.

Sullivan Hanora, (wid.) r. 191 Meek.

Sullivan H. H., grocer and produce dealer, 76 W. Washington, r. 60 N. California.

Sullivan James, works, Rolling Mill, r. cor. Merrill and Missouri.

Sullivan James, brakeman, C. & I. J. R. R., bds. 61 S. Noble.

Sullivan James, lab., r. cor. Helen and Georgia.

Sullivan Johanna, servant, Palmer House.

Sullivan John, lab., r. 5 Bates.

Sullivan John, lab., r. 79 S. East.

Sullivan John, yardman, P. C. & St. L. R. R.

Sullivan John, lab., r. 279 S. West.

Sullivan John, lab., r. 364 W. North.

Sullivan John, plasterer, r, Coburn, bet. East and New Jersey.

Sullivan J. B, (S. & Drew) r. 84 E. Pratt.

Sullivan Maggie Miss, chambermaid, Spencer House. .

Sullivan Margaret, servant, Spencer House.

Sullivan Michael D., railroader, r. 150 Meek.

Sullivan Pat. F., lab., r. 4 Oriental.

Sullivan Peter. lab., I. C. & L. Depot, bds. 209 S Illinois.

Sullivan Sylvester, lab., r. 383 E. Ohio.

Sullivan Thomas, works, Arsenal, r. 190 Harrison.

Sullivan T. L., law student, 57 N. Tennessee.

Sullivan William, carpenter, r. 427 N. Tennessee.

Sullivan William, lab., r. 456 S. East.

Sullivan William, attorney at law, over 47 E. Washington, r. 410 N. Meridian,

Sullivan Wm. J., brakeman I. C. & L. R. R., r. 424 E. Vermont.

SULLIVAN & DREW, (J. B. S. & J. A. Drew) livery, sale and boarding stables, 10 E. Pearl.

Summers Albert B., carpenter, r. 83 N. California.

Summers Geo. W., (col'd) lab., Clinton bet. New Jersey and East.

Summers William, (col'd) lab., r. 27 Douglass.

Summons Martin, porter H. C. Chandler, r. 144 Douglass.

Sumner Eli J., patent dry kiln, r. 1 E. Pratt.

Sumner William, (W. S. & Co.) r. Cincinnati, O.

Sumner William, plasterer, bds. 422 N. New Jersey.

SUMNER WILLIAM & CO. (W. S. & J. R. Wright) general agents Wheeler & Wilson Sewing Machines, 10 W. Washington.

Surbey Jacob S. (Baker & S.) r. 275 E. South.

Surface Goodwin, r. 38 Christian av.

Surface John M., druggist, bds. 95 Jackson.

Surface Lydia, (wid. John R.) r. 40 Christian av.

Surface Milford, r. 38 Christian av.

Suthard George, telegraph operator, r. 274 E. St. Clair.

Sutherland James W., machinist, 48 Greer.

Sutherland Levi, lab., r. 59 E. McCarty.

Sutter James A., salesman Trade Palace, r. 9 Cherry.

Sutter F., physician, 62 E. Washington, r. 290 Virginia av.

Sutter William, carpenter, r. 294 Liberty.

Sutton Joseph M., plasterer, r. 82 Massachusetts av.

Sutton S. L., engineer, C. C. C. & I. R. R., r. 345 N. Noble.

Suabacher Joseph, (S. & Selig) r. 259 N. Illinois.

Suabb Charles Buttler, (A. Reese & Co.) bds. over 225 W. Washington.

Sward Barbara Miss, servant, 32 N. Mississippi.

Swafford Edward, woodhauler, r. Chesapeake, nr. West. .

Swailes John, stonecutter, r. 42 Henry.

Swain David F., bookkeeper, J. C. Burton & Co.. bds. Depot Dining Hall.

Swain George, clk., People's Dispatch, bds. Macy House.

Swain James, clk., People's Dispatch, bds. Macy House.

Swain J. H., carriage painter, 36 S. Pennsylvania.

Swain Lewis, lab, bds. 61 S. Noble.

Swain Mary J. Mrs., (wid. Rufus) r. 41 Fletcher av.

Swain Sallie Miss, clk., R. Sedgewick, r. 184 N. Tennessee.

Swain W. F., boot and shoe dealer, bds. Depot Dining Hall.

Swank Angie Miss, milliner, Mrs. Thomas, bds. Macy House.

Swank S., cancer physician, r. 50 S. Illinois.

Swarns Marion, teamster, r. 62 Bicking.

Sweeney Eugene, r. 347 N. Winston.

Sweeney H., saloon, 81 S. Illinois, r. same.

Sweeney John, cigarmaker, 39 W. Washington, r. 16 S. Mississippi.

Sweeney Sarah, (wid. Patrick) r. 268 S. Tennessee.

Sweeney Thomas, machinist, Sinker & Co., r. 51 E. McCarty.

H. H. LEE

MAKES A SPECIALTY OF

Choice Green, Black & Japan Teas.

Sweetser George M., city distributing clk. P. O., r. N. Pennsylvania.

Sweetser James N., attorney at law, 21 E. Washington, r. 600 N. Pennsylvania.

SWEETSER JOHN, whol. dealer in wines and liquors, 30 S. Meridian, r. 242 N. Meridian.

Swigert Joseph. merchant policeman, r. 40 Douglass.

Sweinhart Andrew, carriage painter, r. St. Joseph bet. New Jersey and Alabama.

Sweinhart Charles, bds. 379 N. Alabama.

Sweinhart Edmond, shoemaker, r. 132 E. St. Mary.

Sweinhart William, cutter, J. Staub, r. 379 N. Alabama.

Sweinhart W. T., clk., P. C. & St. L. freight office, r. 379 N. Alabama.

Swindler Benjamin F., clk., G. P. Tuttles, bds. 225 N. New Jersey.

Swindler John H., blacksmith, r. 225 N. New Jersey.

Swing Dennis, carpenter, r. cor. North and West.

Swing William W. (S. & Dennis) r. 248 N. West.

Swing & Dennis, (W. W. S. and C. C D.) druggists, 4 Martindale's blk.

Swiss Max, tailor, r. 388 E. Market.

Swœnmeyer Henry, cooper, r. 308 N. Noble.

Swohoda Joseph, cabinetmaker, Western Furniture Co.

Sycrup Henry, grocer and produce dealer, 199 Massachusetts av., r. same.

Sylvester David, street contractor, r. 26 Lockerbie.

Sylvia Marion, coachmaker, 84 N. Alabama.

Sym James, machinist, r. 346 S. Alabama.

TACKETT FRANK M., painter, r. over 248 E. Washington.

Taehan William, railroader, r. 156 Huron.

TAFFE GEORGE, City Marshal, r. 175 Spring.

Taffe Hannibal, day policeman, bds. Palmer House.

Taggart Daniel, woodworker Shaw, L. & C., bds. Pyle House.

Taggart John A., bds. Pyle House.

TAGGART SAMUEL, practical millwright and mill furnisher, 132 S. Pennsylvania, r. 118 N. Mississippi.

Taggert Daniel, bakery, 134 S. Meridian, bds. Pyle House.

Tait b. Mrs., Capital Restaurant, 89 E. Market, r. same.

Talbott Charles H. (Richard & Talbott) r. 19 W. Pratt.

Talbott Gabriel, cooper, r. 166 Blake.

Talbott George, (col'd) lab., r. cor. Broadway and Arch.

Talbott Henry, (col'd) lab., r. Elizabeth.

Tolbott Jane. (wid. William) r. 145 N. Mississippi.

Talbott John M., (Richard & T.) r. 114 N. Tennessee.

Talbott Rev Bishop, r. Tinker, bet. Pennsylvania and Delaware.

Talbott Richard, (Patterson, Moore & Talbott) r. 136 E. North.

Talbott R. A. (Alford, T. & Co.) r. 136 E. North.

TALBOTT W. H., president Gatling Gun Co., r. se. cor. Meridian and Ohio.

Tally George, (col'd) dyer, r. 160 W. Tinker.

Tanner Emily, (wid. David) r. 70 Elizabeth.

Tanner James, hackdriver, r. 70 Elizabeth.

Tanner John L. (T. & Pressel) r. 2 Athon.

Tanner Thomas, lab., Long & Joseph.

TANNER & PRESSEL, (J. S. T. and T. J. P.) furniture repairers and upholsterers, 76 Virginia av.

Tapking John F., machinist, r. 123 N. New Jersey.

Tarbutton John H., clk., P. O., bds. 9 S. Mississippi.

Tarkington J. E., clk. Trade Palace, bds. 216 N. Delaware.

Tarkington John S. (Martindale & T.) r. 272 N. Meridian.

Tarkington W. C. (Hibben, T. & Co.) r. 216 N. Delaware.

Tarkington W. W., clk., bds. 216 N. Delaware.

Tarlton J. A., grocer and produce dealer, cor. Illinois and Seventh, r. N. city limits.

Tarlton John, r. 492 N. Tennessee.

Tate James D., steward, Spencer House.

Tate Robert, horseshoer, John Hitchens, bds. 126 N Broadway.

TATE WARREN, manufacturer of sash, doors, blinds, etc., 38 S. New Jersey, bds Pattison, House.

Tattersoll Joseph, stonecutter, r. 186 Virginia av.

Tavis B. H., cooper, r. 351 N. Noble.

Taylor ——, carpenter, bds. 154 E. St. Clair.

Taylor Ben., railroader, bds. 231 W. South.

Taylor Charles, (col'd) fireman, Palmer House.

Taylor Charles P., clk. P. O., r. 357 N. Pennsylvania.

Taylor David M., cashier Indianapolis National Bank, r. 680 N. Illinois.

Taylor Dorsey, (col'd) lab., r. Lafayette Railroad, bet. Fifth and Sixth.

Taylor Edwin, attorney at law, office 4 Brown's bldg., bds. 251 N Alabama.

Taylor Edwin, (col'd) teamster, bds. 435 N. East.

Taylor Franklin, (Chandler & T.) r. 290 W. Vermont.

Taylor George, (col'd) lab., r. Howard, bet. First and Second.

Taylor George, (col'd) lab., r. 68 N. Missouri.

Taylor George W., carpenter, r. 7 Dacota.

Taylor George W., (col'd) lab., bds. 135 Bright.

Taylor Harvey, civil engineer, r. 492 E. Market.

Taylor Henry, (col'd) lab., r. 143 Bright.

Taylor Isaac, r. 120 Massachusetts av.

Taylor Isaac, architect, 14 Delaware, r. 209 N. Liberty.

Taylor Israel H., bookkeeper, Harrison's bank, r. 397 N. Pennsylvania.

Taylor James, moulder, Eagle Machine Works, r. 296 S. Meridian.

Taylor James B., pianoforte maker, r. 79 N. New Jersey.

Taylor Jesse D., r. 485 S. Meridian.

Taylor John, (col'd) lab., r. Howard, between Fourth and Fifth.

Taylor John H., works Osgood, Smith & Co., r. 82 Garden.

Taylor Julia A., matron, Indiana Institute for Deaf and Dumb.

Taylor J. C., brakeman, bds. 58 Benton.

TAYLOR J. F., architectural and ornamental draughtsman and plasterer, 80 Massachusetts av., r. 61 N. New Jersey.

Taylor L. M. Mrs., r. 389 Virginia av.

Taylor M., fashionable milliner, 6½ W. Washington, bds. Palmer House.

Taylor Mary Mrs., r. 76 Fort Wayne av.

Taylor Mary C., (wid.) Joseph, r. 45 Huron.

Taylor Mary J., (wid. Wm. M.,) r. 168 N. Illinois.

Taylor —— Mrs., r. 11 E. New York.

TAYLOR NAPOLEON B., attorney at law, office, 4 Brown's bldg., r. 251 N. Alabama.

Taylor Oliver, (col'd) cook, r. 225 W. Ohio.

BENHAM BRO'S,

36 East Washington St.,

STATE AGENTS

FOR THE

INDIANAPOLIS MANUFACTURING CO.'S

PIANOS.

Taylor P. T., switchman, J., M. & I. R. R., r. 250 Chestnut.

Taylor Phoebe Mrs. (col'd) r. W. end Rhode Island.

Taylor Q., eating house, 42 Indiana av., r. same.

Taylor Samuel, grocer, 77 E. Market, r. E. North.

Taylor Stephen, (col'd) lab., 14 Rhode Island.

Taylor Sophia Miss, (col'd) r. 232 Blackford.

Taylor Thomas, student North Western Christian University.

Taylor T. B. (Bland & T.) 331 N. Pennsylvania.

Taylor William M., r. 168 N. Illinois.

Taylor Wm, moulder Eagle Machine Works, r. 274 S. Delaware.

Taylor Wm., engineer C. C. & I. C. R. R., bds. 58 Benton.

Taylor W. A., salesman Mooney & Co., r. 266 S. New Jersey.

Taylor W. E., bookkeeper Wheeler Sewing Machine Co., bds., 250 Chestnut.

Tebbee Charles, lab. C. C. & I. C. Depot, r. 39 Meek.

Teckenbrock Christian, blacksmith, r. 16 Henry.

Teckenbrock William H., works T. R & I. R. R., r. 445 S. Meridian.

Tedrow Joseph, salesman Strong, Smith & Co., bds. Little's Hotel.

Teeple Herman, blacksmith, r. 330 Virginia av.

Teeters George, (col'd) lab., r. cor. Ray and Maple.

Teeters Jerry, lab., r. cor. Maple and Ray.

Teeters Sonney, lab., r. 558 Maple.

Teil John, wagonmaker, 423 S. Meridian, r. 396 S. Illinois.

Teine Christian, cigarmaker, r. 553 E. St. Clair.

Tellkamp John, blacksmith, r. 232 S. New Jersey.

Temperly John, carpenter, bds. 82 E. St. Clair.

Temple Carter, (col'd) carpenter, r. 248 Minerva.

Temple Wm., railroader, bds. 62 Bicking.

Templer James, carpenter, r. 2 Dougherty.

Teneyck Edward, fireman, J. M. & I. R. R., r 131 E. South.

Teneyck James, bottler, A Reed, bds. 120 Indiana av.

Teneyck Jerry, boot and shoemaker, 340 W. Washington, r. same.

Teneyck John, railroader, r. 213 N. Missouri.

Teneyck John, shoemaker. r. 120 Indiana av.

Teneyck Sarah, (wid.) r. 131 E. South.

Tenfel Carl, cabinetmaker, bds Court Street Boarding House.

Tenman Wm., varnisher, r. 19 Elm.

Terrill Francis, tailor, W. F. Rupp, r. 131 E. Washington.

Terry James, works Osgood, Smith & Co., bds. 217 S. Illinois.

Terry Joel, (Gibson & T.) r. Washington nr. New Jersey.

Terry J. M., marblecutter, r. 27 New Jersey.

Terry Wm. (col'd) lab., r. 160 Douglass al.

Tersey Eliza Miss, weaver, Merritt & Coughlen.

Terwilliger Alvin, blower, glass works, bds. 88 S. Mississippi.

Test C. S., steward, Indiana Hospital for Insane, r. same.

Tetaz Henry L., huckster, r. 323 N. Alabama.

Tewell Ezra Y., piano tuner, bds. 236 N. East.

Thalman Isaac, (C. E. Geisendorff & Co.) r. 330 W. New York.

Thalman Isaac, sr., r. 324 E. Ohio.

Thalman John, baker, 75 N. Alabama, r. same.

Thatcher James, works Osgood, Smith & Co., r. 56 Eddy.

Thatcher Jasper, plowhandle bender, r. 168 Buchanan.

Thatcher John, lab., bds. 27 Hahn.

Thatcher Rebecca, (wid.) r. 182 Meek.

Thatcher William, lab., r. 182 Meek.

THATCHER W. P., steward Indiana Surgical Institute, r. same.

Thatcher W. P. Mrs., matron Indiana Surgical Institute, r. same.

Thayer Daniel W., clk., r. 309 E. Market.

Thayer Frank, clk., 7 W. Washington, r. 309 E. Market.

Thayer George V., grocery and produce, 248 E. Washington, r. 498 N. Pennsylvania.

Thayer M. A., (wid.) r. 309 E. Market.

Themeyer Andrew, moulder, r. 428 S. Missouri.

Theobald F., r. 94 E. Washington.

Theodore Thomas, bricklayer, r. 285 N. East.

Thicke Rudolph, harness maker, r. 60 Morris.

Thiesing Joseph, tanner, r. 518 E. Washington.

Third Street Mission Church, Third street, bet. Tennessee and Illinois.

Thomann John, dealer in candies, tobacco, cigars, &c., 306 Virginia av., r. same.

Thomas Albert, blacksmith, S. Raymond.

Thomas Benjamin, finisher Woolen Mills, r. 26 Douglass.

Thomas Bros., (C. & J. C. T.) grocers, 250 E. Ohio.

Thomas Charles, (T. Bros.) r. 115 N. Noble.

Thomas Daniel L., student, r. 76 Ash.

Thomas Dudley, (col'd) farmer, r. 270 W. Second.

Thomas Frederick, shoemaker, bds. 224 W. Cumberland.

Thomas George, lab., r. 115 N. Noble.

Thomas George, jr., night policeman, r. 115 N. Noble.

Thomas Henry, teamster, r. 160 W. Washington.

Thomas Henry, (col'd) porter, N. Byram.

Thomas Henry P., captain merchant's police, 468 E. Georgia.

Thomas H. H., canvassing agent, r. 44 S. Tennessee.

Thomas James E., bookkeeper Western Union Telegraph, r. 304 E. Georgia.

Thomas John, superintent Rolling Mill, r. 319 S. Meridian.

Thomas John C. (Thomas Bros.) r. 115 N. Noble.

Thomas John Q., student, r. 76 Ash.

Thomas Louis, shoemaker, bds. 224 W. Cumberland.

Thomas L. L., r. 269 S. New Jersey.

Thomas Mary F., doctress, 74½ N. Pennsylvania.

Thomas M. J. Mrs., fashionable milliner, No. 8 W. Washington, r. 704 N. Tennessee.

Thomas Newton, telegraph opearator, bds. 272 Winston.

Thomas O. E., checkman P. C. & St. L. freight depot, r. 69 N. Liberty.

Thomas Oscar, tinner Munson & Johnston, r. cor. New York and West.

Thomas R. Z. (Smith, Reynolds & Thomas) r. 351 E. McCarty.

Thomas Scott, engineer J. M. & I. R. R., bds. 152 Madison av.

Thomas William, bookkeeper, r. 397 E. Georgia.

Thomas Wm., works Stroet R. R. Co., r. 152 Madison av.

Thomas William, (col'd) lab., r. 230 W. Vermont.

Thomas Wm. A. (T. Bros.) r. 115 N. Noble.

Thomas William M., bookkeeper, 38 S. Meridian, r. 397 E. Georgia.

Thompson A. B., clb Bates House.

Thompson A. Mrs , bookstore, 13 N. Pennsylvania, r. 131 N. Alabama.

Thompson D. J., fish market, 107 S. Illinois, r. 55 Massachusetts av.

Thompson E. Mrs., laundress Bates House.

Thompson Eli, (Emerson, Beam & T.) r. 124 N. West.

Thompson Emma Miss, servant, 217 S. Illinois.

Thompson E. P., money order clk. P. O., r. 430 N. Tennessee.

Thompson Frank, (col'd) lab., r. 2 Ann.

Thompson George, lab., Rolling Mill, r. 272 S. Missouri.

Thompson George, (col'd) porter, Palmer House.

Thompson Gideon B., printer, Sentinel office, r. 224 E. Michigan.

Thompson Henry, (col'd) housecleaner, r. 231 W. Ohio.

Thompson James, moulder, Greenleaf & Co., r. 51 Maple.

Thompson James L., clk. W. Clem, r. 353 N. Winston.

Thompson John, blacksmith, r. 14 Dougherty.

Thompson John, engineer, I. C. & L. R. R., r. 393 E. Georgia.

Thompson John, lab., r. 375 W Washington.

Thompson John, saloonkeeper, r. 351 S. Pennsylvania.

Thompson John, (col'd) lab., r. 428 E. St. Clair.

Thompson John W., painter, bds. 276 E. Washington.

Thompson J. G., carpenter, r. 667 N. Illinois.

Thompson J. I., bricklayer, r. 92 Broadway.

THOMPSON J. FRED., proprietor Clipper Saloon, 33 N. Illinois.

Thompson Joseph, moulder, r. 54 Greer.

Thompson Lewis, barber, r. cor. First and Lafayette R. R.

Thompson Milton, carpenter, r. 134 Elen.

Thompson Thomas, lab., bds. 169 S. Tennessee.

Thompson W. Clinton, (T. & Woodburn,) r. 82 N. East.

Thompson William J., stone cutter. r. 31 S. West.

Thompson W. H., harnessmaker, r. 24 S. Delaware.

Thompson W. S., coal screener, r. 280 E. north.

THOMPSON & WOODBURN, (W. C. T. and J. H. W.) physicians and surgeons, 90 N. Illinois.

Thoms Fredrick, (Spiegel, Thoms & Co.) r. 76 N. East.

Thoms Henry, cabinetmaker, Spiegel, Thoms & Co.

Thonison William, physician, 62 Virginia av., r. same.

Thonssen B. E. (Ludorff, L. & Co.) r. 257 N. Mississippi.

Thorn William, helper C. C. & I. C. R. R. shops.

Thorn William, blacksmith, r. Jackson near Cherry.

Thornbrough Allen, policeman, r. 196 N. Mississippi.

Thornbrough John M., clk., 65 S. Illinois, r. same.

Thorne John, meat market, 141 N. Delaware.

Thornley Jasper, machinist, bds. 86 Forest av.

Thornley Orion, machinist, r. 86 Forest av.

Thornton Doc, (col'd) lab., r. Lafayette R. R. bet. Fifth and Sixth.

Thornton Edwin, clk., Bee Hive store, bds. cor. Pratt and Illinois.

Thorny George W., cabinetmaker, r. 173 E. Washington.

Thorpe C. P., commercial traveler, r. 103 N. Alabama.

Thorpe Thomas D, traveling salesman, John Woodbridge, r. 86 E. Pratt.

Thrasher W. M., Prof., N. W. C. University, r. N. of University.

Thretton Eugene, stone mason, r. Chesapeake, nr. West.

Thretton James, stone mason, r. Chesapeake, nr. West.

Throne David, upholster, Hume, Adams & Co., bds. Pyle House.

Thum Charles, lithographer, Braden & Burford, r. 114 Ash.

Thumbert William, shoemaker, r. E. Market.

Thurston C. P., traveler, bds. 79 W. North.

Thurston Edward, expressman, Union Depot.

Thurston Valours, works Emerson, Beam & Co., bds. 180 N. Missouri.

Thurston W. B., jr., clk. 96 Virginia av., r. 79 W. North.

Thurston Wm. B. (Maxwell, Fry & T.) r. r. 79 W. North.

Tibbetts J. I., clk. William W. Wallace, 441 N. Illinois, bds. same.

Tibbi Charles, lab., C. C. & I. C. R. R.

Tierny Martin, machinist, r. 26 Maple.

Tiffany George, traveling agent, Chandler & Co., r. 184 N. Tennessee.

Tilbeny Nehan, works J. H. McKendry, r. 492 N. Mississippi.

TILFORD J. M., Sup't Indianapolis Printing and Pub. Co., r. College av.

Tilford Samuel, r. 95 Broadway.

Tills Benjamin R., carpenter, r. 213 N. Pennsylvania.

Tills Charles, carriage painter, bds. 84 Massachusetts av.

Tilly Herman, printer, Daily Telegraph, r. 17 N. East.

Tilt T. C., salesman, 108 S. Meridian, r. 201 Meek.

Timmons Patrick, delivery man, Frank Wright, r. cor. Minerva and New York.

Tindall Norman, lumber dealer, r. 33 Vine.

Tindall William, wagon maker, r. 33 Vine.

Tiny Margrette, (wid.) r. 70 Railroad.

Tippa James, plasterer, r. over 346 E. Washington.

Tisdale T. P. (Burnham & T.) r. cor. New York and Meridian.

Titcomb Daniel, agent Bigelow Mining Co., r. 183 N. Tennessee.

Toal C. C., clk. Paris Store, bds. Macy House.

Tobias F. L., messenger U. S. Express Co., bds. National Hotel.

Tobin Thomas, moulder Eagle Machine Works, r. 1 Ann.

Tobin Thomas H., lab., r. 474 S. West.

Tobin William, clk., 116 S. Meridian, bds. 424 S. West.

Todd, Carmichael & Williams, (C. N. Todd, J. D. Carmichael and D. G. Williams) whol. and retail dealers in books, stationery, etc., Glenn's blk.

Todd Charles N. (T. C. & W.) r. 228 N Tennessee.

Todd Frank O. (T. & Hoff) r. 19 Massachusetts av.

Todd H. M., salesman New York Store, bds. 65 N. New Jersey.

Todd John M. (J. T. & Co.) r. 31 N. Bright.

TODD JOHN M. & CO. (J. M. T., T. J. Breedlove and C. M. Breedlove) real estate agents, 24½ E. Washington.

Todd R. N. (Todd & Bigelow) r. 78 W. Market.

Todd Samel, fish stand, 107 S. Illinois, r. same.

Todd Samuel A., lab., r. 60 Bright.

TODD & BIGELOW, (R. N. Todd and J. K. Bigelow) physicians, rooms 3 and 4 McCunt's blk.

Todd & Hoff, (F. O. T. and J. E. H.) 19 Massachusetts av.

Toland Kate Mrs., chamber maid Neiman House.

Tomlinson James M. (T. & Cox) r. 410 N. Meridian.

Tomlinson Stephens, r. 27 W. Ohio.

TOMLINSON & COX, (J. M. T. and W. C. C.) druggists, 18 E. Washington.

Tompkins Frank M., lab., bds. 291 Massachusetts av.

Tompkins J. H. F., bookkeeper, Shaw, Lippincott & Conner, r. 291 Massachusetts av.

Tompkins William B., clk., bds. 291 Massachusetts av.

Tonlin Newton, bds. 18 S. Pennsylvania.

Tool John, bartender, Senate Saloon.

Toole John, works Osgood, Smith & Co., bds. Ray House.

Toole Martin, mechanic, r. 281 S. East.

TOUSEY GEORGE, president Indiana National Bank, r. 415 N. Meridian.

Tousey Oliver, (Byram, Cornelius & Co.) r. 182 N. Meridian.

Tousey Omer, salesman, 108 S. Meridian, bds. 786 N. Illinois.

Tousey Ralph, agent Life and Fire Ins. Co., Nos. 2 and 3 Odd Fellows' Hall, r. cor. Tennessee and Third.

Tousey N. G., (Lesh, T. & Co.) 359 N. Illinois.

Tout Nancy C., (wid. Henry F.) r. 336 N. West.

Tout William M., bricklayer, r. 625 N. Meridian.

Touts Peter, wagonmaker, r. West Indianapolis.

Town August, blacksmith, Eagle Machine Works, r. 276 S. Delaware.

Townley George E., bookkeeper, Fred P. Rush, bds. Union Depot Dining Hall.

Townsend A. G., (wid.) confectionery, 321 E. Market, r. same.

Townsend Mrs., r. 142 S. East.

Tracy M. O., (M. O. T. & Co.) bds. 237 E. South.

TRACY M. O. & CO., (M. O. T. & M. D. Losey) publishers and dealers in engravings, 7 Martindale's Blk.

TRADE PALACE, N. R. Smith & Co., proprietors, 26 and 28 W. Washington.

Trask George R., ag't American Express Co., r. 735 N. Meridian,

Trask John F., night policeman, r. 25 Greer.

Traub Charles, painter, r. 201 Jackson.

Traub Conrad, cistern builder, r. 111 Ft. Wayne av.

Traub Israel, grocer and produce dealer, 500 N. Alabama, r. same.

Traub Jacob, painter, r. 500 N. Alabama.

Traub John, confectioner, r. 183 Madison av.

Travan William, pastor African M. E. church, r. 125 N. California.

TRAVER'S BEE HIVE, George M. Traver proprietor, nw. cor. Washington and Meridian.

TRAVER GEORGE M., dealer in dry goods, cloaks and shawls. nw. cor. Washington and Meridian, bds. 112 N. Pennsylvania.

Travis Albert, night policeman, r. 180 N. Missouri.

Tray Thomas, lab. r. 8 Willard.

Trayser L. L., piano manufacturer, 82 E. Market, r. same.

Treat A. A., r. 25 W. Pratt.

Treat A. J., (T. & Claflin) r. 246 N. Meridian.

Treat H. P., Machinist, r. 188 S. Mississippi.

TREAT & CLAFLIN, (A. J. T. and C. C. C.) merchant tailors, 30 N. Pennsylvania,

Treder John, stone mason, r. 310 E. New York.

Trefy Gottlieb Rev., pastor German M. E. church, r. 185 E. New York.

Treon Kate, Mrs., r. 29 S. West.

Trepe Henry, works Osgood, Smith & Co., r. 435 S. Illinois.

Trigg Spencer C., miller, works Sohl Gibson & Co., r. 359 W. Washington.

Troemper John, r. 182 E. Washington.

Troessler William, machinist, Eagle Machine Works, r. 276 W. Michigan.

Trope John, confectioner, r. 185 Madison av.

Trotter John, lab., r. 65 N. East.

TROUTMAN JAMES B., messenger A. M. U. Ex. Co., r. 77 W. Second.

TROXELL J. R., attorney, 4 Talbott & New blk., r. 126 Virginia av.

Truckess John, blacksmith shop, 60 Kentucky av.

Trueblood James capitalist, r. 347 N. Delaware.

BENHAM BRO'S,

36 East Washington St.,

PIANOS, ORGANS, MUSIC.

Best Goods! Lowest Prices!

Trueblood Lidy Miss, (col'd) bds. 175 Douglass al.

Trueblood L. D., clk. 298 N. Pennsylvania, bds. 347 N. Delaware.

Trueblood Newton A., traveling agent, r. 483 N. Mississippi.

Truex Henry, expressman, bds. 132 Maple.

Trumbs Calvin B., joiner, works cor. Tennessee and Georgia, r. 35 Indiana av.

Trump Jacob, brickmason, r. 535 Fort Wayne av.

Trusler Nelson, (Mason & T.) r. 162 N. Illinois.

Trusler Thomas J., Deputy Secretary of State, r. Western av., nr. Christian av.

Trusmiple Frederick, lab., r. 33 Blake.

Tubb ——, lab., r. Tennessee, north of Seventh.

Tuchong Michael, shoemaker, 313 E. Washington.

Tucker ——, r. 50 Fletcher av.

Tucker Duane H., traveling agent, r. 285 N. Michigan.

Tucker H. S. (T. & Smith) r. 306 N. Delaware.

Tucker Joshua, with Hahn & Bals, r. 276 N. Tennessee.

Tucker Maggie Miss, 6 Pearl al.

Tucker Richard S., manufacturer of patent socks, r. 187 W. South.

Tucker Washington H., foreman Water's Steam Factory, r. 430 N. Mississippi.

TUCKER & SMITH, (H. S. T. and Wm. S.) dealers in cloaks, white goods, etc., 9 N. Pennsylvania.

Tuhey Patrick, works Rolling Mill, bds. 300 S. Tennessee.

Tuhm Charles, lithographer, r. 77 Oak.

Tully Edward M., clk. 40 S. Meridian, bds. 60 W. Market.

Tully Eliza A, Mrs., boarding house, 60 W. Market.

Tupper Frank C., huckster, r. 79 Elizabeth.

TURBYVILLE ROBERT, prop'r, farmers and drovers hotel, W. Indianapolis.

Turk Charles, blacksmith, r. 315 Virginia av.

Turk John, laborer, r. Coburn, bet. New Jersey and East.

H. H. LEE'S

WHOLESALE PRICES FOR

TEAS, COFFEES & SUGARS,

ARE THE SAME EACH DAY

As are quoted in the

CINCINNATI DAILY PAPERS.

TURNER A. H., with Nickerson & Downey, r. over 6 W. Washington.

Turner Augustus, (col'd) barber, r. cor. Georgia and Tennessee.

Turner Burton, (col'd) carpenter, r. 174 Douglass al.

Turner C. L., traveler, Indianapolis Journal, r. 115 E. Ohio.

Turner Gerhard, lab., r. 14 Michigan rd.

Turner Hall, 130 E. Maryland.

Turner James, lab., r. 69 Elizabeth.

Turner James, r. 66 Indiana av.

Turner Kate H. Miss, teacher, Fourth Ward School.

Turner Nathan, (col'd) cook, Bates House, r. 232 Blackford.

Turner Moses, teamster, r. 269 N. East.

Turner Nancy Mrs., seamstress, r. 219 N. West.

Turner Robert, lab., r. 185 W. Second.

Turner William, bricklayer, r. 416 N. New Jersey.

Turner William, teamster, r. 269 N. East.

Turner W. H., coal office, 19 Circle, r. cor. Circle and Meridian.

Tuschong Michael, shoemaker, bds. 416 W. Washington.

TUTEWILER BROTHERS, (J. W. T., H. W. T., and C. W. T.) stoves, tinware and house furnishing goods, 74 E. Washington.

Tutewiler Charles W., (T. Bros.) r. 85 Massachusetts av.

Tutewiler Henry, plasterer, r. 85 Massachusetts av.

Tutewiler Henry W., (T. Bros.) r. 166 N. Alabama.

Tutewiler John W., (T. Bros.) r. 85 Massachusetts av.

Tuttle B. T., merchandise broker, r. 496 N. Meridian.

Tuttle G. P., dealer in teas, coffees, sugar and fancy groceries, 1 Martindale's blk., r. 334 N. Meridian.

Tuttle Orien, reel driver, engine No. 1, r. 261 W. Washington.

TWINING WILLIAM, manager Life Association of America, office, Sentinel bldg., bds. Bates House.

Tyer Charles W., lockmaker, r. 139 S. East.

Tyer Geo. W., freight conductor, J. C. & L. R. R., r. 139 S. East.

Tyler Charles, billiard tender, 39 E. Washington, r. 239 N. Illinois.

Tyler C. M., clk., Court House, r. 239 S. Illinois.

Tyler S. E. Miss, with Bowen, Stewart & Co., r. 152 N. Meridian.

Tyler S. S., engineer, bds. 164 W. Maryland.

Tyler Winfield, clk., C. C. C. & I. R. R., r. ne. cor. Mississippi and Market.

Tyner Albert H., clk., P. O., bds. 204 N. Illinois.

Tyner C. E., lab., r. 563 E. St. Clair.

Tyre Charles, machinist, r. 137 S. East.

Tyre Mat., engineer, C. C. & I. C. R. R., r. 139 S. East.

Tyson Ella S. Mrs., teacher, City Academy, bds. 71 W. Michigan.

UBANK ROWLAND, carriagepainter, r. N. Pennsylvania nr. Tinker.

Uhl & Durham, (P. U. and H. E. D.) cigars and tobacco, 19 S. Meridian.

Uhl Matthew physician, office 52 S. Pennsylvania, r. same.

Uhl Peter, (P. & Durham) r. 118 E. Pratt.

Uffman Henry, cigarmaker, with Charles C. Hunt, bds. 89 N. Delaware.

Ulich J. G., salesman, New York Store, bds. 89 S. Illinois.

Underhill Anne A. (wid.) r. 355 N. Alabama.

Union Fire Company, No. 3 engine house, 125 E. South.

UNION HALL BOARDING HOUSE, 135 E. Washington, Wm. Dell, prop'r.

UNION HOUSE sw. cor. Illinois and South; Stephen Sautler, prop'r.

UNION NOVELTY WORKS Manufacturing Co., cor St. Clair and Canal, S. C. Frink, President, H. A. Moore, Secretary.

Union Starch Factory, E. end New York, F. W. Piel, proprietor.

Union Mission Chapel, Blackford, bet. Vermont and Michigan.

United Brethren Church, New Jersey cor. Ohio.

United Presbyterian Church, Ohio bet. Delaware and Pennsylvania.

Universalist Church, ne. cor. Michigan and Tennessee.

Unversaw Andrew, r. 125 E. Merrill.

Unversaw John, meat market, 48 Virginia av., r. 345 S. Alabama.

Updegraff Daniel, saloon, cor. St. Clair and Plum, r. same.

Updegraff Geo., bartender, 255 E. Washington.

Updyke John, plasterer, r. 154 S. Noble.

Updyke Samuel, plasterer, r. 107 Meek.

Upfold Rev. Bishop, r. 477 N. Pennsylvania.

Urban John, lab., r. cor. West and First.

VAILE HENRY, lab., 313 N. Noble.

Vail Sidney, teacher, Deaf and Dumb Asylum, r. E. Washington, nr. Asylum.

Vain John, cooper, r. 126 Union.

Vajen Frank, salesman, 21 W. Washington, r. 128 N. Meridian.

Vajen John H., (J. H. V. & Co.) r. 128 N. Meridian.

Vajen John H., jr., messenger, Citizens' Bank, bds. 128 N. Meridian.

VAJEN J. H. & CO., (J. H. V., J. S. Hildebrand and J. L. Fugate) dealers in hardware, cutlery, etc., 21 W. Washington.

Vajen William, salesman, 21 W. Washington, r. 128 N. Meridian.

Valentine W. H., hoopskirts and corsetts, 34 W. Washington, r. 115 N. Illinois.

Vallmer John, stone mason, r. 474 S. Tennessee.

Van Antwerp G. W., blacksmith, 287 E Washington, r. 175 N. East.

Van Benthuysen J. H., fish market, 149 Virginia av., r. 145 Virginia av.

Van Bergen W. H., carpenter, r. 75 W. Michigan.

Van Blaricum J. M., carriage and wagon manufacturer, 231 W. Washington, r. same.

Van Buren F. A. (Wiley & Van Buren) r. 287 E. Market.

Van Camp C., bookkeeper, bds. 36 California.

Van Camp G. C. (V. & Jackson) r. 36 California.

Van Camp & Jackson, (G. C. V. & T. B. J.) fruit and commission dealers, 69 W. Washington.

Vancampen Wm., brakeman J. M. & I. R. R., r. 144 Union.

Vance George W., carpenter, 226 Dougherty.

Vance John J., watchmaker and jeweler, 410 S. Meridian, bds. 327 E. Vermont.

Vance Mary, (wid.) r. 445 E. Washington.

Vance Samuel C., with Woollen Webb & Co., r. E. end of Market.

Vance Thos. (col'd) r. Howard, bet. Third and Fourth.

Vance Thomas, cabinetmaker, r. 327 E Vermont.

Vance Thomas P., clk., r. 101 Forest av.

Vance W. W., passenger conductor I. C. & L. R R., r. 165 S. Alabama.

Vandegrift W. H., clk. I. C. & L. R. R., bds. Palmer House.

Vanderbilt H. M., agent Domestic Sewing Machine, bds. 496 N. Mississippi.

Vandervort J. O. P., miller at Starch Factory, r. 56 Michigan rd.

23

BENHAM BRO'S,

36 East Washington St.,

PUBLISHERS OF

BENHAM'S MUSICAL REVIEW,

MONTHLY, $1.00 PER ANNUM.

Van Dusan C., roadmaster I. C. & R. R., r. 288 E. South.

Vandyke W. W., with Merrill & Field.

Vandyne G., clk. Hume, Adams & Co., r. 38 W. North.

Vanhorn Nicholas, lawyer, r. 85 Ash.

Vanhouten Cornelius, lab., r. 272 E. North.

Vanhouten J. H., clk., r. 272 E. North.

Vankamp John. jr., carpenter, r. 161 Spring.

Vankamp John, sr., carpenter, r. 161 Spring.

Vankeuren Edward, carpenter, r. 136 W. First.

Vankirk L. M., glass blower, bds. 164 W. Maryland.

VanLandingham Elizabeth, (wid.) r. cor. Vine and Broadway.

VanLandingham L., secretary Gas Company, r. 276 N. Alabama.

Vanmeter B. R. Dr., Indiana Surgical Institute, r. same.

Vannattan Martha, (wid.) r. 133 Rail road.

Vannoy Ward, plasterer, r. 134 W. Michigan.

Van Pelt Louis, auctioneer, r. 18 Fletcher av.

Vanplake Eli, soldier United States Arsenal.

Vanshort J., hostler, bds. 18 Pennsylvania.

Van Siclen Alexander, insurance agent, with E. B. Martindale, bds. R. B. Ducan.

Vanstan John, shoemaker, r. 239 S. Alabama.

Vantyle Abraham, master mechanic C. & I. J. R. R. shops, r. 328 E. Georgia.

Vanvleet Drucilla, Mrs., seamstress, over 272 E. Market.

Vanwenen B. V., carpenter, r. S. E. cor. Ohio and Illinois.

Vanzandt William, cigarmaker, bds. 166 E. Market.

Varner James B., bottler. Wm. Smith, r. 42 Rose.

Varney Carrie. (wid.) r. 291 E. Ohio.

Vater Thomas J. (V. & King) r. 339 N. Tennessee.

VATER & KING, (T. J. V. & J. K.) proprietors Equity Foundry and Machine Works, cor. Canal and Georgia.

Vaughn Dennis, carpenter, r. 75 W. Louisiana.

Vaughn Dennis, inspector I. C. & L. R. R.

Vaughn George W., boarding house, 44 S. Tennessee.

Vaughn Jacob, carpenter, r. 548 N. Mississippi.

Vaustan John, boot and shoe manufacturer, 10 Virginia av., r. 239 S. Alabama.

Vawter Rebecca J. (wid) r. 37 Ellen.

Vawter John A., produce dealer, r. 575 S. Meridian.

Veatch James C., Adjutant General, office State building, r. Rockport Indiana.

Veazey William, r. 146 E. McCarty.

Vehling Fritz, tailor, 170 E. Washington, bds. 191 S. New Jersey.

Vehling Frederick, groceries and produce, 197 E. South, r. same.

Vehling Henry, Cabinet Maker's Union, r. 296 E. Washington.

Vehling Henry, chairmaker, bds. 53 Harrison.

Velvit Cornelius, works rolling mill, bds. 78 W. McCarty.

Verity S. T., piano tuner and repairer, r. 42 Huron.

Verrill H. A., baggage master, P. C. & St. L. R. R.

Verrill William, lab., P. C. & St. L. freight depot.

Vert Josephine, (wid) r. 77 Lockerbie.

Vestal J. N., printer Journal office, r. N. Blackford.

Vestal Newton J., printer works Journal office, r. 140 Bright.

Vick Abbie (col'd wid) r. 248 W. Ohio.

Vickers Edwin, salesman, 127 S. Meridian, r. 303 S. Meridian.

VICKERS W. B., (Harding & V.) editor Saturday Evening Mirror, r. 230 E. New York.

Victor Julius, (L. & V.) bds. Kentucky av.

Victor Kate Mrs. (wid. LeFaut) r. 166 N. Mississippi.

Vielhaber D., boot and shoe manufacturer, 204 E. Washington, r. same.

Vielhaber Daniel, works glass works, bds. Union Hall.

Vielhaber Gustave, shoemaker, 204 E. Washington, r. same.

Viernickel Joseph, bakery and confectionery, 285 E. Washington, r. same.

Vieweg August, painter, r. 125 E. Washington.

Vinable Isam, (col'd) lab., r. 116 Ash.

Vince William, lab., r. 217 Coburn.

Vincent Ann A. (wid.) r. 109 Railroad.

Vincent William A., expressman, r. 61 Russell.

VINCENT WILLIAM H., carpenter and builder, shop rear of 178 N. Davidson, r. same.

Vineyard Thomas, switchman, r. 26 S. West.

VINNEDGE, JONES & CO. (J. D. Vinnedge, A. Jones and W. S. Armstrong) whol. dealers in boots and shoes, 66 S. Meridian.

Vinnedge J. A., r. 704 N. Illinois.

Vinnedge J. A. (Wright & V.) r. se. of city limits.

Vinnedge J. D. (Vinnedge, Jones & Co.) r. 144 E New York.

Vinton A. E. (Keifer & V.) r. N. Meridian, cor. Fifth.

Vinton M. E., clk. Salsbury Paper Mill, bds. N. Meridian, cor. Fifth.

Virgil Henry, with Adams Express Co., r. 164 N. Alabama.

Voegtle Jacob, house furnishing goods, 103 E. Washington.

Vogel Frederick, lab., r. 446 S. West.

Vogel Henry, carpenter, r. 523 E. Market.

Voght Barnard, leader orchestra Academy of Music, r. 242 E. Ohio.

Voght Fred, (H. H. Langenberg & Co.) r. 246 W. Washington.

Voght Joseph, clk. National Hotel billiard rooms, bds. at National Hotel.

Voight David, beltmaker, r. 535 S. Meridian.

Voight Frederick, city express wagon, r. 111 N. Noble.

Voight H. W. (W. J. Holliday & Co.) r. 225 N. Mississippi.

Vollrath Charles, cabinetmaker, works 246 S. Meridian, bds. 64 S. East.

Vollrath Charles A., carpenter, r. 79 S. Liberty.

Volmer Godfrey, butcher, bds. 207 W. Michigan.

Vondergotten Henry, barber, shop 140 S. Illinois, r. 279 N. Liberty.

Vondersaar Wendell, blacksmith and wagonmaker, 144 Fort Wayne av., r. 146 Fort Wayne av.

VONEGUT CLEMENS, dealer in hardware and cutlery, 184 and 186 E. Washington, r. 508 E. Market.

Von Lindenmann Berhard, lab., r. E. city limits.

Voorhees A. L., (wid.) r. 135 N. Illinois.

Voss G. H., (V. & Davis) attorney at law, r. 590 N. Illinois.

Voss & Davis, attorneys at law, 3 Talbott & New's blk. N. Pennsylvania.

Voylie Andrew, clk. 13 N. Pennsylvania, r. 131 N. Alabama.

Voylie Charles, clk. 13 N. Pennsylvania, r. 131 N. Alabama.

WACHS CHARLES, baker, r. 17 Ft. Wayne av.

Wachtstetter Charles, barkeeper, 154 W. Washington, bds. same.

WACHTSTETTER JACOB, saloon, 154 W. Washington, r. same.

Wachtstetter Matthew, bds. 145 W. Washington.

Wacker August, works A. Wiegand, bds. same.

Waddle Samuel, lab., r. 114 Railroad.

Wade Samuel, (col'd) barber, 249 E. South, r. same.

Wade Walker, (col'd) lab., r. 31 Hosbrook.

Wageman Gustave, (Weinberger & W.) r. 88 Union.

Wagner Charles, (Sprengpfeil & Co.) bds. 42 S. Liberty.

Wagner Charles, lab., r. 218 S. New Jersey.

Wagner Conrad, lab., r. 561 S. Meridian.

Wagner C. W. B., foreman rolling mill, bds. California House.

Wagner David, fireman, C. C. C. & I. R. R., bds. 315 E. New York.

Wagner Fred., works J. M. & I. depot, r. 204 Union.

Wagner Geo., with Haskit, Morris & Co., r. 82 S. Delaware.

Wagner George, lab., r. 82 S. Delaware.

Wagner Gottlieb, butcher, works 194 S. Illinois, bds. same.

Wagner G. W., loan office, 66 N. Illinois, r. same.

Wagner Henry, lab., r. 228 N. Winston.

Wagner J. H. lab., r. 62 Bicking.

Wagner Martin, asst. porter, 108 S. Meridian, bds. 23 W. Georgia.

Wagner Theodore A., salesman, C. M. Raschig, bds. Pyle House.

Wagoner Joseph, teamster, r. 191 N. Liberty.

Wagoner Louis, (col'd) cooper.

Wahn Christian, currier, r. 467 S. New Jersey.

Wains Oliver P., carpenter, r. 78 E. New York.

Wainwright Samuel, tinshop, 18 W. Maryland, bds. 278 N. Mississippi.

Wainwright W. H., lettercarrier, r. 23 W. St. Joseph.

WAKEFIELD WM., (Bowman & W.) r. 61 N. Illinois.

Walden Treadwell Rev., rector, St. Paul's Cathedral, r. 257 N. Delaware.

BENHAM BRO'S,

36 East Washington St.,

SHEET MUSIC, VIOLINS,

GUITARS, STRINGS, &c.

Walden Wm. (col'd) whitewasher, r. 223 N. West.

Waldo Charles, tailor, 19 W. Washington, r. 9 E. Washington.

Waldo George, r. 115 W. New York.

Waldo George, tinner, Munson & Johnston.

Waldo Mary Mrs. (wid.) r. 258 N. Mississippi.

Waldo William P., painter, r. 31 Vine.

Waldsman Frederick, pastry cook at Union Depot, r. 133 N. Liberty.

Walk Anthony E, shoemaker, r. E. Market.

Walk Julius C., watchmaker, Bingham & Co., r. 249 W. Washington.

Walk Louis, boarding house, 28 W. Georgia.

Walker A., engineer, r. 128 E. St. Mary.

Walker Austin, (col'd) barkeeper, cor. Tennessee and Kentucky av., r. 147 W. North.

Walker Alex S., general agent, Wheeler & Wilson Sewing Machines, 10 W. Washington, r. 81 W. Vermont.

Walker Edward, stencilcutter, 25 W. Washington, up stairs, r. same.

Walker Frank, (col'd) lab., r. African al. bet. Sixth and Seventh.

Walker George, (col'd) barber, bds. 225 N. Tennessee.

Walker Henry, with McCord & Wheatley, r. 41 Elm.

WALKER H. H., state agent Home Insurance Co., of New York, 3 Martindale's blk., r. se. cor. Western and Home avs.

Walker Isaac, breaksman, r. 173 N. Winston.

Walker Jacob, (col'd) barber, works M. Mason, bds. 207 W. North.

Walker John, (col'd) lab., bds. 355 W. Washington.

Walker John C., painter, r. 48 Bright.

Walker John W., carpenter, bds. 316 E. North.

Walker Joseph B., physician, 276 N. Mississippi, r. same.

Walker L. P. (L. P. W. & Co.) bds. Bates House.

WALKER L. B. & CO., Domestic Sewing Machine Co., 58 N. Illinois.

Walker Mary W. Mrs., dealer in notions and dress trimmings, 40 S. Illinois, bds. Ray House.

THE CHINA TEA STORES

Are very handsomely decorated with

Accurate Views and Scenes

OF

CHINESE LIFE AND SCENERY.

Call and see them before leaving the City

Walker Nathan A. Rev., r. 66 Christian av.

Walker S. W., engineer, I. C. & L. R. R., bds. Ray House.

Walker T. R., salesman, 129 S. Meridian, r, 129 N. Illinois.

Walker Webster, works, Indianapolis Wagon and Agricultural Works, bds. 211 S. Illinois.

Walker William, lab., works California House, bds. same.

Wall A. H., carpenter, r. 278 McCarty.

Wall Charles E., oculist and aurist, 21½ W. Maryland, r. same.

Wall Michael, fireman, I. C. & L. R. R.

Wall Thomas, flagman, r. 154 Stevens.

Wall Thomas, carpenter, bds. Little Hotel.

Wall Thomas, wiper I. C. & L. R. R. shops.

Wallace Andrew, whol. grocer and commission merchant, 52 and 54 S. Delaware, r. 84 N. Delaware.

Wallace Andrew, stonecutter, Scott & Nicholson.

Wallace Frank, works Paper Mill.

Wallace G. C., correspondent, Josselyn Bros. & Co., r. 38 Cherry.

Wallace H. Mrs., r. 167 S. Alabama.

Wallace James, tinsmith, works McOuats, bds. 38 S. Tennessee.

Wallace James, copyist, r. 219 N. Davidson.

Wallace James, stonecutter, r. 167 S. Alabama.

Wallace James, F., physician, McOuats blk, r. 19 W. Maryland.

Wallace Jane, (wid.) r. 158 W. Washington.

Wallace Joseph A., clk., 105 Ash.

Wallace John, shoemaker, r. 329 N. Noble.

Wallace Johnson, stonecutter, r. 167 S. Alabama.

Wallace Jonathan, shoemaker, r. 193 Bates.

Wallace L. A. Mrs., dressmaker, 26 W. Maryland, r. same.

Wallace Oliver J., brickmason, r. 219 N. Davidson.

Wallace Samuel, bricklayer, r. 35 Vine.

Wallace Sarah, (wid. Alex. G.) r. 105 Ash.

Wallace Susan, teacher, Indiana Institution for the Deaf and Dumb.

Wallace William, machinist, r. 258 S. Missouri.

WALLACE WILLIAM, lawyer, No. 4 Odd Fellows' Hall, r. 285 N. Delaware.

Wallace William P., manufacturer and dealer in cigars and tobacco, 28 W. Louisiana, r. 160 E. Market.

WALLACE WILL W., drugs, groceries and liquors, 441 N. Illinois, r. same.

WALLACE W. W., dealer in monuments and tombstones, 120 S. Illinois, r. 2 Indiana av.

Walle John, blacksmith, r. 244 S. Delaware.

Walle Nathan, blacksmith, r. 73 S. Liberty.

Walle M., blacksmith, r. 73 S. Liberty.

Waller Bernhard, boot and shoe shop, 151 Indiana av., r. same.

WALLICK J. F., sup't Western Union Telegraph Co., room 8 Blackford's Block, r. 36 W. Michigan.

Wallingford Catherine Mrs., r. 456 N. Delaware.

Wallingford Florence Miss, teacher, 9th Ward School, r. 456 N. Delaware.

WALLIS NICHOLAS, wholesale brush manufactory, 17 N. Noble, r. 27 Massachusetts av.

Walls Henry, r. 21 E. North.

Walls Wesley L., printer, Sentinel Office, bds. 307 E. McCarty.

Walpole Esther Mrs., (wid. Thomas D.) r. 410 N. Illinois.

Walpole Luke, r. 410 N. Illinois.

Walpole S. P. Miss, r. 127 N. Meridian.

Walsh Margaret, (wid Thomas) r. 334 S. Alabama.

Walsh Michael, lab., r. 334 S. Alabama.

WALSH W. J., saloon, 294 S. Delaware.

Walsman Fred, painter, Shaw L. & C., r. 133 N. Liberty.

Walter Charles, cabinetmaker, r. 200 N. Mississippi.

Walter G., saloon, 248 W. South r. same.

Walter Jacob, brewer Meikel's brewery, bds. 323 W. Washington.

Walter William, boots and shoes, 51 W. Washington.

Walters Alfred, sign painter, 46 Kentucky av. bds. 30½ N. Pennsylvania.

Walters Henry A., works J. H. McKendry, r. N. Mississippi, bet. First and Second.

Walters James, foreman Osgood, Smith & Co., r. 538 S. Meridian.

Walters Louis, (col'd) lab., r. 184 N. Missouri.

Walters Luther M., Rev., r. 309 S. Meridian.

WALTON H. L., branch office London and New York Publishing Company, 20½ N. Delaware.

Walton John F., pianomaker, r. 30½ N. Pennsylvania.

Wambach John, works rolling mill, bds. 78 W. McCarty.

Wamsley Harvey, carpenter, r. 354 N. West.

Wambach William, r. 78 W. McCarty.

Wampler David, railroader, r. 47 Bates.

Wampler William A., railroader, r. 47 Bates.

Wanderly Henry, brickmason, r. 146 N Davidson.

Wandram William, tailor, r. 406 S. Delaware.

Wands Alexander, restaurant, r. 359 N. Pennsylvania.

Wands Alexander W., machinist, r. ne. cor. Graham and McCarty.

Wands John, shoemaker, r. 47 Huron.

Wands John, boot and shoemaker, 28 S. Delaware, r. 65 Greer.

Wands John jr., 28 S. Delaware, r. 47 Huron.

Wands William, physician, 66 E. Market, r. 330 E. Vermont.

Wanes John, boilermaker, r. 85 S. Pennsylvania.

Wann Henry L., millwright, 132 S. Pennsylvania.

Wanoka Christian, soldier U. S. arsenal.

Ward C. D., attorney at law, Talbott and News blk.

Ward B. Dr., drugs and medicines, 397 N. New Jersey, r. 389 N. New Jersey.

Ward D. L., messenger, American M. U. Express Co., r. 81 Walnut.

Ward H., conductor, T. H. & I. R. R., r. 43 Kentucky av.

Ward Marion, clk., B. Ward, bds, 389 N. New Jersey.

Ward Michael, street car driver, r. 417 Virginia av.

Ward Patrick, traveling agent, Prenatt & O'Connor, r. 195 W. South.

Ward Peter H., attorney, 4 Talbott & New's blk., r. 162 N. New Jersey.

WARD'S PORTABLE GAS, A. F. Noble, prop'r, State of Indiana, 28 Kentucky av.

Warden William, lab, r. terminus Docata.

Ware Kate, (wid. Robert) boarding house, 111 W. South.

Warfield Charles, (col'd) lab., 114 Ash.

Warfield Parker, (col'd) lab., works cor. Forest av. and Jackson.

Warmling Henry, machinist, works 244 S. Pennsylvania, r. 330 S. Delaware.

Warne George, r. 59 W. Maryland.

Warne James P., clk, I. B. & L. freight office, r. 275 S. Noble.

Warne Joseph B. (Mayhew, W. & Co.) r. 59 W. Maryland.

Warneling Henry, machinist, r. 330 S. Delaware.

Warner Augustus, works Jackson, Rider & Co.

Warner Edward, painter, r. 208 W. Vermont.

Warner George, clk., Clipper saloon, r. 66 W. Maryland.

Warner Joseph, lab., r. 234 W. Michigan.

Warner Louis, groceries and provisions, 154 Indiana av.

Warner Marcus, bds. Palmer House.

Warner Sarah J. (wid. John) r. 234 W. Michigan.

Warner Thomas, printer, works Journal office, r. 123 N. West.

Warner William, brickmason, r. 511 N. Mississippi.

Warning William, baker, r. 107 E. Washington.

Warren George S. (J. H. Baldwin & Co.) bds. Spencer House.

Warren Joseph, lab., r. 155 High.

Warren Nathaniel, blower, Glass Works, bds. 147 S. Mississippi.

Warren Simon, lumber dealer, office 27 Massachusetts av., r. 136 E. St. Joseph.

Warren True, works Gas Works, r. 64 S. Alabama.

Warrenberg John, teamster, r. 309 E. New York.

Warrenberg Wm., teamster, r. 325 E. New York.

Washburn Calvin, carpenter, r. 348 N. Winston.

Washington David, (col'd) lab., r. N. Mississippi, bet. Third and Fourth, ws.

Washington George, (col'd) works Novelty Works.

WASHINGTON HALL SALOON, 90 and 92 W. Washington, Philip Farbach, prop'r.

Washington Henry, (col'd) lab., r. 223 E. Michigan.

Washington House, cor. West and Maryland, P. Deitz, prop'r.

Washington J. M. (Alcorn & Co.) r. 27 S. Illinois.

Washington Leroy, (col'd) lab., r. 207 W. North.

Washington Louis, (col'd) lab., r. Lafayette Railroad, bet. Second and Third.

Wasson A. W., veterinary surgeon, 42 E. Maryland, r. 72 E. Maryland.

Wasson Charles K., moulder, bds. 175 S. Tennessee.

H. H. LEE,

Dealer in

Teas, Coffees, Sugars & Spices,

No. 7 ODD FELLOWS HALL

AND

ACADEMY OF MUSIC CORNER.

Wasson Hiram P., clk. Bee Hive Store, bds. 177 S. Tennessee.

Wasson M. E, telegraph operator, I. C. & L. R. R., bds. Union Depot Dining Hall.

Wasson Joel, blacksmith, r. 39 Michigan rd.

Wasson Wm. G., machinist, r. 177 S. Tennessee.

Wasson Wm. P., boot and shoe manufacturer, 175 S. Tennessee, r. same.

Wate Abbie R. Miss, teacher Fourth Ward School, bds. 228 N. East.

Waterman Christian, (Berg & W.) r. cor. South and Tennessee.

Waterman Henry, moulder Greenleaf & Co.

Waterman L. D, physician, 68 N. Pennsylvania, r. 377 N. Delaware.

Waters John G., deputy city clk., r. 86 N. Mississippi.

Waters Morris, lab. T. H. & I. R. R., r. 320 S. West.

Waters Samuel D., lab., r. 57 Oriental.

Watkins Ed., painter, Osgood & Chapman. r. 402 S. Tennessee.

Watson E. C., cooper, r. al. bet. New York and Ohio, and Pennsylvania and Mississippi.

Watson Elmer W., breakman, r. 536 E. Georgia.

Watson James, engineer I. C. & L. R. R., r. 92 Bates.

Watson John C., lab., r. 27 Hahn.

Watson John W., machinist, r. 607 E. Washington.

Watson Joseph S, printer, 79 W. Washington, r. 207 W. Maryland.

Watson Morris, musician, r. N. Missouri near Ohio.

Watson Robert J., breakman, r. 607 E. Washington.

Watson Samuel W., bookkeeper Harrison's Bank, r. 504 N. Delaware.

Watson Wm., lab., bds. 68 W. South.

Watson Wm. P., first bookkeeper First National Bank, r. 421 N. Illinois.

Watten John, railroader, r. 138 S East.

Watts William, mantle setter, r. 458 E. Georgia.

Watz Louis, blacksmith, bds. Globe house.

Waugh Daniel, machinist, r. 49 Ellen.

Waugh Daniel, bolt cutter, C. C. & I. C. R. R. shops.

Waugh Henry, lab., C. C. C. & I. R. R.

Way Alfred, guitar teacher, r. cor. Illinois and Fifth.

Way Amanda M. Miss., editress Western Independent, 10 S. Pennsylvania, r. same.

WAY A. M. & LOU, manufacturers of regalias of all orders, 10 S. Pennsylvania.

Way Lou Miss, (A. M. and Lou Way) r. 10 S. Pennsylvania.

Way Stephen, cutter, W. N. Crain bds. Pyle House.

Way Truman, switchman, r. 296 S. Alabama.

Way William, baggage master, I. C. & L. R. R., bds. 296 S. Alabama.

Wayne C., foreman, D. Yandes jr.

Wayne John, works Jackson Rider & Co.

Weakley G. W., operator, W. U. Telegraph, bds. 35 Virginia av.

Weakley J. A., stoves and tin ware, 191 W. Washington, r. 159 W. New York.

Weakley Robert, tinner, r. 179 W. New York.

WEANER JOHN, proprietor Washington House No's 181 and 183 S. Meridian.

Weatherbee A. F., works Jackson Rider & Co.

Weaver Emma F., dressmaker, bds. 199 N. Illinois.

Weaver Frank W., clk., 39 N. Illinois bds. 233 N. Illinois.

Weaver Fred., carpenter, r. 273 N. Noble.

Weaver George, bricklayer, r. 323 N. Liberty.

Weaver Harry, bootmaker, 5 West Washington, bds 276 N. Liberty.

Weaver James, bootmaker, 5 W. Washington, r. 276 N. Liberty.

Weaver Michael, cooper, r. 55 Hellen.

Weaver Thomas, plasterer, r. 232 S. Missouri.

Weaver William W., (W. and Hedges) r. 233 N. Illinois.

WEAVER & HEDGES, (W. W. W. and E. H.) undertakers, 39 N. Illinois.

Webb A. L., seeds and agricultural implements, 83 W. Washington, bds. 64 W. Maryland.

Webb Charles, (col'd) porter, J. R. Marsh, r. 162 Elm.

WEBB ISAIAH, groceries and provisions, 314 Indiana av., r. 312 Indiana av.

Webb John W. (Bell & Webb) r. 19 Maria.

Webb Joseph P., carpenter, r. 456 E. Georgia.

Webb Joshua, r. 55 Ellen.

Webb Laura, (wid. Ira) boarding house, 64 W. Maryland.

Webb W. S. (Woollen, Webb & Co., also, Hibben, Tarkington & Co.) r. 440 S. Meridian.

Weber ———, brass moulder, r. 336 Railroad.

Weber Adam, lab., r. 340 S. Delaware.

Weber David, carpenter, r. 264 Massachusetts av.

Weber David, moulder, r. 278 Vincent.

Weber Elizabeth, (wid.) r. 351 Railroad.

Weber Erhard, clk. Crossland, Hanna & Co., r. 53 California.

Weber Fred, Cabinet Makers' Union, r. 366 N. Noble.

Weber Fred, watchmaker and jeweler, 43 S. Illinois, bds. Illinois House.

Weber George, lab., r. 149 N. Noble.

Weber George il., works Glass Works, r. 430 S. Meridian.

Weber Henry, lab., r. 111 E. Washington.

Weber Henry, works Schneider & Co., r. 336 Railroad.

Weber Henry, waiter, Emenegger's Hotel.

Weber John A., r. cor. Christian av. and Plum.

Weber John W. (col'd) lab., r. 167 Indiana av.

Weber J. F., clk. W. Haerle, bds. 366 N. Noble.

Weber Lewis, barber, shop 182 S. Illinois, r. 309 S. Pennsylvania.

Weber Mary, (wid.) r. 84 S. Liberty.

Weber William, lab., r. 84 Huron.

Weber William, blacksmith, r. 105 Huron.

Webster Abner, r 706 N. Illinois.

Webster Chester, salesman, bds. 305 E. New York.

Webster Geo. C., (Daggett & Co.) r. 140 N. East.

Webster Geo. C., jr., salesman 26 S. Meridian.

Webster George S., machinist, r. 88 California.

Webster J. H., driver hook and ladder trucks, r. 29 N. New Jersey.

Webster Daniel, butcher, r. 424 S. Illinois.

Wecker August, lab., bds. 200 S. Missouri.

Weckerling Frederick, lab. r. 92 Russell.

Wederecht John, cigarmaker, r. 135 E. Washington.

Weegmann C. Hermann, music teacher, r. 259 E. New York.

Weeks George, machinist, r. 174 E. Washington.

Weeks Richard, lab., r. Wabash, bet. East and Liberty.

Weeks William N., bookkeeper 18 W. Pearl, r. 60 S. Pennsylvania.

Weese Christian, turner, r. 81 S. Liberty.

WEGHORST HENRY, florist, and vegetable gardener, Japan, bet. Nebraska and East, r. same.

Weghorst Hermann, lab., r. 467 S. East.

Wehle Conrad, teamster, bds. N. New Jersey.

Wehle Gregor, barkeeper, 12 Louisiana, bds. same.

Wehle Lucas, shoemaker, r. 87 N. New Jersey.

Wehley Conrad, plowmaker, bds. 235 E. Washington.

Wehling Charles, blacksmith, 234 S. Delaware, r. 240 S. Delaware.

Wehling Fred., grocer, 193 E. South, r. same.

Wehling William, cooper, r. 232 Blake.

Wehn Christian, currier, r. 451 S. New Jersey.

Weibel Adolph, baker, r. 376 E. Ohio.

Weidle John, baker, works 178 S. Illinois, r. same.

Weideman John, porter, r. 46 Coburn.

Weigand A., florist, cor. Kentucky av. and South, r. same.

Weigant John, Deputy Marshal Union Depot, r. 444 S. Meridian.

Weiker Henry, lab., r. 272 E. Louisiana.

Weikert Alonzo. clk., Haskit, Morris & Co., bds. 127 Duncan.

Weikert Henry, works 21 and 23 W. Pearl, bds. California House.

Weikert Joseph, carpenter, r. 127 Duncan.

Weikonfoe Ernst, tailor, r. 23 Kentucky av.

Weil William. lab., r. 76 S. Tennessee.

Weilacher John, barkeeper, 20 Kentucky av., bds. 386 N. Tennessee.

Weiland C., yardman, P. C. & St. L. R. R.

Weiland Christian, switchman, I. C. & L. R. R. yard, r. 134 Union.

Weiland William C., clk., 397 S. Meridian, r. 558 S. Illinois.

Weinberger Ernest, r. 297 N. East.

Weinberger Herman, (W. & Waegemann,) r. 138 S. Meridian.

WEINBERGER & WAEGEMANN, (H. W. and G. W.) confectioners and eating house, 10 W. Louisiana.

Weir D. B., mail agent, T. H. & I. R. R.

Weir Jas. L., salesman, New York Store, bds. Macy House.

Weir John, plumber, J. G. Hanning, bds. 17½ Virginia av.

Weir William, (W. & Greenlee) bds. Mozart Hall.

THE CHINA TEA STORES

ARE AT

No. 7 ODD FELLOWS HALL

AND

ACADEMY OF MUSIC CORNER.

WEIR & GREENLEE, (W. W. and E. A. G.) marble works, 44 Virginia av.

Weis George, tailor, G. H. Heitkam, r. Circle restaurant.

Weis John L., Darmstadt Hoff. 401 E. Washington.

Weis Peter, grocer, sw. cor. East and McCarty, r. same.

Weise M. F., pastor, German Lutheran Church, r. 218 Huron.

Weisenheimer F. L., works Jackson, Rider & Co.

Weishaar John, bootmaker, r. 140 Madison av.

Weismann William, lab., r. 433 Virginia av.

Weismeyer John, lab., r. 345 E. McCarty.

Weithouse John, cigarmaker, with C. C. Hunt, bds. 23 Kentucky av.

Welch Edward, weaver, woolen mills, bds. 323 W. Washington.

Welch James, porter, Hume, Adams & Co., r. 255 W. Washington.

Welch James, shoemaker, bds. 199 W. Maryland.

Welch Jenny, domestic, Bates House.

Welch Judson, lab., r. 83 W. Louisiana.

Welch Kattie, (wid. Christ,) r. 152 N. Davidson.

Welch Mary, domestic, Blind Institute.

Welch Michael, porter, J. C Burton & Co., r. 80 Indiana av.

Welch Patrick, lab., r. 30 Helen.

Welch, Patrick, engineer, C. C. & I. C. R. R., bds. 58 Benton.

Weller James, engine tender, Caledonia Paper Mill, r. cor. New York and Blake.

Weller Levi, mailcarrier, Union Depot r. 651 N. Tennessee.

Weller William, blacksmith, Sinker & Davis, r. 281 N. Mississippi.

Welling W. W., mailagent, P. C. & St. L. R. R.

WELLMAN HIRAM B., inventor and patentee of Ozaline Burning Fluid, r. 118 N. Liberty.

Wells A. J., letter carrier, r. 240 N. Illinois.

Wells Edmond, bootmaker, 28 S. Delaware, r. 191 S. New Jersey.

Wells Graham A. (W. & Sullivan) r. 181 N. New Jersey.

Wells James, engineer, r. 4 Hahn

Wells James, engineer, works coffee and spice mills.

Wells John H., carpenter, r. 786 N. Tennessee.

Wells Joseph, clk., r. 38 Cherry.

WELLS MERRITT, dentist, rooms Yohn's blk., r. 112 Plum.

Wells Peter, (col'd) lab., r. cor. Michigan and Missouri.

Wells T. L., boot and shoemaker, 57 N. Illinois, r. 63 W. Ohio.

Wells William F., lab., r. 38 Cherry.

WELLS & SULLIVAN, (G. A. W. and B. W. S.) dentists, over 15 E. Washington.

Welsh B. D., painter, bds. 74 State.

Welsh James, lab., bds. 296 W. New York.

Welsh John, lab., r. 110 N. Davidson.

WELSH MAURICE, prop'r Senate Saloon, 80 W. Washington, r. 355 S. Meridian.

Welsh Michael, porter, J. C. Burton & Co., r. 80 Indiana av.

WELSH PATRICK, Bank Saloon, 23 W. Washington, r. 363 S. Meridian.

Welte Catharine Miss, hoop skirt manufactory, 153 E. Washington, r. 173 E. Washington.

Wemwe Joseph A., traveling agent, r. 374 W. Vermont.

Wempner Henry, checkman, I. C. & L. depot, r. 59 Harrison.

Wenger Frank, barkeeper, 176 E. Washington, r same.

Wenken Ernst, (Bach & W.) r. 178 N. Noble.

Wenken William, painomaker, r. 178 N. Noble.

Wenner John J., varnisher, r. 484 S. New Jersey.

Wennick J. H., lab., r. S. Tennessee.

Wensel Simon, carpenter, r. 323 W. Market.

Wenshorst Henry, hostler, bds. Mozart Hall.

Wentling L. L., clk., 174 E. Washington, bds. 24½ Kentucky av.

WERBE CHARLES, speculator, r. Court, bet. Alabama and New Jersey.

Werbe Christopher G. attorney, 94 E. Washington, r. East. S. of limits.

Werbe Fred L., groceries and notions, 249 W. Washington, r. same.

Werbe Henry G., watchmaker Bingham & Co., r. 249 W. Washington.

Werker Henry, lab., r. 274 E. Louisiana.

Werner S. Miss, teacher of music Indianapolis Young Ladies' Institute, r. Cincinnati, O.

Wernsing Herman, tailor, r. 430 S. Illinois.

Wert E. A., commercial traveler, r. 127 N. Alabama.

Wert Joseph, r. 127 N. Alabama.

Werther Wm., butcher, r. 358 E. New York.

Wertz Jacob, painter, r. 222 S. Missouri.

Wesbey Charles, painter, bds. 324 W. Maryland.

Wesbey Ephram, cooper, r. 324 W. Maryland.

Wesbey Wm. H., printer Sentinel office, bds. 324 W. Maryland.

Wesley Chapel, (Methodist) sw. cor Meridian and New York.

Wesley Charles, (G. W. W. & Son) prop'r Bates House.

WESLEY GEO. W. & SON, prop's Bates House, cor. Illinois and Washington.

Wesling Conrad, drayman, r. 330 N. Noble.

Wesseler John A., wood peddler, 124 N. Winston, r. same.

West Charles M., with Stewart & Morgan, druggists, bds. Bates House.

West Clinton, printer, r. 294 E. Market.

West David, works stave factory, r. 34 Elm.

West George, cooper, r. 179 E. South.

West G. H. (West, Morris & Gorrell) r. 483 N. Tennessee.

West J. C (Scott, W. & Co.) r. 357 N. New Jersey.

West Market Space, bet. Tennessee, Mississippi, Market and Ohio.

WEST, MORRIS & GORRELL, (Geo. H. W., John L. M., and S. W. G.) dealers in china, glass and queensware, 37 S. Meridian.

West William C., printer, r. 294 E. Market.

Westeine Allen, shoemaker, bds. California House.

Westerfeld Conrad, driver delivery wagon for A Ball, 178 S. Illinois, bds. same.

Western Furniture Co, 105 E. Washington, John Weust, President.

Western House, 127 S. Illinois, John C. Clawsen, proprietor.

WESTERN INDEPENDENT, weekly paper, published at 10 S. Pennsylvania, Amanda Way, editress.

WESTERN MACHINE WORKS, Sinker & Davis, proprietors, portable and stationary engines, 125 S. Pennsylvania.

WESTERN MUSICAL REVIEW, monthly, H. L. & A. M. Benham, proprietors, 36 E. Washington.

24

WESTERN PUBLISHING CO., publishers and agents for popular subscription books, etc., M. V. B. Cowen, Manager.

WESTERN UNION TELEGRAPH CO., Chas. C. Whitney, Manager, 11 S. Meridian.

Western J. M., moulder, r. 424 Virginia av.

Westpfall Theodore, lab., 150 Union.

Wetzel Hans P., clk. T. H. & I. freight office.

Weust John, Western Furniture Co., r. 143 Fort Wayne av.

Whalen Dennis, lab., r. 126 Meck.

Whalen Timothy, lab., r. over 280 E. Washington.

Whalen William, cooper, r. 45 Elm.

Whaley Crittenlen, clk. B. G. Stout & Bro., bds. 142 N. Mississippi.

Wheat William C., (W., Fletcher & Co.) r. Franklin, Ind.

Wheat, Fletcher & Co., (W. C. W., L. W. F., and B. Coffin) pork packers, office, 1 Vinton's blk.

Wheatley H. H., manufacturer of doors, sash, frames, etc., shop cor. South and Delaware, r. 311, S. East.

Wheatley John M., bookkeeper, McCord & Wheatley, r. 309 S. East.

Wheatley Martin, (Caylor & Co.,) bds. 379 N. West.

Wheatley Wm. M. (McCord & W.) r. 202 E. Ohio.

Whedon Americus, conductor J. M. &. I. R. R., bds Bates House.

Wheeler Charlotte Mrs., r. 317 W. Market.

Wheeler D. Y., clk. Millner & Sherwood, bds. National Hotel.

Wheeler John, fireman C. C. & I. C. R. R., bds. 58 Benton.

Wheble Lucas, boots and shoes, 235 E. Washington, r. 87 N. New Jersey.

Whelan Josph K., r. 300 Massachusetts av.

Wherritt William, r. 135 W. New York.

Whipple C. W., machinist, r. 48 Forest av.

Whietler George, cigarmaker, with Chas. C. Hunt, bds. 89 N. Delaware.

WHITCOMB E. A., State agent St. Louis Mutual Life Insurance Co., 4 Yohn's blk., r. 300 E. North.

H. H. LEE

MAKES A SPECIALTY OF

Choice Green, Black & Japan Teas.

Whitcomb Jane D. Mrs., boarding house, 164 W. Maryland.

WHITCOMB JEROME G., agent J. M. & I. R. R., office ss. South, bet. Delaware and Pennsylvania, r. 162 E. Market.

White Alfred, (col'd) lab., 77 Ann.

White Allen C., paperhanger, r. 102 Bates.

White Alonzo M., general agent Berkshire Life Insurance Co., r. 377 N. East.

White America Miss, (col'd) servant, 125 N. California.

White A. S. insurance agent, 19 N. Illinois, r. 363 N. Alabama.

White Charles H., works Vater & King, r. 82 Indiana av.

White Charles H., gasfitter, r. 82 Lockerbie.

White C. L., bookkeeper I. & St. L. R. R., r. 109 Virginia av.

White Charles M., State agent Home Insurance Co., of New York, r. 26 W. Pratt.

White George, lab., r. Fifth, bet. Mississippi and Lafayette R. R.

White George W., agent, 42 S. Meridian, r. 171 W. Michigan.

White George W., (col'd) lab., r. 57 N. Noble.

White Hattie Miss, servant, works 169 S. Tennessee.

White Hezekiah, lab. I. C. & L. R. R., r. 182 Bates.

White Hughes W. (W. & Ferguson) r. 138 Virginia av.

White James T., lab., r. 194 Douglass al.

White Jane Mrs., boarding house, r. 75 S. Pennsylvania.

White Joseph, bds. 440 N. East.

White J. B., baggage master, P. C. & St. L. R. R.

White J. M., soldier U. S. Arsenal.

White K. U. Miss, township librarian, 14 N. Delaware, r. N. of city.

White Mary Miss, (col'd) washerwoman, r. 194 Douglass al.

White Margret J. (col'd wid. Stephen) r. 194 Douglass al.

White Michael, car repairer C. C. C. & I. R. R., bds. 153 N. Winston.

White Mr., engineer I. & V. R. R., bds. 58 Benton.

White Rhoda, (wid. Charles) tailoress, r. cor. Madison and McCarty.

White Richard, gas fitter, 130 Michigan road.

White Robert B., superintendent Fletcher farms, r. 251 E. St. Clair.

White Sarah Mrs., (wid. Samuel) r. 117 N. Mississippi

White Susan A. (wid. Milton) r. 494 Virginia av.

White Thomas. works rolling mill, r. 278 S. Tennessee.

White William. carpenter, r. 72 Maple.

White William E. (col'd) lab., r. 194 Douglass al.

White William S., carpenter and builder, r. 68 Plum.

WHITE & FERGUSON, (H. W. White and W. W. Ferguson) custom tailors, room 3 old P. O. building.

Whitehead John, clk., 405 W. Washington. bds. same.

Whitehead Moses S., carriagemaker, r. 357 N. East.

Whitehead Thomas, works Byrkit & Co., r. 160 Ft. Wayne av.

WHITEHEAD WILLIAM, groceries, provisions and saloon, 430 and 432 W. Washington, r. same.

Whiteley Susie, (wid.) r. 336 E. New York.

Whiteside Joel G., chemist, Hannaman & Co., r. 122 N. Delaware.

Whithorf William, works Jackson, Rider & Co.

Whiting T. M., manufacturer and bleacher of straw goods, 26 Kentucky av., r. same.

Whitley H. H., carpenter, r. 311 S. East.

Whitman Charles, carriagemaker, r. 216 E. Market.

Whitman Hannah C., (wid. Freman) r. 195 Jackson.

Whitman H. N., carpenter, r. 101 Bradshaw.

Whitman L. M., r. 493 N. East.

Whitman Peter, woodsawyer, r. 326 Railroad.

Whitman W., traveling man, bds. 144 N. Tennessee.

WHITNEY CHARLES C., manager W. U. Telegraph, r. 94 S. Noble.

Whitney George A., bookkeeper, Jackson, Rider & Co., bds 71 Indiana av.

Whitney J. W., blacksmith, 46 S. Pennsylvania, r. 71 E. Maryland.

Whitney T. D., works Stave Factory, r. 302 N. Blake.

Whitney William, agent C. & I. J. R. R., r. 160 N. Meridian.

Whitney William, boot and shoe manufacturer, 55 and 57 S. Illinois, r. same.

Whitridge Samuel, painter, r 639 N. Illinois.

Whitridge W., r. 363 N. New Jersey.

Whitsitt Benjamin, bricklayer, r. 291 Virginia av.

Whitsitt Court E., contractor, r. 291 Virginia av.

Whitsitt Jesse, bricklayer, r. 291 Virginia av.

Whitsitt John A., contractor, r. 66 Huron.

Whitsitt John B., engineer C. C. & I. C. R. R., res. 43 Bates.

Whittaker John, carriage smith, r. 60 Massachusetts av

Whittaker John, blacksmith, r. 353 N. New Jersey.

Whittaker John, (col'd) lab., r. 530 S. Illinois.

Whittaker T. F., clk., 55 W. Washington, r. 72 W. Maryland.

Whitted John V., lab., r. 153 N. Noble.

Whittemore E. C. (wid.) boarding house, 58 Benton.

Whiting Robert, r. 258 S. Meridian.

Whittlesey S. L, clk., T. H. & I. R. R., r. 74 State.

Whitten E., r. 316 E North

Whitton Robert L., bookkeeper, 61 S. Meridian, r. 258 S. Meridian.

Whoulihan Jerry, lab., works gas works, r. 424 S. Tennessee.

Whoulihan Patrick, lab., works rolling mill, r. 424 S. Tennessee.

Wibke Wm., wagonmaker, with Lou Miller, r. 293 Davidson.

Wichmann Chas. C. L., carriage painter, 25 S. East, r. 216 E. Market.

Wickhoff J. B., carpenter, r. 351 N. Noble.

Wickliff Charles, lab., r. W. Second nr. Lafayette Railroad.

Wicks Richard, porter, Munson & Johnston.

Wiebke H., expressman, J., Robertson & Co.

WIEGAND ANTON, green house and flour garden, cor. Kentucky av. and Canal, r. cor. South and Canal.

Wiegman Christian, baker. r. 202 E. Court.

Wiegman Christian, jr., (Cook & W.) r. 202 E. Court.

Weigand Michael, shoemaker, r. room 6 Marmont Hall.

Wiehelm John, lab., r. 265 S. Alabama.

WIES PETER, grocer, sw. cor. East and McCarty.

Wiese Andrew, carpenter, C. C. & I. C. R. R., r. 168 E. Ohio.

Wiese Anthony F., lab., r. 327 E. Michigan.

Wiese Charles, carpenter. r. 283 E. Ohio.

Wiegemann John, teamster, r. 162 N. Winston.

Wiest Christopher, saloon, cor. Washington and East, r. same.

Wiggins George W., tinner, r. 36 S. Alabama.

Wiggins Joseph. (Foster, Wiggins & Co) r. 79 E. St. Joseph.

Wiggins Lizzie, (wid. John) r. 15 S. Mississippi.

Wiggins Percival E. (D. & W.) r. 31 W. St. Clair.

Wilaman John, porter, 34 S. Meridian, r. 46 Coburn.

Wiland William, works Glass Works, r. 222 Bluff rd.

Wilberger Pleasant, (col'd) lab., r. African al., bet, Sixth and Seventh.

Wilcox C. D. (W. & Means) r. 62 Fletcher av.

Wilcox David, r. 293 W. Blake.

Wilcox George H., pressmen Journal office. r. 9 Vine.

Wilcox John C., butcher, r. 293 Blake.

Wilcox Thomas, machinist, r. cor. South and Virginia av.

Wilcox William, works Jackson, Rider & Co.

Wilcox William H., speculator, r. 154 N. West.

Wilcox & Means, (C. D. W. and T. A. M.) agents Desota Mutual Life Insurance Co., rooms 3 and 4 Wiley's blk.

Wilcoxen Wm. B. cabinetmaker, r. ne. cor. Tennessee and First.

Wild John, stovemoulder, r. 753 N. Mississippi.

WILDER C. P., dealer in books, wall paper, etc., 26 E. Washington, r. 374 N. Tennessee.

Wilderick William E., confectioner, 317 Virginia av., r. same.

Wilding Charles, clk. 23 E. Washington, r. 123 N. East.

Wilding William, shoemaker, r. 123 N. East,

Wiles Bro. & Co., (W. D. Wiles, D. H. Wiles, D. W. Coffin and John J. Morris) whol. grocers and tea and tobacco dealers, 149 S. Meridian.

Wiles C. H., clk., 25 E. Georgia, bds. 224 E. Market.

Wiles D. H. (W. Bro. & Co.) r. 53 Fort Wayne av.

Wiles O. P, bill clk Wiles, Bros. & Co., r. 394 N. New Jersey.

Wiles Theodore, lettercarrier, bds. 64 W. Maryland.

THE CHINA TEA STORES

ARE AMONG THE

Attractions of Indianapolis.

Call and See Them before leaving the City.

WILES THOMAS, stoneware house, 25 E Georgia, r. 224 E Market.

Wiles T. S., clk. 25 E. Georgia, r. 224 E. Market.

Wiles William M., U. S. Assessor Internal Revenue, office P. O. bldg., r. 286 N. Pennsylvania

Wiles W. D. (W., Bros. & Co.) r. 394 N. New Jersey.

WILES & REYNOLDS, (W. M. W. and T. E R.) druggists, 48 N. Pennesylvania.

Wiley Andrew, salesman, bds. 131 N. Alabama.

Wiley Charles, salesman, bds. 131 N. Alabama.

Wiley Delaney, physician, 16½ E. Washington, r. 55 Massachusetts av.

Wiley David, works Rolling Mill, bds. 78 W. McCarty.

Wiley E. W. (W. & VanBuren) r. 287 E. Market.

Wiley Frank A., clk. P. O., bds. 204 N. Illinois.

Wiley H. W., professer N. W. C. University, r. College av., opposite University.

Wiley John S., salesman, r. 36 Cherry.

Wiley M. W. (M. W. W. & ——) r. 308 S. Meridian.

WILEY M. W. & CO., (M. W. W. and ——) druggists and chemists, 408 S. Meridian.

Wiley Wm. Y., Captain and O. S. K., U. S. Arsenal, bds same.

WILEY & VAN BUREN, (E. W. W. and F. A. VanB.) general agents Grover & Baker Sewing Machine Co., 21 E. Washington.

Wilgus Jacob, engineer, r. 302 S. Illinois.

Wilhelm Aug., with McCord & Wheatley, r. 172 W. New York.

Wilhelm Charles, Western Furniture Company, r. cor. St. Mary and Alabama.

Wilhelm Charles, jr., cabinetmaker, r. 517 N. Alabama.

Wilhelm Christ., lab., r. 265 S. Alabama.

Wilhelm Daniel, Western Furniture Company, r. 163 E. St. Mary.

Wilkening Charles, expressman, r. 285 Davidson.

Wilkins John A., (Wilkins & Co.) r. 80 E. Market.

Wilkins & Co., (John A. Wilkins & ——) manufacturers of mattresses, 84 E. Market.

Wilking Henry, shoemaker, r. 22 West.

Wilkins Charles, teamster, r. Pennsylvania or. Tinker.

Wilkins Charles A., machinist, works Greenleaf & Co., bds. 124 S. Meridian.

Wilkins Peter, detective, r. N. Pennsylvania or. Tinker.

Wilkinson D. E., grocery and produce dealer, 44 N. Pennsylvania, r. 412 N. Delaware.

Wilkinson L. W., salesman, New York Store, r. 70 E. Ohio.

Wilkinson James, brakeman, I. C. & L. R. R., bds. Ray House.

Wilkinson John, tailor, 32 N. Illinois, r. 77 Kentucky av.

Wilkinson John, clk., New York Store, r. 70 E. Ohio.

Wilkinson William, r. 85 N. Delaware.

Will Adolphus, clk., with John Mueller, r. 96 N. Noble.

Will Fred., saloon, r. 99 N Noble.

Will John F., city tannery, r. 96 N. Noble.

Willard A. B., (A. G. W. & Co.) r. nw. cor. Alabama and York.

Willard A. G., (A. G. W. & Co.) r. 138 Massachusetts av.

WILLARD A. G. & CO., (A. G. Willard, A. B. Willard and C. P. Wilson) wholesale and retail dealers in pianos, organs and sheet music, 4 and 5 Bates House Block.

Willard Will., blacksmith, r. 281 N. Mississippi.

Willchen Davies, lab., r. 335 N. Winston.

Willer Levi, mail messenger, P. O., r. 651 N. Tennessee.

Willboff George, teamster, Smith's Brewery, r. 212 Madison av.

Williams Amanda Miss, (col'd) servant, 76 N. California.

Williams Angeline, (wid. Thomas H.) r. 131 Huron.

Williams Ann M. (wid. Jacob T.) r. 88 N. California.

Williams August, works Planing Mill, r. 172 W. New York.

Williams Bruns, salesman, 79 S. Meridian, r. 172 W. New York.

Williams Charles C., r. 748 N. Illinois.

Williams Charles, retired, r. 28 W. Michigan.

Williams Dan. (col'd) Bates House.

Williams Daniel, plasterer, r. 277 E New York.

Williams Daniel G., (Todd, Carmichael & W.) r. 512 N. Tennessee.

Williams David, blacksmith, r. 237 W. Merrill.

Williams David B., clk. pension office. r. 80 S. Mississippi.

Williams D. C., moulder, r. 18 Dougherty.

Williams E. (col'd) cook Sherman House.

Williams Edgar, clk. Browning & Sloan, bds. 226 N. Illinois.

Williams Edward C., moulder, r. 18 Dougherty.

Williams Elizabeth Mrs. (wid.) boarding house, 438 S. Illinois.

Williams Edgar H. (Barnes & W.) r. Broadway, nr. Christian av.

Williams George, lab. r. 2d house from New York on Bright.

Williams George B. Superviser of Internal Revenue, Vinton's blk., bds. Bates House.

Williams Giles, telegraph operator, with W. F. Wallick.

Williams Griffith, blacksmith, r. 70 Meek.

Williams H. M. Miss, teacher Indianpolis Young Ladies Institute.

Williams Horace, (col'd) lab., r. 140 Elm.

Williams James Y., machinist, Chandler & Taylor, r. 88 California.

Williams John, iron pudler, r. 314 W. Merrill.

Williams John, works rolling Mill, bds. 441 S. Illinois.

Williams John, carpenter, r. 17 E. North.

Williams John C. (col'd) whitewasher, r. 85 W. Georgia.

WILLIAMS J. D., President State Board of Agriculture, office State House.

Williams John X, heater rolling mill, r. 363 S. Missouri.

Williams J. M., minister, r. Howard, bet. Second and Third.

Williams Lucy, (col'd) washer woman, r. cor. Blake and Rhode Island.

Williams Mary E., (wid.) Ambrose, r. 248 W. Market.

Williams Nicholas M., salesman, bds. 65 N. East.

Williams, Owen, r. 226 N. Illinois.

Williams Rees R., works rolling mill, r. 5 Willard.

Williams Robert, hostler, r. 55 Fayette.

Williams Sue, (wid.) r. 281 E. New York.

Williams Thomas T., bricklayer, r. Broadway, nr. Christian av.

Williams Wallace, (col'd) lab., r. African al., bet. Sixth and Seventh.

Williams William, painter, Shaw, Lippincott & Conner, r. 223 Buchanan.

Williams William, helper, rolling mill, bds. 363 S. Missouri.

Williams William, stone mason, r. 223 Buchanan.

Williams William, Superintendent Rink, r. 44 N. Tennessee.

BENHAM BRO'S,

36 E. Washington St.,

AGENTS FOR THE

INDIANAPOLIS MANUFACTURING CO.'S

PIANOS.

Williams William, policeman, r. 299 S. East.

Williams William S., traveling agent, bds. 33 W. Maryland.

Williams William G., blacksmith, r. 70 Meek.

Williams W. B., agent, G. W. Despatch and E. T. Co., 80 and 82 Virginia av., r. 247 N. East.

Williams W. R., letter carrier, r. cor. Potomac and West.

Williamson Asher, engineer Peg and Last Factory, r. 122 E. Merrill.

Williamson Edward, works Indianapolis Agricultural Works, bds. 438 S. Illinois.

Williamson Leonidas, engineer, bds. 438 S. Illinois.

Williamson L. B., iron rail maker, r. 317 S. East.

Williamson Marshall D., lumber dealer, r. 460 N. Delaware.

Willich Charles, cabinetmaker, r. 163 E. St. Mary.

Willich Daniel, Western Furniture Co. r. 163 E. St. Mary.

Willeg Daniel, cabinetmaker, r. St. Mary bet. Alabama and New Jersey.

Willis Charles, (col'd) barber, 10 S. Delaware, bds. 361 E. New York.

Willis George, express messenger, r. 27 N. Noble.

Willis Henry, prest. and supt. of the Indiana Cement Pipe Co., r. 780 N. Illinois.

Willis Jonathan, tinsmith, shop, 166 Indiana av. r. cor. Smith and Maria.

Willis Robert, brakeman, C. C. & I. C R. R., bds. 58 Benton.

Willis Josiah, cooper, r. 31 Ellen.

Wilson Thomas, clk., r 340 E. New York.

Wilmington Edward M., deputy county auditor, r. 122 St. Mary.

Wilmington L. F., mailagent, I. & V. R. R., r. 426 N. East.

Wilmont Caroline A. (wid.) r. 244½ E. Washington.

Wilson Albert, moulder, bds. Ray House.

Wilson Allie Miss, school teacher, bds. 97 W. Maryland.

Wilson Amanda Miss, r. 188 W. George.

Wilson B. A., r. 686 N. Illinois.

Wilson Benjamin F., works street railroad company. bds. 18 N. Noble.

Wilson Chas., clk., r. 178 S. New Jersey.

H. H. LEE

Makes a Specialty of

CHOICE GOLDEN RIO,

AND

OLD GOVERNMENT JAVA COFFEES.

Wilson Chas., lab., r. 188 N. Winston.

Wilson Charles C., coach painter, 26 S. New Jersey, r. 266 S. Mississippi.

Wilson Charles G. jr., bookbinder, bds. 266 S. Mississippi.

Wilson C. C. (col'd) cook, county jail, r. 145 Bright.

Wilson C. P. (A. C. Williard & Co.) r. 337 S. Meridian.

Wilson David, salesman, New York store, bds. Macy House.

Wilson D. H., clk., New York store, bds. Macy House.

Wilson Frank, lab., r. 18 N. Noble.

Wilson Frank, printer, Sentinel office, r. 26 S. Mississippi.

Wilson Frank, printer, Braden & Burford, bds. 30½ N. Pennsylvania.

Wilson Fred., mantlesetter, Munson & Johnston.

Wilson Geo. W., real estate agent, r. 174 W. Michigan.

Wilson Grace D. Miss, teacher, r. 97 W. Maryland.

Wilson Steven, plasterer, r. 325 S. Alabama.

Wilson Hugh, machinist, works Greenleaf & Co., bds. 169 S. Tennessee.

Wilson James, carpenter, r. 477 W. Michigan.

Wilson James, clk. Adam Bretz, r. 44 W. Louisiana.

Wilson James A., carriage painter, works Miller's carriage shop, bds. 35 W. Georgia.

Wilson James G., carpenter, r. 418 Indiana av.

Wilson James H., clk. Citizens' Street R. R. office., r. 18 N. Noble.

Wilson James H., bookkeeper J. E. Robertson & Co., r. 324 N. Delaware.

WILSON JAMES T. (W. & R.) dealer in liquors and tobacco, No. 3 Spencer House, bds. Globe House.

Wilson James W., lumber dealer, office 27 Massachusetts av., r. 134 E. St. Joseph.

Wilson John, carpenter, r. 25 S. New Jersey.

Wilson John, bricklayer, r. 188 W. Georgia.

Wilson John, finisher, Greenleaf & Co., bds. 169 S. Tennessee.

Wilson John S., carpenter, r. 68 N. East.

Wilson J. T., plasterer, r. 117 S. Benton.

Wilson Joseph, peddler of notions, r. 278 E. Louisiana.

Wilson J. C., manager Union Depot Telegraph Office, bds. 169 N. Illinois.

Wilson J. W., lumber dealer, r. 134 E. St. Joseph.

Wilson J. W., tailor, r. 226 S. Noble.

Wilson George, photographer, 36½ E. Washington, r. same.

Wilson Lizzie Miss, r. 167 W. Washington.

Wilson Louis, (col'd) servant, 172 N, West.

Wilson L. B., r. 97 W. Maryland.

Wilson L. D. attorney at law, 16½ E. Washington, bds. 174 W. Maryland.

Wilson Marion C., lab., r. 340 Indiana av.

Wilson Martin B., lab., r. 533 S. Meridian.

Wilson Mary E. Miss, teacher, bds. 174 Virginia av.

Wilson Mattie Miss, servant, 238 N. West.

Wilson Mattie Mrs., dressmaker, r. 119 W. Vermont.

Wilson M. W., cabinetmaker, bds. California House.

Wilson Napoleon, (col'd) lab., r. 350 W. North.

Wilson O. M., assistant U. S. District Attorney, room 2 Ætna building, r. 73 S. Tennessee.

Wilson Pat Mrs., r. 276 S. Delaware.

Wilson Rebecca, (wid. Hiram) dressmaker and tailoress, 68 S. Illinois.

Wilson Richard, (col'd) lab., r. Lafayette road bet. First and Second.

Wilson S. A. (wid. James B.) r. 239 E. Louisiana.

Wilson Sanford B., r. 623 E. Washington.

Wilson Stephen B., traveling agent, r. 126 E. Walnut.

Wilson Stephen C., cain seat maker, r. 159 Elizabeth.

Wilson Thomas, (col'd) lab., r. cor. Ash and Christian av.

Wilson Thomas E., salesman, r. 324 N. Delaware.

Wilson Thomas S., policeman, r. 178 S. New Jersey.

Wilson William, secretary Indianapolis Cotton Mill Co., r. 324 N. Delaware.

Wimpe Joseph A., agent, r. nw. cor. Vermont and Bright.

Winchenbaugh Emery D., carpenter, r. 374 N. West.

Winchester E. H. (W. & S.) National Hotel.

WINCHESTER & SAPP, (E. H. Winchester and W. D. Sapp) proprietors National Hotel opp. Union Depot.

Winder Alfred, operator W. U. Telegraph, r. 66 N. Peru.

Windsor James E., with B. F. Haugh & Co., r. 324 S. Delaware.

Winder John M., salesman, Boston Store, bds. 68 E. Market.

Wing Thomas, conductor C. C. & I. C. R. R., bds. Spencer House.

Wingate J. F., r. 306 N. Delaware.

Wingate Martha Miss, waiter Neiman House.

Wingate Wm. L., sawmill, S. East, r. 122 Virginia av.

Wink Isabella Miss, millinery, 152 E. Washington, r. same.

Wink Mrs., midwife, r. 195 S. Alabama.

Winkler John, clk. Globe House r. same.

Winkler Mary Miss, works Globe House.

Winkler Valentine, stonemason. bds. Globe House.

Winslow A. B., with J. D. Condit, bds. 54 Circle.

Winter Anthony, lab., r. 169 E. St. Mary.

Winter Edward, painter, r. Gregg, bet. Jackson and East.

Winter Henry F., blacksmith, r. 41 Grant.

WINTER I. N., dealer in second-hand goods, 17 Virginia av., r. 43 Ellsworth.

Winter I. N., cutter, 37 E. Washington, r. 43 Ellsworth.

Winter John A., painter, Hubbard's blk., r. 345 N. Noble.

Winter Rudolph J., dealer in rags and old iron, 244 S. Meridian, r. same

WINTER WILLIAM, local editor Sentinel, bds. 480 N. Mississippi.

Winters ——, bds. Bates House.

Winters Anthony, lab., J. C. Ferguson & Co.

Winters Philip, saloon, bds. Ray House

Winters Philip C., maltster, r. 258 S. Alabama.

Winz Elizabeth Mrs., r. 226 Dougherty.

Wipker Henry, expressman, r. cor. North and Davidson.

Wirt Jno. B., letter carrier, r. 465 Virginia av.

Wirt Wm., salesman r. 127 N. Alabama.

Wirth John, clk., 668 N. Pennsylvania, bds. same.

Wirtz Henry, carriagesmith, Shaw, Lippencott & Connor, r. 503 S. East.

Wirtz Jacob, veterinary surgeon, r. 503 S. East.

Wise A., with B. F. Haugh & Co., r. 573 E. St. Clair.

Wise Christian, lab., 81 S. Liberty.

Wise John, bricklayer, r. 343 N. Delaware.

Wise W. T., barber, r. 299 E. New York.

Wiseman Anna Mrs., r. 199 N. Pennsylvania.

Wiseman Simon, teamster, r. 355 W. Washington.

Wiseman Wm., watchman, r. 214 E. Meek.

Wiser John W., brakeman, C. C. C. & I. R. R., r. 583 E. Washington.

Wishmeir Charles F., works Starch Factory, r. 292 N. Winston.

Wishmeir Christian, fireman, Starch Factory, r. 292 N. Winston.

Wishmeir C. F., miller, r. 258 N. Davidson.

Wisehmeir C. F., fireman, Starch Factory, r. 258 N. Davidson.

Wishmeir George, delivery clk., bds. 274 E. Ohio.

Wishmire Anthony, jr., lab., bds. 274 E. Ohio.

Wissart John, proprietor, Meridian Exchange, 180 S. Meridian, r. same.

Wister Annie E. Miss, r. 97 W. South.

Withers George T., lab., r. S. Mississippi, nr. Rolling Mill.

Witlinger Jacob, grocer, 100 S. Noble, r. same.

Witman H. T., physician, r. 39 Indiana av.

WITT BENNETT F., war claim agent, attorney and notary public and supervising agent Franklin Life Insurance Co., sw. cor. Washington and Meridian, r. 364 N. New Jersey.

WITT & ARBUCKLE, (B. F. W. and M. R.) real estate agents, sw. cor. Washington and Meridian.

Witthof August, cooper, r. 82 S. East.

Withof Henry, cabinetmaker, r. 82 S. East.

Witthoft Frederick, groceries and saloon, 329 Indiana av., r. same.

Wobitz Louis, butcher, bds. 352 S. Delaware.

Wocher John, stonecutter, r. 25 Meek.

Wocker Julius, clk., r. 23 Meek.

Woelz Charles, wholesale and retail confectioner, 149 N. Delaware, r. same.

Wolf Caroline Mrs., r. 255 S. Mississippi.

Wolf Charles, saloon, 176 S. Illinois, r. same.

Wolf George W., painter, 255 S. Mississippi.

Wolf Isaac, cooper, bds. 408 W. Washington.

Wolf Lizzie Mrs. (wid. Jacob) r. 246 Chestnut.

Wolf Moses, salesman, Hays, Rosenthal & Co., r. 144 Virginia av.

THE CHINA TEA STORES

Have the NAME of being the

MOST ATTRACTIVE STORES IN THE WEST.

No. 7 Odd Fellows Hall
AND
ACADEMY OF MUSIC CORNER.

Wolf Philip H., cigarmaker, 36 Virginia av., bds. 176 S. Delaware.

Wolf Samuel, railroader, r. 50 Elm.

Wolf Valentine, boarding house and saloon, 176 S. Delaware, r. same.

Wolfe William A, (S. & W.) r. 196 Virginia av.

Wolfrom Albert T., (Wolfrom Bros.) bds. 201 N New Jersey.

Wolfrom Bros., stoves and tinware, 197 E. Washington.

Wolfrom C. A., foreman press room Journal Office, r. 201 N. New Jersey.

Wolfrom Christian, (Wolfrom Bros.) r. 201 N. New Jersey.

Wolfrom Ernest E, bookkeeper, bds 201 N. New Jersey.

Wolfrom Sarah (wid.) r. 201 N. New Jersey.

Wolson Charles, wiper, C. C. C. & I. R. R. Shops.

Wolsterbaum A., (wid) grocery, 312 N. Illinois, r. same.

Wood A. D., (W. & Hoss) r. 201 N. Delaware cor. Vermont.

Wood Alexander, assistant City Engineer, r. 18 W. Vermont.

Wood Annie, (wid.) r. 53 Hellen.

Wood Cinthia, (wid.) r. 74 N. Liberty.

Wood Daniel L., (Nutting & Wood) r. 417 N. Tennessee.

Wood David A., bookkeeper, Dessar Bros. & Co., r. E. Washington, near city limits.

Wood Edmunson R., carpenter.

Wood Eugene W., teacher, Indiana Institution for the Deaf and Dumb.

Wood Fred, steam fitter, 70 N. Illinois.

Wood Herman, (W. & Mansur) r. 124 N. Tennessee.

Wood James W., carpenter and joiner, r. 124 Bates.

Wood Jenny, domestic, Bates House.

Wood John, cooper, r. 114 S. Noble.

Wood John T., assistant P. M., r. 393 N. Pennsylvania.

Wood John J., carpenter and joiner, r. 124 Bates.

Wood John M., (W. & Foudray) r. 4 Massachusetts av.

Wood L., physician, office, 31 Virginia av., r. 563 N. Mississippi.

Wood Maurice G., clk. Nutting & Wood, bds. 407 N. Pennsylvania.

Wood N. H., conductor, C. C. & I. C. R. R., bds. Bates House.

Wood Nicholas, well and cistern digger, r. 428 E. St. Clair.

Wood S. Mrs., r. 125 N. Pennsylvania.

Wood ——, (wid.) r. E. Washington, nr. Deaf and Dumb Asylum.

Wood William D., clk. H. H. Lee, r. 189 N. Illinois.

Wood William E., stock dealer, r. 442 N. Pennsylvania.

Wood Wm. J., salesman, Stoneman, Pee & Co , r. 304 E. Market.

Wood & Foudray, (J. M. W. and J. E. F.) livery and sale stables, 16 N. Pennsylvania.

WOOD & HOSS, (A. D. W. and John T. Hoss) brokers and real estate agents, Wiley's blk., over 10 N. Pennsylvania.

Wood & Mansur, (Herman W. and Frank M.) livery and sale stable, 21 and 23 W. Pearl.

Woodard Alpheus, conductor, C. C. & I, C. R. R., r. 75 Davidson.

Woodard John T., clk., 2 Palmer House, bds. 25 N. Harrison.

Woodard J. H., correspondent Cincinnati Gazette, r. 197 N. Alabama.

Woodbridge Chas. A., (John Woodbridge & Co.,) r. 147 N. Pennsylvania.

Woodbridge C. L., (John Woodbridge & Co.,) r. 147 N. Pennsylvania.

WOODBRIDGE JOHN, whol. dealer in glassware, queensware, etc., 36 S. Meridian, bds. 147 N. Pennsylvania.

WOODBRIDGE JOHN & CO. (John Woodbridge, Cal. Woodbridge, Chas. Woodbridge and Chas. Jones) queensware, glassware and china, 12 W. Washington.

Woodbridge J. D., engineer, r. 81 E. Michigan.

Woodburn J. H. Dr. (Thompson & W.) r. 264 N. Illinois.

Woodbury Charles, marblecutter, Smith, Ittenbach & Co., bds. E. Georgia.

Woodbury N. T. Dr., dentist, 39½ W. Washington, r. 76 W. Market.

Woodfill George, r. 524 N. Mississippi.

Woodford James, traveling agent, r. 160 N. West.

Woodford J. E, traveling agent, bds. Spencer House.

Woodruff James O., supt. Water Works, bds. 179 N. Alabama.

Woodruff M. W., clk. American Express Co., bds. 475 N. Pennsylvania.

Woodruff Wm., clk. lunch stand Union Depot, bds. same.

Wood Almon, fireman Glass Works, r. 88 S. Mississippi.

Woods B. F., woodhauler, r. 234 Huron,

Woods Daniel, razor grinder, r. 290 W. Washington.
Woods Elvin, supt. Glass Works, bds. 44 S. Tennessee.
Woods George F., blower Glass Works, bds. 147 S Mississippi, cor. Maryland.
Woods J., teamster, bds. 73 Kentucky av.
Woods John, cooper, r. 114 S. Noble.
Woods Maria, (col'd, wid) r 247 N. West.
Woods Thomas, lab., works Osgood, Smith & Co., r. 24 W McCarty.
Woods William J., whol. agent, r. 304 E. Market.
Woodson John S., custom tailor, 72 Virginia av., r. same.
WOOLLEN GREEN V., supt. City Hospital, r. cor. West and Vermont.
Woollen K., (wid.) r. 178 E. Vermont.
Woollen Sarah, (wid. Milton), r. 248 N. West.
WOOLLEN, WEBB & CO., bankers, (W. W. Woollen and W. S. Webb) No. 31 W. Washington.
Woollen William M., dealer in groceries and provisions, 101 Indiana av, r. 288 N. Tennessee
Woollen William W., (Woollen & Ruddell) r. College av.
Woollen William W. (Woollen, Webb & Co.) r. 167 N. Tennessee.
WOOLLEN & RUDDELL, (William W. Woollen and James H. Ruddell,) attorneys at Law, 25½ E. Washington.
Woolley Thomas, bds 369 N. New Jersey.
Woolrich John C., clk. Palmer House, r. same.
Wompner Henry, checkman, P. C. & St. L. Depot, r. 59 Harrison.
Wonnell Louisa, (wid. John A) boarding house, 31 Indiana av.
Worden C. D, (C. J. Worden & Son) r. 218 E. Market.
Worden C. J., (C. J. Worden & Son) r. 89 E. Market.
Worden C. J & Son, agents Empire Mutual Life Insurance Company, 85 E. Market.
Worland William, grocery and feed store and dealer in loose hay and straw, 52 Virginia av, r. same.
Worley William, teamster, r. 325 E. New York.
Worman Charles R., bds. 79 E. Ohio.
Worman W. W., salesman Murphy Johnston & Co, r. 79 E. Ohio.
Worthington Gerhard, r. 405 S. Delaware.
WORTHINGTON L., president C. & I. J. R R., office 110 and 112 Virginia av., r. Cincinnati Ohio.
25

BENHAM BRO'S,

36 East Washington St.,

Pianos, Organs and Melodeons Tuned, Moved and Repaired.

Worthington William H., trunkmaker, Virginia av., r. 23 Douglass.
Wortman Charles, bootmaker, r 358 Virginia av.
Wrede Theodore, clk. Frank Erdlemyer, r 91 E. Washington.
Wredt Charles, bowling alley, 34 W. Georgia. r. same
Wren Edward, wagonmaker, r. 99 S. New Jersey.
WREN THOMAS, contractor, r. 355 S. Tennessee cor. Norwood.
Wrench Fred, stone cutter, r. 139 Stevens.
Wrenick & Burk, (M. W. and J. B.) dress and cloakmakers, 62 Indiana av.
Wright A. L., (Hanna, Adams & Co.) r. 224 N. Alabama.
Wright A. P, night policeman, r. 128 Broadway.
Wright Ben C. (Hamlin & W.) r. 275 N. Delaware.
Wright C. E. (Fletcher & W.) r. 107 N. Alabama.
Wright C. N., pumpmaker, r. 330 S. Noble.
Wright Charles A., real estate agent and notary public, 17½ W. Washington., room 2, bds. Bates House.
Wright C. W., general agent Hartford Life Insurance Co., office 8 E. Washington, r. 477 N Meridian.
Wright Elizabeth, (wid. Alonzo) r. 182 W. Georgia.
Wright Elizabeth Miss, seamstress, r. 160 Indiana av., up stairs.
Wright Frank Miss, r. 37 Douglass al.
WRIGHT FRANK T., painter, r. 361 W Vermont.
Wright Frank, painter, bds. 366 W. Washington.
WRIGHT FRANK, ale brewer cor. Blake and New York, r. 160 N. West.
Wright G S., attorney at law, room 5 Langsdale's blk. r. 275 N. Delaware.
Wright Henry, machinist, Eagle Machine Works, bds. 366 W. Washington.
Wright Hiram N, proprietor Wright House, 366 W Washington.
Wright Jacob, (Hamlin & W.) r. 275 N. Delaware.
Wright J, (col'd) lab., r. 174 Indiana av.
Wright John, (col'd) lab., r. 460 S. Missouri.

Wright John C., r. 32 E Vermont.

Wright John C., fireman C. & I. J. R. R., r. 22 Oriental.

WRIGHT JOHN M., photographer, 39½ E Washington, r. same.

Wright John N, traveling agent, West. Morris & Gorrell, r 477 N Meridian

Wright John R. (William Sumner & Co.) r Cincinnati, O.

Wright John S., lightning rod manufacturer, r. 795 N. Tennessee.

Wright Joseph, bricklayer, r. 171 Virginia av.

Wright Joseph C., millwright, r. 302 W Washington.

Wright J. H., works Vater & King, r. 89 S. Illinois.

Wright J. J., physician, 58½ E. Market, r. 498 N. Pennsylvania.

Wright Levi, grocery and produce dealer 323 N. Alabama, r. 314 N. Alabama

Wright Liddy J., (wid.) r. cor. Cherry and Broadway.

Wright M. H., physician, r. 103 N. Meridian.

Wright Nathan, (col'd) barber, shop 128 S. Illinois, r. 269 Blake.

Wright Peter, (col'd) lab., r. Ninth, near Canal.

Wright Richard M., shoemaker, r. 22 Oriental.

Wright Samuel, clk., bds. 314 N. Alabama.

WRIGHT THEODORE F., (W. & Holman) r. 361 W. Vermont.

Wright Thomas, clk., r. 76 Plum.

Wright Thomas, (col'd) lab., r. 135 Bright.

Wright William B., grocer, r. 83 E. Michigan.

Wright Willis W., (Carber, John & Co) r. E National Road.

Wright William, printer, Journal Office.

Wright W. G., pumpmaker, 36 S. Pennsylvania, r. 274 Virginia av.

Wright W. H., assessor, 52 S. Meridian, r. 83 E. Michigan.

WRIGHT & HOLMAN, (T. F. Wright and B. M. H.) job printers, 33 W. Washington.

Wright & Vinedge, (J. T W. & J. A. V) real estate agents, 62 E. Washington.

Wurst John, turner, r. 143 Ft. Wayne av.

Wundram William, tailor, r. 404 S. Delaware.

Wurringer William, druggist and chemist, 127 E. Washington, r. same.

Wyatt Thomas, r 83 S. Benton.

Wyatt W. D., dealer in groceries and provisions, cor. Noble and Fletcher av., r. 83 Benton.

Wyland Mary Mrs., r. 246 Chestnut.

Wymoth Amos, blacksmith, W. Indianapolis.

Wynn C. C. Mrs., teacher, Institute for the Blind.

Wynn W. S., salesman, Bowen, Stewart & Co., bds. se. cor Walnut and Tennessee.

Wysong Christopher, bricklayer, r. 281 N. Noble.

Wysong Geo, bricklayer, r. 281 N. Noble.

YACMANN MINNIE MISS, clk. 147 W. Washington, bds same.

Yager Godfrey, trunkmaker, 89 S. Illinois, r. 185 N. Noble.

Yandes Daniel jr., dealer in hides and leather, 76 E. Washington, r. N. Tennessee, out city limits.

Yandes D., leather and hides, 76 E. Washington, r 179 E Ohio.

Yandes George B., bds. Bates House.

Yandes Simon, lawyer, 21 E. Washington, bds. Bates House.

Yarbrough Sarah (wid.) r. 153 Meek.

Yarling Peter, tailor, r. 125 McCarty.

Yaw James, lab., r. 302 W. Market.

Yeager Christian, lab., r. 292½ E. Washington.

Yeager Christ., watchman, P. C. & St. L. Freight Depot.

Yeager Marion, fireman, C. & I. J. R. R., bds. 61 S. Noble.

Yeager William, dealer in groceries, provisions, etc., 282 N. Noble, r. 284 N. Noble.

Yeaton L. B., superintendent Fire Alarm Telegraph, r. 74 E. Ohio.

Yeiser Jacob, conductor, C. C. & I. C. R. R., bds. Spencer House.

Yewell Ezra T., pianotuner, r. 202 N. East.

Yewell Frank, conductor, Silver Palace Sleeping Car, r. 338 Chestnut.

Yewell Solomon, bookkeeper, r. 320 Chestnut.

Yewell Solomon, jr., dramatic agent, r. 320 Chestnut.

Yocum Louis, blower Glass Works, bds. California House.

Yohn Albert B., clk. J. B. V. Smith, bds. 206 N. Delaware.

Yohn Charles G., clk. Harrison's Bank, bds 206 N. Delaware.

Yohn James, capitalist, r. 206 N. Delaware

Yohn's Block, cor. Meridian and Washington.

Yorger Clemens C., butcher, r. 361 N. Noble.

Yorger John, (Y. & Bros.) r. Arsenal rd.

Yorger John & Bro. (J Y. and N. Y.) butchers, 245 E. Washington.

Yorger Notz, (Y. & Bro.) r. 17 Arsenal rd.

York R S., bookkeeper, bds 128 N. Tennessee.

Yost J. H. T., stonemason, r 380 S. West.

Yost Thomas, bridge contractor, r. 103 W South.

Yotz Peter, wagonmaker, r. W. Indianapolis.

YOUART JOHN M., physician, 39½ W. Washington, r. 564 N. Tennessee.

Young Annie L, (wid., Nelson R.) r. 232 W. Michigan.

Young Ellen, (col'd) cook, Macy House. bds. same.

Young George, (col'd) barber, 16 S. Meridian, r. same.

Young Jesse (col'd) r. Tennessee N. of Seventh

Young John, attorney at law, 100 E Washington, r. cor. Christian av. and Jackson.

Young Julius, tailor, over 197 E. Washington.

YOUNG MEN'S CHRISTIAN ASSOCIATION, Rev. John B Brandt, Superintendent, rooms 17 and 18 Vinton's blk, and 46½ N. Pennsylvania.

Young Squire, (col'd) lab., r. 259 N. West.

Young Thornton, (col'd) lab., r. 228 N. Noble.

Young William, carpenter, r. 68 Athon.

Yount John, lab, r. 68 Eddy.

Youtsey William, lab, Osgood, Smith & Co.

Youtsey Thomas, works Osgood, Smith & Co., r. 57 Eddy.

ZABLE CHARLES, Cabinet Maker's Union, r. 185 Meek.

Zahm Bernhard, engineer, C. C. & I.C. R. R.

Zambell Andrew, fireman, C. C. & I C R. R., bds. cor. Meek and Noble.

Zapf Edward, cabinetmaker, r. 126 Maple.

Zapf John D., blacksmith, r. 205 N. Winston.

Zapf Philip, servant, Circle Restaurant.

Zeelie Henry, lab. J. C. Ferguson & Co.

Zehringer Landolin, cabinetmaker, r. 164 N. Davidson.

Zellers Henry, mattressmaker, bds Macy House.

Zepf Mathias, lab, r. 19 Meek.

Ziegelmiller G., lab., bds. 323 W. Washington.

Ziegelmiller Herman, saloon, 59 N. Alabama, r. 53 N. Alabama.

Ziegler Charles, lawyer, bds. 396 N. Alabama.

ZIEGLER GEO. H., patent agency, 87 E. Market, r. 346 N. Meridian.

Zimmer Ferdinand, barber, r. 260 S. Delaware.

Zimmer Peter, (Z. & N.) r. 319 S. Delaware.

Zimmer P. M., salesman 29 W. Washington, r. 343 W. Washington.

Zimmer & Neihaus (Peter Z. and Joseph I. N.) dealers in groceries and provisions, 323 S. Delaware.

Zimmerman Benjamin, works Osgood, Smith & Co., r. 266 S. Illinois.

Zimmermann C., slate and metal roofing, 35 S Alabama, r. 604 E. Washington.

Zimmerman Harry, slater, r 130 Spring.

Zimmerman Jacob, cigarmaker, bds. cor. South and Illinois.

Zimmerman James B., slateroofer, r. 424 E. Georgia.

Zimmerman Mary, (wid.) r. 130 N. Spring.

Zogg Ferdinand, (Pfændler & Z) bds. 326 W. Washington.

ZONCADA CARL, professor of vocal and instrumental music, r. 109 E. Washington.

Zoras Mary, (wid. George) r. 313 S. Delaware.

Zschech Gustavus H., asst. supt. Eagle Machine Works, r. 251 S Meridian.

Zscheck Fred'ck, carpenter, r. 90 Union.

Zukunft Weekly paper, printed by Guttenberg Company.

Zumbusch Theodore, jeweler and watchmaker, 93 E. Washington, r. 61 E. Maryland.

Zumpf Emil, musician, r. 172 N. New Jersey.

Zwig William, tailor, r. 356 S. Alabama.

HUTCHINSON'S

CONSTITUTION

BUSINESS DIRECTORY,

FOR 1870,

Embracing a Classified List of the Principal Trades, Professions and Pursuits in the City of Indianapolis, Arranged Alphabetically for Each Trade.

Abstract of Titles.

Elliott Joseph T., Recorder's Office.
MARTIN & BROWN, 10 E. Washington.

Agricultural Implements.

BRADEN J., 75 W. Washington.
CASE & PARKER, 84 W. Washington.
Lukens R. L., 81 W. Washington.
PRIER HENRY J., 203 E. Washington.
SHERWOOD L. Q., 81 N. Illinois.
Stilz J. George, 78 E. Washington.
Webb A. L., 83 Masonic Hall.

Agricultural Seed Stores.

BRADEN J, 75 W. Washington.
Lukens R. L, 81 W. Washington.
Stilz J. George, 78 E. Washington.
Webb A. L, 83 W. Washington.

Ale and Porter Depots.

Baker Charles, 209 Massachusetts av.
Meir V. & Bros, 225 W. Washington.
O'Connor M. J., 54 S. Illinois.

Amusements, Places of.

Academy of Music, cor. Ohio and Illinois.
Indianapolis Skating Rink, cor. Tennessee and Georgia.
Masonic Hall, se. cor. Washington and Tennessee.
Metropolitan Hall, ne. cor. Washington and Tennessee.

Apothecaries.

(See Drugs and Medicines.)

Architects.

BOHLEN D. A., 19 Talbott & New's blk.
Curzon Joseph, 4 Blackford's blk.

H. H. LEE

MAKES A SPECIALTY OF

Choice Green, Black & Japan Teas.

DAGGETT & ROTH, Vinton's blk.
ENOS & HUEBNER, rooms 1 and 2, Eden's blk.
Hodgson I., 4 Brown's blk.
May Edwin, 173 N. Pennsylvania.
Peckham C. H., 6 Blake's row.
Taylor I., 14 N. Delaware.
Taylor J. F., (ornamental) 80 Massachusetts av.

Artificial Limbs.

American Leg and Arm Co., 172 E. Washington, Haywood & Roemer, proprietors.

Artists.

Cox Jacob, 26 W. Washington.
GLESSING T. B., 233 W. New York.
Greuzard Louis, 454 Virginia av.
Hayes B. S., 4 Talbott & New's blk.
Hill John B., 84 N. Alabama.
Lietz T., 45 E. Washington.
STARLING S. S. MRS., 77½ E. Market.

Attorneys.

(*See Lawyers.*)

Auction and Commission Merchants.

Davis & Jones, 88 E. Washington.
Featherston Wm. E., 194 W. Washington.
McCURDY GEORGE W., cor. Virginia av. and Washington.
Rothschild & Co., 97 E. Washington.
SPELLMAN & CO., 111 S. Illinois and 85 E. Washington.

Awning Manufacturer.

Gorham Wm. H., (slate) 16 E. Washington.

Bakeries.

ÆRATED BREAD CO., 14 and 16 E. South.
Balls Anthony, 178 S. Illinois.
Bollman Frederick, 107 E. Washington.
Bossert John, 112 S Meridian.
ERHART FRANK, 112 S. Illinois.
Ferger Charles 93 E. South.
Grein John, 246 E. Washington.
Gross Charles, 264 E. Washington.
Hespelt Charles & Co., 150 W. Vermont.
Hofacker Charles, 277 N. Noble.
Knauf Adam, 257 Massachusetts av.
Kuhn William, 150 N. East.
McFarlane W. K., 12 S. Meridian.
PARROTT, NICKUM & CO., (steam cracker) 188 E. Washington.
Rauser George, 68 S. West.
Taggart Daniel, 134 S. Meridian.
Viernickel Joseph, 285 E. Washington.

Bands.

HAHN'S BAND, office, Washington Hall.
MEYER'S BAND, 96 S. Illinois.

Banks and Bankers.

CITIZENS NATIONAL, 11 and 13 E. Washington
FIRST NATIONAL, se. cor. Washington and Meridian.
FLETCHER S. A. & CO., 30 and 32 E. Washington.
HARRISON'S BANK, 15 E. Washington.
INDIANA BANKING CO., 28 E. Washington
INDIANA NATIONAL, 2 E. Washington.
INDIANAPOLIS BRANCH BANKING CO., sw. cor. Washington and Pennsylvania.
INDIANAPOLIS INSURANCE CO., cor. Virginia av. and Pennsylvania.
INDIANAPOLIS NATIONAL, ne. cor. Washington and Pennsylvania.
Mansur s, 154 E. Washington.
MERCHANTS' NATIONAL, 48 E. Washington.
PETTIT, BRADEN & CO., 3 Bates House.
RITSINGER'S, 14 E. Washington.
WOOLLEN, WEBB & CO., 31 W. Washington.

Barber Shops.

Artis Wm. H. (col'd) 193 W. Washington.

Basket & Reed, (col'd) 10 S. Pennsylvania.

Brayboy John, cor. Meridian and Washington.

Ferling George, se. cor. Meridian and Washington.

GEUTIG HENRY, cor. Wrshington and Pennsylvania.

Harden & Dorsey, 180 W. Washington.

Hill & Carter, (col'd) Bates Haouse.

Jones John, 16 S Meridian.

Jones & Stewart, 29 N Illinois.

KLE N J. G., 2 Martindale's blk.

PERKINSON GEORGE W, 552 S. Meridian

Porter W. M & J T., 1:9 S. Illinois.

Russell & Gulliver, (col'd) 26 N. Pennsylvania.

Vondergotton, 140 S. Illinois.

Bath Houses.

MERIDIAN STREET, bath house cor. Meridian and Circle.

Beer Gardens.

Inwalle's Garden, 367 Virginia av.

Noble Street Garden, 50 N. Noble.

REINMAN REINHARDT, 252 E. Washington.

REITZ FRANK, cor. Alabama and Washington.

Schaub's Garden, 380 Virginia av.

Bell Hangers.

Isensee Albert, 28 N. Illinois.

Kindler Charles, 60 N. Pennsylvania.

Reinhardt P. J., 81 S. Illinois.

Bell Manufacturer.

SCHNEIDER & CO., 26 E Louisiana.

Belting.

(Rubber and Leather.)

FISHBACK JOHN, 125 S. Meridian.

Mooney & Co., 147 S. Meridian.

Bill Posters.

DISHON JAMES M., office Journal bldg.

Billiard Halls.

Balke Charles, 231 E. Washington.

BOHRMAN PETER, 9 W. Washington.

BENHAM BRO'S,

36 East Washington St.,

STATE AGENTS

FOR THE

INDIANAPOLIS MANUFACTURING CO.'S

PIANOS.

BUSSEY JOHN, National Hotel.

FAHRBACH PHILIP, Washington Hall.

Hoefgen Emanuel, nw. cor. Meridian and Maryland.

HUEGELE JOHN, 39 E. Washington.

Rav J. H., 274 E. Washington.

SELKING WILLIAM, 33 N. Pennsylvania.

SHEPHERD J. McB., 179 E. Washington.

Bird Cages.

BALDWIN J. H. & CO., 6 E. Washington.

Jenninger G. & E., 115 S. Illinois.

MAYER CHARLES & CO., 29 W. Washington.

Blacksmiths.

Davis G. M. (col'd) 252 Indiana av.

Ewald Henry, 299 Massachusetts av.

Fleitz Charles, 487 S. Meridian.

Gates John J., 26 S. New Jersey.

Gibson Harry, 291 Kentucky av.

Hillman William, 377 Virginia av.

Moore Thomas C., se. end Virginia av.

Raymond Samuel, 60 E. Maryland.

Renner Christian, 423 S. Meridian.

Roesener Charles, ns. St. Clair bet. broadway and Massachusetts av.

Siebert Samuel M, 302 E Washington.

Smith John G., 36 S. Pennsylvania.

Stirk J. P, 19 N. Alabama.

Stumpf Joseph, Massachusetts av. cor. Plum.

Trucks & Kay, 60 Kentucky av.

Van Antwerp G. W., 287 E Washington.

Vondersaar Wendell, 144 Ft. Wayne av.

Whitney J. W., 46 S. Pennsylvania.

Wehling Charles' 231 S. Delaware

Weymouth Amos, ns. National rd. west of the bridge.

Blacksmiths' Tools.

HOLLIDAY W. J. & CO., 59 S. Meridian.

Maxwell, Fry & Thurston, 34 S. Meridian.

THE CHINA TEA STORES
ARE LOCATED AT
No. 7 ODD FELLOWS HALL
AND
ACADEMY OF MUSIC CORNER.

SAME GOODS SAME PRICES at BOTH

Blank Book Manufacturers.

BRADEN & BURFORD, 24 W. Washington.
JOURNAL BOOK BINDERY, (Douglass & Conner) Market ne. cor. Circle, Journal bldg.
Sheets William, 79 W. Washington.
Smith Julius H. C., Circle se. cor. Meridian.
STATE SENTINEL BOOK BINDERY, R. J. Bright, sw. cor. Circle and Meridian.

Bleachers and Pressers.

CONATY J. B., 44 S. Illinois.
Malpas H. & Co., 17 Miller's blk.
Whiting E. M, 26 Kentucky av.

Boarding Houses.

Adams Alex., 268 E. St. Clair.
Allison Mrs., 52 N. Pennsylvania.
Baker S. E., 392 N. Alabama.
Barkes Sarah, 9 S. Mississippi.
Beard Soloman, 69 W. Market.
BESE ERNEST, 65 S. East.
Brown D. D. Mrs., 54 S. Pennsylvania.
Burges C. N., 98 N East
Conner Mary E., 78 N. Illinois.
Daniels George T., 131 S. Illinois.
Davis C. Mrs., 60 S. Pennsylvania.
Doerr George, 267 E. Washington.
Dunmeyer Sarah, 17 S Illinois.
Egerton Charles, 179 S Meridian.
Elder W. G., 58 S. Pennsylvania.
Emenegger M, 111 E. Washington.
Essman William 183 S. Illinois.
Fenton John, 124 S. Meridian.
Fox Ellen, 199 W. Maryland.
Fry Mrs. 204 N. Illinois.
Hawkins Eliza, 171 Jackson.
Hoyt Harriet Mrs., 84 Massachusetts av.
King John, 35 Circle.
KOLB WILLIAM, 23 Kentucky av.
Martin J., 33 W. Maryland.
Mason Louisa, 23 W. Georgia.
MATTLER STEPHEN, cor. South and Illinois.
Morris Jacob, 18 Circle.
Mount G A., 148 Indiana av.
Nidigh Catherine Mrs., 416 W. Washington.

Neiman Lulu Mrs 130 S. Illinois.
NOBLE W J, 18 and 20 S. Pennsylvania.
Nolen Lavina, 188 S Illinois.
Omera R. 24 W. Georgia.
Porter Wm. H., 74 N. Pennsylvania.
Reed S. A. Mrs., 30½ N Pennsylvania.
Ritch E. Mrs., 17½ Virginia av.
Tolley E. A. Mrs., 60 W. Market.
UNION HALL, 135 E Washington.
Vaugh George W., 44 S Tennessee.
Walk Louis, 28 W. George.
Whitcomb J. Mrs., 154 W Maryland.
White Jane, 75 S. Pennsylvania.
Wright H M., 566 W. Washington.

Boiler Makers.

COX THOMAS J., 24 E Georgia.
Dumont & Roberts, cor. Mississippi and Louisiana.
EAGLE MACHINE WORKS, east end Union Depot.
SINKER & DAVIS, Western Machine Works.

Book Binders.

JOURNAL BOOK BINDERY, (Douglass & Conner) Market ne. cor. Circle, Journal bldg
SENTINEL BOOK BINDERY, (R J. Bright) sw. cor. Meridian and Circle, Sentinel bldg.
Sheets William, 79 W. Washington.
Smith Julius H. C., Circle se. cor. Meridian.
Steinhauser B. A, 168 E. Washington.

Book Sellers and Stationers.

BOWEN, STEWART & CO., 18 W Washington.
BRADEN & BURFORD, 24 W. Washington.
GEHRING CONRAD, 147 E.Washington.
MERRILL & FIELD, 5 E Washington.
PALMER EDWARD L. (Catholic) 60 S. Illinois.
SMITH JAMES H. V., 4 E. Washington.
Thompson Adda Mrs., 13 N. Pennsylvania.
Todd, Carmichael & Williams, Glenn's blk.
WILDER C. P., 26 E. Washington.

Boot and Shoe Manufacturers.

(Retail Dealers.)
Adams J. W., 53 W. Washington.

ALBERSHARDT H. F., 139 E. Washington.
Aldag Charles, 175 E. Washington.
ARDEN J., 65 S. Meridian.
Bair George, 361 S. Delaware.
Barnworth B., 48 Massachusetts av.
Berry D. M., 199 Indiana av.
Bond & Smith, 161 E. Washington.
Bristor Wm. A., 75 E. Washington.
BRONSON & JONES, 17 W. Washington.
Busch Christian, 248 W. Washington.
Christ John, 138 S. Meridian.
Davis J. E., 239 E. Washington.
Dugan Thomas, 136 S. Illinois.
Dunbar M., 2 Palmer House blk.
DURY & HAWK, 3 E. Washington.
Eyman J. H., 11½ N. Illinois.
Furran John, 191 W. Washington.
Fisher George, 119 Ft. Wayne av.
Friedgen C., 26 W. Washington.
Hafner August, 127 W. Washington.
Hanson M., 361 S. Delaware.
Hofacker G., 16 S. Delaware.
Holbrook P. & Co., 9 Odd Fellows Hall.
Karle Christian, 3 E. Washington.
KINGSBURY & CO., 47 S. Illinois.
Matz John, 176 W. Washington.
Maurice & Spahr, 69 N. Pennsylvania.
Mick & Marshall, 13 W. Washington.
Moorbach Peter, 301 S. Delaware.
Norris John, 23 E. Washington.
Peacock & McLain, 298 Blake.
Rahb Sebastian, 9 N. Illinois.
REID, COUNCIL & CO., 25 W. Washington.
Rehling William, 257 S. Delaware.
Resener C. F., E St. Clair.
Resener Henry, 370 Virginia av.
Rheinschild John, 395 N. New Jersey.
Robinus Frank, 223 W. Washington.
Rose J. N., 90 E. Market.
Schildmeyer A., 313 E. Washington.
Schomberg Wm., 218 E. Washington.
SENOUR J. & CO., 5 W. Washington.
Schafer John, cor. Canal and Indiana av.
Sherer Adam, 34 N. Illinois.
Shopp George, 121 S. Illinois.
Siersdorfer L., 41 E. Washington.
SPRENGFIEL & CO., 122 S. Illinois.
Stein Joseph, 406 S. Meridian.
Teneyck J., 340 W. Washington.
Vanstan John, 10 Virginia av.
Vielhaber D., 204 E. Washington.
Waller B., 151 Indiana av.
Walter William, 37 W. Washington.
Wands John, 28 S. Delaware.
Wasson W. P., 175 S. Tennessee.
Wells T. L., 57 N. Illinois.
Whele Lucas, 235 E. Washington.
Whitney William, 55 S. Illinois.
26

BENHAM BRO'S,

36 East Washington St.,

AGENTS FOR THE

BURDETT ORGAN.

Boots and Shoes.

(Wholesale.)

BRONSON & JONES, 17 W. Washington.
BURTON J. C. & CO., 114 S. Meridian.
HENDRICKS, EDMUNDS, & CO., 79 S. Meridian.
KINGSBURY & CO., 47 S. Illinois.
MAYHEW, WARNE & CO., 8 W. Louisiana.
MAYHEW & BRANHAM, 129 S. Meridian
REID, COUNCIL & CO., 25 W. Washington.
VINNEDGE, JONES & CO., 66 S. Meridian.

Bowling Alleys.

KLARE & SCHRAEDER, 588 S. Meridian.
SINGLE ABDEN, 176 E. Washington.
Schaub Henry jr., 334 Virginia av.
Wreidt C., 34 W. Georgia.

Box Manufacturers.

PFÆNDLER & ZOGG, cor. Louisiana and Mississippi.
Wheatley Henry H., cor. South and Delaware.

Brass Founders.

Davis J. W., 110 S. Delaware.
EAGLE BRASS WORKS, 94 S. Delaware, Stierle & Leeper, prop'rs.
Johnson E. & Co., 108 S. Delaware.
PHŒNIX BELL AND BRASS WORKS, Schneider & Co., proprietors, 26 E. Louisiana.

Brewers.

Harting Bros., 7 Norwood.
LEIBER PETER & CO., 313 S. Pennsylvania.
Maus Casper, W. end New York.

H. H. LEE

PURCHASES HIS

Teas, Coffees, Sugars & Spices

DIRECT FROM THE

Importers and Refineries,

THUS SAVING

HIS CUSTOMERS TWO OR THREE PROFITS.

MEIKEL JOHN P., 297 W. Washington.
SCHMIDT C. F., S. end Alabama.
SPONSEL & BALZ, Madison rd.
WRIGHT FRANK, W. end New York.

Bricklayers and Contractors.

Cruse John P., 550 E. Washington.
Fiscus T. W., 280 E. St. Clair.
Lucky George, 75 E. Washington.
Martin John, 133 N. Pennsylvania.
Theodore Thomas, 285 N. East.
Wallace & Gray, 219 N. Davidson.
Whitsitt Court E., sw. cor. Washington and Meridian.

Brokers.

(*Merchandise.*)

Jones & Hasselman, 30 S. Meridian.

Brokers.

(*Note, Stock and Bond.*)

GOODWIN T. A., 79 E. Market.
MARTIN LUTHER R., 10 E. Washington.
MICK, GEYER & CO., 16½ E. Washington.
WOOD & HOSS, Wiley's blk.

Brush Manufacturers.

Schmedel & Fricker, 300 Morris.
Wallace Nicholas, 17 N. Noble.

Butchers.

(*See Meat Market.*)

Cabinet Makers.

See Furniture Manufacturers.)

Cancer Physicians.

Coward E., 92 S. Illinois.
Swank M., 76 N. Pennsylvania.

Candy Makers.

(*See Confectioners.*)

Carpenters and Builders.

Altland S. F., 176 E. Court.
Berry & Flathers, 36 S. Pennsylvania.
BLACK G. H., 368 E. New York.
Boedeker & Nirman, 418 E. North.
BRIGGS & BROS., 98 Indiana av.
BUILDERS' AND MANUFAC-
TURERS' ASSOCIATION,
225 N. Delaware.
Cosly R. M., 317 Massachusetts av.
FATOUT J. L. & M. K., nr. Lafayette depot.
Feary J. E., 318 E. North.
GILKEY & JONES, 48 Kentucky av.
LANG & BLACK, 61 W. Pratt.
Lowe N. H. & Son, 39 S. New Jersey.
Many John B. & Son, 120 Spring.
Monroe & Johnson, 40 W. Market.
Morse T. J., West. nr. New York.
Rafert A. F., 75 E. Walnut.
Rickard Thomas, 127 E. Maryland.
Rouiter Peter, cor. Cedar and Hosbrook.
SHOVER & CHRISTIAN, 124 E. Vermont.
VINCENT WILLIAM H., 178 N. Davidson.

Carpets, Oil Cloth, Etc.

(*Wholesale and Retail.*)

Gall & Rush, 101 E. Washington.
HUME, ADAMS & CO., 26 and 28 W. Washington.
ROLL WILLIAM H., 38 S. Illinois.

Carriage Manufacturers.

DREW SAMUEL W., E. Market Square.
LOWE GEORGE & CO., 26 and 28 S. Tennessee.
LUTHER ROBERT D., 224 E. Washington.
MILLER GEORGE, cor. Kentucky av. and Georgia.
SHAW, LIPPINCOTT & CONNER, 26, 28 and 30 E. Georgia.
SMITH FULLER, proprietor Citizens' Carriage Shop, cor. Liberty and Washington.
Van Blaricum J., 231 W. Washington.

Carriage Materials.

Osgood, Smith & Co., 230 S. Illinois.
SHARE GEORGE K. & CO., 40 S. Meridian.

Castings.

(*See Founders.*)

Chair Manufacturers.

Jackson, Rider & Co., cor. New York and Canal.
Schilling & Bros., 134 E. McCarty.
SPROULE, CONKLIN & LEE, cor. New York and Canal.

China, Glass and Queensware.

(*Wholesale and Retail.*)

Coulon Chas. & Co., 168 E. Washington.
HOLLWEG & REESE, 92 and 94 S. Meridian.
SCHRADER CHRISTIAN, 94 E. Washington.
SCOTT, WEST & CO., 127 S. Meridian.
WEST, MORRIS & GORRELL, 37 S. Meridian.
WOODBRIDGE JOHN, 36 S. Meridian.
WOODBRIDGE JOHN & CO., 12 W. Washington.

China Tea Stores.

LEE H. F., Academy of Music Corner and No. 7 Odd Fellows Hall.

Cigars and Tobacco Manufacturers.

(*Retail Dealers.*)

Back & Wenken, 209 E. Washington.
Campbell John, 11 N. Illinois.
HUNT CHAS. C., 61 E. Washington.
Koster C. J. M., 14 Indiana av.
KRETSCH PETER, 141 S. Illinois.
McGau J. A., 16 N. Illinois.
Mayer Mathias, 96 S. Illinois.
MAYER & BROS., 39 W. Washington.
Mengis F., 182 S. Delaware.
MEYER CHARLES F., 11 N. Pennsylvania.
MEYER GEO. F. & CO., 35 W. Washington.
Meyer Jacob, cor. Maryland and Illinois.
Oliver Chas., 288 W. Washington.
RASCHIG C. M., 11 E. Washington.
Reinken Henry, 266 E. Washington.
Reynolds N. W., 244½ E. Washington.
Rosewinkel Geo., 183 Massachusetts av.
Schmidt R. & Son, 308 E. Washington.
Schutz Henry, 36 Virginia av.
Selking William, 33 N. Pennsylvania.
Sharpe Andrew W., 28 N. Pennsylvania.

BENHAM BRO'S,

36 East Washington St.,

PIANOS, ORGANS, MUSIC.

Best Goods! Lowest Prices!

SOLOMON & GARRATT, 42 W. Washington.
Speckman Henry, 108 S. Illinois.
Uhl & Durham, 21 S. Meridian.
WILSON J. T., 3 Spencer House.

Cigars and Tobaccos.

(*Wholesale.*)

GREEN J. C. & CO., 381 S. Meridian.
HUNT C. C., 61 E. Washington.
Lines J. W., & Co., 4 W. Louisiana.
MAYER & BROS., 39 W. Washington.
MEYER G. F. & CO., 35 W. Washington.
Oliver Charles, 288 W. Washington.
RASCHIG C. M., 11 E. Washington.
Sharpe A. W., 28 N. Pennsylvania.
SOLOMON & GARRATT, 42 W. Washington.
Wallace W. P., 28 W. Louisiana.

Claim Agents.

BLAKE JOHN W., 45 E. Washington.
Hamlin & Wright, 62 E. Washington.
WITT B. F. & CO., sw. cor. Meridian and Washington.

Clocks and Mirrors.

Daumont H. & Co., 15 W. Washington.

Clothing.

(*Retail.*)

GŒPPER F. & CO., 17 E. Washington.
GRAMLING J. & P., 35 E. Washington.
GREISHEIMER M., 1 W. Washington.
Kahn L., 24 W. Louisiana.
KAHN & KAUFMAN, 71 and 133 S. Illinois.
Mitchell J., 2 Bates House blk.
MOSSLER L. I. & BROS., 37 E. Washington.
Rauh Brothers, 1 Palmer House.

H. H. LEE'S

WHOLESALE PRICES FOR

TEAS. COFFEES & SUGARS,

ARE THE SAME EACH DAY

As are quoted in the

CINCINNATI DAILY PAPERS.

Reinheimer N., Palmer House.
Rothschild Henry 125 W. Washington.
Segar Levy, 227 E. Washington.

Clothing.

(Wholesale.)

Dessar Bros. & Co., 60 S. Meridian
HAYS, ROSENTHAL & CO., 64 S. Meridian.
MOSLER L. I. & BROS., 37 E. Washington.

Coal and Coke Dealers.

Bigelow Mining Company, office, cor. Tennessee and Smith.
Funk John 23 Virginia av.
DUTSCH, DIXON & DELL, 27 E. Georgia.
Davis Benjamin & Co., 108 S. West.
ELDER JOHN R., 21 S. Pennsylvania.
Faulkner & Connelly, 24 E. Georgia.
Francis & Co., cor. Market and Canal.
INGLE MARK W., 36 E. Market.
McDonough D. B., 144 S. Alabama.
Rolling Mill Coal Company, office, cor. South and Tennessee.
ROSS J. H., 24 E. Pearl.
Turner W. H. & Co., 19 Circle.

Coffee and Spice Mills.

JUDSON, MAGUIRE & CO., 31 E. Maryland.

Collar Makers.

(Horse.)

Kaufman A. S., 76 S. Delaware.
Schwegel Daniel, 261 S. Pennsylvania.

Collecting Agents.

BLAKE JOHN W., 45 E. Washington.
GOODWIN T A., 78 E. Market.
NICHOL JOSEPH W., 16½ E. Washington.

Commercial Colleges.

KOERNER C. & CO., 5 Ætna bldg.
Bryant, Stratton & Co., se. cor. Washington and Meridian.

Commission Merchants.

Barnes & Williams, 26 N. Illinois,
BUDD & HINSLEY, 18 W. Pearl.
CALDWELL & FRANCIS, 61 S. Illinois.
Elliot & Berry, 21 Circle.
Gallup W. P. & E. P., 43 N. Tennessee.
GLAZIER CHARLES, 146 S. Pennsylvania.
HOLMAN G. G., 6 Bates House blk.
LESH, TOUSEY & CO., 72 and 74 S. Delaware.
NOEL & SON, 86 Virginia av.
Osterman John & Co., 86 W. Washington.
Porter Omer T., 61 S. Meridian.
Rush Fred. P., 99 S. Delaware.
VanCamp & Jackson, 69 W. Washington.
Wallace Andrew, 52 S. Delaware.

Commissioner of Deeds.

MARTIN LUTHER R., 10 E. Washington.

Confectioners and Fruit Stores

Baldwin J. L., 56 N. Illinois.
Balls A., 178 S. Illinois.
BAUER JACOB, 147 W. Washington.
BECKER BROS., 17 N. Pennsylvania.
Bollman F., 107 E. Washington.
CAEVERT CHAS, 143 W. Washington.
Carter C. C., 59 N. Illinois.
Castelle Elizabeth, 105 Massachusetts av.
Conti A., cor. Washington and Illinois.
Coster Mary, 22 N. Delaware.
ERHART FRANK, 112 S. Illinois.
Martin C. Mrs., 80 E. Washington.
Parrisette Joseph, 25 N. Illinois.
SMITH R. L., 40 W. Washington.
Stephens T. D., 164 Indiana av.
Townsend A. G Mrs., 321 E. Market.
Weinberger & Co., 10 W. Louisiana.
Wildrick W. E., 317 Virginia av.

Confectioners.

(Wholesale.)

BECKER F. P. & BROS., 17 N. Pennsylvania.

DAGGETT & CO., 26 S. Meridian.
SMITH R. L. 40 W. Washington,

Coopers.

Baird Wm., west end Maryland.
Burton Daniel, west end New York.
MAY ANDREW, 102 S. East.
McNeely E., 364 W. Washington.
Schwomeyer H., 308 N. Noble.

Copper Dealers.

COTTRELL THOMAS, 177 E.
  Washington.

Coppersmiths.

Johnson E. & Co., 108 S. Delaware.
LANGENSKAMP Wm., 96 S.
  Delaware.

Cotton Factories.

Indianapolis Cotton Factory, west end
  Washington, north of bridge, R. P.
  Duncan, sup't.

Cutlery.

(See *Hardware*.)

Dental Depot.

Strong & Smith, 48 N. Pennsylvania.

Dentists.

Burgess C C., 1 Odd Fellows' Hall.
Heiskel W. L., Martindale's blk.
Hunt P. G C., 76½ E. Market.
Johnston J. F., 19 W. Maryland.
Kilgore J. D., 70 N. Illinois.
Munhall I. W., 35½ E. Market.
Nichols T. M., 25 W. Washington.
Pursell A. E., Martindale's blk.
WELLS & SULLIVAN, 15 E.
  Washington.
WELLS MERRITT, 2 Yohn's blk.
Woodbury W. T., 39½ W. Washington.

Dress Trimmings.

ALLEN NANA M. MRS., 36½ E.
  Washington.
Fairbank & Co., 22 W. Washington.
HAERLE WILLIAM, 4 W. Wash-
  ington.
SPADES H. M., 20 E. Washington.
Walker Mary W. 40 S. Illinois.

BENHAM BRO'S,

36 East Washington St.,

PUBLISHERS OF

BENHAM'S MUSICAL REVIEW,

MONTHLY, $1 00 PER ANNUM.

Dress and Cloak Makers.

ALLEN NANA M. MRS., 36½ E.
  Washington.
Barker Kate, 19 Massachusetts av.
Bissell J. W. Mrs., 24 S. West.
Daugherty E. Miss, 12 Martindale's blk.
Doriand Mrs., 9 E. New York.
Grannis Mary Mrs., 76 Massachusetts av.
HOLLIDAY E. J. MRS., 46 S. Illi-
  nois.
JORDAN ELLA MISS, 186½ W.
  Washington.
Jarrell F. E. Miss, 36 N. Illinois.
Smith Lizzie D., 40 S. Illinois.
Newton M. S. Mrs., 110 S. Illinois.

Druggists.

(*Wholesale.*)

BROWNING & SLOAN, 7 and 9
  E. Washington.
Haskit, Morris & Co., 14 W. Washington.
Kiefer & Vinton, 68 S. Meridian.
PATTERSON, MOORE & TAL-
  BOTT, 123 S. Meridian.
Stewart & Morgan, 40 E. Wahington.

Druggists.

(*Retail.*)

BROWNING & SLOAN, 7 and 9
  E. Washington.
Bryan F. A., cor. Massachusetts av. and
  Vermont.
BRYAN JAMES W., cor. Louisiana
  and Illinois.
Butterfield W. W., 521 N. Illinois.
CAMPBELL & GREEN, 149 W.
  Washington.
Dryer James W., 313 E. Washington.
ERDLEMEYER FRANK, 91 E.
  Washington.
FRAUER I. C., 246 E. Washington.
Hannaman & Co., 100 E. Washington.
HASKIT. MORRIS & CO., 14 W.
  Washington.
Hay Campbell, 48 W. Washington.
LEE H. H., 18 and 20 Bates House.
LOWRY WILEY M., 65 Massachu-
  setts av.

H. H. LEE
HAS BUT
ONE PRICE, SELLS FOR CASH,
And Guarantees all Goods
Sold at the China Tea Stores,
To be as Represented.

MARTIN EMILE, cor. Meridian and McCarty.
METZNER ADOLPH, 127 E. Washington.
Miller E. F., 49 S. Illinois.
MOODY BROS., cor. Tennessee and New York.
Mueller S. H., 187 E. Washington.
Sage Charles, 172 W. Washington.
Snider W. H., cor. Virginia av. and South.
STEWART & MORGAN, 40 E. Washington.
Swing & Dennis, 4 Martindale's blk.
TOMLINSON & COX, 18 E. Washington.
WALLACE W. W., 441 N. Illinois
WILES & REYNOLDS, Vinton's blk.
WILEY M. W. & CO., 408 S. Meridian.

Dry Goods.
(Importers.)

CULLINY PATRICK M., 72 W. Washington.

Dry Goods.
(Retail.)

Adams F. J. & R. F., 180 E. Washington.
Close W. H., 10 E. Washington.
CULLINY P. M., 72 W. Washington.
Deitch Felix, 162 W. Washington.
Eccles Wm. 22 W. Washington.
Fairbanks & Co., 22 W. Washington.
GORDON & HESS, 3 Odd Fellows Hall.
Kahn S. & Bros., 45 E. Washington.
Kahn S. & Bros., 174 E. Washington.
Linter C. H., 184 Indiana av.
Meir, Lewis & Co., 151 Ft. Wayne av.
PETTIS, DICKSON & CO., Glenn's blk.
Prange C. & Co., 318 E. Washington.
Rice C., 164 W. Washington.
Robertson Bros., 95 E. Washington.
Sailors James L., 156 W. Washington.
SMITH N. R. & CO., 26 and 28 W. Washington.
SPADES H. M., 20 E. Washington.

Syrup H., 199 Massachusetts av.
TRAVER GEORGE M., nw. cor. Washington and Meridian.
TUCKER & SMITH, 9 N. Pennsylvania.

Dry Goods.
(Wholesale.)

BYRAM, CORNELIUS & CO., 104 S. Meridian.
HIBBEN, TARKINGTON & CO., 112 S. Meridian.
Landers, Conduitt & Co., 95 S. Meridian.
MURPHY, JOHNSTON & CO., se. cor. Meridian and Maryland.
PETTIS, DICKSON & CO., Glenn's blk.
SMITH N. R. & CO., 26 and 28 W. Washington.

Dye Works.

Smith J. B., 3 Martindale's blk.

Dyers and Scourers.

Bouchett S. Mrs., 42 Kentucky av.
Friedgen C. H., 41 N. Illinois.
Heaft August, 65 N. Illinois.
PROSSER JOHN, cor. Market and Illinois.
Skinner & Bradock, 62 S. Illinois.
Smith John B., 3 Martindale's blk.

Eating Houses.
(See also Restaurants.)

Andrew John B., 32 W. Louisiana.
Back John, 30 W. Louisiana.
Harper James, 34 W. Louisiana.
Keppel Martin, 36 W. Louisiana.

Edge Tool Manufacturer.

Kellogg Newton, 411 W. Washington.

Embroidering and Stamping.

Luders Misses, 74½ E. Market.
Strider T. P., 46 S. Illinois.

Engine Builders.

Chandler & Taylor, 270 W. Washington.
EAGLE MACHINE WORKS. Louisiana, cor. Meridian.
GREENLEAF & CO. 325 S. Tennessee.

WESTERN MACHINE W'KS.
Sinker & Davis, proprietors, cor.
Pennsylvania and Union Railroad.

Engravers.
(Wood and Metal.)

BINGHAM W. P., 50 E. Washington.
CHANDLER H. C. & CO., cor.
Meridian and Pearl.
Perrine T. B., 24 Virginia av.

Engravings.
(Steel.)

TRACY M. O. & CO., 7 Martindale's blk.

Express Companies.

ADAMS EXPRESS CO. J. H.
Ohr, Agent, office in new Sentinel
bldg.
American Merchants' Union Express Co.,
J. Butterfield, Agent, 42 and 44 E.
Washington.

Fancy Goods.
(Retail.)

BALDWIN J. H., 6 E. Washington.
Heninger G. & E., 115 S. Illinois.
MAYER CHARLES & CO., 29 W.
Washington.

Fancy Goods.
(Wholesale.)

BALDWIN J. H. & CO., 6 E. Washington.
MAYER CHARLES & CO., 29 W.
Washington.

Fast Freight Lines.

Empire Line, J. A. Murray, agent, 96
Virginia av.
ERIE TRANSP'TN CO., W. B.Williams, agent, 80 and 82 Virginia av.
Great Western Despatch, T. A. Lewis,
superintendent, 82 Virginia av.
MERCHANTS' DESPATCH, S.
T. Scott, agent, 19 Virginia av.
PEOPLE'S DESPATCH, S. T.
Scott, agent, 19 Virginia av.
STAR UNION LINE, S. F. Gray,
agent, 85 Virginia av.
WHITE LINE CO., Alabama, cor.
Railroad.

BENHAM BRO'S,
36 East Washington St.,
SHEET MUSIC, VIOLINS,
GUITARS, STRINGS, &c.

Feathers.

Sherman & Comingore, 21 W. Maryland.

Ferreotypes.

Hall Alfred, 16½ E. Washington.

Files and Rasps.

Drotz & Stienbauer, 136 S. Pennsylvania.

Fish Markets.

Sowders & Jacoby, 26 W. Pearl.
Todd Samuel, 107 S. Illinois.
Van Benthusian J. H., 149 Virginia av.

Fishing Tackle.

BALDWIN J. H. & CO., 6 E.
Washington.
BALLWEG AMBROSE, 129 W.
Washington.
BECK SAMUEL, 62 E. Washington.
MAYER CHARLES & CO., 29
W. Washington.

Florist.
(See Nurserymen.)

Flour and Feed.

Altman H. & Co., cor. Ray and Meridian.
Bell & Webb, 78 Massachusetts av.
Booker & Co., 46 Virginia av.
Caldwell H. W., 149 Indiana av.
Caylor & Co., 185 Indiana av.
COOK & WEIGMAN, 253 E. Washington.
Dehene & Bros., 300 E. Washington.
Fahrion George, 90 E. South.
GLAZIER CHARLES, 146 S. Pennsylvania.
GOTH, BROWN & CO., 489 N
New York.
Hoffmeister N., 150 N. Noble.
Langenberg H. H. & Co., 244 W. Washington.
McFarland R., 155 W. Washington.
Osterman John & Co., 86 W. Washington.

THE CHINA TEA STORES

Are very handsomely decorated with

Accurate Views and Scenes

OF

CHINESE LIFE AND SCENERY.

Call and see them before leaving the City.

ROBISON ANTHONY W., 201 Indiana av.

Rush Fred. P., 99 S. Delaware

STOLTE & COOK, 253 E. Washton.

Stolte & May, 365 S. Delaware.

WEBB A. L., 83 W. Washington.

Flouring Mills.

Carlisle Henry, 200 W. Maryland.

Carlisle John, 200 W. Market.

Geisendorff & Co., west end Washington.

HECKMAN & SHEESLEY, 354 E. Washington.

Orme C. & Bros., S. Meridian out city limits.

RESENER & BROS., Cumberland, bet. Delaware and Alabama.

Skillen James, 354 W. Washington.

SOHL, GIBSON & CO., 352 W. Washington.

Foundries and Machine Shops.

Chandler & Taylor, 379 W. Washington.

EAGLE MACHINE WORKS, east end Union Depot.

GREENLEAF & CO., 319 S. Tennessee.

Hetherington B. F. & Co., 244 S. Pennsylvania.

Russell David, cor. Benton and Market.

UNION NOVELTY WORKS. cor. Canal and St. Clair.

VATER & KING, cor. Canal and Georgia.

WESTERN MACHINE W'KS, 125 S. Pennsylvania.

Fruit House.

VanCamp & Jackson, 69 W. Washington.

Furniture.

(*Dealers.*)

BAKER N. S., 78 E. Washington.

Burk, Earnshaw & Co., 67 W. Wasington.

CABINET MAKERS' UNION, 426 to 450 E. Market.

DOHN PHILIP, 246 S. Meridian.

GEBHARD AUGUST, 117 E. Washington.

Helweg Charles, 115 E. Washington.

Joze N., 8 S. Pennsylvania.

MASTERS JOHN H., 141 W. Washington.

MITCHELL, RAMMELSBERG & CO., 38 E. Washington.

SPEIGEL, THOMS & CO., 71 and 73 W. Washington.

Marott John, 87 E. Washington.

Western Furniture Co., 105 E. Washing.

Furniture.

(*Manufacturers.*)

Burk, Earnshaw & Co., 67 W. Washington.

CABINET MAKERS' UNION, 450 E. Market.

DOHN PHILIP, 246 S. Meridian.

Jackson, Rider & Co., cor. New York and Canal.

MITCHELL, RAMMELSBERG & CO., 38 E. Washington.

Ott John, terminus Dacota.

SPEIGEL, THOMS & CO., 71 and 73 W. Washington.

Western Furniture Co., 105 E. Washington.

Furs.

(*Dealers.*)

BAMBERGER H., 16 E. Washington.

DAVIS ISAAC & CO., 12 E. Washington.

Lelewer D. & Bros., 56 S. Meridian.

Gregory Denis, 33 S. Illinois.

Furs.

(*Manufacturers and Dealers.*)

Lelewer D. & Bros., 56 S. Meridian.

Gas and Steam Fitters.

(*See also Plumbers.*)

Amos & Co., 21 Massachusetts av.

Davis Joseph W., 110 S. Delaware.

HANNING JOHN G., 82 W. Washington.

Karney John, 78 Virginia av.

NEAB CONRAD, 70 N. Illinois.

Gents' Furnishing Goods.

GRIESHEIMER M., 1 W. Washington.

PARKER R. R., 30 W. Washington.

SMITH & FOSTER, 22 E. Washington.

Glue Manufacturers.

Goss & Co., Michigan rd., opposite Camp Morton.

Grocers.
(*Wholesale.*)

ALFORD, TALBOTT & CO., 123 S. Meridian.
CROSSLAND, HANNA & CO., sw. cor. Meridian and Maryland.
FOSTER, WIGGINS & CO., 68 and 70 S. Delaware.
HOLLAND, OSTERMEYER & CO., 27 and 29 E. Maryland.
ROBERTSON J. E. & CO., 74 and 76 S. Meridian.
SEVERIN, SCHNULL & CO., 55 and 57 S. Meridian.
Wallace Andrew, 52 and 54 S. Delaware.
Wiles Bros & Co., 149 S. Meridian.

Grocers and Produce Dealers.

Adams John H., 198 W. South.
Affanger S. J., 199 Indiana av.
ALTMAN H. & CO., cor. Ray and Meridian.
Baker & Surbey, 199 Virginia av.
Basdœfer George, 546 E. Washington.
Bass & Henderson, 143 N. Delaware.
Baxter & Davis, 250 W. Washington.
Berg & Waterman, 193 S. Tennessee.
Blatz Catherine, 440 S. Illinois.
Boechter George, 52 S. California.
Bothwell H., 530 N. Mississippi.
Bretz Adam, 44 W. Louisiana.
Brinker August, 174 W. New York.
Brown A., 387 S. Delaware.
BROWN F. M., 59 W. Washington.
Brown John G., 300 N. New Jersey.
Brown John J., 202 E. Washington.
Brunner John, 684 N. Mississippi.
Cady & Hendricks, 523 N. Illinois.
CALDWELL H. W., 149 Indiana av.
CARR THOMAS, 276 S. Missouri.
CLEM AARON, cor. Delaware and Massachusetts av.
Coble D. & G., 152 W. Washington.
COMER STEPHEN, 668 N. Tennessee.
Cook W. & Co., 249 E. Washington.
COORS AUG. F., 151 W. Washington.
CORBALY & COSSELL, 414 W. Washington.
Culver E., 240 Indiana av.
Cussick Joseph, 75 S. West.
Deppel L., 557 Virginia av.
Dietz J. & L., cor. Alabama and Ft. Wayne av.

27

BENHAM BRO'S,

36 East Washington St.,

AGENTS FOR THE

BURDETT ORGAN.

Donnelly Francis, 347 S. Delaware.
Draper J. H., 213 E. Washington.
DUNN & WIGGINS, cor. Indiana av. and New York.
Eagle John H., cor. Delaware and Ft. Wayne av.
Farmer A. B., 251 N. Illinois.
Folken M., 674 N. Mississippi.
FRICK JOHN, cor. Massachusetts av. and St. Clair.
GAHM JOHN, 196 Indiana av.
George Robert, 184 W. Washington.
Gimbel M., 329 S. East.
Goe H. M., 352 W. New York.
Gold Adam, 405 W. Washington.
GOTH, BROWN & CO., 489 N. New Jersey.
HAGERHORST C. F. & CO., 223 W. Ohio.
Haneman J. & T., 135 Massachusetts av.
HARLAN GEORGE W., cor. Massachusetts av. and New Jersey.
Harmoming C., 288 S. Delaware.
Hanley John, 340 Virginia av.
Healey Patrick, 225 S. Tennessee.
Hilgemeir C., cor. Delaware and McCarty.
Hill James, 314 W. New York.
Hoffman Philip, cor. Sixth and Tennessee.
Hoffmeister Nicholas, 150 N. Noble.
Hoover D., 149 Blake.
HORN HENRY J., 174 W. Washington.
Huff J. T., 298 N. Pennsylvania.
Hutchins E. S., 407 N. Alabama.
Jasper F. W., 333 Virginia av.
Johnson H. A., 339 N. New Jersey.
Johnson R. J. & Co., 399 N. Illinois.
JONES & PICKERILL, cor. Cherry and Broadway.
Jordan John, 158 W. Washington.
Kalb F., 310 N. Winston.
Kassler Fred., cor. Plum and Massachusetts av.
Kensil George, cor. West and McCarty.
KETTENBACH, NEWMEYER & CO., 173 Massachusetts av.
Kevere John H., 525 N. Mississippi.
Koch H. H., 192 S. Noble.
Kœhl Peter, 188 S. Illinois.
Kothe Wm., 130 N. Davidson.
KRUG G. C. & CO. 296 E. Georgia.
Kuhlman E., 1 Buchanan.
Langenberg H. H. & Co., 244 W. Washington.
Lawless & Curran, 138 S. Noble.

H. H. LEE,
Dealer in
Teas, Coffees, Sugars & Spices,
No. 7 ODD FELLOWS HALL
AND
ACADEMY OF MUSIC CORNER.

Lawrence A. V., 173 W. Washington.
Lawyer & Hall, 49 S. New Jersey.
Lehr Philip, cor. Noble and Massachusetts av.
Lemon D. H., 188 W. Washington.
LINDERMAN FRANK, 206 E. Washington.
Linter A. H., 182 Indiana av.
Lyneaner C, 380 Virginia av.
MAJOR STEPHEN T., 342 E. Washington.
Manu James B., 283 Virginia av.
Many John, cor. Noble and Virginia av.
Mardyck James Y., 399 E. Georgia.
Marshall & Sons, cor. Cherry and Broadway.
Morgemech V., 21 Chatham.
MUELLER EDWARD, 141 E. Washington.
Morrison J. B., cor. New Jersey and Virginia av.
Murphy Timothy, 396 W. North,
MUSSMAN W. & D.544 S. Meridian.
Naughton Patrick, 291 E. Washington.
Newcomb W. C., 302 N. Illinois.
Ostermeyer C. F., 350 E. Ohio.
Patterson J. & Co., 45 Virginia av.
Pfailing Theodore, cor. Mississippi and Vermont.
Poehler Louis, cor. Ray and Meridian.
PRANGE & CO., 318 E. Washington.
Quaintance Daniel, 68 Virginia av.
RAU & BOMBARGER, 46 Indiana av.
Reasner & Schildmeyer, 593 E. Washington.
Redmond Thomas, 246 W. Washington.
Reese Henry, 113 W. Washington.
Reider E. C., 298 E. Washington.
Rextock Edward, 172 S. Illinois.
Rentsch Herman, 141 E. Washington.
Richter Wm., 410 Virginia av.
Richter & Schrosluck, cor. Illinois and Russell.
Ripley & Gates, 47 N. Illinois.
Rodewald Henry, 441 Virginia av.
Ropka Helen Mrs., cor. McCarty and Pennsylvania.
Rosenrock F. W, 178 Virginia av.
Rupp John, 201 Kentucky av.
Sagehorn Jacob, 122 E. Washington.
Sahm R., 142 Ft. Wayne av.
Santo Ed., cor. Indiana av. and North.
SCHETTER CHRISTIAN, 99 E. South.

Schlathauer Adam, 248 N. Liberty.
Schrader Christian, 389 Virginia av.
Schrader & Harting, 299 S. Delaware.
Schœder Christian, 401 Virginia av.
Shreer H. H., 260 S. Alabama.
SCHURICH FRED., W. Indianapolis.
SCHUTTER CHRISTIAN, 239 S. Meridian.
Schwear & Spear, 576 E. Washington.
Schwicks Charles, 524 S. Meridian.
Schwomeyer Charles, 307 S. Meridian.
Seibert Geo. W., 51 N. Noble.
Sexauer Edward, 125 E. Washington.
Sheets David, 241 W. McCarty.
Showater S., 257 Indiana av.
Shuh John, 322 Virginia av.
Simon Fred., 188 N. Noble.
SIMPSON JOHN, cor. Illinois and Georgia.
Simpson Nicholas, 235 S. Delaware.
SMITH BUTLER K. jr., 94 N. Illinois.
Smith F. E, 164 W. Michigan.
Smith Fred., cor. Vermont and Mississippi.
Socwell H. M., 232 E. Washington.
SPENCER MILTON, 192 E. Washington
SPONSEL HENRY, 355 S. Delaware.
Stiegman Charles, 150 Madison av.
Stalle & Mays, 365 S. Delaware.
STOUT BEN. G. & BROS., 7 and 8 Bates House blk.
Stuckmeyer J. H., 358 Virginia av.
Swart J. B., 219 Massachusetts av.
Sullivan H. H., 76 W. Washington.
Tarlton A. J., cor. Illinois and Seventh.
Taylor Samuel, 77 E Market.
Thayer George V., 218 E. Washington.
Traub Israel, 509 N. Alabama.
Vehling Fred., 197 E. South.
WALLACE W. W., 441 N. Illinois.
Warner Louis, 154 Indiana av.
WEBB ISAIAH, 314 Indiana av.
WEIS PETER, sw. cor. East and McCarty.
WHITEHEAD WILLIAM, 430 and 432 W. Washington.
Wilkinson D. E., 44 N. Pennsylvania.
Wittinger Jacob, 109 S. Noble.
Witthoff Fred., 329 Indiana av.
Wolsterbaum A. (wid.) 312 N. Illinois.
Woolen Wm. M, 101 Indiana av.
Worland William, 52 Virginia av.
Wright Levi, 323 N. Alabama.
Wyatt W. D., cor. Noble and Fletcher av.
Zimmer & Neihaus, 323 S. Delaware.

Guns and Pistols.

BALLWEG AMBROSE, 129 W. Washington.

BECK SAMUEL, 63 E. Washington.
VAJEN J. H. & CO., 21 W. Washington.

Gunsmiths.

BALLWEG A., 129 W. Washington.
BECK CHRISTIAN, 12 S. Pennsylvania.
BECK SAMUEL, 63 E. Washington.

Hair Workers and Braiders.
(Also Human Hair Goods.)

SPADES H. M., 20 E. Washington.
Mahorney J. T., 235 Blake.
Medina F. J., 34 W. Washington.

Hair and Bristle Works.

Indianapolis Hair and Bristle Works, S. end West, F. Miller superintendent.

Hardware.
(Wholesale.)

ANDERSON, BULLOCK & SCHOFIELD, 62 S. Meridian.
KIMBAL, AIKMAN & CO., 110 S. Meridian.
OVER E. & CO., 82 and 84 S. Meridian.

Hardware.
(Retail.)

Fowler J. P., 203 Massachusetts av.
Frees Chas. & Co., 27 W. Washington.
Layman J. T. & Co., 64 E. Washington.
MANKEDICK BROS., 123 E. Washington.
POTTAGE CHARLES, 77½ W. Washington.
VAJEN J. H. & CO., 21 W. Washington.
VONEGUT CLEMENS, 184 and 186 E. Washington.

Harness and Saddlemakers.

Andra John, 178 E. Washington.
Armholder H. & Bros., 225 E. Washington.
FRAUER, BEILER & CO., 109 E. Washington.
Hereth Ad., 24 N. Delaware.
HUFFER JAMES W., 23 S. Meridian.
Jemison John, 428 S. Meridian.
Marsh W. J., 182 W. Washington.

BENHAM BRO'S,
36 East Washington St.,
Pianos, Organs and Melodeons
FOR
CASH OR ON TIME.

Nicoli C., 326 E. Washington.
Sellers & Co., 11 S. Meridian.
SULGROVE JAMES, 20 W. Washington.
Shawver C. J., 297 Indiana av.

Harness and Saddlery Hardware.

FRAUER, BEILER & CO., 109 E. Washington.
SHARE GEORGE K., 40 S. Meridian.
SULGROVE JAMES, 20 W. Washington.

Hat and Bonnet Frames.
(Retail.)

Copeland J. W., 8 E. Washington.

Hats, Caps and Furs.
(Retail.)

BAKER JAMES M., 194 E. Washington.
BAMBERGER H., 16 E. Washington.
DAVIS ISAAC & CO., 12 E. Washington.
Obermeyer W. M., 2 Palmer House.
Seaton E. A., 25 N. Pennsylvania.

Hats, Caps and Furs.
(Wholesale.)

CARR & ALVEY, 6 W. Louisiana.
Donaldson & Stout, 54 S. Meridian.
Rickard & Talbott, 78 S. Meridian.

Hides and Leather.

DIETZ & RIESNER, 17 S. Delaware.
FISHBACK JOHN P., 125 S. Meridian.
Frenzel John P., cor. Washington and Davidson.
Sharpe J. K., 47 S. Delaware.
Yandes D., 76 E. Washington.

Homœopathic Physician.

CORLISS C. F., room 5, Miller's blk.

THE CHINA TEA STORES

ARE AT

No. 7 ODD FELLOWS HALL

AND

ACADEMY OF MUSIC CORNER.

Hoop Skirts and Corsets.

Glick & Schwartz, 54 N. Illinois.
Mossler A. L., 59 S. Illinois.
Newman P. Mrs., 95 E. Washington.
Valentine W. H., 34 W. Washington.
Welte Catharine, 153 E. Washington.

Horse Shoers.

(See also Blacksmiths.)

Clark John T., 27 N. Tennessee.
Gates John G., 26 S. New Jersey.
HITCHINS JOHN, 44 E. Maryland.
Smith John G., 36 S. Pennsylvania.

Hosiery.

PARKER R. R., 30 W. Washington.
PETTIS, DICKSON & CO., Glenn's blk.
SMITH N. R. & CO., Trade Palace.
Valentine W. H., 34 W. Washington.

Hot Air Furnaces.

Frankem I. L., 34 E. Washington.
MUNSON & JOHNSTON, 62 E. Washington.

Hotels.

BATES HOUSE, Wesley and Son, Washington n. w. cor. Illinois.
BICKING HOUSE, W. Hebble, 89 S. Illinois.
CALIFORNIA HOUSE, A. Kistner, 184 S. Illinois.
CHICAGO HOUSE, Fred. Sietz, 117 S. Illinois.
Concordia House, F. Mottery, 200 S. Meridian.
Emeneggers Hotel, 111 and 113 E. Washington.
GLOBE HOUSE, H. Greunet, 166 S. Illinois.
Grant House, cor. Illinois and South.
ILLINOIS HOUSE, W. Essmann, 183 S. Illinois.
JEFFERSON HOUSE, F. H. Greunert, 61 E. South.

Lafayette House, George Hoppe, 179 S. Meridian.
LITTLE'S HOTEL, G. Longfellow, Washington se. cor. New Jersey.
MACY HOUSE, A. W. Melsheimer, 45 N. Illinois.
Martin House, Jesse Martin, 33 W. Maryland.
MASON HOUSE, B. Mason & Son, 71 to 75 S. Illinois.
NATIONAL HOTEL, Sapp & Winchester, McNabb, opp. Union Depot.
Neiman House, Mrs. Neiman, 130 S. Illinois.
PALMER HOUSE, Jeff. K. Scott, Illinois, se. cor. Washington.
Pattison House, J. B. Bell, 63 N. Alabama.
Pyle House, John Pyle, 95 N. Meridian.
Ray House, J. M. Lambert, South, se. cor. Delaware.
RICHMOND TEMPERANCE HOUSE, J. G. Collius, 35 W. Georgia.
SHERMAN HOUSE, W. M. Hawkins, Louisiana, opp. Union Depot.
SPENCER HOUSE, J. W. Gray, ne. cor. Louisiana and Illinois.
STANRIDGE HOUSE, Henry J. Stanridge, 41 W. Maryland.
UNION HOUSE, Stephen Mattler, 202 S. Illinois.
Washington House, Peter Deitz, cor. West and Maryland.
Washington House, John Weauer, 181 S. Illinois.
Western House, John Clawson, 127 S. Illinois.

House Furnishing Goods.

ADAMS G. F. & CO., 32 S. Meridian.
Frankem I. L., 34 E. Washington.
MUNSON & JOHNSTON, 62 E. Washington.
TUTEWILER BROS., 74 E. Washington.
Vœgtle Jacob, 103 E. Washington.

Ice Cream Saloons.

(See also Confectioners.)

BECKER F. P. & BROS., 17 N. Pennsylvania.
Carter C. C., 59 N. Illinois.
SMITH R. L., 40 W. Washington.
Martin Mrs., 80 E. Washington.
Parisette Joseph, 25 N. Illinois.

Ice Dealers.

BURKHART GEORGE F., cor. Mississippi and Michigan.

BUTSCH JOSEPH, 68 W. South.
Pitts George W. 370 N. Tennessee.

Insurance Agents.

ABROMET A., room 1, Ætna bldg.
Barnard J., Sentinel bldg.
BEARDSLEY R. E., 11 N. Meridian.
BIEDENMEISTER C. A., 139 E. Washington.
Boyles M. W., 6 Odd Fellows Hall.
Caldwell W. W., 42 W. Washington.
Childers J. R., 4 Blackford's blk.
CONKLIN H. N., 16½ E. Washington.
Curtis H. R., 4½ W. Washington.
Davis C. B. C., Old Fellows Hall.
DUNLOP J. S. & CO., 2 W. Washington.
Folsom E. S., 14 Talbott and News blk.
GIBSON WM. T., Secretary, 6 Odd Fellows Hall.
Gilbert Edward, 4 Blackford's blk.
Green E. S., office, Citizens Nat. Bank.
GREENE & ROYSE, 10 Blackford's blk.
Haehl & Anker, 20 S. Delaware.
Haley W. D., 75 E. Market.
HAMMOND & GRUBBS, 1 Citizens Bank bldg.
Hay William, 6 Blackford's blk.
McCarty, McDonald & Co., Odd Fellows Hall.
McGILLIARD & BROWN, 11 S. Meridian.
MARTIN & HOPKINS, New Journal bldg.
METZGER ALEXANDER, 6 Odd Fellows Hall.
Murphy Tobias M., 9 Martinsdale blk.
NORTHROP W. W., 2 Blake's Row.
Nutting & Wood, 17½ W. Washington.
Olin C. C., 2½ W. Washington.
Ransford & Denton, cor. Meridian and Washington.
Rorison B., Citizens Bank bldg.
SHORTRIDGE W. C., 4 Citizens Bank bldg.
SNYDER D. E. & CO., 13 E. Washington.
Tousey Ralph, 2 Odd Fellows Hall.
TWINING WILLIAM, Sentinel bldg.
WALKER H. H., 3 Martinsdale blk.
WHITCOMB E. A., 4 Yohn's blk.
White A. M., 19 N. Meridian.
White A. S., 19 N. Illinois.
White C. M., 19 N. Meridian.
Wilcox & Means, 3 and 4 Wiley's blk.
Worder C. J. & Son, 85 E. Market.

Iron Railings.

HAUGH B. F. & CO., 74 S. Pennsylvania.

Iron and Steel Warehouses.

(Wholesale.)

HOLLIDAY W. J. & CO., 59 S. Meridian.
Maxwell, Fry & Thurston, 34 S. Meridian.
OVER E. & CO., 82 & 84 S. Meridian.

Jewelry.

BINGHAM W. P., 50 E. Washington.
CRAFT & CUTTER, 24 E. Washington.
FRENCH C. C., 13 N. Meridian.
McLENE & HERRON, 1 Bates' house blk.
Phipp Bros., 32 W. Washington.

Justices of the Peace.

BOGGESS H. H., 96 E. Washington.
Curtis Andrew, 85 E. Washington.
Doepfner Charles, 68 E. Washington.
FISHER CHARLES, 4 Yohn's blk.
Seerest Charles, 45½ E. Washington.

Lamp Trimmings.

HOLLIDAY W. & C. F., 15 S. Meridian.

Lamps, Chandeliers, Etc.

HOLLIDAY W. & C. F., 15 S. Meridian.
SCOTT, WEST & CO., 127 S. Meridian.

Land Warrant Broker.

MARTIN L. R., 10 E. Washington.

Lath and Shingles.

Coburn & Jones, cor. Mississippi and Georgia.
ISGRIGG & BRACKEN, 180 W. Market.
McCORD & WHEATLEY, 186 S. Alabama.

H. H. LEE

MAKES A SPECIALTY OF

Choice Green, Black & Japan Teas.

Laundry.
(Steam.)

SPAULDING J. L., office, 74 E. Market.

Lawyers.

Adams Samuel, 17½ W. Washington.
BARBOUR & JACOBS, 14 N. Delaware.
BARTHOLOMEW P. W., 20½ N Delaware.
Beck A. T., 20½ N. Delaware.
BERNHAMER W. F. A., 83 E. Washington.
BILLS J. M., Parker's blk.
BLAKE JOHN W., 45 E. Washington.
BOWLES THOMAS H., 60 E. Washington.
Brown Ignatius, 8 E. Washington.
Browne T. M., P. O. bldg.
Burns D. V., 62 E. Washington.
CARTER GEORGE E., 96 E. Washington.
DENNY A F., 94 E. Washington.
DUNCAN R. B. & J. S., 3 Brown's blk.
Dye & Harris, 8 and 9, Talbott & New's blk.
ELLIOTT & HOLSTEIN, 24½ E. Washington.
Finch T. M. & J. A., 6 Talbott & New's blk.
GORDON GEORGE E., 6 Odd Fellows' Hall.
Gordon J. W., 4 Talbott & New's blk.
Guffin & Parker, 10 Talbott & New's blk.
Hammond & Judah, 64 E. Washington.
HANNA & KNEFLER, Parker's blk., N. Delaware.
Harrison Reuben E., 17½ W. Washington.
HARRISON TEMPLE C., 17½ W. Washington.
HARVEY JOHN S., 101 E. Washington.
Hazelton William, 4 Ætna bldg.
HELLER JAMES E., 20½ N. Delaware.
HENDRICKS, HORD & HENDRICKS, 24½ E. Washington.
HOLMAN JOHN A., 12 Talbott & New's blk.

JOHNSON EDWARD T., 9 Blackford's blk.
JOHNSON THOMAS E., 42 E. Washington.
JORDAN LEWIS, 1 and 2, Talbott & New's blk.
KLINGENSMITH & HINES, 115½ E. Washington.
Leary P. C., 87½ E. Market.
LEATHERS W. W., 3 Odd Fellows' Hall.
Logan & Brown, 4½ W. Washington.
LOWE WILLIAM A., 16½ E. Washington.
McDonald & McDonald, 3 Ætna bldg.
Martindale & Tarkington, Martinsdale's blk.
Miller J., 94 E. Washington.
MORROW & TRUSLER, 6 Vinton's blk.
Morton George T., Talbott & News blk.
Negley P. G., 24½ E. Washington.
NEWCOMB, MITCHELL & KETCHAM, over 21 E. Washington.
NICHOL J. W., 16½ E. Washington.
PARKER & BLOOMER, 32½ E. Washington.
Patterson William, 98 E. Washington.
Peelle S. J., 68 E. Washington.
PERKINS, BAKER & PERKINS, room 4 Ætna bldg.
Perrin George K., 45 E. Washington.
PORTER, HARRISON & FISHBACK, 5 Yohn's blk.
Rand & Hall, 24½ E. Washington.
Ray John W., 42½ E. Washington.
Ray Martin M. & W. S., 12 Talbott & News blk.
RITTER & IRVING, 24½ E. Washington.
Roach A. L., 3 Ætna bldg.
Roberts Joseph T., 3 Kinder's blk.
SCOTT JOHN N., 32½ E. Washington.
Smith C. W., 5 Yohn's blk.
SPAHR & DAILY, 20½ N. Delaware
KIMBALL E. W., 46 E. Washington.
Sullivan William, 47 E. Washington.
Sweetser James N., 21 E. Washington.
Taylor Edwin, 4 Brown's blk.
TAYLOR NAPOLEON B., 4 Brown's blk.
Voss & Davis, 3 Talbott & News blk.
WALLACE WILLIS, 4 Odd Fellows Hall.
Ward C. D. & P. H., Talbott & News blk.
Wilson L. D., 16½ E. Washington.
WITT B. F., cor. Washington and Meridian.
WOOLEN & RUDDELL, 25½ E. Washington.

Yandes Simon, 21 E. Washington.
Young John, 100 E. Washington.

Lead Pipe and Sheet Lead.

COTTRELL THOMAS, 177 E. Washington.

Leather and Findings.

DEITZ & REISNER, 17 S. Delaware.
FISHBACK JOHN, 125 S. Meridian.
MOONEY & CO., 147 S. Meridian.
Sharpe J. K., 47 S. Delaware.
Yandes D., 76 E. Washington.

Lightning Rod Manufacturers.

INDIANAPOLIS COPPER
LIGHTNING ROD WORKS,
David Munson, Prop., 62 E. Washington.

Lime, Plaster and Cement.

BUTSCH, DICKSON & DELL, 27 E. Georgia.
Fawkner & Connelly, 24 W. Maryland.
McDonough D. B., 144 S. Alabama.

Linseed Oil Manufacturers.

Evans I. P. & Bros., 124 S. Delaware.

Liquors.
(Wholesale.)

BEISER AUGUST, 106 S. Illinois
BENDER, TOBIAS & CO., 189 E. Washington.
Bess William K., 284 W. Washington.
GAPEN & CATHERWOOD, 118 S. Meridian.
HAHN & BALS, 25 S. Meridian.
HORN H. J., 174 W. Washington.
Kaufman A. S., 116 S. Meridian.
KAUFMAN CHARLES, 23 W. Maryland.
Kaufman Moses, 42 W. Louisiana.
LANG LOUIS, 29 S. Meridian.
MUELLER JOHN, 306 E. Washington.
Rikhoff & Bros., 80 S. Meridian.
RYAN T. F., 143 S. Meridian.
RYAN & HOLBROOK, 48 S. Meridian.
SCHWABACKER & SELIG, 41 S. Delaware.
Stout & Son, 160 W. Washington
SWEETSER JOHN, 30 S. Meridian.
WILSON JAMES T., 3 Spencer House.

Lithographers.

BRADEN & BURFORD, 24 W. Washington.

Livery, Sale and Feed Stables.

ALLEN HENRY, 25 E. Pearl.
BRUNDAGE E. C., 223 E. Washington.
Bucksot William, rear Palmer House.
Caffey John H., Wabash al.
Conrad C. P., 19 S. Delaware.
EXCHANGE STABLES, Wm. Hinesly, proprietor, 33 N. Illinois.
GATES & PRAY, E. Market Square.
Hetselgesser & Co., cor. Illinois and South.
Landis Jacob, 30 S. Pennsylvania.
Mills & Hollingsworth, 277 W. Washington.
Stout & Son, 163 W. Washington.
SULLIVAN & DREW, 10 E. Pearl.
Wood & Foudray, 16 N. Pennsylvania.
Wood & Mansur, 21 W. Maryland.

Locksmiths and Bell Hangers.

(See Bell Hangers.)

Looking Glasses.

Daumont H. & Co., 15 W. Washington.
LIEBER H. & CO., 60 E. Washington.
Meyer C. F., 7 Martindale's blk.

Looms.

Howe & Converse, 372 W. Washington.

Lumber Dealers.

BUNTE & DICKSON, 387 E. Market.
Coburn & Jones, cor. Mississippi and Georgia.
Donnellan Charles, office, 6 Blake's row.
Eberts & Owens, 44 Kentucky av.
EMERSON, BEAM & THOMPSON, 225 to 229, W. Market.
HILL GEORGE W., 110 S. East.

JOHN SENOUR. WILL SENOUR.

J. SENOUR & CO.,

CITY SHOE STORE,

No. 5 West Washington St.,

Indianapolis, Ind.

HILDEBRAND & KEPPLE, cor. Indiana av. and Canal.
ISGRIGG & BRACKEN, 180 W. Market.
King Cornelius, cor. St. Clair and Peru.
Long & Joseph, cor. Walnut and Lafayette R. R.
Marsee J. & Son, New Jersey, nr. Washington.
McCORD & WHEATLEY, 186 S. Alabama.
Pressley J. T., cor. Louisiana and West.
STREIGHT & WOOD, office, Yohn's blk.
TATE WARREN, 58 S. New Jersey.
Warne Simon, office, 27 Massachusetts av.

Malt Manufacturers.

Munday & Snyder, 214 S. Delaware.

Mantles.

MUNSON & JOHNSTON, 62 E. Washington.

Marble Workers and Dealers.

Carpenter B. O., 36 E. Market.
DAME JASON, 69 E. Washington.
Lewis W. H., 50 Kentucky av.
MAXWELL G. W., 66 Virginia av.
Roberts & Hiltebrand, 46 Virginia av.
WALLACE W. W., 120 S. Illinois.
WEIR & GREENLEE, 44 Virginia av.

Mathematical Instruments.

(*Manufacturers of.*)

Steffins E. F., sw. cor. Washington and Meridian.

Meat Markets.

Beall J. W., 316 W. Washington.
Beck Fred., cor. McCarty and Meridian.
Boecher Henry, 122 S. Meridian.
Coleman Herman, 300 N. West.
DAVIS E. W., 153 W. Washington.
Dietz & Borst, 104 S. Illinois.
Dobbins M., 751 N. Illinois.

ESSIGKE RICHARD, 170 S. Illinois.
Grafenstein F., 660 N. Tennessee.
Hahn Jacob, 95 W. South.
Heid Louis, cor. Michigan and Noble.
Heryd F., 234 E. Washington.
Jacobi A., 387 S. Delaware.
Kaufman Louis, 32 Virginia av.
KAUFMAN MORITZ, cor. West and North.
Keiser Charles, Fourth, nr. Tennessee.
KELLISCH MARTIN, Bates House blk.
Klepfer A. J., 313 Massachusetts av.
Kramer Henry, 80 Fort Wayne av.
Kuhn Charles, 207 W. Michigan.
Leible A., cor. Plum and Cherry.
Leuisser J., 131 Massachusetts av.
MAGLEY JACOB, 186 W. Washington.
Mayer Michael, 220 S. Meridian.
Moser George, 295 S. Missouri.
Shafer John, 92 N. Illinois.
Sindlinger G., 194 S. Illinois.
SPITZFADDEN PETER, 71 E. Washington.
Stillwagon John, 442 S. Illinois.
Thorne J., 141 N. Delaware.
Unversaw John, 48 Virginia av.
Yorger John & Bros., 245 E. Washington.

Merchant Tailors.

(*See Tailors.*)

Midwives.

Despa Minna, 50 Lockerbie.
Wink Theresa, 195 S. Meridian.

Mill Furnishing Goods and Millwright.

TAGGART SAMUEL, 132 S. Pennsylvania.

Millers.

(*See Flouring Mills.*)

Milliners and Milliners' Goods.

Baker B. Mrs., 244 E. Washington.
Baker E. C. Miss, 194 E. Washington.
CATLIN M. J. MRS., 46 W. Washington.
CONATY J. B., 44 S. Illinois.
COPELAND J. W. & CO., 8 E. Washington.
Goodman Mary J., 23 Massachusetts av.
HOLLIDAY E. J. MRS., 46 S. Illinois.

Kirk E. Mrs. 73 N. Pennsylvania.
Kunz M. A. Miss, 9 S. Alabama.
Lenders L. Misses, 74½ E. Market.
Taylor Madam, 6½ W. Washington.
Thomas M. J. Mrs., 8 W. Washington.

Millinery Goods.
(*Whol sale.*)

Copeland J. W. & Co., 89 S. Meridian.
FAHNLEY & McCREA, 131 S.
Meridian.

Mineral Water Manufacturers.

Dausen & Scribner, 17 Circle.
Reed Anson & Co., 276 W. Washington.
SMITH WILLIAM, 222 E. Wash
ington.

Mouldings.

Dumont & Co., 15 W. Washington
LIEBER H. & CO., 60 E. Washing-
ton.
Meyer C. F, 7 Martindale's blk.

Music Publishers.

BENHAM BROS., 36 E. Washing-
ten.

Music Teachers.

Black J. S., 35½ E. Washington.
Bergstein Carl, 11 Martindale's blk.
Griffith Abie Miss, 42 S Mississippi.
Hess Charles, 263 S Meridian.
Pearsol P. R., 24 W. New York.
SCHELLSCHMIDT A., 173 E.
Washington.
Smith Attlie, 141 Buchanan.

Music and Musical Instru-
ments.

BENHAM BROS., 36 E. Washing-
ton
SCHELLSCHMIDT A., 173 E.
Washington.
WILLARD A. G. & CO., 4 and 6
Bates House.

Newspaper and Periodical
Depots.

Aftune Andrew, 26 S. Delaware.
Barth L. A., Union Depot.
Beltz H. A., Spencer House.
Hindman Robert, Palmer House.

28

BENHAM BRO'S,
36 E. Washington St.,
AGENTS FOR THE
INDIANAPOLIS MANUFACTURING CO.'S
PIANOS.

PALMER EDWARD L., 60 S.
Illinois.
Pyburn H. Wm., P. O. News Stand.

Newspapers and Publica-
tions.
(*See Appendix.*)

Notary Public.
(*See also Lawyers.*)

CAMPBELL GEORGE H., 3 Odd
Fellows Hall.
Franklin G E., 3 Ætna bldg.
HARRISON TEMPLE C., 17½ W.
Washington.
House Ben D., 62 E. Washington.
LOWE WM. A., 16½ E Washington.
MARTIN L. R., 10 E. Washington.
Mathews J F., 62 E. Washington.
May A. D., Sentinel Office.
Moore J. G., 6 Talbott & New's blk.
NICHOL J. W, 16½ E. Washington.
WITT B. F., cor. Washington and
Meridian.

Note and Bill Broker.

MARTIN L. R., 10 E. Washington.

Notions.
(*Wholesale.*)

BYRAM CORNELIUS & CO.,
101 S. Meridian.
FAHNLEY & McCREA, 131 S.
Meridian.
FORTNER, FLOYD & CO., 75
S. Meridian.
**HIBBEN, TARKINGTON &
CO.,** 112 S. Meridian.
Landers, Conduitt & Co., 95 S. Meridian.
Ludorf L. & Co., 42 S. Meridian.
MURPHY, JOHNSTON & CO.,
101 S Meridian.
PETTIS, DICKSON & CO.,
Glenn's blk.
STONEMAN, PEE & CO., nw. cor.
Meridian and Louisiana.
TRAVER GEORGE M., cor. Meri-
dian and Washington.

H. H. LEE

Makes a Specialty of

☐☐ICE GOLDEN RIO,

AND

☐ GOVERNMENT JAVA COFFEES.

Notions.

(Retail.)

☐WMAN & WAKEFIELD, 61
  N. Illinois.
☐LINY D. B., 72 W. Washington.
☐MER & BÖLLINGER, 259
  N. Washington
☐ERLE WILLIAM, 4 W. Wash-
  ington.
☐☐ Robert, 151 E. Washington.
☐☐ Joseph, 115 E. Washington.
☐☐ & Foley, 60 N. Illinois.
☐☐☐ R., 68 N. Illinois.
☐ADES H. M., 20 E. Washington.
☐☐CKER & SMITH, 9 N. Pennsyl-
  vania.

Notions and Fancy Goods.

☐ALDWIN J. H. & CO., 6 E.
  Washington.
☐WMAN & WAKEFIELD, 61
  N. Illinois.
☐☐ & Schwartz, 54 N. Illinois.
☐☐ck R., 68 N. Illinois.
☐ADES H. M., 20 E. Washington.

Nurserymen.

☐☐wood Nursery, J. F Hill, Michigan
  rd., east of city.
☐☐mack John. West Indianapolis.
☐☐GHORST HENRY, Japan, S.
  city limits.
☐☐and Anton, cor. Kentucky av. and
  Canal.

Oculists.

☐☐ H. & Son. 2 Miller's blk.
☐☐ CHARLES E., 21½ W. Maryland.

Oil Manufacturers.

☐☐ J. P. & Co., 124 S. Delaware.

Opticians.

☐☐Y GEORGE W., 498 E. Washington.

Moses L. W., 50 E. Washington.
Semmons H., 43 S. Illinois.

Oysters, Fish and Game.

DeRUITER D., 65 S. Illinois.
Randall Nelson A., 29 S. Illinois.
Sharp & Long, 119 S. Illinois.

Painters.

(House and Sign.)

Anhorn E., cor. St. Clair and Spring.
Chivalier A., 23 S. East.
Cook T. V., 58 N. Pennsylvania.
Cornelius & Melville, 31 Kentucky av.
Egger & Muecke, cor. Washington and
  Alabama
ELVIN & FOX, 58 N. Pennsylvania.
Fertig Frank, 21 S. Illinois.
Helle Louis, 248 S. Pennsylvania.
Jenkins E., 43 Massachusetts av.
Knotts Nim K., 32 S. New Jersey.
Lupton W. C. 79 N. Pennsylvania.
McElvano John, 46 Kentucky av.
Osgood & Chapman, cor. Virginia av.
  and Washington
RYAN BROTHERS, 18 S. Meridian.
Traub Jacob, 500 N. Alabama.

Paints, Oils and Glass.

BOYD FRANK A, 22 S. Meridian.
BROWNING & SLOAN, 7 and 9
  E. Washington.
CAMPBELL & GREEN, 149 W.
  Washington.
Sage Charles, 172 W. Washington.
Stewart & Morgan, 40 E. Washington.

Paper Bags.

CHANDLER & CO., 24 S. Meridian.

Paper Box Manufacturer.

Steinhauser B. A., 164 E. Washington.

Paper Dealers.

(Wholesale.)

BOWEN, STEWART & CO., 18
  W. Washington
CALEDONIA PAPER MILL,
  265 W. Washington.
CHANDLER & CO., 24 S. Meridian.
SALSBURY & CO., W. end Mary-
  land.
SEAMAN E. & CO., (wrapping
  paper,) 79 W. Washington.

Paper Hangers.
(See Also Painters.)

Cornelius & Melville, 31 Kentucky av.
Gall & Rush, 101 e. Washington.
Hume, Adams & Co., 26 and 28 W. Washington.
Marshall N. F., 37 Indiana av.
MESSICK T. B., 194 W. Vermont.
Roll W. H., 38 S. Illinois.

Paper Manufacturers.

CALEDONIA PAPER MILL, office, 265 W. Washington.
SALSBURY & CO., W. end Maryland.

Patent Medicines.
(Manufacturers of.)

Alcon & Co., 27 S. Illinois.
BUELL C H., 75 E Market.
FERREE T. M., 81 E. Market.

Patent Right Agents & Dealers

FOY OWEN, 74 Virginia av.
NOBLE A. F., (Ward's gas light) 34 Kentucky av.
NELLMAN H. B., patentee burning fluid, 118 N. Liberty.
ZIEGLER G. H., 87 E. Market.

Patent Solicitors.

Indianapolis Patent Agency, 87 E. Market, G. H. Ziegler, Manager.
MAYHEW O. F., office, State House bldg.

Paving---Concrete.
(Burns' Patent.)

SIMS & HOSKINS, ws. Canal, bet. Georgia and Louisiana.

Pawn Brokers.

SOLOMON J. & M., 25 S. Illinois.
Stephens Hattie Mrs., 28 S. Illinois.
Wagner G. W., 66 N. Illinois.

Photographers.

Abbott J. D., 94 E. Washington.
Adams & Davis, 2 W. Washington.
Andrew S. B., 162½ Indiana av.
Boston Ferrotype Company, 33 W. Washington.

BENHAM BRO'S,
36 East Washington St.,
PIANOS, ORGANS, MUSIC.

Best Goods!   Lowest Prices

BRUENING E. & J., over Washington.
CLAFLIN DAVID B., 32½ E. Washington.
Elliott J. P., 8 E. Washington.
HALL ALFORD, 16½ E. Washington, E. Judkins, Manager.
INGRAHAM C. B., 32½ E. Washington.
Miller A. R., 45 E. Washington.
Otis & Fowler, 24½ E. Washington.
Wilson George, 36½ E Washington.
WRIGHT JOHN M., 39½ E. Washington.

Photographers' Stock.

Daumont H. & Co., 15 W. Washington.
Hudson S., 196 E. Washington.
LIEBER H. & CO., 60 E. Washington.

Physicians.

ABBETT L. & C. H., 35 Virginia av.
Allen H. R., Surgical Institute.
ATHON JAMES,
Avery J. P., 1 Mass.
Bacon R. H., cor. Washington.
BARNES R. H., 62 Virginia av.
Barney Jacob, 245 N. Davidson.
BENNETT P. S., 33 Virginia av.
BOYD J. T., 14½ S. Pennsylvania.
Bullard W. R., 72 E. Market.
Burnham & Tisdale, 38 W. Market.
Butterfield S. A., 366 N. East.
Davis A. W., 130 N. Pennsylvania.
DUNLAP J M., 2 McOuats blk.
Evans B. F., 201 N. Delaware.
EWING DAVID, 33 Virginia av.
FARNSWORTH T. W., 21 Maryland.
FERREE F. M., 81 E. Market.
FLETCHER & WRIGHT, 107 Alabama.
Foley W. W., 53 Indiana av.
Gaston John M., 66 E. Market.
Gustin L., cor. Illinois and Louisiana.
Harlan L. D., 178 Virginia av.
Homburg R., 194 E. Washington.
JAMESON & FUNKHOUSE, 35 E. Market.

KENDRICK WM. H., 73 N. East.
King J. S., 13 S. Mississippi.
KIRKPATRIC JOHN, 35 W Market.
KITCHEN J. M, Vinton's blk
Lewis G. H., cor. Liberty and Washington
Looper F., 192 E. Washington.
MOODY JOHN B , cor. Indiana av. and Tennessee.
Moore S. H., 72 E. Washington.
Moore Wm. G , 262 Massachusetts av.
New G. W., 15 Miller's blk.
NEWCOMER F. S., 6 Blake's blk.
Oliver D H., 82 E. Market.
Parvin T, 135 N. Alabama.
Patterson A. W., 125 N Alabama.
PICKERILL GEORGE W., 30½ N. Pennsylvania.
Prunk D H., 30 N. Mississippi.
RICH T. C, 58 E. Market.
Selman A. G., 21 Virginia av.
Siddall J. P., 166 Virginia av.
Smith F. M., 40 N. Illinois.
STEVENS THAD. M., over 15 E. Washington.
Sutter F. 62 E Washington.
THOMPSON & WOOLBURN, 90 N. Illinois.
Thomson Wm, 62 Virginia av.
TODD & BIGELOW, 3 and 4 McOmat's blk.
Uhl Nathan, 52 S. Pennsylvania.
Wallace J. F., McOmat's blk.
Woods Wm, 66 E. Market.
Weterman L. D., 68 N. Pennsylvania.
Wiley Delaney, 16½ E. Washington.
Wood L., 31 Virginia av.
Wright J. J., 58½ E. Market.
Wright M. H., 103 N. Meridian.
YOUART JOHN M., 39½ W. Washington.
Walker J. B., 276 N. Mississippi.

Physicians.
(Cancer.)

Howard E. & Son, 92 S. Illinois.
Swank M., 76 N. Pennsylvania.

Physicians.
(Throat and Lungs.)

HALE JUDSON, 1 Miller's blk.

Piano Dealers.

PENHAM BROS., 36 E. Washington.
SOEHNER CHARLES, 83 N. Illinois.
Stowel M. A., 46 N. Pennsylvania.
WILLARD A. G. & CO., 4 and 5 Bates House blk

Piano Manufacturers.

INDIANAPOLIS PIANO MANUFACTURING CO., 159 and 161 E. Washington
Kappes J. H. & Co. 216 S. Illinois.
Schroer H. H., 141 W. Washington.

Pictures and Picture Frames.

Dannent H. & Co, 15 W. Washington.
Hudson S., 106 E Washington.
LEIBER H. & CO., 60 E. Washington.
Meyers C. F., 7 Martindale's blk.

Planing Mills.

BUILDERS' AND MANUFACTURERS' ASSOCIATION, 2 5 N. Delaware
BYRKITT & SONS, cor. Tennessee and Georgia.
EMERSON, BEAM & THOMPSON, 2 5 W. Market.
HILL GEORGE W., cor. East and Georgia.
McCORD & WHEATLEY, 186 S. Alabama.
TATE WARREN, 38 S. New Jersey.

Plasterers.
(Ornamental.)

TAYLOR JOHN F., 80 Massachusetts av.

Platers, Gold and Silver.

FULMER FREDERICK, 30 Virginia av.
Higgins W. B., 75 E. Washington.
Jennison A. F., Talbott and News blk.

Plow Handles.
(Manufacturers.)

Osgood, Smith & Co, 230 S. Illinois.

Plow Manufacturers.

Beard & Kimbal, 39 S. Tennessee.
BUCHANAN J. M., 27 S. East.

Plumbers.

(See also Gas and Steam Pipe Fitters.)

Davis Joseph W., 110 S. Delaware.
Dunn John C., 22 Kentucky av.
HANNING JOHN G., 82 W. Washington.
Karney John, 78 Virginia av.
NEAB CONRAD, 70 N. Illinois.

Pork Packers.

Ferguson J. C. & Co., W. end Georgia.
LESH, TOUSEY & CO., 72 and 74 S. Delaware.
KINGAN & CO., terminus W. Maryland.

Powder Dealers.

BALLWEGG A., 129 W. Washington.
BECK SAMUEL, 63 E. Washington.

Printers, Book and Job.

(See also Publishers.)

BRADEN & BURFORD, 24 W. Washington.
BRIGHT R. J., New Sentinel blds. sw. cor. Meridian and Circle.
Cameron Wm. S., 8 E. Pearl.
CHANDLER H. C. & CO., cor. Meridian and Pearl.
INDIANAPOLIS JOURNAL CO., Journal bldg., ne. cor. Market and Circle.
Indianapolis Printing and Publishing House, se cor Meridian and Circle.
Pettibone & Burke, Talbott and News blk.
WRIGHT & HOLMAN, 33 W. Washington.

Produce and Provision Dealers.

(See Grocers and Produce Dealers.)

Publishers.

(See also Newspapers and Publications.)

Bland & Taylor, 83 E Market.
BŒTTICHER JULIUS, 164 E. Washington.
BRIGHT R. J, Daily and Weekly Sentinel, Sentinel bldg
DOUGLASS & CONNER, new Journal bldg.
DOWLING W. W., office in Journal bldg.

BENHAM BROS,

36 East Washington St.,

PUBLISHERS OF

BENHAM'S MUSICAL REVIEW,

MONTHLY, $1 00 PER ANNUM.

Grafton J. J., cor. Meridian and Circle.
GUTENBERG PUBLISHING CO, se. cor. Meridian and Circle.
HANN J. B., o.hee. Journal bldg.
VICKERS W. B., se. cor. Meridian and Circle.
HUTCHINSON C. P., 16½ E. Washington.
LEE M. G., ne. cor. Washington and Illinois.
MORTON & RICKER, old Journal bldg.
STREIGH P A D., office, Yohn's blk.
WALTON H. L., (branch office, New York and London) 29½ N. Delaware.

Pump Makers.

DURBON R. A., (wood) 107 S. Meridian.
HANNING J. G. (iron), 82 W. Washington.
NEAB CONRAD, (iron) 70 N. Illinois.
Wright W. G. (wood) 36 S. Pennsylvania.

Queensware.

(See China, Glass and Queensware.)

Railings.

(Wrought and Cast.)

HAUGH B. F. & CO., 74 S. Pennsylvania.

Real Estate Agents.

Alexander G. W., 2 W. Washington.
Anderson G. P., 2 W. Washington.
Barnitz C., 115 E. Washington
Boyles M. W., 6 Odd Fellows' Hall.
BURNHAM S. W., 9 N. Illinois.
CARTER JOHN & CO., nw. cor. Washington and Delaware.
Colden & Johnson, Talbott & New's blk.
Daubenspeck N., 121 N. Delaware.
ELDRIDGE & CO., 16½ E. Washington
FRANK JAMES, 35½ E. Washington.
GOODWIN T. A., 79 E. Market.
Jones J., 17½ W. Washington.
Lehr T. A., 83 E. Washington.
LINDLEY & CO., 8 E. Washington

H. H. LEE

HAS BUT

ONE PRICE, SELLS FOR CASH,

And Guarantees all Goods

Sold at the China Tea Stores,

To be as Represented.

LOVE WILLIAM & CO., 1 Talbott & New's blk.

McKERNAN J. H., 2 Blake's blk.

MARTIN LUTHER R., 10 E. Washington.

MICK, GEYER & CO., 16½ E. Washington.

MINICK D. C. & CO., 17½ W. Washington.

SEIDENSTICKER ADOLPH & CO., 14 S. Delaware

SHOEMAKER & DURFIELD, 16½ E. Washington.

Smith Frank, 31 W. Washington.

SPANN JOHN S. & CO., Brown's blk., nw. cor. Pennsylvania and Washington.

STAPP JAMES H., 10 S. Pennsylvania.

TODD JOHN M. & CO., 24½ E. Washington.

WITT & ARBUCKLE, sw. cor. Washington and Meridian.

WOOD & HOSS, Wiley's blk.

Wright & Vinnedge, 62 E. Washington.

Rectifyers and Distillers.

BENDER T. & CO., 189 E. Washington.

GAPEN & CATHERWOOD, 118 S. Meridian.

Hahn & Balls, 25 S Meridian.

RYAN T. F., 143 S. Meridian.

SWEETSER JOHN, 30 S. Meridian.

Restaurants.

BAUER JACOB, 147 W. Washington.

BECKER BROS., 17 N. Pennsylvania.

CIRCLE, (Mrs. Geo. Rhodius) 15 N. Meridian.

CRYSTAL PALACE, 44 W. Washington.

Parrisette Joseph, 25 N. Illinois.

Randall Berry, 29 S. Illinois.

UNION DEPOT, T. B. Spratt, Supt.

WEINBERGER & WAGEMANN, 10 W. Louisiana.

Rolling Mills.

Indianapolis Rolling Mill Co., J. M. Lord, Prest. Office, Citizens' Bank bldg.

BUTSCH, DICKSON & CO., office and salesroom, 96 and 98 S. Meridian.

Roofers.

(Composition)

SIMS & HOSKINS, cor. Canal and Georgia.

Roofers.

(Slate and Metal.)

Zimmermann C., 35 S. Alabam.

Saddles and Harness.

(See Harness and Saddle Makers.)

Saloons.

ACADEMY OF MUSIC, under Academy.

Altman H. & Co., cor. Ray and Meridian.

Anderson R., 191 E. Washington.

ARMBRUSTER FRANK E., 439 W. Washington.

Armbruster J. J., 215 W. Maryland.

Asmus Louis, 199 Indiana av.

Baker Charles, 209 Massachusetts av.

Balke Charles, 231 E Washington.

BARLOW THOMAS, 79 E. Washington.

BECK EDWARD, 44 W. Washington.

BEHRINGER JOSEPH, 145 W. Washington.

BESS WM. K., 284 W. Washington.

BOHRMAN PETER, 9 W. Washington.

Buersdœrfer George, cor. Indiana av. and Illinois

Burk George, 24 W. Pearl.

Butsch George M., 243 S. Delaware.

BUSSEY JOHN, 29 W. McNabb.

Carr Thomas, 276 S. Missouri.

Carroll & Britt, 152 S. Illinois.

Carter Wm. E., 87 S. Illinois.

Christy A., 26 W. Louisiana.

DELL WM., 135 E. Washington.

Deppell L., 557 Virginia av.

DESCHLER JOSEPH, 15 N. Pennsylvania.

Dickman Carl, 208 E. Washington.

Dietz P., 249 W. Maryland.

Dietz Fred & Co., 133 E. Washington.

Dietz & Haug, 255 E. Washington.

Dugan N., 52 S. Illinois.
Dunningberg J., 89 E. South.
EURICH JOHN L., 17 N. Illinois.
FAHRBACH PHILIP, Washington Hall.
FITCH D. H., 23 N Illinois.
GAHM JOHN, 196 Indiana av.
Geis John, 62 S. Delaware.
Geis Lawrence. 99 E. Washington.
GEM. P. Bothman, Prop'r, 9 W. Washington.
GINZ MICHAEL, 185 E. Washington.
Griffith T.. 48 S. Pennsylvania.
Grobe Charles. 12 W. Louisiana.
GRUENERT JNO. H.. 61 E. South.
GRUENERT HENRY, 164 S. Illinois.
Hartnett P. E., 101 S. Illinois.
Hartrodt H., 249 Kentucky av.
Hang Michael, 138 S. Pennsylvania.
Heiser Charles, 76 S. Delaware.
HELM JOHN, 272 Winston.
HUEGELE JOHN, 39 E. Washington.
Huppertegraft D., cor. Massachusetts av. and St. Clair
ILG GEORGE, 323 W. Washington.
Inwalle B J., 367 Virginia av.
KISSEL FREDERICK, cor. McCarty and Russell.
KLARE & SCHRŒDER, 588 S. Meridian.
Knozer George, 60 S. Delaware.
KŒHLER JOHN, 247 N. Noble.
KŒNIGER GEORGE, 338 S. Meridian.
LANG LOUIS. 29 S. Meridian.
LAUER CHARLES, 202 E. Washington.
Laupheimer August, 139 S. Illinois.
Lee & Replogle, 346 E. Washington.
LEHRITTER CONRAD, 92 E. Washington.
LEHRITTER GEORGE, 143 E. Washington.
LEONARD & VICTOR, 65 W. Washington.
McAndrews, 251 W. Washington.
McBRIDE JOHN C., 195 W. Washington.
McCARTY SIMON, Bates House.
McGrarty John, 116 S. Illinois.
McGrimes, cor. South and Meridian.
McLaughlin Wm., 344 S. West.
Marmont Hugo, cor. Illinois and Georgia.
MATTLER STEPHEN, cor. South and Illinois.
Mayer Charles, 133 E. Washington.
Merl Nicholas, 286 W. Washington.
MINICK HIRAM, Palmer House.
Moninger Conrad, 167 W. Washington.
MONINGER DANIEL, 20 Kentucky av.

BENHAM BRO'S,

36 East Washington St.,

SHEET MUSIC, VIOLINS,

GUITARS, STRINGS, &c.

MUELLER CHARLES G., 25 S. Delaware.
Murphy T., 396 W. North.
NALTNER JOSEPH, 134 S. Meridian.
NALTNER MARTIN, 207 Virginia av.
NATIONAL HOTEL SALOON, J. Bussey, proprietor.
O'Leary Jeremiah, 103 S. Illinois.
Oehler David, 48 Russell.
PARLOR SALOON, 179 E. Washington.
PEARSON JOHN & CO. (House of Lords), 78 W. Washington.
Poehler L., cor. Ray and Meridian.
POLSTER FREDERICK, 144 Indiana av.
Quin John T., 245 W. Maryland.
Redmond Thomas, 346 W. Washington.
Reichwein P., 50 N. Noble.
REINMAN REINHART, 252 E. Washington.
REITZ FRANK R., 156 E. Washington.
RENARD EUGENIE, 299 E. Washington.
RHODIUS MRS. GEORGE, 15 N. Meridian.
Richter Wm., 418 Virginia av.
Rosebrook T. W., 178 Virginia av.
Rupp John, 201 Kentucky av.
Santo Edward, cor. Indiana av. and North.
Schaub Henry, 168 W. Washington.
SCHETTER CHRISTIAN, 99 E. South, cor. Delaware.
SCHURICH FRED., W. Indianapolis
Schericho Charles, 524 S. Meridian.
Schwomeyer Charles, 397 S. Meridian.
Seidensticker Frederick, 248 N. Noble.
Seiman Fidel, 211 W. Washington.
Seitz Charles, 110 S. Illinois.
SEITZ FRED., 117 S. Illinois.
SELKING WILLIAM, 33 N. Pennsylvania
SHEPHERD JAS. McB., 179 E. Washington.
SINGLE ABDEN, 176 E. Washington.
SMITH HENRY, 131 W. Washington.
Sponsel George, 231 S. Delaware.
Sweeney H., 81 S. Illinois.

THE CHINA TEA STORES

Are very handsomely decorated with

Accurate Views and Scenes
of

CHINESE LIFE AND SCENERY.

Call and see them before leaving the City.

THOMPSON J. FRED. (ipper),
33 N. Illinois.
Updegraff D., cor. St. Clair and Plum.
WACHSTETTER JACOB, 154 W.
Washington.
WALSH W. J. 291 S. Delaware.
Walter George. 248 N. South.
WASHINGTON HALL, Philip
Farbach proprietor.
WELSH MAURICE, (Senate), 80
W. Washington.
WELSH PATRICK, (Bank), 23 W
Washington.
Whitehead William, 430 W. Washington
Witthoff F., 329 Indiana av.
Wolf C., 176 S. Illinois.
Zeigelmuller H., 59 N. Alabama.

Sash, Doors and Blinds.

(See also Planing Mills and Lumber Dealers.)

BUILDERS' AND MANUFAC-
TURERS' ASSOCIATION,
225 N. Delaware.
BYRKITT M. & SONS, cor. Geor-
gia and Tennessee.
EMERSON, BEAM & THOMP-
SON, 225 W. Market.
HILL GEORGE W., cor. Georgia
and East.
TATE WARREN, 38 S. New Jersey.
Wheatley H. H., cor. South and Delaware.

Saw Manufacturers.

SHEFFIELD SAW WORKS, 210
to 216 S. Illinois, E. C. Atkins & Co.,
proprietors.
SINKER ALFRED T., proprietor
American Saw Works, cor. Pennsylvania and Georgia.

Saw Mills.

HILDEBRAND & KEPPLE, cor.
Indiana av. and Canal.
Long & Joseph, cor. Walnut and Lafayette
R. R.
MARSEE J. & SON, New Jersey,
nr. Railroad.
Pressley J. T., cor. Louisiana and West.

Saw Mills.

(Manufacturers of.)

Chandler & Taylor, 370 W Washington.
EAGLE MACHINE WORKS, E.
end Union Depot.
WERTERN MACHINE W'KS,
125 S. Delaware.

Saws.

(Muley, Circular and Cross Cut.)

ATKINS E. C. & CO., 210 S, Illinois.
SINKER ALFRED T., cor. Pennsylvania and Georgia.

Scales and Balances.

Gallup E. P. & W. P., 42 N. Tennessee.

Second-Hand Stores.

Appleby R., 171 W. Washington.
Benson David, 206 S. Illinois.
Cohen A., 31 S. Illinois.
Garratt A., 257 n. Washington.
Marot John R., 87 E. Washington.
Smith G. B., 78 S. Delaware.
WINTER I. N., 17 Virginia av.

Seed Stores.

(See Agricultural and Seed Stores.)

Sewing Machines.

BUTTON HOLE, (over seaming)
Fagan & Ross, agents, 18 N. Dela-
ware.
DOMESTIC, L. B. Walker, agent, 58
N. Illinois.
FLORENCE, J. W. Smith, agent, 27
N. Pennsylvania.
GROVER & BAKER, Wiley & Van
Buren agents, 21 E. Washington.
HOWE, Olin & Foltz, agents, 21 N
Pennsylvania.
SINGER, Josselyn Brothers, dealers,
74 W. Washington.
WEED, James Skardon & Son, agents,
42 N. Pennsylvania.
WHEELER & WILSON, William
Sumner & Co., agents, 10 W. Wash-
ington.

Sheet Iron Dealers.

COTTRELL THOMAS, 177 E.
Washington.
COX THOMAS, 24 E. Georgia.

Sheet Iron Worker.

COX THOMAS, 24 E. Georgia.

Show Case Manufacturers.

Berkhofer G., 5 Virginia av.
KAUFMAN CHARLES, 14 N.
Delaware.

Silver-Plated Goods.

ADAMS G. F. & CO., 32 S. Meridian
WOODBRIDGE JOHN & CO.,
12 W. Washington.

Silver Platers.

(See also Platers in Silver and Gold.)

Soap Manufacturers.

Bergman Frank, S. end West.

Soda Water Manufacturers.

(See Mineral Water.)

Stair Builders.

Aldrich John D., 73 E. Washington.
Des Jardins Joseph, 464 Virginia av.
SHOVER & CHRISTIAN, 124 E.
Vermont.

Starch Manufactory.

Union Starch Factory, E. end New York.

Staves and Headings.

Bunte & Dickson, 387 E. Market.
Carey J. S. & Co, W. end Georgia.
McKendry J., cor. Pratt and Lafayette
R. R.
MAY ANDREW, 102 S. East.

Steam Engines.

(See Engine Builders.)

Stencil Cutters.

Walker Edward, 25 W. Washington.

Stocking Manufacturers.

Funke F. W., 90 E. Washington.
Rause & Riemenschneider, 84 E. Washington.
29

Stone Masons.

Renard John, 321 E. New York.
Richter & Bros., 310 Virginia av.
Yost Thomas, cor. Tennessee and South.

Stone Yards.

Farman Frank, Kentucky av. nr. Canal.
Goddard Samuel, cor. Georgia and Missis-
sippi.
Scott & Nicholson, cor. Kentucky av. and
Canal.
SMITH, ITTENBACH & CO.,
two squares E. of Noble, bet. Harri-
son and Lord.

Stone and Crockery Ware.

HOLLWEG & REESE, 90 and 92
S. Meridian.
WILES THOMAS, 25 E. Georgia.

Storage and Commission.

(See Commission Merchants.)

Stoves.

(Manufacturers.)

ROOT D. & CO., Foundry, 183 S.
Pennsylvania; Wareroom, 66 E.
Washington.

Stoves and Tin-Ware.

(See also Tin, Copper and Sheet-Iron
Workers.)

Adams G. F. & Co., 32 S. Meridian.
Cox Charles, 57 W. Washington.
Engle & Hunt, 405 N. Alabama.
Frankem I. L., 34 E. Washington.
KUNZ & RICHMOND, 229 E.
Washington.
Lamatte Joseph, 192 Massachusetts av.
McOUAT R. L. & A. W., 61 and 63
W. Washington.
Martin & Meyers 157 W. Washington.
MUNSON & JOHNSTON, 62 E.
Washington.
ROOT DELOSS & CO., 66 E. Wash-
ington.

THE CHINA TEA STORES

Have the NAME of being the

MOST ATTRACTIVE STORES IN THE WEST.

No. 7 Odd Fellows Hall

AND

ACADEMY OF MUSIC CORNER.

TUTEWILER BROS., 74 E. Washington.
VŒGTLE JACOB, 103 E. Washington.
Wolfrom Bros., 197 E. Washington.

Straw Goods.
(*Wholesale.*)

CARR & ALVEY, 6 W. Washington.
COPELAND J. W. & CO., 116 S. Meridian.
FAHNLEY & McCREA, 131 S. Meridian.

Straw Goods.
(*Wholesale and Retail.*)

BAMBERGER H., 16 E. Washington.
COPELAND J. W., 8 E. Washington.
DAVIS ISAAC & CO., 12 E. Washington.
Seaton E. A., 25 W. Washington.

Surgical Institute.

INDIANA SURGICAL INSTITUTE, ne. cor. Georgia and Illinois.

Surgical Instruments.

BROWNING & SLOAN, 7 and 9 E. Washington.
Steffins E., Hubbard's blk.

Tailors.
(*Merchant.*)

BECKER & HUBER, 77 E. Washington.
Bristol A., 170 E. Washington.
Budenz Louis, Mozart Hall.
Clark William H., 58 N. Illinois.
CRAIN W. N., 32 W. Washington.
Engas H., 113 S. Illinois.
GRISTNER A. J., 171 E. Washington.
GŒPPER F. & CO., 17 E. Washington.

GRAMLING J. & P., 35 E. Washington.
GRAY GEORGE W., 27 Kentucky av.
GRAY STEPHEN & CO., 14 N. Pennsylvania.
Green George, 32 N. Pennsylvania.
HALL E. A., 31 N. Pennsylvania.
HEITKAM GEORGE H., 8 W. Washington.
Holtz George & Co., 124 S. Illinois.
HURRLE IGNATZ, 170 E. Washington.
Jachman Herman, 257 E Washington.
KELLY P., 40 S. Illinois.
Melville R. B., 24 Kentucky av.
MORITZ BROTHERS, 19 W. Washington.
MOSSLER L. I. & BROTHERS, 37 E. Washington.
Peterson Brothers, 258 S. Delaware.
PORTER THEO. R., over 24 W. Washington.
ROTH & MEIER, 198 E. Washington.
RUPP WILLIAM F., 38 W. Washington.
Sailers J. M., 156 W. Washington.
Schildmeyer Fred., 182 E. Washington.
STAUB JOSEPH, 2 Odd Fellows' Hall.
Steinman John, 32 Virginia av.
Trent & Claflin, 30 N. Pennsylvania.
WHITE & FERGUSON, room 3 Blackford's blk.

Tanners' Oil.

Dietz & Reisner, 17 S. Delaware.
Fishback John, 125 S. Meridian.
Mooney & Co., 147 S. Meridian.

Tanners and Curriers.

DOUGHERTY M. & CO., S. city limits, opp. Underhill's mill.
Fishback John, Michigan rd., nw. city limits.
Frenzel J. P., cor. Meek and Benton.

Teas.
(*Wholesale.*)

LEE H. H., cor. Illinois and Ohio, and 7 Odd Fellows' Hall.
Millner & Sherwood, 27 McNabb.
Wiles Brothers & Co., 149 S. Meridian.

Teas.
(*Retail.*)

HORN HENRY J., 174 W. Washington.

LEE H. H., 7 Odd Fellows' Hall, and under Academy of Music.
Tuttle G. P., cor. Market and Pennsylvania.

Telegraph Companies.

PACIFIC & ATLANTIC CO., 22 S. Meridian.
WESTERN UNION, Blackford's blk., branch office, Union Depot.

Tin, Copper and Sheet Iron.

COTTRELL THOMAS, 177 E. Washington.
COX THOMAS J., 24 E. Georgia.
Stumpf H. A., 94 Indiana av.

Tobacco Manufacturers.

(*See also Cigars and Tobacco.*)

MADDEN THOMAS, 172 W. Cumberland.
Oliver Charles, 288 W. Washington.
SMITH, REYNOLDS & THOMAS, 85 and 87 E. South.

Toys and Notions.

(*Wholesale and Retail*)

BALDWIN J. H., 6 E. Washington.
Henninger G. & E. 115 S. Illinois.
MAYER CHARLES & CO., 29 W. Washington.

Trunks, Traveling Bags and Valises.

(*Manufacturers and Dealers.*)

Bogart James, 2 N. Meridian.
Burton Martin, 39 S. Meridian.
Forby C. H., 109 S. Illinois.
ROBINSON BROS., 20 and 22 Virginia av
SHILLING L. R., 55 W. Washington.
Smith R. L. & Co., 16½ S. Meridian.

Turners.

(*Wood.*)

KOLB LOUIS, 23 E. South.
Ingersoll Frank, 259 E. Washington.
Meyer Martin, 19 S. Alabama.

Umbrella Makers.

Mayer John, 69 E. Washington.

BENHAM BRO'S,

36 East Washington St.,

Pianos, Organs and Melodeons Tuned, Moved and Repaired.

Undertakers.

Grinsteiner George, 276 E Market.
Herman F. J., 26 S. Delaware.
LONG MATHEW, 15 Circle.
WEAVER & HEDGES, 30 N. Illinois.

Upholsterers.

(*See also Furniture Mnfrs. and Dealers.*)

BAKER N. S., 73 E. Washington.
GEBHARD AUGUST, 117 E. Washington.
Gibbs Wm. P., 78 E. Market.
TANNER & PRESSEL, 76 Virginia av.
Wilkins & Co., 84 E. Market.

Varnish Manufacturers.

MEARS & LILLY, cor. Mississippi and Kentucky av.

Veterinary Surgeons.

Alleby James, 21 E. Pearl.
Navin John M, 163 W. Washington.
Wasson A. W., 42 E. Maryland.

Vinegar Manufacturers.

Brand & Kreis, 198 E. Washington.
Wright Frank, W. end New York.

Wagon Makers.

(*See also Carriage Builders.*)

DREW S. W., E. Market Square.
Ewald William, end Massachusetts av.
Feil John, 423 S. Meridian.
INDIANAPOLIS WAGON & AGRICULTURAL WORKS, 172 S. Tennessee.
Miller Lewis, 478 E. Washington.
Munsell Henry, cor. Massachusetts av. and Plum.
Van Blaricum Jesse, 231 W. Washington.
Van Iassar W., 144 Fort Wayne av.
Wheling C., 234 S. Delaware.

H. H. LEE'S

WHOLESALE PRICES FOR

TEAS, COFFEES & SUGARS,

ARE THE SAME EACH DAY

As are quoted in the

CINCINNATI DAILY PAPERS.

Wagon Yards.

(See also Livery and Feed Stables.)

Gates, Pray & Co., E. Market Square.
Mills & Hollingsworth, 277 W. Washington.
Stout F. & Son, 163 W. Washington.

Wagon and Carriage Material

Case, Parker & Co., 84 W. Washington.
Osgood, Smith & Co., 230 S. Illinois.

Wall Paper & Window Shades.

Gall & Rush, 101 E. Washington.
Hume, Adams & Co., 26 and 28 W. Washington.
ROLL WM. A., 38 S. Illinois.
WILDER C. P., 26 E. Washington.

Watches, Clocks and Jewelr.

BINGHAM W. P., 50 E. Washington.
CRAFT & CUTTER, 24 E. Washington.
Davis George, 39 W. Washington.
Deitrick Charles, 60 N. Pennsylvania.
FELLER GEORGE, 226 E. Washington.
Ferguson C. A., 7 W. Washington.
Forbes J. R., 34 Virginia av.
FRENCH C. G., 13 N. Meridian.
Keifer L. F. & Son, 2 Odd Fellows Hall.
McLENE & HERRON, 1 Bates House bldg.
Oehler Andrew, 20 S. Delaware.
Oehler Roman, 183 W. Washington.
PAULMAN E. L., 114 S. Illinois.
Phipps Bros., 32 W. Washington.
Slusher Henry, 190 W. Washington.
Vance J. J., 410 S. Meridian.
Weber F., 43 S. Illinois.
Zumbush T., 93 E. Washington.

Wigs, Toupees, Etc.

Medina J. F., 32 W. Washington.

Willow Ware.

(Wholesale and Retail.)

MAJOR STEPHEN T., 342 E. Washington.
MAYER CHARLES & CO, 29 W. Washington.
Ohleyer George, 456 S. Meridian.

Window Glass.

(Wholesale and Retail.)

BROWNING & SLOAN, 7 and 9 E. Washington.
OVER E. & CO., 82 and 84 S. Meridian.

Wood Carver.

Ludwig Louis, 269 E. Washington.

Wood Yard.

Aldrich & Gay, cor. Indiana av. and Canal.

Wool Dealers.

Geisendorff & Co., 402 W. Washington.
Merritt & Coughlen, W. end Washington.

Woolen Mills.

Geisendorff & Co., 402 W. Washington.
Merritt & Coughlen, W. end Washington.

Woolen Mill Machinery.

Dickson C. & Co., 49 N. Tennessee.
Howe & Converse, 372 W. Washington.
Merritt & Coughlen, W. end Washington.

Zinc, Copper, Etc.

Cottrell Thomas, 177 E. Washington.

APPENDIX.

UNITED STATES GOVERNMENT.

The twenty-first Presidential term of four years begun on the 4th of March, 1869, and will expire on the 3d of March, 1873.

U. S. GRANT, of Illinois, President.
SCHUYLER COLFAX, of Indiana, Vice President.
HAMILTON FISH, of New York, Secretary of State.
GEORGE S. BOUTWELL, of Massachusetts, Secretary of the Treasury.
WILLIAM W. BELKNAP, of Iowa, Secretary of War.
GEORGE M. ROBESON, of New Jersey, Secretary of the Navy.
J. D. COX, of Ohio, Secretary of the Interior.
JOHN A. J. CRESWELL, of Maryland, Postmaster General.
E. R. HOAR, of Massachusetts, Attorney General.

UNITED STATE OFFICES IN INDIANAPOLIS.

United States Internal Revenue, Sixth District, Indiana.

Assessor—William M. Wiles.
Assistants—L. M. Phipps and Love H. Jameson.
Chief Clerk—H. J. Craft; Office, room 14 P. O. building.
Collector—Charles F. Hogate.
Deputy—James King; Office, room 15 P. O. building.
Register—Edmund Browning; Office, room 8 P. O. building.
Receiver—G. M. Ballard.

United States Marshal's Office.

United States Marshal—Benjamin J. Spooner; Office, room 6 P. O. building.
Deputies—I. S. Bigelow, W. C. David, John C. Spooner and H. N. Bigelow.
United States Commissioner—Eben W. Kimball; Office, 46 E. Washington.
Supervisor Internal Revenue, (For Indiana),—G. B. Williams; Office, room 4 Vinton's block.

3]

INDIANA STATE GOVERNMENT.

CONRAD BAKER, Governor.
WILLIAM CUMBACK, Lieutenant Governor.
JOHN COMMONS, Governor's Secretary.
MAX F. A. HOFFMAN, Secretary of State.
JOHN D. EVANS, Auditor of State.
NATHAN KIMBALL, Treasurer of State.
B. C. HOBBS, Superintendent of Public Instruction.
M. G. McLAIN, State Librarian.
D. E. WILLIAMSON, Attorney General.
JOHN G. GREENWALT, Adjutant General.

Indiana Courts.

SUPREME COURT meets at the Supreme Court Rooms (State Building) sw. cor. Washington and Tennessee, on the 4th Mondays in May and November. Chief Justice, Charles A. Ray, Indianapolis; Judges, J. T. Elliott, Newcastle, James S. Frazer, Warsaw, Robert Gregory, Lafayette; Attorney General, D. E. Williamson, Greencastle; Sheriff, Cyrus J. Dobbs, Indianapolis; Deputy, ——; Clerk, Theodore W. McCoy, Jeffersonville; Deputy, J. M. Judah, Vincennes; Reporter, James B. Black, Indianapolis.

UNITED STATES CIRCUIT COURT meets 1st Tuesdays in May and November at the United States building. Circuit court held by Hon. David Davis, Asst. Justice of the United States Court, Hon Thomas Drummond and Hon. W. Q. Gresham, District Judges, Clerk, John H. Howland.

UNITED STATES SUPREME COURT meets same time and place.

County Officers.

Clerk—Wm. C. Smock.
Deputies—C. F. Rooker, D. C. Greenfield, R. W. Smock, S. L. Harvey and R. C. Corbaley.

THE CHINA TEA STORES

ARE AT

No. 7 ODD FELLOWS HALL

AND

ACADEMY OF MUSIC CORNER.

Sheriff—Geo. W. Parker.
Deputies—J. Elliott and H. C. Adams.
Treasurer—Frank Erdelmeyer.
Deputy—B. F. Riley.
Auditor—George F. McGinnis.
Deputies—F. W. Hamilton and E. M. Wilmington.
Recorder—Wm. J. Elliott.

Board of County Commissioners.

Joseph K. English, Center township; Lorenzo VanScyoc, Washington township; Aaron McCray, Wayne township. *Court Bailiffs*—J. R. Shea, T. D. Amos, L. L. McFadden.

Township Trustees.

Center—Cyrus C. Heizer.
Decatur—J. J. Billingsley.
Franklin—James L. Thompson.
Lawrence—Samuel Cory.
Perry—John E. Griffith.
Pike—James H. Kennedy.
Warren—William Hunter.
Washington—H. A. Haverstick.
Wayne—Alexander Jameson.

County Courts.

MARION CIVIL CIRCUIT COURT meets 3d Monday in every February, 4th Monday in May, 3d Monday in September, and 1st Monday in December at the Court House; length of term six weeks; Judge, Cyrus C. Hines; Prosecuting Attorney, —— Howe, Clerk, W. C. Smock.

MARION CRIMINAL CIRCUIT COURT meets 1st Mondays in January and July at the Court House. Judge, Geo. H. Chapman; Prosecuting Attorney, John S. Duncan; Clerk, Wm. C. Smock.

COMMON PLEAS COURT meets 1st Mondays in February, April, September and November at the Court House; length of term six weeks. Judge, Solomon Blair; Prosecuting Attorney, William Irvin; Clerk, Wm. C. Smock.

CITY GOVERNMENT.

DANIEL MACAULEY, Mayor. (*Term Expires May*, 1871.)

CITY OFFICERS.

Clerk—Daniel M. Ransdell.
Deputies—J. R. Clinton and J. G. Waters.
Treasurer—Robert S. Foster.
Deputy—John W. Coons.
Attorney—Byron K. Elliott.
Engineer—R. M. Patterson.
Assessor—William Hadley.
Marshal—George Taffe.
Street Commissioner—August Bruner.
Chief Fire Engineer—Daniel Glazier.
Chief of Police—Henry Paul.
Lieutenant of Police—James N. Stevens.
Gas Inspector.—George H. Fleming.
Market Master—James Y. Mardyck.
Sealer—S. B. Morris.
Sexton—James H. Hedges.
Printer—J. G. Douglass.

CITY COUNCILMEN.

First Ward—Leon Kahn and John S. Newman.
Second Ward—T. C. Harrison and D. W. Wiles.
Third Ward—J. H. Woodburn and W. W. Weaver.
Fourth Ward—Erie Locke and Isaac Thalman.
Fifth Ward—Edward Reagan and James B. McShepherd.
Sixth Ward—Austin H. Brown and R. Kennington.
Seventh Ward—J. Marsee and Thomas Cottrell.
Eighth Ward—C. E. Whitsitt and Christopher Heckman.
Ninth Ward—John Pyle and Frederick Thoms.

STANDING COMMITTEES.

Accounts and Claims—James H. Woodburn, L. Kahn, and C. Heckman.
Benevolence and Hospitals—J. H. Woodburn, W. W. Weaver, and E. Reagan.
Bridges—Erie Locke, J. L. Marsee, and Austin H. Brown.
Finance—J. S. Newman, J. H. Woodburn, T. Cottrell, A. H. Brown, and Isaac Thalman.
Fire Department—John L. Marsee, Isaac Thalman, and Edward Reagan.
Gaslight—W. D. Wiles, Leon Kahn, and R. Kennington.
Judiciary—J. S. Newman, T. C. Harrison, and Thomas Cottrell.
Markets—John Pyle, W. W. Weaver, and Robert Kennington.

Police—John Marsee, J. H. Woodburn, and W. D. Wiles
Printing and Stationery—Fred Thoms, T. C. Harrison, and A. H. Brown.
Public Buildings—W. W. Weaver, John Pyle, and J. B. McShepherd.
Public Schools—T. C. Harrison, Isaac Thalman, and C. E. Whitsitt.
Railroads—W. D. Wiles, Fred Thoms, and J. B. McShepherd.
Revision of Ordinances—T. C. Harrison, Erie Locke, and Thomas Cottrell.
Sewerage—J. L. Marsee, Erie Locke, and C. E. Whitsitt.
Streets and Alleys—Isaac Thalman, J. L. Marsee, and C. Heckman.
Water Works—L. Kahn, W. D. Wiles, and C. Heckman.

INDIANAPOLIS BOARD OF TRADE.

OFFICERS.

W. C. TARKINGTON, President.
JAMES C. FERGUSON, First Vice Pres't.
GEORGE MERRITT, Second Vice Pres't.
JOHN FISHBACK, Third Vice Pres't.
J. BARNARD, Secretary.
JOHN W. MURPHY, Treasurer.

BOARD OF DIRECTORS.

Joseph D. Pattison.
Thomas D. Kingan.
John M. Caldwell.
E. B. Martindale.
David Gibson.
E. T. Sinker.
Milton M. Landis,
George K. Share.
John W. Murphy.
Robert Connelly.
S. V. B. Noel.
W. D. Wiles.

Police Department.

HENRY PAUL, Chief.
JAMES N. STEVENS, Lieutenant.

POLICEMEN—DAY.

First Ward—Robert B. Barbee.
Second Ward—Jesse T. Murphy.
Third Ward—Hannibal Taffe.
Fourth Ward—William Bolen.
Fifth Ward—John L. Brown.
Sixth Ward—Omer B. Boardman.
Seventh Ward—Thomas S. Wilson.
Eighth Ward—William Williams.
Ninth Ward—Laven M. Russell.

POLICEMAN—NIGHT.

First Ward—Thomas Dain, Samuel Barker.
Second Ward—George Buser, John A. McKinney.
Third Ward—Allen Thornbrough, Isaac N. Aldrich.
Fourth Ward—Charles D. McCoy, Albert Travis.

Fifth Ward—Samuel Buser, Asbury P. Wright
Sixth Ward—Robert Campbell, Joseph P. Duvall.
Seventh Ward—Hubbard S. Adams, George Sponsel.
Eighth Ward—Abel E. Catterson, Michael Looney.
Ninth Ward—George Thomas, Paulin Lendormie.

FIRE DEPARTMENT.

DANIEL GLAZIER, Chief.
Engine Co. No. 1, south side Washington bet. West and California.
Engine Co. No. 2, junction New York, Delaware and Massachusetts av.
Engine Co. No. 3, south side South bet. Delaware and Alabama.
Hook and Ladder Co. east side New Jersey bet. Market and Washington.

Fire Alarm Telegraph Signals.

L. B. YEATON, Superintendent.

SIGNAL NUMBERS.

2 No. 2 Engine House, cor. Massachusetts av. and New York.
3 Corner East and New York.
4 Hook and Ladder house, New Jersey nr. Washington.
5 Spiegel, Thoms & Co's factory, S. East.
5 Corner Washington and Noble.
7 Corner Davidson and New York.
1—2 Corner Noble and Michigan.
1—3 Corner Noble and Massachusetts av.
1—4 Corner East and Massachusetts av.
1—5 Corner New Jersey and Fort Wayne av.
1—6 Corner Delaware and Ft. Wayne av
1—7 Corner Pennsylvania and Pratt.
1—8 Blind Asylum.
2—1 Corner Tennessee and St. Clair.
2—3 Michigan bet. Meridian and Illinois.
2—4 Tennessee bet. Vermont and Michigan.
2—5 Corner Illinois and Indiana av.
2—6 Corner New York and Canal, Helwig's Mill.
2—7 Corner West and Indiana av.
2—8 Corner Lafayette R. R. and St. Clair.

H. H. LEE

MAKES A SPECIALTY OF

Choice Green, Black & Japan Teas.

3–1 No. 382 Indiana av.
3–2 Corner Blake and Michigan.
3–4 Corner Douglass and New York.
3–4 Frank Wright's Brewery.
3–5 Cotton Factory nr. River.
3–6 Geisendorff's Woolen Factory nr. River.
3–7 No. 1 Engine House, Washington bet. West and California.
4–1 Corner West and Kentucky av.
4–2 Corner Georgia and Mississippi, Coburn & Jones' Lumber Yard.
4–3 Corner Washington and Tennessee.
4–5 Corner Illinois and Louisiana, Spencer House.
4–6 Illinois and Garden, Osgood & Smith's.
4–7 Corner Illinois and McCarty.
5–1 Corner Meridian and Ray.
5–2 Corner Delaware and McCarty.
5–3 Corner East and Bicking.
5–4 Corner Virginia av. and Bradshaw.
5–6 Corner Virginia av. and Noble.
5–7 Corner Georgia and Benton.
6–1 No. 16 Fletcher av.
6–2 No. 3 Engine House, South bet. Delaware and Alabama.
6–3 Gas Works.
5–4 Corner Pennsylvania and Georgia.
6–5 Watch Tower, Glenn's Block.
6–7 Corner Delaware and Washington.
7–1 No. 185 New Jersey, Chief Engineer's.

SCHOOLS.

PUBLIC.

The city free schools are under the general management of a Board of three Trustees, elected by the Common Council, A. C. Shortridge being clerk of the Board and Superintendent of the public schools. Office of the Board and Superintendent, in the High School building, corner Market and Circle.

SCHOOLS AND TEACHERS.

First District, cor. Vermont and New Jersey. Ruth Morris, Principal.
Second District, Delaware, bet. Vermont and Michigan, Jennie L. Lindley, Principal.

Third District, New York, bet. Illinois and Tennessee, Ada B. Plum, Principal.
Fourth District, (old house, col'd) Market, bet. West and California, M. L. Mahurin, Principal.
Fourth District, (new house) cor. Michigan and Blackford, A. P. Funnelle, Principal.
Fifth District, Maryland, bet. Canal and Mississippi, E. T. Ford, Principal.
Fifth District, (new house) Root, nr. West, M. A. McEnally, Principal.
Sixth District, (new) Union, bet. Merrill and McCarty, Helen A. Davis, Principal.
Sixth District, (old col'd) Pennsylvania, nr. South, Sarah Douglass, Principal.
Seventh District, East, nr. Louisiana, Mary Ingersol, Principal.
Eighth District, Virginia av., cor. Huron, Maria H. Jones, Principal.
Ninth District, (new) cor. Davidson and Michigan, Mary E. Perrott, Principal.
High School, cor. Market and Circle, William Bell, Principal.
Court House School, old Court House bldg., Henrie Colgen, Principal.

SCHOOLS—(Colored.)

Allen Chapel, Broadway, nr. Cherry.
Fourth Ward, Market, bet. West and California.
Public School, 180 W. Georgia.
Mississippi School, 642 N. Mississippi.

SCHOOLS—(Private.)

German English, Maryland, bet. Delaware and Alabama.
German Evangelical, cor. East and Stevens.
German Lutheran, cor. East and Georgia.
St. John's, (for boys) Georgia, bet. Illinois and Tennessee.
St. John's, (for girls) cor. Tennessee and Georgia.
St. Mary's, (German Catholic) Maryland, bet. Delaware and Pennsylvania.
St. Peter's, Dougherty, nr. Virginia av.

CHURCHES.

BAPTIST.

First Baptist Church, ne. cor. New York and Pennsylvania. Rev. Henry Day, pastor.
Garden Mission, ne. cor. Washington and Canal (up stairs.) Sabbath School at nine o'clock A.M. H. Knippenberg, Supt.
Mission Chappel, cor. Noble and South.
African Baptist Church, Michigan, bet. Indiana av. and West.

CATHOLIC.

St. John's (Roman) Georgia, bet. Illinois and Tennessee. Rev. Father Bessonies, pastor.

St. Mary's, (German), Maryland, bet. Pennsylvania and Delaware. Rev. Father S. Siegrest, pastor.

St. Peter's, Dougherty, nr. Virginia av. Rev. J. R. Fitz Patrick, pastor.

CHRISTIAN.

Christian Chapel, cor. Ohio and Delaware. Elder W. F. Black, pastor.

Second Christian Church, cor. Mississippi and First. Rev. Mr. Conrad, pastor.

Third Christian Church, Rev. A. Council, pastor.

Fourth Christian Church, 330 Indiana av.

CONGREGATIONAL.

Mayflower Congregational Church, St. Clair cor. East. Rev. C. M. Saunders, pastor.

Plymouth Congregational Church, cor. Circle and Meridian.

EPISCOPAL.

Grace Church, se. cor. St. Joseph and Pennsylvania. Rev. C. B. Davidson, D. D., rector.

Christ Church, cor. Meridian and Circle. Rev. B. Franklin, rector.

Church of the Holy Innocents, Fletcher av., ne. cor. Cedar. Rev. Geo. B. Engle, rector.

St. Paul's Cathedral, cor. Illinois and New York. Rev. Treadwell Walden, rector.

FRIENDS.

Friends' Church, cor. Delaware and St. Clair. Enos G. Pray, pastor.

GERMAN EVANGELICAL.

St. Paul's, New Jersey bet. Ohio and Market.

German Reformed, Alabama bet. Washington and Market.

Zion's, Ohio bet. Meridian and Illinois.

HEBREW.

Jewish Synagogue, Market bet. East and New Jersey. Morris Messing, Rabbi.

LUTHERAN.

St. Paul's cor. East and Georgia.

First English, cor. Alabama and New York. Rev. W. W. Criley, pastor.

METHODIST.

Ames Methodist Episcopal Church, cor. Madison av. and Merrill. Rev. L. M. Walters, pastor.

Allen Chapel, (African), Broadway bet. Christian av. and Cherry.

Asbury Chapel, New Jersey, bet. Louisiana and South.

Bethel Chapel, (African), 180 W. Georgia.

Grace Methodist Episcopal Church, cor. Market and East. Rev. J. W. Locke, D. D., pastor.

Robert's Tabernacle, cor. Delaware and Vermont. Rev. F. C. Holliday, pastor.

Strange Chapel, cor. Michigan and Tennessee. Rev. J. W. T. McMullen, pastor.

Trinity Methodist Episcopal Church, cor. Alabama and North. Rev. J. M. Crawford, pastor.

Third Street Church, bet. Illinois and Tennessee.

German Methodist, cor. New York and New Jersey. Rev. G. Trefz, pastor.

Meridian Street Church, cor. Meridian and New York. Dr. Bowman, President of Asbury University, pastor.

PRESBYTERIAN.

First Church, sw. cor. Pennsylvania and New York. Rev. R. D. Harper, D.D., pastor.

Second Church, cor. Pennsylvania and Vermont. Rev. Hanford A. Edson, pastor.

Third Church, cor. Illinois and Ohio. Rev. Robert Sloss, pastor.

Fourth Church, cor. Delaware and Market. Rev. W. W. Sickles, pastor.

Fifth Church, Blackford, nr. Michigan. Rev. W. B. Chamberlain, pastor.

Sixth Church, (Olivet Mission), se. cor. Union and McCarty. Rev. L. A. Aldrich, pastor.

Seventh Church, Elm, nr. Cedar. Rev. J. B. Brandt, pastor.

Reformed Church of Covenanters, South bet. East and Noble. Rev. John Crozier, pastor.

United Church, Ohio, bet. Pennsylvania and Delaware.

United Brethren, cor. New Jersey and Ohio. Rev. B. F. Morgan, pastor.

H. H. LEE,
Dealer in
Teas, Coffees, Sugars & Spices,
No. 7 ODD FELLOWS HALL
AND
ACADEMY OF MUSIC CORNER.

Memorial Chapel, cor. Bellefontaine and Christian av.

UNITARIAN.

Unitarian services at the Academy of Music, Sunday morning at half-past ten A.M. Rev. Henry Blanchard, pastor.

UNIVERSALIST.

Murray Church, Masonic Hall.
Second Church, Michigan, bet. Illinois and Tennessee.

MISSION.

Illinois Street Church, cor. of Illinois and Phipps.

YOUNG MEN'S CHRISTIAN ASSOCIA-TION.

Prayer meetings every evening in the week from eight to a quarter of nine o'clock, at the rooms of the Young Men's Christian Association, in Vinton's blk., sw. cor. Pennsylvania and Market, (up stairs.)

CEMETERIES.

Catholic, one mile S. of city, on Bluff rd., adjoining Hebrew.
City, ws. Kentucky av., S. of South.
Crown Hill, two miles nw. of city, entrance Michigan rd.
Green Lawn, ws. Kentucky av., bet. Louisiana and River.
Hebrew, one mile S. of city, on Bluff rd.

POST OFFICE DEPARTMENT.

Indianapolis Post Office.

POST OFFICE BUILDING.

Located southeast corner Pennsylvania and Market. Open from 7:30 A.M, to 6:30 P.M.; Sundays from 9 A.M. to 10 A.M.
Post Master—W. R. Holloway.
Assistant Post Master—John F. Wood.
Money Order Clerks—E. P. Thompson and Geo. C. Brooks.
Local Mail Agent—William Boaz.

Registry Clerks—B. F. Conner and E. K. Hart.

Mail Carriers.

FREE DELIVERY SYSTEM INAUGURATED JULY 1st, 1869.

Henry J. Brittain, Newton Hume, N. B. Meek, Wm. B. Dowdney, Andrew J. Wells, J. B. Sulgrove, M. D. Hamilton, E. M. Spicer, W. H. Wainwright, J. D. Eagle, S. McHugh, T. B. Stapp, H. C. Evans, J. T. Plummer, J. B. West, W. F. Homberg, Geo. W. Sulgrove, W. R. Williams.

Time of Arrival and Closing of Mails.

All Mails are assorted for delivery, immediately upon their arrival at the office.

East.

VIA COLUMBUS & INDIANAPOLIS R. R.—New York, Washington, Philadelphia, Harrisburg, Pittsburg, close 6:30 and 10 P.M.
Wheeling and Baltimore, close 10 P.M.
Richmond, Columbus, O., and Dayton, O., close 11:30 A.M. and 10 P.M.
VIA BELLEFONTAINE R. R.—Cleveland, Buffalo, Albany, Boston, all of New England and Northern Ohio, close 9 A.M. and 6:30 P.M.

West.

VIA TERRE HAUTE R R.—St. Louis, all Kansas, Colorado, Arizona, Idaho, New Mexico, California, Missouri, Southern and Central Illinois and Terre Haute, close 6:30 A. M. and 6:30 P.M.
TERRE HAUTE WAY—Evansville, Vincennes and Southwestern Indiana, close 10 and 12:30 P.M.

North.

VIA PERU R. R.—All Michigan, Iowa, Wisconsin, Minnesota, Oregon, Montana, Utah, Chicago, Northern Illinois, Nebraska, Peru, Kokomo, Logansport, Detroit and Canada, close 10:30 A.M. and 6:30 P.M.
VIA LAFAYETTE R. R.—Quincy, Springfield, Decatur, Bloomington, Peoria, Jacksonville, Attica, Covington, close 10:30 A.M. and 6:30 P.M.
Lafayette, Fort Wayne and Toledo, close, 6:30 P.M.

South.

VIA JEFFERSONVILLE R R.—All Texas Louisiana, Alabama, Georgia, Mississippi, South Carolina Arkansas, Louisville, New Albany, Jeffersonville, Madison and Seymour, close 9 A.M. and 6:30 P.M.

VIA CINCINNATI R. R.—All Southern Ohio and Eastern Kentucky, close 9 A. M. and 6.30 P.M.

VIA VINCINNES R. R.—Martinsville, West Newton, Valley Mills, Spencer, Gosport, Mooresville, Brooklyn, etc., close 12:30 P.M.

VIA JUNCTION R. R.—Connersville, Rushville, Beech Grove, Morristown, Hamilton, O., Oxford, O., Sugar Creek, Davisvill, Carrsville and Kinder, close 12:30 P.M.

Horse Mails.

WAVERLY WAY—Waverly, Bluff Creek, and Glenn Valley, daily, close, 7 A.M.

CRAWFORDSVILLE WAY—Brownsv'le, Clermont, daily, close 12 M.

New Ross, New Elizabeth Junction, Pittsboro' and Orth, Tuesdays and Fridays, close 12:30 P.M.

Rates of Postage.

Letters to any part of the United States, 3 cents, for each ½ ounce or part thereof.

Drop letters, 2 cents per each ½ ounce. Advertised letters, 1 cent, in addition to the regular rates.

Valuable letters may be registered on application at the office of mailing, and the payment of a registration fee, not exceeding 20 cents.

Transcient newspapers, periodicals, pamphlets, blanks, proof sheets, book manuscripts, and all mailable printed matter, (except circulars and books,) 2 cents for each and every 4 ounces; double these rates are charged for books.

Unsealed circulars, (to one address), not exceeding three in number, 2 cents, and in the same proportion for a greater number.

Seeds, cuttings, roots, etc., 2 cents for each 4 ounces or less quantity.

All packages of mail matter, not charged with letter postage, must be so arranged that the same can be conveniently examined by the Postmasters; if not, letter postage will be charged.

No package will be forwarded by mail which weighs over 4 pounds.

All postage matter, for delivery within the United States, must be PREPAID by stamps, except duly certified letters of soldiers and sailors.

Weekly newspapers, (one copy only), sent to actual subscribers, within the county where printed and published, free.

Letters to Canada and other British-North American Provinces, when not over 3000 miles, 10 cents for each ½ ounce. When over 3000 miles, 15 cents, pre-payment optional.

Letters to Great Britain or Ireland, 12 cents. Prepayment optional.

Letters to France, 15 cents for each ½ ounce. Prepayment optional.

Letters to other foreign countries, vary in rate, according to the route by which they are sent, and the proper information can be obtained of any Postmaster in the United States.

BANKS AND BANKING HOUSES.

CITIZENS' NATIONAL BANK, W. C. Holmes, President, J. R. Haugh, Cashier, 11 and 13 E. Washington.

FIRST NATIONAL BANK, W. H. English, President, J. C. New, Cashier, se. cor. Washington and Meridian.

FLETCHER'S BANK, (Fletcher & Co.) 32 E. Washington.

HARRISON A. & J. C. S., 15 E. Washington.

INDIANA BANKING CO., A. W. Davis, President, 28 E. Washington.

INDIANA NATIONAL BANK, Geo. Tousey, President, D. M. Taylor, Cashier, ne. cor. Washington and Meridian.

INDIANAPOLIS BRANCH BANKING CO., (Sharpe & Fletcher), proprietors, 49 E. Washington.

INDIANAPOLIS INSURANCE COMPANY'S BANK, cor. Virginia av. and Pennsylvania.

INDIANAPOLIS NATIONAL BANK, J. P. Haughey, President, A. F. Williams, Cashier, ne. cor. Washington and Pennsylvania.

MANSUR'S BANK, Isaiah Mansur, proprietor, 154 E. Washington.

MERCHANTS' NATIONAL BANK, J. S. Newman, President, F. Baggs, Cashier, 48 E. Washington.

PETTIT, BRADEN & CO., 3 Bates' House.

RITZINGER'S BANK, J. B. Ritzinger, proprietor, 14 E. Washington.

WOOLEN, WEBB & CO., 31 W. Washington.

SECRET AND BENEVOLENT ASS'NS.

MASONIC.

Ancient and Honorable Order of Free and Accepted Masons.

THE GRAND LODGE—Meets in the city of Indianapolis, at the Grand Masonic Hall, West Washington street, southeast corner Tennessee, Tuesday after the fourth Monday in May, annually. Grand Secretary's office in Grand Masonic Hall. John M. Bramwell, R. W. G. S. of Indianapolis; Charles Fisher, R. W. G. T. of Indianapolis.

THE GRAND CHAPTER—Meets annually on the third Wednesday in October.

GRAND COUNCIL—R. and S. Masters. —Meets annually, on Tuesday before the third Wednesday in October.

GRAND COMMANDERY—Meets on the first Tuesday in April. Charles Fisher, of Indianapolis, G. T.; John M. Bramwell, of Indianapolis, G. R.

Subordinate Lodges in Indianapolis.

A. AND A. SCOTTISH RITE—Meets in Yohn's blk.

CENTRE LODGE, NO. 23—Meets on the first Wednesday in each month, in the Ætna bldg. Joseph Solomon, W. M.; Charles Fisher, Sec.

MARION LODGE, NO. 35—Meets on the third Wednesday in each month, in Masonic Hall. J. Saylor, W. M.; John M Bramwell, Sec.

TEUTONIA LODGE, NO. 178—Meets on the second Wednesday in each month, in Mason Hall. Louis Helle, Sec.

CAPITAL CITY LODGE, NO. 312— Meets on the first Tuesday in each month, in Mason Hall. G. H. Fleming, Sec.

ANCIENT LANDMARKS LODGE, NO. 319—Meets on the first Thursday in each month, in Ætna bldg. E. Hartwell. Sec.

MYSTIC TIE LODGE, W. D—Meets on the fourth Monday in each month, in Masonic Hall. W. S. Cone, Sec.

INDIANAPOLIS CHAPTER, NO. 5— Meets on the first Friday in each month, in Masonic Hall. C. Fisher, Sec.

INDIANAPOLIS COUNCIL, NO. 2.— Meets on the first Monday in each month, in Masonic Hall. C. Fisher, Rec.

RAPER COMMANDERY, NO. 1—Meets on the fourth Wednesday in each month, in Masonic Hall. Charles Fisher, Rec.

ODD FELLOWS

Independent Order of Odd Fellows.

THE GRAND LODGE OF INDIANAPOLIS—Holds its semi-annual communication at Odd Fellows Hall, in the city of Indianapolis, on the third Tuesday of May and November, of each year.

CAPITAL LODGE, NO. 124—Meets every Friday evening at Odd Fellows Hall. C. Roeap, Sec.

CENTER LODGE, NO. 18—Meets every Tuesday evening, at Odd Fellows Hall. George P. Anderson, Sec.

GERMANIA LODGE — Meets every Thursday evening at Odd Fellows Hall. P. Lehr, Sec.

MARION ENCAMPMENT—Meets on the second and fourth Monday in each month at Odd Fellows Hall. J. F. Wallick, Secretary.

METROPOLITAN ENCAMPMENT, No. 5.—Meets every first and third Monday in each month at Odd Fellows Hall. George D. Staats, Scribe.

OLIVE BRANCH, (Rebecca Degree) LODGE, NO. 6.—Meets every Saturday evening. George D. Staats, Sec.

PHILOXENIAN LODGE, No. 44—Meets every Wednesday evening at Odd Fellows Hall. W. S. Coen, Secretary.

GOOD TEMPLARS.

INDEPENDENT ORDER OF GOOD TEMPLARS—RIGHT WORTHY GRAND LODGE.

RIGHT WORTHY GRAND LODGE OFFICERS.

R. W. G. T.—J. H. Orne, Massachusetts
R. W. G. C.—W. S. Williams, C. W.
R. W. G. V. T.—Fanny Woodberry, Ill.
R. W. G. S.—J. Spencer, Ohio.
R. W. G. Tr.—John Campbell, Mo.
R. W. G. Ch.—Rev. M. Parkhurst, Mass.
R. W. G. M.—J. J. Hickman, Ky.
R. W. G. D. M.—Lillie J. Robinson, Wis.
R. W. G. I. G.—A. R. Leonard, Wis.
R. W. G. O. G.—D. R. Pershing, Ind.

GRAND LODGE OFFICERS.

G. W. C. T.—S. T. Montgomery, Kokomo.

G. W. C.—J. R. Randall, Wabash.

G.W.V. T.—Mollie Flanner, Knightstown.

G. W. S.—D. R. Pershing, Warsaw.

G. W. Tr.—S. Johnson, Centerville.

G. W. Ch.—W. H. Myers, Greensburg.

G. W. M.—J. R. Bohmie, Logansport.

G. W. D. M.—Amanda Stewart, Ireland.

G. W. I. G.—J. G. McPheters, Bloomington.

G. W. O. G.—J. Simpson, Folsomville.

The next session to be held in Indianapolis, the third Tuesday in October, 1870.

INDIANA STATE TEMPERANCE ALLIANCE.

Prest.—Col. J. W. Ray, Indianapolis.

Cor. Sec.—Rev. J.V. R. Miller, Richmond.

Rec. Sec.—Sylvester Johnson, Centerville.

Treas.—J. B. Abbett, Indianapolis.

Gen. Agt.—C. Martindale, Indianapolis.

I. O. G. T.—NIGHTS OF MEETING.

The following are the times and places of meeting of the different Lodges in this city. Good Templars visiting the city, should avail themselves of the opportunity to attend.

Gough Lodge—Monday evening. Southwest corner of Washington and Pennsylvania streets.

Centre Lodge—Tuesday evening. Southwest corner of Washington and Pennsylvania streets.

Northern Star Lodge—Wednesday evening. Southwest corner of Washington and Pennsylvania streets.

Marion Lodge—Friday evening. Over Seventh Ward Grocery, corner New Jersey and Virginia avenue.

Charity Lodge—Wednesday evening. Church between Illinois and Russel avenue.

Way Lodge—Saturday evening. Southwest corner of Washington and Pennsylvania streets.

Franklin Lodge—Saturday evening. Southwest corner of Broadway and Cherry streets.

DRUIDS.

OCTAVIAN GROVE NO. 3, U. O. A. D.—Meets every Monday evening at 27 S. Meridian. A. Dickman, Sec'y.

HUMBOLT GROVE NO. 8, U. O. A. D.—Meets Wednesday evening of each week, at 27 S. Meridian. Geo. Fabrion, Sec'y.

SOCIETIES AND ASSOCIATIONS.

BUTCHERS' ASSOCIATION. — Meets every Thursday evening. F. Borst, Sec'y.

32

BENHAM BRO'S,

36 East Washington St.,

AGENTS FOR THE

BURDETT ORGAN.

ECLECTIC MEDICAL ASSOCIATON. G. W. Pickerill, Sec'y; L. Abbett, Treas.

GERMAN TURNERS' GYMNASTIC ASSOCIATION.—Charles Koehne, Prest; J. W. Loeper, Sec'y. Meets first Wednesday in every month at Turner Hall.

GERMAN TURN-VEREIN (Gymnastic Society)—John Rosenberg, Prest.

HARMONIA (German Musical)—Meets on Monday and Wednesday evenings of each week at Marmont Hall. Aug. Mueller, Director.

HOME FOR FRIENDLESS WOMEN.—Tennessee, north of limits. Officers: James Smith, Supt.; Sarah J. Smith, City Missionary; Susan L. Horney, Matron.

INDIANAPOLIS ACADEMY OF MEDICINE.—Meets at the rooms of the Young Men's Christian Association, Tuesday evening of each week. J. A. Comingore, Prest.; Charles Wright, Sec'y.

INDIANAPOLIS MÆNNERCHOR SOCIETY (German Musical)—Theodore Dingeldey, Prest.; F. Merz, Sec'y. Meets at Miller's Hall, corner of Delaware and Pearl, on Tuesday evening of each week.

LADIES' WORKING BAND (Connected with the Y. M. C. A.)—Mrs. R. C. Wiles, Prest.; Mrs. A. Clark, Sec'y.

MENDELSSOHN SOCIETY (Musical) —Organized September, 1867.—Regular meeting Wednesday evening at room 11 Martindale's blk. W. H. Churchman, Prest.; H. L. Benham, Sec'y.

ORPHAN ASYLUM.—Mrs. Anna M. Johnson, Matron. 711 N. Tennessee.

ST. JOHN'S HOME FOR INVALIDS. —Under charge of the Sisters of Providence, 127 and 129 S. Tennessee.

YOUNG MEN'S CHRISTIAN ASSOCIATION.—Rooms 16, 17, 18 and 19 Vinton's blk., opp. Postoffice; organized November, 1854. W. A. Bell, Prest.; J. B. Brandt, Supt.

KNIGHTS OF PYTHIAS.

OFFICERS FOR THE YEAR 1870.

GRAND LODGE.

John B. Stumph, V. G. P.; John Caven, G. C.; John L. Brown, V. G. C.; Charles P. Carty, G. P. and C. S.; Geo. F. Meyer, G. B.; John B. Ryan, G. G.; George H. Swain, G. I. S.; Charles Johns, G. O. S.

THE CHINA TEA STORES

Have the NAME of being the

MOST ATTRACTIVE STORES IN THE WEST.

No. 7 Odd Fellows Hall
AND
ACADEMY OF MUSIC CORNER.

MARION LODGE NO. 1.

Meets every Friday Evening.

John Caven, V. P.; Charles P. Carty, W. C.; George Brown, V. C.; Charles H. Cox, R. and C. S.; O. A. Burtch, F. S.; Wm. M. Obermeyer, Banker; M. L. Seddlemeyer, Guide; J. L. Boston, J. S.; Morris Mosler, O. S.

OLIVE BRANCH LODGE, No. 2.

Meets every Saturday Evening.

A. R. Miller, V. P.; Jot Elliott, W. C.; J. H. Smithers, V. C.; Y. F. Miller, R. and C. S.; N. S. Potter, F. S.; Henry Phillips, Banker: G. C. Webster, Guide; Jesse D. Haven, O. S.

STAR LODGE, NO. 7.

Meets every Teusday Evening.

W. M. Davis, V. P.; W. H. Hazelton, W. C.; Fred. J. Prail, V. C.; Henry S. Keely, R. and C. S.; J. H. Lendlum, F. S.; Carlin Hamlin, Banker; Wm. Wicks, Guide; Cyrus B. Blue, I. S.; Joseph Kingham, O. S.

KŒRNER LODGE, NO. 6.

Meets every Monday Evening.

John B. Stumph, V. P.; Geo. F. Meyer, W. C.; Charles Lauer, V. C.; Otto Boetticher, R. and C. C.; Charles Schmidt, F. S.; Wm. Shenneman, Banker; Wm. Hansa, Guide; Henry Paul, I. S.; Charles Johns, O. S.

AGRICULTURAL.

Indiana State Board of Agriculture.

Hon. J. D. Williams, President.
John Sutherland, Vice-President.
Joseph Poole, Secretary.
Carlos Dickson, Treasurer.
J. S. Ronson, General Superintendent.

MEMBERS OF THE STATE BOARD OF AGRICULTURE.

First District, L. A. Burke, New Harmony.

Second District, Hon. J. D. Williams, Wheatland.

Third District, John C. Shoemaker, Cannelton.

Fourth District, G. A. Buskirk, Bloomington.

Fifth District, Benjamin North, Rising Sun.

Sixth District, T. V. Mitchell, New Salem.

Seventh District, Jacob Muntz, Edinburg.

Eighth District, Hon. W. C. Donaldson, Montezuma.

Ninth District, Hon. A. D. Hamrick Hamrick's Station.

Tenth Distrcit, Alexander Heron, Connersville.

Eleventh District, Wm. Crim, Anderson.

Twelfth District, Joseph Poole, Attica.

Thirteenth District, H. Caldwell, Wabash.

Fourteenth District, Stephen Davidson, Rochester.

Fifteenth District, John Sutherland, Laporte.

Sixteenth District, I. D. G. Nelson, Fort Wayne.

Fair Grounds of the Indiana State Agricultural Society, terminus N. Delaware Street.

The Eighteenth Annual State Fair, will be held at Indianapolis, commencing October 3d.

Indianapolis Agricultural, Mechanical and Horticural Association.

OFFICE: BOARD OF TRADE ROOM.

Lewis W. Hasselman, President.
E. S. Alvord, Vice-President,
John B. Sullivan, Superintendent.
Elisha J. Howland, Treasurer.
J. George Stilz, Secretary.
W. H. Loomis, Assistant Secretary.

BOARD OF DIRECTORS.

Joseph D. Pattison.   Fielding Beeler.
Thomas B. McCarty.   W. C. Holmes.
Richard J. Bright.   John Fishback.
John T. Francis.   E. S. Alvord.
Lewis W. Hasselman.

The First Annual Exhibition of the Indianapolis Agricultural, Mechanical and Horticultural Association, will be held at Indianapolis, commencing Monday, September 5th.

Newspapers and Publications.

AMERICAN HOUSE WIFE, (monthly).
COMMERCIAL, (daily evening), M. T. Lee, editor, cor. Illinois and Washington.

FUTURE, (German Weekly), issued by the Gutenberg Publishing Co., Meridian, se. cor. Circle.

HEART AND HAND, (monthly), Rev. E. P. Ingersoll, editor; A. A. Barnes & Co., publishers; office, 38 E. Washington.

INDEPENDENT, (monthly), S. T. Montgomery, editor, 10½ S. Meridian.

INDIANA MASONIC HOME ADVOCATE, (monthly), F. M. Blair, editor and publisher. 44 N. Pennsylvania, Vinton's blk.

INDIANA SCHOOL JOURNAL, (monthly), G. W. Hoss and Thomas Charles, editors and proprs.

INDIANA TEACHER, (monthly), John B. Allen, editor and propr.

INDIANA VOLKSBLADT, (weekly), J. Bœtticher, editor and propr., 164 E. Washington.

INDIANAPOLIS JOURNAL, Republican, (daily except Sunday, weekly, Friday), Douglas & Conner, publishers, Market, se. cor. Circle. (Journal bldg.)

JOLLY HOOSIER, (monthly), A. C. Roach, editor and publisher.

JOURNAL OF COMMERCE, (weekly), Morton & Ricker, proprs., ne. cor. Meridian and Circle.

LADIES' CHRISTIAN MONITOR, (montly), Mrs. M. M. B. Goodwin, editor and propr.

LADIES' OWN MAGAZINE, (monthly), Mrs. M. Cora Bland, editor. Bland & Taylor, publishers.

LITTLE CHIEF, (monthly), Shortridge & Alden, editors and proprietors.

LITTLE SOWER, (weekly), W. W. Dowling, editor and propr.

MASONIC ADVOCATE, (monthly).

MIRROR, (Saturday evening), 19 N. Meridian.

MOCKING BIRD, (German weekly, Sunday), issued by the Gutenburg Publishing Co., Meridian, se. cor. Circle.

MORNING WATCH, (monthly), W. W. Dowling, editor and propr.

NEWS, (daily evening), J. R. Holliday, editor and publisher, Sentinel bldg.

MOTHER'S MONITOR, (monthly), Mrs. M. M. B. Goodwin, editor and propr.

NORTHWESTERN, (monthly), Martin & Hopkins, editors and publishers, Market, ne. cor. Circle. (Journal bldg.)

ODD FELLOWS' TALISMAN, (monthly), R J. Strickland, editor and publisher, 30 S. Meridian.

ROACH'S WESTERN MUSEUM, (monthly), A. C. Roach, editor and publisher.

SATURDAY ADVERTISER, (weekly), published by the Indianapolis Printing and Publishing House.

SPARKLING GEM, (monthly), Mrs. M.

BENHAM BRO'S,

36 East Washington St.,

Pianos, Organs and Melodeons Tuned, Moved and Repaired.

M. R. Goodwin, editor, A. Q. Goodwin, publisher. 30 S. Meridian.

STATE SENTINEL, (daily except Sunday, weekly Wednesday), R. J. Bright, propr., new Sentinel bldg., sw. cor. Meridian and Circle.

SUNBEAM, (monthly), William Travis, editor.

TELEGRAPH, (German), published daily and weekly by the Gutenberg Publishing Co., C. Beyschlag, editor. Office, Meridian, se. cor. Circle.

WESTERN FIRESIDE, (monthly), F. C. Holliday, editor; R. R. City Printing Co., proprs., 55½ E. Market, Vinton's blk.

WESTERN MUSICAL REVIEW, (monthly), Benham Bros, editors and publishers.

Public Halls, Blocks, and Buildings.

ACADEMY OF MUSIC, se. cor. Illinois and Ohio.

ÆTNA BUILDING, es. Pennsylvania bet. Washington and Market.

ALVORD'S BLOCK, sv. cor. Meridian and Georgia.

BATES HOUSE BLOCK, nw. cor. Washington and Illinois.

BISMARK HALL, Virginia av. nr. McCarty.

BLACKFORD'S BLOCK, Washington se. cor. Meridian.

BLAKE BLOCK, ss. Washington bet. Illinois and Tennessee.

BROWN'S BLOCK, Pennsylvania nw. cor. Washington.

CITIZENS' NATIONAL BANK BUILDING, 11 and 13 E. Washington.

CITY OFFICES, Cottrell & Knight's new building.

COTTRELL & KNIGHT'S BLOCK, Washington bet. Alabama and New Jersey.

COUNTY BUILDINGS, Court House Square, ns. Washington bet. Delaware and Alabama.

COUNTY OFFICES, Court House Square, ns. Washington bet. Delaware and Alabama.

EDEN'S BLOCK, ss. Market bet. Pennsylvania and Delaware.

EMENEGGER HALL, ss. Washington bet. Delaware and Alabama.

H. H. LEE'S

WHOLESALE PRICES FOR

TEAS, COFFEES & SUGARS,

ARE THE SAME EACH DAY

As are quoted in the

CINCINNATI DAILY PAPERS.

FATOUT'S BLOCK, ss. Washington bet.
Mississippi and Canal.
GALLUP'S BLOCK, Tennessee se. cor.
Market.
GLENN'S BLOCK, ss. Washington bet.
Meridian and Pennsylvania.
GOOD TEMPLARS HALL, sw. cor. Meridian and Washington.
GYMNASIUM HALL, nw. cor. Meridian
and Maryland.
HERETH'S BLOCK, N. Delaware opp.
Court House.
HUBBARD'S BLOCK. Washington sw.
cor. Meridian.
INDIANA SURGICAL INSTITUTE, ne.
cor. Georgia and Illinois.
JOURNAL BUILDING, Market ne. cor.
Circle.
KNIGHTS OF PYTHIAS HALL, fourth
story Citizens' National Bank bldg.
MARMONT HALL, 102, 104 and 106 S.
Illinois.
MARTINDALE'S BLOCK, Pennsylvania
ne. cor. Market.
MASONIC HALL, Washington se. cor.
Tennessee.
METROPOLITAN THEATER, Washington ne. cor. Tennessee.
MILLER'S BLOCK, nw. cor. Illinois and
Market.
MILLER'S HALL, cor. Delaware and
Pearl.
MOZART HALL, es. Delaware bet.
Washington and Maryland.
MOORE'S HALL, 64 E. Washington.
NATIONAL GUARD'S HALL, Washington bet. Delaware and Alabama.
NEW'S BLOCK, 10 and 12 E. Washington.
NORWOOD BLOCK, ws. Illinois bet.
Washington and Market.
ODD FELLOWS HALL AND BUILDING,
ne. cor. Pennsylvania and Washington.
PARKER'S BLOCK, cor. Delaware and
Court.
ROBERT'S BLOCK, es. Louisiana opp.
Depot.
SCHNULL'S BLOCK, sw. cor. Meridian
and Maryland.
SEIDENSTICKER'S BLOCK, opp. ss.
Union Depot.
SENTINEL BUILDING, sw. cor. Meridian and Circle.

SHERMAN HOUSE BLOCK, Louisiana
opp. Depot.
STATE HOUSE, full square, bet. Washington and Market, and Tennessee
and Mississippi.
SUPERVISOR OF INTERNAL REVENUE, (State), G. B. Williams, room
4 Vinton's blk.
SUPREME COURT AND STATE OFFICE
BUILDING, sw. cor. Washington and
Tennessee.
TALBOTT & NEW'S BLOCK, es. Pennsylvania bet. Washington and Market.
TEMPERANCE HALL, ns. Washington
bet. Illinois and Meridian.
THORP'S HALL AND BLOCK, ss. Market bet Pennsylvania and Delaware.
WASHINGTON HALL, ns. Washington
bet. Illinois and Tennessee.

STAMP DUTIES.

AGREEMENT, or contract, for
every sheet or piece of paper
upon which or either of the same
shall be written...................... $ 05
ASSIGNMENT of a mortgage lease
or policy of insurance requires
the same stamp as the original.
BANK CHECK, draft, or order at
sight or on demand..... 02
BILL OF EXCHANGE, draft or
order not exceeding one hundred dollars, or any
PROMISSORY NOTE for a sum
not exceeding one hundred dollars...... 05
For every additional hundred
dollars...... 05
BILL OF EXCHANGE not exceeding one hundred dollars.......... 02
For every additional hundred
dollars...... 02
BILL OF LADING, or receipt...... 10
BILL OF SALE 05
BOND (indemnity) of one thousand dollars or less........... 50
For every additional thousand
dollars...... 50
BOND for the due execution or
performance of the duties of any
office 1 00
BOND of any other description..... 25
BOND (personal). See mortgage.
COUNTY, city or town bonds, railroad and other corporation bonds
and scrip, are subject to stamp
duty. See mortgage.
CERTIFICATE of stock in any incorporated company................. 25

CERTIFICATE of deposit of any sum of money in any bank or trust company, if for a sum not exceeding one hundred dollars.. 02
For a sum exceeding one hundred dollars............ 05
CERTIFICATE of any other description 05
CHARTER PARTIES. — Tonnage not exceeding one hundred and fifty tons........ .... 1 00
Exceeding one hundred and fifty tons and not exceeding three hundred tons................ .... 3 00
Exceeding three hundred tons and not exceeding six............ 5 00
Exceeding six hundred tons...... 10 00
CONTRACT, broker's note or memorandum of sale of dry goods or merchandise, stock bonds, exchange notes of land, real estate or property................ 10
CONVEYANCE, deed, instrument or writing, when the actual consideration or value does not exceed five hundred dollars........ 50
When the consideration exceeds five hundred dollars, and does not exceed one thousand... .... 1 00
And for every additional five hundred dollars, or fractional part thereof, in excess of one thousand dollars.... 50
INSURANCE, (life) not exceeding one thousand dollars. 25
Exceeding one thousand dollars, and not exceeding five thousand............ 50
Exceeding five thousand dollars. 1 00
INSURANCE, (marine, inland or fire) where premiums do not exceed ten dollars............ 10
Exceeding ten, and not exceeding fifty dollars............ 25
Exceeding fifty dollars...... 50
LEASE, of three hundred dollars per annum or less............ 50
For every additional two hundred dollars, or fractional part. 50
MANIFEST, for custom house entry or clearance, or cargo of any ship, vessel or steamer for a foreign port, if the registered tonage of such ship, vessel or steamer does not exceed three hundred tons 1 00
Exceeding three hundred tons, and not six hundred tons 3 00
Exceeding six hundred tons...... 5 00
MORTGAGE, TRUST, DEED, BILL, OR SALE OF PERSONAL BOND, exceeding one hundred dollars, and not exceeding five hundred dollars............ 50

BENHAM BRO'S.
36 East Washington St.,
KEEP
THE VERY BEST
VIOLIN AND GUITAR STRINGS.

And for every additional five hundred dollars, or fractional part thereof, in excess of five hundred dollars 50
POWER OF ATTORNEY, to transfer stock.............. 25
POWER OF ATTORNEY OR PROXY............ 10
POWER OF ATTORNEY, to receive or collect rent............ 25
POWER OF ATTORNEY, to convey or sell real estate............ 1 00
POWER OF ATTORNEY, for any other purpose............ 50
PROBATE OF WILL, not exceeding the value of two thousand dollars........ $1 00
For every additional one thousand dollars or fractional part thereof............ 50
PROTEST,............ 25
RECEIPTS, for the payment of any sum of money, or for the payment of any debt due, exceeding twenty dollars............ 02
Warehouse receipts, for property, goods, wares or merchandise, not exceeding in value five hundred dollars........ 10
Exceeding in value, five hundred dollars and not exceeding one thousand dollars............ 20
Exceeding in value $1,000, for every additional $1,000.......... 10
Warehouse receipts, for any goods, merchandise, etc.,.......... 25
RENEWALS of charter, party contract or agreements, require the same stamp as the original instrument............
PROPRIETARY, for and upon every packet, box, bottle, etc., not exceeding in value the sum twenty-five cents............ 01
Exceeding in value twenty-five cents and not exceeding fifty... 02
Exceeding in value fifty cents and not exceeding seventy-five. 03
Exceeding in value seventy-five cents and not exceeding one dollar............ 04
For each additional fifty cents... 02
Exceeding in value one dollar... 02
FRICTION MATCHES, each parcel or package 01

THE CHINA TEA STORES

ARE LOCATED AT

No. 7 ODD FELLOWS HALL

AND

ACADEMY OF MUSIC CORNER.

SAME GOODS, SAME PRICES at BOTH.

When in parcels or packages
containing more than one hundred, for each parcel or package.   02
PHOTOGRAPHS, not exceeding
the retail price of twenty-five cts.   02
Exceeding the retail price of
twenty-five cents.....................   03
Exceeding the retail price of
fifty cents...............   05
Exceeding the retail price of
one dollar............................   07
For every additional dollar......   05
PLAYING CARDS, when the retail
price per pack does not exceed
eighteen cents.......................   02
Exceeding the retail price of
eighteen cents.......................   04
Exceeding the retail price of
twenty-five cents...................   10
Exceeding the retail price of fifty cents.............................   15
For every additional fifty cents.   05
CANNED MEATS, &c.—For and
upon every can, bottle, or single
package, containing sauces, syr-
ups, prepared mustard, jams, or
jellies contained therein, and
packed, or sealed, made prepared
and sold, or offered for sale, or
removed for consumption in the
United States, on and after, the
first day of October, eighteen
hundred and sixty-six, when
such a can, bottle, or other single
package, with its contents, shall
not exceed two pounds in weight,
the sum of one cent..............   1
When such can, bottle, or other
single package, with its contents,
shall exceed two pounds in
weight, for every additional
pound or fractional part thereof,
one cent..............................   1

WARD BOUNDARIES.

FIRST WARD.—All that part of the city
bounded on the south by New York
street, on the north by North street,
(from Meridian street east to the ter-
mination of North street, thence east
on the continuation of the line from
the center of North street to the corporation line), and on the east by the
corporation line, shall constitute the
First Ward.

SECOND WARD.—All that part of the city
bounded on the south by the northern
boundary of the First Ward, on the
west by Meridian street, and on the
north and east by the corporation line,
shall constitute the Second Ward.

THIRD WARD.—All that part of the city
bounded on the north by Washington
street, (from Meridian street to Mississippi street), on the west by Mississippi
street, from Washington street north to
the intersection of Indiana avenue,
thence northwest by Indiana avenue to
West street, thence north by West
street to the corporation line, and on
the east by Meridian street and Circle
street, (running east of the Governor's
Circle), shall constitute the Third
Ward.

FOURTH WARD.—All that part of the city
bounded on the south by Washington
street, on the west by White River and
the corporation line, and on the east
by the western boundary of the Third
Ward, shall constitute the Fourth Ward.

FIFTH WARD.—All that part of the city
bounded on the north by Washington
street, on the west by White River, on
the east by Illinois street and South
street, and south by the corporation line,
shall constitute the Fifth Ward.

SIXTH WARD.—All that part of the city
bounded on the north by Washington
street, on the west by Illinois street, on
the east by Delaware street, and on
the south by the corporation line, shall
constitute the Sixth Ward.

SEVENTH WARD.—All that part of the city
bounded on the north by Washington
street, on the west by Delaware street,
on the east by East street, and on the
south by the corporation line, shall constitute the Seventh Ward.

EIGHTH WARD.—All that part of the city
bounded on the north by Washington
street, on the west by East, and on the
east and south by the corporation line,
shall constitute the Eighth Ward.

NINTH WARD—All that part of the city
bounded on the south by Washington
street, (from the corporation line west
to Meridian street), on the west by
Meridian street and Circle street, (running east of the Governor's Circle), on
the north by New York street, and on
the east by the corporation line, shall
constitute the Ninth Ward.

SHIPPER'S GUIDE.

EMBRACING

STATIONS AND ROUTES ON ALL RAILROADS

DIVERGING

FROM INDIANAPOLIS

STATIONS.	RAILROADS.	STATIONS.	RAILROADS.
Acton, Ind	I. C. & L.	Cable, O	C. C. & I. C.
Adams, Ind	I. C. & L.	Caledonia, O	C. C. C. & I.
Alford, Ind	C. C. C. & I.	Cambridge City, Ind	C. C. & I. C.
Amity, Ind	J. M. & I.	Carrollton, Ind	C. & I. J.
Amo, Ind	T. H. & I.	Cartersburg, Ind	T. H. & I.
Anderson, Ind	C. C. C. & I.	Cary's, O	C. C. C. & I.
Anderson's Ferry, O	I. C. & L.	Cassville, Ind	I. P. & C.
Anoka, Ind	I. P. & C.	Castleton, Ind	I. P. & C.
Arcadia, Ind	I. P. & C.	Centerton, Ind	I. & V.
Arnold's, O. (Harrison's Branch)	I. C. & L.	Centerville, Ind	C. C. & I. C.
Ashmore, Ill	T. H. A. & St. L.	Charleston, Ill	T. H. A. & St. L.
Augusta, Ind	I. C. & L.	Charlottsville, Ind	C. C. & I. C.
Austin, Ind	J. M. & I.	Chesterfield, Ind	C. C. C. & I.
Batesville, Ind	I. C. & L.	Chicago, Ill	I. P. & C.
Becknell, Ind	I. & V.	Chicago, Ill	I. C. & L.
Becks, Ind	I. P. & C.	Cicero, Ind	I. P. & C.
Beeler's, Ind	I. & V.	Cincinnati, O	C. & I. J.
Bellefontaine, O	C. C. C. & I.	Cincinnati, O	I. C. & L.
Bellville, Ind	T. H. & I.	Clark's Hill, Ind	I. C. & L.
Bennett's, Ind	I. P. & C.	Clayton, Ind	T. H. & I.
Bethalto, Ill	T. H. A. & St. L.	Clermont, Ind	I. B. & W.
Big Spring, O	C. C. C. & I.	Cleaves, O	I. C. & L.
Brandon, Ind	C. & I. J.	Cleveland, Ind	C. C. & I. C.
Brantwood, Ind	I. P. & C.	Cleveland, O	C. C. C. & I.
Brazil, Ind	T. H. & I.	Cleveland, O	C. C. & I. C.
Bridgeport, Ind	T. H. & I.	Cloverland, Ind	T. H. & I.
Bright's, Ind	J. M. & I.	Coatsville, Ind	T. H. & I.
Britton's, Ind	I. P. & C.	Coffin's, Ind	C. C. & I. C.
Brookfield, Ind	I. C. & L.	Colfax, Ind	I. C. & L.
Brookland, Ind	I. & V.	College Corner, Ind	C. & I. J.
Browns, Ind	I. P. C. &	Columbus, Ind	J. M. & I.
Brownsburg, Ind	I. B. & W.	Columbus, O	C. C. & I. C.
Brownsville, Ind	C. & I. J.	Connersville, Ind	C. & I. J.
Bruceville, Ind	I. & V.	Conover, O	C. C. & I. C.
Bryant's, O	C. C. C. & I.	Cottage Grove, Ind	C. & I. J.
Buena Vista, Ind	I. P. & C.	Covington, O	C. C. & I. C.
Bunker Hill, Ind	C. & I. J.	Crawfordsville, Ind	I. B. & W.
Bunker Hill, Ind	I. P. & C.	Crestline, O	C. C. C. & I.
Bunker Hill, Ill	T. H. A. & St. L.	Crothersville, Ind	J. M. & I.
Burk's, O. (Harrison's Branch)	I. C. & L.	Crown Point, Ind	I. P. & C.
Burlington, Ind	C. & I. J.	Culver's, Ind	I. C. & L.
Butler, Ill	T. H. A. & St. L.	Cumberland, Ind	C. C. & I. C.
Butler's, Ind	J. M. & I.	Dallas, O	C. C. & I. C.

STATIONS.	RAILROADS.	STATIONS.	RAILROADS.
Dalton, Ill	I. P. & C.	Henryville, Ind	J. M. & I.
DeGraff, O	C. C. & I.	Hilliard's, O	C. C. & I. C.
Delhi, O	I. C. & L.	Hillsboro, Ill	T. H. A. & St. L.
Devau's, O	I. C. & L.	Holme's, Ind	I. C. & L.
Dixon, Ind	I. & V.	Holmes, Ind	I. B. & W.
Dublin, Ind	C. C. & I. C.	Houston, O	C. C. & I.
Dudley's, Ill	T. H. A & St. L.	Howland, Ind	I. P. & C.
Du Point, Ind	J. M. & I.	Hynd's, Ind	I. & V.
Eagle Creek, Ind	T. H. & I.	Jackson, Ind	I. P. & C.
Eagle's, Ind	T. H. & I.	James, Ind	I. P. & C.
East St. Louis	T. H. A. & St. L.	Jamestown, Ind	I. B. & W.
Edinburgh, Ind	J. M. & I.	Jeffersonville, Ind	J. M. & I.
Edwardsport, Ind	I. & V.	Jones' Mills, O	C. C. C. & I.
Elizabethtown, Ind	J. M. & I.	Joliet Crossing, Ind	I. P. & C.
Elizabethtown O	J. C. & L.	Jonesville, Ind	J. M. & I.
English Lake, Ind	I. P. & C.	Kansas, Ill	T. H. A. & St. L.
Fairfield, Ind	I. P. & C.	Knightstown, Ind	C. C. & I. C.
Fairland, Ind	I. C. & L.	Kokomo, Ind	I. P. & C.
Farmington, Ind	J. M. & I.	Koute's, Ind	I. P. & C.
Farmington, Ind	C. & I. J.	Layfayette, Ind	I. C. & L.
Farmland, Ind	C. C. C. & I.	Lancaville, Ind	C. C. & I.
Fillmore, Ind	T. H. & I.	Langdon, Ind	J. M. & I.
Fletcher, O	C. C. & I. C.	Lansing, Ill	I. P. & C.
Fortville, Ind	C. C. C. & I.	Lardosa, Ind	C. & I. J.
Franklin, Indiana	J. M. & I.	Larue, O	C. C. C. & I.
Frederick, Ind	I. B. & W.	Lawrenceburg, Ind	I. C. & L.
Freedom, Ind	I. & V.	Lebanon, Ind	I. C. & L.
Friends' Woods, Ind	I. & V.	Lewisville, Ind	C. C. & I. C.
Fountainetown, Ind	C. & I. J.	Liberty, Ind	C. & I. J.
Fulton, O	C. C. C. & I.	Lotus, Ind	C. & I. J.
Gallion, O	C. C. C. & I.	Lincoln, Ind	I. P. & C.
Gallaudet, Ind	I. C. & L.	Litchfield, Ill	T. H. A. & St. L.
Galveston, Ind	I. P. & C.	Logansport, Ind	I. P. & C.
Gebhardt, Ind	I. P. & C.	London, Ind	I. C. & L.
Germantown, Ind	C. C. & I. C.	Loramie, O	C. C. C. & I.
Gettysburg, O	C. C. & I. C.	Louisville, Ky	J. M. & I.
Gillespie, Ill	T. H. A. & St. L.	Lowell, Ind	J. M. & I.
Gosport, Ind	I. & V.	Lyons, Ind	C. & I. J.
Greencastle, Ind	T. H. & I.	Lyons, Ind	I. & V.
Greencastle Junction, Ind	T. H. & I.	McGord's, Ind	C. C. & I.
Greenfield, Ind	C. C. & I. C.	McCoy's, Ind	I. C. & L.
Greensburg, Ind	I. C. & L.	McDonald's, O	C. & I. J.
Greenville, O	C. C. & I. C.	McGonigle's, O	C. & I. J.
Greenwood, Ind	J. M. & I.	Madison, Ind	J. M. & I.
Guilford, Ind	I. C. & P.	Marco, Ind	I. & V.
Gurley's, O	C. C. & I. C.	Marion, O	C. C. C. & I.
Gwinnes	C. & I. J.	Marshfield, Ind	J. M. & I.
Hagenbaugh's, O	C. C. & I. C.	Martinsville, Ind	I. & V.
Hamilton, O	C. & I. J.	Matthews, Ind	I. & V.
Hamrick's, Ind	T. H. & I.	Mattoon, Ill	T. H. A. & St. L.
Hanover, O	C. & I. J.	Memphis, Ind	J. M. & I.
Hardentown, Ind	I. C. & L.	Miama, Ind	I. P. & C.
Harden, O	C. C. & I.	Milford, O	C. C. & I. C.
Harman's, Ind	I. C. & L.	Mooresville, Ind	I. & V.
Harmony, Ind	T. H. & I.	Morehouse, Ind	C. & I. J.
Harper, O	C. C. C. & I.	Morris, Ind	I. C. & L.
Harrison, O.(Harrison's Branch)	I. C. & L.	Morristown, Ind	C. & I. J.
Harrison Junction, O	I. C. & L.	Morristown, Ind	C. C. C. & I.
Harrisonville, Ind	C. C. & I.	Mt. Victory, O	C. C. C. & I.
Harvey's, Ind	C. C. & I. C.	Muncie, Ind	C. C. C. & I.
Hastings, Ind	I. & V.	Munday's, Ind	I. & V.
Hazelrigg, Ind	I. C. & L.	New Britton, Ind	I. P. & C.
Hebron, Ind	I. P. & C.	Newbury, Ind	T. H. & I.

STATIONS.	RAILROADS.	STATIONS.	RAILROADS.
New Elizabethtown, Ind	I. B. & W.	Shelbyville, Ind	I. C. & L.
New Madison, O	C. C. & I. C.	Shelbyville, Ill	T. H. A. & St. L.
New Paris, O	C. C. & I. C.	Sidney, O	C. C. C. & I.
New Point, Ind	I. C. & L.	Simonson, O., Harrison's br'ch	I. C. & L.
Newton, Ind	I. C. & L.	Slick's, O	C. C. C. & I.
Noblesville, Ind	I. P. & C.	Smithfield, Ind	C. C. C. & I.
Nokomis, Ill	T. H. A. & St. L.	Smith's Crossing, Ind	I. C. & L.
North Judson, Ind	I. P. & C.	Southport, Ind	J. M. & L.
North Madison, Ind	J. M. & I.	South Side, Ind	I. C. & L.
North Vernon, Ind	J. M. & I.	Spades, Ind	I. C. & L.
North Western Junction, Ill	I. P. & C.	Spencer, Ind	I. & V.
Oakland, Ind	C. C. & I.	Spounton, Ind	T. H. & L.
Ogden, Ind	C. C. & I. C.	Stockwell, Ind	I. C. & L.
Ogleton, O	C. & I. J.	Strawn's, Ind	C. C. & I. C.
Oxford, O	C. & I. J.	Sulphur Springs, Ind	C. & I. J.
Palistine, Ind	C. & I. J.	Summit, Ind	T. H. & I.
Pana, Ill	T. H. A. & St. L.	Sunman, Ind	I. C. & L.
Paragon, Ind	I. & V.	Switz City, Ind	I. & V.
Paris, Ill	T. H. A. & St. L.	Taylorsville, Ind	J. M. & I.
Pemberton, O	C. C. C. & I.	Terre Haute, Ind	T. H. & I.
Pendleton, Ind	J. M. & I.	Thorntown, Ind	I. C. & L.
Peru, Ind	I. P. & C.	Tipton, Ind	I. P. & C.
Philadelphia, Ind	C. C. & I. C.	Trautman's, O	I. C. & L.
Piqua, O	C. C. & I. C.	Tyner's, Ind	C. & I. J.
Pittsboro, Ind	I. B. & W.	Union, Ind	C. C. C. & I.
Plainfield, Ind	T. H. & I.	Unionville, O	C. C. C. & I. C.
Pleasant Valley, O	C. C. & I. C.	Urbana, O	C. C. & I. C.
Poplar Grove, Ind	I. C. & L.	Valley City, Ind	I. B. & W.
Prairie, Ind	T. H. & I.	Valley Mills, Ind	I. & V.
Prescott, Ind	I. C. & L.	Van Wedden's, Ind	I. C. & L.
Queensville, Ind	J. M. & I.	Vernon, Ind	J. M. & I.
Quincy, O	C. C. C. & I.	Versailles, O	C. C. C. & I.
Raysville, Ind	C. C. & I. C.	Vorsland, Ind	I. P. & C.
Reelsville, Ind	T. H. & I.	Vienna, Ind	J. M. & I.
Retreat, Ind	J. M. & I.	Vienna, Ind	C. & I. J.
Richmond, Ind	C. C. & I. C.	Vincennes, Ind	I. & V.
Richmond Junction, O	C. C. & I. C.	Waldron, Ind	I. C. & L.
Ridgeway, O	C. C. C. & I.	Walesboro', Ind	J. M. & I.
Riffners, O., Hamilton branch	I. C. & L.	Walton, Ind	I. P. & C.
River Side, O	I. C. & L.	Waynesville, Ind	J. M. & I.
Rock Creek, Ind	J. M. & I.	Weaver's, Ind	T. H. & I.
Rockford, Ind	J. M. & I.	Weaver's, O	C. C. & I. C.
Rock Island, Ill	I. P. & C.	Weisburg, Ind	I. C. & L.
Rosedale, Ind	I. P. & C.	Westville, O	C. C. & I. C.
Royal Center, Ind	I. P. & C.	West Newton, Ind	I. & V.
Rushsylvania, O	C. C. C. & I	Wheatland, Ind	J. M. & I.
Rushville, Ind	C. & I. J.	Whitestown, Ind	I. C. & L.
St. Louis, Mo	T. H. A. & St. L.	Wiggs, Ind	J. M. & I.
St. Louis, Ill	I. P. & C.	Wiley's, O	C. C. & I. C.
St. Paul, Ind	I. C. & L.	Williams, Ind	T. H. & I.
St. Paris, O	C. C. & I. C.	Winchester, Ind	C. C. & I.
Sanford's, Ill	T. H. A. & St. L.	Windsor, Ill	T. H. A. & St. L.
Sandburn, Ind	I. & V.	Winnamac, Ind	I. P. & C.
Scarboro', Ind	I. P. & C.	Woodbury, Ind	C. C. C. & I.
Scioto, O	C. C. & I. C.	Woods, O	C. & I. J.
Scipio, Ind	J. M. & I.	Wood's Mill, Ind	T. H. & I.
Sedamsville, O	I. C. & L.	Woodstock, O	C. C. & I. C.
Sellersburg, Ind	J. M. & I.	Worthington, Ind	I. & V.
Seymour, Ind	J. M. & I.	Worthsville, Ind	J. M. & I.
Shakapee, Ind	I. P. & C.	Yorktown, Ind	C. C. C. & I.
Sharpsville, Ind	I. P. & C.	Zionville, Ind	I. C. & L.

33

INDIANA POST-OFFICES,

COMPILED BY COUNTIES, AND REVISED FOR 1870.

ADAMS.

Canoper.
Desatur, (c. h.)
Kirkland.
Limber Lost.

Linn Grove.
Monmouth.
Pleasant Mills.

ALLEN.

Arcola.
Chamberlain.
East Liberty.
Fort Wayne, (c. h.)
Hall's Corners.
Harlan.
Heller's Corner's
Leo.
Little River.
Maples.
Massillon.

Monroeville.
New Haven.
Nine Mile.
Perry.
Phelps.
Po.
Randall.
Ridge Road.
Root.
St. Vincent.
Woodburn.

BARTHOLOMEW.

Azalia.
Burnsville.
Clay Hill.
Clifford.
Columbus, (c. h.)
Elizabethtown.
Hartsville.
Hope.
Jonesville.
Kansas.
Lowell Mills.

Moore's Vineyard.
Mount Healthy.
Newbern.
Rock Creek.
St. Louis Crossing.
South Bethany.
Taylorsburg.
Taylorsville.
Wailesborough.
Waynesville.

BENTON.

Catalpa Grove.
Parish Grove.

Oxford, (c. h.)

BLACKFORD.

Dundee.
Hartford City, (c. h.)
Montpelier.

Priam.
Scott.

BOONE.

Dover.
Elizaville.
Jamestown.
Lebanon, (c. h.)
Northern Depot.
Northfield.

Reese's Mill.
Royalton.
Thorntown.
White Lick.
Whitestown.
Zionsville.

BROWN.

Bean Blossom.

Nashville, (c. h.)

Cleona.
Elkinsville.
Gold Creek.
Mount Liberty.
Mount Moriah.

New Bellsville.
Oak Farm.
Ridge Woof.
Spearsville.

CARROLL.

Burlington.
Burrows.
Camden.
Carroll.
Cornucopia.
Deer Creek.
Delphi, (c. h.)
Fetherhuff's Mills.

Lockport.
Mount Jefferson.
Pittsburg.
Prince William.
Pyrmont.
Rockfield.
Wild Cat.

CASS.

Amsterdam.
Anoka.
Crittenden.
Curveton.
Fitch.
Galveston.
Gerphart.
Hubbard.
Lewisburg.
Lincoln.

Logansport, (c. h.)
Metea.
Montez.
New Waverly.
Onward.
Royal Center.
Spring Creek.
Twelve Mile.
Twin Corners.
Walton.

CLARK.

Bennettsville.
Bethlehem.
Blue Lick.
Charlestown, (c. h.)
Henryville.
Hibernia.
Jeffersonville.
Memphis.
Muddy Fork.

New Providence.
New Washington.
Oregon.
Polk Run.
Sellersburg.
Slate Cut.
Sylvan Grove.
Utica.

CLAY.

Ashborough.
Belle Air.
Bowling Green, (c. h.)
Brazil.
Center Point.
Christy's Prairie.
Cloverland.
Coffee.

Farm.
Harmony.
Howesville.
Martz.
Poland.
Staunton.
Van Buren.

CLINTON.

Berlin.
Budget's Corner.

Michigantown.
Middle Fork.

Colfax.
Edna Mills.
Frankfort, (c.h.)
Geetingsville.
Jefferson.
Kirk's Cross Roads.

Mulberry.
Pickard Mill.
Ramessa.
Rossville.
Russiaville.

CRAWFORD.

Alton.
Down Hill.
Elkton.
English.
Fredonia.
Grantsburgh.
Leavenworth, (c.h.)
Magnolia.

Marengo.
Mifflin.
Milltown.
Mount Prospect.
Nebraska.
Pedoria.
Pilot Knob.
Wickliffe.

DAVIESS.

Alfordsville.
Black Oak Ridge.
Bogard.
Clark's Prairie.
Epsom.
Glendale.
High Rock.

Hudsonville.
Montgomery's St'n.
Owl Prairie.
Plainville.
Raglesville.
Washington, (c.h.)

DEARBORN.

Aurora.
Bright.
Cochran.
Dillsborough.
Farmer's Retreat.
Guilford.
Guionsville.
Holman.
Jones' Station.
Kelso.
Lawrenceburg, (c.h.)

Lawrenceville.
Logan.
Manchester.
Moore's Hills.
New Alsace.
Saint Leon.
Sparta.
Weisburg.
Wilmington.
Wright's Corners.
Yorkville.

DECATUR.

Adams.
Alert.
Clarksburg.
Clifty.
Forest Hill.
Greensburg, (c.h.)
Jackson.
Kingston.
McCoy's Station.
Millhousen.
Rossburg.

Saint Morris.
Saint Omer.
Saint Paul.
Sardinia.
Smyrna.
Spring Hill.
Waynesburg.
Westport.
Williamstown.
Wintersville.

DE KALB.

Arctic.
Auburn, (c.h.)
Butler.
Coburn's Corners.
Cole's Corners.
Corunna.

Jarvis.
Mount Hope.
Newville.
Smithfield.
Spencerville.
Taylor's Corners.

Fairfield Center.
Iba.

Victor.
Waterloo City.

DELAWARE.

Albany.
Anthony.
Daleville.
Eaton.
Grantville.
Harrison.
Muncie, (c.h.)

New Burlington.
New Corner.
Richwoods.
Selma.
Sharon.
Wheeling.
Yorktown.

DUBOIS.

Birdseye.
Bretzville.
Celestine.
Ditney Hill.
Ferdinand.
Haysville.
Hilham.

Holland.
Huntingsburg.
Ireland.
Jasper, (c.h.)
Ludlow.
Porterville.

ELKHART.

Benton.
Bristol.
Elkhart.
Fish Lake.
Goshen, (c.h.)
Locke.
Middleberry.

Millersburg.
Mount Olive.
New Paris.
South West.
Vistula.
Wakarusa.
Waterford Mills.

FAYETTE.

Alquina.
Bentonville.
Columbia.
Connersville, (c.h.)
Everton.
Falmouth.

Harrisburg.
Longwood.
Lyon's Station.
Null's Mills.
Orange.
Waterloo.

FLOYD.

Edwardsville.
Floyd Knobs.
Galena.
Georgetown.

Greenville.
New Albany,(c.h.)
Scottsville.

FOUNTAIN.

Attica.
Buell.
Cole Creek.
Covington, (c.h.)
Fountain City.
Harveysburg.
Headley's Mills.

Hillsboro.
Newton.
Portland.
Rob Roy.
Steam Corner.
Wallace.

FRANKLIN

Andersonville.
Blooming Grove.
Blue Creek.

Mixersville.
Mount Carmel.
New Trenton.

Brookville, (c.h.)   Oak Forest.
Cedar Grove.   Oldenburg.
Drewersburg.   Peppertown.
Enochsburg.   Saint Peters.
Fairfield.   South Gate.
Haymond.   Springfield.
Jennings.   Stipp's Hill.
Laurel.   Whitcomb.
Metamora.   Wynn.

FULTON.

Akron.   Indian Field.
Aubbeenaubbee.   Kewanna.
Bloomingsburg.   Lake Sixteen.
Blue Grass.   Mill Ark.
Bruce's Lake.   *Rochester,* (c.h.)
Fulton.   Sidney.
Green Oak.

GIBSON.

Bovine.   Oakland City.
Buckskin.   Owensville.
Fort Branch.   Patoka.
Haubstadt.   *Princeton,* (c.h.)
Hazleton.   Somerville.
Marsh Creek.   West Buna Vista.

GRANT.

Arcana.   Mier.
Fairmount.   New Cumberland.
Grant.   Oak Wooks.
Greenbush.   Point Isabel.
Holt.   Rigdon.
Jadden.   Slash.
Jalapa.   Trask.
Jonesboro'.   Winthrop.
Marion, (c.h.)

GREENE.

Bloomfield, (c.h.) Owensburg.
Buck Creek.   Pleasant Ridge.
Hobbieville.   Point Commerce.
Jasonville.   Scotland.
Linton.   Silver Creek.
Lone Tree.   Solsberry.
Marco.   Worthington.
Newberry.   Wright.

HAMILTON.

Arcadia.   Engletown.
Boxley.   New Britton.
Carmel.   *Noblesville,* (c.h.)
Cicero.   Sheilville.
Clarksville.   Strawtown.
Deming.   Westfield.

HANCOCK.

Charlottesville.   Philadelphia.

Cleveland.   Sugar Creek,
Eden.   Walpole.
Fortville.   Warrington.
Greenfield, (c.h.) Westland.
Kinder.   Willow Branch.
McCordsville.   Woodbury.
Mount Comfort.

HARRISON.

Barren.   Mauckport.
Bradford.   New Amsterdam.
Byrneville.   New Middletown.
Cedar Spring.   New Salisbury.
Corydon, (c.h.)   Palmyra.
Crisps Cross Roads.   Rosewood.
Elizabeth.   Sharp's Mills.
Fairdale.   Spring Dale,
Hancock.   Valley City.
Knob Creek.   West Boston.
Laconia.   White Cottage.
Lanesville.

HENDRICKS.

Amo.   New Winchester.
Belleville.   North Salem.
Brownsburg.   Pecksburg.
Cartersburg.   Pittsboro'.
Clayton.   Plainfield.
Contesville.   Springtown.
Danville, (c.h.)   Stilesville.
New Elizabeth.

HENRY.

Ashland.   Mechanicsburg.
Blountsville.   Middletown,
Cadiz.   Millville.
Coffin's Station.   *New Castle,* (c.h.)
Dan. Webster.   New Lisbon.
Devon.   Ogden.
Greensboro'.   Raysville.
Honey Creek.   Rogersville.
Knightstown.   Spiceland.
Lewisville.   Sulphur Springs.
Luray.

HOWARD.

Alto.   New London.
Blair.   Oakford.
Cassville.   Poplar Grove.
Center.   Russiaville.
Greentown.   Shanghi.
Jerome.   Vermont.
Kokomo, (c.h.)   West Liberty.

HUNTINGTON.

Antioch.   Markle.
Branch Creek.   Mount Etna.
Huntington, (c.h.) Roanoke.
Mahon.   Warren.

JACKSON.

Baker's Mills.
Brownstown, (c.b.)
Conlogue.
Cortland.
Crane's Mills.
Crothersville.
Dudley.
Ewing.
Findlay's Mills.
Freetown.
Houston.
Medora.

Mooney.
New Farmington.
Reddington.
Retreat.
Rockford.
Seymour.
Sparksville.
Tampico.
Valley Farm.
Vallonia.
White Creek.
Woodville.

JASPER.

Carpenter's Creek.
Cathcart.
Pleasant Grove.

Remington.
Rensselaer, (c. h.)
Walkersville.

JAY.

Balbec.
Bear Creek.
Bluff Point.
Boundary.
College Corner.
Dunkirk.
Gillum.
Greene.
Half Way.

Hector.
Joy, (c. h.)
Jordon.
Monroe.
New Corrydon.
New Mt. Pleasant.
Pennville.
Salamonia.
Winchester.

JEFFERSON.

Barbersville.
Bryantsburg.
Cannan.
Dupont.
Graham.
Hanover.
Home.
Kent.
Lancaster.

Madison, (c. h.)
Manville.
Mud Lick.
North Madison.
Saluda.
Stony Point.
Swanville.
Volga.
Wirt.

JENNINGS.

Denville.
Brewersville.
Brooksburg.
Butlerville.
Cana.
Hopewell.
Montgomery.
Nebraska.
Oakdale.
Otto Creek.

Paris.
Queensville.
San Jacinto.
Scipio.
Six Mile.
State.
Storm's Creek.
Tripton.
Vernon, (c. h.)
Zenas.

JOHNSON.

Amity.
Bargersville.
Bluff Creek.
Edinburg.

Needham's Station.
Nineveh.
Trafalgar.
Whiteland.

FRANKLIN, (c. h.)

Franklin, (c. h.)
Greenwood.
Musselman.

Winneyville.
Worthsville.

KNOX.

Bruceville.
Busseron.
Decker's Station.
Edwardsport.
Elm.
Emerson's Station.
Freelandville.
Griswold.

High Point.
Lovely Dale.
Oak Station.
Pond Creek Mills.
Spaldingville.
Vincennes, (c. h.)
Wheatland.

KOSCIUSKO.

Atwood.
Beaver Dam.
Boydston's.
Claypool.
Clear Spring.
Etna Green.
Leesburg.
Milford.
North Galveston.
Oneida.
Orion.

Oswego.
Palestine.
Pierceton.
Rose Hill.
Sevastopol.
Silver Lake.
Syracuse.
Warsaw, (c. h.)
Wooster.
Yellow Creek.

LA GRANGE.

Brighton.
Brushby Prairie.
Greenfield's Mills.
Haw Patch.
La Grange, (c. h.)
Lima.
Marcy.

Mongoquinong.
Mount Pisgah.
Ontario.
Ringgold.
South Milford.
Walcotteville.

LAKE.

Brunswick.
Cedar Lake.
Clark's Station.
Crown Point, (c. b.)
Deep River.
Dyer.
Eagle Creek.
Gibson's Station.
Hanover.
Hobart.
Lake Station.

Lowell.
Merrillville.
Miller's Station.
Orchard Grove.
Gutley.
Ross.
Saint John.
Schererville.
Tolleston.
West Creek.
Winfield.

LA PORTE.

Bigelow's Mills.
Big Springs.
Calino.
Crossing.
Door Village.
Hannah Station.
Haskell.
Hudson.
Kingsbury.

La Porte, (c. h.)
Michigan City.
New Durham.
Rolling Prairie.
Roselle.
Union Mills.
Wanatah.
Westville.

LAWRENCE.

Bedford, (o. h.)
Bono.
Bryantsville.
Erie.
Fayetteville.
Fort Ritner.
Georgia.
Guthrie.
Heltonville.
Huron.
Juliet.

Lawrenceport.
Leatherwood.
Leesville.
Mitchell.
Morgiana.
Pinhook.
River Vale.
Silverveille.
Spring Mill.
Springville.
Tunnelton.

MADISON.

Alexandria.
Alfont.
Anderson, (c. h.)
Bock's Mills.
Branson.
Chesterfield.
Curtis.
Duck Creek.
Fishersburg.
Florida.
Forestville.
Frankton.

Huntsville.
Markleville.
Mendon.
Mercury.
Oceola.
Ovid.
Pendleton.
Perkinsville.
Prosperity.
Rigdon.
Summitville.
Zinsburg.

MARION.

Acton.
Adair.
Augusta Station.
Bridgeport.
Broad Ripple.
Carrsville.
Castleton.
Clermont.
Cumberland.
Fall Creek.

Gallaudette.
Germantown.
Glenn's Valley.
Indianapolis, (c. h.)
James' Switch.
Lawrence.
Millersville.
Southport.
Valley Mills.
West Newton.

MARSHALL.

Alden.
Argos.
Bourbon.
Bremen.
Fairmount.
Inwood.
Marmont.

Maxinkuckee.
Plymouth, (c. h.)
Sligo.
Tippecanoetown.
Tyner City.
Walnut Hill.
Yellow River.

MARTIN.

Dover Hill, (c. h.)
Dye.
Halbert's Bluff.
Keck's Church.
Loogootee.
McCameron.

Mountain Spring.
Mount Pleasant.
Natchez.
South Martin.
Trinity Springs.
Willow Valley.

MIAMI.

Bennett's Switch.

Paw Paw.

Bunker Hill.
Cary.
Chili.
Five.Corners.
Gilead.
Mexico.
Miami.
Niconza.

Perrysburg.
Peru, (c. h.)
Reserve.
Santa Fe.
Stockdale.
Wawpecong.
Wheatville.
Xenia.

MONROE.

Bloomington, (c. h.)
Bryant's Creek.
Ellittsville.
Harrodsburg.
Miller.

Mount Tabor.
Smithville.
Stanford.
Stinesville.
Unionville.

MONTGOMERY.

Alamo.
Ashley's Mills.
Beckville.
Brown's Valley.
Clowser's Mills
Crawfordsville, (c. h.)
Darlington.
Ladoga.
Linden.
Mace.
New·Richmond.
New Ross.

Orth.
Parkersburg.
Pleasant Hill.
Potatoe Creek.
Prairie Edge.
Shannondale.
Sugar River.
Waveland.
Waynetown.
Wesley.
Whitesville.
Yountsville.

MORGAN.

Brooklyn.
Centerton.
Center Valley.
Eminence.
Hall..
Martinsville, (c. h.)

Monrovia.
Mooresville.
Morgantown.
Sheasville.
Waverly.

NEWTON.

Adrience, (c. h.)
Beaver City.
Brook.
Goodland.

Kent.
Morocco.
Pilot Grove.

NOBLE.

Albion, (c. h.)
Avilla.
Bourie.
Cold Springs.
Cromwell.
Heela.
Kendallsville.
Ligonier.
Lisbon.
Merriam.

Noble.
Northport.
Port Mitchell.
Simon's Corner.
Springfield Mills.
Swan.
Wawaka.
Wilmot.
Wolf Lake.

OHIO.

Abberdeen.
Bear Branch.

Hartford.
Rising Sun, (c. h.)

ORANGE.

Campbell.   Orangeville.
Chambersburg.   Orleans.
French Lick.   *Paoli*, (c. h.)
Green Brier.   Stamper's Creek;
Leipsic.   Valeene.
McDonald's.   West Baden.
Newton Stewart.

OWEN.

Alligator.   Hausertown.
Arney.   Jordan Village.
Atkinsonville.   Patricksburg.
Cataract.   Quincy.
Cuba.   *Spencer*, (c. h.)
Deem.   Stockton.
Freedom.   Vandalia.
Gosport.   White Hall.

PARKE.

Annapolis.   Howard.
Armiesburg.   Lick Branch.
Banner Mills.   Mansfield.
Bellmore.   Montezuma.
Bethany.   Numa.
Bloomingdale.   Parkville.
Bridgeton.   *Rockville*, (c. h.)
Bruin's Cross Roads.   Rosedale.
Carlin.   Rossville.
Clinton Lock.   Russell's Mills.
Delta.   Sylvania.
Gallatin.   Waterman.
Hollandsburg.   Wright's Mills.

PERRY.

Adysville.   Oil Creek.
Cannelton, (c. h.)   Rock Island.
Derby.   Rome.
Don Juan.   Rono.
Foster's Ridge.   Tell City.
Leopold.   Tobinsport.
Lilly Dale.   Troy.
Lusher's.

PIKE.

Delectable Hill.   Union.
Hawthorn Mills.   White Oak Grove.
High Bank.   Winslow.
Petersburg, (c. h.)

PORTER.

Bengal.   Jackson Center.
Boon Grove.   Porter's Cross Roads.
Coffee Creek.   Salt Creek.
Foster.   Tassinong Grove.
Furnessvill.   *Valparaiso*, (c. h.)
Hebron.   Wheeler.
Hickory Point.

POSEY.

Black Hawk Mills.   New Harmony.
Blairsville.   Parker's Settlement.
Cynthiana.   Poseyville.
Farmersville.   Saint Wendels.
Grafton.   Stewartsville.
Hickory Branch.   Wadesville.
Mt. Vernon, (c. h.)

PULASKI.

Francisville.   Pulaski.
Ganson.   Star City.
Medarysville.   Strawberry Ridge.
Monterey.   Two Mile Prairie.
Oak.   *Winnamac*, (c. h.)

PUTNAM.

Bainbridge.   Johnsville.
Brunerstown.   Manhattan.
Cairo.   Morton.
Carpentersville.   Mount Meridian.
Cloverdale.   New Maysville.
Fillmore.   Portland Mills.
Greencastle, (c. h.)   Putnamville.
Groveland.   Reelsville.
Hamrick's Station.   Russellville.

RANDOLPH.

Arba.   Mar's Hill.
Balaka.   Neff.
Bartonia.   New Pittsburg.
Bloomingsport.   Parker.
Cerro Gordo.   Ridgeville.
Deerfield.   Snow Hill.
Emmettsville.   Spartanburg.
Fairview.   Trenton.
Farmland.   Union City.
Harrisville.   *Winchester*, (c. h.)
Losantville.   Windsor.
Lynn.

RIPLEY.

Ballstown.   North Hogan.
Batesville.   Olean.
Benham's Store.   Osgood.
Bross Plain.   Piercerville.
Delaware.   Poston.
Elrod.   Rei.
Hart's Mills.   Spade's Depot.
Hermann.   Stringtown.
Holton.   Sunman.
Milan.   Titusville.
Morris.   *Versailles*, (c. h.)
Napoleon.   Way.
New Marion.

RUSH.

Beech Grove.   Moscow.
Bloom.   New Salem.

Carthage.
Groves.
Hannegan.
Homar.
Manilla.
Melrose.
Milroy.

Raleigh.
Richland.
Rushville, (c. h.)
Smelser's Mills.
Star.
Steele's.
Sumner.

ST. JOSEPH.

Cottage Hill.
Lakeville.
Mishawaka.
New Castle.
North Liberty.
Notre Dame.
Osceola.

Richardson.
Soth Bend, (c. h.)
Sumption Prairie.
Terre Coupee.
Walkerton.
West York.
Woodland.

SCOTT.

Afton.
Alpha.
Austin.

Lexington, (c. h.)
Vienna.
Woosterton.

SHELBY.

Blue Ridge.
Boggstown.
Brookfield.
Conn's Creek.
Davisville.
Fairland.
Flat Rock.
Freeport.
Lewis Creek.
London.
Marietta.

Moral.
Morristown.
Mount Auburn.
Noah.
Pleasant View.
Prescott.
Shelbyville, (c. h.)
Smithland.
Sulphur Hill.
Wintertown.

SPENCER.

Buffalo.
Dale.
Enterprise.
French Island.
Fulda.
Gentryville.
Grand View.
Lake.

Mariah Hill.
Midway.
New Boston.
Newtonville.
Oakland.
Rockport, (c. h.)
Saint Meinrad.
Santa Claus.

STARKE.

Clear Lake.
English Lake.
Grover Town.
Hamlet Station.
Knox, (c. h.)

Lake City.
North Bend.
North Judson.
San Pierre.
Toto.

STEUBEN.

Alvarado.
Angola, (c. h.)
Crooked Creek.
Fish Creek.
Flint.

North East.
Orland.
Pleasant Lake.
Salem Center.
Sandy Ridge.

Fremont.
Hamilton.
Mets.

Turkey Creek.
York Center.

SULLIVAN.

Ascension.
Bateham.
Black Creek.
Brick Mill.
Carlisle.
Currysville.
Graysville.
Hymera.

Merom.
New Lebanon.
Paton's.
Shelburn.
Sprontt's.
Sullivan, (c. h.)
Turman's Creek.

SWITZERLAND.

Allensville.
Bennington.
Craig.
Florence.
Grant's Creek.
Jacksonville.
Moorefield.

Mount Sterling.
Patriot.
Pleasant.
Quercus Grove.
Rutherford.
Sugar Branch.
Vevay, (c. h.)

TIPPECANOE.

Americus.
Battle Ground.
Chauncey.
Clark's Hill.
Colburn.
Concord.
Culver's Station.
Dayton.
Farmers' Institute.
Lafayette, (c. h.)

Montmorency.
Octagon.
Pettit.
Romney.
Shawnee Mound.
Stockwell.
Sugar Grove.
Transitville.
West Point.
Wyandot.

TIPTON.

Curtisville.
Groomsville.
Jackson Station.
Nevada.
New Lancester.
Normanda.

Prairie.
Sharpsville.
Tetersburg.
Tipton. (c. h.)
West Kinderhook.
Windfall City.

UNION.

Beechy Mire.
Billingsville.
Brownsville.
Clifton.
Cottage Grove.

Dunlapsville.
Liberty, (c. h.)
Lotus.
Quakertown.

VANDERBURG.

Armstrong.
Cypressdale.
Evansville, (c. h.)
Kasson.

McCutchanville.
Nash Depot.
Oakdam.
Saundersville.

34

VERMILLION.

Clinton.
Eugene.
Highland.
Jones.

Newport, (c. h.)
Perrysville.
Quaker Hill.
Toronto.

TIGO.

Cookerly.
Ellsworth.
Fruit Hill.
Lewis.
New Goshen.
Pimento.

Prairie Creek.
Prairieton.
Saint Marys.
Sandford.
Terre Haute, (c. b.)
Wauhoo.

WABASH.

America.
Belden.
Dora.
Emmaus.
La Fontaine.
La Gro.
Laketon.
Liberty Mills.
Lodi.

New Holland.
New Madison.
North Manchester.
Rich Valley.
Roann.
Somerset.
Urbana.
Wabash, (c. h.)

WARREN.

Baltimore.
Independence.
Marshfield.
Pine Village.

Rainsville.
State Line.
West Lebanon.
Williamsport, (c. h.)

WARRICK.

Booneville, (c. h.)
Canal.
Crowville.
Hartsboro'.
Lee.

Lynnville.
Newburg.
Polk Patch.
Wheatonville.
Yankeetown.

WASHINGTON.

Beck's Mills.

Little York.

Campbellsburg.
Canton.
Chestnut Hill.
Claysville.
Fhrabee's Station.
Flower Gap.
Fredericksburg.
Hardinsburg.
Harristown.
Heffren.
Hitchcock's Station.
Kossuth.

Livonia.
Martinsburg.
Millport.
New Philadelphia.
New Retreat.
Organ Spring.
Pekin.
Prowsville.
Salem, (c. h.)
Saltilloville.
South Boston.
Texas.

WAYNE.

Abington.
Benson.
Bethel.
Boston.
Cambridge City.
Centerville, (c. h.)
Chester.
Cox's Mills.
Dalton.
Dublin.
East Germantown.
Economy.
Green's Fork.

Hagerstown.
Jacksonburg.
Kalorama.
Milton.
Neil's Station.
New Garden.
Olive Hill.
Richmond.
Walnut Level.
Webster.
White Water.
Williamsburg.

WELLS.

Brookston.
Buffalo.
Burnett's Creek.
Cathcart.
Chalmers.
Flowerville.

Idaville.
Monon.
Monticello, (c. h.)
Reynolds.
Seafield.
Wolcott.

WHITLEY.

Cherubusco.
Coesse.
Collamer.
Columbia City, (c. h.)
Fuller's Corners.
Hecla.

Laud.
Saturn.
South Cleveland.
South Whitley.
Summit.
Washington Center.